Gandhāran Buddhist Texts, Volume 2

Gandhāran Buddhist Texts

Series editor: Richard Salomon

The Gandhāran Buddhist Texts series presents text editions and studies of the birch bark scrolls in the British Library's Kharoṣṭhī manuscript collection, dating from about the first century A.D. These texts are being published under the auspices of the British Library/University of Washington Early Buddhist Manuscripts Project. The series will also include studies of related textual materials from other collections.

Ancient Buddhist Scrolls from Gandhāra: The British Library Kharoṣṭhī Fragments, by Richard Salomon

A Gāndhārī Version of the Rhinoceros Sūtra: British Library Kharoṣṭhī Fragment 5B, by Richard Salomon, Gandhāran Buddhist Texts, vol. 1

Three Gāndhārī Ekottarikāgama-Type Sūtras: British Library Kharoṣṭhī Fragments 12 and 14, by Mark Allon, Gandhāran Buddhist Texts, vol. 2

Three Gāndhārī Ekottarikāgama-Type Sūtras

British Library Kharoṣṭhī Fragments 12 and 14

Mark Allon

with a contribution by Andrew Glass

UNIVERSITY OF WASHINGTON PRESS

Seattle and London

Printed in the United States of America

ISBN (cloth): 0-295-98185-7

The paper used in this publication is acid-free and recycled from 10 percent postconsumer and at least 50 percent preconsumer waste. It meets the minimum requirements of American National Standard for Information Sciences—Permanence of Paper for Printed Library Materials, ANSI Z39.48–1984.

For my mother and father

The nature of this kind of work is that it brings profit to everyone,
and the only person to suffer hardship is the one who undertakes to do it.
The reader who freely runs through all these books does not realise
that sometimes we were held up for days by a single word.

Erasmus

Contents

Illustrations and Tables

Plates *(following p. 102)*

Figures

Tables

Preface

This volume is the second to be published in the Gandhāran Buddhist Texts (GBT) series, the first being *A Gāndhārī Version of the Rhinoceros Sūtra: British Library Kharoṣṭhī Fragment 5B* (Seattle: University of Washington Press, 2000), by Richard Salomon, with a contribution by Andrew Glass. The principal goal of the GBT series is to publish editions and studies of the texts of the British Library's collection of Kharoṣṭhī manuscript fragments and of similar collections of Gandhāran manuscripts that have recently come to light (see the series introduction in Salomon 2000: xi–xiii). This and related activities are being carried out under the auspices of the British Library/University of Washington Early Buddhist Manuscripts Project (EBMP).

A detailed overview of the British Library's Kharoṣṭhī manuscript collection was presented in *Ancient Buddhist Scrolls from Gandhāra: The British Library Kharoṣṭhī Fragments* (Salomon 1999), to which the reader is referred for further information. (The reader is also referred to the EBMP's website [http://depts.washington.edu/ebmp/], where background information to the project and images of the manuscripts published to date are available.) In brief, this collection was acquired by the British Library in 1994 along with several inscribed earthenware pots, including the one in which the manuscripts were originally buried. The collection consists of twenty-nine birch bark fragments that constitute the remains of at least twenty-one different original scrolls and at least twenty-three separate texts. All of the texts in this collection are Buddhist, encompassing a diversity of genres, and all but one are written in the Kharoṣṭhī script and the Gāndhārī language. The original provenance of these manuscripts is unknown, but they are thought to have come from a site in or around Haḍḍa in the Jalalabad Plain of eastern Afghanistan (Salomon 1999: 20–2). The manuscripts were evidently not new when they were placed in earthenware pots in antiquity and ritually interred in a sacred place (Salomon 1999: 69–86). The collection has been provisionally affiliated with the Dharmaguptaka school (Salomon 1999: 21, 171–5, 214–7) and dated to the early first century A.D, most likely between A.D. 10 and 30 (Salomon 1999: 141–55).

The present volume consists of an edition and study of the three Ekottarikāgama-type sūtras preserved on British Library Fragments 12 and 14. As was the case in the first volume in the GBT series (Salomon 2000), the paleographic analysis (§§ 4.1–7) is written by Andrew Glass. I have chosen to publish this text from among the several in the British Library collection for two reasons. The first is my fondness for canonical Buddhist sūtras and a more-than-passing interest in the composition and stylistic features of this genre (Allon 1997). The second is more practical: two of these three Gāndhārī sūtras have Pali and Chinese parallels. The Pali parallels in particular provide much needed assistance in the reading and interpretation of the often fragmentary and difficult Gāndhārī text. Further, given the formulaic and repetitive nature of Buddhist literature of this genre, even when a particular Gāndhārī expression differs from that of the corresponding Pali sutta, parallels for it could usually be found either elsewhere in the Pali canon or in Buddhist Sanskrit literature. Typically it was only upon finding these parallel expressions in Pali or Sanskrit that the Gāndhārī text could be accurately interpreted.

The following further publications for the GBT series are currently in progress:

A New Version of the Gāndhārī Dharmapada and a Collection of Previous-Birth Stories: British Library Kharoṣṭhī Fragments 16 and 25 (GBT 3), by Timothy Lenz.

A Gāndhārī Abhidharma Text: British Library Kharoṣṭhī Fragment 28 (GBT 4), by Collett Cox.

A Gāndhārī Version of the Songs of Lake Anavatapta (Anavatapta-gāthā): British Library Kharoṣṭhī Fragment 1 (GBT 5), by Richard Salomon.

Further volumes of editions of the British Library and other texts will follow these in the future.

Not long after the British Library acquired its Kharoṣṭhī manuscript fragments, two other collections of ancient Gandhāran Buddhist manuscripts came to light and were acquired by private collectors. These manuscript collections are referred to as the Senior collection and Schøyen collection, after their owners. The Senior collection, which is comparable in size and antiquity to the British Library collection, consists of twenty-four birch bark scrolls. The texts are all canonical sūtras, many with parallels in the Saṃyutta-nikāya/Saṃyuktāgamas, though it has yet to be determined whether this collection actually represents a portion of a Gāndhārī Saṃyuktāgama. A preliminary reading of these manuscripts was made by Richard Salomon as they were being conserved, and a more detailed reading of several sūtras in the collection has been undertaken by the EBMP team at our regular group meetings. A preliminary survey article on this collection by Richard Salomon (parallel to Salomon 1997) will soon be published, and a survey and sample of this collection by members of the EBMP (parallel to Salomon 1999) will follow in the GBT series.

Not surprisingly, the three Ekottarikāgama-type sūtras edited here have many phrases and formulas in common with the sūtras in the Senior collection, and I have made use of these parallels wherever possible. The Senior material has greatly improved the linguistic and formulaic analysis of the text of the British Library Ekottarikāgama-type sūtras; in some case it has enabled me to reconstruct a missing or damaged portion of the text. The Senior manuscripts have also been important to this study of the Ekottarikāgama-type sūtras on other levels, for instance in the discussion (§ 2.2) of the tendency of the scribe of the Ekottarikāgama-type sūtras to give the text in full where the scribe of the Senior manuscripts frequently abbreviates common formulas. In short, the Senior manuscripts have proved invaluable to the study of the sūtras presented in this volume.

The Schøyen manuscript collection consists predominantly of fragments of Sanskrit Buddhist texts written in Brāhmī script, mostly on palm leaf but sometimes on birch bark or vellum. However, it also includes numerous small fragments of texts in the Gāndhārī language and Kharoṣṭhī script, written on palm leaf. These Gāndhārī fragments, which are probably slightly younger than those in the British Library and Senior collections, are particularly relevant to the work of the EBMP. As with the Senior collection, I have found these Schøyen Kharoṣṭhī fragments valuable for the present study. The first Kharoṣṭhī fragments in the Schøyen collection, in this case fragments of a Gāndhārī Mahāparinirvāṇa-sūtra, were recently published by Allon and Salomon (2000). Further Gāndhārī fragments in this collection will be published in due course by members of the EBMP team in the Buddhist Manuscripts in the Schøyen Collection series.

As the present volume shows, the study of the Senior and Schøyen Kharoṣṭhī manuscript fragments in conjunction with those belonging to the British Library is not only fruitful but essential. Given the orthographic and paleographic peculiarities of this material, as well as the fragmentary nature of the manuscripts and the inherent difficulty of the language, it is often the case that the key to understanding a word or phrase in one Gāndhārī text, or to interpreting a particular akṣara (graphic syllable), is to be found in another text in the rapidly increasing corpus of Gāndhārī manuscripts. Thus, the scope of the EBMP has by necessity expanded to include all available Gāndhārī manuscripts written in the Kharoṣṭhī script.

Some four or five centuries after the death of the Buddha, a Buddhist monk in Gandhāra made a copy of a collection of sūtras that recorded the Buddha's words: ink, pen, and birch bark fixing the sacred. After almost 2000 years hidden away from the eyes of men, plus a mere four years of my labor, this manuscript can once again be read and studied, albeit by a very different audience than that for which it was originally intended. Making this ancient Gandhāran text available to this twenty-first-century audience, few of whom are familiar with this monk's language or the script he used, would not have been possible without the assistance of numerous individuals and several institutions. First and foremost among the individuals is Richard Salomon, who invited me to participate in this exciting and important project. He has been an inspiring guide in the labyrinth of Gāndhārī/Kharoṣṭhī studies and I have learned much from him. The standard of this work has certainly been improved by his careful reading and learned comments on it. Further, through the generosity and hospitality of both Richard and Carol Salomon, the stay of my family in Seattle has been made a happier one.

Besides writing the paleographic analysis presented in §§ 4.1–7 of this volume, Andrew Glass has provided, with characteristic enthusiasm, much-needed and valued assistance in the technical aspects of handling this and related material, in producing the images and figures, and in preparing the manuscript for publication. He has also improved the reading of the manuscript in many places. His contributions to this volume and to the EBMP as a whole have been indispensable.

Other members of the EBMP team, namely Collett Cox, Timothy Lenz, Tien-chang Shih, and Jason Neelis, have also made important contributions to this publication. Our work on these documents is very much a team effort, with our regular group meetings during which we read and discuss each others' texts being particularly valuable. I have also enjoyed the personal support and friendship of these individuals.

A special thanks is due to Tien-chang Shih, who made the Chinese parallels to these Gāndhārī sūtras available to me. Once again, the EBMP is lucky to have such an enthusiastic student. Collett Cox and Jan Nattier (Indiana University) provided references to Chinese material relevant to sections of this study, and Paul Harrison (University of Canterbury) provided an English translation of An Shigao's Chinese translation of the Prahāṇa-sūtra (the contributions of these individuals are also acknowledged in the relevant sections). During the course of this study I have frequently had the pleasure of drawing on the language and linguistic expertise of several colleagues in the Department of Asian Languages and Literature, University of Washington. They include Michael Shapiro, Zev Handel, Jeffrey Schoening, and Ulrich Pagel (now at the School of Oriental and African Studies, London). I have enjoyed working with such talented individuals.

Several German scholars who are involved in the publication and study of the Sanskrit fragments of Buddhist texts from Gilgit and Central Asia have been particularly generous with their time and learning. Among them are Klaus Wille, Siglinde Dietz, and Jens-Uwe Hartmann. They were also helpful during my brief research visit to Göttingen in 1998. I am also indebted to Jens-Uwe Hartmann for his comments on the first chapter of this book.

Throughout the course of this research my doctoral advisor, Professor K. R. Norman, provided learned responses to my many inquires. Professors O. von Hinüber, Peter Skilling, Anne Blackburn, Fumio Enomoto, and Jonathan Silk, to name but a few, have also provided information. Once again, the contributions of each are acknowledged where appropriate.

This work would not have been possible without the financial support of the EBMP's anonymous benefactor. His continued interest in the outcome of my research as well as that of the other EBMP team members has been very encouraging, and I have appreciated his patience and understanding. May he enjoy the results of my research as much as I have enjoyed undertaking it.

Two institutions have also provided substantial financial support to the EBMP. They are the National Endowment for the Humanities (Program for Collaborative Research) and the Henry Luce Foundation. At the latter institution, we are particularly indebted to Michael Gilligan, Program Director for Theology, for his assistance. We wish to thank both institutions for helping us to make these ancient and sacred documents available to a wider audience.

Central to the success of the EBMP has been the ongoing support of the British Library and its staff. Individuals who have been particularly helpful are Graham Shaw, Deputy Director, Oriental and India Office Collections; Michael O'Keefe, Head of the South Asian Collection; Elizabeth Hunter, Photographer; Mark Barnard, Head of Conservation Studios; John Burton, Senior Conservation Officer; and Robert Davies, Conservation Officer. I have also enjoyed working closely with these people during my research visits to the British Library.

From its inception the EBMP has been fortunate enough to have received the full support of the University of Washington. In particular we are grateful to the College of Arts and Sciences and its Divisional Dean of Arts and Humanities, Professor Michael Halleran; to the Graduate School and its Dean, Professor Marsha Landolt; and to the South Asia Center and its Director, Professor Frank Conlon. The project has continued to receive practical and moral support from the Department of Asian Languages and Literature, and in particular from its former and present chairs, Professors David Knechtges, Michael Shapiro, and William Boltz. On a personal level, my stay in the United States and presence in the department have been skillfully facilitated by Youngie Yoon, the department's administrative assistant.

Without doubt, this volume would not have seen the light of day without the support and publishing skills of the staff of the University of Washington Press. In particular we would like to thank Pat Soden, Director, Naomi Pascal, Associate Director and Editor-in-Chief, and Michael Duckworth, Acquisitions Editor. I am also indebted to Pamela J. Bruton, whose editing skills have been essential to the standard and production of this volume. You know you have a good editor when she picks up spelling inconsistencies in your Pali or Sanskrit!

Adobe Systems, Inc., generously provided our project with several of its products, including Adobe Photoshop 5.5, Acrobat 4.0, and InDesign 1.5. As the original manuscripts are too fragile to be moved from the British Library, the bulk of our research is undertaken with digital images. Adobe Photoshop has been essential to the manipulation of these images and the creation of the reconstructions and figures for this volume.

Finally, two individuals in my home life have kept me sane as I wrestled with birch bark fragments and the orthographic whims of Gandhāran scribes. The first is my wife, Louise. Without her understanding, patience, and companionship this research and its publication would not have been possible. Yet again she has endured a long stint in a foreign land as I pursued my career in Buddhist studies. The second is our daughter, Holly, who was born as this volume took shape. What better way to relax after a day on the manuscript than playing with such a delightful little being.

Format, Transcription, and Citation System

For various reasons it was felt that the three-part format of the first volume in the GBT series (Salomon 2000) was not appropriate for this volume. Rather, this volume consists of ten chapters. Chapters 1 to 6 provide an introduction to the text being edited, a discussion of its relationship to related literature in other languages, a description of the manuscript, and detailed paleographic and linguistic analyses of the text. Chapter 7 contains the text as it appears in the manuscript, the reconstructed text, and a translation of the reconstructed text. The three sūtras preserved on this manuscript are discussed in detail in chapters 8, 9, and 10, respectively. Each of these three chapters consists of the following: an introductory discussion of the sūtra and its parallels in other languages, if any, and a detailed commentary on the text. Within the text commentary, the sūtra is divided into distinct events, which usually correspond to distinct formulas.

All bibliographic citations are by author's name and date, referring to the entries in the references at the end of the book. However, Pali Text Society editions of Pali texts cited are not included in the reference list, unless they differ from those given in Bechert 1990.

The conventions of transcription, the citation system, abbreviations, and other conventions follow those adopted in GBT 1 (Salomon 2000), with a few minor changes. In citing Pali texts, references to line numbers now follow the system commonly used for Buddhist Sanskrit texts. For example, AN II 37.23 refers to Aṅguttara-nikāya, volume II, page 37, line 23. Two abbreviations have changed. In Salomon 1999 and 2000 the abbreviation for the Khotan Dharmapada (Brough 1962) was KDhp, replacing GDhp of previous scholarship. For this and subsequent volumes in the GBT series it is Dhp-G^{K}. The abbreviation for the Gāndhārī Dharmapada fragment in the British Library (London) collection of Kharoṣṭhī manuscripts, which will be published in volume 3 of the GBT series, is Dhp-G^{L}. This brings the abbreviation of these texts into line with Khvs-G (= Gāndhārī version of the Khaggaviṣāṇa-sutta; Salomon 2000). Similar abbreviations are adopted for other Gāndhārī texts in the British Library collection: AG-G (= Gāndhārī version of the Anavatapta-gāthā); EĀ-G (= the text edited here); and Saṅg-G (= Gāndhārī version of the Saṅgīti-sūtra). Although EĀ-G has been adopted as the abbreviation for the three Ekottarikāgama-type sūtras presented in this volume, it is yet to be proven that these sūtras originally formed a section of a complete Gāndhārī Ekottarikāgama (see §§ 1.3–6). Finally, the abbreviation for the Pali Text Society's Pali-English Dictionary is PTSD rather than PED of Salomon 2000.

The symbols and conventions used to represent the transcribed text in this volume are the following:

[ ]	An unclear or partially preserved akṣara (graphic syllable) whose reading is not certain.
(*)	A lost or completely illegible akṣara that has been conjecturally restored on the basis of the context.
<* >	An akṣara that has been omitted by the scribe and conjecturally restored.
.	A missing portion (consonantal or diacritic vowel sign) of a partially legible akṣara. For example, *.e* transcribes an akṣara in which the diacritic vowel *e* is visible, but the consonant to which it was attached is lost or illegible, while *g.* represents an akṣara whose consonantal element is legible as *g* but which is incompletely preserved so that it cannot be determined which vowel diacritic, if any, was attached to it. The notation *r..* marks an akṣara in which the preconsonantal *r* sign is visible, but both the consonant that followed it and the vowel of the akṣara are illegible. The notation *a.* indicates an independent vowel sign (𐨀 = *a*), sometimes referred to as "alif" or vowel carrier sign, which is similarly incomplete, so that it cannot be determined whether a diacritic sign (indicating the independent vowel *i, u, e,* or *o*) was originally attached to it.
?	A visible or partially visible but illegible akṣara.
+	A missing akṣara that would have appeared on a lost or obscured portion of the manuscript. A series of these signs indicates the number of lost akṣaras (calculated in verse texts, usually estimated in prose).
///	Beginning or end of an incompletely preserved line.
·, ◦	A small dot or circle placed on or above the line in the original text as a mark of punctuation, indicating a word, sentence, or verse unit division.
O	A larger circle, a design composed of several circles, or some other such major punctuation symbol used in the original text to mark a sectional division.
=	A word break within an akṣara: for instance, in a phrase such as *evam=eva* in which the final consonant of the preceding word and the initial vowel of the following word are written together as a single syllabic unit (e.g., 𐨨𐨅 *me*).
–	Metrically long syllable.
⏑	Metrically short syllable.
⏓	Metrically long or short syllable.

Abbreviations

For complete citations to text editions, see References. For Pali texts, see Bechert 1990.

Ā.	ātmanepada
abbrev.	abbreviated
abl.	ablative
abs.	absolutive
acc.	accusative
adj.	adjective
adv.	adverb
AG-G	Gāndhārī Anavataptagāthā (BL Fragment 1, ed. Salomon, forthcoming)
AG-Skt.	Sanskrit Anavataptagāthā (ed. Bechert 1961)
AKBh(P)	Abhidharmakośabhāṣya (ed. Pradhan 1975)
AKV	Abhidharmakośavyākhyā (ed. Wogihara 1932–6)
Amg.	Ardhamāgadhī
AN	Aṅguttara-nikāya
aor.	aorist
Ap	Apadāna
Apa.	Apabhraṃśa
Ap-a	Apadāna-aṭṭhakathā, Visuddhajanavilāsinī
As	Atthasālinī, Dhammasaṅganī-aṭṭhakathā
Avś	Avadānaśataka (ed. Speyer 1906–9)
BBh	Bodhisattvabhūmi (ed. Wogihara 1930–6)
BBS	Ernst Waldschmidt, *Bruchstücke buddhistischer Sūtras aus dem zentralasiatischen Sanskritkanon* (Leipzig, 1932)
B[e]	Burmese (Chaṭṭhasaṅgāyana) edition(s) of Pali texts (= VRI-CD unless otherwise stated; page references are to the printed edition given by the VRI-CD)
BhīKaVā(R/LVP)	Bhikṣuṇīkarmavācanā (ed. Ridding and LaVallée Poussin 1920)
BhīVin(Mā-L)	Bhikṣuṇī-vinaya (ed. Roth 1970)
BHS	Buddhist Hybrid Sanskrit
BHSD	Franklin Edgerton, *Buddhist Hybrid Sanskrit Dictionary* (New Haven, 1953)

BHSG	Franklin Edgerton, *Buddhist Hybrid Sanskrit Grammar* (New Haven, 1953)
Bil	Ernst Waldschmidt, "Zu einigen Bilinguen aus den Turfan-Funden" (1955)
BimbSū	Bimbasāra-sūtra (ed. Waldschmidt 1932: 114–48)
BL	British Library
BSR	*Buddhist Studies Review*
bv.	bahuvrīhi compound
Bv	Buddhavaṃsa
Bv-a	Buddhavaṃsa-aṭṭhakathā, Madhuratthavilāsinī
card.	cardinal number
caus.	causative
C^e	Sri Lankan edition(s) of Pali texts
Chin.	Chinese
comm./comms.	commentary, commentaries
CP	*Collected Papers*
Cp-a	Cariyāpiṭaka-aṭṭhakathā, Paramatthadīpanī VII
CPD	*A Critical Pāli Dictionary,* 2 vols. to date (Copenhagen, 1924–)
CPS	Catuṣpariṣat-sūtra (ed. Waldschmidt 1952–62)
DĀ	Dīrghāgama
Daśo	Daśottara-sūtra (ed. Mittal 1957 and ed. Schlingloff 1962)
dat.	dative
DBhS	Daśabhūmika-sūtra (ed. Rahder 1926)
DBhS(V)	Daśabhūmika-sūtra (ed. Vaidya 1967)
DbSū(1)	Daśabala-sūtra 1 (ed. Waldschmidt 1932: 207–25)
DbSū(2)	Daśabala-sūtra 2 (ed. Waldschmidt 1958)
dem. pron.	demonstrative pronoun
denom.	denominative
Dhk-CD	Dhammakaya CD-ROM = PTS edition of Pali texts (*Pali Text Version 1.0* [Khlong Luang: Dhammakaya Foundation, 1996])
Dhp	Dhammapada (ed. von Hinüber and Norman 1994)
Dhp-a	Dhammapada-aṭṭhakathā
Dhp-G^K	Gāndhārī Khotan Dharmapada (= "Gāndhārī Dharmapada," ed. Brough 1962; formerly KDhp in Salomon 1999, 2000)
Dhp-G^L	Gāndhārī London Dharmapada (BL Fragments 16+25; ed. Lenz 1999)
Dhs	Dhammasaṅgaṇī
Dhsgr	Dharmasaṅgraha (ed. Müller and Wenzel 1885)
Dhsk	Dharmaskandha (ed. Dietz 1984)
Divy	Divyāvadāna (ed. Cowell and Neil 1886)
DN	Dīgha-nikāya
DPPN	G. P. Malalasekera, *Dictionary of Pāli Proper Names,* 2 vols. (London, 1937–8)

dv.	dvandva compound
EĀ	Ekottarikāgama/Ekottarāgama
EĀ-G	Gāndhārī Ekottarikāgama (= three Ekottarikāgama-type sūtras, ed. Allon, present publication)
EĀ-Skt.$^{Gil.}$	Sanskrit Gilgit Ekottarikāgama (ed. Tripāṭhī 1995)
EBMP	British Library/University of Washington Early Buddhist Manuscripts Project
E^e	European (Pali Text Society) edition(s) of Pali texts
f.	feminine
fasc.	fascicle
fig./figs.	figures(s)
fl.	flourished
fut.	future
G	Gāndhārī
gdv.	gerundive
gen.	genitive
Gv	Gaṇḍavyūha-sūtra (ed. Suzuki and Idzumi 1934–6)
impf.	imperfect
impv.	imperative
ind.	indeclinable
inf.	infinitive
instr.	instrumental
interr. pron.	interrogative pronoun
It	Itivuttaka
It-a	Itivuttaka-aṭṭhakathā, Paramatthadīpanī II
Jā	Jātaka, together with Jātakatthavaṇṇanā
KaVā	Karmavācanā (ed. Härtel 1956)
kdh.	karmadhāraya compound
Khvs-G	Gāndhārī *Khargaviṣaṇa-sutra (ed. Salomon 2000)
Kv	Kathāvatthu
l./ll.	line(s)
Lal	Lalitavistara (ed. Lefmann 1902–8)
Lal(H)	Lalitavistara (ed. Hokazono 1994)
Lal(M)	Lalitavistara (ed. Mitra 1877)
Lal(V)	Lalitavistara (ed. Vaidya 1958)
loc.	locative
m.	masculine
MĀ	Madhyamāgama
Mah-CD	Mahidol CD-ROM = Thai edition of Pali texts (*Budsir on CD-ROM: A Digital Edition of Buddhist Scriptures* [Bangkok: Mahidol University Computing Center, 1994])
MAV	Mahāvadāna-sūtra (ed. Waldschmidt 1953–6)
MBh	Mahābhārata (Critical Edition; Poona, 1933–41)

Mg.	Māgadhī
MIA	Middle Indo-Aryan
Mil	Milindapañha
MKV	Mahākarmavibhaṅga and Karmavibhaṅgopadeśa (ed. Lévi 1932)
MN	Majjhima-nikāya
Mp	Manorathapūraṇī, Aṅguttaranikāya-aṭṭhakathā
MPS	Mahāparinirvāṇa-sūtra (ed. Waldschmidt 1950–1)
Mp-ṭ	Manorathapūraṇīṭīkā, Sāratthamañjūsā (ed. Pecenko 1996–9)
ms./mss.	manuscript(s)
MSV	Mūlasarvāstivāda-vinaya (ed. Dutt 1984)
Mvu	Mahāvastu-avadāna (ed. Senart 1882–97)
Mvy	Mahāvyutpatti (ed. Sakaki 1926)
MW	Monier Monier-Williams, *A Sanskrit-English Dictionary* (Oxford, 1899)
n.	neuter
Nett-a	Nettipakaraṇa-aṭṭhakathā
NIA	New Indo-Aryan
Nidd I	Mahāniddesa
Nidd II	Cullaniddesa
Nidd-a I	Mahāniddesa-aṭṭhakathā, Saddhammapajjotikā I
NidSa	Nidāna-saṃyukta (ed. Tripāṭhī 1962)
no./nos.	number(s)
nom.	nominative
OIA	Old Indo-Aryan
opt.	optative
P	Pali
P.	parasmaipada
p./pp.	page(s)
pass.	passive
Paṭis	Paṭisambhidāmagga
Paṭis-a	Paṭisambhidāmagga-aṭṭhakathā, Saddhammapakāsinī
PDhp	Patna Dharmapada (ed. Roth 1980)
pers.	person
Peṭ	Peṭakopadesa
Pj II	Paramatthajotikā, Suttanipāta-aṭṭhakathā
Pkt.	Prakrit
pl.	plural
pl./pls.	plates
P.N.	proper noun
pp.	past participle
Pp	Puggalapaññatti
pres.	present
pres. part.	present participle

pret.	preterite
pron.	pronoun
pron. adj.	pronominal adjective
Ps	Papañcasūdanī, Majjhimanikāya-aṭṭhakathā
PSPP(D)	Pañcaviṃśatisāhasrikā Prajñāpāramitā (ed. Dutt 1934)
Ps-pṭ	Papañcasūdanī-purāṇaṭīkā, Līnatthapakāsinī II
PTC	F. L. Woodward et al., *Pāli Tripiṭakaṃ Concordance,* 3 vols. (London, 1952–84)
PTS	Pali Text Society
PTSD	T. W. Rhys Davids and William Stede, *The Pali Text Society's Pali-English Dictionary* (London, 1921–5)
Pv	Petavatthu
Pv-a	Petavatthu-aṭṭhakathā, Paramatthadīpanī IV
PW	Otto Böhtlingk and Rudolph Roth, *Sanskrit-Wörterbuch,* 7 vols. (St. Petersburg, 1855–75)
r	recto
RP	Rāṣṭrapālaparipṛcchā (ed. Finot 1901)
SĀ	Saṃyuktāgama
SĀ(LVP)	Saṃyuktāgama (ed. La Vallée Poussin 1913)
Saṅg-G	Gāndhārī Saṅgīti-sūtra and commentary (BL Fragment 15)
Saṅg-Skt.	Sanskrit Saṅgīti-sūtra (ed. Stache-Rosen 1968)
ŚBh	Śrāvakabhūmi
ŚBh(S)	Śrāvakabhūmi (ed. Shukla 1973)
ŚBh(T)	Śrāvakabhūmi (ed. Śrāvakabhūmi Study Group, Taishō University, 1998)
SBhV	Saṅghabhedavastu (ed. Gnoli 1977–8)
S[e]	Thai (King of Siam) edition(s) of Pali texts (= Mah-CD unless otherwise stated; page references are to the printed edition given by the Mah-CD)
sg.	singular
SHT	*Sanskrithandschriften aus den Turfan-Funden*, 8 vols. to date (Göttingen, 1965–)
Śikṣ	Śikṣāsamuccaya (ed. Bendall 1902)
Sinh.	Sinhalese
Skt.	Sanskrit
Sn	Suttanipāta
SN	Saṃyutta-nikāya
Sp	Samantapāsādikā, Vinaya-aṭṭhakathā
SP	Saddharmapuṇḍarīka (ed. Kern and Nanjio 1908–12)
Spk	Sāratthapakāsinī, Saṃyuttanikāya-aṭṭhakathā
Spk-pṭ	Sāratthapakāsinī-purānaṭīkā, Līnatthapakāsinī III
Sp-ṭ	Samantapāsādikā-ṭīkā, Sāratthadīpanī
ŚSPP(G)	Śatasāhasrikā Prajñāpāramitā (ed. Ghoṣa 1902–13)

Sv	Sumaṅgalavilāsinī, Dīghanikāya-aṭṭhakathā
Sv-pṭ	Sumaṅgalavilāsinī-purāṇaṭīkā, Līnatthapakāsinī I
SWTF	Heinz Bechert, ed., *Sanskrit-Wörterbuch der buddhistischen Texte aus den Turfan-Funden*, 1 vol. to date (Göttingen, 1994–)
T	J. Takakusu and K. Watanabe, eds., *Taishō Shinshū Daizōkyō*, 100 vols. (Tokyo, 1924–34)
Th	Theragāthā
Th-a	Theragāthā-aṭṭhakathā
Tib.	Tibetan
Toch.	Tocharian
tp.	tatpuruṣa compound
ts.	tatsama
Ud	Udāna
Ud-a	Udāna-aṭṭhakathā, Paramatthadīpanī I
udd.	uddāna
Uv	Udānavarga (ed. Bernhard 1965–8)
v	verso
v./vv.	verse(s)
Vibh	Vibhaṅga
Vibh-a	Vibhaṅga-aṭṭhakathā, Sammohavinodanī
Vin	Vinayapiṭaka
Vism	Visuddhimagga (ed. Rhys Davids 1920–1)
Vism-mhṭ	Visuddhimagga-mahāṭīkā, Paramatthamañjūsā
Vism(W)	Visuddhimagga (ed. Warren 1950)
v.l./vv.ll.	varia lectio/variae lectiones
voc.	vocative
VRI-CD	Vipassana Research Institute CD-ROM = Burmese Chaṭṭhasaṅgāyana edition of Pali texts (*Chaṭṭha Saṅgāyana CD-ROM from Dhammagiri, Version 3.0* [Igatpuri: Vipassana Research Institute, 1999])
Vv	Vimānavatthu
Vv-a	Vimānavatthu-aṭṭhakathā
w.r.	wrong reading

Three Gāndhārī Ekottarikāgama-Type Sūtras

British Library Kharoṣṭhī Fragments 12 and 14

CHAPTER 1

British Library Kharoṣṭhī Fragments 12 and 14

1.1. The Contents of British Library Kharoṣṭhī Fragments 12 and 14

Fragments 12 and 14 of the British Library (BL) Kharoṣṭhī manuscripts (Or.14915.25, Or.14915.24, and Or.14915.28 = frames 25, 24, and 28) were first described by Richard Salomon in *Ancient Buddhist Scrolls from Gandhāra: The British Library Kharoṣṭhī Fragments* (1999: 48–9). They constitute the lower part of a scroll, with no loss of text between the two fragments and with the original bottom of the scroll intact (see pls. 5–7). The upper part of the scroll has not survived. The scroll as preserved contains two distinct texts, written by different scribes. The first text occupies the bulk of the recto side of the scroll and consists of three sūtras, or rather the remnants of three sūtras, as the beginning of the first is missing and the end of the third must have been on a separate scroll, which has not survived. That the third sūtra was continued on a new scroll is proven by the fact that the scribe chose to discontinue the writing of this text on this scroll at an appropriate juncture in the third sūtra, that is, after the description of the third of four concepts, leaving space for approximately seven more lines of text at the bottom of the scroll (see Salomon 1999: 91). It appears that the scribe of this first text did not favor writing to the very bottom of a scroll. As will be discussed in greater detail below, the fact that all three sūtras are relatively short and have a numerical association with the number 4 suggests that these sūtras formed part of a Catuṣka-nipāta, a "Section of Fours," of a Gāndhārī Ekottarikāgama (EĀ).

The second text on the scroll consists of the skeletal outlines of a series of avadāna-type stories, a genre that is particularly well represented in the BL collection. Most of the avadānas in this collection were written by the same scribe (see Salomon 1999: 35–9). The scribe of this second text began where the scribe of the first text left off, writing five lines in the blank space at the bottom of the scroll before turning the scroll over and continuing on the verso. It appears that this second text was written some time after the first, though it is impossible to determine how long after. It seems that this "avadāna" scribe was in effect scavenging blank areas of scroll, as shown by the many other fragments in the collection where this has occurred.

The subject of the present publication is the first text, the series of three sūtras on the recto of this scroll. The publication and study of the second text, which apparently has no relationship to the first, will be undertaken in the future, most likely by another member of our team and perhaps in conjunction with other texts of this genre. For the interest of the reader a provisional reading and translation of the first avadāna are presented in appendix 2.

1.2. The Three Gāndhārī Ekottarikāgama/Aṅguttara-nikāya-Type Sūtras and Their Parallels and Titles in Other Languages

The manuscript lacks a colophon, as is to be expected since this series of three sūtras represents neither the beginning nor the end of the collection to which it belongs. None of the sūtras bears a title (i.e., no title appears between the first and second or between the second and third sūtras), which indicates that titles were probably also not attached to the other sūtras of the collection. It is also unfortunate that there is no remnant of an uddāna, for, as is well known, there is a close connection between the title of a sutta/sūtra and its uddāna entry (see, e.g., Feer 1884: x; Waldschmidt 1980: 144–5). The absence of an uddāna suggests that these three sūtras did not cross any divisional boundaries, such as the end of one vagga/varga and the beginning of the next, where uddānas commonly occur in Buddhist texts.

Only one example of a colophon has been identified among the BL Kharoṣṭhī manuscripts (see Salomon 1999: 40–2), but this absence may primarily be due to the fact that the beginnings of most scrolls, where colophons normally occur, have not survived (see Salomon 1999: 22). Similarly, there is only one example of an uddāna in the collection. This is in the "Rhinoceros Sūtra," the G version of the P Khaggavisāṇa-sutta of the Suttanipāta (35–75), but in this case it is an uddāna to individual verses of the poem (see Salomon 2000: 34–7). In many instances the avadāna texts include what are in effect their titles. For example, the first avadāna story on this scroll (presented in appendix 2) begins with *puniga avadano,* "The Puniga avadāna." Other examples are seen in the pūrvayoga texts, which depict the past lives of individuals, an example of which is presented in Salomon 1999: 38–9 and begins *anadasa pr[uva](*yo)ge,* "The previous birth of Ānanda."[1]

In some cases the title of a G text can be anticipated with some degree of probability on the basis of the titles of the parallel versions in other languages. For example, there are now three versions of the Rhinoceros Sūtra: Pali, Sanskrit, and Gāndhārī. The P version in the Suttanipāta is referred to as the Khaggavisāṇa-sutta based on the occurrence of the word *khaggavisāṇa* in the refrain of each of the poem's verses (the uddāna entry is the abbreviated *visāṇaṃ;* Sn p. 38; see Norman 1992a: xxvi), while the title of the BHS version in the Mahāvastu appears to be Khaḍgaviṣāṇa-gāthā based on the postscript *sarvā khaḍgaviṣāna-gāthā vistareṇa kartavyā* (see Salomon 2000: § 1.4.1). The title of the G version is not preserved in the manuscript, but in light of the P and Skt. titles, it is quite likely that the title of the G version was either *Khargaviṣaṇa-sutra or *Khargaviṣaṇa-gas̱a (see Salomon 2000: 10). Since our manuscript contains no titles, the titles of the three G sūtras presented here have likewise been constructed on the basis of the titles of their parallels in other languages or, failing that, on the basis of a key word.

The absence of individual titles in our manuscript is worthy of further comment. In the case of P manuscripts, it seems to be the norm for the titles of the suttas within the Dīgha-nikāya (DN) and Majjhima-nikāya (MN) to be given after each sutta; that is, each

[1] See also Salomon 2000: § 1.4.1 and his commentary on verse 1, p. 117.

sutta within these collections concludes with a phrase stating, for example, that the sutta of such-and-such a name has ended or that the sutta of such-and-such a name is, say, the first of the vagga. Examples are *mahāparinibbānasuttantaṃ niṭṭhitaṃ* (DN II 168) and *mūlapariyāyasuttaṃ paṭhamaṃ* (MN I 6). In these nikāyas, vagga titles correspondingly occur after the last sutta of each vagga, for example, *mahāvaggo* (DN II 358) and *mūlapariyāyavaggo paṭhamo* (MN I 63). Not unexpectedly, there is much variation in the manuscripts in the reading of such entries. In contrast to this tradition for the DN and MN, it seems that in manuscripts of the Saṃyutta-nikāya (SN) and Aṅguttara-nikāya (AN) individual sutta titles are not given but are to be inferred from the uddāna entry that usually occurs at the end of each vagga.[2] In other words, among the four main nikāyas, titles to individual suttas are given after each sutta only in the two collections that contain fewer and longer suttas, namely, the DN and MN.[3]

In the case of the Central Asian (Turfan) manuscripts, the state of affairs is more difficult to determine due to their fragmentary nature, but it appears that only some aspects of the basic pattern observed for P texts hold true for these manuscripts. In some manuscripts of Dīrghāgama (DĀ) sūtras, for example, the sūtra titles occur at the ends of sūtras. For example, SHT V 1351, a fragment of the Ambāṣṭa-sūtra of the DĀ, ends with *// ambāṣṭasūtraṃ samā(*ptaṃ) // 10* (R6).[4] In one manuscript of the Catuṣpariṣat-sūtra, the sūtra concludes with *catuṣparīṣasūtraṃ* [sic] *samāptaḥ* [sic] (see CPS § 28g.6), while the first of the two sūtras preserved on SHT IV 165 frag. 29, a fragment of the DĀ, concludes with *māyājāl(*a)ḥ* [sic] *sū(*traṃ samāptaṃ)* (Vb). However, I am informed by Jens-Uwe Hartmann that in Central Asian manuscripts of DĀ sūtras as well as in the new DĀ manuscript from Gilgit (see Hartmann 2000), it is more common for the sūtra titles to occur in uddānas. For example, SHT V 1290, which contains the remnants of four sūtras from the DĀ, includes an uddāna after the second surviving sūtra (c R8) that preserves

---

2 There is some variation in the mss. in the placement of the uddānas, in whether or not the vagga titles and uddānas are given, and in their reading. For example, in the Sinh. mss. used for the E^e of the AN, the uddānas to the first three nipātas are given at the end of the Tika-nipāta (see Morris 1961: viii), while the vagga titles are given after each vagga. In the case of the Catukka-nipāta, the Burmese mss. used for the E^e give the vagga titles and uddānas throughout, while the Sinh. mss. give the vagga titles and uddānas for the first ten vaggas only (Morris 1888: iii). An example of ms. variation in the uddāna entry for a given sutta is seen in the case of the entry for sutta 36 of the Catukka-nipāta of the AN, which is the P parallel to the first G sūtra in this collection. These variations in the uddāna entry, combined with the fact that the "title" by which a particular sutta or text is referred to in other P texts, such as the commentaries, does not always match its uddāna entry, indicate that the uddāna entry provided but one possible source for the title of a sutta or text.

3 Number and size may not, in fact, be the determining factors, at least, not the only ones. Function, for example, may also play a part. A survey of the entries in Somadasa 1987 indicates that in mss. containing a few selected suttas and texts the titles are not always given. I am indebted to Professor O. von Hinüber for providing information on sutta titles in P mss., particularly the old northern Thai mss.

4 It is not certain that this sūtra fragment is part of a DĀ ms. Among other things, the presence of the number 10 after the title is problematic (Jens-Uwe Hartmann, personal communication).

the titles of the previous two sūtras, which are evidently part of a group of five: *śoṇatāṇṭhyaś ca kūṭatāṇṭhyena paścimāḥ 1*.[5] In the case of Madhyamāgama (MĀ) fragments, such as SHT IV 412, examples of sūtra titles or uddānas are not preserved.

In light of the extensive remnants of the Nidāna-saṃyukta of the Saṃyuktāgama (SĀ), it appears that, as is the case with P manuscripts of the SN, the sūtra titles are to be inferred from the uddānas (Tripāṭhī 1962: 10–1; see also SHT VI 1399, first published in Waldschmidt 1980: 144–5).[6] This is also the case with the sūtras in the Skt. fragment of the Mūlasarvāstivādin EĀ from Gilgit (see Tripāṭhī 1995: 21–4).

In view of these observations, the absence of a title after each sūtra in this G collection of sūtras is consistent with the P and Skt. manuscripts of the SN/SĀ and AN/EĀ collections. The similar lack of sūtra titles in the Senior manuscripts (see Preface), a collection of G sūtras that may be a section of a G SĀ, appears to provide further evidence that in manuscripts of the SN/SĀ and AN/EĀ, titles to individual suttas/sūtras were given only in uddānas.

A detailed discussion of the contents of the three G sūtras preserved on this scroll, along with their parallels in other languages and their titles, is presented in the introduction to the study of each sūtra (§§ 8.1, 9.1, and 10.1). A brief summary of that information for the purpose of the present discussion follows.

The first sūtra in the collection records a discussion between the Buddha and a brahman named Dhoṇa in which the brahman asks the Buddha four questions. The sūtra concludes with three, possibly four, verses spoken by the Buddha. The P parallel to this sūtra, which was first identified by Richard Salomon (1999: 24, 48), is sutta 36 of the Catukka-nipāta, or Section of Fours, of the AN (II 37–9). As in the G sūtra, the brahman asks the Buddha four questions. The P sutta concludes with two verses. No Skt. version has so far come to light, nor does there seem to be a Tibetan translation, but three Chinese translations of this sūtra have been identified by Tien-chang Shih. The first appears in the Zengyi ahan jing, the EĀ (T 2 no. 125 [sūtra 38.3] fasc. 31, pp. 717c18–718a12). In contrast to the P version, which is in the "fours" section of the AN because of the four questions Dona asks the Buddha, this Chinese version appears in the Section of Sixes of the EĀ, based, it seems, on the six sense bases mentioned. The other two Chinese versions appear in the Saṃyuktāgamas, the first in the Za ahan jing (T 2 no. 99 [sūtra 101]

---

[5] See Hartmann 1989: 40. The titles of several sūtras preserved in SHT IV 32, which was formerly identified as an anthology of mostly MĀ sūtras (Schlingloff 1961: 33 ff.; Sander 1979: 4.61–2, 1980: 6–14) but is now believed to be part of the DĀ (Jens-Uwe Hartmann, personal communication), are preserved in an uddāna (frag. 66 Bl.183 V5–6). Hartmann also brings to my attention a further fragmentary DĀ uddāna preserved in SHT III 978.

[6] Several anthologies of Skt. sūtras in the Central Asian material contain sūtra titles, either at the end of each sūtra or within an uddāna. In the case of fragment SHT I 581, an anthology of sūtras from different āgamas, the titles of two of the seven sūtras have survived at the end of the relevant sūtras: *bimb(*asāra)sūtraṃ samāptaḥ* and *mahāsamājasūtraṃ samāptaḥ* (see Waldschmidt 1980: 162). It is therefore likely that titles were included after each of the sūtras in this collection. Further examples of fragments containing colophons and uddānas giving sūtra titles and of sūtra titles within texts can be found by searching the indexes to the SHT (s.vv. *sūtra, samāpta,* and *uddāna*).

p. 28a20–b18), the second in the Beiyi za ahan jing (T 2 no. 100 [sūtra 267] p. 467a26–b24). In the first (T no. 99), the brahman asks the Buddha ten questions, while in the second (T no. 100), he asks him eight. Both versions conclude with verse.

Like the G sūtra, the three Chinese versions lack titles. Both the P sutta and its commentary lack titles in the European editions (E^e), but the Burmese and Thai editions give this sutta the title Doṇa-sutta because of the uddāna entry *doṇo* in those editions (the E^e has *loke,* following the Sinh. manuscripts). As the sutta is referred to as the Doṇa-sutta in the P tradition (see § 8.1.2 for details), and as the main character in the G sūtra is the brahman Dhoṇa, I will refer to the G text throughout this study as the Dhoṇa-sutra.[7]

The second G sūtra in this collection, like the third, depicts the Buddha preaching to the monks. The topic of the Buddha's discourse in the second sūtra is *budhabayaṇa,* which is the equivalent of P and Skt. *buddhavacana,* literally, "the word of the Buddha" but also "the instruction or teaching of the Buddha or Buddhas," which the Buddha declares to be easy to enact under certain conditions. The structure of this sūtra is based on the four postures: walking, standing, sitting, and lying down awake. The sūtra does not include any verses. No P or Skt. versions of this sūtra, nor Tibetan or Chinese translations, have so far been identified. As the key term in this sūtra is *budhabayaṇa,* I will refer to it as the Budhabayaṇa-sutra.

The topic of the Buddha's discourse in the third sūtra is the four efforts (or abandonings): G *prasaṇa*/P *padhāna*/Skt. *pradhāna, prahāṇa.* As mentioned, the sūtra is incomplete. The description of the last of the four efforts and the conclusion to the sūtra were written on a separate scroll, which has not survived. A P parallel was first identified by Salomon (1999: 24, 48). It is sutta 14 of the Catukka-nipāta, the Section of Fours, of the AN. Judging from what survives of the G text, the main difference between the two versions is the order in which the four *prasaṇa/padhāna*s are presented. As the P version concludes with a verse spoken by the Buddha, it is likely that the G version also contained at least one verse. No complete Skt. parallel survives, but the remnant of a sūtra dealing with the same topic found in the Central Asian (Turfan) collection (SHT V 1445+1447), which was brought to my attention by Paul Harrison, probably represents a parallel to the G sūtra. Two Chinese translations of this sūtra have been identified by Paul Harrison (1997: 272), and further Chinese sūtras dealing with the same topic have been

---

[7] I adopt the spelling *sutra* rather than *sūtra* here and in the G titles proposed for the other two sūtras because this is the expected and attested G form of the word as written in Kharoṣṭhī script. Skt. *sūtra* appears in G as *sutra* in an abhidharma text in the BL collection in the phrase *nasti śadehi sutrehi anuyujidavo* (Frag. 28 [= frame 52], v86), "it is not the case that [this view] is confirmed in hundreds of sūtras," and *eva śad[e]hi sutrehi anuyujidava* (Frag. 28 [frame 52], v87), "[this view] is thus confirmed in hundreds of sūtras." (I am indebted to Collett Cox, who is currently editing these mss., for providing these references.) The word also appears as such in the Niya documents (Boyer, Rapson, and Senart 1920–9: index, s.v. *sutra*), mostly in the original sense of "string" (e.g., 209 obv.3, 420 obv.8), though it may have the Buddhist technical sense in *suvaṃniya nama sutra* (390 obv.6; see Thomas 1933: 60). See Salomon 2000: § 1.4.1 for the proposed title *Khargaviṣaṇa-sutra for the G version of the P Khaggavisāṇa-sutta.

brought to my attention by Jan Nattier. The first parallel is in the Za jing sishisi bian, An Shigao's anthology of EĀ sūtras (T 2 no. 150a p. 877b27–c15, [sūtra 11 according to the T edition, sūtra 26 according to the numbering of Harrison 1997: 272]). The second is in the Za ahan jing, the SĀ (T 2 no. 99 [sūtra 879] p. 221b16–c5). Both are quite close to the G and P versions, the main difference being once again the order in which the four *prahāṇa*s are listed. Like the Pali, the Chinese sūtras end in verse, though An Shigao's translation is in prose form.

Neither the G, Skt., nor Chinese versions of the sūtra bear titles. The E[e] of both the P sutta (AN II 16–7) and its commentary likewise have no titles, but the Burmese and Thai editions give the title Saṃvara-sutta to this sutta, based on the entry *saṃvaraṃ* in the uddāna. The title Padhāna-sutta, based on the uddāna entry *padhānaṃ* (E[e]), *padhānāni* (B[e] and S[e]), is given to the preceding sutta, no. 13 in the Catukka-nipāta, which deals with the same topic but defines the four *padhāna*s differently. A second AN sutta, no. 69 in the Catukka-nipāta (AN II 74), which differs from sutta 14 of the Catukka-nipāta (AN II 16–7) only in the definitions given, is also entitled Padhāna-sutta in the Burmese and Thai editions, based on the uddāna entry *padhānaṃ*. As the main topic of this G sūtra is the four *prasaṇa*s, the G sūtra will be referred to as the Prasaṇa-sutra, and the P parallel will be referred to as the Saṃvara-sutta.

1.3. The Three Sūtras as Part of an Ekottarikāgama Collection

As noted above, the P parallel to the first G sūtra on this scroll, the Dhoṇa-sutra, is sutta 36 of the Catukka-nipāta of the AN, while the P parallel to the third G sūtra, the Prasaṇa-sutra, is sutta 14 of the Catukka-nipāta. Although the second G sūtra, the Budhabayaṇa-sutra, has no P parallel, it is interesting that the structure of the sūtra is provided by the four postures, which also provide the structure of suttas 11 and 12 of the P Catukka-nipāta. As discussed in greater detail in § 9.1, the theme of these two P suttas is *viriya,* "energy," which is synonymous with *padhāna,* "effort," the topic of suttas 13 and 14 of the Catukka-nipāta. In suttas 11 and 12 of the Catukka-nipāta the concept of *viriya* is elaborated in two distinct ways around the frame of the four postures, and suttas 13 and 14 provide two different definitions of the four *padhāna*s, one general and one specific. In the G Budhabayaṇa-sutra the central concepts are *budhabayaṇa,* "the word or teaching of the Buddha," and *sato kamatu,* which can be taken to mean either "good action" or "the practice of mindfulness," and whether or not it is easy to perform in each of the four postures. Therefore, there seems to be no overt thematic connection between this G sūtra and suttas 11 and 12 of the P Catukka-nipāta, the G Prasaṇa-sutra, or suttas 13 and 14 of the P Catukka-nipāta, the last five of which deal with energy and effort. Similarly, there seems to be no thematic relationship between the G Dhoṇa- and Budhabayaṇa-sutras, for the theme of the former appears to be the Buddha's identity and his status in the world, central to which is the destruction of the "influxes" or "taints" (P *āsava*/BHS *āsrava, āśrava;* the actual word has not survived in the Gāndhārī but must have been present in the intact scroll).

Because all three G sūtras have an association with the number 4, and because two of the sūtras have parallels in the Catukka-nipāta, while the third, the Budhabayaṇa-sutra, is structurally parallel to at least two suttas of the Catukka-nipāta, it is tempting to see this collection of G sūtras as part of a Section of Fours (Skt. *Catuṣka-nipāta*) of a G Ekottarikāgama (more will be said about this title below). Further, as the latter part of the third sūtra was presumably continued on a second scroll, it is possible that the surviving scroll was part of a multivolume Section of Fours and perhaps also part of a multivolume Ekottarikāgama (see Salomon 1999: 24, 90–1). The recent discovery of the Senior manuscripts, which may represent a portion of a G Saṃyuktāgama (see Preface), supports the hypothesis that we are dealing with a section of a G āgama since it proves the existence of āgamas in Gāndhārī, or at least of manuscripts containing large numbers of sūtras from a particular āgama (see Salomon 1999: 6–7, 57–8; Salomon and Schopen 1984: 120–1). There are, however, alternative interpretations. But in order to explore these alternatives, it is first necessary to discuss what survives of the EĀ/AN collections and to document the character of this material.

1.4. The Survival of Ekottarikāgama/Aṅguttara-nikāya Collections

The three sūtras presented in this publication may be the first G EĀ-type sūtras to come to light and may even represent the first fragments of a G EĀ, but they are not necessarily the first examples of EĀ material in the G language. Salomon and Schopen have argued that a passage in the G inscription of the Apraca king Indravarman referring to establishing relics of the Buddha is a quotation from "some redaction of the *Ekottarāgama*" (1984: 120) written in Gāndhārī and that this example of a quoted passage, "and by extension some version of the *Ekottarāgama,* had wide currency in the Kharoṣṭhī area around the beginning of the Christian era, and perhaps somewhat earlier" (1984: 121). Although this remains speculative (see the criticism in Fussman: 1989: 442 n. 21), the BL Kharoṣṭhī documents and the Senior manuscripts prove beyond doubt that a great variety of Buddhist texts, including collections of sūtras, were in use in the Gandhāran region at this period. The epigraphic "quotation" or paraphrase provides further evidence that certain sectors of the Gandhāran population were familiar with such textual sources.

The P AN of the Theravādins (or, more precisely, the Theravādins of the Mahāvihara in Sri Lanka) is the only complete EĀ/AN collection to survive in an Indic language.[8] Although presented as a complete text, the exact structure of the AN is by no means fixed, with the exact number of suttas it contains being uncertain.[9] In his preface to his edition of volume V of the AN, Hardy stated: "If we are to judge from our MSS., we may fairly assume three different versions of the Aṅguttara, a Sinhalese, a Burmese, and a Siamese" (1900: iii).

---

[8] For bibliographic information on the E^{e} and translations, see Norman 1983: 54 n. 136 and von Hinüber 1996: 38–9, to which should be added the English translation of books 1–3 by Gooneratne (1913) and of book 4 by Jayasundere (1925).

[9] See von Hinüber 1996: § 77; Warder 1961: xii; and the introductions to each volume of the E^{e} of the AN.

The literal meaning of the P title is "the by-one-limb-more collection" (Norman 1983: 54; cf. von Hinüber 1996: § 76). It was C. A. F. Rhys Davids (1932: vi) who coined the now standard English title *The Book of the Gradual Sayings* for the AN in her introduction to Woodward's translation of volume I, whereas Jayasundere entitled his 1925 translation of the Catukka-nipāta *The Book of the Numerical Sayings*. The German translation by Nyanatiloka bears the title *Die Lehrreden des Buddha aus der angereihten Sammlung Anguttara-nikāya* (3rd ed., 1969).

The title Aṅguttara-nikāya is particular to the Theravādins, whereas other schools seemed to have used Ekottarikāgama or Ekottarāgama (see, e.g., Lamotte 1988: 149 ff.). P equivalents to the latter are encountered in noncanonical P sources. Apart from the well-known examples in the P Milindapañha (Mil), where the AN is referred to as the Ekuttaranikāya (362.17–8) and Ekuttarikanikāya (392.2), noncanonical P sources also attest Ekuttara(-Saṃyuttaka), Ekuttarika, and Ekuttariya (see CPD, s.vv. for references). Further, the word *ekautiraka-baṇaka* (= Skt. *ekottarika-bhāṇaka*) is recorded in a Sinh. inscription (see Norman 1989b: 33 n. 26 [= CP, vol. IV, p. 97 n. 3]). The terms *ekuttaranikāya* and *ekuttarikanikāya* in the Mil and *ekuttarika* in the Peṭakopadesa (Peṭ) have been interpreted by Bechert (1955–7: 352–3) as an indication of the non-Theravādin origins for these two texts.

No complete Skt. EĀ survives. The most extensive surviving portion of an EĀ comes from the Gilgit manuscripts and consists of sections of the nipātas on the ones and twos. These were first edited by Yusen Okubo (1982).[10] All fragments were then definitively edited by Chandrabhāl Tripāṭhī (1995), who attributes this text to the Mūlasarvāstivādins (1995: 28, 35).

Several Central Asian (Turfan) sūtra fragments published in the *Sanskrithandschriften aus den Turfan-Funden* (SHT) have been identified as "Fragmente aus dem Einer-Abschnitt (*ekanipātā*) des Ekottarāgama" (SHT III 974, 975, 1000; see Waldschmidt 1980: 169–74; Tripāṭhī 1995: 19), and several other fragments are tentatively assigned to the EĀ: SHT I 590 (see VII, p. 308), III 952 (Trika-nipāta), VI 1395 (Eka-nipāta), V 1108 (Pañcaka-nipāta).[11] In some cases fragments are merely identified by the editors as Skt. parallels to P AN suttas: SHT I 620R (see IV, p. 339) (Ekādasaka-nipāta),[12] III 977 (Tika-nipāta), V 1031a (Tika-nipāta), VI 1326 Bl.212 (Navaka-nipāta), 1341 (Chakka-nipāta),

---

[10] The Ujjain leaves of the ms. were first published by Sudha Sengupta (1975) (mentioned by Okubo 1982: 120 and Tripāṭhī 1995: 12 n. 5).

[11] Harrison (1997: 269, 274) draws attention to the fact that the Skt. fragments SHT VII 1732 and V 1108 provide parallels to sūtras 9 and 35 of An Shigao's anthology, respectively.

[12] The parallel is given as AN no. 11.16 (V 342) of the Ekādasa-nipāta. However, since the same list, minus three items, also occurs in the Aṭṭhaka-nipāta, AN no. 8.1 (IV 150), it may have belonged to the latter section. Similarly, SHT I 620V was identified as a sūtra with a parallel in the Skt. MPS § 41.12–4 (cf. § 41.5–9) that lists the four places of pilgrimage. However, the P parallel to the similar MPS § 41.5–9 occurs at AN no. 4.118 (II 120) within the Catukka-nipāta. As this fragment contains two distinct sūtras and as the number of items listed in each is not certain (despite the P parallels), it is therefore possible that they belong to the EĀ.

1360 (Chakka- or Dasaka-nipāta), and 1379 (Navaka-nipāta).[13] Other fragments that have been identified as belonging to the SĀ or to other texts may in fact belong to the EĀ, for example, SHT V 1445+1447 (see below, pp. 19–20). Further, given that Buddhist sūtra literature is so repetitive, the Skt. equivalents of some EĀ sūtras may be found in texts such as the Skt. Mahāparinirvāṇa-, Daśottara-, or Saṅgīti-sūtras of the DĀ, since many of their component elements have parallels in the P AN, although texts included in the P AN did not necessarily form part of a Skt. EĀ. These Central Asian sūtra fragments are normally attributed to the Sarvāstivādins.

Finally, some EĀ sūtras are quoted in noncanonical Skt. sources. For example, the Saptamaithunasaṃyukta-sūtra, which has a parallel in the P AN and in the Chinese EĀ, is quoted in the Śikṣāsamuccaya (see Hahn 1977), while quotations from the EĀ or, at least, from passages with parallels in the Chinese EĀ and/or P AN are also found in such texts as the Abhidharmakośabhāṣya (see Pāsādika 1989: 135, index).[14]

None of the Gilgit or Central Asian fragments preserve titles for either the component sūtras or for the āgama itself. The forms Ekottarikā and Ekottarikāgama for the title of the āgama are, however, attested in several other Skt. sources. In the Mūlasarvāstivāda-vinaya (MSV), also found among the Gilgit manuscripts, we find *vistareṇa vairaṃbhyasūtram ekottarikāgame catuṣkanipāte* (MSV I 45.19). In the Divyāvadāna (Divy) there appears *ekottarikā. ayaṃ tāvat khustikayā ekottarikayā dharmaṃ deśayati* (329.2–3; cf. 329.6–7), while the Mahāvyutpatti (1421) lists the title as *ekottarikāgamaḥ*. The Karmavibhaṅgopadeśa (Lévi 1932) has *bhagavatā sūtram uktam ekottarike* (153.11–2), *yathaikottarikāgratāsūtra uktam* (157.9–10), and *atraikottarikāsūtraṃ* (167.2). Further Skt. examples are *ekottarikāgama* in the Abhidharmakośavyākhyā (188.25) and possibly *ekotta(*r)[i]* in the Central Asian (Turfan) fragment (see SWTF, s.v.; Tripāṭhī 1995: 20 n. 28). In contrast, I have not been able to find any examples of the form *ekottarāgama* in Skt. sources. Neither form seems to be attested in Indian inscriptions (excluding Sri Lanka), Skt. or otherwise; the word is not listed in Tsukamoto 1996–8.

Contemporary scholars disagree as to whether the proper title of the āgama is Ekottarāgama or Ekottarikāgama. Despite the absence of textual or epigraphical examples, the form Ekottarāgama is favored by, among others, Lamotte in his *History of Indian Buddhism* (1988: e.g., 150 ff.), the editors of the Central Asian fragments (SHT III 974, 975, 1000; VI 1395), and the editors of the Gilgit EĀ fragment (Okubo 1982; Tripāṭhī 1995); Tripāṭhī employs this form despite being aware of the occurrence of *ekottarikāgama* in the Gilgit MSV (1995: 20 n. 28). In contrast, the form Ekottarikāgama is preferred by Waldschmidt (1980: 136 ff., 169 ff.; cf. 174, where he refers to the Gilgit fragment of the EĀ with this term, despite Tripāṭhī's use of Ekottarāgama) and Harrison (1997). The same variation in the title of this āgama is encountered in references to the

---

[13] Cf. Tripāṭhī 1995: 19; see also SHT V 1161, identified as containing SĀ sūtras with a P parallel in the Tika-nipāta.

[14] Lamotte (1967: 106n) notes that the EĀ is frequently quoted in the Mahākarmavibhaṅga and its commentary (Lévi 1932).

Chinese translation.[15] As only Ekottarikāgama is attested, I adopt that title throughout this study. (For the proposed G form, see pp. 24–5.)

Besides the P AN, which represents the only complete EĀ/AN to have survived in an Indic language, a complete EĀ is extant in Chinese translation. This is the Zengyi ahan jing (T no. 125) translated in A.D. 384–5 by Dharmanandin and revised by Gautama Saṅghadeva in A.D. 397–8 (see Mayeda 1985: 102; Waldschmidt 1980: 137 n. 4, 169 n. 168). This Chinese EĀ is said to contain many Mahāyāna additions (Lamotte 1967, 1988: 154; Harrison 1997: 279–80; cf. Mayeda 1985: 103). Although often associated with the Mahāsaṅghikas (see Harrison 1997: 279 n. 55 for references), it has also been attributed to the Dharmaguptakas and other schools (Mayeda 1985: 103). A translation of this Chinese EĀ has been appearing in installments in *Buddhist Studies Review,* initially in French, now continued in English (Huyên-Vi 1984–).

Apart from the Zengyi ahan jing (T no. 125), there is also an anthology of forty-four EĀ sūtras in Chinese, the Za jing sishisi bian, which was compiled and translated by An Shigao. This is a much earlier translation than the Zengyi ahan jing. The original arrangement of this text was established by Harrison, who proposed a Sarvāstivādin affiliation (1997: 280). That it is an anthology is proven by the fact that the numerical sequence is incomplete, with no sūtras from the Sections of Ones, Sixes, Sevens, or Tens (or Elevens), and by the small number of sūtras from any one section (see Harrison 1997: 276).[16]

Finally, although there is no equivalent to the EĀ in Tibetan,[17] there are a number of Tib. versions of EĀ/AN sūtras. For example, Skilling (1993) has drawn attention to Tib. translations of three AN suttas (pp. 117–8 [1.6.A], 119 ff. [1.7.A], 123–4 [1.8]). Also, Tib. equivalents of EĀ/AN sūtras occur as quotes within other texts, for example, the Tib. translation of the Saptamaithunasaṃyukta-sūtra quoted in the Sikṣasāmuccaya (see Hahn 1977: 215 ff.), or as components of longer texts, similar to the Skt. material discussed above.[18]

---

[15] It is referred to as the Ekottarāgama by, e.g., Lamotte (1988: 154), Nakamura (1980: 39), and Mayeda (1985: 102–3), but as the Ekottarikāgama by, e.g., Hahn (1977), Waldschmidt (1980: 169–74), and Harrison (1997: 279–80).

[16] The absence of any sūtras dealing with eleven things may reflect the lack of such a section in the original EĀ (see Norman 1983: 56–7).

[17] In a catalog of translated works from the beginning of the ninth century, a translation of a/the gCig las 'phros pa'i lung in 18 Bampo is listed. This title corresponds to *ekottar(ik)āgama,* but the work is apparently lost (see Lalou 1953: no. 274). I am indebted to Jens-Uwe Hartmann for bringing this reference to my attention.

[18] The Tib. translations of a number of the EĀ sūtras in An Shigao's anthology (T no. 150a) found in texts such as Śamathadeva's Abhidharmakośopāyikā are noted throughout Harrison 1997 (e.g., 269 n. 26, 270 n. 29, 271 nn. 32, 33).

1.5. The Character of EĀ/AN Sūtras/Suttas and the Organizational Principles of the EĀ/AN Collections

Whereas a number of important studies have been undertaken on the character and formation of the Vinaya- and Abhidhamma-/Abhidharma-piṭakas and, among the nikāyas/āgamas, on the DN/DĀs, MN/MĀs, and SN/SĀs, there is a relative paucity of research on the AN and EĀs. The most comprehensive surveys or overviews of the P AN to date are van Zeyst's 1965 article "Aṅguttara Nikāya" in the *Encyclopaedia of Buddhism* (1.629–55) and Hardy's series of appendixes in volume 5 of the PTS edition (Hardy 1900: 370–422).[19] Pande (1974: especially 230–47) attempts to identify strata in the AN. Tripāṭhī (1995: especially 25) provides some discussion of the Gilgit fragment of the EĀ edited by him, while Harrison's 1997 article on An Shigao's anthology of forty-four EĀ sūtras in Chinese translation establishes the order of the original text, thus providing a basis for further research, and offers some insights on the nature of the collection. Research on the Chinese EĀ, the Zengyi ahan jing (T no. 125), has primarily been conducted by Japanese scholars. For example, Akanuma (1958: 120–56) provides a list of the contents of the Zengyi ahan jing, and Mayeda (1964: 663–73) discusses the formation of the AN/EĀ collections.[20] Further studies by Japanese scholars relevant to the EĀ are mentioned in Mayeda 1985: 102–3 and Nakamura 1980: 38–9. General outlines of the Zengyi ahan jing in English can be found in the two articles on āgama in the *Encyclopaedia of Buddhism* already mentioned (Chêng 1963: 242 [left column], 243–4; Kumoi 1963: 247 [left column]), while studies of individual sūtras by Lamotte (1967), Hahn (1977), and Waldschmidt (1980: 169–74) comment on the character of the āgama as a whole.

The principle of organization in the AN/EĀs is numerical. Suttas/sūtras that are deemed to have an association with a particular number are grouped together into nipātas, "sections," "chapters," or "books," which are arranged in ascending order from the section on the ones up to the tens or elevens. Although the word *nipāta,* which is used throughout the P AN, does not occur in the Skt. fragments of the EĀ from Gilgit or Central Asia, it is attested in the Gilgit manuscripts of the MSV in *vistareṇa vairaṃbhyasūtram ekottarikāgame catuṣkanipāte* (I 45.19).[21]

---

[19] Others are Winternitz 1983: 58–64; Law 1933: 1.180–93; Norman 1983: 54–7; von Hinüber 1996: 38–41; Webb 1991: 24–7. Further information can be gained from the introductions to each volume of the edition and translation of the AN. Hazra 1994: 1.249–70 is useless, being for the most part a verbatim quote of van Zeyst's 1965 *Encyclopaedia of Buddhism* article, but without proper acknowledgment.

[20] I am indebted to Fumio Enomoto for bringing this reference to my attention. Unfortunately, its contents are not accessible to me.

[21] For *nipāta,* see Norman 1992a: xxv; Wright 1995: 221; von Hinüber 1996: 39n. Von Hinüber (1996: § 77) translates *ekanipāta* as "chapter containing of the ones." Norman 1983: 54 and the BHSD, s.v., prefer "section." In the English translation of the AN by Woodward and Hare, each nipāta is entitled "The Book of the Ones," "The Book of the Twos," etc., while in the concluding statement to each of the first three nipātas, Woodward refers to each nipāta as the "Section of the Ones," etc. (e.g., vol. I, p. 41).

With reference to the sūtras in An Shigao's Chinese EĀ anthology, Harrison (1997: 265) states that "nearly all of them display what we might call the *Ekottarikāgama* style (i.e., they approach their subject numerically)." Certainly, one of the most common types of sutta/sūtra in the AN/EĀs is that in which the numbered item or items that form the subject of the sutta/sūtra are introduced as such at the beginning; for example, "Monks, these two bright dhammas protect the world. What two?" followed by the enumeration and elaboration of the two bright dhammas,[22] or "Monks, there are these four efforts. What four?"[23] Also relatively common in, say, the Section of Ones (Eka-nipāta) are suttas/sūtras based on statements such as "Monks, I do not know of another single thing which thus developed is as workable as the mind."[24] However, there are also many suttas/sūtras where, although a numerical association is discernible, the items are not explicitly listed or where, although apparent, the numerical association could be with more than one number. For example, in the second nipāta of the Gilgit EĀ (EĀ-Skt.$^{Gil.}$ §§ 23 ff.), we find many sūtras in which the Buddha describes opposites. A translation of § 23.1a–b, which has no direct parallel in the P AN, is "Monks, I will teach you about the unrighteous and righteous assembly. . . . What is the unrighteous assembly? The assembly that engages in killing, stealing, sexual misconduct, and intoxicants is said to be unrighteous." The description of the righteous assembly is then presented in opposite terms. In other words, this sūtra has been included in the Section of Twos of this EĀ because the Buddha is teaching opposites, but since four things are being listed (killing, stealing, sexual misconduct, and intoxicants), it could also have been included in the Section of Fours (Catuṣka-nipāta).[25]

Although many suttas/sūtras in the AN/EĀs are explicitly numerical, it is probably too limiting to speak of an AN or EĀ style in the singular, for many suttas/sūtras within these collections are differently structured. In many cases the numerical association is based on secondary factors. For example, sutta 68 of the Catukka-nipāta, or Section of Fours, of the AN (II 73) is included in the Section of Fours on account of the four similes that illustrate a particular point (the similes and verse occur at Vin II 188, and the verse occurs at SN I 154). Suttas 11 and 12 of the Catukka-nipāta (AN II 13–5) are included in this nipāta based on the four postures that provide the basic structure to these suttas. Sutta 36 of the Catukka-nipāta (AN II 37–9), the Doṇa-sutta, is included in this nipāta because of the four questions the brahman Doṇa asks the Buddha, and sutta 74 (AN II 78) is included in the same nipāta based on the four types of people a new wife and a new monk feel embarrassed in front of.

Occasionally the reason for the inclusion of a sutta/sūtra in a particular nipāta is not obvious. The Catukka-nipāta of the AN provides a number of examples. One of the best

---

[22] AN no. 2.1.9 (I 51); see Harrison 1997: 269 (no. 9) for the Chinese and Skt. parallels.

[23] AN no. 4.14 (II 16); see pp. 247–9, below, for the Chinese and Skt. parallels. The G parallel is the third in our collection, the Prasaṇa-sutra.

[24] AN no. 1.3.2 (I 5); cf. similar Skt. sūtras in the Gilgit EĀ (EĀ-Skt.$^{Gil.}$ §§ 2–3).

[25] However, as the Catuṣka-nipāta of this Skt. EĀ has not survived, it cannot be determined whether it included such a sūtra.

is sutta 48 (AN II 51 = SN II 280). In this sutta the monk Visākha preaches to the monks (*sandasseti samādapeti samuttejeti sampahaṃseti*) in a skilled manner (the content of the discourse is not mentioned). The Buddha praises his manner of delivery, then utters two verses, consisting of four śloka pādas. Nowhere are four concepts or things mentioned. Is, then, the association with the number 4 based on the four synonymous verbs (*sandasseti,* etc.) or the four pādas of śloka verse? Examples of suttas in the Catukka-nipāta where the number association is only marginally more evident are the following. Sutta 39 (AN II 42–3; the verses occur at SN I 76) seems to be included on the basis of the four types of sacrifice mentioned in the first pāda of the verses[26] or perhaps on the basis of the statement in the prose section that in sacrifice cows (1), goats and sheep (2), and chickens and pigs (3) are killed and various kinds of creatures (4) are destroyed (*yaññe gāvo haññanti ajeḷakā haññanti kukkuṭasūkarā haññanti vividhā pāṇā saṅghātaṃ āpajjanti*); sutta 40 is similar but with different verses. Sutta 70 (AN II 74–6) seems to be included in the Catukka-nipāta on the basis of the four social groups mentioned (*rājāno, rājaputtā, brāhmaṇagahapatikā, negamajānapadā*). Sutta 76 (AN II 79–80 = DN II 154–5) has been included either because the Buddha asks the monks four times (the last time in slightly different wording) whether any of them have doubt concerning the Buddha, Dhamma, Saṅgha, path, or way (five things), or on the basis of the description of a monk that concludes the sutta: (*bhikkhu*) *so sotāpanno avinipātadhammo niyato sambodhiparāyano*.

Further, since the enumeration and categorization of virtually every conceivable thing—concepts, states of mind, objects of meditation, ascetic practices, types of people, attainments, causes of earthquakes, foods, virtues, types of speech, to name but a few—are so dominant a characteristic of Buddhist literature, whole suttas/sūtras or large sections of suttas/sūtras that approach their subject numerically are extremely common in all nikāyas/āgamas. The P Satipaṭṭhāna-sutta of the MN (no. 10) along with its expanded version, the Mahāsatipaṭṭhāna-suttanta of the DN (no. 22), and the Chinese counterpart in the MĀ (T 1 no. 26 [sūtra 98]) are good examples.[27] No doubt the P Satipaṭṭhāna-suttas were excluded from the P AN because of their size, though size alone is not the sole determining factor for exclusion from the AN/EĀ collections, for there are many suttas in the P AN, for example, that are as large as some MN suttas. For example, the first and second suttas of the MN, the Mūlapariyāya (I 1–6) and Sabbāsava (I 6–12), take up five and a half pages each in the E^{e}, while the third and seventh suttas, the Dhammadāyāda (I

[26] The first two lines of AN II 42–3 read *assamedhaṃ purisamedhaṃ sammāpāsaṃ vācapeyyaṃ, niraggalaṃ mahārambhā na te honti mahapphalā* (at SN I 76 the reading is *vājapeyyaṃ, niraggaḷaṃ*). The words *assamedhaṃ purisamedhaṃ sammāpāsaṃ vācapeyyaṃ, niraggaḷaṃ* occur at Sn 303, which Norman (1992a: 33, 206) takes as five sacrifices. The same list occurs at Dhp-G^{K} 196 (see Woodward 1933: 50 n.1; Brough 1962: 242; Norman 1992a: 206).

[27] In contrast, the structure of the P Saṅgīti- and Dasottara-suttantas of the DN (nos. 33 and 34) and their Skt. (Stache-Rosen 1968; Mittel 1957; Schlingloff 1962) and Chinese (Chinese DĀ, T 1 no. 1 [sūtras 9 and 10]) counterparts, the Saṅgīti- and Daśottara-sūtras of the DĀ, is the same as the AN/EĀs, covering an extended number range.

12–6) and Vatthūpama (I 36–40), take up four pages each (though of course the abbreviations need to be filled out to establish the full text in each case).[28] The P AN has several suttas that are a similar size or larger, though these are admittedly not the norm. For example, within the Mahāvaggas of the Catukka-nipāta and Chakka-nipāta, sutta no. 4.198 (II 205–11) is six pages long (this sutta is parallel to the latter part of sutta 51 of the MN [I 343–9]); no. 6.55 (III 374–9) is five pages; no. 6.60 (III 392–9) is seven pages; and nos. 6.62–3 (III 402–17) are seven and a half pages each. Although these figures are imprecise, with the complete text of each sutta once again needing to be established, these examples nonetheless illustrate the point that not all suttas in the P AN are short.

If we turn to the Skt. EĀ fragment from Gilgit, which includes most of the first and second nipātas, we find that all of the sūtras are short, as are the suttas of the same nipātas in the P AN, though it is impossible to know what was included in the higher nipātas of this EĀ. In contrast, the Chinese EĀ (T no. 125) seems to represent quite a different collection from the P AN and the Skt. EĀ from Gilgit, containing many long sūtras whose P parallels are found in other nikāyas. Examples of sūtras in the Chinese EĀ (T no. 125) with parallels in the P MN are the following: a parallel to part of the Satipaṭṭhāna-sutta (MN no. 10);[29] a parallel to the Vatthūpama-sutta (MN no. 7);[30] and a parallel to the Dhammadāyāda-sutta (MN no. 3).[31] The relatively small size of the last two MN suttas was mentioned above. Further examples are listed in Akanuma's catalog (1958: 120–56).

Although no complete MN or DN suttas appear in the P AN, there are many examples of the same P sutta occurring in both the AN and the SN and in other canonical texts such as the Udāna and Itivuttaka as well. Examples are AN no. 4.45 (II 47–9) = SN no. 2.3.6 (I 61–2); AN no. 4.48 (II 51) = SN no. 21.7 (II 280); and AN no. 9.70 (IV 308–13) = SN no. 51.10 (V 258–63) = Ud 62 = DN II 102–7. AN no. 10.89 (V 170–4) combines SN suttas 6.1.9 and 10 (I 149–53).[32] In other words, these suttas, which are comparatively short, have been included in the SN on the basis of their subject matter and in the AN on the basis of their numerical association. Yet, as noted by Norman, even here there is a "blurring of distinction between the Saṃyutta-nikāya and the Aṅguttara-nikāya" that "can be seen in the way in which some *vaggas* [of the AN] contain *suttas* which all deal with one and the same subject, so that they resemble a *saṃyutta*" (Norman 1983: 56, cf. 50; see also Rhys Davids 1910: viii). Norman gives the following examples: "The ten *suttas* of *vagga* (1.1) deal with the relationship between husband and wife; *vagga* (1.14) has 80 *suttas* giving the names of the most prominent male and female disciples and their

---

[28] In Allon 1997: 274–5, I established the full text of the Udumbarikasīhanāda-suttanta of the DN (no. 25). When abbreviations were restored, the complete text was 34% larger than the text of the E[e].

[29] T 2 no. 125 pp. 567c–569b; the French translation appears in BSR 6.1 (1989): 39–46.

[30] T 2 no. 125 pp. 573c–575a; the French translation appears in BSR 8.1–2 (1991): 131–9.

[31] T 2 no. 125 pp. 587c–589a; the English translation appears in BSR 12.1 (1995): 51–7.

[32] A list of some AN passages found elsewhere in the canon is given by Hardy (1900: viii note) in his preface to vol. V of his edition of the AN. See also Rhys Davids and Rhys Davids (1959: 72).

virtues; *vagga* (1.20) contains 262 suttas on different kinds of meditation leading to *nibbāna; vagga* (5.18) has ten *suttas* about *upāsakas"* (1983: 56).

In summary, the characteristic that defines the AN/EĀ collections and distinguishes them from the other three major nikāyas/āgamas is the principle of organizing suttas/sūtras according to a numerical arrangement, a principle used elsewhere in Buddhist literature and in Indian literature generally (see Norman 1969a: xxiii–xxiv, 1983: 28; Gombrich 1990: 23–4; von Hinüber 1996: § 78). In the case of the P AN, at least, this is combined with a tendency to exclude long suttas, though suttas as long as the shorter suttas of the MN are occasionally found. In the case of the Chinese EĀ (T no. 125) the tendency to exclude longer sūtras seems to have been relaxed at some stage or, perhaps, was never operational. And although many suttas/sūtras of the AN/EĀ collections "approach their subject numerically," that is, have an explicit numerical association, such suttas/sūtras cannot be considered to be the norm, for in the case of the P AN, at least, the numerical association of many of its suttas is vague and based on an extensive range of alternative factors. In view of the above, and given that Buddhist sutta/sūtra literature is characteristically enumerative and classificatory and is pervaded by a tendency to proliferate similar elements (e.g., to give four similes rather than one), it can be seen that virtually the entire corpus of discourses attributed to the Buddha and his monks could qualify for inclusion in this nikāya/āgama.

Subject matter is another factor that seems to have been operational in the formation of the P AN and that may have limited the nature of the material that could be included in the AN. As noted by Norman (1983: 55–6), such well-known Buddhist concepts as the three refuges (*saraṇa*), the three characteristics of existence (*lakkhaṇa*), and the Noble Eightfold Path are missing from the AN, though they are present in the SN.[33] C. A. F. Rhys Davids's remarks are of some interest here: "We see that most of the doctrines, taught in the Anguttara through the mnemonic of numbering heads or features, are in nearly every case *not* the numbered lists with which we are most familiar. These were so important that the number needed no emphasis, and, further, that they were allotted each of them an entire Saṃyutta. The Anguttara lists, on the other hand, refer very largely to analyses of social and individual character, and of phases and stages of mental culture." The "main tenets," she continues, "like the Paṭicca-samuppāda, Four Satipaṭṭhānas, Eightfold Path, Jhānas and Khandhas, are very fully dealt with in the Saṃyutta, but are nearly negligible quantities in the Anguttara" (1910: vii). And based on a cursory review of the subjects dealt with in the AN and SN, which shows that they do not cover the same topics, Rhys Davids further proposed that it was not unreasonable to conclude that these two nikāyas "were not independently compiled" (1910: viii; see also Norman 1983: 50, 56).

Where does all this leave our three G sūtras? As we have seen, the first and third sūtras, the Dhoṇa-sutra and Prasaṇa-sutra, have parallels in the P AN (the Doṇa- and Saṃvara-suttas), while the second, the Budhabayaṇa-sutra, is structurally similar to two

---

[33] See von Hinüber 1996: § 82 and the review of von Hinüber 1996 by Cousins (1998: 155). Rhys Davids (1910: vi–viii) makes a number of interesting comments based on the indexes to the AN.

AN suttas that precede the P Saṃvara-sutta. This being the case, and given that one of the three Chinese translations of the Dhoṇa-sutra is found in the EĀ, and one of the two Chinese translations of the Prasaṇa-sutra is found in An Shigao's anthology of EĀ sūtras, it would perhaps seem pointless to ask whether these G sūtras could be anything other than EĀ sūtras. But given that there is a blurring of distinction between the P AN and SN, at least, and given that the other two Chinese translations of the Dhoṇa-sutra and the second of the two translations of the Prasaṇa-sutra are found in the SĀs, the question is indeed appropriate. The answer, of course, is that it is highly unlikely that these three sūtras belonged to a SĀ, for, as we have seen, there seems to be no thematic relationship between them. Rather, their grouping is based on a numerical factor, namely, on the number 4.

In the course of the above discussion Norman's observation that the P AN contains whole vaggas whose suttas deal with the same topic was noted. In fact, the organizational principle of grouping suttas of similar subject matter together within the P AN is far more extensive than Norman's statement suggests. As noted by a number of scholars, there is a tendency in the P AN for two, or occasionally more, suttas that deal with the same topic to be placed together (Rhys Davids 1933: v, 1934: vi; Winternitz 1983: 2.59; van Zeyst 1965: 629 [right column]–630 [left column], then throughout the remainder of the article). For example, in the first two vaggas of the Catukka-nipāta we find the following pairings: the first two suttas (nos. 4.1–2) deal with virtue, concentration, understanding, and liberation (*sīla, samādhi, paññā, vimutti*); the next two suttas (nos. 4.3–4) concern the untaught fool (*bālo avyatto asappuriso*); the fifth and sixth suttas (nos. 4.5–6) each describe four types of individual who are found in the world (*cattāro puggalā*); the seventh (no. 4.7) is concerned with the four types of individual who are, among other things, confident (*visārada*), while the topic of the eighth (no. 4.8) is the four confidences (*vesārajja*) of a Tathāgata; the connection between the ninth (no. 4.9) and tenth (no. 4.10) is less apparent, but it seems to be *taṅhā* (no. 4.9) and *kāma* (no. 4.10), with *saṃsāra* occurring in the verses of both. As I have already noted above, no. 4.11 and no. 4.12, the first and second suttas of the second vagga (the Cara-vagga), deal with energy (*viriya*) within the framework of the four postures, while the next two suttas (nos. 4.13–4) define the four efforts (*padhāna*). Since *viriya* and *padhāna* are synonymous, the first four suttas of the second vagga of the Catukka-nipāta are thematically linked. The connection between nos. 4.15 and 4.16 is not so obvious, but the topic of the remaining four suttas of the vagga (nos. 4.17–20) is rebirth states (*gati*).

This thematic linking, particularly pairing, of suttas is for the most part consistent throughout the remainder of the Catukka-nipāta.[34] In some cases the pairing consists of suttas that deal with the same topic, one in brief, the other in full. Particularly interesting are suttas 4.161 and 4.162, which deal with the four *paṭipadā;* the uddāna entries for

[34] The results of my study of the Catukka-nipāta will be published in the future.

these two suttas are *saṅkhittaṃ,* "brief," and *vitthataṃ,* "expanded" (AN II 157).[35] More common are the pairs or longer sequences of suttas that deal with the same topic in different ways, as in nos. 4.13 and 4.14, already mentioned, where effort (*padhāna*) is defined first in general terms and then in specific terms (see chap. 10 for details).[36] The principle of arranging suttas within the AN primarily on a numerical basis but with a secondary tendency to group suttas within each numbered section (*nipāta*) thematically parallels the organization of verses within the Theragāthā and Therīgāthā (Norman 1969a: xxiii–xxv, 1971: xxii–xxiv).

Another organizational principle that seems to be operational in the P Catukka-nipāta, at least, is the grouping of suttas with verses at the beginning of the nipāta (see van Zeyst 1965: 634 [left column]). The suttas of the first seven vaggas, that is, the first 70 of the 271 suttas of the Catukka-nipāta (according to the numbering in the E[e]), conclude with one or more verses.[37] This is parallel to the SN, where the first vagga, the Sagātha-vagga, consists entirely of mixed prose-verse suttas, a genre referred to as *geyya* in Pali, *geya* in Sanskrit.[38]

Despite being few and fragmentary, the Central Asian Skt. fragments of EĀ sūtras suggest that the organizational tendencies observed in the P AN were operational in that EĀ too. The three fragments SHT III 974, 975, and 1000, identified as "Fragmente aus dem Einer-Abschnitt (*ekanipāta*) des Ekottarāgama," contain sūtras based on the expression "I know of no single thing" (*nāham ekadharmam api samanupaśyāmi*) (cf. SHT VI 1395), parallel to the suttas of the first vaggas of the P Eka-nipāta and to several vargas and sūtras of the Skt. EĀ from Gilgit (EĀ-Skt.[Gil.], e.g., §§ 2–3). Of those fragments that may belong to the EĀ, SHT V 1108 is the most interesting for our purposes. It contains a number of "sūtras" that deal with different topics and that are all associated with the number 5, and most of them appear to be in thematically linked pairs. Finally, as shown in the study of the Prasaṇa-sutra (chap. 10), fragment SHT V 1445+1447, which was identified by the editor, E. Waldschmidt, as a "Fragment aus dem Prahāṇasūtra (II) des Saṃyuktāgama" on the basis of the Chinese parallel in the SĀ, in fact contains the remnants of two sūtras, rather than one, both dealing with the topic of effort (*prahāṇa*). These two sūtras are probably parallel to suttas 13 and 14 of the Catukka-nipāta of the AN. Noting that An Shigao's anthology of EĀ sūtras (T no. 150a) contains a translation

---

[35] A list of such pairs in the AN is given by Hardy (1900) as appendix III in his edition of the AN (vol. V, p. 420), to which can be added nos. 4.146–7 from the Catukka-nipāta, as well as nos. 4.161–2 just mentioned.

[36] Examples in the Catukka-nipāta of groups of more than two suttas dealing with the same topic are the following: nos. 4.87–90 (4.91–100 similarly list types of individuals), 4.123–6, 4.151–5, 4.161–8, 4.201–6, 4.247–50.

[37] In some cases it is unclear whether the concluding "verse" is, in fact, metrical, as in no. 4.13 (AN II 15).

[38] For *geyya/geya,* see Norman 1983: 15; Lamotte 1988: 144; Kalupahana 1965: 617 (left column); Mayeda 1964: 24 ff. In some sūtras in the Gilgit fragment of the EĀ only the verses are written, the prose being left to be supplied by the reciter based on the preceding sūtra. The uddāna entry for these sūtras is *sagīyakaṃ* (EĀ-Skt.[Gil.] §§ 15.0, 15.4, cf. 33.4; see Tripāṭhī 1995: 25).

of the Prahāṇa-sūtra parallel to sutta 14 of the P Catukka-nipāta, Harrison (1997: 272) suggests that Waldschmidt's ascription of this fragment to the SĀ "must now be reconsidered"; that is, the fragment should possibly be assigned to the EĀ. If the two sūtras on this fragment do in fact belong to the EĀ, they provide yet another example of a thematically linked pair of sūtras in the Skt. EĀ of the Sarvāstivādins.

The organization of the sūtras in the Skt. EĀ fragment from Gilgit, which preserves most of the Section of Ones and Section of Twos (Eka- and Dvika-nipātas), seems to closely match that of the parallel sections of the P AN. As already noted, sūtras based on the phrase "I know of no single thing" (*nāham ekadharmam api samanupaśyāmi*) are grouped together (EĀ-Skt.[Gil.], e.g., §§ 2–3), while many sūtras in the second nipāta involve opposites and are based on the phrase "Monks, I will teach you *x* and *y*" (*vo bhikṣavaḥ . . . deśayiṣyāmi;* EĀ-Skt.[Gil.], e.g., §§ 23 ff.) (see Tripāṭhī 1995: 25).

The case of An Shigao's Chinese anthology of EĀ sūtras (T no. 150a) discussed by Harrison (1997) is an interesting one, for in this anthology of forty-four sūtras that were probably selected from a complete EĀ, thematic or other connections between the sūtras are discernible. According to the ordering of the forty-four sūtras established by Harrison, we find the following connections: the first eight sūtras (nos. 1–8) each list two types of persons who are either hard to find in the world, easy to satisfy in the world, or hard to surpass in the world (these can be grouped into pairs: nos. 1–2, 3–4, 5–6, 7–8); sūtra nos. 10 and 11 both share the phrase "body, speech, and mind"; nos. 16 and 17, whose parallels are grouped together in the P AN (nos. 3.68–9), both deal with evil; nos. 23–5 each list four types of persons; nos. 30 and 31 deal with gifts; nos. 37 and 38 deal with five undesirable consequences of certain things; nos. 39 and 40, which are also grouped together in the P AN (nos. 5.215–6), present the five disadvantages of certain things; and nos. 43 and 44 are perhaps connected by "boils" (?).[39] Of course, it cannot currently be determined whether these connections reflect the organizational tendencies of the collection upon which this anthology was based or An Shigao's own inclinations.

Several scholars have commented on the fact that the Chinese EĀ (T no. 125) differs from the P AN, Skt. fragments of the EĀs belonging to the Sarvāstivādins and Mūlasarvāstivādins, and An Shigao's anthology of EĀ sūtras in Chinese translation (T no. 150a) in a number of its characteristics, including Mahāyānist influences and the addition of comparatively long sūtras and sūtras of a composite nature (Chêng 1963: 244; Kumoi 1963: 247 [left column]; Lamotte 1967: 106, 116; Waldschmidt 1980: 171, 173–4; Tripāṭhī 1995: 35; Harrison 1997: 279–80). As far as I can determine from those sections of this work that have so far been translated into French and English (all of the Section of Ones and most of the Section of Twos; BSR 1.2–, 1984–) and from the entries in Akanuma's catalog (1958: 120–56), it nonetheless seems that the organizational principles of the other AN/EĀs outlined above are also evident in at least some sections of the Chinese collection. As in the P AN, whole "parts" (品), or "vargas," consisting of sūtras dealing with a similar topic are encountered. For example, the second part (varga)

[39] These comments are tentative, as they are based on my reading of Harrison's English summary. They need to be verified by those working with Chinese Buddhist texts.

of the text consists of ten sūtras that each list one of the ten things to be remembered, *"Les dix commémorations,"*[40] and the third part consists of ten sūtras elaborating each of these ten things to be remembered.[41] The fourth, fifth, sixth, and seventh parts consist of sūtras that list the foremost among the Buddha's monks, nuns, and male and female lay followers, respectively.[42] All but the first of the ten sūtras of the eighth part describe the Tathāgata. The P parallels to some of these are grouped together in the Ekapuggala-vagga, which precedes the Etadagga-vagga, the vagga that contains the series of suttas just mentioned that list the foremost monks, etc.[43]

Similarly, pairs of sūtras, small runs of sūtras on a common theme, and sūtras that share some element in common are also encountered in the Chinese EĀ. For example, the fifth sūtra of the sixteenth "part" lists a series of ten opposites, the first bad, the second good,[44] while the sixth sūtra lists a series of eight opposites, the first false, the second correct.[45] The topic of the tenth sūtra of the same part is Rāhula's practice, a sūtra that has no parallel in Pali,[46] and the next sūtra, the first of the seventeenth part, is the Chinese version of the P Mahārāhula-sutta, which occurs in the MN (no. 62).[47] These two sūtras are without equivalents in any other AN/EĀ collection (P, Skt., or An Shigao's anthology) but have been grouped together in the Chinese EĀ, albeit across varga boundaries,[48] because they both are accounts of the same monk. The second and third sūtras of the seventeenth part both present two things that are rare in the world, parallel to a number of suttas in the P Puggala-vagga,[49] while the fifth and sixth sūtras of this part deal with false

---

[40] T 2 no. 125 pp. 552c–553b; French translation: BSR 3.1 (1986): 31. According to Akanuma's catalog and Huyên-Vi's French translation, there is no P parallel.

[41] T 2 no. 125 pp. 554a–556c; French translation: BSR 3.1 (1986): 32–6 (the page numbers given here and in the following do not include the endnotes). There is no P parallel.

[42] T 2 no. 125 pp. 557a–560a; French translation: BSR 3.2 (1986): 132–41; 4.1 (1987): 47–57. P parallel: AN no. 1.14 (I 23–6).

[43] T 2 no. 125 pp. 560c–561c; French translation: BSR 4.2 (1987): 127–31. P parallel to some: AN no. 1.13 (I 22–3).

[44] T 2 no. 125 (16.5) p. 580a; French translation: BSR 10.1 (1993): 86–7. No P parallel.

[45] T 2 no. 125 (16.6) p. 580b; French translation: BSR 10.1 (1993): 87–9. No P parallel.

[46] T 2 no. 125 (16.10) p. 581b–c; French translation: BSR 10.1 (1993): 94.

[47] T 2 no. 125 (17.1) pp. 581c–582c (581b29 ff. according to Huyên-Vi and Pāsādika in the BSR translation); English translation: BSR 10.2 (1993): 213–22.

[48] Unless we should understand the text division differently. Cf. the translators' note (BSR 11.1 [1994]: 50 n. 1). Should sūtras 9 and 10 of the sixteenth part (16.9–10) be grouped together on the grounds that they both concern monks (the ninth, Aniruddha; the tenth, Rāhula) and that the "Mahā-Rāhulasutta" was inserted later because it also describes Rāhula? If so, this would explain the anomaly that the seventeenth part has eleven sūtras.

[49] T 2 no. 125 (17.2–3) pp. 582c–583a; English translation: BSR 11.1 (1994): 50–1. P parallels to some: AN no. 2.6. For the P parallels see the translators' notes in BSR 11.1 (1994): 50–1.

views and right views, respectively, the P parallels of which also appear together in the AN.[50]

Although the above examples illustrate that the organizational principles of the other AN/EĀs are discernible in sections of the Chinese EĀ (T no. 125), these findings are very tentative. A thorough investigation of this collection by someone with the necessary skills is a desideratum but is beyond the scope of the present study.

1.6. Interpretations of the Structure of the Gāndhārī Sūtra Fragment

Applying these observations on the organizational principles of the various AN/EĀ collections, we can draw some tentative conclusions about our collection of three G sūtras. If these sūtras do represent a portion of a Section of Fours, a Catuṣka-nipāta, of a G EĀ, it would appear that the sūtras in this EĀ were not arranged according to the same organizational principles that are encountered in the other AN/EĀ collections. This is particularly true with reference to the P AN. There seems to be no thematic or other connection between the three G sūtras other than the numerical factor. In contrast, the P parallel to the third G sūtra, sutta 14 of the P Catukka-nipāta, is paired with the preceding sutta, sutta 13, which also defines effort (*padhāna*), but in general rather than specific terms, while these two suttas are in turn thematically connected with the preceding two suttas (nos. 11–2), which themselves constitute a pair based on topic (*viriya*) and structure (the four postures). Further, it has been noted that the P parallels to the first and third G sūtras (nos. 4.36 and 4.14) and the two P suttas that are structurally similar to the second G sūtra (nos. 4.11–2) all conclude with verse and therefore have been placed at the beginning of the P Catukka-nipāta, that is, within the first seven vaggas, the suttas of which are all *sagātha*-. But the second G sūtra on this scroll, the Budhabayaṇa-sutra, lacks verses, which indicates that this organizational principle was probably not followed by the compilers of this G collection, though of course the very small size of our G text renders this statement highly speculative.

Although the absence of the organizational principles that are observed in the P, Skt., and Chinese AN/EĀs may merely indicate that such organizational principles were not employed in this G EĀ or, at least, in this section of the text, it nonetheless raises the possibility that our scroll was not part of a multivolume Catuṣka-nipāta and EĀ but rather belonged to a different type of collection. An examination of P and Central Asian Skt. manuscripts containing collections of suttas/sūtras is particularly instructive in this regard, for although manuscripts of the complete AN are common, and although the Skt. manuscript of a portion of the (Gilgit) EĀ survives, a diverse range of other types of collections are also encountered.[51]

---

[50] T 2 no. 125 (17.5–6) p. 583a–b; English translation: BSR 11.1 (1994): 52–3. P parallel: AN no. 1.17.9–10 (I 32). It is possible that sūtra 5 is connected with sūtra 4, because both mention the "karmically unwholesome."

[51] In the case of P mss. the following catalogs are useful: Somadasa 1987, 1996; Pruitt and Bischoff 1998; Bechert et al. 1979; Braun et al. 1985, 1996. I have checked the original of a number of the

The first alternative interpretation is that this collection of three sūtras is a fragment, not of a complete EĀ, but of an anthology of EĀ sūtras parallel to An Shigao's anthology of forty-four EĀ sūtras (T no. 150a). An Shigao's anthology, as restored by Harrison (1997), contains nine sūtras from the twos, eight sūtras from the threes, eleven sūtras from the fours, fourteen sūtras from the fives, and one sūtra each from the eights and nines. The remnants of numerous manuscripts of the Skt. Ṣaṭsūtraka-nipāta, a collection of six DĀ sūtras that seem to have been highly popular in Central Asia (see Hartmann 1994, 1999: 125 ff.), provide a parallel example of an anthology of sūtras from another āgama. However, in this case the "anthology" seems to represent an actual section of the Sarvāstivādin DĀ; that is, these six sūtras are grouped together in the DĀ itself (see Hartmann 1994, 1999: 125 ff.), which suggests that the arrangement of sūtras within the Sarvāstivādin DĀ resulted in part from an anthologizing activity.[52] There are also examples of P manuscripts containing selections of AN suttas. For example, a nineteenth-century Sinh. manuscript in the BL, Or.6599(25),[53] that belonged to a monk by the name of Nivandanagoma Dhammarakkhita thera contains the following six AN suttas or parts of suttas: sutta 156 and the first part of sutta 157 of the Catukka-nipāta (nos. 4.156 and 4.157.1); sutta 19 of the Aṭṭhaka-nipāta (no. 8.19); sutta 17 of the same nipāta (no. 8.17); sutta 42 of the Tika-nipāta (no. 3.42), minus the verse; and the second part of sutta 129 of the Tika-nipāta (no. 3.192.2). These six suttas are followed by an incomplete *anumodanā gāthā,* or verse text in praise of giving. Of interest is the fact that the suttas are not in traditional numerical order (suttas from the threes follow those from the eights, and no. 8.17 follows no. 8.19) and that in some cases only parts of the sutta are given.

A second alternative is that this scroll represents a section of a multivolume anthology of sūtras selected from various sources, that is, an anthology of EĀ and non-EĀ sūtras, or even mixed sūtra and non-sūtra texts. For example, Sinh. manuscript Or.6600(15) in the BL contains four texts: a SN sutta, a bilingual P-Sinh. version of this sutta, a second SN sutta, and an AN sutta. A Skt. manuscript from Central Asia, first published by Waldschmidt (1932),[54] contains seven canonical sūtras selected from different āgamas and other sources, followed by the *pratītyasamutpāda* formula. Although these two examples, the first Pali, the second Sanskrit, contain only a small number of suttas/sūtras, it is likely that manuscripts containing larger selections of suttas/sūtras from different collections, including a number of suttas/sūtras from one section of an AN/EĀ, were created.

Some P manuscripts suggest yet another alternative. BL manuscript Or.6599(32) (eighty-four folios written in Mūl [Cambodian] script) contains two texts (both incom-

---

BL mss. (Somadasa 1987). The Central Asian mss. are listed in the SHT with further documentation in secondary sources.

[52] SHT IV 32, which was formerly thought to represent an anthology of mostly MĀ sūtras (Schlingloff 1961: 33 ff.; Sander 1979: 4.61–2, 1980: 6–14), has been identified by Jens-Uwe Hartmann as belonging to the DĀ (personal communication).

[53] These and the following BL mss. are listed in Somadasa 1987.

[54] SHT I 581. Further documented with additions by Waldschmidt 1980: 137–62 and Sander 1987.

plete): the Pañcama-nipāta of the Vinaya commentary Samantapāsādikā and the Duka-nipāta of the AN. A Burmese manuscript of twelve folios in the Wellcome Institute (WMS. Burmese-Pāli 46) also contains two texts (both incomplete): a part of the Cha(kka)-nipāta of the AN and a part of the Yamaka of the Abhidhamma-piṭaka. Although it is probably less likely, given the scroll format of the BL Kharoṣṭhī manuscripts, these examples suggest that a section of a Catuṣka-nipāta of a G EĀ, or even a complete Catuṣka-nipāta, could have been combined with another text or part of another text, rather than with the rest of the EĀ.

The above examples show that although these three G sūtras could represent a section of a multivolume Catuṣka-nipāta, which itself was a portion of a G EĀ, we cannot be certain of this. It could equally have belonged to a multivolume anthology of EĀ sūtras or of mixed EĀ and non-EĀ sūtras. Strictly speaking, we can only say that it represents a collection of EĀ-type sūtras with an association with the number 4.

Another factor needs to be taken into consideration here. If these three G sūtras represent a section of the Catuṣka-nipāta of a G EĀ, then the volume of scrolls that constituted the complete EĀ must have been truly massive, especially since this scribe did not use the verso of the scrolls and never abbreviated repetitive passages. Given the volume of scrolls required to write a complete EĀ, it is unlikely that one scribe was ever responsible for copying the complete āgama. It is more likely that scribes copied sections of the collection as the need arose, say, the Sections of Ones and Twos or the Section of Fours. It is therefore quite probable that our scribe was only responsible for copying the Catuṣka-nipāta of the EĀ, if indeed these three G sūtras are part of the Catuṣka-nipāta. This is supported by the relatively small size of the other two texts written by this scribe, the Dharmapada fragment (BL Frags. 16+25) and the Anavataptagāthā (BL Frag. 1). Salomon estimates that the complete Dharmapada would have occupied approximately six scrolls (1999: 90), and he estimates that the complete Anavataptagāthā would have occupied about three or four scrolls (personal communication).

Finally, if this collection of three sūtras does represent a section of the Catuṣka-nipāta of a G EĀ, the G equivalents of the P and Skt. titles Catukka-nipāta/Catuṣka-nipāta and Aṅguttara-nikāya/Ekottar(ik)āgama need to be considered. First, although I have been referring to a "Gāndhārī Ekottarikāgama," we cannot be certain that the G equivalent of Skt. *ekottar(ik)āgama* was actually applied to this collection at this time in Gandhāra. But since this is the title given to this collection in all "Northern" sources, and since the terms *aṅguttara* and *nikāya* as equivalents of *ekottar(ik)a* and *āgama* seem to have been particular to the Theravādins (see, e.g., Lamotte 1988: 152–3), it is highly likely that the G title reflected Skt. *ekottar(ik)āgama* rather than P *aṅguttaranikāya*.

The G equivalents of Skt. *catuṣkanipāta* and *ekottar(ik)āgama* and their components are not attested. The equivalents of Skt. *catuṣka* could be **caduka, *catuka,* or **caüka,* depending on the scribe.[55] The equivalents of Skt. *nipāta* could be **ṇipada, *ṇivada,* or **ṇiäda,* with the initial dental nasal also being possible (e.g.,**nipada, *nivada,* or **niäda*)

[55] For the conjunct *-ṣk-* in G, see Salomon 2000: § 6.2.2.4.

and with *-t-* remaining unvoiced (e.g., **nipata, *nivata,* or **ṇiäta*). Although, as we have seen, *ekottarika* is the form attested in Skt. sources, *ekottara* is supported by such examples as *ekuttaranikāya* (besides *ekuttarikanikāya*) and *ekuttara-saṃyuttaka* in P sources. We therefore cannot be certain whether the G title would have reflected Skt. *ekottara* or *ekottarika*. The G equivalent of Skt. *ekottara* would be **ekutara* or **ekotara* (with such variants as **egutara* also possible), while the equivalent of Skt. *ekottarika* would be **ekutariga, *ekotariga, *ekutaria,* or **ekotaria*. Skt. *āgama* would appear as **agama* or, in the orthography of the scribe of our scroll, as **aghama*. Obviously, it is pointless to attempt to extract a full title from this plethora of possible spellings.

CHAPTER 2

Comparison of the Gāndhārī, Pali, Sanskrit, and Chinese Versions

2.1. General Comments

As noted in chapter 1, parallels to the Dhoṇa- and Prasaṇa-sutras, the first and third sūtras preserved on this manuscript, are found in Pali and Chinese (the Skt. fragment that may represent a parallel to the Prasaṇa-sutra is too small and fragmentary to allow a secure identification), while a parallel to the Budhabayaṇa-sutra has not so far been identified in any language. The existence of P parallels to two of the three G sūtras is particularly fortuitous for, besides providing much needed assistance for the reading and interpretation of the G text, the structure, diction, and grammar of two Middle Indic versions of early Buddhist suttas/sūtras can thereby be compared. Although the lack of Skt. parallels is regrettable, the formulaic nature of Buddhist sūtra literature means that many of the component elements of these G sūtras, including the Budhabayaṇa-sutra, have one or more Skt. equivalents. This makes it possible to undertake a detailed comparison of the G, P, and various Skt. versions of these formulas, which sheds further light on the peculiarities of each and their relationships, on the status of the G text, and on the development of the diction of Buddhist literature of this genre. The Chinese translations are also valuable, but mainly in terms of structure, the course of events depicted, and general wording. They are of limited value for a detailed comparison of the diction and grammar of these texts.

With reference to the G, P, and Skt. versions of the Khargaviṣaṇa-sutra/Khagga-visāṇa-sutta/Khaḍgaviṣāṇa-gāthā, Salomon (2000: 38) noted that the relationships among these three versions are "quite complex" and that "as all too often is the case among parallel versions of Buddhist canonical texts in different Indic languages . . . , they do not divide into clear and neat groupings." As the following analysis will show, this statement is equally true for the relationship between the G, P, and Chinese versions of the Dhoṇa- and Prasaṇa-sutras, as well as for the relationship between the G, P, and Skt. versions of particular formulas. The G text, for example, parallels the P version with reference to some features but differs from the P version and parallels the Chinese or Skt., or both, with reference to others. Differences are discernible on virtually all levels: the course of events and information given, details of diction, and, to a lesser extent, grammar.

2.2. Abbreviation

Several types of abbreviation are commonly encountered in Buddhist manuscripts, including the abbreviation or omission of common formulas, the abbreviation of well-known lists, and the abbreviation of repetitive sections of the text. However, with a few possible exceptions, which will be discussed below, abbreviation is absent in this manuscript. In comparison, abbreviation seems to be the norm in published editions and in the manuscripts used for such editions of, say, the P AN, which of course includes the parallels to the G Dhoṇa- and Prasaṇa-sutras (the Doṇa- and Saṃvara-suttas), as well as suttas that are partially similar to the G Budhabayaṇa-sutra. For example, the P Doṇa-sutta, as presented in the editions, lacks the opening phrase *evaṃ me sutaṃ*. Undoubtedly, this phrase was included when the sutta was chanted, as indicated by its presence in the first sutta in the editions of the Catukka-nipāta, to which section this sutta belongs (see p. 135). Although this section of the G Dhoṇa-sutra is missing due to damage to the manuscript, the other two sūtras preserved on this manuscript include this standard introductory phrase, which implies that it was also present in the Dhoṇa-sutra. Similarly, whereas the G Budhabayaṇa- and Prasaṇa-sutras have the full Śrāvastī nidāna (*eva me rśoda eka samaya bhayavadu śavastie viharadi jedavaṇo aṇasapiḍiasa aramu. tatra ya* . . .), the P parallel to the latter lacks a nidāna. The Central Asian Skt. fragment of a sūtra that may represent a parallel to the G Prasaṇa-sutra is too fragmentary to determine whether a nidāna was included. As mentioned in the discussion of this passage (text commentary to ll. 37–9), the majority of the suttas that depict the Buddha preaching to the monks (like the Prasaṇa- and Budhabayaṇa-sutras) lack nidānas in the editions of the P AN. It appears that the nidāna was to be added when such suttas were recited, as indicated by the presence of nidānas in AN suttas found in manuscripts containing selections, or anthologies, of suttas or mixed sutta/non-sutta texts. Again, the G Dhoṇa-sutra includes the common formula that introduces verses spoken by the Buddha (*(*ida)m u bhayavadu ida vadita sughadu hasavaro idam avaï śastu*), while the P Doṇa-sutta lacks it. But as seen in my discussion of this section of the G text (text commentary to ll. 15–6, pp. 178, 183), the corresponding P formula (*idam avoca bhagavā idaṃ vatvā sugato athāparaṃ etad avoca satthā*) does introduce the Buddha's verses in the first sutta of the nipāta. Further, whereas the G Dhoṇa-sutra has an appropriate conclusion, with Dhoṇa being converted and expressing his delight in the Buddha's words, the P Doṇa-sutta ends with the Buddha's verses, leaving the sutta without an explicit conclusion. In this case, if a conclusion was added when this sutta was recited, it is unclear what form it would have taken, for the Chinese translations end with the brahman expressing his delight in the Buddha's words and departing, with no mention of his conversion (see text commentary to ll. 20–5, pp. 203–5, and ll. 25–6, pp. 219–20). Similarly, the Budhabayaṇa-sutra ends with the common formula that depicts the monks delighting at the Buddha's words (*idam u <*bhayavadu> atamaṇa te bhikh(*u bhayavadeṇa bhaṣido) abhiṇadi*). Although there is no P parallel to this sūtra, most P suttas of this class, such as the Saṃvara-sutta, the P parallel to the G Prasaṇa-sutra, lack such a conclusion in the editions and manuscripts used for the editions. But once again, as this formula (P *idam avoca bhagavā. attamanā te bhikkhū bhagavato bhāsitaṃ abhinandun ti*) is commonly found attached to such suttas when they occur in manuscripts of anthologies of suttas or mixed sutta/non-sutta texts, the phrase was presumably included when such suttas were recited. This is also supported by the occurrence of the formula in the last sutta of the first volume of the E^{e} of the AN (see p. 220). Finally, in the G Prasaṇa-sutra the highly repetitive definitions of *sabara-* and *bhavaṇa-prasaṇa* (= P *saṃvara-* and *bhāvanā-padhāna*) are given in full, while in the P editions they are abbreviated, as they are also in all Skt. versions of these formulas (see text commentary to ll. 40–60 and ll. 63–73).

As mentioned above, there are three instances where abbreviation may have occurred in the manuscript. In the Dhoṇa-sutra, after the Buddha's verses, the brahman declares his faith in the Buddha. In my analysis of this passage (text commentary to ll. 20–5, p. 207) I show that in P texts this conversion formula is usually preceded by a formula indicating a change of speaker (*evaṃ vutte* [name] *brāhmaṇo bhagavantam etad avoca*). As this formula does occur in a similar passage that concludes a G sūtra in the Senior manuscripts, which contain a collection of sūtras in Gāndhārī, its absence in the Dhoṇa-sutra may be an instance of abbreviation. However, given that this would be the only example of this kind of abbreviation in this manuscript, alternative explanations are possible. For example, the omission may have resulted from a scribal error, or it may have occurred when a scribe who wished to give a complete version of the sūtra copied the text from a manuscript in which such formulas were commonly abbreviated or omitted. Although he managed to give a complete version of this and the other sūtras in all other respects, the necessity to include this phrase perhaps escaped him. Of course, it is also possible that the omission occurred at the oral-written interface, when a monk first wrote the sūtra down from memory.

The second instance where abbreviation may have occurred is in the nidāna *tatra ya bhayavadu bhikhu amatredi. te bhikhu bhayavadu pracarśoṣu,* which begins the Budhabayaṇa- and Prasaṇa-sutras (ll. 27–8, 38). Since the P parallel (*tatra kho bhagavā bhikkhū āmantesi bhikkhavo ti. bhadante ti te bhikkhū bhagavato paccassosuṃ*) includes the vocatives (*bhikkhavo ti. bhadante ti*) and since similar formulas found in Buddhist Skt. texts (excluding the opening nidāna) also include such vocatives, it is possible that they were omitted by the scribe in both occurrences (see pp. 231–2). Further G examples are necessary to clarify this issue.

The third possible instance of abbreviation is the list of perceptions of the body in various states of decay found in the definition of the "effort of protecting" (*aṇorakṣaṇa-prasaṇa*) in the Prasaṇa-sutra (ll. 60–3). However, as the manuscript is damaged at this point and the reading problematic, the matter remains unresolved (for full discussion, see p. 287). Thus, none of these passages is a definite example of abbreviation, and the fact that the text of these G sūtras is complete in all other respects suggests that they are not in fact abbreviations.

The Chinese translations of the Dhoṇa- and Prasaṇa-sutras include full introductions (nidānas), the formula introducing the Buddha's verse(s), and concluding formulas. Judging from the French and English translations of the Chinese EĀ (T no. 125; see Huyên-Vi 1984–) and from Harrison's description of the sūtras in An-Shigao's anthology of EĀ sūtras (Harrison 1997), it appears that the Chinese translations always include these formulas, presenting full versions of each sūtra. However, the Chinese translators apparently did not favor giving repetitive passages in full, as seen, for example, in An Shigao's translation of the Prahāṇa-sūtra (T no. 150a p. 877b27–c15).

In the Skt. manuscript of the EĀ edited by Tripāṭhī (1995), the omission or abbreviation of the introductory and concluding formulas is the norm: the full nidāna occurs once (§ 28.01), is abbreviated once (§ 14.01), and is omitted in the remainder of the sūtras. A similar state of affairs is found in Skt. manuscripts of the SĀ (for full references and discussion, see text commentary to ll. 26–8, p. 227). Although the abbreviation or omission of common formulas and the abbreviation of repetitive passages are regular in these and other Skt. manuscripts, in yet other Skt. manuscripts formulas and repetitive passages are given in full (Waldschmidt 1956: 214). In this respect the sūtras in the Senior manuscripts, many of which have parallels in the P SN, provide an excellent contrast to the manuscript edited here. In these Kharoṣṭhī manuscripts abbreviation of the opening and closing formulas, and perhaps also of other formulas and repetitive passages, is common, if not the norm (see text commentary to ll. 26–8). Among the BL Kharoṣṭhī manuscripts a similar diversity in abbreviating tendencies is encountered. The repetitive refrain that concludes all but one of the verses in the Khvs-G (e.g., v. 27, *eko care khargaviṣaṇagapo;* see Salomon 2000: 105–12) is always given in full, as is the refrain which occurs in most of the verses in the Dhp-G^{L} fragment (e.g., v. 10, *uragha jiṇam iva tvaya puraṇo*). In contrast, abbreviation seems to occur in some of the Abhidharma manuscripts (Collett Cox, personal communication).[1]

2.3. Structure, Sequence of Events, and Details of Description

In the Dhoṇa-sutra/Doṇa-sutta, the G sutra parallels the P sutta rather than the Chinese translations on several points. For example, whereas in the G and P versions the brahman asks the Buddha four questions ("Is the Buddha a god, *gandharva, yakṣa,* or human?"), in the three Chinese versions the number of questions is extended by including *asura, nāga,* Brahmā, and others: in the EĀ (T no. 125) version he asks five questions; in the version in the first SĀ (T no. 99) he asks ten questions; and in the sūtra in the second SĀ (T no. 100) he asks eight questions (see text commentary to ll. 9–15, pp. 174–5). But in other respects the G sutra parallels the Chinese. For example, the G and Chinese versions omit the lengthy prose response of the Buddha found in the P version (see pp. 171–2), and both include a concluding description of the brahman's delight in the Buddha's words, which is lacking in the P version (see text commentary to ll. 25–6). The G and Chinese versions also differ from the Pali in first describing the Buddha sitting under a tree and then the brahman seeing his footprints on the road, rather than vice versa (see text commentary to ll. 5–6). But then, the P and Chinese versions are similar in contrast to the G on several points. For example, the Pali and Chinese lack the description of the brahman's conversion found in the Gāndhārī (see text commentary to ll. 20–5), while the Gāndhārī seems not to include the description of the brahman's thoughts

[1] The abbreviation of most of the avadāna texts in the BL collection is of a different type (for an example, see appendix 2).

concerning the Buddha's footprints, which is found in the P and Chinese versions (see text commentary to ll. 5–6, p. 150). There are also instances where all versions of this sutta/sūtra differ, as seen, for example, in the number and content of the verses spoken by the Buddha (see text commentary to ll. 16–20). Finally, although the two Chinese SĀ versions are quite close, they are not identical, while the Chinese EĀ version diverges in several important respects from the G, P, and the two Chinese SĀ versions. In other words, although these five versions of the Dhoṇa-sutra/Doṇa-sutta preserve what is basically the same story and have similar structures, they differ as to the order of events and whether or not certain items of information are included. No two versions are identical.

This is also true for the four complete versions of the Prasaṇa-sutra (G, P, and two Chinese translations), which, in presenting a discourse given by the Buddha to the monks, represents a very different class of sutta/sūtra from the Dhoṇa-sutra. The order of the four *prasaṇa/padhāna/prahāṇa*s differs in each (except that in the two Chinese translations the order is the same; see § 10.1.3), certain phrases are omitted in some, and the definitions of each of the "efforts" vary. Differences of this kind are the norm in comparisons of parallel versions of early Buddhist texts preserved in different languages.

2.4. Diction

Canonical sutta/sūtra texts are formulaic, regularly expressing the same idea in identical or similar wording (Allon 1997: 9–14). Buddhist literature is also highly repetitive, with the same story, verse, or collection of verses commonly occurring in more than one text. Thus, despite the lack of Skt. parallels to these G sūtras, the formulaic and repetitive character of this literature means that many sections of the G text have one or more Skt. equivalents, which enables the diction of the G text to be better understood. Of course, unlike P texts, Buddhist Skt. literature does not represent a homogeneous tradition. Differences between the prose formulas and parallel verses are common in different Skt. texts. It appears that this is also true for Buddhist texts in Gāndhārī, for a preliminary study of the G sūtras preserved in the Senior manuscripts shows that the diction of this second set of G sūtras is not identical to that of our three sūtras.

Differences between the G, P, and Skt. versions of particular formulas are numerous and various. Although expressing the same idea, the same formulas found in texts belonging to different traditions and preserved in different Indic languages are rarely identical. In some cases the differences are minor. For example, a different synonym or particle may be used, or there may be differences in grammar (e.g., of verb tense). But in other cases the differences are more substantial. As was shown to be the case in the previous section with reference to the overall sequence of events and the information included in each version, the relationship between parallel versions of the same formula found in Gāndhārī, Pali, and Sanskrit is complex: the G version is sometimes parallel to the Pali, sometimes to the Sanskrit, and sometimes represents an independent tradition. The conversion formula, which occurs at the end of the Dhoṇa-sutra, provides a particularly good illustration of this complexity. As shown in my analysis of this passage (see text commentary to ll. 20–5), the formula parallels the Pali in the first part, including a long simile passage, but parallels the Skt. version, which is virtually identical in all Skt. texts, in the final section (see below). It is also likely that the G version parallels the P version in the initial exclamation.

It is odd that the simile passage, which consists of a sequence of four similes likening the Buddha's words to the uncovering of what was covered, etc., does not occur in any Skt. text (it also appears to be absent in Tibetan texts). This situation is further complicated by the absence of this simile passage in a second G version of the formula found in the Senior manuscripts, though in this case the omission of the initial exclamation, which is present in all versions, suggests that the scribe may have abbreviated the formula. The abbreviation of other formulas in the Senior manuscripts (e.g., the nidāna; see text commentary to ll. 26–8) further supports this interpretation. Further investigation, particularly of Chinese and Tibetan texts, is needed to explain the absence of this simile passage in Skt. texts.

The Skt. version of the formula that begins the Budhabayaṇa- and Prasaṇa-sutras, namely the Śrāvastī nidāna, provides an interesting parallel to the Skt. version of the conversion formula in that the Skt. version of this nidāna is also briefer than the corresponding G and P versions and seems to have resulted from an abbreviating process (see text commentary to ll. 26–8). The G, P, and Skt. versions of the formula are virtually identical in the first half, but in the latter part, where the G version has *tatra ya bhayavadu bhikhu amatredi te bhikhu bhayavadu pracarśoṣu. bhayavadu eghad uya* (based on the reading of the occurrences in ll. 26–8 and 37–9) and the P version has *tatra kho bhagavā bhikkhū āmantesi bhikkhavo ti. bhadante ti te bhikkhū bhagavato paccassosuṃ. bhagavā etad avoca*, Skt. texts merely have *tatra bhagavān bhikṣūn āmantrayati sma*. As noted in the discussion of this formula, the phrase Skt. *tatra bhagavān bhikṣūn āmantrayati sma*/P *tatra kho bhagavā bhikkhū āmantesi,* which lacks these latter units, commonly occurs within sūtras/suttas. It is therefore possible that in Skt. texts this shorter formula replaced the lengthier formula in the opening of sūtras. It was also noted that *tatra kho bhagavā bhikkhū āmantesi* is a common abbreviation of *tatra kho bhagavā bhikkhū āmantesi bhikkhavo ti. bhadante ti te bhikkhū bhagavato paccassosuṃ. bhagavā etad avoca* in P manuscripts. In other words, it is also possible that the briefer Skt. version resulted from a tendency to abbreviate this formula in manuscripts. As mentioned above (§ 2.2), the absence of the vocatives (P *bhikkhavo ti. bhadante ti*) in the G version may also represent an abbreviation.

The description of the Buddha's calm appearance provides another instance where the G version parallels the P version in some respects, but the Skt. versions in others (see text commentary to ll. 6–8). In this case the first half of the description is closer to the Pali, while the latter part parallels the various Skt. versions in including at least one simile (the Skt. versions vary as to the number and nature of the similes given). This simile, which occurs in other contexts in the P canon, likens the Buddha's appearance to a serene pond. The G version also parallels the P version in some respects but the Skt. version in others in the rhetorical question and concluding statement that bracket the definitions of each of the *prasaṇa*s. Here the Gāndhārī parallels the Pali in the wording of the former but parallels the Sanskrit in the latter (see text commentary to ll. 40–60, pp. 266–9). Further examples are found in the definitions of *sabara-prasaṇa* (text commentary to ll. 40–60) and *aṇorakṣaṇa-prasaṇa* (text commentary to ll. 60–3).

To return to the latter part of the conversion formula, which, as mentioned above, parallels the Skt. version rather than the P version, the three versions are

P *upāsakaṃ maṃ bhavaṃ gotamo dhāretu ajjatagge pāṇupetaṃ saraṇaṃ gatan ti*
G *u(*asaghu) mi ṣ(*a)ma(*ṇe ghuda)m(*e) dharedu ajavaghreṇa yavajivu praṇouviade śaraṇo <*ghade> abhiprasaṇe*
Skt. *upāsakaṃ ca māṃ dhārayādyāgreṇa yāvajjīvaṃ prāṇopetaṃ śaraṇaṃ gatam abhiprasannam*

The G version parallels the Skt. version in the instrumental *ajavaghreṇa* = Skt. *adyāgreṇa* against the locative of the P version, and in including the words *yavajivu* = Skt. *yāvajjīvaṃ* and *abhiprasaṇe* = Skt. *abhiprasannam*. As seen in the discussion of this passage (text commentary to ll. 20–5), *yāvajjīvaṃ* or similar expressions occur in the P Apadāna and in P commentarial glosses and Sinh. sannayas on *pāṇupetaṃ,* while *abhiprasannam,* "out of faith," is inherent in the act of conversion and is articulated in several Apadāna and P commentarial passages. In other words, the expanded wording of the G and Skt. versions is expressed in P commentaries and in a late canonical text such as the Apadāna. It is, however, not certain that the inclusion of these two expression in the G and Skt. versions represents a later development—another instance of glosses and ideas found in P commentarial material finding their way into the canonical text—because the more wordy version of the G and Skt. versions may have been known at the time the redactors of the P canon adopted the simpler formula as the standard one for their canon (see below).

The Gāndhārī also differs from the Pali and parallels at least some Skt. texts in the description of the Buddha's footprints (see text commentary to ll. 3–5). The G, P, and multiple Skt. versions all begin with a string of epithets that are also applied to the cakravartin's wheel-treasure (e.g., P *sahassārāni sanemikāni sanābhikāni*). In the G sutra this is followed by three further epithets. The interpretation of the first of these is problematic, but if it means "golden," this would parallel the inclusion of such an epithet in the description of the wheel-treasure found in some Skt. texts. The next two epithets, meaning "bright" and "shining" (G *aceata prabh(*a)śp(*a)ra* = Skt. *arciṣmant-prabhāsvara-*), are applied to the wheel-marks on the Buddha's feet in such texts as the Lalitavistara, while two similar epithets (*surucira darśanīya*) appear in a parallel passage in the Gaṇḍavyūha. The more elaborate description in the G text, which is found in some Skt. texts, parallels the more elaborate description in the G text of the Buddha's serene appearance, already mentioned. Unlike the Pali, but parallel to a passage found in the Mahāvastu, the G passage includes a simile that likens the Buddha to a serene pond.

Further examples of the Gāndhārī being parallel to the Sanskrit rather than the Pali are the following: (1) The G phrase that describes the Buddha seated at the root of a tree is *añadaro rokṣamulo ṇiṣae (*ṇiṣaṇo)*, which parallels the Skt. expression *anyataraṃ vṛkṣamūlaṃ niśritya niṣaṇṇa-*, rather than P *aññatarasmiṃ rukkhamūle nisinnaṃ,* in including the postpositional absolutive *ṇiṣae* = BHS *niśrāya* constructed with the accusative (see text commentary to ll. 5–6). (2) In contrast to P *pakāsito* the G sūtra has *sapraghaśide,* which is the equivalent of Skt. *saṃprakāśitaḥ,* the form found in Skt. texts (see text commentary to ll. 20–5). In Buddhist Skt. texts there is a tendency for verbal prefixes to be multiplied (see below). (3) The phrase *citam arśaveti,* with the verb constructed with *citam* = Skt. *cittam* as direct object, parallels *cittam anusravanti,* etc., of the Sanskrit rather than P *anvāssaveyyuṃ* (see below for references). (4) The present indicative *amatredi* parallels the Skt. *āmantrayati* rather than the P preterite *āmantesi* (see text commentary to ll. 26–8, p. 231).

There are also instances where the G text parallels one or other of the Skt. versions but not all of them. Examples are G *ida vadita,* parallel to *idaṃ vaditvā* of the Saddharmapuṇḍarīka-sūtra rather than to P *idaṃ vatvā* and *idam uktvā* of all other Skt. examples (see text commentary to ll. 15–6); G *abhija domaṇastu,* parallel to *abhidhyā daurmanasyam* of the Mahāvastu (a noncompounded form as determined from context), in contrast to the P and other Skt. versions, which have a dvandva compound, P *abhijjhādomanassā,* Skt. *abhidhyādaurmanasye* (see text commentary to ll. 40–60, p. 273); and the interrogative pronoun *kadara* = Skt. *katara* found in some Skt. texts, contrasting with *katama* used in canonical P and in other Skt. texts. Although *katara* is found in Pali, it is primarily found in paracanonical texts (see text commentary to ll. 40–60, pp. 267–8).

There are also instances where the G text parallels the Pali rather than the Sanskrit. In the nidāna to the second and third sūtras, where Gāndhārī and Pali have the enclitic form of the pronoun (G *eva me rśodu,* P *evaṃ me sutaṃ*), Sanskrit has the nonenclitic form (*evaṃ mayā śrutam*); and the accusative case in G *eka samaya* and P *ekaṃ samayaṃ* contrasts with the locative in Skt. *ekasmin samaye* (see text commentary to ll. 26–8). In the definition of *sabara-prasaṇa* the G and P texts construct the sense object in the singular (e.g., G *ruvo,* P *rūpaṃ*), while the Skt. examples have a plural form (e.g., *rūpāṇi*). The exception is the Mahāvastu, which has the singular in the case of *rūpaṃ* but the plural for the other five sense objects (see text commentary ll. 40–60, pp. 270, 276).

There are also instances where the Gāndhārī parallels the Pali and some, but not all, Skt. versions of particular formulas. For example, the G form of the approach formula as preserved in both this BL manuscript (*((*yeṇa bha)yavadu teṇa uasakrami uasakramita*) and in the Senior manuscripts is the same as the P version (*yena bhagavā ten' upasaṅkami upasaṅkamitvā*) and that of some Skt. texts, but it contrasts with innovations such as *upajagāma upetya* found in other Skt. texts (see text commentary to ll. 8–9). The form parallel to G *dharma-vie-* and P *dhamma-vicaya-* in the Central Asian (Turfan) manuscripts is *dharma-vicaya-,* which contrasts with *dharma-pravicaya-* encountered in most other Skt. texts (see text commentary to ll. 63–73, pp. 294–5).[2]

The use of various synonyms, or the expression of the same idea in different wording, is commonly encountered when multiple versions of the same Buddhist sūtra, verse, or text are compared. A study of these G sūtras and their parallels provides many examples.

---

[2] Cf. the discussion of the pāda *taśpi budho mi bramaṇa* (ll. 16–20, pp. 199–200).

Several occur in the conversion formula (see text commentary to ll. 20–5): G *maghu praghaśe,* P *maggaṃ ācikkheyya* (the two synonyms occur together in some P texts); G *adhagharo aloka va* <**dharae*>, P *andhakāre vā telapajjotaṃ dhāreyya;* and G *krirṇo śukro dharmu akhade vivaḍe sapraghaśide,* P *anekapariyāyena dhammo pakāsito.* Although occurrences of the word *buddhavacana,* the P and Skt. equivalent of G *budhabayaṇa,* which appears in the Budhabayaṇa-sutra, are rare in P canonical and in comparable Skt. texts but common in P paracanonical works, similar expressions, such as *bhagavato vacana-, buddhānaṃ sāsana-, satthu sāsana-,* are found in canonical works (see text commentary to ll. 28–36, pp. 237–9). In the definition of *sabara-prasaṇa* in the Prasaṇa-sutra we find the phrase *pavea akuśala dharma citam arśaveti,* where the P version has *pāpakā akusalā dhammā anvāssaveyyuṃ* and the various Skt. versions have *aneke pāpakāḥ akuśalā dharmāḥ cittaṃ anuprāvensuḥ, anye vā pāpakā akuśalā dharmāś cittam anuprāpnuyuḥ,* and *loke pāpakā akuśalā dharmāś cittam anusravanti,* to list but three. The equivalent of G *arśaveti* (from *ā* + √*sru*) does not occur in P canonical texts but does appear in commentarial glosses of similar phrases (see text commentary to ll. 40–60, pp. 273–4). In the same passage we find G *maṇase dharmu añadu* (absolutive in *-tu* from *ā* + √*jñā*), which contrasts with P *manasā dhammaṃ viññāya* and Skt. *manasā dharmān vijñāya.* Once again, the basis for this substitution of synonyms is seen in other canonical P passages and in lists of synonyms found in the canonical, but commentarial, Niddesa (*jānāmi ājānāmi vijānāmi . . .*) (see pp. 277–8). The G definition of *aṇorakṣaṇa-prasaṇa* concludes with the phrase *tae aṇorakṣae sapadedi.* The P definition has no equivalent of this phrase, but parallel expressions are found in Pali, for example, *te ārakkhena guttiyā sampādeti,* where G *aṇorakṣae* (= P *anurakkhāya*) and P *ārakkhena* are clearly synonymous (see text commentary to ll. 60–3).

In the introduction to the Dhoṇa-sutra the wording used to describe the Buddha traveling on the road, which is incomplete, is *-hoṭo magheṇa ghatva* (*-hoṭo* probably is the remnant of a place-name in the accusative). The P version has *ekaṃ samayaṃ bhagavā antarā ca ukkaṭṭhaṃ antarā ca setabbyaṃ addhānamaggapaṭipanno hoti.* An expression similar to the Pali appears in Skt. texts. The P equivalent (*maggena gantvā*) of G *magheṇa ghatva* is not found in canonical texts but is encountered in commentaries (see text commentary to ll. 1–3; cf. also the discussion of *to magho,* l. 3).

Similarly, in the Dhoṇa-sutra, Dhoṇa is first introduced with the expression *teṇa ceva samaeṇa dhoṇo ṇama bramaṇo.* The P parallel has *doṇo pi sudaṃ brāhmaṇo.* Although a formula similar to the G formula is found in canonical P (*tena kho pana samayena* [person's name] *nāma* [person's social status]) and in comparable Skt. texts, a closer parallel is found in P commentaries (*tena ca samayena . . .* ; see text commentary to l. 3).

Many of the G expressions cited above are alien to P canonical sutta texts but are encountered in paracanonical or late canonical P literature. Some other examples are not attested at all in Pali. Further examples of this kind are the following: (1) The combination of the particle *re* = P *re/are* with the interrogative pronoun in the question *ku re bhu bhaviśasi,* where the Pali has *atha kho ko carahi bhavaṃ bhavissatī ti.* The particle is more common in P commentaries (see text commentary to ll. 9–15, pp. 176–7). (2) The inclusion of the phrase *satu savijamaṇa loghaśpi* in the initial listing of the four *prasaṇas* (*catvarime bhikṣave prasaṇa ∘ satu savijamaṇa loghaśpi ∘*), where the P has *cattār' imāni bhikkhave padhānāni*. In P texts the corresponding phrase *santo saṃvijjamānā lokasmiṃ* only occurs when animate things are listed (see text commentary to ll. 39–40). (3) The employment of *sayasavi* = P *seyyathāpi* in the definition of *aṇorakṣaṇa-prasaṇa* as a means of introducing a list of perceptions. Lists are normally introduced by *seyyathīdaṃ* in P and *sayyathīdaṃ* or *tadyathā* in Buddhist Skt. texts, though occasionally *seyyathāpi/sayyathāpi* is so employed in P and Skt. texts (see text commentary to ll. 60–3, p. 281). (4) The employment of *yavad eva* both in the definition of *sabara-prasaṇa,* where the P and Skt. versions have *yato* (see text commentary to ll. 40–60, pp. 271–2), and in the conversion formula (see text commentary to ll. 20–5).

On a more minute, though perhaps no less significant, level there are numerous instances where the G and P versions (and Skt. version or versions where they exist) differ in the use of the indeclinable particles. Two examples have already been mentioned. The first is G *teṇa ceva samaeṇa*. The P parallel has *doṇo pi sudaṃ brāhmaṇo,* but the phrase corresponding to the Gāndhārī occurs elsewhere in the P canon as *tena kho pana samayena* and in Skt. texts as *tena khalu (punaḥ) samayena*, while *tena ca samayena* is found in P commentaries. The second is G *ku re bhu bhaviśasi,* P *atha kho ko carahi bhavaṃ bhavissatī ti.*[3] In both of these examples the equivalent of the Skt. particle *khalu,* P *kho,* is absent, as it appears to be throughout this manuscript. Other examples are G *ṇaho bramaṇa maṇośu bhaviśe* (ll. 9–15), where the P has *na kho ahaṃ brāhmaṇa manusso bhavissāmī ti* (taking G *ṇaho* as the equivalent of Skt. *nāham*); G *evam eva* (l. 23) against P *evam eva kho;* and G *tatra ya* (ll. 27 and 38) against P *tatra kho* (for details, see text commentary to ll. 9–15, pp. 169–70). Although this is complicated by the omission of *kho* in these passages in some P manuscripts, the absence of this indeclinable in this G manuscript is nonetheless significant, because in canonical P prose *kho* and other indeclinable particles are extremely common, frequently functioning as markers of new sentences and clauses. Parallel to this is the complete absence of the quotative particle *iti* in this manuscript (for details, see pp. 170–1); the absence of the equivalent of the particle *nu* in G *maṇośu bhu bhaviśasi,* where the P parallel has *manusso no bhavaṃ bhavissatī ti* (see p. 169); the omission of the conjunctive *ca* in the rhetorical question that begins the definitions of the *prasaṇa*s, for example, G *kadara bhikṣave a(*ṇo-rakṣaṇaprasa)ṇe,* P *katamañ ca bhikkhave anurakkhanappadhānaṃ* (pp. 266–9);[4] and the omission of vocatives in several passages. Examples of the latter are the apparent lack of the second vocative in *(*abhikatu) bhu ghodama abhikatu,* where the P has *abhikkantaṃ bho gotama abhikkantaṃ bho gotama* (see text commentary to ll. 20–5); G *tatra ya bhayavadu bhikhu amatredi te bhikhu bhayavadu pracarśoṣu,* where the P has *tatra kho bhagavā bhikkhū āmantesi bhikkhavo ti. bhadante ti te bhikkhū bhagavato paccassosuṃ* (see text commentary to ll. 26–8); and the lack of the vocative in each of the statements that conclude the definitions of the three *prasaṇa*s, for example, G *aï bucadi sabara-*

[3] A further example is G *bhavidavu p(*i) bh(*a)vi(*du),* P *bhāvetabbañ ca bhāvitaṃ* (see text commentary to ll. 16–20).

[4] See also the omission of the disjunctive *va* = P/Skt. *vā* in *ṇiujidu ukuje,* where the P has *nikkujjitaṃ vā ukkujjeyya* (see text commentary to ll. 20–5).

prasaṇo, P *idaṃ vuccati bhikkhave saṃvarappadhānaṃ* (see text commentary to ll. 40–60, pp. 266–9). The Skt. parallels to each of these phrases similarly lack vocatives.

In P sutta texts vocatives and indeclinables such as *kho* are extremely common. They appear to function as markers of new sentences and clauses and, in the case of vocatives, as indicators of who is speaking. It is also likely that the proliferation of such repetitive elements is yet another means by which dissimilar material is rendered more similar (Allon 1997: 349–50). Such features would have been important in an oral and oral/aural context, facilitating the audience's understanding of the text and assisting those who wished to memorize it. They are thus indicative of the oral and oral/aural phases of this literature. It is therefore interesting that the tendency to omit vocatives and particles such as *khalu* and *iti* is a common feature of many Skt. texts (see below). However, a more complete evaluation of these features of this manuscript awaits the further study and publication of other G texts in the BL collection, particularly those of the same genre, as well as of the sūtra collection preserved in the Senior manuscripts.

The G, P, and Skt. versions of the verses of the G Dhoṇa-sutra exhibit several of the kinds of differences documented above for the prose portions. While some pādas are identical in all versions, other pādas show differences in word order or word choice, though without much difference in meaning. For example, where the Gāndhārī has *puḍar(*io) yasa phulo,* "just as a flowering lotus," the Pali has *puṇḍarīkaṃ yathā vaggu,* "just as a beautiful lotus." As seen in the study of this verse, *phulla* is frequently applied to lotuses in P literature, though apparently not to *puṇḍarīka,* and is often found in the same position within the pāda. Again, where the Gāndhārī has *virbhasta bhiriḍighama,* the Pali has *viddhastā vinaḷīkatā,* showing differences that typically arise in the course of oral transmission (see text commentary to ll. 16–20; for similar comments on the verses of the Khvs-G, see Salomon 2000: 38–52).

Thus, a study of the diction of these three G sūtras shows that they represent an independent textual tradition. The wording of the G text sometimes parallels the Pali, at other times one or other of the Skt. versions, and not uncommonly differs from all attested versions. However, certain features of the G text tend to ally it more closely with Skt. texts.

In his study of the diction of three canonical Skt. sūtras (MPS, CPS, and MAV) belonging to the Sarvāstivādin school, von Simson (1965: §§ 18–23) showed that the prose of these Skt. texts is frequently more elaborate than that of the corresponding P texts. The wording is often expanded through the proliferation of synonyms or through the addition of elements that clarify the meaning or add extra information. Although this is not a regular feature of the G text, there are at least three examples of it: the inclusion or "addition" of *yavajivu* and *abhiprasaṇe* in the latter part of the conversion formula and the more elaborate descriptions of the Buddha's footprints and of his calm appearance. There is also a tendency in these Skt. texts for words to be expanded through the addition of verbal prefixes (von Simson 1965: § 19.5–6), which is reflected in this manuscript in *sapraghaśide,* where the P has *pakāsito.* As in this G manuscript, the quotative particle *iti* is not favored in these Skt. texts (von Simson 1965: § 12.30), and vocatives and the indeclinable *khalu* tend to occur less frequently than in P texts. Thus, although the diction of these G sūtras does not match that of any group of comparable Skt. texts, it shows signs of developments that are common in Buddhist Skt. literature. In this respect it appears to represent a stage somewhere between P and Skt. texts. This is particularly interesting because a comparison of the G, P, and Skt. versions of the Khargaviṣaṇa-sutra/Khaggavisāṇa-sutta/Khaḍgaviṣāṇa-gāthā showed that, although "the overall structure and contents of the Gāndhārī text resemble the Pali version fairly closely and diverge widely from the Sanskrit, . . . the actual readings of the Gāndhārī text are consistently closer to the Sanskrit" (Salomon 2000: 38, cf. 40–1).

2.5. Grammar

For the most part, the differences in grammar between the G and P texts, and Skt. parallel passages where they exist, are not significant. Several have already been mentioned. Grammatical differences include the following:

1. Finite versus nonfinite verb forms: G *maghade abhikrami* (pret.), P *maggā okkamma* (abs.) (see pp. 138–9); G *alitu śpi* (pp.), P *upalippāmi* (pres.) (pp. 198–9).
2. Different verbal tense: G *dhrekṣatu* (fut. impv. or pres. impv.), P *dakkhinti* (fut.) (p. 213); G *amatredi* and Skt. *āmantrayati* (pres.), P *āmantesi* (pret.) (pp. 230–1); and G *arśaveti* (pres.), P *anvāssaveyyuṃ* (opt.), Skt. *anuprāpnuyuḥ* (opt.), *anusravanti* (pres.), etc. (pp. 273–4).
3. Different forms of the absolutive: G *añadu* (abs. in *-tu*), P *viññāya,* Skt. *vijñāya* (pp. 277–8).
4. Different grammatical person (verbs): G *maṇośu bhu bhaviśasi* (2nd sg.), P *manusso no bhavaṃ bhavissatī ti* (3rd sg.) (p. 169).
5. Different number (nouns): G *ruvo* (sg.), P *rūpaṃ* (sg.), Skt. *rūpāṇi* (pl.) (p. 170).
6. Different case: G *ajavaghreṇa* and Skt. *adyāgreṇa* (instr.), P *ajjatagge* (loc.) (pp. 216–7); G *bhayavadeṇa* (instr.), P and Skt. *bhagavato* (gen.) (pp. 222–3).

Of these, the uncommon absolutive in *-tu* (*añadu*) may be significant, as the employment of diverse absolutives seems to be characteristic of some G texts (see pp. 277–8). The instrumental construction in *bhayavadeṇa bhaṣido abhiṇadi,* where the P and Skt. texts have the genitive (e.g., P *bhagavato bhāsitaṃ abhinandi*), is also of interest, as is *dhrekṣatu,* which is either the rare future imperative or the present imperative (the Pali has the future *dakkhinti*). Not mentioned above but also worthy of note is the use of the enclitic pronoun *mi* = P/Skt. *me* for the accusative, where the Pali has *maṃ* and the Sanskrit has *māṃ* (p. 216). But perhaps the most significant new development encountered in this text is the use of the historic locative termination in *taśpi* for the ablative, where the ablative appears in the P *tasmā* and Skt. *tasmād* as demanded by the context. As noted in the discussion of this word and similar examples (pp. 277–8), the ablative, genitive, and locative singular of the pronoun have collapsed in Gāndhārī, so that any one historical form could be used for any of these three oblique cases. This attests a later stage of a process first recorded in Pali and other Prakrits. Further instances of this phenomenon appear in at least one other BL Kharoṣṭhī manuscript and in the Senior manuscripts.

2.6. Clues to the Underlying Source Dialect: Language and Translation

Salomon (2000: 48) refers to the language of the Khvs-G as "'Gāndhārī translationese,' that is, the sort of semi-Gāndhārī that characterizes texts, whether manuscript or epigraphic, that have clearly been translated or calqued from other MIA dialects with typical midland features broadly similar to those of Pali." He quotes Brough, who refers to the G and P versions of the Dharmapada/Dhammapada as "word-for-word transpositions of their original rather than as translations in the usual sense" (Brough 1962: 113). It goes without saying that these statements are equally applicable to the text of these three G sūtras and also to their P parallels. All surviving versions of Buddhist texts of this genre in Indic languages are translations or transpositions from another dialect.

When verse texts such as the Dharmapada/Dhammapada or Khaggavisāṇa-sutta/Khaḍgaviṣāna-gāthā were translated into Gāndhārī, the meter would have inhibited the adoption of a more colloquial Gāndhārī, which presumably would have involved changes in syntax and word order and the adoption of different word forms and a different vocabulary. Transposition is indeed the most appropriate term for the translation of such texts, for it was primarily a matter of "adjusting the words to G phonetics" (Salomon 2000: 48). Although metrical constraints were not an issue in the translation of prose, the religious status of the text, as well as other factors, would have inhibited profound changes, as the style of the G text reveals. For the most part, the text conforms to the style of P and Skt. canonical sutta/sūtra texts, though there are some interesting exceptions. The most obvious one is the phrase *maghena ghatva,* which appears in the opening section of the Dhoṇa-sutra (ll. 2, 6) in the description of the Buddha traveling on the road. Such an expression is not found in P or Skt. canonical sutta/sūtra texts in such a context but is in keeping with P commentarial usage (see pp. 136–8). However, it is unclear whether this should be interpreted as an example of a more colloquial Gāndhārī, since the building up of complete sentences by stringing together sequences of nonfinite clauses is common in sutta/sūtra prose. At present our knowledge of G Buddhist literature is not mature enough to enable us in a text such as this to identify stylistic and syntactic features and elements of vocabulary that could be said to be specifically G features (see Salomon 1999: 138–40).

In contrast, the phonology and morphology of the language are comparatively well documented (see chaps. 5 and 6). It is thus possible to identify phonetic and morphological features that are not typical for Gāndhārī and that reflect the underlying dialect from which these texts were translated or through which they were at one time transmitted (Salomon 2000: 48–9). Examples of words containing phonetic features that appear to have been carried over from the source dialect, or from a dialect through which the text passed, are the following:

1. *Bhikhu* = P *bhikkhu*/Skt. *bhikṣu* with *kh* (= *kkh*) for the OIA cluster *kṣ* (normally retained in G) in all examples of the word except the vocative plural *bhikṣave* (for details, see p. 95).
2. The prefix *paḍi-* = P *paṭi-*/Skt. *prati-* with retroflex stop (§ 5.2.2.3) and postconsonantal *r* not written.
3. Other instances where postconsonantal *r* is not written, for example, *ghaṇa-* = P *ghāna-*/Skt. *ghrāṇa-* (see § 5.2.3.4).
4. The reflex of OIA *r̥* as *u* in *phuṣita* = P *phusitvā*/BHS *spr̥śitvā* and as *a* in *vivaḍe* = P *vivaṭa-*/Skt. *vivr̥ta-*. G reflexes of OIA *r̥* normally include *r,* for example, G *proṭhu* = P *puṭṭha-*/Skt. *pr̥ṣṭa-* (see § 5.1.9).
5. The dental sibilant in *suda* = P *sota-*/BHS *śrota-*/Skt. *śrotra-,* which appears alongside the more common G spelling *ṣuda*. The former spelling reflects a source dialect in which the OIA cluster *śr-* appeared as *s-,* as in Pali (see § 5.2.3.6, p. 93).
6. *Śpayita,* which, if the reading is correct, reflects a form such as P *sāyitvā* rather than BHS *svādayitvā* (with intervocalic dental) (see p. 83, n. 4). There are no examples in this manuscript of the elision of intervocalic dental stops (§ 5.2.2.4).

Also of interest are the following:

7. *Abhiñae,* which seems to have been understood to be an absolutive (= Skt. *abhjñāya*), where the Pali and Sanskrit have the past participle (P *abhiññātaṃ*/Skt. *abhijñātam*). It therefore appears that an underlying form such as **abhiñaya(ṃ)* or **abhiñaï*/**abhiñae,* with elision of intervocalic *-t-,* was not recognized as a past participle (see pp. 200–1).
8. *Praṣadha-* = P *pasaddhi-*/BHS *praśrabdhi-*/*prasrabdhi-* and *arśaveti* from *ā* + √*sru,* which both show the alternation of *sr* and *śr* that is common in Buddhist Sanskrit, particularly in the case of derivatives of √*sru* and √*śru* (see pp. 274, 296).
9. *Vipuao,* which reflects a spelling such as BHS *vipūyaka-* rather than P *vipubbaka-* (see p. 285).

Virtually all of the above phonetic features are attested in other G texts and documents (see the above references). Examples 1–6 are in keeping with P phonology. The apparent elision of intervocalic *-t-* in *abhiñae* (7) may not reflect the source dialect but could rather represent a development that occurred during the transmission of the text in Gāndhārī (see p. 201). The alternation of *sr* and *śr* evident in *praṣadha-* and *arśaveti* (8) occurs even in Sanskrit (BHSG, § 2.58) and therefore is probably not to be traced to the source dialect. Thus, the majority of these examples suggest that the source dialect of this G text was something broadly akin to Pali, though not necessarily identical with it (Salomon 2000: 51–2).

2.7. Conclusion and Comments on Sectarian Affiliation

In terms of their grouping and ordering, this collection of three G sūtras has no counterpart in surviving Buddhist literature, whether in an Indic language or in Chinese or Tibetan translation. A comparison of the G, P, and Chinese versions of the Dhoṇa- and

Prasaṇa-sutras and a comparison of the G, P, and Skt. versions of certain formulas show that these G texts belong to an independent tradition. In particular, the diction of these sūtras does not match that of any Buddhist text which survives in an Indic language, though this is not surprising, given that the literature of only a limited number of Buddhist sects has survived to date. Based on the research undertaken so far, it has therefore not been possible to identify a likely sectarian affiliation for these sūtras. But this is not to say that such an identification is impossible to determine. Based on a variety of factors, Salomon (1999: 166–82) proposed a Dharmaguptaka affiliation for most, if not all, of the BL Kharoṣṭhī manuscripts. Although Chinese translations are of limited value in a formulaic analysis of Buddhist texts, a detailed comparison of the formulas of the G sūtras with their counterparts in Chinese texts of supposed Dharmaguptaka affiliation may still prove fruitful. But this must be left to those with the appropriate language skills.

CHAPTER 3

Physical Description of the Manuscript

3.1. Description of the Manuscript

The scroll containing the EĀ-type sūtras came to the British Library in a modern glass jar (jar no. 6; for a description of the initial condition and preservation of the BL Kharoṣṭhī manuscripts, see Salomon 1999: 15–20). In the process of unraveling this scroll, it was determined to consist of two major "Fragments." These were allocated BL Fragment numbers 12 and 14 and preserved in three glass frames (frames 24, 25, and 28; BL accession nos. Or.14915.24, Or.14915.25, and Or.14915.28). The upper section of Fragment 12 is preserved in frame 25, and its lower section is preserved in frame 24. Fragment 14 is preserved in frame 28 (see Salomon 1999: 48–9). In addition, thirty-one small fragments belonging to this manuscript were found among the loose bits of bark and dust collected from the bottom of the glass jar in which the scroll was brought to the BL. These are preserved in a separate glass frame (currently without an accession number). The debris from each glass jar was initially collected in separate boxes (Salomon 1999: 52–3; for an illustration of one box, see Salomon 2000: pl. 7). As these fragments came from glass jar no. 6, they are referred to as "debris box 6 fragments."

The manuscript consists of many "subfragments," of varying sizes, referred to as "fragments" throughout this study (in contrast to "Fragment," with uppercase F, used to refer to the major Fragments, 12 and 14). The "subfragments," or fragments, within each frame were designated by the frame number followed by a lowercase letter or letters according to their location in the frame; thus 25a (= frame 25, fragment a), 25b, and so on, and 28a, 28b, and so on. Within each frame, letter designations (see figs. 1–3) were first assigned to the larger fragments, beginning at the top left and continuing to the bottom right, then to the smaller fragments following the same method, ending with the small fragments that adhere to the verso and are only visible from the verso. Although the horizontal splitting of the manuscript has caused it to break up into many separate horizontal sections of bark, these are taken to be part of the same fragment as long as they are in their correct order. The debris box fragments are designated D6 (= debris box no. 6), followed by a lowercase letter (D6a, D6b, etc., to D6ee), starting from the top left and finishing at the bottom right as they are preserved in the glass frame. (For detailed descriptions of each fragment, see § 3.3.)

The portion of the manuscript preserved in frame 25 (see pl. 5), which is the top of the surviving section of the manuscript (i.e., the outer layers of the rolled-up scroll), is the most fragmentary. It consists of ten larger fragments (frags. 25a–25j) and twenty-four smaller fragments (25k–25hh). The larger fragments as they appear in the unreconstructed manuscript can be divided into three main sequences: 25a–25b at the top of the frame, 25c–25f in the middle, and 25g–25j at the bottom. Although the fragments within each sequence are in their correct order, the three main sequences, or sections, are not, so that in the reconstructed manuscript the order is 25g–25j, 25c–25f, 25a–25b. As the remainder of the manuscript consists of two large fragments (24a and 28a), which are in their correct order, it is unlikely that this manuscript was rolled up for interment with sections of the manuscript out of order, as may have been the case with the Khvs-G manuscript (Salomon 2000: 21–3). It seems that the fragments of frame 25 came to be out of order during the process of unraveling the scroll. Because the outside of the scroll was highly fragmented, it was impossible for the conservators to determine where the scroll actually began, and some sections of the scroll fell off as the scroll was exposed to moisture in the initial stages of the unraveling process.

The sections of the manuscript preserved in frames 24 and 28 (pls. 6–7) represent the bulk of the manuscript. Each of these two frames contains one main, large fragment (frags. 24a and 28a, respectively) and several much smaller fragments (frags. 24b–24dd and 28b–28g). Most of the smaller fragments in frame 24, some of which are upside down and/or back to front, appear in the upper left region. The correct location of most of these fragments is further down the manuscript. It appears that, since the left margin of the manuscript was highly fragmented, fragments belonging to layers further inside the scroll tended to drop out as it was unrolled.

3.2. Reconstruction of the Scroll

3.2.1. Size and Format

The dimensions for the unreconstructed manuscript (see pls. 5–7) were first given in Salomon 1999: 48–9. BL Fragment 12 (comprising frames 25 and 24, in that order) is, at its maximum points, 14.5 cm wide and 57 cm high. The width given by Salomon (1999: 48) was 16.5 cm, but this included fragment 24n, which butts up against the main fragment (24a) and gives the illusion of being a part of the main fragment. Fragment 14 (frame 28) is 14.5 cm wide and 27.7 cm high. The maximum height for the reconstructed manuscript (see pls. 1–4) is 76 cm, and the maximum width is 14.5 cm (in two places the measurement is 15 cm, but in both instances this occurs where the placement of a free-floating fragment is inexact).

Line 22 is one of the few complete lines of text in the manuscript. The left edge of the manuscript falls immediately to the left of the original last akṣara of the line. Therefore, only the blank left margin is missing at this point. The width of the original left margin is uncertain, as it nowhere survives intact. If it was the same as the right margin, which is 1 cm wide on average, then, since the surviving portion of the manuscript is 14.5 cm wide at this location (l. 22), the original undamaged manuscript must have been about 15.5 cm wide here. Although the width of the manuscript may have varied slightly along its length, the difference in width is unlikely to have been great. This measurement is toward the lower end of the range of widths established for the manuscripts of the BL Kharoṣṭhī manuscript collection (14–25 cm) but is approximately the same as that for the manuscript of the Anavataptagāthā, which was also written by our scribe (BL Frag. 1; see

Salomon 1999: 88). The Dharmapada manuscript (BL Frags. 16 and 25), again written by the same scribe, was probably slightly more than 20 cm wide (Timothy Lenz, personal communication).

As with most of the BL Kharoṣṭhī manuscripts, the original height of our manuscript is impossible to determine (Salomon 1999: 88–9, 91). Salomon (1999: 88–90) estimated the original length of several scrolls in the BL collection. For example, the manuscript containing the Saṅgīti-sūtra and its commentary (BL Frag. 15), the surviving portion of which is 115 cm long, is likely to have originally been 230–50 cm long, while the original length of the scroll containing the first two vargas of the Dharmapada (BL Frags. 16 and 25, written by our scribe) was "roughly 125 cm." Lenz (1999: § 1.1.5), who has undertaken further study of the latter manuscript, estimates the original length at 130.5 cm. The original length of the scroll containing the Anavataptagāthā (BL Frag. 1, written by our scribe) has not yet been established. The surviving portion of that manuscript, which probably represents about two-thirds of the original scroll, is 154.8 cm. The original scroll may therefore have been roughly 230 cm long (Richard Salomon, personal communication). Finally, the original length of the Khaḍgaviṣāṇa-sūtra manuscript must have been not much more than the 44.4 cm established for the reconstructed manuscript (Salomon 2000: 23–4). This is one of the shorter manuscripts in the BL collection, the smaller size being due to the nature of the text (Salomon 2000: 23–5).

The original length of the above scrolls can be calculated because the approximate size of each of these four texts (Saṅg-G, Dhp-G^{L}, AG-G, and Khvs-G) can be estimated with some degree of certainty by comparison with extant versions in other languages. In contrast, although it is likely that this collection of three EĀ-type sūtras formed part of a multivolume collection of sūtras, it is impossible to determine how many sūtras the collection contained. Further, since the length of the sūtras varies considerably (as illustrated by the three surviving sūtras), and since this scribe found it acceptable to begin a sūtra at the bottom of one scroll and finish it on the next, there is no way of determining how many sūtras preceded the three surviving ones on this scroll. Finally, although the width (14.5 cm) of the AG-G is more or less the same as the width of our scroll, suggesting that the length of our scroll may have been approximately the same, and therefore also the same as the original length of the Saṅg-G scroll (230–50 cm), the Dhp-G^{L}, which also was written by our scribe, was apparently only about 130 cm long. Thus, we simply cannot say what proportion of the original scroll the surviving 76 cm of manuscript represents.

Like most of the scrolls in the BL collection, this one was constructed of several sections of bark glued together, with each additional section of bark slightly overlying the preceding section (for details of the construction technique, see Salomon 1999: 92–6, 107–8). The surviving portion of this manuscript consists of three sections of bark, which are clearly visible in the photo of the unreconstructed manuscript (pls. 5–7) since the sections have separated, exposing the blank areas of bark that were once glued together. The blank, glue areas at the bottom of the first and second sections of bark are both about 2 cm wide. The original length of the first section of bark, which contains lines 1–32 of the surviving text, is uncertain because its top border is missing; the length of its surviving portion in the reconstructed manuscript is about 30 cm. The second section of bark, which contains lines 33–53, is approximately 23.5 cm long. The third and final section, containing lines 54–73, is 27 cm long. The above measurements show that the sections of bark used to construct this scroll were not of uniform length. Also, the size of these sections of bark contrasts with the much larger sections used to construct the AG-G scroll, where each section was about 45 cm, except for the bottom section, which was about 30 cm (Salomon 1999: 92–4). In contrast to the unusually fine, thin quality of the bark of the Khvs-G manuscript (Salomon 2000: 23–4), the bark of this manuscript is relatively thick, like the majority of the BL scrolls.

The right margin of this manuscript, and undoubtedly the left margin also, were sewn with a single row of stitching, like most of the manuscripts in the BL collection (Salomon 1999: 94–6, 2000: 25). Both the needle holes and some remnants of the dark brown thread are clearly visible along the length of the right margin, which for the most part has survived intact. The line of sewing is 0.5–1.0 cm from the edge of the manuscript, and the holes are approximately 0.5 cm apart. Some needle holes appear to be spherical, with a diameter of about 0.1 cm, while others are irregular in shape, perhaps resulting from the splitting of the bark. The composition of the thread is yet to be identified. The purpose of the sewing was apparently to prevent the horizontal splitting of the manuscript and to hold the manuscript together in the event of such splitting (Salomon 1999: 94).

The scribe of the first text on this scroll, the collection of EĀ-type sūtras, left an area of about 6.5–7 cm blank at the bottom of the recto of the manuscript and did not write on the verso at all. As mentioned in § 1.1, the third surviving sūtra in this collection is not complete and must have been continued on another scroll, indicating that this manuscript was part of a multivolume collection of scrolls. The other two manuscripts written by this scribe, BL Fragments 1 (the AG-G) and 16 and 25 (the Dhp-G^{L}), similarly originally belonged to multivolume collections of scrolls, and the bottom of the recto and the entire verso were also left blank on both of them (Salomon 1999: 87–8). However, in contrast to the AG-G and Dhp-G^{L}, it is not possible to calculate the number of scrolls used to write this text, since the exact size and nature of the original text of which these sūtras formed a part are not known (see § 1.6). The practice of writing a single text on several scrolls may have resulted from a desire to avoid using the verso with its inferior writing surface. Also, multiple, relatively short volumes may have been more convenient to handle than a single long scroll (Salomon 1999: 90–1).

Two small oblong holes, about 0.27 cm in diameter at their widest point, appear in the blank bottom margin of the scroll (see pl. 4). The hole on the left side of the recto is about 2.5 cm from the original bottom margin of the manuscript, and the hole on the right is about 1.4 cm from the bottom. Salomon (1999: 101) suggested that these may represent pin marks, indicating that the bottom of the manuscript was originally fastened to a roller, which facilitated the use and preservation of the scroll. If so, the bark would have been pinned onto the roller from the verso side, which formed the original outside of the scroll.

Apart from the blank vertical margins and the much wider blank area at the bottom of the manuscript, the text of our manuscript covers the recto of the surviving portion of the scroll in an even and, for the most part, uninterrupted manner. Each line is written to the left margin, with the exception of lines 32, 53, and 73. Lines 32 and 53 occur directly above the raised line of bark created when two sections of bark were glued together. Because the scribe's line of writing tended to slant slightly down to the left as he wrote, he chose not to complete these two lines so as to avoid writing across this raised area (Salomon 1999: 92). The short line 73 is the last line of the EĀ-G text on this scroll. At the same location in two consecutive lines (ll. 33 and 34), the scribe left a blank space the width of one akṣara, which suggests that he was avoiding a rough section of bark. There also appears to be a space of two akṣaras left blank toward the end of line 7. In another location (l. 61, third akṣara), it appears that the ink of an akṣara that was written on a knot in the bark ran and was subsequently erased by the scribe. For reasons that are yet to be determined, the majority of the smudged akṣaras found on this manuscript appear in the last ten or so lines (see § 4.6). It is unlikely that this was due to some physical difficulty in writing at the bottom of the scroll, for a similar smudging is not seen in other manuscripts in the BL collection.

With the exception of the two short lines just mentioned (ll. 32 and 53), which have twenty-six and eighteen akṣaras, respectively, and the last line of writing in this scribe's hand on the recto (l. 73), which has only twelve akṣaras, the number of akṣaras per line of the reconstructed text ranges from twenty-eight (ll. 28, 49) to thirty-eight or thirty-nine (l. 9), including punctuation marks. The lines that appear to be complete, and that were written to the left margin, are line 9 (twenty-eight or twenty-nine akṣaras), line 18 (thirty-one akṣaras), line 22 (thirty-four akṣaras), line 26 (thirty-two or thirty-three akṣaras), and line 49 (twenty-eight akṣaras). In those sections of the manuscript where the text is repetitive and the lacunae can be completed with certainty, the akṣara count can also be determined. For example, the original number of akṣaras on lines 10–4 was 35, 33, 34, 37, 34, and for lines 27–38 it was 34, 28, 34, 32, 30, 26 (the short l. 32), 30 (plus a blank space), 30 (plus a blank space), 30, 34, 35, 35. The average number of akṣaras per line is about thirty-two. Where the missing text can be reconstructed with some degree of accuracy, the number of akṣaras missing per line ranges from one to ten, mostly from the left margin. Due to substantial damage to the upper left margin of the manuscript, the number of akṣaras missing from lines near the beginning of the text exceeds ten in several instances.

The area at the bottom of the recto and the entire verso, which were originally left blank by the scribe of the first text on this scroll (scribe no. 1), were subsequently used by a second scribe (no. 2) to write the unrelated avadāna text, probably at a much later date (see § 1.1). This second scribe wrote the first avadāna (see appendix 2) in the blank space at the bottom of the recto, then turned the scroll over lengthwise and continued the text, starting with the second avadāna. The writing on the verso thus goes in the reverse direction to the writing on the recto (Salomon 1999: 87). The style of the scribe who wrote the avadāna text is quite different from that of the first scribe (Salomon 1999: 54). His hand is large and flowing, with large spaces between each letter and between each line. His line of writing slopes downward to the left more steeply than that of the first scribe.

3.2.2. Patterns of Damage

Several scrolls in the BL collection sustained substantial damage due to the practice of folding the rolled-up scroll in half. As the scroll dried out, it eventually broke into two halves, or two vertical sections, with loss of text on either side of the divide. Scrolls in the BL collection that have been damaged in this way include the manuscripts of the Khvs-G (BL Frag. 5B) and Dhp-G^{L} (BL Frags. 16 and 25), the latter written by our scribe (see Salomon 2000: 26). Fortunately, the manuscript of the EĀ-G was not so folded, which means that, in contrast to these two manuscripts, the vertical middle of the manuscript is entire. The patterns of damage to the EĀ-G scroll thus differ somewhat from those of the Khvs-G described by Salomon (2000: 25–7).

This scroll has sustained four types of damage that have resulted in loss of text. The first is horizontal splitting (see Salomon 1999: 105, 2000: 25–6). As a rolled-up birch bark scroll dries and ages, it tends to crack horizontally, which often results in further splintering and loss of material on either side of the crack. The pattern of cracking tends to coincide with half the circumference of the rolled-up scroll, presumably because the scroll was slightly flattened by the pressure of other scrolls when they were interred together in the clay pot. In the case of a long scroll such as this one, the cracks tend to be closer together toward the bottom of the scroll, which corresponds to the inside of the scroll when it was rolled up.

The loss of text due to the horizontal splitting of the manuscript is relatively minor compared to that which resulted from damage to the left margin of the scroll and from the disintegration of the outer layers of the scroll. Damage to the left margin probably resulted from this end of the rolled-up scroll pressing against the inside of the clay pot during interment and absorbing moisture, for the right margin of the scroll is virtually intact. Further damage of this kind may have occurred when the scrolls were taken out of the clay pot and placed in modern glass jars. Further, the outer layers of a rolled-up scroll were inevitably exposed to damage, both when the scroll was in use in the monastery and being stored in the library and when it was interred in the clay pot (see Salomon 1999: 104–5). Once again, further damage of this kind may have occurred after the discovery of these scrolls. The result is that a substantial portion of the top of the scroll is missing (see § 3.2.1), while the upper section of what has survived of the scroll, particularly the upper left margin, is badly damaged and fragmentary. Finally, the written surface of the manuscript has deteriorated in many locations, making a reading of the text difficult. Such damage no doubt resulted in part from the use of the manuscript in antiquity.

3.2.3. The Reconstructed Text

The first sūtra on the surviving section of this scroll, the Dhoṇa-sutra, occupies lines 1–26 of the reconstructed manuscript. The beginning of the sūtra, that is, a portion of the nidāna, the opening formula, is now lost. The original text probably occupied twenty-seven or twenty-eight lines. Further loss of text has occurred due to damage to the left margin. Although some sections of this sūtra are repetitive, allowing some of the missing wording to be reconstructed, much of it is not. Therefore, the reconstruction of many of the lacunae of the text of this sūtra is tentative.

The second sūtra, the Budhabayaṇa-sutra, occupies lines 26–37, starting immediately after the punctuation mark that marks the end of the first sūtra. Taking up only twelve lines (or, rather, eleven lines of actual text, since the first and last lines are half lines), this sūtra is the shortest of the three that have survived on this manuscript. Although some loss of text has resulted from damage to the left margin, all of the lacunae can be restored with a high degree of certainty, since this sūtra consists of a nidāna identical to that of the third sūtra, a highly repetitive short discourse by the Buddha, and a closing formula which is the same as that of the first sūtra. The text of this sūtra is therefore in effect virtually complete.

The third and final sūtra, the Prasaṇa-sutra, occupies lines 37–73 (thirty-seven lines). But as mentioned elsewhere, the sūtra is incomplete because the scribe wrote the final part of the text on a separate scroll that has not survived. The sections of the P version of this sūtra corresponding to these missing sections of the G sūtra represent approximately 23% of the whole text (see pp. 296–7). Since the P and G versions are quite similar, the complete Prasaṇa-sutra must have been by far the longest of these three G sūtras. Like the Budhabayaṇa-sutra, this sūtra is highly repetitive, so that most of the lacunae resulting from damage to the left margin can be reconstructed with some degree of certainty.

3.3. Descriptive List of the Subfragments of BL Fragments 12 and 14

The system of numbering the fragments, or subfragments, within each frame was explained in § 3.1. As mentioned, the fragments preserved in frame 25 represent the top of the reconstructed manuscript, while those in frames 24 and 28 are the middle and lower sections, respectively. The fragment numbers will therefore be presented here in that order (25, 24, 28). Unless otherwise stated, the description of the position of each fragment refers to its location when viewed from the recto of the frame.

3.3.1. Frame 25

25a: Large fragment at the upper center of the frame, currently not in its correct position. It belongs between fragments 25f and 24a in the reconstructed manuscript.

25b: Medium fragment at the lower left corner of fragment 25a, from which it has become separated. Approximately in correct location.

25c: Medium fragment at the center left of frame. In correct position in relationship to fragments 25d, 25e, and 25f.

25d: Long narrow fragment correctly located between fragments 25c and 25f.

25e: Medium fragment in its correct position to the right of fragments 25c and 25d.

25f: Large fragment occupying the center of the frame. In correct position in relationship to fragments 25c, 25d, and 25e.

25g: Medium fragment that has flipped over and overlies the left end of fragment 25h. Parts of several akṣaras of the recto are visible on the verso of the frame. Located below fragment 25h in the reconstructed manuscript (l. 2).

25h: Medium fragment whose entire upper edge is overlain by fragment 25f. Parts of akṣaras belonging to two lines, the first representing the first line of text of the reconstructed manuscript. Its correct location is the upper left corner of fragment 25j.

25i: Medium fragment whose entire upper edge is overlain by fragment 25f. Parts of akṣaras of lines 2 and 3. Its correct location is the upper right edge of fragment 25j.

25j: Large fragment at the lower center of frame, currently not in its correct position. It belongs at the very top of the reconstructed manuscript.

25k: Small fragment that has flipped over, at extreme upper left corner of the frame. Parts of two akṣaras of line 17.

25l: Small fragment at the upper left corner of the frame. Parts of an uncertain number of illegible akṣaras. Unable to be located in the reconstructed text.

25m: Small, upside-down fragment, top center. Bottoms, or possibly tops, of three, possibly four, illegible akṣaras. Unlocated.

25n: Small fragment, top center. Bottom of what appears to be a single illegible akṣara. Unlocated.

25o: Small, upside-down fragment, upper right of frame. Tops of four akṣaras of line 31.

25p: Cluster of two small fragments; the larger one has fragmented and moved since the old black-and-white photo was taken. It is perhaps now located under the tape that binds the edge of the glass frame. The second splinter remains visible at the far left in the color photo. The original fragment is reproduced from the black-and-white photo and included in plate 8. Parts of four akṣaras, at least one of which is legible (for reading, see appendix 1). Unlocated.

25q: Small fragment. Present in old black-and-white photo, now missing (reproduced in pl. 8). Part of one or two illegible akṣaras. Unlocated.

25r: Small fragment overlying the top right edge of fragment 25a. Part of one illegible akṣara. Unlocated.

25s: Small fragment mostly obscured by lower left edge of fragment 25a. Part of one illegible akṣara. Unlocated.

25t: Small fragment partly obscured by upper edge of fragment 25b. Part of one akṣara. Tentatively located in line 16.

25u: Small, distorted fragment in the middle of the frame at the juncture of fragments 25a, 25c, and 25e, partly obscured by these fragments. Tops of three akṣaras of line 17.

25v: Small fragment between fragments 25d and 25f, partly obscured by them. Part of one akṣara or perhaps only a blemish from the inner bark. Located in line 7 on the basis of the reading of the text on the verso.

25w: Small, flipped-over fragment obscured by top right corner of fragment 25f. Parts of akṣaras belonging to two lines, some of which also appear on fragment 25x (for reading, see appendix 1). Unlocated.

25x: Small, flipped-over fragment obscured by top right corner of fragment 25f. Parts of two akṣaras. The bottom of the second akṣara appears on fragment 25w (for reading, see appendix 1). Unlocated.

25y: Small fragment adhering to the upper left region of fragment 25f. Parts of two or three illegible akṣaras belonging to two lines. Unlocated.

25z: Small fragment adhering to the upper left region of fragment 25f. Parts of akṣaras of lines 8 and 9.

25aa: Small fragment adhering to upper right of fragment 25i. Top of one akṣara of line 12.

25bb: Small, upside-down fragment at lower left of frame. Parts of akṣaras of lines 2 and 3.

25cc: Small, upside-down fragment at bottom of frame. Parts of three akṣaras of line 12.

25dd: Small, upside-down fragment at bottom of frame. Parts of akṣaras of lines 12–4.

25ee: Small, upside-down fragment at bottom of frame. Parts of five akṣaras of line 12.

25ff: Small fragment at lower right edge of fragment 25j, more intact in the old black-and-white photo. Parts of akṣaras of two lines (for reading, see appendix 1). Unlocated.

25gg: Small fragment at bottom right of frame. Parts of akṣaras of lines 6 and 7.

25hh: Small, flipped-over fragment at bottom right of frame. Parts of akṣaras of lines 16 and 17.

25ii: Tiny fragment adhering to upper left edge of verso of fragment 25f. Part of one illegible akṣara. Unlocated.

25jj: Tiny fragment adhering to upper left edge of verso of fragment 25f. Part of one illegible akṣara. Unlocated.

25kk: Tiny fragment adhering to upper right edge of verso of fragment 25f. Part of one illegible akṣara. Unlocated.

3.3.2. Frame 24

24a: Very large fragment representing the bulk of the manuscript in frame 24.

24b: Medium fragment at upper left of fragment 24a, from which it has broken away. Lies to left of its correct location. Contains the remnants of lines 18–20.

24c: Very small fragment, mostly obscured by the upper left corner of fragment 24b. Parts of two illegible akṣaras. Unlocated.

24d: Small, slender, flipped-over fragment at upper left of frame. Parts of two illegible akṣaras. Unlocated.

24e: Small, flipped-over fragment at upper left of frame. Parts of akṣaras of lines 16 and 17.

24f: Very small fragment to right of fragment 24e. Parts of two or three illegible akṣaras. Unlocated.

24g: Small fragment at upper left of frame. Parts of akṣaras of lines 18 and 19.

24h: Small, flipped-over fragment at upper left of frame immediately above fragment 24i. Bottoms of three akṣaras of line 44.

24i: Small fragment immediately below fragment 24h. Parts of akṣaras of lines 36 and 37.

24j: Small fragment at upper left of frame forming a cluster with fragments 24k and 24l. Parts of akṣaras of lines 42 and 43.

24k: Very small fragment pressed up against right corner of fragment 24j. Part of one illegible akṣara. Unlocated.

24l: Very small fragment pressed up against right edge of fragment 24j. Parts of one or two illegible akṣaras. Unlocated.

24m: Very small fragment that appears to the left of fragment 24n in the old black-and-white photo but has since disappeared (reproduced in pl. 8). Part of one akṣara belonging to line 48.

24n: Small fragment at upper left of the frame, butting up against fragments 24o, 24p, 24q, and 24a. Contains parts of akṣaras of lines 48 and 49.

24o: Small fragment butting up against upper right edge of fragment 24n. Parts of akṣaras of lines 42 and 43.

24p: Very small fragment compressed between fragments 24n, 24o, and 24a. Part of one akṣara of line 48.

24q: Small fragment butting up against fragments 24n and 24a. Parts of akṣaras of lines 42 and 43.

24r: Very small fragment located between fragments 24q and 24a. Part of one akṣara of line 44.

24s: Very small fragment located between fragments 24q and 24a. Parts of two akṣaras of line 44.

24t: Small, blank, flipped-over fragment immediately below fragment 24q, opposite large blank glue area of fragment 24a. Belongs to blank glue area between lines 53 and 54.

24u: Small, flipped-over fragment lying along left edge of fragment 24a, center of frame. Parts of akṣaras of lines 37 and 38.

24v: Small fragment wedged between fragments 24u and 24a. Parts of akṣaras of lines 36 and 37.

24w: Very small fragment embedded in deep crack in fragment 24a (to right of frag. 24v). Part of one akṣara of line 37.

24x: Very small fragment partly obscured by fragment 24a, center left of frame. Parts of three akṣaras of line 41.

24y: Very small fragment adhering to fragment 24a, lower left section. Part of one akṣara of line 45.

24z: Very small fragment mostly obscured by fragment 24a, lower left section. Part of one illegible akṣara. Unlocated.

24aa: Very small free-floating fragment, lower left of frame. Appears attached to fragment 24a in the old black-and-white photo. Part of one akṣara of line 45.

24bb: Very small fragment at lower left of frame. Part of one illegible akṣara. Unlocated, may belong to line 50 near its present position in the unreconstructed manuscript.

24cc: Very small, flipped-over fragment at lower left of frame, partly obscured by fragment 24a. Parts of two akṣaras of line 52.

24dd: Very small, upside-down fragment adhering to lower section of fragment 24a. Parts of two akṣaras that may belong to the recto (for reading, see appendix 1). Unlocated.

3.3.3. Frame 28

28a: Very large fragment representing the bulk of the manuscript in frame 28.

28b: Very small fragment at upper left of frame. Attached to fragment 28a in the old black-and-white photo. Part of one akṣara of line 54.

28c: Very small fragment at lower left edge of first horizontal section of fragment 28a. Part of one akṣara of line 54.

28d: Small fragment butting up against upper left margin of fragment 28a and upper margin of fragment 28e. Parts of akṣaras of two lines (for reading, see appendix 1). Unlocated.

28e: Small fragment butting up against the lower edge of fragment 28d. Parts of two akṣaras (for reading, see appendix 1). Unlocated.

28f: Small fragment partly obscured by the right edge of fragment 28a (middle section). Part of one illegible akṣara. Unlocated.

28g: Small fragment off lower left edge of fragment 28a. Attached to fragment 28a in old black-and-white photo. Part of one akṣara of the first line of the Puniga avadāna (presented in appendix 2).

3.3.4. Debris Box Fragments (pl. 8)

All the debris box fragments are small.

D6a: Parts of two akṣaras of line 19.

D6b: Parts of akṣaras of lines 9 and 10.

D6c: Tops of three akṣaras of line 44.

D6d: It is unclear which side is the recto and which the verso. Both are therefore reproduced in plate 8 as D6d-A and D6d-B. Both contain parts of akṣaras (for reading, see appendix 1). Unlocated.

D6e: Parts of akṣaras of lines 26 and 27.

D6f: Part of one akṣara (for reading, see appendix 1). Unlocated.

D6g: Parts of three illegible akṣaras. The orientation of the fragment is uncertain. Unlocated.

D6h: Parts of two akṣaras (for reading, see appendix 1). Unlocated.

D6i: Parts of akṣaras of lines 1 and 2.

D6j: Parts of akṣaras of lines 25 and 26.

D6k: Parts of three akṣaras (for reading, see appendix 1). Possibly to be located in line 51.

D6l: Parts of two illegible akṣaras. Unlocated.

D6m: Parts of akṣaras of lines 12 and 13.

D6n: Part of one illegible akṣara. Unlocated.

D6o: Parts of two akṣaras (for reading, see appendix 1). Unlocated.

D6p: Parts of three akṣaras of line 18.

D6q: Parts of three, possibly four, illegible akṣaras. Unlocated.

D6r: Tops of eight akṣaras of line 16.

D6s: Part of one or two akṣaras (for reading, see appendix 1). Unlocated.

D6t: Part of two akṣaras (for reading, see appendix 1). Unlocated.

D6u: Part of one akṣara of line 21.

D6v: Parts of akṣaras of lines 18 and 19.

D6w: It is unclear which side is the recto and which the verso (reproduced in pl. 8 as D6w-A and D6w-B). Both contain parts of illegible akṣaras. Unlocated.

D6x: Parts of four akṣaras of line 21.

D6y: Parts of two illegible akṣaras. Unlocated.

D6z: Parts of two akṣaras (for reading, see appendix 1). Unlocated.

D6aa: Parts of two akṣaras (for reading, see appendix 1). Unlocated.

D6bb: Parts of three akṣaras of line 31.

D6cc: Part of one illegible akṣara. Unlocated.

D6dd: Parts of akṣaras of lines 23 and 24.

D6ee: Parts of akṣaras of two lines (for reading, see appendix 1). Unlocated.

CHAPTER 4

Paleography and Orthography

The scribe of BL Fragments 12 and 14 also wrote two other manuscripts in the collection: Fragment 1, containing portions of the Anavataptagāthā (Salomon 1999: 31–3), and Fragments 16 and 25, containing part of a text corresponding to the end of the Bhikhu-varga of the Dhp-G^K (Salomon 1999: 35). He is referred to as BL scribe 1 or "big hand" (see Salomon 1999: 54–5). For the purposes of this chapter only the script of the present manuscript will be discussed in detail. Throughout this chapter references are given to akṣaras by line number and syllable number from right to left (which includes punctuation marks); for example, 40.7 refers to line 40 of the edition, seventh visible character from the right.

4.1. The Writing Instrument

This manuscript was written with a broad-edged reed pen, or *calamus*. Unlike the scribe of the Khvs-G (see Salomon 2000: § 5.1), this scribe did not recut the nib frequently. This resulted in a gradual softening of the nib's fibers, so that the thickness of the strokes increases slightly from line to line and the distinction between the thick and thin strokes has become blurred. This is clearly seen at the beginning of the third sūtra of this text (l. 37), where the scribe recut the nib or changed to a new pen. In line 37 the nib width[1] is 0.7 mm and the depth 0.3 mm. After writing ten lines, the nib has increased to a width of 1.2 mm and a depth of 0.6 mm (l. 47). It is not clear if the nib was split, as is believed to have been the normal practice for reed pens, though not for the Indian wooden pen (*varṇikā*) (Sircar 1965: 82).

4.2. General Features of the Hand

The script of the present manuscript has a bold, upright appearance. The scribe has worked slowly, forming each character with care. This is indicated by his preference for multiple-stroke forms rather than the more economical cursive ones. The pen angle varies from 30° to 37°. Since this is also the natural pen angle for a right-handed person, it is probable that the nib was cut square. The verticals are, in most cases, written perpendicular to the line of writing. The curvature of the lines indicates that the scribe did not rule lines, in common with the other manuscripts in the BL collection. Interline spacing is about 1 cm. The height of the central part of the letters between the ascenders and descenders, or "x-height," is about 5 mm, giving a letter weight of about 1:5, which is slightly more elongated than the letters in the Khvs-G (see Salomon 2000: § 5.2).

[1] All measurements have been taken from the right side of the manuscript, as the left side has shrunk slightly due to moisture damage.

4.3. Foot Marks

One of the characteristics of Kharoṣṭhī writing is the foot marks, or flourishes, which appear at the base of the vertical stems. The fact that different types of foot marks are associated with different akṣaras has been known for some time (Dani 1963: 264), and this is often helpful in determining readings for badly damaged characters. Only three types of foot marks have been identified here, as opposed to eight in the Khvs-G (Salomon 2000: § 5.4).

A hook to the left (e.g., *a* 58.5) is found attached to the independent vowels (excluding *u;* see § 4.4.1.3), *ka, kha, gha, ca, cha, ja, ña, ṭha, ṭ́ha, ḍa, ḍh, ta, da, dha, pa, pha, ba, bha, ra, la, va, śa, ṣa,* and *sa*. This mark is the same as the type 4 foot mark of the Khvs-G (Salomon 2000: § 5.4), although there appears to be very little overlap between the two manuscripts in its application to specific letters.

The leftward hook takes a variety of subforms, but since these all reflect the same basic pen movement, no further classification has been attempted. The range of such subforms is seen in the following examples of the independent vowel *a:* (40.7), (45.13), (48.1), (58.5), (58.24). In the case of *a* (45.13), the hook appears to have been added with a second stroke rather than as a continuation of the first. If the presence or absence of a foot mark is not related to the phonetic value of the character, as was seen to be the case in the Khvs-G (Salomon 2000: § 5.4), it is unclear why the scribe would have taken the care to add a mark to a letter secondarily, although incidental marks often come to be regarded as intrinsic parts of a letter and may be written with separate strokes—for example, the serifs of Roman capitals and the top line of Devanāgarī.

A slight hook to the right (e.g., *ṇa* 26.17) is found only with *ṇa*. This is similar to the type 7 foot mark of the Khvs-G (Salomon 2000: § 5.4), although the scribe of the Khvs-G does not write *ṇa* with the type 7 foot mark.

In addition to these two foot marks a number of akṣaras appear with straight stems as opposed to distinct foot marks (e.g., *a* 35.1); this is the "type zero" foot mark in the Khvs-G (Salomon 2000: § 5.4). The independent vowels, *ḍe, ṇa, ta, dha, ya, ra, va, śa,* and *sa* all appear with a straight stem.

4.4. Analysis of Individual Letters (Table 1)

For the purposes of this discussion, those characters which vary with respect to the presence or absence of a foot mark will be called "forms," while those characters in which there is a structural difference in terms of stroke order or direction will be referred to as "types."

4.4.1. Independent Vowels

4.4.1.1. *a*

The independent vowel *a* has two basic forms: the more common one with a hook at the base (40.7), the other without (35.1). Otherwise, this letter is the standard Kharoṣṭhī type (see also *a* in § 4.6). In some cases this letter looks very similar to a rounded *va*, for example, (27.12; see § 4.4.2.29).

Table 1. Kharoṣṭhī script as written by the scribe of British Library Fragments 12 and 14

Basic Characters

	a	*i*	*u*	*e*	*o*
Independent vowels § 4.4.1	35.1 40.7 45.13 48.1 58.5 58.24	13.29 36.17	9.6	26.20 39.1 56 17	8.6 62.16
k- § 4.4.2.1	32.22 33.18		52.8		
kh- § 4.4.2.2	23.20		28.6		
g- § 4.4.2.3					
gh- § 4.4.2.4	34.11 39.2		19.1 67.6	6.4	21.2
c- § 4.4.2.5	39.6 60.13	43.3 52.14		5 9	
ch- § 4.4.2.6	44.8		8.16		

* An asterisk denotes characters that are incomplete due to fragmentation of the manuscript.

	a	*i*	*u*	*e*	*o*
j- § 4.4.2.7	46.19 60.7	53.8		27.10	
j̄- § 4.4.2.8					
ñ- § 4.4.2.9	57.15		20.11	19.20	
ṭ- § 4.4.2.10					2.2 6.2
ṭh- § 4.4.2.11	54.5		13.3		
ṭ́h- § 4.4.2.12		31.3 62.20			
ḍ- § 4.4.2.13		27.18 38.1		* 23.24	
ḍh- § 4.4.2.14	22.2				
ṇ- § 4.4.2.15	26.17 32.9 33.5	33.11 50.2 65.10		32.18 40.6	29.7 40.8
t- § 4.4.2.16	29.8 33.6	46.8	33.19	28.4 30.12	34.2
th- § 4.4.2.17					

	a	*i*	*u*	*e*	*o*
d- § 4.4.2.18	16.7 20.3 46.11	12.3 13.30 54.18 60.8	27.1	26.9 71.10	44.9
dh- § 4.4.2.19	25.2 33.2 49.1 69.13				26.1
n- § 4.4.2.20					
p- § 4.4.2.21	52.4	27.17	62.14		
ph- § 4.4.2.22			54.7		
b- § 4.4.2.23	40.2		33.1		
bh- § 4.4.2.24	26.6 62.1	33.7 51.19 53.5	21.1		
m- § 4.4.2.25	26.4	19.10	24.6	39.9	
y- § 4.4.2.26	17.8 33.4	56.27		54.2	

	a	*i*	*u*	*e*	*o*
r- § 4.4.2.27	34.12 40.9	39.8	65.8	25.3	5.3 6.19 31.9 33.17
l- § 4.4.2.28	56.1 62.11	19.3		32.8	6.22
v- § 4.4.2.29	3.9 4.8 26.8 26.12	10.11 27.6	73.3	10.1 33.9	
ś- § 4.4.2.30	27.2 52.9	23.28	11.11 23.15	34.6	
ṣ- § 4.4.2.31	33.12 69.12	26.13 70.1	44.10		
s- § 4.4.2.32	3.10 27.20 40.1	58.6	33.15	57.11	

	a	*i*	*u*	*e*	*o*
h- § 4.4.2.33	27.7	20.6 42.5 51.4		44.18	11.18 13.13

Conjunct Characters (§ 4.4.3)

kra 4.14	*kri* 23.13	*kro* 23.16	*kṣa* 40.10	*kṣi* 18.1	*kṣu* 11.4
ghra 42.4 51.3	*ghre* 25.8	*tra* 38.9	*tre* 28.2	*tva* 39.7	*dhra* 10.7
dhri 50.3	*dhre* 22.32	*dhro* 47.7	*pra* 40.4 69.6	*pro* 54.4	*bra* 19.11
bro 48.14 51.23	*rṇo* 23.14	*rva* 20.10	*rbha* 18.4	*rma* 49.2 56.3	*rmu* 23.18
rvo 10.8	*rśa* 49.7	*śpa* 64.14	*śpi* 19.5 * 19.7	*sta* 18.5	*sti* 27.4
stu 52.3					

Punctuation (§ 4.5)

39.5	37.5	26.19	73.12

Corrections (§ 4.6)

a 73.1	*khu* 38.16	*tva* 44.11	*pra* 40.12	*ya* 29.6	*śa* 10.12

4.4.1.2. *i*

This character also appears in two forms: with a hook at the base (36.17) and without (13.29). The horizontal stroke has been written from left to right against the direction of writing (see Salomon 2000: § 5.5.1.2).

4.4.1.3. *u*

The independent *u* vowel has a closed loop (e.g., 9.6). This is the usual type from the Saka period onward. Since the base is taken up with the loop, it cannot have a foot mark.

4.4.1.4. *e*

There are two types of the independent *e* vowel. The first has two strokes and a straight stem (39.1) or, less often, a hook or enlarged base (26.20). The second type is made with a single stroke (56.17). The same two types occur in the Khvs-G (see Salomon 2000: § 5.5.1.4). Although in the present manuscript there is no clear pattern for their distribution, in the Khvs-G the types vary according to whether or not they are in pāda-initial position.

4.4.1.5. *o*

The independent *o* vowel appears in two forms: once with the leftward foot mark (8.6) and once without (62.16).

4.4.2. Consonants

4.4.2.1. *ka*

The type of *ka* found in this manuscript is made with two strokes. The first stroke forms the top line and the right arm; the second stroke adds the stem and bottom hook (e.g., 33.18). This type of *ka* has been identified as a secondary development and associated with the Kuṣāṇa period (Salomon 2000: § 5.5.2.1). The syllable *ku* has been constructed in the same way, except that the bottom hook forms a closed loop (52.8). In one instance the right arm of *ka* has curled around far enough that it touches the stem to form a closed loop on the right (32.22).

4.4.2.2. *kha*

This character appears only in the syllables *kha* (23.20) and *khu* (28.6). In all cases it is contained more or less within the line of writing rather than rising high above it as in the Khvs-G and Dhp-G^{K} (Salomon 2000: § 5.5.2.2). See also *khu* in § 4.6.

4.4.2.3. *ga*

This scribe does not write *ga*. See § 4.8.1.1.

4.4.2.4. *gha*

The *gha* is consistently drawn with two strokes. The first begins at the top left, forms the loop at the top right, descends to the base, and finishes with a hook to the left. The second stroke adds the arm on the right side of the stem. In a few cases the right arm has formed a closed loop: for example, *gha* (34.11) and *ghu* (67.6).

4.4.2.5. *ca*

The type of *ca* found in this manuscript is typical of the middle and later periods of Kharoṣṭhī (see Salomon 2000: § 5.5.2.5). It appears once in a somewhat contorted form, (60.13), so that it resembles *sa* .

4.4.2.6. *cha*

Like *ca,* the shape of *cha* is typical of middle to later Kharoṣṭhī (e.g., 44.8; see Salomon 2000: § 5.5.2.6). It is formed with two strokes. The first makes the top line, forms a loop at the top right, and descends to form the stem and bottom hook. The second stroke adds the rounded crossbar from left to right.

4.4.2.7. *ja*

There are two types of *ja* in this manuscript. The first is an older type made with two strokes: first the left arm, then the right arm and stem (e.g., 46.19). The second, more common type is a cursive development in which a rounded single stroke forms both the left and right arms, before descending to form the stem (e.g., 60.7).

4.4.2.8. *ǰa*

There are no examples of *ǰ*- in this text. See § 4.8.1.

4.4.2.9. *ña*

The top of the stem of this character has a pronounced hook (e.g., 57.15). This feature is perhaps associated with the more curved top of *ña* (e.g.,) seen in inscriptions from the Aśokan period to the Takht-i-Bāhī inscription of the year 103 (ca. A.D. 46). The tight hook of our manuscript is also seen in a relatively late inscription, the Jamālgaṛhī inscription of the year 359 of the so-called Old Sāka era, which is likely to represent approximately A.D. 200 (see Salomon 1998: 181), *ñe* (*rañe;* Konow 1929: pl. 22.1, l. 2), but seldom in between. The character is written with two strokes; first the stem, then the right arm.

4.4.2.10. *ṭa*

This rare character occurs only in the syllable *ṭo*. It has two types. The radical of the first type is made cursively with a single stroke (e.g., 2.2), the *o*-vowel diacritic being added secondarily. In the second type the first stroke makes the left arm, and the second makes the vertical and right arm. In the second type the vowel stroke is added lower down on the stem (e.g., 6.2).

4.4.2.11. *ṭha*

This character is found in the syllables *ṭha* (54.5) and *ṭhu* (13.3). It is formed with two strokes; first the top line and stem, then the left arm.

4.4.2.12. *ṭ́ha*

This character occurs twice, both times with the *i*-vowel diacritic (e.g., 62.20). The radical of *ṭ́ha* is distinguished from *ṭha* by a short vertical that begins the left arm. For details on the relationship between these two characters, see Brough 1962: 76–7.

4.4.2.13. *ḍa*

This character has two types, both occurring with the *i*-vowel diacritic. The first is formed with a single stroke and is very similar to the cursive form of *ja:* compare *ji* (53.8) and *ḍi* (27.18). The second type is made with two strokes; first the left arm, then the stem (e.g., 38.1). The lower portion of the only occurrence of *ḍe* is damaged, so that it appears in table 1 without a foot mark, but in fact it probably had a leftward hook.

4.4.2.14. *ḍha*

This rare character occurs only once (22.2). It is formed with two strokes: a crossbar at the top and a stem descending from the crossbar's midpoint and ending with a leftward hook.

4.4.2.15. *ṇa*

There are two forms of *ṇa*. The first has a straight stem (e.g., 33.5). The second, less common form has a rightward foot mark (e.g., 26.17). This foot mark is first seen in an inscription of the Kaniṣka year 41, for example, (*matarapitaraṇa;* Konow 1929: pl. 32.1, l. 4). The rightward hook is also found in *ṇe* (32.18; in this case it is barely distinct from the stem) and *ṇo* (29.7) but has not been observed in the combination *ṇi*. It cannot occur with *ṇu,* as there the foot is taken up with the loop of the *u*-vowel diacritic. The *i*-vowel stroke in *ṇi* is sometimes written so that it does not touch the radical (e.g., 65.10).

4.4.2.16. *ta*

In this manuscript *ta* is clearly distinguished from *da*, with which it can be confused in some hands. In one case the right shoulder of the form is pointed, (29.8). This character also appears with a small leftward foot mark (e.g., 33.6).

4.4.2.17. *tha*

There are no examples of *th-* in the text. See § 4.8.1.

4.4.2.18. *da*

This consonant appears in the normal *s*-shaped form with only slight variations in the amount of curvature at each end, from the flattened *di* (54.18) to the rounded *do* (44.9). The angle of the vowel stroke of *di* ranges from horizontal (e.g., 12.3) to strongly oblique, such that it contacts the rounded tips of the top and bottom (e.g., 13.30). In *de* (71.10) the vowel stroke, drawn from the top right downward to the left, has extended over the central line of the radical.

4.4.2.19. *dha*

There are two types of *dha*. The first is a careful angular form (e.g., 49.1), which also occurs without the foot mark in (69.13). The second is a more rounded, cursive form, (25.2), similar to the form found in the Aśokan inscriptions (e.g., *dha*). However, since this is the only example of the rounded type, it is likely that the form has been miswritten rather than being a genuine archaism.

4.4.2.20. *na*

There are no examples of *n-* in the text. See § 4.8.1.

4.4.2.21. *pa*

This character appears in the normal two-stroke form (e.g., 52.4). The first stroke forms the stem and ends in the leftward hook, and the second stroke adds the right arm from the middle of the stem extending out to the right and downward. In the single example of *pi,* (27.17), the *i* vowel appears in the usual position, as a vertical stroke through the middle of the right arm.

4.4.2.22. *pha*

This character occurs in this text only in the syllable *phu* (e.g., 54.7). It is distinguished from *pu* (e.g., 62.14) only by the slight extension of the right arm on the left side of the stem.

4.4.2.23. *ba*

This character appears in all cases with its characteristic pronounced double hook at the top (e.g., 40.2). The scribe has thus avoided the confusion with *ra* or *ta* that can occur in more cursive writing (see Salomon 2000: § 5.5.2.22).

4.4.2.24. *bha*

This consonant has three types. The first (e.g., 26.6) is made with three strokes: the top line is drawn from left to right; the second stroke descends from the midpoint of the first line before turning rightward to make a hook; the last stroke adds the lower half of the stem and the hook to the left. Thus the character differs only slightly from *ka* (see § 4.4.2.1). The second, more cursive type is constructed in exactly the same way as *ka* (e.g., *bhi* 53.5). In the third type the first stroke forms the top line and the full stem, while a second stroke adds the right arm (e.g., *bhi* 51.19).

4.4.2.25. *ma*

This character appears in the usual high position with regard to the line of writing. The right vertical rises a little higher than the left (e.g., 26.4); compare *ma* (Khvs-G 38a7) with the balanced *ma* (Dhp-G^{K} 107d3). The shape of the radical in the syllable *mi* differs slightly from the basic form in that the two sides curl inward: (19.10). The stroke of the *i* vowel is written with a hook to the left at the bottom. This scribe writes the ligatured type of *mu* (e.g., 24.6). This type is the standard from the Indo-Greek period onward (cf. in the Bajaur casket inscription). The syllable *me* is formed with two strokes (e.g., 39.9), first the radical beginning at the tip of the left arm, and then the *e*-vowel diacritic drawn upward. This contrasts with the single-stroke type seen in the Khvs-G (29b2), in which the right arm hooks back into the middle of the character in lieu of the vowel marker.

4.4.2.26. *ya*

This scribe always writes the older, pointed type of *ya* (e.g., 33.4) rather than the later, flat-topped form that is generally found from the Kuṣāṇa period onward (e.g., Dhp-G[K] 106b5; see Salomon 2000: § 5.5.2.25). It is written with two strokes from the midpoint down to each side. In one example of the syllable *ye* (54.2) the stroke order has been changed, so that the second stroke forms both the *e*-vowel diacritic and the right arm from the top. See also *ya* in § 4.6.

4.4.2.27. *ra*

This character appears in two forms, with and without the leftward foot mark (e.g., 34.12 and 40.9). The syllable *ro* may be written with a straight stem (e.g., 33.17) or with a bent stem (e.g., 6.19). The akṣara (5.3) could be read as *ro* or *so*.

4.4.2.28. *la*

There are two types of *la*. In the first, the stem is drawn with a downward stroke and the left arm is added with a separate stroke (e.g., 56.1). In the second, more cursive type, the scribe starts with the left arm, draws the pen rightward, and loops up to the top of the stem before descending (e.g., 62.11); compare Khvs-G (23b2).

4.4.2.29. *va*

Our scribe writes two forms of *va*, with and without the rightward hook (e.g., 26.8 and 3.9). It is sometimes written with a slightly rounded head (e.g., 27.12), so that it resembles the independent vowel *a* (e.g., 48.1; see § 4.4.1.1).

4.4.2.30. *śa*

This letter is written with two strokes (e.g., 52.9). The first forms the top line and right leg; the second makes the left leg from the top downward. This is similar to the *śa* written by the scribe of the Khvs-G (see Salomon 2000: § 5.5.2.29). The right leg may have a slight hook to the left (e.g., 27.2). See also *śa* in § 4.6.

4.4.2.31. *ṣa*

This letter is made with two strokes (e.g., 33.12). The stem is apparently formed with the first stroke, and the looped top with the second. The two strokes do not always meet at the top of the stem (e.g., 69.12).

4.4.2.32. *sa*

In this manuscript we find only the late, open type of *sa* (e.g., 40.1), generally associated with the Kuṣāṇa period. For a discussion of the various types of *sa* and their chronological implications, see Salomon 2000: § 5.5.2.32. It occurs once without the leftward hook, (27.20). The akṣara (5.3) could be read as *ro* or *so*.

4.4.2.33. *ha*

This character appears in the standard one-stroke form throughout this manuscript (e.g., 27.7). There are two types of the combination *hi*. The first is a two-stroke form, the *i* vowel being added with a second stroke (42.5). The second type is a cursive, single-stroke form, in which the *i* vowel has been added by extending the rightward foot back across the center of the character (e.g., 20.6).

4.4.3. Conjunct Consonants

4.4.3.1. *kṣa*

This character, conventionally transcribed as *kṣa,* appears in this manuscript in the usual form (e.g., 40.10). The stem has the leftward foot mark in all cases. See also *kṣa* in § 4.6.

4.4.3.2. Preconsonantal *r*

The sign for preconsonantal *r* is formed by continuing the stem of the radical with a clockwise spiral (e.g., *rva* 20.10). It also occurs in this text in the following combinations: *rṇo* (23.14), *rbha* (18.4), *rvo* (10.8), and *rśa* (49.7). In the combination *rma* it takes a special form since the radical has no downward stem on which the mark can be affixed (*ma*). Therefore, the right arm is extended and the spiral is added to the top of the character, but in a counterclockwise direction (e.g., *rma* 49.2). This sign plus *ṇ* is used occasionally to represent the reflex of OIA *-ṣṇ-* (see § 4.8.1).

4.4.3.3. Postconsonantal *r*

The mark of a postconsonantal *r* shows considerable variation in this text, from the short, flat mark at the base of *dhra* (10.7) to the large, curved hook of *bra* (19.11). Despite the size of this mark in the last example, there is no risk of confusion with postconsonantal *v,* which is much bigger still (see § 4.4.3.4). The syllable *ghra* has two types. In the first (e.g., 51.3), the stroke order has been rearranged so that the first stroke forms the top line, right loop, and top half of the stem; the second stroke begins at the tip of the right arm and loops around to form the bottom of the stem and the postconsonantal *r* mark in a single turn. In the second type, found only in (42.4), the first stroke forms the top, upper part of the stem, and right arm, and the second stroke adds the lower part of the stem and the *-r-* mark at the base. See also *pra* in § 4.6.

4.4.3.4. Postconsonantal *v*

This mark appears as a large hook extending above the top line of the syllable. It is found in this manuscript only in the combination *tva* (e.g., 39.7). See also *tva* in § 4.6.

4.4.3.5. *śpa*

This sign is conventionally transcribed as *śpa* but is used variously to represent the equivalents of Skt. *śpa, śva, sma,* and *spa* (there are no examples of *spa* in this text; for details see

Brough 1962: § 55; and below, § 5.2.3.6). There are two types, both occurring almost side by side in line 19. The first is similar to *ka,* formed with the top and right loops in a single stroke, the lower portion of the stem and leftward foot mark being added with a second stroke (e.g., *śpi* 19.5). In the second type the top loop and stem are formed with the first stroke, and the right arm is added secondarily (e.g., *śpi* 19.7, the top of this character is damaged).

4.4.3.6. *sta*

This character appears in its usual two-stroke form (e.g., 18.5). The stem has a leftward foot mark.

4.5. Punctuation

Three types of punctuation marks appear in this manuscript. The first is a small circle (e.g., 39.5) used to mark the end of a phrase (5.7) or sentence (3.5). It is also used to mark the end of a pāda in the verses (ll. 16–20). For further comments on the use of this mark, see § 4.8.2.

The second punctuation mark is a large circle (e.g., 37.5) marking the end of a sūtra. At the end of the first sūtra, it appears that the scribe first wrote a small circle and then corrected it to a large circle, (26.19).

The third punctuation mark occurs at the end of the last sūtra, (73.12). It appears that our scribe's usual large circle was later expanded with two larger circles by the scribe who wrote the following text on this piece of bark. Presumably this was done with the intention of making a clear distinction between the two works.

4.6. Corrections

This scribe has corrected the text by making interlinear additions where characters had been omitted and by overwriting incorrect letters. The interlinear additions, which are always written beneath the line to which they refer, are as follows: *va* (8.14), *ṇe* (40.14), *asiaraṇame(*va)* (42.11 ff.), *e* (63.7), and *de* (66.22, 71.4). In one case (22.10), a faint unexpected akṣara of uncertain reading (perhaps *a*) appears below the line. Of the several cases of overwriting in this manuscript, the incorrect letter is sometimes visible underneath the correct letter. In *budhabayaṇo* ( ) in line 29, the scribe originally omitted the *ya* and wrote *budhabaṇa* ( ) before realizing his mistake and making the right leg of the *ya* from the tip of the *ṇa*, that is, *ya* (29.6). The *khu* in 38.16 was first written as a plain *kha,* and the *u*-vowel loop was added subsequently. Other examples where the scribe modified an incorrect character include *śa* (10.12), where the scribe corrected what he probably originally wrote as *va*. Similarly, the *ji* in 51.18 seems to have been corrected from an original *ci*. In *tva* (44.11), the scribe wrote a normal *ta* before separately adding a postconsonantal *v*. Likewise in *pra* (40.12), the postconsonantal *r* was added secondarily. In *a* (73.1), it is not clear whether the scribe overwrote an incorrect form or whether there was too much ink on his nib. The latter is likely since this is the first character in the line, and he may have just dipped his pen before starting it. The *kṣa* in 31.20 is faint, and there is a faint trace of a *va* beneath it. The scribe may have smudged out a *va* and written the *kṣa* over it. In other parts of the manuscript the scribe has apparently smudged a character in order to erase it (see *ma,* 17.7; *bha,* 26.10; *a,* 61.3, 64.14, 69.3, 69.4, 72.2, 72.3, 73.5, 73.8, 73.9).

4.6.1. Incidental Marks

In addition to the corrections mentioned above, a few traces of ink appear to be extraneous. There is a horizontal line beneath *ha* in 3.3, (the top of this character is missing). Such a mark is not normal in Kharoṣṭhī and has not been observed previously in combination with this letter. Its value, if any, is therefore uncertain. A short joining stroke between the punctuation mark in 4.15 and the following *sa*, , is certainly a hypercursive stroke formed when the scribe did not lift his pen between forming the punctuation mark and starting the *sa*. A large ink mark in the right margin (l. 33) is likely to be a smudged drip of ink. There is a trace of ink preceding the first character of line 73.

4.7. Paleographic Dating

In the Kharoṣṭhī script the letters *ka, ca, cha, ya,* and *sa* are the best indicators of script development. Table 2 shows a comparison of these characters taken from the present manuscript (EĀ-G) with equivalents from the Khvs-G.

	ka	*ca*	*cha*	*ya*	*sa*
EĀ-G	(33.18)	(39.6)	(44.8)	(33.4)	(40.1)
Khvs-G	(18b4)	(28a4)	(5b3)	(28a6)	(1a1)

Table 2. Comparison of test letters in the EĀ-G and the Khvs-G.

With the exception of the differences in the scribes' use of foot marks and the slight clockwise rotation of the *ya* in the Khvs-G, the basic letter types are the same. The chronological range for each of the test letters is discussed in their corresponding sections above. In the discussion of the date of the Khvs-G (Salomon 2000: § 5.8), which also took into account historical evidence provided by other manuscripts and inscribed pots in the BL collection (Salomon 1999: 141–55), a date in the first half of the first century A.D. was considered to be the most likely. The evidence of the present manuscript is in agreement with those findings and it can be assigned to the same period.

4.8. Orthography

A general outline of the orthography of the BL manuscripts appears in Salomon 1999: 120–4; the orthography of the first of the BL Kharoṣṭhī manuscripts to be published, the Khvs-G, is discussed in Salomon 2000: § 5.9.

As is characteristic of scribes writing the Gāndhārī language in Kharoṣṭhī script, several orthographic features are specific to our scribe. These are consistently encountered in all three texts written by him, namely, the three EĀ-type sūtras, the Anavataptagāthā (AG-G) fragment being edited by Richard Salomon, and the Dharmapada fragment (Dhp-G^{L}) being edited by Timothy Lenz (see Lenz 1999: § 4.4 for the orthography of the Dhp-G^{L} fragment). Within our text a high degree of consistency is seen in the spelling of most words. Examples are *arśaveti* (= BHS *āsrāvayanti/āśrāvayanti*), *avajadi* (= Skt. *āpadyate*), *asiaraṇam eva* (= Skt.

adhikaraṇam eva), *ṇiṣida-* (= BHS *niśrita-*), *domaṇastu* (= Skt. **daurmanastvam*), *pavea* (= Skt. *pāpakāḥ*), *prasaṇa-* (= Skt. *pradhāna-*, *prahāṇa-*), *bramaṇa-* (= Skt. *brāhmaṇa-*), *bhayavada-* (= Skt. *bhagavant*), *bhaviśasi* (= Skt. *bhaviṣyasi*), *bhikṣave* in the vocative (= Skt. *bhikṣavaḥ*), *bhikhu* in all other cases, *bhu* (= Skt. *bhoḥ*), *vivasagha-* (= BHS *vyavasarga-*), *vivea-* (= Skt. *viveka-*), *śavastie* (= Skt. *śrāvastyām*), *ṣamaṇa-* (= Skt. *śramaṇa-*), and *sabujagha-* (= BHS *saṃbodhyaṅga-*), all of which occur several or many times (see the word index for occurrences). Except for the variation in final vowels, which is virtually universal in Gāndhārī, alternative spellings for the same word are relatively uncommon. In most cases these involve well-attested alternations. Examples are *vucadi/bucadi* (= P *vuccati*), *dharma-/dhama-* (= Skt. *dharma-*), *ghudama-/ghodama-* (= P *gotama-*), *eghad uya/eghad oya* (= P *etad avaca*), *ca/ya* (= Skt. *ca*), *a/ba/va* (= Skt. *vā*), *pariṇama-/prariṇama-* (= Skt. *parināma-*), *[p](*i)/avi* (= Skt. *api*), *mi/śpi* (= Skt. *asmi*), *sabara-/savara-* (= Skt. *saṃvara-*), and *sarva-/sava-* (= Skt. *sarva-*). This overall consistency in orthography, with occasional examples of variant spellings in the case of certain words, seems to hold true for the Dhp-G^L as well, whereas the orthography of the AG-G awaits satisfactory documentation. In the Dhp-G^L, the only example of a word with alternating spellings is *ti/di* (= Skt. *iti*) (2d, 9b).

The three texts written by our scribe are on separate scrolls. No doubt these were written on separate occasions. It is also likely that the exemplars of each text that he copied were written by different scribes. This being the case, the fact that our scribe's orthography is more or less consistent in all of the texts written by him indicates he must have ignored the orthographic tendencies of the manuscripts he copied, having his own notion of "correct" spelling.[2]

4.8.1. Orthographic Peculiarities

Aspirated *gh* is invariably written for etymological *g* and *gh* (see Salomon 1999: 127–8). Examples in initial position are *ghudama-/ghodama-* = P *gotama-* (ll. 21, 24, etc.) and *ghadharva-* = Skt. *gandharva-* (ll. 10, 12, etc.). Examples in medial position are *viragha-* = Skt. *virāga-* (ll. 66, 67, etc.) and *sugha[du]* = Skt. *sugataḥ* (l. 16). (See § 5.2.2.1 for further details.)

Similarly, *dh* is occasionally written for etymological *d* in both initial and medial positions, usually in environments with original *r/r̥* (see Salomon 1999: 127–8). Examples of the former are *[dhr]i[śpa]ṇa* = P *disvāna*/Skt. *dr̥ṣṭvā* (l. 41), *dhrekṣatu* = Skt. **drakṣayantu* (l. 22) or P *dakkhanti*, and *dhoṇa-* = P *doṇa-*/Skt. *droṇa-* (ll. 3, 4, 26). An example of the latter is *cakṣidhri* = P *cakkhundriyaṃ*/Skt. *cakṣurindriyam* (l. 43), for which compare *sodhroba(*lo)* = P *sudubbalaṃ* in Dhp-G^L 6b, written by the same scribe. (See Brough 1962: §§ 43, 49; Burrow 1937: § 26; Fussman 1989: 482. For Pali and MIA see Geiger 1994: §§ 40, 60; von Hinüber 1986: § 185.)

[2] There is one example of similar words spelled differently in separate texts written by him, which may reflect the spellings he encountered in his exemplar: *bhiriḍighama* = P *vinaḷīkatā* (l. 18) and *[ṇaḍa]sedo* = P *naḷasetuṃ* (Dhp-G^L 6b). Cf. also *hasavaro* = Skt. *athāparam* (l. 16) and *oraparo* = P *oraparaṃ* (Dhp-G^L 7c, etc.), although the retention of *p* in *oraparo* may be due to its word-initial position. Also of interest is the spelling *ti* (= Skt. *iti*), besides *di*, in the Dhp-G^L (9b), where the spelling in our text is *idi* (e.g., ll. 12–4). A satisfactory assessment of such examples will be possible only upon the publication of the AG-G and Dhp-G^L fragments.

The distinction between retroflex (*ṇ*) and dental (*n*) nasals found in some Kharoṣṭhī documents (see Salomon 1999: 121, 124, 2000: §§ 5.9, 5.9.1) is absent in the texts written by this scribe, the retroflex nasal consonant being used throughout for both etymological *ṇ* and *n* (Salomon 1999: 121). This parallels the orthography of the scribe of the Khvs-G (see Salomon 2000: §§ 5.9, 5.9.1).

The "special," or modified, sibilant *s̱* ( ) is never written. This letter typically occurs in other Kharoṣṭhī documents, such as the Dhp-G[K] and Khvs-G (see Salomon 1999: 121, 2000: § 5.9.2), to represent the original genitive singular ending *-sya* and the reflex of original dental aspirates *th* and *dh* in intervocalic position (see Salomon 1999: 121). In our text regular dental *s* ( ) invariably appears in such instances. Examples of the former usage are *aṇasapiḍiasa* = P *anāthapiṇḍikassa*/Skt. *anāthapiṇḍadasya* (l. 27) and *muḍhasa* = Skt. *mūḍhasya* (l. 22). Examples of the latter are *aṇasapiḍiasa* (l. 27, third syllable) and *ṇirusa-* = Skt. *nirodha-* (ll. 65, etc.).

Like several other scribes represented in the BL collection, our scribe never writes anusvāra (see Salomon 1999: 120–1, 2000: § 5.9.3).

There are no examples of the indirect notation of geminate consonants with subscript *r* as encountered in some BL Kharoṣṭhī manuscripts, as in *kharga-* = P *khagga-*, *uparno* = Skt. *utpannaḥ, pradivarno* = Skt. *pratipannaḥ,* and *bhirno* = Skt. *bhinnam* (see Salomon 1999: 122–3, 2000: § 5.9.4).

There are no instances of the diacritic additions to consonant signs that are encountered elsewhere in Kharoṣṭhī documents (see Salomon 1999: 121–2, 2000: § 5.9.5) and that are used "either to represent modified pronunciations or to mark abbreviated forms of consonantal clusters" (Salomon 1999: 121). For instance, in Kharoṣṭhī documents retroflex *ṣ* with horizontal diacritic above (*ṣ̄*) is commonly used to represent the sound corresponding to the Skt. cluster *ṣṇ,* as in *taṣ̄a* = Skt. *tṛṣṇā* in the Dhp-G[K] (84a) and Khvs-G (35b). In contrast, this phoneme appears as *rṇ* (*rṇo*) in the documents written by our scribe. Examples are *krirṇo* = Skt. *kṛṣṇaḥ* (l. 23) and *tarṇa* = Skt. *tṛṣṇām* (Dhp-G[L] 7a) (see pp. 92–3 for further discussion). A similar use of the preconsonantal *r* is seen in *parcimia* = BHS *paścimika-* in the AG-G (l. 12), written by the same scribe. The G reflex of original *śc* is commonly represented by *c̄* ( ) (Burrow 1937: § 49) or *ch* (*pacha* = Skt. *paścāt,* Dhp-G[K] 34, etc.). Again, whereas *j̄* ( ) is often encountered in Kharoṣṭhī documents in positions corresponding to P *(j)jh* < Skt. *dhy,* as in *j̄aṇa-* = P *jhāna-*/Skt. *dhyāna-* (Salomon 1999: 122, 2000: § 5.9.5), this phoneme is represented by ordinary *j* in this text. Examples are *abhija* = P *abhijjhā*/Skt. *abhidhyā* (ll. 42, 45, etc.), and *-sabujaghu* = P *-sambojjhaṅgaṃ*/BHS *-saṃbodhyaṅgam* (ll. 64, etc.). However, *j̄* occurs once in the AG-G (l. 52).

There are no instances of rare vowel signs, such as the syllabic vowel *ṛ,* or of the notation of long vowels, which are sporadically encountered in Kharoṣṭhī documents, including the BL manuscripts (see Salomon 1999: 123).

In this manuscript original *śr* appears as *ś, ṣ,* or *s,* but in three cases it is written as *rś* ( ): *arśaveti* = BHS *āsrāvayanti/āśrāvayanti* (ll. 43, 46, etc.), *pracarśoṣu* = Skt. *pratyaśrauṣuḥ* (l. 28), and *rśoda-* = Skt. *śruta-* (ll. 26, 37). (See § 5.2.3.6 for further details.)

The conjunct *śp* is used to represent the reflexes of original *śv, sm,* and *sv* indiscriminately. (See pp. 93, 95–6 for further details.)

4.8.2. The Employment of the Small Punctuation Mark

The use of the small punctuation mark (⊙) in this manuscript is in some respects relatively consistent, in others inconsistent (see § 4.5 for a physical description). The definition of the effort of development (*bhavaṇaprasaṇa*), consisting of seven parallel structures corresponding to the seven "factors of enlightenment" (ll. 63–73), provides a good illustration of several ways in which this small punctuation mark is employed by this scribe, as well as of the degree of consistency associated with each type of employment:[3]

a. *ka(*dara bhikṣave bha)vaṇaprasaṇe ◦*
   1. *aï bhikṣave bhikhu śpadisabujaghu bhavedi ◦ vi(*veaṇiṣide vi)raghaṇiṣide ◦ ṇirusaṇiṣide vivasaghapariṇame ◦*
   2. *dharmaviesa(*bujaghu bha)vedi ◦ viveaṇiṣide viraghaṇiṣide ◦ ṇirusaṇiṣide vivasagha(*pariṇame ◦)*
   3. *(*vi)riasabujaghu bhavedi viveaṇiṣida ◦ viraghaṇiṣide ṇirusaṇiṣid(*e vivasagha)pariṇamu ◦*
   4. *prid(*i)sabujaghu bhavedi viveaṇ(*i)ṣid(*e) viraghaṇiṣide ṇi(*rusaṇiṣi)de vivasaghaprariṇamu ◦*
   5. *praṣadhasabujaghu bhavedi ◦ viveaṇiṣide (*viraghaṇi)ṣide ṇirusaṇiṣide ◦ vivasaghapariṇamu ◦*
   6. *samasisabujaghu bhav(*edi (◦) vive)aṇiṣide viraghaṇ<*i>ṣide ṇirusaṇiṣide vivasaghaprariṇamu ◦*
   7. *uekṣa(*sabuja)gh(*u) bhavedi viveaṇiṣide viraghaṇiṣide ṇirusaṇiṣide vivasagha(*pariṇamu ◦)*

b. *aï vucadi bhavaṇaprasaṇe* ○[4]

In this passage the punctuation mark is written after the opening rhetorical question (a), after the concluding statement (b), and after each of the seven parallel sentences (nos. 1–7, after *-pariṇame/-pariṇamu/-prariṇamu*), marking off major syntactic units. It is used in a similar consistent fashion in the repetitive passage in which Dhoṇa asks the Buddha four questions and then restates these four, before concluding with another question (ll. 9–15). Here punctuation occurs after the finite verb (*bhaviśe* ◦) in all but the last of the eight repetitions. Punctuation does not occur between the last *bhaviśe* and the interrogative sentence (*bhaviśe ku re bhu bhaviśasi,* l. 15). This marking of major syntactic units is the most common and most consistent way in which this scribe employs the small punctuation mark. Despite this, there are instances where apparently major syntactic units are not punctuated. For example, the opening nidāna formula in the second and third sūtras, the sentence "And there the Bhagavat addressed the monks," is not separated from the following sentence, "Those monks responded to the Bhagavat," though punctuation is written after this and the following sentence, "The Bhagavat

---

[3] In this and in the following examples, the reconstructed text is quoted.

[4] The ○ is the third type of punctuation mark described in § 4.5. The scribe of the sūtras wrote a large punctuation mark, which was then encircled with two larger circles by the scribe of the avadāna text.

said this": *tatra ya bhayavadu bhikhu amatredi te bhikhu bhayavadu pracarśoṣu ◦ bhayavadu eghad oya* ◦ (ll. 27–8, 38–9).[5]

The small punctuation mark is used less consistently to separate distinct grammatical units within a sentence or clause. For example, within each of the seven parallel sentences of the "effort of development" passage quoted above, punctuation is written after the finite verb *bhavedi,* "he develops the enlightenment factor *x,*" in three of the six cases where this section of the text survives (sentence no. 6 is reconstructed). This separates the main clause from the following string of four attributes that qualify the grammatical object. A similar usage of punctuation is seen in the sentence *catvarime bhikṣave prasaṇa ◦ satu savijamaṇa loghaśpi* ◦ (l. 39), "Monks, these four efforts are found existing in the world."[6] Similarly, in five of the six occurrences of the clause *abhija domaṇastu pavea akuśala dharma ◦ citam arśaveti* ◦ (ll. 42 etc.), the grammatical subject, "evil, unprofitable states of covetousness and grief," is marked off from the predicate, "overpower the mind."[7]

Finally, in the "effort of development" passage punctuation is used quite inconsistently to separate the components of the string of four adjectival compounds (*viveaṇiṣide viraghaṇiṣide ṇirusaṇiṣide vivasaghapariṇamu*) that qualify the grammatical object. In the first and second sentences it occurs between the second and third compounds, in the third sentence between the first and second, and in the fifth sentence between the third and fourth, while in the fourth and seventh sentences punctuation does not occur. Similarly, in the list of four "efforts," punctuation occurs between the third and fourth efforts only: *sabaraprasaṇe aṇorakṣaṇaprasaṇe bhavaṇaprasaṇo ◦ prasaṇaprasaṇo* ◦ (l. 40).[8]

The small punctuation mark is also used to mark the end of each "line" (or sixteen syllables) of śloka verse in the Dhoṇa-sutra (ll. 16–20), that is, after pādas b, d, and f. The limited examples in our manuscript suggest that the scribe consistently punctuated his verses. However, this contrasts with the punctuation in the verses of the Dhp-G^L fragment, written by the same scribe. According to Lenz (1999: § 4.3), two types of punctuation are used in the Dhp-G^L. The first is a small circle that "is invariably used to mark the end of a verse," and the second is a

---

[5] Cf. the following: the lack of punctuation after the finite verb in *uasakrami uasakramita* (l. 9) and the occurrence of punctuation after the finite verb in *abhikrami ◦ aña(*daro)* (l. 2), but its absence in the second occurrence of the same phrase *abhikrami añadaro* (l. 6). Again, while punctuation occurs after the definition of the first "effort" in the Prasaṇa-sutra, i.e., after the final finite verb and before the summary statement (*avajadi ◦ aï bucadi sabaraprasaṇo* ◦, l. 60), it is missing in the same location in the definition of the second "effort" (*sapadedi idi vucadi aṇorakṣaṇaprasaṇo* ◦, l. 63).

[6] Cf. the description of the wheel-marks on the Buddha's footprints (*cakra ◦ sahasahara s(*aṇemia saṇabhia) savarovaghada*, ll. 4–5), where the punctuation separates the noun from the following string of epithets of the wheel.

[7] The small punctuation mark appears after the infinitive *katu* in only one of the three complete occurrences of the four repetitions of *sukaro katu ◦ tatu paḍideṇa ṇa baleṇa* ◦, "is easy to perform, but only by a wise man, not a fool" (ll. 30–5). There is only one instance of punctuation after an absolutive, *dhriśpaṇa* (l. 41), whereas punctuation is lacking after the absolutives in the following parallel structures (ll. 44–60).

[8] Cf. the punctuation in the description of a corpse in various states of decomposition (*sayasavi viṇilaü vipuao a ◦ aṭhisaña va p(*uḍavayasaña va),* l. 62), in the epithets of the wheel-marks on the Buddha's footprints (ll. 4–5), and in the description of Buddha's appearance (ll. 7–8).

small dot that "is sporadically used to mark pāda breaks" (1999: § 4.3; the meter is aupacchandasika).

Finally, in a few instances a punctuation mark is used where we would not expect one, for example, after the vocative *bhikṣave* in line 33.

CHAPTER 5

Phonology

Although this text provides some unusual and previously unattested phonological features, some of which are due to the orthographic peculiarities of this scribe, the phonology for the most part conforms to that encountered in other Gāndhārī documents of what is referred to as the middle period (Salomon 1999: § 6.4, 2000: 79).

5.1. Vowels

5.1.1. Palatalization of *a*

For previous discussions, see Konow 1929: xcvi; Burrow 1937: §§ 6, 8, 9; Brough 1962: § 22a; Fussman 1989: §§ 19.3, 28, 30.2; Salomon 2000: § 6.1.1.

There are numerous instances in this manuscript of the palatalization of *a* in a palatal environment, a phenomenon well documented in Gāndhārī. It appears that all examples in this manuscript occur in the environment of *y*. Most instances can be summarized by the formula *ya, yaṃ, ay* > *e/i*. To this can be added the related phenomenon of the contraction of *aya* to *e*. Examples of *ya* > *e* include the reflexes of Skt. absolutives in *-āya* (*[a]bhiñae* = Skt. *abhijñāya,* l. 19; and *ṇiṣa[e]* = BHS *niśrāya,* l. 6) and dative singular masculine and feminine terminations, and possibly also the instrumental singular feminine of a pronoun: *aṇorakṣa[e]* = P *anurakkhāya*/Skt. *anurakṣayā* (l. 63; dat. sg. f.), *sabarae* = P/Skt. *saṃvarāya* (ll. 43, etc.; dat. sg. m.), and *tae,* probably = P *tāya* (l. 63; dem. pron., instr. sg. f.). In *aṇovejaṇa-* = P/Skt. *anuvyañjana-* (ll. 47, etc.) the most likely development is *-vya-* > **-vye-* > *-vve-* (written as *-ve-*). Parallel is *vivasagha-* = P *vossagga-*/BHS *vyavasarga-*[1] (ll. 66, etc.), with the development *vyava-* > **vyeva-* > **vveva-* > *viva-* (see p. 294 for further discussion).

Examples of *-yaṃ* > *e/i* are *aï* = P/Skt. *ayaṃ* (ll. 60, 73, etc.), *abhiñehi* = Skt. *abhijñeyam* (l. 19; gdv., nom. sg. n.), and *śavastie* = P *sāvatthiyaṃ*/Skt. *śrāvastyām* (ll. 27, 37; loc. sg. f.).

The development *ay* > *e* is attested in *śeaṇeṇa* = Skt. *śayānena* (ll. 34, 34–5). The same development results from secondary *ay* (*-akāḥ* > *-ayā* > *-eā,* written as *ea*) in *pavea* = Skt. *pāpakāḥ* (ll. 42, etc.). In the Dhp-G^K the same word appears as *pavaka-* (see Brough 1962: index, s.v.). A possible example of *ay* > *i* may be *-uviade* (l. 25) if this word represents *-upayātam* (see text commentary to ll. 20–5).

[1] The PTSD (s.vv. *vossagga* and *vavassagga*) derives P *vossagga-* from *ava* + √*sṛj,* while it derives *vavassagga,* for which it gives a different definition, from *vi-ava* + √*sṛj.* The BHSD (s.v. *vyavasarga*) gives *vavassagga* as the P equivalent of BHS *vyavasarga.*

The contraction of *aya* > *e* is seen in *vie* = P/Skt. *vicaya* (l. 65), probably influenced by its position in a compound (*dharma-vie-sa(*bujaghu)* = BHS *dharma-vicaya-saṃbodhyaṅgam*), with elision of *c* (*vicaya* > **vice* > *vie*). Alternatively, the development may have been *vicaya* > **viceya* > **viye* > *vie*, with the dropping of the final syllable *ya* as seen elsewhere in this manuscript (see § 5.5). If so, this would be an example of the palatalization of *a* in the environment of *c*. *A[va]ï* (l. 16) may be a further example of the palatalization of *a* in the environment of *c* if this word is the equivalent of P and BHS *avaca* rather than of BHS *avaci, avacī* (see text commentary to ll. 15–6).

The contraction of *aya* > *e* in causative and denominative verbs is the norm throughout this manuscript, as in MIA generally: *amatredi* = Skt. *āmantrayati/~te* (ll. 27–8, 38), *arśaveti* = BHS *āsravayanti/āśravayanti* (ll. 43, etc.), *dharedu* = Skt. *dhārayatu* (l. 25), *bhavedi* = Skt. *bhāvayati* (ll. 64, etc.), and *sapadedi* = Skt. *saṃpādayati* (l. 63). There are no examples of the development *aya* > *eya,* which is encountered in the Niya documents (Burrow 1937: § 6).

Examples where palatalization in a *y* environment has not occurred are *sama[ya]* = P *samayaṃ* (l. 37), *samaeṇa* = Skt. *samayena* (l. 3), *v[i]puao* = BHS *vipūyakam* (l. 62), and *(*vi)ria-* = P *viriya-*/Skt. *vīrya-* (ll. 66–7). This is probably due to the avoidance of sequences of similar vowels (see Brough 1962: §§ 30, 37), so that *samaeṇa* is preferred to **sameeṇa* and *(*vi)ria-* to **virie-*.

5.1.2. Alternation of *a* and *i*

P/Skt. *nimitta* appears as *ṇimiti* throughout this manuscript as prior member in the compound *ṇimiti-ghrahe* = Skt. *nimitta-grāhī* (ll. 41, etc.) and probably as final member in *sama[si]-ṇimi[ti] ///* (l. 61), where the P and Skt. parallels have *samādhi-nimittaṃ*. The final *-i/-e* of *-ghrahe* = Skt. *-grāhī* and *samasi-* = Skt. *samādhi-* may have influenced the spelling *ṇimiti*. Two further possible examples of the representation of original *a* as *i* are *idi* (l. 63), if this is the equivalent of Skt. *idam* rather than *iti* (see text commentary to ll. 40–60), and *bhiriḍi-ghama* = P *vinaḷīkatā* (l. 18; see text commentary to ll. 16–20). (See Konow 1929: xcvi.)

Examples of the development of *i* > *a* are *praṣadha-* = BHS *praśrabdhi-,* which appears in *praṣadha-sabujaghu* = BHS *praśrabdhi-saṃbodhyaṅgam* (l. 69) and in *ruaṇa* = Skt. *rūpāni* (l. 22) (see Brough 1962: §§ 23–4). Both instances occur in unstressed syllables (see Fussman 1989: § 27.1–3). A further example may be *-ṇaṣide* = BHS *-niśritam* (l. 71), but as all other occurrences read *-ṇiṣide* (ll. 66, etc.), this may be a scribal error. As is often the case with Gāndhārī, the distinction between orthographic and phonological phenomena is not always straightforward.

5.1.3. Alternation of *ă* and *e* (?)

There is one doubtful example of *e* in place of original *ā*. This is *maṇase* (l. 57), where the parallel P has *manasā* (instr. sg. n.), and where the instrumental is required. Although *e* for original *ā* in final position (which is unattested to my knowledge) could represent a similar phenomenon to final *o* for *ā* (see § 5.1.5), it is also possible that the text should be emended to *maṇase*<**ṇa*>. An alternative explanation is that *maṇase* represents an accusative or locative singular (equivalent to P *mānasaṃ* or *mānase*) used for the instrumental (see text commentary to ll. 40–60).

In *dhrekṣatu* (l. 22), which is either the third-person plural future imperative of √*dr̥ś* (= Skt. **drakṣyantu*) or present imperative (= P *dakkhantu*), *re* represents a regular G development of OIA *r̥* rather than an example of *e* for *a* in medial position (see § 5.1.9).

5.1.4. Alternation of *ă* and *u* (?)

A possible example of *u* for *ā* is *jagharadu* (ll. 34, 35), if this represents the instrumental singular of the present participle of √*jāgr̥* (see text commentary to ll. 28–36). A further doubtful example is *suyasavi* = P *seyyathāpi*/BHS *sayyathāpi* (l. 21), which appears alongside *sayasavi* (l. 62). The former spelling is unexpected, and it may be the case that the scribe mistook a more cursive tail on the initial *s* akṣara of his exemplar for a *u* diacritic. In *sarvañu* = Skt. *sarvajñaḥ* (l. 20), *-ñu* = Skt. *-jña* is the expected MIA form, parallel to P *sabbaññū,* rather than a true example of *u* for original *a*.

5.1.5. Alternation of *ā* and *o*

For previous discussions, see Brough 1962: § 22; Salomon 2000: § 6.1.3.

If the reading is *[yaso]* rather than *[yasa]* = Skt. *yathā* (l. 18; see text commentary to ll. 16–20), this would be an example of the alternation of *ā* and *o* attested elsewhere in Gāndhārī in both medial and final positions.

5.1.6. Alternation of *ĭ* and *e*

For previous discussions, see Konow 1929: xcvi–xcvii; Burrow 1937: §§ 1, 3; Brough 1962: § 21; Fussman 1989: § 30.1; Salomon 2000: § 6.1.4.

There are several examples of *i* in place of etymological *e,* and of *e* in place of original *ĭ*. Examples in final position are *-ghrahe* (ll. 41, etc.) besides *-ghrahi* (ll. 42, etc.) = Skt. *-grāhī,* and *mi* (ll. 20, 24) besides *me* (ll. 26, 37) = P/Skt. *me*. Examples in medial position are *aceata* = P *accimantāni*/Skt. *arciṣmanti* (l. 5; adj., nom. pl. n.), *aṇa[vela]* = Skt. *anāvilam* (l. 8; reading uncertain), and *bhavidavu* = P *bhāvetabbaṃ* (l. 19), where the context demands the causative as seen in the P and Skt. parallel verses (metrical considerations do not give assistance since the word is the first word of a śloka pāda). The reading and interpretation of *i[va]* (l. 8) are uncertain; the word may represent either Skt. *iva* or *eva*.

5.1.7. Alternation of *i* and *u* (?)

In view of further examples in the Senior manuscripts discussed in the text commentary to ll. 36–7, it appears that *[a]bhiṇadi* = P *abhinandun* (l. 37) represents a regular G third-person plural preterite taken over from the third-person singular form rather than an instance of *i* in place of etymological *u*. (Cf. *phuṣamu* and *kariṣamu* in the Dhp-G^{K}, discussed by Brough 1962: 83, 275–6, where the P and Skt. parallels have the singular; for *-u* > *-i,* see Fussman 1989: § 30.1.)

5.1.8. Alternation of *ū̆* and *o*

For previous discussions, see Konow 1929: xcvii; Burrow 1937: §§ 2, 4; Brough 1962: § 21; Fussman 1989: § 30.1; Salomon 2000: § 6.1.2.

Instances of *o* in place of etymological *u* or *ū* and conversely of *u* in place of etymological *o* are numerous in this manuscript. In some cases the spelling alternates between *u* and *o* in the same word: *ghudama-* (ll. 21, 24) besides *ghodama-* (ll. 21, 23) = P *gotama-*/Skt. *gautama-* (cf. *godama* in Dhp-G[K] 288d, 100–5), and *tatu* (ll. 29, etc.) besides *(*ta)to* (ll. 31–2), probably representing Skt. *tat tu*.

There is one example of *u* where we would expect *o* in final position: *bhu* = P *bho*/Skt. *bhoḥ* (ll. 9, etc.). In contrast to the Khvs-G, where the locative plural masculine/neuter is regularly *-eṣo* (Salomon 2000: § 6.1.2), this termination appears as *-eṣu* in this manuscript, though there is only one example: *padeṣu* = Skt. *pādeṣu* (l. 4).

Examples of original *u* appearing as *o* in medial position are *aṇorakṣa[e]* = P *anurakkhāya* (l. 63), *aṇorakṣaṇa-* = Skt. *anurakṣaṇā-* (ll. 40, 63), *aṇovejaṇa-* = Skt. *anuvyañjana-* (ll. 44, etc.), *maṇośu* = Skt. *manuṣyaḥ* (ll. 11, etc.), and *rśoda-* = Skt. *śruta-* (ll. 26, 37; cf. *ṣuda* in the Khvs-G 24b and Dhp-G[K] 244d, 254ab, 255c). A further example may be *rova* = Skt. *rūpa* (l. 5; cf. *[r]u[v]o,* l. 41), if this is the correct reading, the alternative reading being *sova<*ṇa>* = Skt. *sauvarṇa*. The appearance of the prefix *anu-* as *aṇo-* in this manuscript contrasts with the Dhp-G[K] and Khvs-G, where the regular spelling for both the prefix *anu-* and the sequence *anu-* in initial position is *aṇu-* (though it does appear as *aṇo* once, in Dhp-G[K] 88a, *aṇośea* = Skt. *anuśayāḥ*). In fact, the spelling *maṇośu* = Skt. *manuṣyaḥ* in this manuscript, which appears as *maṇuśa-* in the Dhp-G[K] (47c, 150a, etc.) and Khvs-G (38ab), may have resulted from the tendency on the part of the scribe of our manuscript to write *aṇo* for the sequence *anu* in any position. This is supported by the absence of the sequence *aṇu* anywhere in this manuscript, as well as in the Dhp-G[L] fragment, which was also written by this scribe.

Besides *ghudama-* referred to above, which appears alongside *ghodama-,* representing *au > o/u,* in four words original *o* consistently appears as *u* in medial position: *ṇirusa-* = Skt. *nirodha-* (ll. 65, etc.), *ṣuda-* (l. 44) and *suda-* (ll. 45, etc.) = P *sota-*/Skt. *śrotra-*, and *-sabujaghu* = BHS *-saṃbodhyaṅgam* (ll. 64, etc.).

The leveling of the original phonetic distinction between *ū̆* and *o* in Gāndhārī, which leads "to one or the other of the original sounds being generalized, apparently at the whim of the individual scribe" (Salomon 2000: § 6.1.2), is well illustrated by the above examples. A general consistency in the spelling of most words, such as *nirusa-, -sabujaghu,* etc., and in the prefix and sequence *anu* always appearing as *aṇo*, contrasts with occasional alternations in the spelling of other words, such as *ghudama-/ghodama-* = Skt. *gautama-, tatu/tato* = Skt. *tat tu,* and *ṣuda-/suda-* = Skt. *śrotra-* contrasting with the related *rśoda-* = Skt. *śruta-*.

Further examples of *ū̆/o* alternation are reflected in *ro* as a development of original *r̥,* where *ru* appears in the corresponding P word (see § 5.1.9 below), and in the reduction of *ava* to *u* or *o* (§ 5.1.10).

5.1.9. Developments of Old Indo-Aryan *r̥*

For previous discussions, see Konow 1929: xcvii; Burrow 1937: § 5; Salomon 2000: § 6.1.5.

Reflexes of OIA *r̥* in this manuscript are the following: *a* in *vivaḍe* = P *vivaṭo*/Skt. *vivr̥taḥ* (l. 23), *śpadi-* = P *sati-*/Skt. *smr̥ti-* (l. 64; cf. *spadi,* Dhp-G^{K} 98b), and possibly *-ghada* = P *-katāni*/Skt. *kr̥tāni* (l. 5; cf. *kita-,* Khvs-G 38a, and *kada/kida/gada* in the Dhp-G^{K}, index s.v.);[2] *u* in *phuṣita* = P *phusitvā*/BHS *spr̥śitvā* (l. 54; cf. *phuṣad(*i)* = Skt. *spr̥śati* or *spr̥śanti*, Dhp-G^{K} 128c), though this may be derived from **sparśitvā* with subsequent labialization (cf. *proṭhabu* = P *phoṭṭhabbaṃ,* l. 54); *ri* in *kriṛno* = P *kaṇho/kiṇho*/Skt. *kr̥ṣṇaḥ* (l. 23), *[dh]r[iśpa]ṇa* = P *disvāna*/Skt. *dr̥ṣṭvā* (l. 41; cf. *dispa/diṣpaṇi,* Dhp-G^{K} 154–5, 203–6, and *driṭhi-* = P *diṭṭhi*/Skt. *dr̥ṣṭi,* Khvs-G 30a); *re* in *dhrekṣatu* = Skt. **drakṣyantu* (3rd pl. fut. impv.) or P *dakkhantu* (3rd pl. impv.) (l. 22); and *ro* in *asabroda-* = P *asaṃvuta-*/Skt. *asaṃvr̥ta-* (ll. 42, etc.; cf. *asavudu,* Dhp-G^{K} 217b, *savrudu,* Dhp-G^{K} 23c), *proṭhu* = P *puṭṭho*/Skt. *pr̥ṣṭaḥ* (ll. 12, etc.; cf. *phuṭha,* Dhp-G^{K} 226c), and *rokṣa-* = P *rukkha-*/Skt. *vr̥kṣa-* (ll. 2, 6; cf. *rukha/rakṣa/rakhkṣa* in the Dhp-G^{K}, index s.vv.). It is worthy of note that the reflex *ru* is absent in this manuscript, *ro* appearing instead in a labial environment, including *rokṣa-* = Skt. *vr̥kṣa-,* where the development must have been *vr̥* > **vru* > *ru,* also written as *ro.*

Except for the *ru/ro* distinction, in only a few cases does the vowel element of the reflex differ from that found either elsewhere in Gāndhārī or in the corresponding Pali. In contrast, the preservation of the *r* element in all but four of the above examples (*-ghada, phuṣita, vivaḍe,* and *śpadi-*) is characteristic of Gāndhārī (Salomon 2000: § 6.1.5), though *r* is retained in such situations more consistently in this manuscript than in the Dhp-G^{K} and Khvs-G manuscripts. Further, in the case of *śpadi-* = Skt. *smr̥ti-,* the absence of *r* may be due to the preceding consonant group (*sm*), as no examples of **śpradi, *spradi,* or the like are attested in Gāndhārī, while *vivaḍe* = P *vivaṭo*/Skt. *vivr̥taḥ* and *phuṣita* = P *phusitvā*/BHS *spr̥śitvā* may have been influenced by the source dialect of the original exemplar (see Salomon 2000: § 6.1.5).

5.1.10. Reduction of *ava*

For previous discussions, see Konow 1929: xcvii; Burrow 1937: § 7; Salomon 2000: § 6.1.6

The original sequence *ava* is commonly contracted to *o* in Gāndhārī, as in MIA generally, most commonly in the prefix *ava* or in the stem forms of √*bhū* but also elsewhere, for instance, in *budhoruma-* besides *budhavaruma-* = Skt. *buddhavarma-* in Kharoṣṭhī inscriptions (Konow 1929: index, s.vv.). The one example of a word containing the reflex of the original prefix *ava* in this manuscript is *vivasagha-* = BHS *vyavasarga-* (ll. 66, etc.). In this case the sequence *vya* has been reduced to *vi* by palatalization (see § 5.1.1). In this manuscript the sequence *ava* in derivatives of √*bhū* remains: *bhavadi* = Skt. *bhavati* (ll. 44, etc.). This contrasts with the Dhp-G^{K} and Khvs-G, where the spelling is regularly *bhodi,* etc. (Brough 1962: index, s.vv. *bhavadi, bhodi;* Salomon 2000: index,

[2] Cf. *tarṇa* (Dhp-G^{L} 7a) and *taṣa* (Khvs-G 35b) = P *taṇhāṃ*/Skt. *tr̥ṣṇām.*

s.v. √*bhū*). There are, however, three examples where the sequence *ava* has been reduced to either *o* or *u* in preterites of √*vac: oya* (l. 39), *[uya]* (ll. 9, 28), and *u* (ll. 16, 36), which are the equivalents of P *avaca*/BHS *avaca*. The forms *oya* and *[uya]* appear in the phrase *eghad oya/eghad uya,* where the P parallel text has *etad avoca,* while *u* occurs in *idam u,* where Pali has *idam avoca*. It appears that the contraction of the sequence *ava* in these cases is related to their occurrence in these fixed locutions (further examples are found in the Senior manuscripts; see pp. 163–5 for further discussion). The same development has not occurred in *idam a[va]ï* (l. 16), where *a[va]ï* is the equivalent of P/BHS *avaca,* with palatalization, or of BHS *avaci, avacī*. The forms *[uya]* and *u* provide further illustration of the leveling of the distinction between *u* and *o* (see § 5.1.8).

For contraction of *aya* > *e,* see § 5.1.1; for dropping of the syllable *ya,* see § 5.5.

5.2. Consonants

5.2.1. Consonants in Initial Position

Single consonants in word-initial position normally remain unchanged in Gāndhārī (Brough 1962: § 29). Purely orthographic changes are seen in *gh-* for original *g-* and *gh-*, *ṇ-* for *n-* (see § 4.8.1), in initial and in medial position, and *dh* occasionally for original *d,* in initial and medial positions (see § 4.8.1). Besides these, there are several examples in this manuscript where an original *v-* in initial position is represented by either *b-, d-,* or *bh-,* and one example of original *ś-* appearing as *ch-*.

There are several examples of the alternation of *v* and *b* in this manuscript, in both initial and noninitial positions, a change that is attested elsewhere in Gāndhārī (see, e.g., Burrow 1937: § 20; Salomon 2000: § 6.2.1.5): *bucadi* (l. 60) besides *vucadi* (ll. 63, 73) = P *vuccadi;* enclitic *ba* (l. 17) besides *va* (ll. 17, etc.) and *a* (ll. 21, 62) = Skt. *vā* (for elision of *v* in *vā* > *a,* see below); *-bayaṇo* = Skt. *-vacanam* (ll. 29, 36) and *-bayaṇata* = Skt. *-vacanatva-* (ll. 30, etc.; interpretation uncertain), both at compound juncture; and *sabara-* (ll. 40, etc.) besides *savara-* (l. 57) = Skt. *saṃvara-*.

Original *v-* appears as *d-* in *dihaghama* = Skt. *vihaṃgamaḥ* (l. 17) and as *bh-* in *bhiriḍi-ghama* = P *vinaḷīkatā* (l. 18). Neither development has been attested in other G documents to my knowledge. As both words occur in the same verse at the end of pādas b and f, respectively, it is possible that the changes are related. The writing of *di-* for *vi-* may be nothing more than a scribal error, while *bhiriḍi-* for P *vinaḷī-* is problematic on a number of levels (see the text commentary to ll. 16–20 for the discussion of these forms).

In *chado* = Skt. *śabdam* (l. 44) original *ś-* appears as *ch-*. The same word occurs as *chada* in Dhp-G[K] 37a. The occurrence of this word in the manuscript being edited here was discussed by Salomon (1999: 135), who drew attention to the discussions by Brough (1962: 101) and Buddruss (1975). Thus our manuscript provides further confirmation that this is the normal G form. According to Norman (1979b: 321–4 = CP, vol. II, pp. 71–6), a similar spelling occurs in Pali in the compound *vivatta-chadda,* which he takes to be equivalent to Skt. **vivr̥tta-śabda* (see also von Hinüber 1983: 32–3).

The behavior of initial consonants of enclitics is variable; the consonant is sometimes treated as initial, sometimes as intervocalic. For example, original *ca* becomes *ya* in *tatra ya* = Skt. *tatra ca* (ll. 27, 38) but elsewhere remains: *teṇa ceva* = Skt. *tena caiva* (l. 3) and *dhama ca bhikhusagha ca* = Skt. *dharmaṃ ca bhikṣusaṃghaṃ ca* (l. 24). The Skt. enclitic *vā* appears as *a, ba,* and *va,* while Skt. *api* appears as *p(*i)* and *avi,* the latter in *sayasavi* = P *seyyathāpi*. For convenience, enclitics are treated here under intervocalic consonants (§ 5.2.2). (See Brough 1962: §§ 68, 70.)

5.2.2. Developments of Intervocalic Consonants

The G reflexes of original single intervocalic consonants encountered in this manuscript are summarized in the following chart (compare the corresponding charts in Salomon 1999: 125, 2000: § 6.2.1). This includes the reflexes of initial consonants of enclitic words, namely *a* = Skt. *vā* and *ca* = Skt. *ca*. Where there is more than one reflex, they are listed in order of frequency. Intervocalic *r, l, ś,* and *s,* which remain unchanged, as is the norm in Gāndhārī, are not listed. No reflexes of original *kh, gh, jh, ṭh, ph,* and *b* occur in this manuscript.

Original OIA Consonant	Reflex(es) in the EĀ-G
k	*ø, gh* (graphic for *g*), *k*
g	*gh* (in writing), *y*
c	*y, ø, c* (only in enclitic *ca*)
(c)ch	*ch*
j	*j* (one example of uncertain reading)
ṭ	*ḍ*
ḍ	*ḍ*
ḍh	*ḍh*
ṇ	*ṇ*
t	*d, gh* (possibly graphic for *g;* one problematic example)
th	*s*
d	*d*
dh	*s*
n	*ṇ, r* (one problematic example)
p	*v, ø, p*
bh	*bh*
m	*m, ø*
y	*ø, y*
v	*v, m, ø, b*
h	*h, s*

The majority of the above developments are either regular in Gāndhārī or have been previously attested. Those that have not been attested before are *-gh-* for *-t-*, *-r-* for *-n-*, elision of *-m-*, and *-s-* for *-h-*.

5.2.2.1. Velars

For previous discussions, see Konow 1929: xcviii–xcix; Burrow 1937: § 16; Brough 1962: §§ 30–1, 38, 41; Fussman 1989: 457; Salomon 2000: § 6.2.1.1.

Original *-k-* is either elided (six words); represented as *-gh-,* which is graphic for *-g-* (five words); or retained (four words):

aṇasapiḍiasa = P *anāthapiṇḍikassa* (ll. 27, 38)
asiaraṇam = Skt. *adhikaraṇam* (ll. 42, etc.)
ṇiujidu = P *ni(k)kujjitaṃ*/Skt.**nikubjitam* (l. 21)
viṇilaü = P/BHS *vinīlakaṃ* (l. 62; cf. *viṇi[lao]* in AG-G, l. 35)
v[i]puao = BHS *vipūyakam* (l. 62)
vivea- = P/Skt. *viveka-* (ll. 66, etc.)

[adhagha]ro = Skt. *andhakāre* (l. 22)
-ghada probably = Skt. *-kṛtāni* (l. 5)
praghaśe = Skt. *prakāśet* (l. 22)
logha- = Skt. *loka-* (ll. 18–9, 39)
*[s](*a)praghaśi[d]e* = Skt. *saṃprakāśitaḥ* (l. 23)

akuśala = Skt. *akuśalāḥ* (ll. 42, etc.)
[a]l[oka] = Skt. *āloka-* (l. 22; reading and interpretation uncertain)
eka = Skt. *ekam* (ll. 26, 37)
sukaro = Skt. *sukaram* (ll. 29, etc.)

Original *-k-* appears as *-gh-,* which is graphic for *-g-,* at compound juncture (*[adhagha]ro, -ghada*), in words based on the root √*kāś* (*praghaśe, [s](*a)praghaśi[d]e;* cf. *avaǵaja* = Skt. *avakāśa* and *praǵaśita* = Skt. *prakāśita* listed by Burrow 1937: § 16, from the Niya documents), and in *logha-* = Skt. *loka-*. The spelling of this last word contrasts with *[a]l[oka]* = Skt. *āloka-* (l. 22), where *-k-* remains, although the reading and interpretation of this word remains uncertain. The word appears as *loka-* throughout the Dhp-G^{K} (index, s.v.) and as *loga-* in the Khvs-G (see index, s.v.).

Four of the six cases where *-k-* is elided involve the suffixal element *-ka* or *-k-* in stem-final position, which parallels the pattern established for the Dhp-G^{K} (Brough 1962: § 38) and Khvs-G (Salomon 2000: § 6.2.1.1). In *asiaraṇam* and *ṇiujidu* the elision of *-k-* has occurred after a short *i* vowel. Fussman (1989: 457) notes that *-k-* develops to *y,* which is left unwritten in the environment of *i* or *e*. In *viṇilaü* and *v[i]puao* in this manuscript *y* < *k* is left unwritten outside the environment of *i* or *e*.

The preservation of original *-k-* in *eka* = Skt. *ekam* is regular in Gāndhārī, as in MIA generally, for reasons summarized by Salomon (2000: § 6.2.1.1). The preservation of original *-k-* in words where it is preceded by the negative prefix *a-,* such as in *akuśala* = Skt. *akuśalāḥ* in this manuscript, that is, at a morpheme boundary, is also expected, with the Dhp-G^{K} providing many parallel examples: *akadaggadi* = P *akathaṃkathī, akadaño* =

Skt. *akr̥tajña-, akaroda* = P *akarontaṃ, akijaṇa* = Skt. *akiñcana,* etc. (see Brough 1962: index, s.vv.). This also applies to *sukaro* = Skt. *sukaram.*

No words containing the reflex of orginal *-kh-* or *-gh-* occur in this manuscript. There are three examples of the reflex of original *-g-*. In two cases it remains, written as *gh*: *viragha-* = Skt. *virāga-* (ll. 66, etc.) and *sugha[du]* = Skt. *sugataḥ* (l. 16). Parallel examples appear in the AG-G (Salomon 1999: 127). But in *bhayavada-* = *bhagavant-* (ll. 4, etc.) original intervocalic *-g-* becomes *y*. Although this word occasionally appears as *bhaǵavato* or even *bhaḱavato* in the Kharoṣṭhī inscriptions (see Konow 1929, index, s.vv.), where *-ǵ-* and *-ḱ-* imply *y* (Fussman 1989: § 20), the spelling of this word is normally conservative in Gāndhārī, where it most commonly appears as *bhagava, bhagavato,* etc. (see § 6.1.4.5 for examples; cf. *bhaghava-* in an inscription edited in Salomon 1995: 136, 137–8). *Bhayavada-* in the manuscript edited here appears to be the first example of this spelling in Gāndhārī, though the spelling is the same throughout the Senior manuscripts (see § 6.1.4.5 for examples).

5.2.2.2. Palatals

For previous discussions, see Konow 1929: xcix–c; Burrow 1937: § 17; Brough 1962: § 32; Salomon 2000: § 6.2.1.2.

Original *-c-* is represented as *-y-* in three cases and as *ø* twice:

-bayaṇo = Skt. *-vacanam* (ll. 29, 36) and *-bayaṇata* = Skt. *-vacanatva-* (?) (ll. 30, etc.)
[uya] and *oya* = P/BHS *avaca* (ll. 9, 28, 39)
ya = Skt. *ca* (ll. 27, 38; cf. *ca,* l. 24)

a[va]ï = P/BHS *avaca* or BHS *avaci, avacī* (l. 16)
vie = P/Skt. *vicaya* (l. 65)

Besides *[uya], oya,* and *a[va]ï,* the preterite of √*vac* also appears as *u* (in *idam u,* ll. 16, 36). In this case the entire final syllable has been dropped (see § 5.5). The only example of *-c-* remaining is in the enclitic *ca* = Skt. *ca* (l. 24) and *ceva* = Skt. *caiva* (l. 3), which also appears as *ya* (ll. 27, 38). The above developments are regular for Gāndhārī (see Salomon 2000: § 6.2.1.2).

Original *-ch-,* which is properly a cluster (*cch;* see Konow 1929: c), remains, written as *ch: achu, ghachami, [ghache], ghachateṇa, paḍ[i]chaṇo* (see index for references; see also Salomon 2000: § 6.2.1.2).

There is only one example of a word containing the reflex of original intervocalic *-j-: [abaji]* = P *abbaje,* first-person singular optative P. of *ā* + √*vraj* (l. 17). However, the reading is not certain due to damage to the manuscript. Intervocalic *-j-* invariably becomes *-y-* in the Dhp-G[K] (Brough 1962: § 32) and in the Khvs-G (Salomon 2000: § 6.2.1.2), though there are exceptions; for example, *ayujadu* = P *ayojayaṃ* (Dhp-G[K] 266b). In view of other derivatives of √*vraj* found in other G sources (e.g., *vayadi, [pravaya]di, -pravaï* in the Dhp-G[K]), where *-j-* never remains, we would have expected **abaye* or **abayi.*

Words containing the reflexes of original *-jh-* are absent in this manuscript.

5.2.2.3. Retroflexes

For previous discussions, see Konow 1929: c; Burrow 1937: § 18; Salomon 2000: § 6.2.1.3.

The OIA prefix *prati-* appears as *paḍi-* in *paḍ[i]chaṇo* = P *paṭicchannaṃ*/Skt. *praticchannam* (l. 21) but as *pradi-* in *pradivajadi* = P *paṭipajjati*/Skt. *pratipadyate* (l. 43). Although the spelling *paḍi-* could have been taken over from the non-Gāndhārī MIA dialect of the source text (see Salomon 2000: § 6.2.1.3), the regular occurrence of both *paḍi-* and *pradi-* in the same text, here as in the Dhp-GK (besides *paḍi-* and *prati-* in the Niya documents), suggests that *paḍi-* was a regular G form, even though it may have originally been inherited from another MIA dialect or dialects.

Besides *paḍ[i]chaṇo,* intervocalic *-ṭ-* is voiced in this text in *vivaḍe* = P *vivaṭo*/Skt. *vivr̥taḥ* (l. 23), as normally in Gāndhārī.

Original *-ḍ-* remains in *bhiriḍi-ghama* = P *vinaḷīkatā* (l. 18), the interpretation of which is problematic. The Skt. equivalent **vinalīkr̥ta-* or **vinālīkr̥ta-* is not recorded, but the spelling of the related "reed" word fluctuates in Sanskrit between *naḍa, naḷa,* and *nala* (see Turner 1966: § 6936). It appears as *naḍa-* in Dhp-GK 85b, where the P parallel has *naḷa-setuṃ* (Sn 4b). The same verse appears in Dhp-GL 6b, a text written by the same scribe as the one presented here, where the reading appears to be *[ṇaḍa]sedo* but could also be *[ṇala]sedo.*

There are no examples of words containing reflexes of original *-ṭh-* and only one example of the reflex of original *-ḍh-*. Here, as expected, *-ḍh-* remains: *muḍhasa* = P *mūḷhassa*/Skt. *mūḍhasya* (l. 22).

5.2.2.4. Dentals

For previous discussions, see Konow 1929: c–ci; Burrow 1937: §§ 19, 50; Brough 1962: §§ 33, 42–3; Salomon 2000: § 6.2.1.4.

Original intervocalic *-t-* is invariably voiced: *akhade* = Skt. *ākhyātaḥ* (l. 23), *añadaro* = Skt. *anyataram* (l. 6), etc. This parallels the treatment of *-t-* in the Dhp-GK (Brough 1962: § 33) but contrasts with the Khvs-G, where *-t-* frequently remains (Salomon 2000: § 6.2.1.4). There is one example where *-t-* is apparently represented by *-g-* or *-gh-,* written as *-gh-*. This appears in the problematic *eghad* in the set locution *eghad uya/oya* (ll. 9, 28, 39), where the parallel expression is *etad avoca* in Pali and *idam avocat* in Sanskrit. For reasons outlined in the discussion of this word (see pp. 163–4)—in particular the occurrence of the same phrase in the Senior manuscripts as *eḋaḋ aya*, *eḋavaya*, and *eḋavayi*—*eghad* is unlikely to represent *eka-* but must be the equivalent of the demonstrative pronoun *etad.* This is unlikely to represent the phonetic development of *-g-/-gh-* for original *-t-* and is probably a textual problem. The development is yet to be satisfactorily explained.

There are no examples of the elision of intervocalic *-t-* or *-d-* in this text (see Salomon 1999: 125–6, 152, 2000: 85), though Salomon (1999: 126) gives two examples from the

AG-G, a text written by our scribe.[3] Further examples are found in the Dhp-G^L, which is also written by this scribe, for example, *upaïda* = Skt. *utpatitam* (5a). There is, however, one example in the manuscript presented here of a word that may be based on an archetype where intervocalic *-t-* was elided.[4] This is *[a]bhiñae* (l.19; occurring in pāda a of a śloka verse), which was probably understood to be an absolutive (= Skt. *abhijñāya*). The P and Skt. parallels of this verse preserve the past participle, P *abhiññātaṃ*/Skt. *abhijñātam,* while the structure of pādas b and c in the G, P, and Skt. versions is past participle + gerundive (or vice versa). This being the case, it is possible that an archetype of the G version where intervocalic *-t-* was elided (e.g., **abhiñaya-*) was mistaken for an absolutive, which makes sense in this context but disturbs the structural symmetry of the verse (see Brough 1962: § 33; Bailey 1946: 783; Norman 1991: §§ 9–10; and see pp. 200–1 for further discussion).

Original intervocalic *-d-* always remains: *idam* = Skt. *idam* (ll. 36, etc.), etc. This parallels the Dhp-G^K (Brough 1962: § 33) but again contrasts with the Khvs-G, where it regularly appears as *-t-* (Salomon 2000: 85). But in some instances, usually in environments with original *r/r̥, d* appears as *dh* in this scribe's orthography: *[dhr]i[śpa]ṇa, dhrekṣatu, dhoṇa,* and *-idhri;* see §§ 4.8.1, 5.1.9.

The dental aspirates *-th-* and *-dh-* in intervocalic position are invariably represented by regular dental *-s-:*

aṇasapiḍiasa = P *anāthapiṇḍikassa* (l. 27)
[yasa] = Skt. *yathā* (l. 18; the reading may be *[yaso]*)
sayasavi (l. 62) and *suyasavi* (l. 21) = P *seyyathāpi*/BHS *sayyathāpi*
hasavaro = Skt. *athāparam* (l. 16)

asiaraṇam = Skt. *adhikaraṇam* (ll. 42, etc.)
ṇirusa- = Skt. *nirodha-* (ll. 65, etc.)
[da]masa = Skt. *damatha* (l. 7)
prasaṇa = P *padhāna*/Skt. *pradhāna* or *prahāṇa* (ll. 39, 40, etc.)
śamasa = Skt. *śamatha* (l. 7)

This is a common development in Gāndhārī, though in texts such as the Khvs-G the phoneme is represented by the special graph *s̱* (ʃ). For further discussion, see Bailey 1946: 776–7; Brough 1962: § 43; Fussman 1989: § 35.3,5 and p. 464 n. 42; and Salomon 1999: 121, 2000: 85.

5.2.2.5. Labials

For previous discussions, see Konow 1929: ci; Burrow 1937: § 20; Brough 1962: §§ 34–6, 44; Fussman 1989: § 18.3; Salomon 2000: § 6.2.1.5.

---

[3] Salomon (personal communication) now reads the second example, *ṇaï[ti]ru,* differently. *Piu* = Skt. *pitur* therefore remains as the only example.

[4] The spelling *[śp](*ay)i[ta]* = P *sāyitvā*/BHS *svādayitvā* (l. 50; reading and reconstruction uncertain), with the elision of *-d-,* reflects the source dialect (see Lüders 1954: § 111; Geiger 1994: § 36).

Original intervocalic *-p-* appears as *-v-* in eight words, is elided in five words, and remains in three cases (including the enclitic *api*):

avajadi = Skt. *āpadyate* (ll. 50, etc.)
*(*u)[avati]* = P/Skt. *upapatti* (l. 16)
-uviade (perhaps a scribal error; for *uvide* = P/Skt. *-upetaṃ,* or representing *-upayātam* [?] in *praṇo-uviade,* where the P and Skt. parallels have *pāṇupetaṃ/prāṇopetam*) (l. 25)
pavea = Skt. *pāpakāḥ* (ll. 42, etc.)
pradivajadi = Skt. *pratipadyate* (l. 43)
[r]u[v]o = Skt. *rūpam* (l. 41) and *-rova-* = Skt. *rūpa* (l. 5; but the reading could be *-sova<*ṇa>-* = Skt. *sauvarṇa*); cf. *ruaṇa* = Skt. *rūpāni* (l. 22)
sayasavi (l. 62) and *suyasavi* (l. 21) = P *seyyathāpi*/BHS *sayyathāpi*
hasavaro = Skt. *athāparam* (l. 16)

*(*u)[avati]* = P/Skt. *upapatti* (l. 16)
uasakrami = P *upasaṅkami* (l. 9)
uasakramita = P *upasaṅkamitvā* (l. 9)
uekṣa- = Skt. *upekṣā-* (l. 71)
ruaṇa = Skt. *rūpāni* (l. 22); cf. *[r]u[v]o* = Skt. *rūpam* (l. 41)

aṇasapiḍiasa = P *anāthapiṇḍikassa* (l. 27)
*[p](*i)* = P *pi/api* (l. 19)
v[i]puao = BHS *vipūyakam* (l. 62)

In general, the development of original *-p-* in our text is typical for Gāndhārī. The variability in the treatment of *-p-* in the enclitic *api,* which appears in this manuscript as *[p](*i)* (if this is the correct reading) and as *avi* in *sayasavi,* is common in Gāndhārī. Original *api* appears as *vi, bi,* and *mi* in the Dhp-G^{K} (Brough 1962: index, s.v. *vi*) and as *pi* and *vi* in the Khvs-G (Salomon 2000: index, s.vv.). This parallels the variability in the spelling of the enclitic *ca* and *vā*.

There are no examples of the reflexes of original intervocalic *-ph-* or *-b-*. Original intervocalic *-bh-* remains in all instances: *abhikatu* = P *abhikkantaṃ* (l. 21), *abhija* = Skt. *abhidhyā* (ll. 42, etc.), etc.

5.2.2.6. Nasals

For previous discussions, see Konow 1929: cii–civ; Burrow 1937: § 34; Brough 1962: §§ 36, 45; Salomon 1999: 121, 2000: § 5.9.1.

As discussed in § 4.8.1, throughout this text, as in the other two texts written by the same scribe, the retroflex nasal appears for both etymological *ṇ* and *n*. As the phonetic distinction between the two nasals had been leveled well before the time of these documents, it became a matter of scribal whim which graph was used (Salomon 2000: § 5.9.1).

Original *-n-* apparently appears as *-r-* in the problematic *bhiriḍi-ghama* = P *vinaḷīkatā*/Skt. **vinălīkṛta-* (l. 18), though the reading of this akṣara is not certain (see text commentary to ll. 16–20 for full discussion).

Although original intervocalic *-m-* normally remains in Gāndhārī, as in virtually all cases in this manuscript, there are two instances where it is apparently elided: *aceata* = P *accimantāni*/Skt. *arciṣmanti* (l. 5; nom. pl. n.) and *cakṣu[a]tu* = P *cakkhumanto*/Skt. *cakṣuṣmantaḥ* (l. 22; nom. pl. m.). Both involve the suffix *-mant* and reflect the MIA forms, such as Pali, where the suffix is added to *-i/-u* stems rather than *-is/-us* stems (cf. BHS *arcimant,* which appears as a proper noun; BHSD, s.v.). It is likely that the elision of *-m-* in these two words is related to the alternation of *m* and *v,* discussed at length by Brough (1962: § 36), who noted that in nasal environments original *-v-* commonly appears as *-m-* (e.g., *ema* = P/Skt. *evaṃ,* discussed below), as in the strong forms of *-vant* stems; for example, *śilamada* = Skt. *śīlavantam* (acc. sg.) but *śilavada* = Skt. *śīlavatā* (instr. sg.). Although *-m-* is retained in all words with the suffix *-mant* in the Dhp-G[K], the converse of certain developments are occasionally encountered in Gāndhārī. In other words, *-v-* for original *-m-* (perhaps in a nasal environment) is theoretically possible. This could then be treated as a glide and left unwritten between dissimilar vowels (cf. *a* for the enclitic *vā* discussed below, § 5.2.2.7).

5.2.2.7. Semivowels

For previous discussions, see Konow 1929: cv–cvi; Burrow 1937: § 50; Brough 1962: §§ 36–9; Fussman 1989: § 19.2; Salomon 2000: § 6.2.1.6.

Original intervocalic *-y-* is elided or "left unwritten" (Salomon 2000: § 6.2.1.6) in five words, besides the numerous instances where palatalization of a preceding or following *a* has occurred (see § 5.1.1). It remains in three, possibly four, words:

-idhrio = Skt. *-indriyam* (l. 8)
gha[ĭ]ta = P *ghāyitvā*/BHS *ghrāyitvā* (l. 47)
v[i]puao = BHS *vipūyakam* (l. 62)
*(*vi)ria-* = P *viriya-*/Skt. *vīrya-* (ll. 66–7)
samaeṇa = Skt. *samayena* (l. 3)

kayidhri = P *kāyindriyaṃ* (ll. 55, 56) and *kayeṇa* = Skt. *kāyena* (l. 54)
*(*to)[yo]* = P/Skt. *toye* (l. 18; reading uncertain)
sama[ya] = P *samayaṃ* (l. 37)

In *sayasavi* (l. 62) and *suyasavi* (l. 21) = P *seyyathāpi*/BHS *sayyathāpi, -y-* probably represents a geminate as in Pali and Buddhist Sanskrit. Although most of the above examples conform to the pattern noted by Brough (1962: § 37) and Salomon (2000: § 6.2.1.6), with *-y-* retained between two *a* vowels but left unwritten between dissimilar vowels (e.g., *sama[ya]* but *samaeṇa*), *kayidhri* and *kayeṇa* do not. In the case of *(*to)[yo],* the reading and reconstruction of which are tentative, *-y-* apparently functions to avoid hiatus of similar vowels.

There are no examples in this manuscript of *-k-* appearing for original *-y-,* like those discussed by Brough (1962: § 38), but there is one example of *-h-* functioning as a syllable divider where original *-y-* has been elided (see Brough 1962: § 39). This is in the gerundive *abhiñehi* = Skt. *abhijñeyam* (l. 19), where *a* in the final syllable has been palatalized and *-h-* written to avoid the hiatus of similar vowels, parallel to *deśehi* = Skt. *deśayet* in the Dhp-G[K] (see Brough 1962: § 39). A similar use of *h* appears in *sahasa-h-ara* = Skt. *sahasrārāni* (l. 4), though this is at a compound juncture. However, in *ramahi* = P *damayaṃ* quoted by Brough (1962: § 39) as the second example of this phenomenon, *-h-* separates dissimilar vowels, while examples such as *idrieṣu* in the Dhp-G[K] (Brough 1962: § 37) indicate that hiatus between "similar" vowels such as *ĭ* + *e* or *e* + *ĭ* was tolerated.

For instances of the dropping of final *ya,* see § 5.5.

As is the norm in Gāndhārī, the semivowels *r* and *l* remain unchanged in this manuscript. Original intervocalic *-v-* also remains in most instances, but in *ema* = Skt. *evam* (ll. 12, etc.), which occurs alongside *eva* and *evam* (ll. 18, 23, etc.), it appears as *-m-*. This development is well attested in the Dhp-G[K], while the forms *ema, emam,* and *emu,* besides *eva, evam,* etc., for Skt. *evam,* appear elsewhere in Gāndhārī (Brough 1962: § 36). The enclitic *vā* appears twice as *a* (ll. 21, 62), showing elision of *-v-* in intervocalic position. It also appears as *[ba]* once (l. 17), besides *va* (ll. 17, etc.), showing the common *b/v* alternation.

5.2.2.8. Sibilants and *h*

For previous discussions, see Konow 1929: cviii; Burrow 1937: §§ 21–3, 28, 33; Brough 1962: §§ 39, 50; Salomon 2000: § 6.2.1.7.

Leaving aside the exceptional *chado* = Skt. *śabdam* (see § 5.2.1), the three OIA sibilants are preserved throughout this manuscript in both intervocalic and initial positions, as is characteristic of Gāndhārī. (For *-ṣ-* in *phuṣita* = P *phusitvā*/BHS *spr̥śitvā*/Skt. *spr̥ṣṭvā,* see § 5.2.3.6, *rś* > *ṣ*.)

Intervocalic *-h-* also remains in all cases with the exception of one, where it appears as *-s-: [pra]saṇa-* = P *pahāna-*/Skt. *prahāṇa-* (l. 40). This occurs in the compound *[pra]saṇa-prasa[ṇo],* where the P and Skt. parallels have *pahāna-ppadhānaṃ* and *prahāṇa-prahāṇam,* respectively. It is likely that the spelling *[pra]saṇa-* = P *pahāna-*/ Skt. *prahāṇa-* developed under the influence of *pra[sa]ṇa-* = P *padhāna-*/Skt. *pradhāna-*/ *prahāṇa-* (see text commentary to ll. 39–40 for full discussion). However, there is a persistent tendency in Gāndhārī for phonetic changes involving the leveling of distinctions between certain sounds in certain environments to be graphically represented by what seems to be the opposite change. For example, the phonetic change of *-k-* > *-y-* conditions spellings like *viyaka* = *vijaya*. Thus, although *s* for *h* has not been previously recorded in Gāndhārī to my knowledge, Lenz (1999: § 2.2.1.8) lists a number of examples in Gāndhārī of *h* appearing for a sibilant. For example, where Dhp-G[K] 87a (cf. 86a) has *yo necasari na precasari,* corresponding to P *yo nāccasārī na paccasārī* (e.g., Sn 8a), Dhp-G[L] 9a (with reconstruction based on 10a) has *(*yo ṇa a)[ca]hari ṇa pracahari.*

Similarly, *mahasa* = Skt. *māsasya* occurs in the Uṇḍ inscription (Konow 1929: 170–1), where the more regular spelling in the inscriptions is *masasa*.

5.2.3. Consonant Clusters

The development of OIA consonant clusters in this text is summarized in the chart below. Original geminates (e.g., *tt* written as *t*), clusters consisting of homorganic nonaspirated + aspirated stops (e.g., *tth, ddh,* which appear as *th, dh,* etc. in writing), and clusters of nasal + homorganic stop (e.g., *paḍideṇa* = Skt. *paṇḍitena*) where the nasal is not written (since our scribe never writes anusvāra) have not been included, though the latter are discussed below. Where two or more reflexes of the same cluster are attested, they are given in order of frequency. Where the reflex is a geminate written as a single consonant, as is the norm in Kharoṣṭhī, the unwritten member of the cluster appears in parentheses.

Original OIA Cluster	Reflex(es) in the EĀ-G
kt	*k*(*k*)
kr	*kr, k*(*k*)
kṣ	*kṣ,* (*k*)*kh*
kṣy	*kṣ*
khy	(*k*)*kh*
gr	*gr*
ghr	*gh*
cy	*c*(*c*)
jñ	*ñ*(*ñ*)
ty	*c*(*c*)
tr	*tr, d*
tv	*t*(*t*), *tv*
dy	*j*(*j*)
dr	*dh*
dhy	*j* (= *jh* ?)
ntr	*tr*
ndr	*dhr*
ny	*ñ*(*ñ*)
pt	*t*(*t*)
pr	*pr, p*
bj	*j*(*j*)
bd	*d*(*d*)
bdh	(*d*)*dh*
br	*br*
bhr	*rbh* (perhaps graphic only)
rg	*gh* (= *gg*)
rc	*c*(*c*)
rt	*t*(*t*)

rm	*m*(*m*), *rm*
ry	*riy*
rv	*rv*, *v*(*v*)
rś	*ś*(*ś*), *ṣ*(*ṣ*)
vy	*v*(*v*), *b*(*b*)
vr	*b*(*b*)
śr	*ṣ*(*ṣ*), *rś*, *ś*(*ś*), *s*
śv	*śp*
ṣṭ	(*ṭ*)*ṭh*, *st* (one problematic example)
ṣṇ	*rṇ* (= *ṣ̄*)
ṣy	*ś*(*ś*)
st	*st*
stv	*st*
sth	(*ṭ́*)*ṭ́h*
sp	*ph* (word initial)
spr	*pr* (word initial)
sm	*śp*, *m*
sy	*s*(*s*)
sr	*ṣ* (via *śr/sr* confusion), *s*(*s*)
sv	*śp*
hm	*m* (= *mm* ?)
hr	*r* (word initial)
hv	(*b*)*bh*

5.2.3.1. Nasal + Stop

For previous discussions, see Konow 1929: civ–cv; Burrow 1937: §§ 45–7; Brough 1962: §§ 7–8, 10a, 46–7; Salomon 1999: § 6.4.3, 2000: § 6.2.2.

In this scribe's orthography a nasal before a homorganic stop is never written (anusvāra being completely absent in the manuscript), while the stop remains unchanged. Examples from each class are *-sagha* = P/Skt. *-saṃghaṃ* (l. 24), *aṇovejaṇa-* = Skt. *anuvyañjana-* (ll. 44, etc.), *paḍideṇa* = P/Skt. *paṇḍitena* (ll. 29, etc.), *cakṣu[a]tu* = Skt. *cakṣuṣmantaḥ* (l. 22), *śata-* = Skt. *śānta-* (l. 7), *ghadharva-* = Skt. *gandharva-* (ll. 10, etc.), *sapadedi* = Skt. *saṃpādayati* (l. 63), and *-sabujaghu* = BHS *-saṃbodhyaṅgam* (ll. 64, etc.). This absence of any sound changes involving nasal + stop of the kind regularly found in the Dhp-G^{K} (e.g., *-ṅk-* > *-g-*, *-ṅg-* > *-ǵ-*, *-ñj-* > *-ñ-*, *-ṇḍ-* > *-ṇ-*, *-nt-* > *-d-*, *-nd-* > *-n-;* see Brough 1962: § 46) is characteristic of the BL collection as a whole (Salomon 1999: § 6.4.3). The Khvs-G, for example, differs from our text only in that the nasal is regularly indicated in that text by anusvāra (Salomon 2000: § 6.2.2).

An original nasal + semivowel follows the same pattern as that for nasal + stop: *sabara-*, *savara-* = P/Skt. *saṃvara-* (ll. 40, etc.) and *savijamaṇa* = Skt. *saṃvidyamāna-* (l. 39). The exception is *ny,* for which see § 5.2.3.4.

5.2.3.2. Stop + Nasal

For previous discussions, see Konow 1929: cv; Burrow 1937: § 44; Bailey 1946: 768–9; Brough 1962: §§ 10, 14.

The only instance of the reflex of an original stop + nasal in this text is *ñ* (= *ññ*) for *jñ*, which appears in derivatives of √*jñā* (see Salomon 2000: § 6.2.2.2): *añadu* (abs. of *ā* + √*jñā* in *-tu*, l. 57), *[a]bhiñae* = Skt. *abhijñāya* (l. 19), *abhiñehi* = Skt. *abhijñeyam* (l. 19), *sarvañu* = P *sabbaññū*/Skt. *sarvajñaḥ* (l. 20), and *saña* = Skt. *saṃjñā-* (l. 62). This follows the regular pattern for Gāndhārī.

For semivowel + nasal, see § 5.2.3.5; for sibilant + nasal, see § 5.2.3.6; for *h* + nasal, see § 5.2.3.7.

5.2.3.3. Stop + Stop Clusters

For previous discussions, see Burrow 1937: § 35; Brough 1962: § 51; Salomon 2000: § 6.2.2.1.

As in other MIA dialects, clusters involving stop + stop undergo assimilation, resulting in a geminate, represented graphically by a single consonant. The conjunct *tk* appears as *k* (= *kk*) in *ukuje*, the optative of the denominative **utkubjaya-*, P *ukkujjeyya* (l. 21). The conjunct *pt* becomes *t* (= *tt*) in *alitu* = P *alitto*/Skt. *aliptaḥ* (l. 19), *[gh]u[t]u* = P *guttaṃ*/Skt. *guptam* (l. 8), *p[r]atu* = P *pattaṃ*/Skt. *prāptam* (l. 7), and possibly *atamaṇa* = P *attamanā*/BHS *āttamanasas/āptamanasas* (l. 36). The cluster *bj* appears as *j* (= *jj*) in *ukuje*, just noted, and in the related *ṇiujidu* = P *ni(k)kujjitaṃ*/Skt.**nikubjitam* (l. 21). The conjunct *bd* becomes *d* (= *dd*) in *chado* = P *saddaṃ*/Skt. *śabdam* (l. 44), while *bdh* appears as *dh* (= *ddh*) in *praṣadha-* = P *passaddhi-*/BHS *praśrabdhi-* (l. 69).

5.2.3.4. Consonant + Semivowel Clusters

For sibilant + semivowel clusters, see § 5.2.3.6; for *h* + semivowel clusters, see § 5.2.3.7.

Examples in this manuscript of clusters with *y* as the latter member follow the pattern common in Gāndhārī and MIA in general, whereby *y* is assimilated to the preceding consonant and, if the consonant is a dental, palatalizes it (see Konow 1929: cvi; Burrow 1937: §§ 41–2; Salomon 2000: § 6.2.2.2):

- *kṣy* > *kṣ*: *dhrekṣatu* = Skt. **drakṣyantu* (3rd pl. fut. impv.) or P *dakkhantu* (3rd pl. impv.) (l. 22)
- *khy* > *kh* (= *kkh*): *akhade* = P *akkhāto*/Skt. *ākhyātaḥ* (l. 23)
- *cy* > *c* (= *cc*): *bucadi, vucadi* = P *vuccati*/Skt. *ucyate* (ll. 60, etc.)
- *ty* > *c* (= *cc*): *pracarśoṣu* = P *paccassosuṃ*/Skt. *pratyaśrauṣuḥ* (l. 28)
- *dy* > *j* (= *jj*): *ajavaghreṇa* = Skt. *adyāgreṇa* (l. 25), *avajadi* = P *āpajjati*/Skt. *āpadyate* (ll. 50, etc.), *pradivajadi* = Skt. *pratipadyate* (ll. 43, etc.), *savijamaṇa* = Skt. *saṃvidyamāna-* (l. 39)
- *dhy* > *j* (= *jh* ?): *abhija* = P *abhijjhā*/Skt. *abhidhyā* (ll. 42, etc.), *-sabujaghu* = BHS *-saṃbodhyaṅgam* (ll. 64, etc.) (see Brough 1962: §§ 6, 6a, 6b)
- *ny* > *ñ* (= *ññ*): *añadara-* = P *aññatara-*/Skt. *anyatara-* (ll. 61, etc.)

vy > *v/b* (= *vv/bb*): *aṇovejaṇa-* = Skt. *anuvyañjana-* (ll. 44, etc.), *prahadavu* = P *pahātabbaṃ*/Skt. *prahātavyam* (l. 20), *proṭhabu* = P *phoṭṭhabbaṃ*/BHS *spraṣṭavya-* (l. 54), *bhavidavu* = P *bhāvetabbaṃ* (l. 19), *vivasagha-* = P *vossagga-*/ BHS *vyavasarga-* (ll. 66, etc.)
ry: see § 5.2.3.5

In clusters with *r* as the latter member, *r* is usually retained:

kr: abhikrami (preterite of *abhi* + √*kram,* ll. 2, 6), *uasakrami* (preterite of *upa-sam* + √*kram,* l. 9), *uasakramita* = BHS *upasaṃkramitvā* (l. 9), *cakra* = Skt. *cakrāṇi* (l. 4), *śukro* = Skt. *śukraḥ* (l. 23)
gr (written *ghr*): *ajavaghreṇa* = Skt. *adyāgreṇa* (l. 25), *-ghrahi/-ghrahe* = Skt. *-grāhī* (ll. 41, 42, etc.)
tr: tatra = Skt. *tatra* (ll. 27, 38)
ntr: amatredi = Skt. *āmantrayate* (ll. 27–8, 38)
ndr (written *dhr*): *-idhri, -idhrio* = P/Skt. *indriya-* (ll. 8, 45, etc.)
pr: abhiprasaṇe = Skt. *abhiprasannam* (l. 25), *praghaśe* = Skt. *prakāśet* (l. 22), *pradivajadi* = Skt. *pratipadyate* (ll. 43, etc.), etc.
br: bramaṇa- = Skt. *brāhmaṇa-* (ll. 3, etc.)

But in several instances *r* is assimilated or at least left unwritten. In the majority of these cases this probably reflects the source dialect (see Salomon 2000: 89):

kr > *k* (= *kk*): *abhikatu* = P *abhikkantaṃ*/Skt. *abhikrāntam* (l. 21; see text commentary to ll. 20–5)
ghr- > *gh-: gha[ï]ta* = P *ghāyitvā*/BHS *ghrāyitvā* (l. 47) and the related *ghaṇa-* = P *ghāna-*/Skt. *ghrāṇa-* (ll. 47, 48, 50)
tr > *t* > *d: ṣuda-* (l. 44) and *suda-* (ll. 45, etc.) = P *sota-*/BHS *śrota-*/Skt. *śrotra-*
dr- > *d-* (written *dh-*): *dhoṇa-* = P *doṇa-*/Skt. *droṇa-* (ll. 3, 4, 26)
pr- > *p: paḍ[i]chaṇo* = P *paṭicchannaṃ*/Skt. *praticchannam* (l. 21)
vr > *b* (= *bb*): *[abaji]* = P *abbaje*/Skt. *āvrajeyam* (l. 17; reading uncertain)

This pattern whereby *r* is generally retained in such clusters but is sporadically assimilated (the norm in other MIA dialects) is typical of Gāndhārī (Konow 1929: cvii–cviii; Burrow 1937: §§ 36b, 37b; Brough 1962: § 51; Salomon 2000: § 6.2.2.2). In one case (*virbhasta* = Skt. *vibhraṣṭāḥ*, l. 18) metathesis has apparently occurred, although this could be merely graphic (see § 5.3, and *rś* written for *śr,* § 5.2.3.6).

For consonant + *r* clusters originating from original syllabic *r̥,* see § 5.1.9.

There are no examples of *l* as the final member of a cluster. Clusters consisting of a stop + *v* are restricted to *tv,* including the absolutive ending Skt. *-tvā,* the abstract suffix Skt. *-tva,* and an original cluster *tv* in a noun stem. In the case of the absolutives, *v* is retained in two instances: *ghatva* = P/Skt. *gatvā* (ll. 2, 6) and *ṣutvaṇa* = Skt. *śrutvā* (l. 44). All other examples are based on the ending *-itvā,* which appears as *-ita* (*-itvā* > *-itta,* written as *-ita*): *uasakramita* = P *upasaṅkamitvā* (l. 9), *gha[ï]ta* = P *ghāyitvā*/BHS *ghrāyitvā* (l. 47), *phuṣita* = P *phusitvā*/BHS *spr̥śitvā*/Skt. *spr̥ṣṭvā* (l. 54), *vadita* = BHS *vaditvā* (l. 16), and *[śp](*ay)i[ta]* = P *sāyitvā*/BHS *svādayitvā* (l. 50). This variation in the treatment of *v* in the absolutive ending is paralleled in the Khvs-G (see Salomon 2000: § 6.2.2.2 for further comments). In all instances of the reflex of the OIA abstract suffix *-tva, v* is assimilated to the preceding consonant (*-tva* > *-tta,* written as *ta*): *domaṇastu* = P *domanassaṃ*/Skt. **daurmanastvam* (ll. 42, etc.), *[maṇ](*o)śata* = Skt. *manuṣyatvam* (l. 17), *yakṣatu* = Skt. *yakṣatvam* (l. 17). The interpretation of *-bayaṇata,* which could be the equivalent of Skt. *-vacanatva-* (ll. 30, etc.), is problematic. Original *v* remains in *catvara-* = Skt. *catvāra-* (l. 39). (See Konow 1929: cviii; Burrow 1937: § 43; Brough 1962: §§ 62–3; Salomon 2000: § 6.2.2.2.)

For *rv,* see § 5.2.3.5; for "intrusive" *r,* see § 5.3.

5.2.3.5. Semivowel + Consonant Clusters

For semivowel + sibilant clusters, see § 5.2.3.6.

Instances of original clusters consisting of the semivowel *r* + consonant follow the regular G pattern; that is, *r* is usually assimilated, but in the clusters *rm* and *rv,* it occasionally remains (Konow 1929: cvi–cvii; Burrow 1937: §§ 36a, 37a, 42; Fussman 1989: §§ 26.2, 37.6; Salomon 2000: § 6.2.2.3).

A prior *r* is assimilated in the following clusters:

rg > *g,* written as *gh* (= *gg*): *magha-* = P *magga-*/Skt. *mārga-* (ll. 2, etc.), *vivasagha-* = P *vossagga-*/BHS *vyavasarga-* (ll. 66, etc.)
rc > *c* (= *cc*): *aceata* = P *accimantāni*/Skt. *arciṣmanti* (l. 5)
rt > *t* (= *tt*): *katu/kato,* which is probably the equivalent of Skt. *kartum* (ll. 30, etc.)

The original cluster *rm* sometimes becomes *m* (= *mm*) but sometimes remains: *domaṇastu* = P *domanassaṃ*/Skt. **daurmanastvam* (ll. 42, etc.; cf. *dormanasta* in Kharoṣṭhī inscriptions; see text commentary, p. 273) and *dhama-* (l. 24) besides *dharma-* (ll. 23, etc.) = Skt. *dharma-*. The interpretation of *kamatu/kamato*, which may be the equivalent of Skt. *karmānta-* (ll. 29, etc.), remains uncertain (see text commentary to ll. 28–36).

The cluster *rv* usually remains but occasionally becomes *v* (= *vv*): *ghadharva-/ghadhrarva-* = P *gandhabba-*/Skt. *gandharva-* (ll. 10, etc.) and *sarva-* = P *sabba-*/Skt. *sarva-* in *sarvañu* and *sa[rvadaśa]vi* (l. 20), but *sava-* in *sava-rova-ghada* (l. 5).

The cluster *ry* is resolved by epenthesis in *(*vi)ria-* = P *viriya-*/Skt. *vīrya-* (ll. 66–7; see § 5.4 for further remarks).

5.2.3.6. Clusters with Sibilants

For previous discussions, see Konow 1929: cix–cxi; Burrow 1937: §§ 38, 41, 48–9; Brough 1962: §§ 52–60; Salomon 2000: §§ 6.2.2.2–4.

Original *śr* appears as *ṣ, rś, ś,* and *s,* in order of frequency. In other G documents original *śr* usually becomes *ṣ,* occasionally remains, and rarely becomes *ś* (see Konow 1929: cix; Burrow 1937: § 38; Brough 1962: § 56; Salomon 2000: § 6.2.2.2).

Original *śr* appears as *ṣ* in word-initial (*śr- > ṣ-*) and medial positions (*śr > ṣ = ṣṣ*). Examples of the former are *ṣamaṇa-* = Skt. *śramaṇa-* (l. 23), *ṣutvaṇa* = Skt. *śrutvā* (l. 44), and *ṣudeṇa* = P *sotena*/BHS *śrotena* (l. 44). Examples of the latter are *ṇiṣida-* = P *nissita-*/BHS *niśrita-* (ll. 65, etc.) and *ṇiṣa[e]* = P *nissāya*/BHS *niśrāya* (l. 6). As will be discussed in greater detail below, *praṣadha-* (l. 69) reflects the variant Buddhist Skt. spelling *praśrabdhi-* rather than Skt. *prasrabdhi-*.

In two cases OIA *śr* appears as *rś: pracarśoṣu* = Skt. *pratyaśrauṣuḥ* (l. 28) and *rśoda-* = Skt. *śruta-* (ll. 26, 37); *arśaveti* reflects BHS *āśrāvayanti* rather than *āsrāvayanti* (ll. 43, etc.). Further examples occur in the AG-G, written by the same scribe: *arśamu* = Skt. *āśramam* (l. 43) and *bahorśodu* = Skt. *bahuśrutaḥ* (l. 96). The Kharoṣṭhī ligature transcribed here as *rś* is (*rśa*), which is quite distinct from *śr* as in *śra* and differs from the regular Kharoṣṭhī ligature used to represent *rśa* (; e.g., Dhp-G^{K} 175a4; see Glass 2000: § 3.2.2) in that the preconsonantal *r* diacritic is attached to the left vertical of *ś* rather than the right. In the one example of the reflex of the original cluster *rś* in this manuscript, the reflex is *ś* rather than *rś* (*-[daśa]vi* = Skt. *-darśāvī,* l. 20). However, in the AG-G an etymologically cognate word is written *-darśiṇa* = Skt. *-darśinā* (l. 96), where the same unusual ligature is used. In other words, the ligature (*rśa*), not previously attested in Kharoṣṭhī, is used by this scribe to represent both the original cluster *rś* and, occasionally, the reflex of *śr*. These are also the first examples of original *śr* appearing as *rś* in Gāndhārī.

This phenomenon, however, may be merely graphic; that is, a subscript preconsonantal *r* was written in place of a postconsonantal *r*. Examples such as *athra* = Skt. *artha, savra* = Skt. *sarva,* and others (listed in Burrow 1937: § 39) in the Niya documents and *savrasi* = P *sabbadhi* in the Dhp-G^{K} (Brough 1962: 235) may represent further instances of this phenomenon, as may *virbhasta* = Skt. *vibhraṣṭāḥ* (l. 18) in this manuscript. However, these may also be examples of the metathesis of postconsonantal *r*. The absence of the ligature *śr* () in the manuscripts written by this scribe supports the conclusion that *rś* for *śr* in this scribe's orthography is merely graphic. Still, the correct explanation may be more complex, for in the manuscripts written by this scribe we find instances of preconsonantal *r* appearing in place of the sibilant in an original sibilant + consonant cluster: *krirṇo* = Skt. *kr̥ṣṇaḥ* in our manuscript (l. 23), *tarṇa* = Skt. *tr̥ṣṇām* in the Dhp-G^{L} (7a), and *parcimia* = BHS *paścimika-* in the AG-G (l. 12).[5] Since the G reflexes of the original clusters *ṣṇ* and *śc* are commonly represented by the modified characters *ṣ̄* () and *c̄* () (see Bailey 1946: 774–5) in Kharoṣṭhī documents, it appears that preconsonantal *r* in *rṇ* of *krirṇo* and *tarṇa* and in *rc* in *parcimia* has the same function as the horizontal diacritic in these modified characters (see § 4.8.1), though in *krirṇo* and *tarṇa* it is the nasal rather than the sibilant that is retained as the main character of the

---

[5] Although related, the appearance of *rv* for *dv* in *rvara* = Skt. *dvāra* (l. 57) and *bharvayo* = Skt. *bharadvājaḥ* (l. 86) in the AG-G requires a different explanation. For the use of preconsonantal *r* as geminate marker, see Salomon 1999: 122–3, 2000: § 5.9.4.

syllable. In fact, with the exception of one example of *j̄* in the AG-G (l. 52), the more usual modified characters such as *s̱̄* and *c̄* are absent in the manuscripts written by this scribe. It is therefore likely that the preconsonantal *r* in *rś* in positions corresponding to Skt. *śr* has a similar function, though the phonetic value of this graph is uncertain.

Besides *ṣ* and *rś,* original *śr* appears as *ś* in *śavastie* = Skt. *śrāvastyām* (ll. 27, 37) and as *s* in *suda-* = P *sota-*/BHS *śrota-*/Skt. *śrotra-* (ll. 45, 46). The spelling *śavasti* also occurs throughout the Senior manuscripts (see the text commentary to ll. 26–8), suggesting that this was the regular G spelling for this word, probably reflecting the spelling in the source dialect. The appearance of the dental sibilant in *suda-,* along with the more regular G spelling *ṣuda-* (l. 44), is surprising. This seems to be the first example in Gāndhārī of *s* appearing for original *śr*. Most likely this spelling is a direct borrowing from an MIA source dialect in which Skt. *śr-* in initial position appeared as dental *s-,* as in Pali. Several parallel examples are found in the Dhp-G^K^: *nisedhe* = Skt. *niṣedha-, nisedara* = Skt. *niṣeddhāram, saya* = Skt. *śayyā, suyi* and *śuyi* = Skt. *śuci,* and others (see Brough 1962: § 50).

As original *śv* regularly appears as *śp* in Gāndhārī, besides *śv* and *ś* (see Konow 1929: cix; Burrow 1937: 21; Brough 1962: § 55), it is likely that *śp* in *[dh]r[iśpa]ṇa* = P *disvāna*/Skt. *dr̥ṣṭvā* (l. 41) is to be understood as a reflex of *śv*. The same word occurs in the AG-G as *dhriśpa* (l. 41) and *dhriśpaṇa* (l. 45). The underlying form thus seems to be **dr̥śvā(na)*. In contrast, the spelling in the Dhp-G^K^ is *diṣpa* (203–6) and *diṣpaṇi* (154–5) with the retroflex sibilant, presumably to be understood as *ṣp* for *ṣv* (see Brough 1962: §§ 55, 58), reflecting **dr̥ṣvā.*

Von Hinüber (1982: 137, 1986: §§ 260, 499, 1988: 16–7) and Norman (1989a: 386 = CP, vol. IV, p. 67) have proposed that P *disvā* is to be derived from Skt. *dr̥śya* (attested in the Mahābharata according to Norman 1989a: 386) rather than from *dr̥ṣṭvā* (to which P *daṭṭhā* and *diṭṭhā* correspond), representing an artificial form based on an "incorrect" Sanskritization of the original P form **dissa, *dissā,* corresponding to Pkt. *dissā, dissa, dissaṃ*. Norman also notes that the appearance of *diṣpa* in the Dhp-G^K^ indicates that "there must have been a North Indian dialect, or dialects, where the same change of **dissā* > *disvā* had taken place, as part of the general process of Sanskritisation" (1989a: 386), and that the word *disvā* must have existed in a North Indian dialect "at some date earlier than the 2nd century A.D. when the copy of the GDhp [= Dhp-G^K^] we possess was probably written" (1993b: 94 = CP, vol. V, p. 162; see also Norman 1984: 4 = CP, vol. III, p. 37). He further maintains that, in the case of P texts, "it is possible that the introduction of Sanskritisms began to take place after the end of Aśoka's reign, and was probably fixed at the stage it had reached by the time the Pāli canon was committed to writing . . . in the first century B.C." (1984: 4; see also Norman 1983: 5).

The examples of *dhriśpa* and *dhriśpaṇa* in the new BL Kharoṣṭhī manuscripts, which have been provisionally dated by Salomon to the early first century A.D. (Salomon 1999: § 7.3), now provide us with the earliest attestations of such forms, which in turn implies that similar forms were probably in existence well before this date. This would support Norman's interpretation, as cited above.

In this manuscript the absolutive of √*spr̥ś* appears as *phuṣita* = P *phusitvā*/BHS *spr̥śitvā*/Skt. *spr̥ṣṭvā* (l. 54). The retroflex sibilant is problematic. As *ṣ* (= *ṣṣ*) is a common G reflex of original *rś* (Konow 1929: cix; Brough 1962: § 58; Salomon 2000: § 6.2.2.3), the underlying form would seem to be **sparśitvā,* with labialization of the root vowel. In the Dhp-G^K derivatives of √*spr̥ś* are *phaṣa* = Skt. *sparśān* (37b), *phaṣaï* = Skt. *sparśayet* (114d; Brough [1962: 212] gives *sparṣayet*), and *phuṣad(*i)* = Skt. *spr̥śati* or *spr̥śanti* (Dhp-G^K 128c). The latter form, *phuṣad(*i),* reflects BHS *sparśati* (see BHSG, p. 237, s.v. *spr̥ś*), which corresponds to P *phassati* (only encountered in the opt. *phasse*) rather than the regular P *phusati,* with labialization of the root vowel. Parallel to *phuṣad(*i),* but with lack of labialization of the root vowel, is *sammaṣadi* = P *sammasati*/Skt. *sammr̥śati* in the Dhp-G^K (56a), which implies an underlying **sammarśati*.

In the case of *-[daśa]vi* = P *-dassāvī*/Skt. *-darśāvī* (l. 20), original *rś* appears as *ś,* though the reading is not certain (cf. *-darśiṇa* = Skt. *-darśinā* in the AG-G, l. 96).

Original *ṣṭ* appears as *ṭh* (= *ṭṭh*) in *proṭhabu* = P *phoṭṭhabbaṃ*/BHS *spraṣṭavyam* (l. 54) and *proṭhu* = P *puṭṭho*/Skt. *pr̥ṣṭaḥ* (ll. 12, etc.), as is normal in Gāndhārī (Konow 1929: cix–cx; Burrow 1937: 20; Brough 1962: § 60; Salomon 2000: § 6.2.2.4), though the phonology and paleography of this conjunct, as well as of the related *st* and *ṭ́h,* are problematic (see Brough 1962: §§ 18, 18a, 18b). The dental cluster in *virbhasta* = Skt. *vibhraṣṭāḥ* (l. 18) is problematic but probably arose under the influence of the semantically similar *vidhvasta-* (see text commentary to ll. 16–20).

While the OIA cluster *ṣṇ* regularly appears as *ṣ̄* in Gāndhārī (Konow 1929: cx; Salomon 2000: § 6.2.2.4), in this scribe's orthography it is represented by *rṇ: krirṇo* = Skt. *kr̥ṣṇaḥ* in this manuscript (l. 23) and *tarṇa* = Skt. *tr̥ṣṇām* in the Dhp-G^L (7a). As noted above in the discussion of *rś* written for *śr,* the preconsonantal *r* in *rṇ* as the reflex of original *ṣṇ* seems to function in the same way as the diacritical mark in *ṣ̄* for *ṣṇ*. Brough (1962: § 9) took the diacritical mark in *ṣ̄* to represent the presence of the nasal. If this is so, the preconsonantal *r* in *krirṇo* = Skt. *kr̥ṣṇaḥ* and *tarṇa* = Skt. *tr̥ṣṇām* would, by the same logic, indicate the presence of the sibilant, implying that the OIA cluster *ṣṇ* remained more or less intact in Gāndhārī, but this may not be the actual situation. Konow (1929: cx, 153) interpreted the diacritic to indicate an aspiration or other reflex of the sibilant, but this view has been criticized by Brough (1962: 63 n. 2). As with other consonant clusters in Gāndhārī, the actual phonetic value of the G reflex of the OIA cluster *ṣṇ* remains problematic.

Original *ṣy* goes to *ś* (= *śś*);[6] that is, the cluster undergoes palatalization, as happens when *y* follows a dental stop (see § 5.2.3.4): *bhaviśasi* = Skt. *bhaviṣyasi* (ll. 9, etc.), *bhaviśe* = Skt. *bhaviṣye* (ll. 10, etc.), *maṇośu* = Skt. *manuṣyaḥ* (ll. 11, etc.), *[maṇ](*o)śata* = Skt. *manuṣyatvam* (l. 17) (see Konow 1929: cx; Burrow 1937: § 41; Brough 1962: § 59). The future endings *-iśasi* and *-iśe,* with palatal sibilant, parallel the forms of the future in Aśokan inscriptions and Niya documents but contrast with the *-iṣidi, -iṣadi,* futures in the Dhp-G^K (Brough 1962: § 59; Caillat 1977–8).

---

[6] Hitch (1984: 194) argues against taking *ś* < *ṣy* as a geminate (*śś*). However, in metrical texts such as the Dhp-G^K the meter clearly demands the geminate.

As is regular in Gāndhārī, original *kṣ* remains in writing in all positions (Konow 1929: cx–cxi; Burrow 1937: § 48; Brough 1962: § 52; Salomon 2000: § 6.2.2.4), though the phonetic value of the Kharoṣṭhī graph remains a matter of speculation (Bailey 1946: 770–5; Brough 1962: § 16; Hitch 1984: 198–200; Salomon 2000: § 6.2.2.4): *aṇorakṣa[e]* = Skt. *anurakṣayā* (l. 63), *uekṣa-* = Skt. *upekṣā-* (l. 71), etc. (for further examples, see the word index, s.vv. *aṇorakṣaṇa-, kṣiṇa, cakṣu-, cakṣu[a]tu, dhrekṣatu, bhikṣave, yakṣatu, yakṣu, rakṣadi, rokṣa-*). The exception is *bhikhu-* = P *bhikkhu-*/Skt. *bhikṣu-* (ll. 27, etc.), which is so spelled in all grammatical numbers and cases recorded in this text with the exception of the vocative plural, where the spelling is *bhikṣave* = P *bhikkhave*/Skt. *bhikṣavaḥ* (ll. 30, etc.). A similar distinction between *bhikṣave* for the vocative plural but *bhikhu-* for all other forms appears in the Dhp-G^{K}, which has *bhikṣavi* for the vocative plural (Brough 1962: § 52). Although the vocative singular does not occur in our text, it appears in the Dhp-G^{K} and the Dhp-G^{L} as *bhikhu* (Dhp-G^{K} 77c = Dhp-G^{L} 1c). According to Brough (1962: § 52), the spelling *bhikhu-* for this technical term is to be attributed to the source dialect, as are other words where *kh* appears for original *kṣ* in the Dhp-G^{K}. However, it is still not clear why the conjunct *kṣ* should appear in the vocative plural only of this word.

There are two examples of the reflex of the OIA cluster *st,* both in noninitial position. In both cases *st* remains, as elsewhere in Gāndhārī (Konow 1929: cxi; Burrow 1937: 20; Brough 1962: § 60; Salomon 2000: § 6.2.2.4): *śavastie* = P *sāvatthiyaṃ*/Skt. *śrāvastyām* (ll. 27, 37) and *ś[astu]* = Skt. *śāstā* (l. 16). In *domaṇastu* = P *domanassaṃ*/Skt. **daurmanastvam* (ll. 42, etc.), original *stv* appears as *st.*

In *aṭ́hi-* = P *aṭṭhi-*/Skt. *asthi-* (l. 62) and *ṭ́hideṇa* = P *ṭhitena*/Skt. *sthitena* (l. 31), original *sth* appears as *ṭ́h* (= *ṭṭh* or *ṭh*), which is regular for Gāndhārī, though once again the phonology and paleography of this and related clusters are problematic (Brough 1962: §§ 18, 18a, 18b; Konow 1929: cxi; Burrow 1937: 20).

The OIA cluster *sp* appears as *ph* in initial position in *phuṣita* = P *phusitvā*/BHS *spr̥śitvā* (l. 54), while initial *pr* in *proṭhabu* = P *phoṭṭhabbaṃ* (l. 54) reflects the BHS form *praṣṭavya-* rather than *spraṣṭavya-* (see Konow 1929: cxi; Brough 1962: § 54).

Original *sm* appears as *śp* throughout this manuscript: *taśpi* = Skt. *tasmin* (ll. 19, 20), *[lo]gha[śpi]* = Skt. *lokasmin* (l. 39), *śpadi-* = Skt. *smr̥ti-* (l. 64), *śpi* = P/Skt. *asmi* (l. 19). The only exception is *mi* = P/Skt. *asmi* (ll. 15, etc.), which is found alongside *śpi*. *Satu/sato* (ll. 29, etc.), which may be the equivalent of Skt. *smr̥ta-,* is problematic since the equivalent of Skt. *smr̥ti* is *śpadi* elsewhere in this manuscript (see text commentary to ll. 28–36). In contrast to the above, OIA *sm* appears as *sm, sv,* or *s* (= *ss*) in the Dhp-G^{K} (Brough 1962: § 53) and as *sv* or *s* (= *ss*) in the Khvs-G (Salomon 2000: § 6.2.2.4). In the Kharoṣṭhī inscriptions the reflexes of original *sm* are *s, m,* or *mr* in locative terminations (Konow 1929: cxi), while in the Niya documents the reflex is *m* in locatives and *sm* elsewhere (Burrow 1937: 20). In the Aśokan inscriptions original *sm* appears as *sp* in locatives (Burrow 1937: 20).[7]

---

[7] E.g., Shāhbāzgaṛhī, rock edict VI, l. 14: *orodhanaspi grabhagaraspi vracaspi vanitaspi uyanaspi.*

Besides being a reflex of orginal *śv* and *sm* (discussed above), *śp* also appears in this manuscript for original *sv* in *prabh(*a)[śp](*a)ra* = BHS *prabhāsvarāṇi* (l. 5) and *[śp](*ay)i[ta]* = P *sāyitvā*/BHS *svādayitvā* (l. 50; reading and reconstruction tentative). In the Niya documents the reflexes of original *sv* are *sv, śv,* and *śp* (Burrow 1937: 21), while in the Dhp-G^{K} the reflexes are *sv* and *s* in the text but *sp* in *sparga-* = Skt. *svarga-* in a verse written in a different hand from that of the main text (Brough 1962: § 55).

In the AG-G, written by the same scribe as the text presented here, *śp* also appears for original *śm* in *śpaśaṇa-* = Skt. *śmaśāna-* (l. 54) and for original *ṣp* in *puśpu* = Skt. *puṣpam* (l. 123), besides being written for original *śv, sm,* and *sv*. Thus, in manuscripts written by this scribe, OIA clusters consisting of a sibilant + the labials *p, m,* or *v* (*śm, śv, ṣp, sm,* and *sv*) all appear as *śp*. The only exception is *sp-* in initial position, whose reflexes, as noted above, are *ph-* in derivatives of √*spr̥ś* (Brough 1962: § 54) and *sm* in the first-person pronoun, Skt. *asmi,* which appears as both *mi* and *śpi* (see above). In other words, this scribe leveled all sibilant + labial clusters to *śp,* a development that is also reflected in the Dhp-G^{L} fragment written by this scribe, where Skt. *tvacam* appears as *śpaya* in the first half the text but as *tvaya* in the second half. As noted by Lenz (1999: notes to v. 11, l. 13r), the scribe apparently initially mistook *tva* () of his exemplar for *sva* (), taking the word to be the equivalent of Skt. *svayam* rather than *tvayam,* which he automatically changed to *śpaya* according to his own dialect and/or orthography, before realizing his mistake and reverting to *tvaya*.

This leveling of the spelling contrasts with the situation found in other Kharoṣṭhī documents, that is, in the Dhp-G^{K}, Khvs-G, and Niya texts, as well as in the Kharoṣṭhī inscriptions (including those of Aśoka). Here, in writing at least, when the reflex of an original sibilant + labial cluster is a sibilant + labial, the labial was liable to change, with *m* appearing as *m* or *v* (just as the cluster *tm* regularly appears as *tv*), *p* appearing as *p* or *v,* and *v* appearing as *v* or *p* (Konow 1929: cix–cxi; Burrow 1937: § 49; Brough 1962: §§ 53–5; Salomon 2000: §§ 6.2.2.3–4).[8] For example, in the Dhp-G^{K} original *śv* appears as *śv, śp,* and *ś;* original *sm* appears as *sv* and *s;* original *sp* appears as *sv* (besides *ph*); and original *sv* appears as *sv, sp,* and *s* (cf. *ṣp* in *diṣpa* = Skt. *dr̥ṣ(ṭ)vā;* see Brough 1962: §§ 53–5). However, although the labial was liable to change, the sibilant remained as in the underlying OIA cluster, with the exception that original *sv* appears as *śv* and *śp,* besides *sv,* in the Niya documents (Burrow 1937: § 49). As the representation of the G reflexes of original sibilant + labial clusters in this scribe's orthography differs from that of other G documents, it is unlikely that his tendency to represent all such clusters with *śp* means that he did not discern any phonetic distinction in these instances. Rather, this seems to be another instance of this scribe standardizing his orthography, parallel to his writing of *gh* for etymological *g* or *gh* throughout his manuscripts. Of course, the true phonetic value of the G reflexes of OIA sibilant + labial clusters is yet to be determined.

As usual in Gāndhārī, original *sy* becomes *s* (= *ss*) (often written as *s̱* in other G documents) in the genitive singular terminations *aṇasapiḍiasa* = Skt. *anāthapiṇḍadasya*

[8] Note that there seem to be no examples of original *v* or *p* appearing as *m* in such clusters, though such a change is found in *ema* for Skt. *evam* (see p. 86), where original *v* is intervocalic.

(ll. 27, 38) and *muḍhasa* = Skt. *mūḍhasya* (l. 22) (Konow 1929: cxi; Burrow 1937: § 41; Brough 1962: § 13; Salomon 2000: § 7.1.1.2).[9]

Finally, original *sr* appears as *s* (= *ss*) in *sahasa-* = Skt. *sahasra-* (l. 4) (see Brough 1962: § 57). As noted above, the G spellings *arśaveti* = BHS *āsrāvayanti/āśrāvayanti* (ll. 43, etc.) and *praṣadha-* = P *passaddhi-*/BHS *prasrabdhi-/praśrabdhi-* (l. 69) reflect an underlying *śr* rather than *sr* in words that in Buddhist Sanskrit show the common alternation between *śr* and *sr* (especially between derivatives of √*sru* and √*śru*). Parallel examples occur in the Dhp-G^K^: *aṇuvaṣuda* = Skt. *anavasruta, viśravadeṇa* = Skt. *visravant-*, and *śravadiṇa* = Skt. *sravantīnām,* though the equivalents of Buddhist Skt. *āsrava/āśrava* and *srotas/śrotas* are *asava* and *sodu* in the Dhp-G^K^ (Brough 1962: § 57; Norman 1991: § 5.3 = CP, vol. V, pp. 60–1).

5.2.3.7. Clusters with *h*

OIA *hm* appears as *m* in *bramaṇa-* = Skt. *brāhmaṇa-* (ll. 3, etc.), a regular spelling for this word in Gāndhārī. In the Dhp-G^K^, for example, the spellings are *bramaṇa* and *brammaṇa* (Brough 1962: index, s.v.; see § 14 for the orthography of *mm*). The latter spelling suggests that *m* in *bramaṇa* of the text edited here represents a geminate. Although original *hm* regularly becomes *mh* in other Prakrits (Pischel 1965: § 330; see Turner 1966: s.v. *brāhmaṇá-*), it appears that the G reflex of original *hm* (*m/mm*) did not involve an aspirate (Bailey 1946: 787–9; Fussman 1989: § 35.1).

Original *hr* in word-initial position is simplified to *r* in *rada* = Skt. *hrada-* (l. 8), the spelling also found in the Dhp-G^K^ (225a). This contrasts with P *rahada-,* where epenthesis and metathesis have occurred (see Geiger 1994: § 49.2), though in at least two cases where this word appears in P verses (Dhp 82a and Sn 721d) the meter requires that the svarabhakti vowel be ignored. In contrast, the same cluster is resolved through epenthesis in G *hirimada* = P *hirīmatā*/Skt. *hrīmatā* (Dhp-G^K^ 222a) and in all related words in the Dhp-G^K^ (cf. *hiri* 98a, 260b, and *ahirieṇa* 221a), where the meter requires this epenthetic form. Epenthesis of the cluster is more common in other Prakrits (see Pischel 1965: § 332).

Original *hv* appears as *bh* in *jibha* = P *jivhā*/Skt. *jihvā* (ll. 50, 51, 53), comparable to Prakrit *jibbhā* (Pischel 1965: § 332). The same word appears in the Senior manuscripts as *jibha* and *cibha* (20 r4,8).

5.3. Metathesis and Intrusive *r*

For previous discussions, see Brough 1962: § 64; Salomon 2000: § 6.3.

In this manuscript there are no clear examples of the metathesis of consonants other than the liquid *r*. The metathesis of the liquid *r,* which has been shown to be an areal feature of both the ancient and the modern languages of the northwest (Morgenstierne 1947), is well documented for Gāndhārī (Bailey 1946: 769, 791; Norman 1991: §§ 3, 15; Salomon 2000: § 6.3). Common examples are *dhrama-* = Skt. *dharma-, dru-* for the

[9] Hitch (1984: 192–5) argues against understanding *s* < *sy* as a geminate (*ss*); see pp. 194–6 for his discussion of the pronunciation.

prefix *dur-,* and *par-* for the prefix *pra-*.[10] Apparent examples in this manuscript are probably better classed as instances of intrusive or even anticipatory *r* rather than metathesis. These are *ghadhrarvo* = Skt. *gandharvaḥ* (l. 10), which occurs alongside *ghadharvo* (ll. 10, etc.), *ghadhro* = Skt. *gandham* (l. 47) (a spelling not previously attested in Gāndhārī), and *-prariṇamu* = Skt. *-pariṇāmam* (ll. 69, 71), which occurs alongside *-pariṇamu* (ll. 68, etc.). *Ghadhro* = Skt. *gandham* is a clear example of intrusive *r,* following a tendency for postconsonantal *r* to develop with the voiced dental stops. However, it is unclear whether the postconsonantal *r* in *ghadhrarvo* and *-prariṇamu* should be classed as intrusive or anticipatory. Examples parallel to *-prariṇamu* occur in the Dhp-G^{K} (*pruju* = Skt. *pūjya-, prodhu* = P *poso,* and *praṇiṇa* = Skt. *pāṇiṇā*), which Brough (1962: § 51) took to be examples of the intrusion of *r* as a "learned" spelling, based on a familiarity with the correspondence between *pa-* of the source dialect and G *pra-*.

The interpretation of *virbhasta* = Skt. *vibhraṣṭāḥ* (l. 18) is also uncertain. This may be an example of the metathesis of postconsonantal *r* with the preceding consonant, or it may represent a mere graphic transposition parallel to *athra-* = Skt. *artha-, savra-* = Skt. *sarva-,* etc., discussed above (§ 5.2.3.6). It is unlikely that the preconsonantal *r* in *virbhasta* is an indirect indicator of a conjunct, as in *rṇ* for original *ṣṇ* (see § 5.2.3.6). The writing of *rś* for the original cluster *śr* is probably unrelated (see § 5.2.3.6).

5.4. Epenthesis (Svarabhakti Vowels)

There is only one example in this manuscript of epenthesis, that is, the resolution of a consonant cluster by means of a svarabhakti vowel: *(*vi)ria-* = P *viriya-*/Skt. *vīrya-* (ll. 66–7) (see Fussman 1989: § 26.2). Although epenthesis is not uncommon in Gāndhārī, this is the first example of the epenthetic form of this word in Gāndhārī to my knowledge (see text commentary to ll. 63–73), though Salomon (2000: 130, 192) suggests that *aradhavirya* in an uddāna verse in the Khvs-G should be read as *aradhavir(i)ya,* as indicated by the meter. However, in view of the P parallel, it is likely that it was read as *aradhavirya* in the actual verse (see Salomon 2000: 130).

5.5. The Contraction of Syllables Involving *ya*

For the contraction *aya* > *e,* see § 5.1.1; for the contraction *ava* > *o,* see § 5.1.10.

The final syllable *ya* has been dropped in the following words (apocopic *ya*): *idhri* = P/Skt. *indriya,* which occurs as the final member of a compound in *cakṣidhri, jibhidhri,* etc. (see index for references; cf. *[vu]didhrio,* l. 8); *u* (in *idam u*) = P/BHS *avaca* (ll. 16, 36), which appears to be a further contraction of the forms *oya* and *uya,* also found in this manuscript (see pp. 179–80); *jibh(*a)* = P *jivhāya*/Skt. *jihvayā* (l. 50); and possibly *(*prasada)ṇi* = Skt. *prasādanīyam* (l. 7), though the reconstruction remains speculative. In the case of *vie* = P/Skt. *vicaya* (l. 65), which occurs in the compound *dharma-viesa(*bujaghu),* the development could have been *vicaya* > **vice* > *vie,* with *aya* > *e* and

---

[10] Examples of the latter are *parvahaï* and *parvaïdo,* probably from *pra* + √*vah,* in the Dhp-G^{K} (16cd) and *parvaïdu* = Skt. *pravrajitam* in the AG-G (l. 101).

elision of *-c-,* or *vicaya* > **viceya* > **viye* > *vie,* with the dropping of final *ya* as in the examples above.

Further examples appear in the Dhp-G^L fragment discussed by Lenz (1999: notes to v. 11): *aghamaṇa* = P *āgamanāya* (11b), where the Dhp-G^K has *akamaṇaï* (88b); and *viṇivadha* = P *vinibandhāya* (Dhp-G^L 12b), where the Dhp-G^K has *viṇavanaü* (89b). A possible example in nonfinal position of the dropping of secondary *yi* is *viṇ.* (Dhp-G^L 4b), where the Dhp-G^K has *(*v)iyi(*ṇ)i* (81b) and the Pali Dhp has *vicinaṃ.*

Similar examples are noted by Burrow (1937: §§ 9, 70) among the Niya documents, for example, *dharmapri* = Skt. *dharmapriya* (cf. also *ni* < *niya* < *nija,* "own," noted by Burrow [1937: § 17], and *dviti* = Skt. *dvitīya-* and *triti* = Skt. *tṛtīya-;* see Boyer, Rapson, and Senart 1920–9: index, s.vv.). With reference to the Niya material, Burrow (1937: § 70) states that nouns originally in *ya* and *iya* are indistinguishable from nouns in *-i.* Brough (1962: § 27) discusses two possible examples of the "coalescence" of a syllable in nonfinal position, namely, *asa* = P *āyasaṃ* and *vidi* = P *vijite* (see also his notes on *ratri* = P *rattiyā* in Dhp-G^K 343a, p. 281), though he considers it possible that these could be scribal errors. Fussman (1989: §§ 18.4, 26.1) provides further examples and discussion, while *aśoraya-* in the "Aśoraya" inscription (Bailey 1982: 149), which is probably the equivalent of Skt. *aśoka-rāja-,* may provide yet another example. The same phenomenon is occasionally encountered in other Prakrits (Pischel 1965: §§ 149–50); for example, *indi* = Skt. *indriya,* which provides a direct parallel to *idhri* in our text, occurs in the Amg. Jaina Bṛhat-kalpa-niryukti (Bollée 1998) in *panc'-indī* (3661), *pancendī* (3662), *vigalendī* (3662), and *eg'-indi-vigala-panc'-indiehi* (651). In the first three examples *ya* is dropped at the end of compounds, as in *idhri* in our text. Also, the contraction of *aya* and *āya* to *ā* and *iya* to *ī* in both word-internal and word-final positions is encountered in Pali (Geiger 1994: §§ 27.1–2,7, 81.1; Norman 1992a, see the notes to vv. 110 and 148 for examples).

It therefore appears that the contraction of syllables involving *ya,* whether original or secondary, in both word-internal and word-final positions, is attested in MIA from an early period. The G examples so far collected include the following: the oblique singular feminine and dative singular masculine/neuter terminations; the final syllable of the stem of words occurring as final members of compounds (with which *idam u* = Skt. *idam avaca* is closely related); and possibly nonfinal syllables (including the syllable *yi* < *ci/ji*) and final syllables of words in compounds in nonfinal position (Bailey 1946: 789–91). The P and Pkt. examples indicate that the final *-i* in *-idhri* is probably long.

5.6. Sandhi Phenomena

For the most part the external sandhi found in this G text parallels that encountered in Pali, with a few interesting exceptions.[11] In some cases, although the development found in the P parallel text differs from the Gāndhārī, the same developments are attested elsewhere in Pali, for example, G *cakṣidhri* for P *cakkhundriya* (§ 5.6.2); G *catvarime,* if this is the equivalent of P *cattāro 'me* (§ 5.6.2); and G *sahasa-ṅ-ara* for P *sahassārāni*

[11] For an overview of sandhi in MIA, see von Hinüber 1986: §§ 262–85.

(§ 5.6.5). In contrast, the example of G *aja-v-aghreṇa* for P *ajja-t-agge* (§ 5.6.5) and the examples of G *teṇa uasakrami* for P *ten' upasaṅkami,* G *bhaviśasi idi* for P *bhavissatī ti,* and G *sapadedi idi* for P *sampādetī ti* (§ 5.6.1), all show developments that differ from those normally encountered in Pali.

5.6.1. Vowel Hiatus

As in other MIA dialects, vowel hiatus is normally tolerated in Gāndhārī. Due to the weakening or loss of the nasalization in final nasalized syllables, the instances of hiatus are greatly increased. Examples are *bhaṣido abhiṇadi* = P *bhāsitaṃ abhinandi* (l. 26) and *rśodu eka* = P *sutaṃ ekaṃ* (l. 37). There are a few examples where the G usage differs from the corresponding Pali. Thus in *teṇa uasakrami* (l. 9), vowel hiatus is retained, whereas in the corresponding Pali expression, *-a* is normally elided: *ten' upasaṅkami.* The sandhi treatment of the particle *iti* also differs from Pali, as in *bhaviśasi idi* (ll. 12, 13, 14) = P *bhavissatī ti* and *sapadedi idi* (l. 63), representing what would appear in Pali as *sampādetī ti.* Here Gāndhārī maintains the bisyllabic form of the particle and tolerates hiatus where Pali contracts it to *ti* with lengthening of the final short vowel of the preceding word (Norman 1993a: 207 n. = CP, vol. V, p. 173 n. 6).

5.6.2. Vowel Sandhi

Although vowel hiatus is the norm in G, examples of vowel sandhi are also regularly encountered, as is characteristic of MIA in general. A small number of examples of external vowel sandhi in the Khvs-G have been documented in Salomon 2000: § 5.9.6. Many more examples are found in the manuscript presented here. They include the following (C = consonant; N = nasal):

1. Examples not involving compounds:

-ă + ă- > -ā- (assumed on historical grounds, because long vowels are not marked in Kharoṣṭhī): *sayasavi, suyasavi* = P *seyyathāpi* (< *-yathā + api*) (ll. 21, 62), *hasavaro* = P/Skt. *athāparaṃ* (*atha + apara;* see Pischel 1965: § 172) (l. 16), and *ṇaho* = P/Skt. *nāhaṃ* (*na + aham*) (ll. 10, 11, etc.).

-a + e- > -e-: ceva = P *ceva*/Skt. *caiva* (< *ca + eva*) (l. 3).

Elision is seen in the following:

-o/-u + a- > -o-: budho mi = P *buddho 'smi* (< *buddho + asmi*) (ll. 19, 20) and *alitu śpi,* probably the equivalent of a P *alitto 'smi* (< *alitto + asmi*) (l. 19).

It is unclear whether *catvarime* (l. 38) represents the sandhi combination of *catvaro/catvaru + ime,* representing *-o/-u + i- > -i-,* or *catvari + ime,* representing *-i + i- > -i-* (presumably with short *i,* following P *cattār' imāni*) (see below).

2. Examples of elision at compound junctures:

-a + i(N)CC- > -i(N)CC-: kayidhri = P *kāyindriya* (ll. 55, 56), *ghaṇidhri* = P *ghānindriya* (ll. 48, 50), *maṇidh(*r)i* = P *manindriya* (l. 58), *[vu]didhrio* = P **vutindriya*/Skt. *vṛ̥tendriya* (l. 8), *śatidhri* = P *santindriyaṃ* (l. 7), and *sudidhri* = P *sotindriya*

(ll. 45, 46). In these and the following examples, it is unclear whether the initial vowel in *idhri* (= P/Skt. *indriya*) is nasalized.

-ā + i(N)CC- > -i(N)CC-: jibhidhri = P *jivhindriya* (< *jivhā* + *indriya*) (ll. 51, 53).

-u + i(N)CC- > -i(N)CC-: cakṣidhri, where the Pali generally has *cakkhundriya* (< *cakkhu* + *indriya*) (ll. 42, 43).

In at least one of the above examples the development differs from the corresponding Pali. Where the Gāndhārī has *cakṣidhri,* the Pali has *cakkhundriya,* with the development *-u + iNCC- > -uNCC-*. However, a similar development is seen in Pali in *su + idha > sīdha,* representing *-u + i- > -ī-* (Norman 1993a: 207 = CP, vol. V, p. 174), where the E^e of DN III 225–6 reads *cakkhindriya,* perhaps following the Sinh. manuscripts. The G example finds a parallel in Amg. *cakkhindiya,* though Pischel (1965: § 162) derives this from *cakkha* = Skt. *cakṣas* + *indriya*. A further example of the Gāndhārī showing a sandhi development that differs from the Pali may be *catvarime* if this represents *catvaro/catvaru + ime* rather than *catvari + ime* (see text commentary to ll. 39–40). In P *cattāro 'me* (< *cattāro + ime*), the development is *-o + i- > -o-*. If *catvarime* represents *catvaro/catvaru + ime,* then this is an example of the contrary development *-o/-u + i- > -i-*. But again, the same development is also seen in Pali, for example, in *mokkho + ito > mokkhito* (Norman 1993a: 210 = CP, vol. V, p. 176). At least one, if not both, of the above examples suggests that Gāndhārī (or at least the Gāndhārī of this text) tends to elide the prior vowel, while Pali tends to elide the latter vowel.

5.6.3. Original Final *m* Remaining before Vowels

For previous discussions, see Brough 1962: § 71; for Pali, see Geiger 1994: § 71.2b; for MIA, see Pischel 1965: § 349.

Examples are *ṇam i[va]* (l. 8), possibly representing P *nam iva; idam a[va]ï* (l. 16), where the P expression is *etad avoca; idam u* = P *idam avaca,* where the P parallel has *idam avoca* (ll. 16, 36); *[eva]m eva* = P *evam eva* (l. 23); *asiaraṇam eva* = Skt. *adhikaraṇam eva* (ll. 42, etc.); *citam arśaveti* = BHS *cittam āsrāvayanti* (ll. 43, etc.); and *sabaram avajadi* = Skt. *saṃvaram āpadyate* (ll. 49, etc.).

5.6.4. Organic Sandhi Consonants

For Pali, see Geiger 1994: § 72. For MIA, see Pischel 1965: § 353; von Hinüber 1986: § 271.

An example of *t* is final *t* of the pronoun *tat* in *tatu, tato* = Skt. *tat tu* (ll. 29, etc.). Examples of the preservation of original *d* are *egha[d uya], eghad oya* = P *etad avaca,* where the P parallel has *etad avoca* (ll. 9, 28, 39); and *yavad eva* = P *yāvad eva* (ll. 22, 42, etc.).

The initial *v* in G *vucadi, bucadi* = P *vuccati*/Skt. *ucyate* (ll. 60, 63, 73) may represent a fossilized sandhi form (Geiger 1994: § 66.1). However, others take P *vuccati* to be derived from the guṇa grade of the root (see Norman's n. 5 to Geiger 1994: § 66.1; and von Hinüber 1986: § 270).

5.6.5. Inorganic Sandhi Consonants

For Pali, see Geiger 1994: § 73. For MIA, see von Hinüber 1986: §§ 270 ff.

There are three examples of inorganic sandhi consonants, each differing from the corresponding Pali. In *aja-v-aghreṇa* = Skt. *adyāgreṇa* (l. 25), the sandhi consonant is *v* where the corresponding P phrase, *ajja-t-agge*, has *t*.[12] In Pali and MIA the sandhi consonant *v* normally appears only in the environment of *u* or *o* (see Geiger 1994: § 72.2; von Hinüber 1986: § 270). There are two examples of the sandhi consonant *h*. The first is *sahasa-h-ara* (l. 4), where the corresponding P *sahassārāni* (representing *sahassa* + *ara*) has contraction of similar vowels instead of an inserted consonant. In several of the P examples of sandhi consonant *h* given by Norman (1979b: 323–4 = CP, vol. II, pp. 75–6), *h* similarly appears as a sandhi consonant at morpheme boundaries, for example, *su-h-uṭṭhita, sa-h-indaka,* and *su-h-uju*. The second example is *abhiñehi* = P *abhiññeyyaṃ*/Skt. *abhijñeyam* (l. 19), where *-h-* is "written in place of alif or *-y-* as a syllable-divider" (Brough 1962: § 39; see also Bailey 1946: 791–3; Norman 1991: § 16).[13] *Hasavaro* = P *athāparaṃ* (l. 16) in our manuscript represents a different phenomenon (see text commentary to ll. 15–6).

---

[12] This phrase has also been derived from *ajjato agge* (CPD, s.v. *ajjatagge*).

[13] For the discussion of *abhiñehi,* see the text commentary to ll. 16–20. For glide *h* in P and Pkt., see Norman 1979b: 323–4 = CP, vol. II, pp. 75–6; 1992a: note to v. 143; Geiger 1994: § 73.7; von Hinüber 1986: § 274.

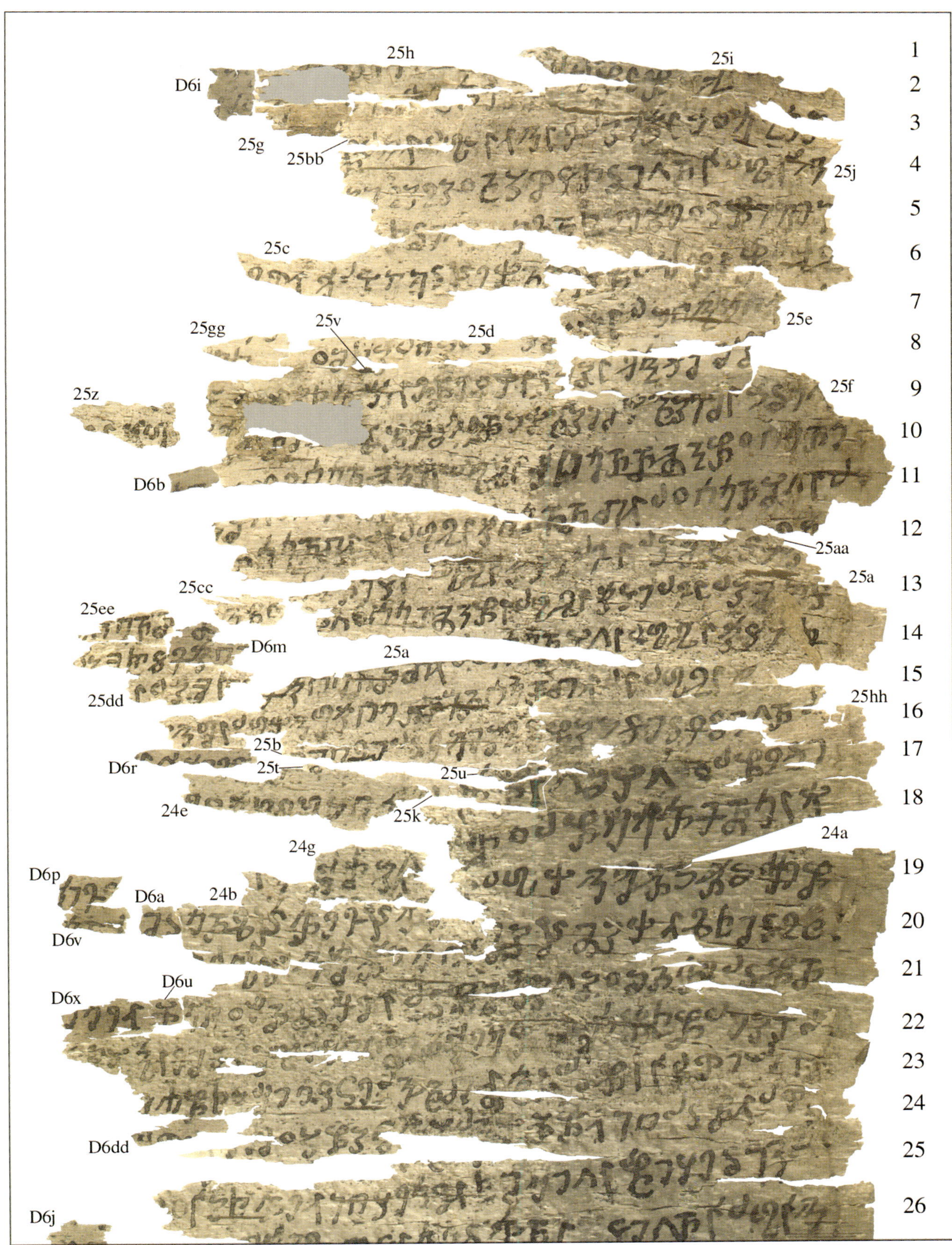

Pl. 1. Reconstructed manuscript, lines 1–26. Scale actual size. (Gray areas represent portions of the original surface of the scroll concealed by overlying fragments.)

Pl. 2. Reconstructed manuscript, lines 22–45. Scale actual size.

Pl. 3. Reconstructed manuscript, lines 40–62. Scale actual size.

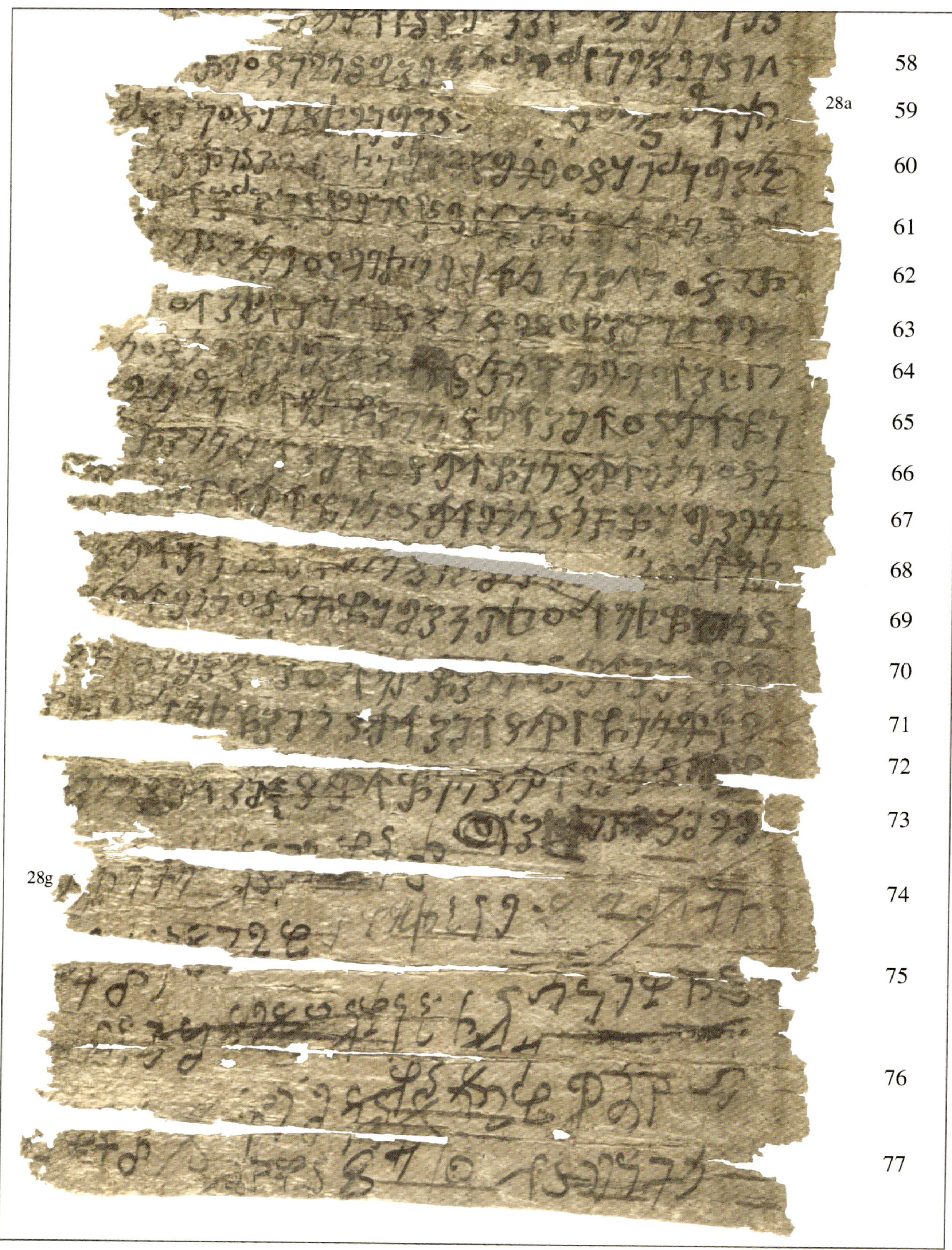

Pl. 4. Reconstructed manuscript, lines 58–77. Scale actual size.

Pl. 5. British Library Kharoṣṭhī Fragment 12 (frame 25), unreconstructed; recto. Scale 75% of actual size.

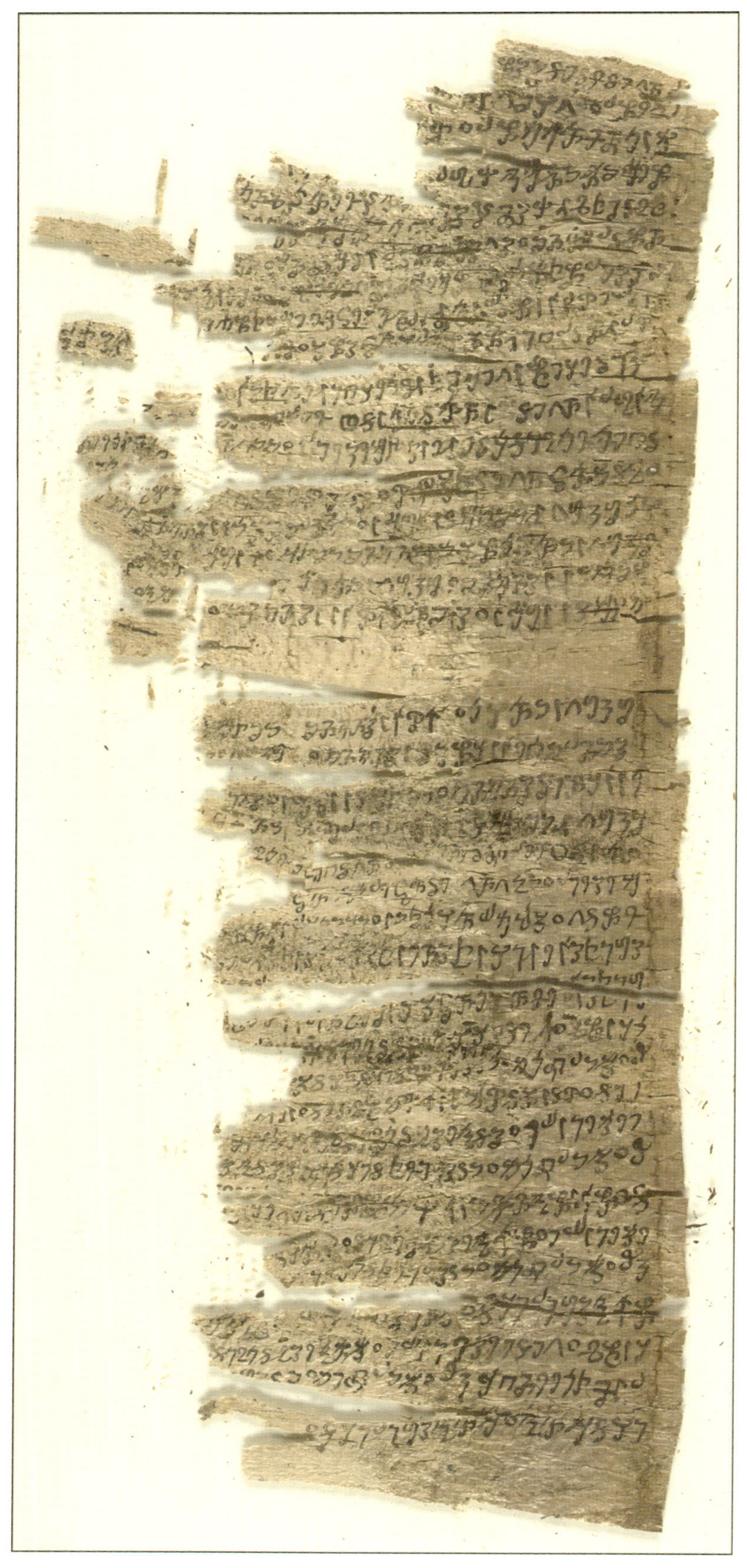

Pl. 6. British Library Kharoṣṭhī Fragment 12 (frame 24), unreconstructed; recto. Scale 50% of actual size.

Pl. 7. British Library Kharoṣṭhī Fragment 14 (frame 28), unreconstructed; recto. Scale 75% of actual size.

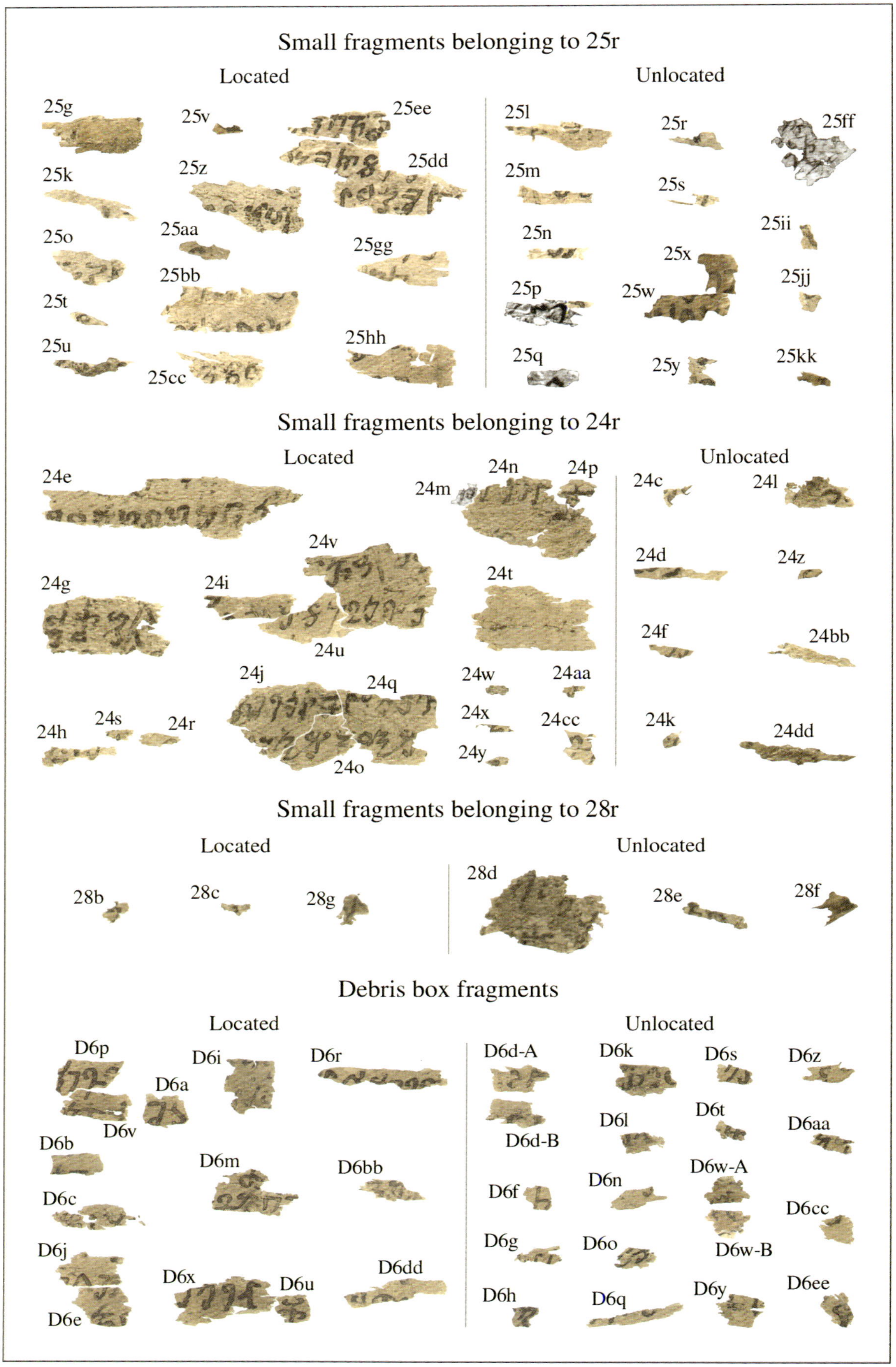

Small fragments belonging to 25r

Located

25g 25v 25ee 25k 25z 25dd 25o 25aa 25gg 25bb 25t 25u 25cc 25hh

Unlocated

25l 25r 25ff 25m 25s 25ii 25n 25x 25jj 25p 25w 25q 25y 25kk

Small fragments belonging to 24r

Located

24e 24n 24p 24m 24v 24g 24i 24t 24u 24j 24q 24w 24aa 24s 24h 24r 24x 24cc 24y 24o

Unlocated

24c 24l 24d 24z 24f 24bb 24k 24dd

Small fragments belonging to 28r

Located

28b 28c 28g

Unlocated

28d 28e 28f

Debris box fragments

Located

D6p D6i D6r D6a D6v D6b D6m D6bb D6c D6j D6x D6u D6dd D6e

Unlocated

D6d-A D6k D6s D6z D6l D6t D6d-B D6aa D6w-A D6n D6f D6cc D6g D6o D6w-B D6h D6q D6y D6ee

Pl. 8. Small fragments misplaced on the scroll and from the debris box. Scale actual size.

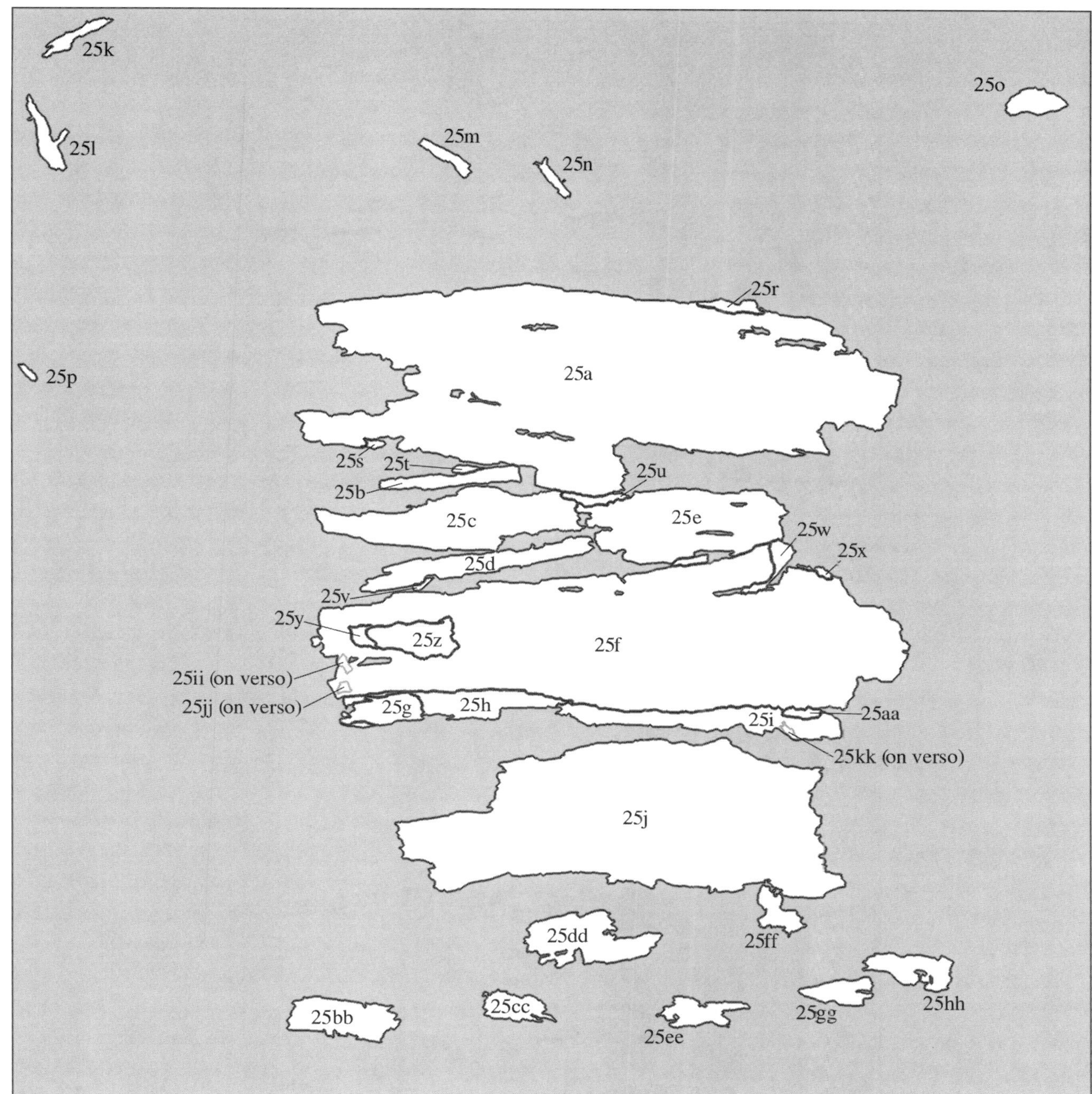

Fig. 1. Key to plate 5.

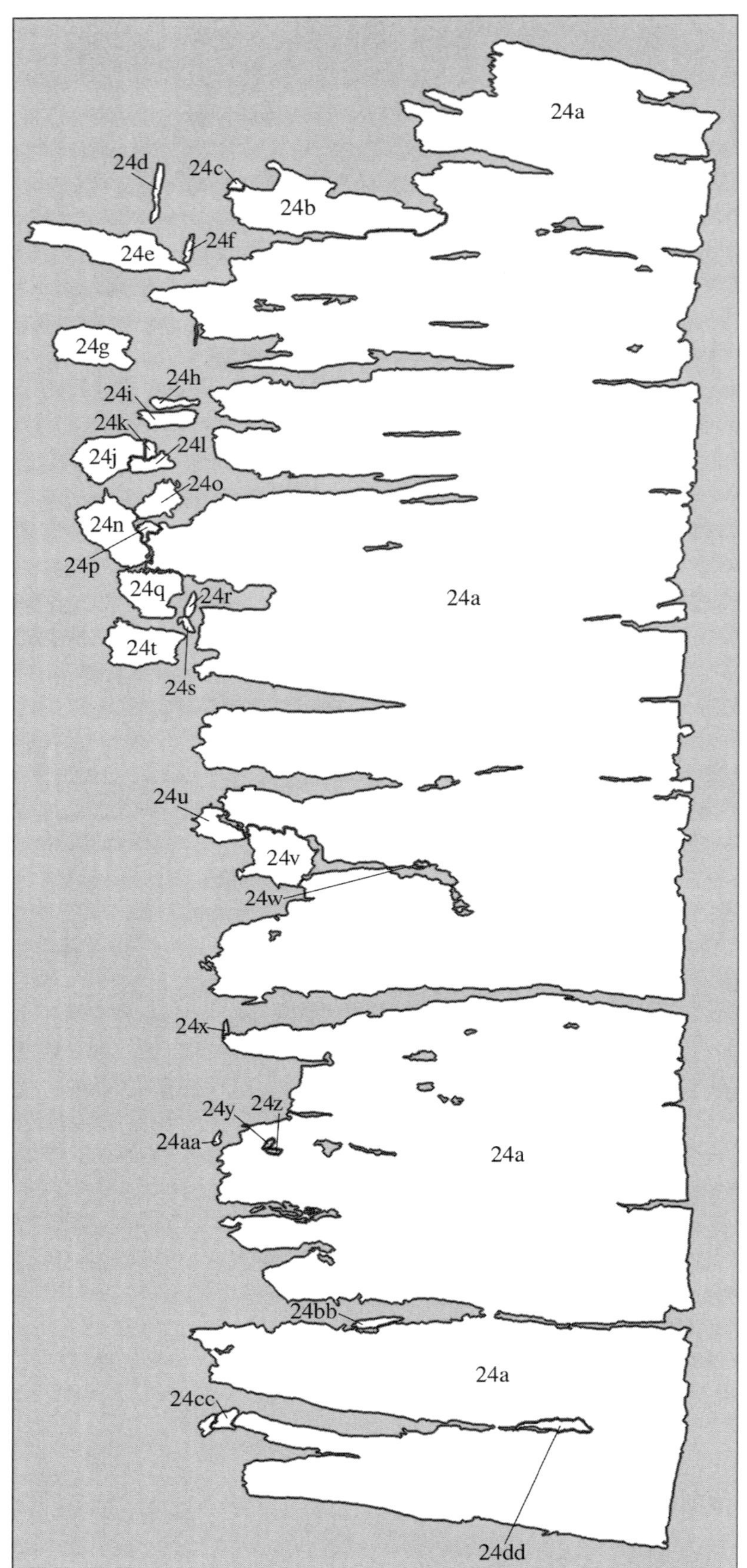

Fig. 2. Key to plate 6.

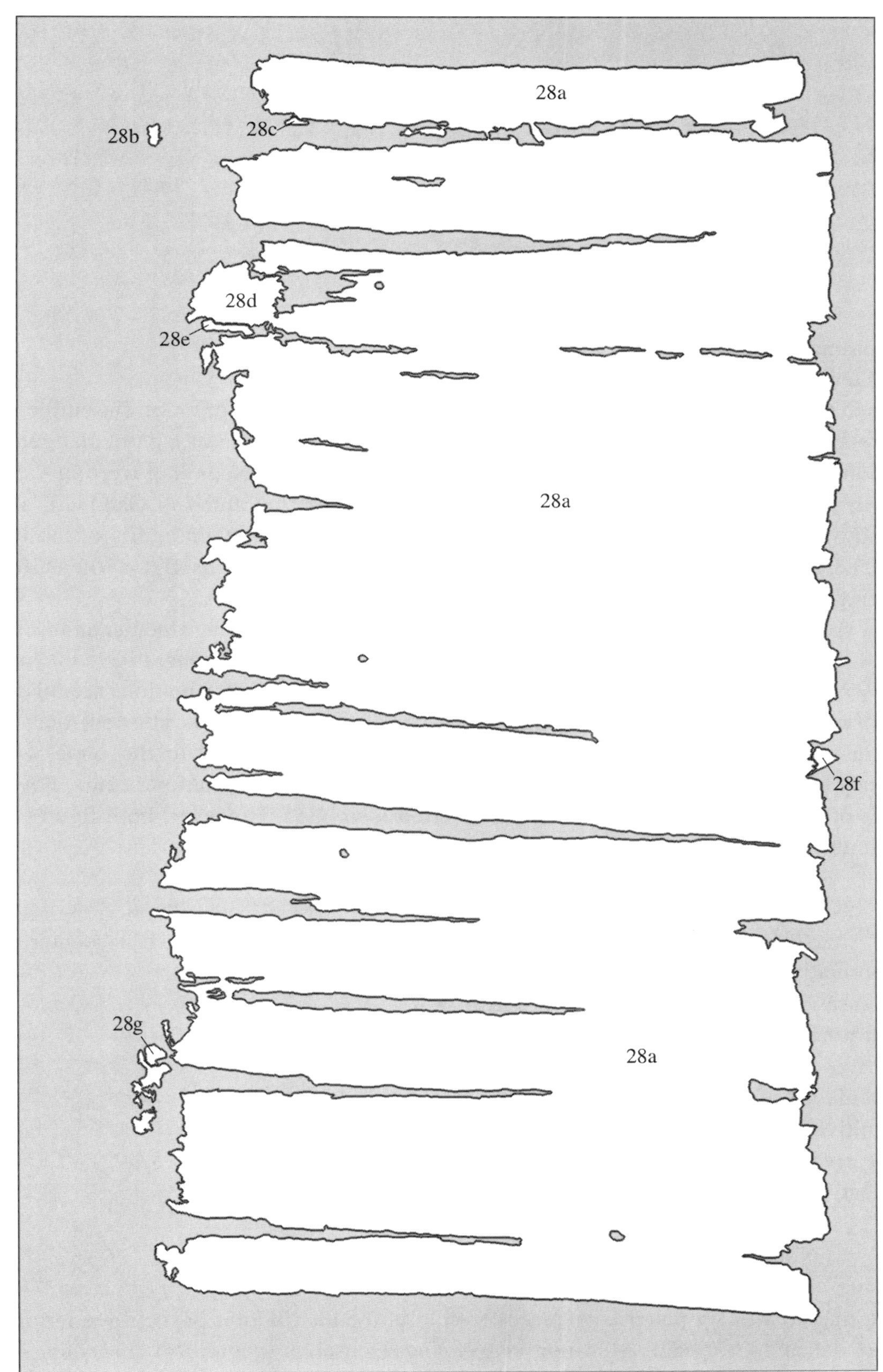

Fig. 3. Key to plate 7.

CHAPTER 6

Morphology

6.1. Nominal Forms

6.1.1. Stems in *-a,* Masculine and Neuter

Since the distinction between the nominative and accusative forms of masculine and neuter stems in *-a* begins to break down in Gāndhārī, the allocation of a particular gender to a noun in a G text is primarily based on the gender of the corresponding word in Pali or Sanskrit. Moreover, shifting between genders was no doubt common in Gāndhārī, as in Pali and Sanskrit, though it is more difficult to identify due to the ambiguity of terminations. There is, however, at least one possible example in this manuscript of the shifting between genders (see § 6.2.2.2; also Salomon 2000: § 7.1.1).

The following chart summarizes the inflections of masculine and neuter nouns and adjectives of stems in *-a*. Details are presented in the following sections. I have excluded words whose grammatical status is ambiguous and words whose terminations are missing or whose reading is uncertain. Where more than one termination is attested, they are given in order of frequency. As different terminations are applied to the same word, frequency is determined according to the number of times a termination occurs, not the number of different words to which a termination is applied. However, both figures are given in the following sections.

	Singular		Plural	
	Masculine	Neuter	Masculine	Neuter
Nominative	*o, e, u, a*	*o, u, a*	*a*	*a*
Accusative	*u, a, o, am, e*	*e, u, o, am, a, i*	*a*	*a, aṇa*
Instrumental	*eṇa*		—	
Dative	*ae*		—	
Ablative	*de*		—	
Genitive	*sa*		—	
Locative	*o, u, śpi*		*eṣu*	
Vocative	*a*		—	

6.1.1.1. Nominative and Accusative Singular

In his cursory study of the morphology of the Dhp-G[K], Brough (1962: §§ 75–7) showed that significant patterns were discernible in the distribution of the three terminations *-o, -u,* and *-a* used for the nominative and accusative singular of masculine and neuter stems in *-a*. He determined that the nominative singular masculine is normally *-o/*

-u (taking *-u* to represent a weakening of *-o*), rarely *-a,* while the accusative singular masculine is normally *-a,* occasionally *-u* (taking *-a* and *-u* to be variants of *-aṃ*), and rarely *-o*. Similarly, the nominative and accusative singular neuter are most regularly *-a* or *-u,* rarely *-o*. According to Salomon (2000: §§ 7.1.1, 7.1.1.1–4) patterns of distribution are similarly discernible in the Khvs-G^K, where, in contrast to the Dhp-G^K and other G documents, only two terminations are encountered, *-o* and *-a*. In this case the nominative singular masculine is normally *-o* for nouns and adjectives but *-a* for participles, while the accusative singular masculine ending is more commonly *-a* or *-aṃ,* less commonly *-o*. In other words, both Brough and Salomon determined that the distribution of the terminations used for the nominative and accusative singular of masculine and neuter stems in *-a* in the two texts edited by them (the Dhp-G^K and the Khvs-G) was not entirely random.

In contrast to the Dhp-G^K, where three terminations (*-o, -u,* and *-a*) are encountered, and the Khvs-G, where two terminations (*-o* and *-a*) are employed, in our manuscript the terminations used for the nominative/accusative singular masculine/neuter are *-o, -u, -e, -a,* and *-am*. The termination *-am* occurs in the accusative singular masculine and neuter when the following word begins with a vowel (e.g., *sabaram avajadi,* ll. 50, etc.). Although absent in the Dhp-G^K and Khvs-G, the ending *-e* is common elsewhere in Gāndhārī (see Fussman 1989: § 34.1).

Whether or not similar patterns are discernible in the text edited here depends on how we interpret the termination *-u*. Brough (1962: §§ 75–7) took final *-u* to represent an alternative to *-o* in the case of the nominative singular masculine, but in the case of the accusative singular masculine and nominative/accusative singular neuter he took it as an alternative to *-a,* both being the equivalent of *-aṃ*. If we adopt this distinction, meaningful patterns in the distribution of the terminations can be discerned in this manuscript also. In the masculine singular the terminations are *-o*/*-u* or *-e,* rarely *-a,* for the nominative, but *-u*/*-a*/*-am,* occasionally *-o,* and rarely *-e,* for the accusative. In the neuter singular the terminations are *-o* or *-u,* rarely *-a,* for the nominative, but *-e* and *-u*/*-a*/*-am,* occasionally *-o,* for the accusative. Leaving aside the occurrence of *-e,* and with the exception of the nominative singular neuter, this parallels the pattern documented by Brough for the Dhp-G^K. However, Brough's schema with reference to the treatment of *-u* seems suspect, for each termination should be taken as a separate alternative. If Brough's schema is rejected, the above patterns all but disappear. In the singular masculine the terminations are equally *-o, -u,* or *-e,* rarely *-a,* for the nominative, and *-o, -u,* or *-a,* in approximately equal proportions, rarely *-e,* for the accusative. In the singular neuter the terminations are *-o* or *-u,* rarely *-a,* in the nominative, and *-e, -u, -a, -o,* or *-am,* rarely *-a,* for the accusative. In other words, apart from the generally infrequent use of *-a,* the distribution of terminations appears under this interpretation to be a matter of scribal whim. The only discernible pattern is the tendency on the part of this scribe to use the same termination for sequences of nouns and adjectives that are in concord, as in *dhoṇo ṇama bramaṇo* (l. 3) but *dhoṇe bramaṇe* elsewhere (ll. 4, 26). Similarly, in the phrase *krirṇo śukro dharmu akhade vivaḍe [s](*a)praghaśi[d]e* (l. 23), the two adjectives that precede *dharmu* end in *-o,* while the string of past participles that follow end in *-e*.

6.1.1.1.1. Nominative Singular Masculine

The endings encountered for the nominative singular masculine are *-o, -e, -u,* and *-a:*

-o (ten words, fifteen occurrences): *aṇorakṣaṇa-prasaṇo* (l. 63), *krirṇo* (l. 23), *ghadharvo/ghadhrarvo* (ll. 10, 10, 13), *dhoṇo* (l. 3), *[pra]saṇa-prasa[ṇo]* (l. 40), *budho* (ll. 15, 15, 19, 20), *bramaṇo* (l. 3), *bhavaṇa-prasaṇo* (l. 40), *śukro* (l. 23), *sabara-prasaṇo* (l. 60).

-e (nine words, fifteen occurrences): *akhade* (l. 23), *aṇorakṣaṇa-prasaṇe* (ll. 40, 60–1), *deve* (ll. 9–10, 12), *dhoṇe* (ll. 4, 26), *bramaṇe* (ll. 4, 26), *bhavaṇa-prasaṇe* (ll. 63–4, 73), *vivaḍe* (l. 23), *[s](*a)praghaśi[d]e* (l. 23), *sabara-prasaṇe* (ll. 40, 40–1).

-u (six words, fourteen occurrences): *alitu* (l. 19), *dharmu* (l. 23), *proṭhu* (ll. 12, 13, 13, 14), *maṇośu* (ll. 11, 11, 14, 15), *yakṣu* (ll. 10, 11, 14), *sugha[du]* (l. 16).

-a (two words, four occurrences): *dihaghama* (l. 17), *samaṇa* (ll. 12, 13, 14).

The terminations *-o, -e,* and *-u* occur with approximately equal frequency, but if, as discussed above, *-u* is taken as a variant, weaker, form of *-o* (Brough 1962: 114), then the main contrast is between *-o/-u* and *-e,* with the former being the more frequent. The termination *-a* is rare for the nominative singular masculine, occurring with only two words. Although one of these latter words is the present participle *samaṇa,* the pattern discerned by Salomon for the Khvs-G that participles tend to have the ending *-a* does not hold true for this manuscript; compare, for example, the past participle *proṭhu* that precedes *samaṇa* (*proṭhu samaṇa,* ll. 12, etc.) and the string of past participles just quoted: *akhade vivaḍe [s](*a)praghaśi[d]e* (l. 23).

Salomon (2000: § 7.1.1.1.1) suggests that the absence of *-e* and the prevalence of the termination *-o* in the nominative/accusative singular masculine/neuters in the Khvs-G may reflect "the influence of the underlying dialect of the source text from which the Khvs-G was translated into Gāndhārī," perhaps a dialect like Pali. But the alternation between *-o, -u,* and *-e* in the manuscript edited here, which belongs to the same collection but is not written by the same scribe, suggests that the presence or absence of the termination *-e* may not be a valid indicator of the dialect of the source text, the employment of the terminations being rather a matter of scribal convention or preference. It may even be the case that the *-o* and *-u* terminations tend to be the most common for no other reason than that, because the pen finishes at the tail in the execution of the majority of akṣaras, the *o* and *u* diacritics are consequently the easiest to write. That the termination used is influenced by ease of execution of the vowel diacritic may be supported by the fact that the usual termination in nouns ending in *-ma* is *-mu* (e.g., *aramu, ghodamu, dharmu, -pariṇamu*), with the ending *-e* occurring only once (*-pariṇame*), for the akṣara *mu* (𐨨𐨂) requires only one stroke, whereas *me* (𐨨𐨅) and *mo* (𐨨𐨆) require two strokes.[1]

[1] Examples of *-me* are found in pronouns (*ime* and *me/mi*), where alternative terminations are not expected.

6.1.1.1.2. Nominative Singular Neuter
The terminations are *-o, -u,* and *-a:*

- *-o* (five words, thirteen occurrences): *prahiṇo* (l. 20), *[phulo]* (l. 18), *budha-bayaṇo* (ll. 29, 36), *v[i]puao* (l. 62), *sukaro* (ll. 29, 30, 31, 31, 32, 33, 34, 35).
- *-u* (six words, ten occurrences): *abhikatu* (l. 21), *domaṇastu* (ll. 42, 45, 48, 51–2, 55), *prahadavu* (l. 20), *bhavidavu* (l. 19), *rśodu* (l. 37), *viṇilaü* (l. 62).
- *-a* (two words, two occurrences): *aṭhi-saña* (l. 62), *[rśoda]* (l. 26), and possibly also *[a]l[oka]* (l. 22).

The frequency of *-o* and *-u* is approximately the same. As with the nominative singular masculine, *-a* is comparatively rare. This is contrary to the pattern encountered in both the Dhp-G^K and the Khvs-G, where *-a* is the more regular ending for the nominative singular neuter (Brough 1962: §§ 75–7; Salomon 2000: § 7.1.1.2). It is unclear what weight should be attached to the absence of the termination *-e,* for this may be only coincidental, since *-e* is the most frequently used termination in the accusative singular neuter (see below).

6.1.1.1.3. Accusative Singular Masculine
The terminations are *-u, -a, -o, -am,* and *-e:*

- *-u* (eight words, eight occurrences): *achu* (l. 8), *[gh]u[t]u* (l. 8), *ghudamu* (l. 24), *ṇasu* (l. 8), *dharmu* (l. 57), *-p[r]atu* (l. 7), *maghu* (l. 22), *rasu* (l. 50).
- *-a* (six words, six occurrences): *aṇa[vela]* (l. 8), *dhama* (l. 24), *bhikhu-sagha* (l. 24), *rada* (l. 8), *[v]ip(*ra)[s](*a)ṇ(*a)* (l. 8), *sama[ya]* (l. 37).
- *-o* (five words, five occurrences): *ghadhro* (l. 47), *chado* (l. 44), *magho* (l. 3), *[vu]didhrio* (l. 8.), *ṣamaṇo* (l. 24).
- *-am* (one word, four occurrences): *sabaram/savaram* (+ *avajadi*) (ll. 50, 53, 57, 60).
- *-e* (one word, one occurrence): *abhiprasaṇe* (l. 25).

In compounds ending in *idhri* = Skt. *indriya* and possibly also in *(*prasada)ṇi* = Skt. *prasādanīyam*, *-a* stems have in effect become *-i* stems through the loss of final *-ya* (see § 5.5).

The terminations *-u, -a,* and *-o* occur with approximately equal frequency, while *-am* remains when followed by a vowel. If *-u* is taken as the equivalent of *-a* (= *-aṃ*), following Brough (1962: 114), then the usual termination is *-u/-a/-am,* with *-o* being less common and *-e* being rare. This would parallel the pattern established for both the Dhp-G^K (Brough 1962: 114) and the Khvs-G (Salomon 2000: § 7.1.1.1.3). However, as stated earlier, Brough's schema is highly suspect.

6.1.1.1.4. Accusative Singular Neuter
The terminations are *-e, -u, -o, -am, -a,* and *-i:*

-e (two words, eighteen occurrences): *-ṇiṣide* (ll. 64–5, 65, 66, 66, 66, 67, 68, 68–9, 69, 69–70, 70–1, 70, 71, 71, 72, 72, 72), *-pariṇame* (l. 65).
-u (five words, thirteen occurrences): *ṇiujidu* (l. 21), *-pariṇamu/prariṇamu* (ll. 67–8, 69, 70, 71, 72), *proṭhabu* (l. 54), *yakṣatu* (l. 17), *-sabujaghu* (ll. 64, 66–7, 68, 69, 70).
-o (five words, six occurrences): *paḍ[i]chaṇo* (l. 21), *bhaṣido* (l. 26), *[r]u[v]o* (l. 41), *rokṣa-mulo* (l. 6), *śaraṇo* (ll. 24, 25).
-am (one word, six occurrences): *citam* (+ *arśaveti*) (ll. 43, 46, 49, 52, 56, 59).
-a (two words, two occurrences): *[maṇ](*o)śata* (l. 17), *-ṇiṣida* (l. 67).
-i (one word, one occurrence): *abhiñehi* (l. 19).

In terms of occurrences, as opposed to the number of different words to which the termination is applied, *-e* is the most common ending. Under Brough's schema, which takes *-u, -a,* and *-am* to be equivalents, the frequency of *-u/-a/-am* is approximately the same as *-e*. If Brough's schema is rejected, as I am inclined to do, then *-e, -u,* and *-o* occur with approximately equal frequency, and *-a* is rare, contrary to the pattern established by Brough. The termination *-i,* which only occurs in *abhiñehi* = Skt. *abhijñeyam,* results from palatalization (see § 5.1.1).

6.1.1.1.5. Nominative and Accusative Plural Masculine and Neuter

The distinction between the nominative and accusative and between the masculine and neuter has virtually disappeared in the plural forms, the termination being *-a* throughout. The old plural neuter ending *-āni* appears only once, as *-aṇa,* with final vowel unwritten, in the accusative neuter. (See Konow 1929: 3; Fussman 1989: §§ 27.3, 34.3.)

Nominative Plural Masculine (eight words, seventeen occurrences): *akuśala* (ll. 52, 55–6, 58–9), *kṣiṇa* (l. 18), *dharma* (ll. 42–3, 45–6, 49, 52, 56, 59), *pavea* (ll. 42, 48, 52), *pra[sa]ṇa* (l. 39), *bhiriḍi-ghama* (l. 18), *virbhasta* (l. 18), *savijamaṇa* (l. 39).

Accusative Plural Neuter: in *-a* (four words, four occurrences), *cakra* (l. 4), *prabh(*a)[śp](*a)ra* (l. 5), *sava-rova-ghada* (l. 5), *sahasa-h-ara* (l. 4); in *-aṇa* = *aṇi* (one word, one occurrence), *ruaṇa* (l. 22).

6.1.1.2. Oblique Cases

Instrumental Singular: The ending is *-eṇa:* (m. in ten words, twenty-three occurrences) *kayeṇa* (l. 54), *gho[da]meṇa* (l. 23), *ṭ́hideṇa* (ll. 31, 31), *ṇiṣaṇeṇa* (ll. 32, 33), *paḍideṇa* (ll. 29, 30, 32, 33, 35, 36), *baleṇa* (ll. 29, 30, 32, 35, 36), *magheṇa* (ll. 2, 6), *śeaṇeṇa* (ll. 34, 34–5), *ṣamaṇeṇa* (l. 23), *samaeṇa* (l. 3); (n. in two words, two occurrences) *ghaṇeṇa* (l. 47), *ṣudeṇa* (l. 44). *Maṇase* (l. 57) as the instrumental singular neuter, where the P parallel has *manasā,* is problematic. Perhaps it should be emended to *maṇase<*na>,* or alternatively, it could represent an example of *e* for *ā* (see § 5.1.3).

Dative Singular: The ending is *-ae,* which occurs only in the masculine *sabarae* (ll. 3, 46, 49, 52, 56, 59).

Ablative Singular: The ending is *-de,* attested only in the masculine *maghade* (ll. 2, 6).

Dative/Genitive Singular: The ending is *-sa,* attested only in the masculine: *aṇasapiḍiasa* (ll. 27, 37–8) and *muḍhasa* (l. 22).

Locative Singular (see Fussman 1989: §§ 31, 34.2): The endings are *-o, -u,* and *-śpi: [adhagha]ro* (m., l. 22), *jedavaṇo* (n., l. 27), *(*to)[yo]* (n., l. 18), *aramu* (m., ll. 27, 38), *[l](*o)ghu* (m., ll. 18–9), *[lo]gha[śpi]* (m., l. 39). *Asabrodu/asabrodo* (ll. 42, 45, 48, 51, 55, 58) could be nominative or locative singular masculine.

Vocative Singular: The ending is *-a,* occurring in *ghudama/ghodama* (ll. 21, 21) and *bramaṇa* (ll. 10, 10–1, 11, 12, 13, 14, 15, 15, 19, 20).

Locative Plural: The ending is *-eṣu,* occurring only once: *padeṣu* (l. 4).

6.1.2. Feminine Stems in Original *-ā*

The nominative singular is *-a* (for *-ā*), with one example: *abhija* (ll. 42, 45, 48, 55). The instrumental singular is probably *-ae* (for *-āe*), which appears in *aṇorakṣa[e]* (l. 63), although the reading and interpretation of this word remain uncertain (see text commentary to ll. 60–3). If the reading *ji[bh](*a)* = P *jivhāya* (l. 50) is correct, this would be an example of the instrumental singular in *-a* (for *-ā*) with loss of final *ya* (see § 5.5).

6.1.3. Other Vocalic Stems

6.1.3.1. Stems in Original *-i* and *-ī*

The nominative singular feminine of an original *-i* stem appears as *-i* in *(*u)[avati]* (l. 16), though the reading and reconstruction remain uncertain (see text commentary to ll. 16–20). The locative singular feminine of an original *-ī* stem appears as *-ie* in *śavastie* = P *sāvatthiyaṃ*/Skt. *śrāvastyāṃ* (ll. 27, 37).

6.1.3.2. Stems in Nonoriginal *-i*

An original *-a* stem has become an *-i* stem through the loss of final *-ya* in words ending in *-iya* and possibly also in *-īya*. The first example is *idhri* = P/Skt. *indriya,* which occurs as the final member of a compound in *kayidhri, ghaṇidhri, cakṣidhri, jibhidhri, maṇidh(*r)i, śatidhri,* and *sudidhri* (see index, s.vv., for references). Where the text is complete, *kayidhri, ghaṇidhri, cakṣidhri, jibhidhri, maṇidh(*r)i,* and *sudidhri* each occur three times: once in the accusative singular neuter; once in the locative singular neuter; and once in an adverbial accusative or instrumental singular. *Śatidhri* (l. 7) is a bahuvrīhi compound declined in the accusative singular masculine. The contracted *idhri* form of the above examples contrasts with *[vu]didhrio* (l. 8), which is a bahuvrīhi compound declined in the accusative singular masculine. The word *(*prasada)ṇi* = P *pasādanīyaṃ* (l. 7) is reconstructed on the basis of the P parallel. If this reconstruction is correct, it would represent another example of the same phenomenon, being declined in the accusative singular masculine. As discussed in greater detail in § 5.5, such contracted forms of *-a* stems are occasionally encountered in Gāndhārī as well as other MIA dialects. The examples in other MIA dialects (where the manuscripts mark vowel length) indicate that the final *-i* in such forms is long (*-ī*); that is, we should understand *-idhrī*. With reference to the examples in the Niya documents, Burrow (1937: § 70) states that such nouns are indistinguishable from nouns in *-i,* quoting, for example, *muli, muliyena,* and *muliyaṃmi*. But the above examples of compounds ending in *-idhri* indicate that, in this manuscript at least, the oblique cases of the singular masculine and neuter are also *-idhri*.

6.1.3.3. Stems in Original *-u*

The masculine is attested for *bhikhu-* = Skt. *bhikṣu-:*

Singular: nominative *bhikhu* (ll. 41, 64); instrumental *bhikhuṇa* (l. 61).
Plural: nominative *bhikhu* (ll. 28, 38); accusative *bhikhu* (l. 38); vocative *bhikṣave* (ll. 28–9, 30, etc.; see § 5.2.3.6).

The neuter is attested in the instrumental singular: *cakṣ[u]ṇa* (l. 41).

6.1.3.4. Stems in Nonoriginal *-u*

As in other MIA dialects, *sarvañu* = P *sabbaññū*/Skt. *sarvajñaḥ* (l. 20, nom. sg. m.) appears to be a *-u* stem, though the word is unattested elsewhere in Gāndhārī to my knowledge.

6.1.3.5. Stems in Original *-tr̥*

The nominative singular masculine appears as *ś[astu]* = Skt. *śāstā* (l. 16), though the reading of the final vowel is uncertain (see text commentary to ll. 15–6). The nominative singular appears as *śaste* in the AG-G (l. 64), which is written by the same scribe, and the accusative singular there is *śastu* (l. 64).

6.1.4. Original Consonant Stems

6.1.4.1. Stems in Original *-in*

The nominative singular masculine of the adjective *ghrahi-* = Skt. *grāhin* appears as *ghrahi* and *ghrahe* in the compounds *aṇovejaṇa-ghrahi* (ll. 41–2, etc.) and *ṇimiti-ghrahe* (ll. 41, etc.), which occur in the same sentence (. . . *ṇa ṇimitighrahe bhavadi ṇa aṇovejaṇaghrahi* ◦). Although in several cases the latter part of the word is lost, in those occurrences where the reading is certain, the distinction between final *-e* in *ṇimitighrahe* and final *-i* in *aṇovejaṇaghrahi* is maintained. Presumably, this represents nothing more than a scribal whim.

6.1.4.2. Stems in Original *-vin*

The nominative singular masculine of the adjective *[daśa]vi* = Skt. *darśāvin* appears in *sa[rva-daśa]vi* (l. 20).

6.1.4.3. Stems in Original *-an*

The accusative singular of an *-an* stem (used adverbially) appears in *ṇama* = Skt. *nāma* (l. 3).

6.1.4.4. Stems in Original *-ant*

The contracted vocative singular masculine equivalent to Skt. *bhoḥ* (from *bhavant*) appears as *bhu* (ll. 9, etc.). All other examples of *-ant* stems are present participles: *ghachateṇa* (ll. 29, 30), instrumental singular masculine of √*gam*, which, like the P *gacchantena,* is based on the stem *gacchanta-; jagharadu* (ll. 34, 35), instrumental or genitive singular masculine of √*jāgr̥* (see text commentary to ll. 28–36); and *sat[u]* = Skt. *santaḥ* (l. 39), nominative plural masculine of √*as*. The interpretation of *viharadi* (ll. 42, 45, etc.) is problematic. It could be either a finite verb or a present participle in the locative singular masculine (see text commentary to ll. 40–60).

6.1.4.5. Stems in Original *-mant* and *-vant*

There are two examples of original stems in *-mant:* the nominative plural masculine *cakṣu[a]tu* = P *cakkhumanto* (l. 22) and the nominative plural neuter *aceata* = P *accimantāni* (l. 5).

Stems in original *-vant* are attested in the equivalent of the Skt. masculine noun *bhagavant*. All forms are singular:

Nominative: *bhayavadu* = P *bhagavā*/Skt. *bhagavān* (ll. 9, etc.).
Accusative: *bhaya[va]du* = P/Skt. *bhagavantaṃ* (l. 9).
Instrumental: *bhayavadeṇa* = P *bhagavatā/bhagavantena*/Skt. *bhagavatā* (l. 26).
Dative/genitive: *bhayavadu* = P *bhagavato/bhagavantassa*/Skt. *bhagavataḥ* (ll. 4, 5, 28).

(*Bhavadu* in l. 37 and *bha[ya]va[ṣu]* in l. 28 are both scribal errors for the nominative *bhayavadu*.) Forms of the same word found in other Gāndhārī documents are as follows (all in the singular):

Nominative: *bhagava* (e.g., avadāna no. 1 on this scroll, see appendix 2; Niya document 511; Mahāparinirvāṇa-sūtra fragment 44b+c r2, additional fragment r3, v2, 109 r1, Allon and Salomon 2000), *bhayava* (Senior 20 r11, v13).
Accusative: *bhagavaṃtaṃ* (Mahāparinirvāṇa-sūtra fragment, additional fragment v3, Allon and Salomon 2000), *bhayavada* (Senior 20 r2,15).
Instrumental: *bhagavata* (Niya document 204), *bhaǵavada* (Kurram casket, l. 2, Konow 1929: 155), *bhayavada* (Senior 20 r11, although this could also be gen. sg.).
Dative/genitive: *bhagavato* (Indravarman casket inscription, l. 4, Salomon and Schopen 1984: 108; Mahāparinirvāṇa-sūtra fragment 44b+c r2, Allon and Salomon 2000), *bhagavado* (e.g., Senavarma inscription, ll. 3b, 4b, Salomon 1986: 264–6), *bhayavada* (Senior 19 r1, v8), *bhaǵavatasa* (Kurram casket inscription, l. 1, Konow 1929: 155).

Since an original unvoiced dental stop when preceded by a nasal (*-nt-*) is never voiced in this manuscript (as in *cakṣu[a]tu* and *aceata* just quoted), the stem throughout this text must be *bhayavada-*, which represents a vowel stem based on the original weak stem *bhagavat*. This contrasts with Pali and the other Prakrits, where such forms are based on the strong stem, as in P *bhagavanta-* (Geiger 1994: § 96; Pischel 1965: §§ 396–8), though isolated instances based on the weak stem are listed by Pischel for the Prakrits (1965: § 398). This also contrasts with the occurrences of this word elsewhere in Gāndhārī as listed above. For example, in the Kurram casket inscription the old instrumental singular *bhaǵavada* = Skt. *bhagavatā* (l. 2) appears alongside the newer vowel stem, genitive singular *bhaǵavatasa* = P *bhagavantassa* (l. 1). Similarly, vowel stem extensions of other *-ant* stems encountered in Gāndhārī also appear to be based on the strong form, for example, *ghachateṇa* in this text (see § 6.1.4.4) and *arahatasa* = P *arahantassa* in the AG-G (l. 111). Konow (1929: cxiv) draws attention to *puyayaṃto, mahaṃtasa,* and other examples in the Kharoṣṭhī inscriptions.[2] The morphology and inflection of *bhayavadu* in the manuscript edited here therefore appear to be anomalous, and the use of the extended stem in the nominative singular contrasts with *bhagava/bhayava* found in other G documents. (For the phonology of *bhayavada-*, see § 5.2.2.1.)

6.1.4.6. Stems in Original *-as*

There is one clear example of a stem in *-as:* the nominative plural masculine *atamaṇa* (l. 36) = P *attamanā*/BHS *attamanasas,* etc. *Maṇase* (l. 57) is problematic. According to the P parallel, *manasā,* this should be an instrumental singular neuter. As noted in § 5.1.3 and the text commentary to lines 40–60, this may be an example of final *-e* for original *-ā*. Alternatively, it may need to be emended to *maṇase<*ṇa>,* the scribe having omitted the final *-ṇa*.

6.1.5. Nominal Compounds

Virtually all of the compounds in this text are G equivalents of the forms found in the parallel P texts and no doubt represent straightforward translations or "transpositions" of what was encountered in the source text. Examples are *aṇovejaṇa-ghrahi* = P *anuvyañjana-ggāhī* (ll. 41–2, etc.), *bhikhu-sagha* = P *bhikkhu-saṅghaṃ* (l. 24), *samasi-sabujagh[u]* = P *samādhi-sambojjhaṅgaṃ* (l. 70), and *sa[rva-daśa]vi* = P *sabba-dassāvī* (l. 20). The exception is the problematic *praṇo-uviade* (l. 25), which may be a pseudo-compound. The P and Skt. equivalents are *pāṇopetaṃ* and *prāṇopetam,* respectively (see text commentary to ll. 20–5 for further details). In three instances the sandhi at the compound juncture differs from the corresponding Pali. They are *aja-v-aghreṇa* (l. 25), *cakṣi[dhri]* (ll. 42, 53), and *sahasa-h-ara* (l. 4) (see §§ 5.6.2, 5.6.5).

---

[2] Since the development of nasal + stop clusters is peculiar in the Dhp-G^{K}, forms such as the accusative singular *śilamadu* and *vadamada* there (see Brough 1962: index, s.vv.) do not provide parallels to our *bhagavadu*.

6.2. Pronouns, Pronominals, and Numerals

6.2.1. Personal Pronouns

The nominative singular is *aho* in *ṇaho* = Skt. *nāham* (ll. 10, 11, etc.). In view of the P parallel *na kho ahaṃ,* it is also possible, though less likely, that this represents P *kho*/Skt. *khalu* (see text commentary to ll. 9–15). The enclitic singular form appears as *mi* or *me:* accusative *mi* (l. 24), instrumental *me* (ll. 26, 37), and instrumental or genitive *mi* (l. 20).

6.2.2. Third-Person/Demonstrative Pronouns

6.2.2.1. *tad* and *etad*

In the singular the forms are *to* (acc. m., l. 3), *teṇa* (instr., ll. 3, 9), and *taśpi* (abl., ll. 19, 20). *Taśpi* represents a locative form used for the ablative (see text commentary to ll. 16–20). The nominative plural masculine is *te* (ll. 28, 36). The interpretation of *tae* (l. 63) is uncertain; it may represent the instrumental singular feminine P *tāya*/Skt. *tayā* (see text commentary to ll. 60–3). *Tatu/tato* (ll. 29, etc.) is probably the equivalent of Skt. *tat tu.*

The accusative singular neuter of original *etad* appears as the problematic *eghad* in *eghad [uya]* and *eghad oya* (ll. 9, 28, 39).

6.2.2.2. *idam*

The accusative singular neuter is *ida* (l. 16) and *idam* (ll. 16, 36). The nominative singular masculine is *aï* (ll. 60, 73) in *aï bucadi sabaraprasaṇo* (l. 60) and *aï vucadi bhavaṇaprasaṇe* (l. 73), where the P parallel has, for example, *idaṃ vuccati saṃvarappadhānaṃ.* The gender of *prasaṇa-* = P *padhāna-* appears to be masculine in this text. In contrast, *idi* appears in place of *aï* in the parallel phrase *idi vucadi aṇorakṣaṇaprasaṇo* (l. 63). In this context, *idi* could represent either Skt. *idam* or *iti* (see text commentary to ll. 40–60, 60–3). If the former, this would be an example of the inconsistency in the employment of genders (see § 6.1.1). At the beginning of the same sūtra, the nominative plural *ime* appears in *catvarime pra[sa]ṇa* (l. 39) where the P parallel has the neuter plural *cattār' imāni padhānāni,* though the masculine occurs elsewhere in Pali (see text commentary to ll. 39–40). It would be natural to take *ime* as nominative plural masculine in this passage, following its more usual usage as such, providing further evidence that *prasaṇa-* is masculine in this text. Although *ime* appears in some inscriptions with the historically neuter noun *śarira-* = Skt. *śarīra-* (e.g., *pratiṭhaviḋa ime śarira śakamuṇisa bhaǵavato* in the Swāt Meridarkh inscription [Konow 1929: 4] and *ime bhagavato śakyamuṇisa śarira pradiṭhaveti* in the Indravarman casket inscription [l. 4, cf. l. 1; Salomon and Schopen 1984: 108]), which suggests that *ime* may also be a neuter plural, *śarira* could in fact be masculine in these passages (see Fussman 1989: 459, 485 n. 63). The evidence is therefore inconclusive, and *ime* in *catvarime pra[sa]ṇa* in the manuscript edited here could be neuter or masculine.

The status of *aï* (ll. 41, 61, 64), which is no doubt the equivalent of P/Skt. *ayaṃ,* is problematic, for P and Skt. parallels have *idha* and *iha,* respectively (see text commentary to ll. 40–60).

6.2.3. Relative Pronoun

The instrumental singular neuter appears as *yeṇa* (ll. 16, 17).

6.2.4. Interrogative Pronouns

6.2.4.1. *kad*

The nominative singular masculine appears as *ku* (l. 15).

6.2.4.2. *katara-*

The nominative singular masculine (or, perhaps, neuter) appears as *kadara* (ll. 40, 60) where the P parallel has *katamaṃ* and the Skt. has *katarat,* both neuter (see text commentary to ll. 40–60).

6.2.5. Pronominally Declined Adjectives

The only example of a pronominal adjective that bears a termination is *añadara-* = Skt. *anyatara-,* which occurs in two contexts. The first is the accusative singular neuter *añadaro* (l. 6). The second is *añadara añadara,* which could also be taken as a compound *añadara-añadara* (l. 61), where the termination or terminations are nominative singular neuter.

6.2.6. Numerals

There are two examples: the accusative singular *eka,* which appears in *eka samaya* (ll. 26, 37), and *catvara-,* which appears in *catvarime* (l. 39), where the termination is obscured by sandhi.

6.3. Verbal Forms

6.3.1. Present Tense

First-Person Singular: The ending is *-mi: ghachami* (l. 24); *mi* (ll. 15, 15, 19, 20) and *śpi* (l. 19), both = P/Skt. *asmi.*

Second-Person Singular: The ending is *-si: vadesi* (ll. 12, etc.) (but this could alternatively represent a preterite).

Third-Person Singular: The ending is *-di: amatredi* (ll. 27–8, 38), *avajadi* (ll. 43–4, etc.), *pradivajadi* (ll. 43, etc.), *bhavadi* (ll. 44, etc.), *bhavedi* (ll. 64, etc.), *rakṣadi* (ll. 43, etc.), *viharadi* (ll. 27, 37; *viharadi* in ll. 42, 45, 48, 51, 55, and 58 may be a present participle), *vucadi/bucadi* (ll. 60, 63, 73), *sapadedi* (l. 63).

Third-Person Plural: The ending is *-ti* (for *-nti*): *arśaveti* (ll. 43, etc.).

6.3.2. Optative

First-Person Singular: *[abaji]* = P *abbaje* (l. 17; reading uncertain). In view of the Pali, the voice is probably parasmaipada.

Third-Person Singular Parasmaipada: *ukuje* (l. 21), *[ghache]* (l. 17), *praghaśe* (l. 22).

The reconstruction of *viv(*are)* = P *vivareyya* (l. 21) is based on the above forms.

There are no examples of optatives in *ea,* which are very common in other G texts (see Brough 1962: 79; Salomon 2000: § 7.3.2).

6.3.3. Imperative

The only example is *dharedu* (l. 25), the third-person singular of the causative. (See § 6.3.5.)

6.3.4. Future

There are two examples: the first-person singular ātmanepada *bhaviśe* (ll. 10, etc.) and the second-person singular parasmaipada *bhaviśasi* (ll. 9, etc.).

6.3.5. Future Imperative

There is one example of what appears to be a future imperative. This is the third-person plural *dhrekṣatu* (l. 22), which would correspond to a Skt. **drakṣyantu*. The P parallel has the future form *dakkhinti*. The alternative explanation is that it represents a present imperative (= P *dakkhantu;* see text commentary to ll. 20–5).

6.3.6. Preterites

Second-Person Singular: *vadesi* (ll. 12, etc.; this could also be a 2nd sg. pres.).

Third-Person Singular: *abhikrami* (ll. 2, 6), *abhiṇadi* (l. 26), *a[va]ï* (l. 16), *uasakrami* (l. 9), *u* = P *avaca* (ll. 16, 36), *[uya]* and *oya* = P *avaca* (ll. 9, 28, 39). The interpretation of *[vi]hari* (l. 3) is uncertain. It could be a preterite or a noun form (see text commentary to ll. 1–3).

Third-Person Plural: *[a]bhiṇadi* (l. 37) and *pracarśoṣu* (l. 28). As noted in the text commentary on *[a]bhiṇadi* (see text commentary to ll. 25–6), it appears that the singular form has been transferred to the plural, as the same form is used for the plural in the Senior manuscripts. The P parallel has *abhinandun*.

6.3.7. Absolutives (Gerunds)

A diverse range of absolutives are encountered in this manuscript, including forms based on original *-ya, -tvā, -itvā,* the extended non-Sanskritic *-tvāna* form, and *-tu*. This diversity seems to be characteristic of G texts (Brough 1962: § 80; Salomon 2000: § 7.3.3).

Original *-ya* forms appear as *-e,* with palatalization (see § 5.1.1): *[a]bhiñae* (l. 19) and *ṇiṣa[e]* (l. 6; used as a postposition). Forms in original *-tvā* appear as *-tva* (for *-tvā*): *ghatva* (ll. 2, 6). The extended *-tvāna* form, which is common in Pali, appears as *-tvaṇa* in *ṣutvaṇa* (l. 44) and probably also in *[dh]r[iśpa]ṇa* = P *disvāna* (l. 41) (see § 5.2.3.6). Forms in original *-itvā* appear as *-ita: uasakramita* (l. 9), *gha[ï]ta* (l. 47), *phuṣita* (l. 54), *vadita* (l. 16), and *[śp](*ay)i[ta]* (l. 50). There is one example of the uncommon absolutive in *tu,* namely, *añadu* (l. 57; based on *ā* + √*jñā*).[3]

---

[3] Cf. the appearance of absolutives in *-ti,* which represent Vedic *-tvī,* in the Dhp-G^K (Brough 1962: § 80).

6.3.8. Infinitives

The infinitive of √*kr̥* appears as *katu/kato* (ll. 30, etc.). This is the only example of an infinitive in this text.

6.3.9. Participles

6.3.9.1. Present Participles Parasmaipada in *-ant*

Examples are *ghachateṇa* (ll. 29, 30), *jagharadu* (ll. 34, 35; see § 5.1.4), *sat[u]* (l. 39). The interpretation of *viharadi* (ll. 42, etc.) is uncertain; it is either a present participle or a finite verb (see text commentary to ll. 40–60). (For the declension of present participles in *-ant,* see § 6.1.4.4.)

6.3.9.2. Present Participles Ātmanepada in *-āna* and *-māna*

There is one example of an ātmanepada present participle in *-āna* (*śeaṇeṇa* = Skt. *śayānena,* ll. 34, 34–5) and one in *-māna* (*savijamaṇa* = Skt. *saṃvidyamāṇa-,* l. 39).

6.3.9.3. Past Participles

There are numerous examples of past participles, functioning both as adjectives and as nouns. All correspond to those found in Pali and, to a large extent, Sanskrit.

Forms in original *-na:*

abhiprasaṇe = Skt. *abhiprasannam* (l. 25)
kṣiṇa = Skt. *kṣīṇāḥ* (l. 18)
ṇiṣaṇeṇa = Skt. *niṣaṇṇena* (ll. 32, 33)
prahiṇo = Skt. *prahīṇam* (l. 20)
*[v]ip(*ra)[s](*a)ṇ(*a)* = Skt. *viprasanna-* (l. 8)

Forms in original *-ta/-ita:*

akhade = Skt. *ākhyātaḥ* (l. 23)
abhikatu = Skt. *abhikrantam* (l. 21)
alitu = Skt. *aliptaḥ* (l. 19)
asabroda- = Skt. *asaṃvr̥ta-* (ll. 42, etc.)
-uviade = Skt. *-upetam* (?) (l. 25)
-ghada = Skt. *-kr̥tāni* (l. 5)
[gh]u[t]u = Skt. *guptam* (l. 8)
ṭ́hideṇa = Skt. *sthitena* (l. 31)
ṇiujidu = P *nikujjitaṃ*/Skt. **nikubjitam* (l. 21)
ṇiṣida- = P *nissita-*/BHS *niśrita-* (ll. 65, etc.)
-p[r]atu = Skt. *prāpta-* (l. 7)
proṭhu = Skt. *pr̥ṣṭaḥ* (ll. 12, etc.)
budho = Skt. *buddhaḥ* (ll. 15, etc.)
*bh(*a)[vi](*du)* = Skt. *bhāvitam* (l. 19)
bhaṣido = Skt. *bhāṣitam* (l. 26)

muḍhasa = Skt. *mūḍhasya* (l. 22)
rśoda- = Skt. *śruta-* (ll. 26, 37)
virbhasta = Skt. *vibhraṣṭāḥ* (l. 18)
vivaḍe = Skt. *vivr̥taḥ* (l. 23)
[vu]didhrio = Skt. *vr̥tendriya-* (l. 8)
śata- = Skt. *śānta-* in *śatidhri* and *śata-maṇa[s.]* (l. 7)
*[s](*a)praghaśi[d]e* = Skt. *saṃprakāśitaḥ* (l. 23)
sugha[du] = Skt. *sugataḥ* (l. 16)

6.3.9.4. Future Passive Participles (Gerundives)

There is one example of a future passive participle in original *-ya: abhiñehi* = Skt. *abhijñeyam* (l. 19). There are three examples in original *-tavya: proṭhabu* = P *phoṭṭhabbaṃ*/ BHS *spraṣṭavya-* (l. 54), *prahadavu* = Skt. *prahātavyam* (l. 20), and *bhavidavu* = P *bhāvetabbaṃ* (l. 19).

CHAPTER 7

Transcribed Text, Reconstruction, and Translation

In § 7.1 the text is presented as it appears in the reconstructed manuscript. The fragment or fragments on which each portion of the text is found are indicated by small superscript fragment numbers, separated by a thin vertical line. For the descriptions and details of the separate fragments, see § 3.3. For explanation of the format of the transcription, including the symbols indicating incomplete or uncertain akṣaras and the like, see pp. xviii–xix.

The reconstructed text and the translation of the reconstructed text appear on facing pages in § 7.2, with each sūtra presented separately. The reconstructed portions of the text and the translation of these reconstructed portions appear in parentheses, prefixed with an asterisk (*).

7.1. Transcribed Text

1. [25h]/// ? ? ? ? ? ? ? [D6i]ta s. ? ///

2. [25i]? ṭo [25i+25j]magh.ṇa ghatva ma[ghade] [25j+25h]a[25j+25h+25bb]bhi[kra][25h+25bb]mi ∘ a[ña] [25g]? + [25h+25g][r]o[D6i]kṣ.mul. ///

3. [25i+25j][s. vi][25j]hari ∘ teṇa ceva samaeṇa dhoṇo ṇama [25j+25bb]bramaṇo to magho ///

4. [25j]/// dhoṇe bramaṇe bhayavadu padeṣu cakra ∘ sahasahara [s.] ///

5. /// savarovaghada ∘ aceata prabh.[25j+25c][śp.]ra [∘ bha]yavadu p.[.e] ///

6. [25j]/// hoṭo [25j+25e]magheṇa ghatva magha[25e][de [25e+25c]abhi][25c]k[r]ami añadaro rokṣamulo [25c+25gg]ṇiṣa[e] ///

7. [25j]/// ? + + [25e]ṇi śatidhri śatamaṇa[s. ∘ [25d]utamada][25d+25f]masa[25f|25d]śama[25d+25f]sa[25v]p[r][25d+25f]atu [25d]∘ [25gg]p. r. [m.] ///

8. [25e+25f]/// [gh]u[t]u [vu]didhrio [25f]ṇasu rada ṇam=i ∘ [va] achu aṇa[vela v]ip..[s.]ṇ. [∘] ? ? [25z]+ ? ///

9. [25f]/// yavadu teṇa uasakrami uasakramita bhaya[vad]u egha[d=u] + + + [v. bhu bha] ? [śasi ṇa] + [25z]bra[ma]ṇ. [d.] ///

10. [25f]ve bhaviśe ∘ ghadhrarvo bhu bhaviśa[s]i ṇaho bramaṇa [25f+25a][gha]dharvo bhaviśe ∘ yakṣu [bh. [D6b]bh.vi] ///

| 25f | 25f+25a | 25a

11. maṇa yakṣu bhaviśe ∘ maṇośu bhu bhaviśasi ṇaho bramaṇa maṇośu bhaviśe [∘] ///

| 25f+25a | 25aa+ 25a | 25a+ 25f | 25a | 25cc | 25cc+ D6m | D6m+ 25ee

12. /// + si idi proṭhu samaṇa ema vadesi ṇaho bramaṇa dev[e bhaviśe] ∘ gh.ḍh.[rv.] bhu

| 25ee+25dd

bhaviśa[si] ///

| 25a | D6m | D6m+25dd

13. di p[r]oṭhu samaṇa ema vadesi ṇaho bramaṇa ghadharvo bhaviśe ∘ ya[kṣ.] + + [vi]śasi idi

| 25dd

proṭh[u sama] ///

| 25a | 25dd

14. ema vadesi ṇaho bramaṇa yakṣ[u] bhaviśe [∘] maṇośu bhu bhaviśasi [id.] proṭhu samaṇa

[e] ///

| 25a+24a | 25a

15. /// s[i] ṇaho bramaṇa maṇośu bhaviśe ku re bhu bhaviśasi budho mi b[r]amaṇa budho

[mi] ///

| 24a+25hh | 24a | 25a | 25a+25b | 25b+ 24e+ 25t | 25b+ 24e | 24e | D6r | 24e+ D6r | D6r

16. m=u bhayavadu ida vadita sugha[du] hasavaro idam=a[va]ï ś[astu ∘] ? ? [a.a.vati]

yeṇa ? ///

| 25hh+ 24a | 24a | 24a+25u+25a | 25k+ 24e | 24e

17. va dihaghama ∘ [ma] yakṣatu yeṇa [ghache maṇ.]śata [ba abaji] ∘ [a.] ///

| 24a | 24g | 24g+24b | 24b | D5p | D6p+ D6v | D6p

18. kṣiṇa virbhasta bhiriḍighama ∘ pu[ḍar.] + [yasa phulo] + [yo ṇ.] + + + + + [◦] eva [l.] ///

| 24a | 24b | 24g+24b | 24b | D6a | D6v

19. ghu alitu śpi taśpi budho mi brama[ṇa] + [a]bhiñae abhiñehi bhavidavu [p.] bh.[vi] ///

| 24a | 24a+24b | 24b

20. prahadavu prahiṇo mi sarvañu sa[rvadaśa]vi taśpi budho [mi bramaṇa] ///

| 24a | D6u+ D6x | D6x

21. bhu ghodama abhikatu ∘ suyasavi [bhu] ghudama ṇiujidu ukuje ∘ paḍ[i]chaṇo a viv. ///

| 24a

22. muḍhasa va maghu praghaśe ? ∘ [adhagha]ro [a]l[oka va] ∘ ya[va]d=eva cakṣu[a]tu ruaṇa

dhrekṣatu ∘

| 24a+ D6dd | 24a

23. [eva]m=eva ṣamaṇeṇa gho[da]meṇa krirṇo śukro dharmu akhade vivaḍe [s.]praghaśi[d]e ///

| D6dd

24. ṣamaṇo ghudamu śaraṇo ghachami dhama ca bhikhusagha ca ∘ u ? ? ? [mi ṣ.]ma ///

| 24a | D6j

25. [m.] dharedu ajavaghreṇa yavajivu praṇouviade śaraṇo abhiprasaṇe ∘ [i] /// /// ? ///

| 24a | D6j+D6e

26. dhoṇe bramaṇe bhayavade[bha]ṇa bhaṣido abhiṇadi ○ eva me [rśoda eka] /// /// bhaya[v.] ///

| 24a | D6e

27. du śavastie viharadi jedavaṇo aṇasapiḍiasa aramu ∘ ta[tra] ya bha[ya] + [d.] bhi ///

| 24a

28. matredi te bhikhu bhayavadu pracarśoṣu ∘ bha[ya]va[ṣu] egha[d=uya ∘ su] ///

29. kṣave budhabayaṇo tatu paḍideṇa [ṇa] baleṇa ∘ sato kamatu [ghacha]teṇa ṇa sukaro ka ///

30. budhabayaṇata bhikṣave ghachateṇa s[u]karo katu tatu paḍideṇa ṇa bal[eṇa] ∘ [sa] ///

| 25o | 25o+ D6bb | D6bb

31. matu ṭ́hideṇa ṇa sukaro katu ∘ budhabayaṇata bhikṣave [ṭ́h.] + ṇa s[u]k.ro k. ///

|24a
32. to [pa]ḍideṇa ṇa baleṇa ∘ satu kama[t]u ṇiṣaṇeṇa ṇa sukaro kat[u] ∘

33. budhabayaṇata bhikṣave ∘ ṇiṣaṇeṇa sukaro katu tatu paḍide ///

34. sato kamato śeaṇeṇa jaghara[du] ṇa sukaro kato ∘ budhabayaṇa[ta] ///

35. aṇeṇa jagharadu sukaro kato ∘ ta[tu] paḍideṇa ṇa [ba]l[e]ṇa ∘ sukar. ///

|24a+ 24v |24a |24i
36. budhabayaṇo tatu paḍideṇa ṇa ba[le]ṇa ∘ idam=u atamaṇa te bhi[kh.] /// /// + + + ? ///

|24a |24w |24a+ 24v |24v |24v+ 24u |24u |24u+ 24i |24i
37. [a]bhiṇadi O eva me rśodu eka sama[ya ∘] bhayadu śavastie viharadi [jedavaṇ.] ///

|24a |24u
38. ḍiasa aramu ∘ tatra ya bhayavadu bhikhu amat[r]edi bhikhu ? ? ? ? ? ///

|24a
39. eghad=oya ∘ catvarime bhikṣave pra[sa]ṇa ∘ sat[u] savijamaṇa [lo]gha[śpi ∘] ///

40. sabaraprasaṇe aṇorakṣaṇaprasa[ṇe] bhavaṇaprasaṇ[o ∘ pra]saṇaprasa[ṇo] ∘ ka[da] ///

|24a+24x
41. baraprasaṇe ∘ aï bhikṣave bhikhu cakṣ[u]ṇa [r]u[v]o [dh]r[iśpa]ṇa ∘ ṇa ṇ[i]mitighra[he] ///

|24a |24a+24q
42. vejaṇaghrahi ∘ yavad=eva [asi]araṇa[m=e] + cakṣi[dhri asabro]du viharad[i] ∘ abhija

|24q+ 24j+ 24o |24j
domaṇastu pavea aku ///

|24a |24a+ 24q |24q |24q+ 24o |24o |24o+ 24j |24j
43. rma ∘ citam=arśaveti ∘ ta[da saba]ra[e pra]divajad[i] rakṣadi cakṣidhri ∘ cakṣidhri sa[ba] ///

|24a |24a+ 24r |24a+ 24s |24s+ D6c+ 24h |D6c+24h
44. [va]jadi ∘ ṣudeṇa chado ṣutvaṇa ṇa ṇimitighrahe bhavadi ∘ ṇa aṇo[ve]jaṇaghra ///

|24a |24a+ 24y |24a+24aa
45. va asiaraṇam=eva ∘ sudidhri asabrodu viharadi ∘ [a]bhi[ja do]maṇastu [pa] ///

|24a
46. rma ∘ citam=arśaveti ∘ tada sabarae pradivajadi rakṣadi sudidhri s[u] ///

47. di ∘ ghaṇeṇa ghadhro gha[ï]ta ṇa ṇimitighrahe bhavadi ṇa aṇovejaṇa[ghra] ///

|24p |24n |24m
48. asiaraṇam=eva ∘ ghaṇidhri asabro[d]u viharadi ∘ abhija doma ? stu [p.v.a ak.] ///

|24a |24n
49. dharma ∘ citam=arśaveti ∘ tada sabarae pradivajadi rakṣadi ? ? + [∘] ///

|24a
50. ghaṇidhri sabaram=avajadi ∘ ji[bh.] rasu [śp.].i[ta ṇa ṇimiti]ghrahe bhavadi ///

51. jaṇaghrahi ∘ yavad=eva asiaraṇam=eva ∘ jibhidhri asabrodo viharadi ? ///

|24a+ 24cc |24cc
52. maṇastu pavea akuśala dharma ∘ citam=arśaveti ∘ tada saba[ra]e ///

|24a
53. rakṣadi ji[bhi]dhri ∘ ji[bhi]dhri sabaram=avajadi ∘

|28a |28a+ 28c |28a+28b
54. kayeṇa proṭhabu phuṣita ṇa ṇimitighrahe bhavadi ṇa aṇo[ve] ///

|28a
55. va asiaraṇam=eva kayidhri asabrodo viharadi ∘ abhija domaṇastu [pa] ///

56. la dharma ◦ citam=arśaveti ◦ tada sabarae pradivajadi rakṣadi kayi[dh..] ///

57. savaram=avajadi ◦ maṇase dharmu añadu ṇa ṇimitighrahe bhavadi ṇa [a] ///

58. yavad=eva asiaraṇam=eva maṇidh.i asabrodu viharadi ◦ abh[i] ///

59. śala dharma citam=arśa[veti ◦] tada sabarae pradivajadi ◦ rakṣadi ma ? ///

60. dhri sabaram=avajadi ◦ aï bucadi sabaraprasaṇo ◦ kadara bhikṣave [a] ///

61. ṇe ◦ [a] aï bhikṣave bhikhuṇa añadara añadara samas[i]ṇimi[ti] ///

62. bhavadi ◦ sayasavi viṇilaü v[i]puao a ◦ aṭ́hisaña [va] p. ? ///

63. tae aṇorakṣa[e] sapadedi idi vucadi aṇorakṣaṇaprasaṇo ◦ [ka] ///

64. vaṇaprasaṇe ◦ aï bhikṣave bhikhu śpadisabujaghu bhavedi ◦ [vi] ? ///

65. raghaṇiṣide ◦ ṇirusaṇiṣide vivasaghapariṇame ◦ dharmavie[sa] ///

66. vedi ◦ viveaṇiṣide viraghaṇiṣide ◦ ṇirusaṇiṣide vivasagha ///

67. riasabujaghu bhavedi viveaṇiṣida ◦ viraghaṇiṣide ṇirusaṇi[ṣid.] ///

68. pariṇamu ◦ [prid.sabujaghu bhave]di [viveaṇ.ṣid. vira]ghaṇiṣide [ṇi] ///

69. de vivasaghaprariṇamu ◦ praṣadhasabujaghu bhavedi ◦ viveaṇiṣide ///

70. ṣide ṇirusaṇiṣide ◦ vivasaghapariṇamu ◦ samasisabujagh[u] bhav. ///

71. aṇiṣi[de] viraghaṇaṣide ṇirusaṇiṣide vivasaghap[r]ariṇamu ◦ uekṣa ///

72. gh. [bhave]di viveaṇiṣide viraghaṇiṣide ṇirusaṇiṣide vivasa[gha] ///

73. aï vuca[di] bhava[ṇapra]saṇe ○ (*the line continues with the avadāna text*) ///

7.2. Reconstruction and Translation of the Text

7.2.1. The "Dhoṇa-sutra"

[1] (*???) ta s. (*??? [2] *ho)ṭo magh(*e)ṇa ghatva maghade abhikrami ◦ aña(*daro) rokṣ(*a)mul(*o ṇiṣae ṇiṣaṇo diva)[3]s(*a) vihari ◦ teṇa ceva samaeṇa dhoṇo ṇama bramaṇo to magho (*pradivaṇo bhavadi ◦ adhrekṣi) [4] dhoṇe bramaṇe bhayavadu padeṣu cakra ◦ sahasahara s(*aṇemia saṇabhia) [5] savarovaghada ◦ aceata prabh(*a)śp(*a)ra ◦ bhayavadu p(*ad)e(*ṣu cakra ???) [6]hoṭo magheṇa ghatva maghade abhikrami añadaro rokṣamulo ṇiṣae (*ṇiṣaṇo ◦ prasadiu [7] prasada)ṇi śatidhri śatamaṇas(*a) ◦ utamadamasaśamasapratu ◦ p(*a)r(*a)m(*a ??? [8] datu) ghutu vudidhrio ṇasu rada ṇam iva ◦ achu aṇavela vip(*ra)s(*a)ṇ(*a) ◦ (*??? dhriśpaṇa yeṇa [9] bha)yavadu teṇa uasakrami uasakramita bhayavadu eghad u(*ya ◦ de)v(*e) bhu bha(*vi)śasi ṇa(*ho) bramaṇ(*a) d(*e)[10]ve bhaviśe ◦ ghadhrarvo bhu bhaviśasi ṇaho bramaṇa ghadharvo bhaviśe ◦ yakṣu bh(*u) bh(*a)vi(*śasi ṇaho bra)[11]maṇa yakṣu bhaviśe ◦ maṇośu bhu bhaviśasi ṇaho bramaṇa maṇośu bhaviśe ◦ (*deve bhu bhavi[12]śa)si idi proṭhu samaṇa ema vadesi ṇaho bramaṇa deve bhaviśe ◦ gh(*a)dh(*a)rv(*o) bhu bhaviśasi (*i)[13]di proṭhu samaṇa ema vadesi ṇaho bramaṇa ghadharvo bhaviśe ◦ yakṣ(*u bhu bha)viśasi idi proṭhu sama(*ṇa) [14] ema vadesi ṇaho bramaṇa yakṣu bhaviśe ◦ maṇośu bhu bhaviśasi id(*i) proṭhu samaṇa e(*ma va[15]de)si ṇaho bramaṇa maṇośu bhaviśe ku re bhu bhaviśasi budho mi bramaṇa budho mi (*??? ida)[16]m u bhayavadu ida vadita sughadu hasavaro idam avaï śastu ◦

(*devo u)avati yeṇa (*ghadharvo) [17] va dihaghama ◦
yakṣatu yeṇa ghache maṇ(*o)śata ba abaji ◦
(*ede mi asava) [18] kṣiṇa virbhasta bhiriḍighama ◦
puḍar(*io) yasa phulo (*to)yo ṇ(*a ualipadi) ◦
eva l(*o)[19]ghu alitu śpi taśpi budho mi bramaṇa (*◦)
abhiñae abhiñehi bhavidavu p(*i) bh(*a)vi(*du ◦)
[20] prahadavu prahiṇo mi sarvañu sarvadaśavi taśpi budho mi bramaṇa (*◦

abhikatu) [21] bhu ghodama abhikatu ◦ suyasavi bhu ghudama ṇiujidu ukuje ◦ paḍichaṇo a viv(*are ◦) [22] muḍhasa va maghu praghaśe ◦ adhagharo aloka va <*dharae> ◦ yavad eva cakṣuatu ruaṇa dhrekṣatu ◦ [23] evam eva ṣamaṇeṇa ghodameṇa krirṇo śukro dharmu akhade vivaḍe s(*a)praghaśide (*◦ eṣaho) [24] ṣamaṇo ghudamu śaraṇo ghachami dhama ca bhikhusagha ca ◦ u(*asaghu) mi ṣ(*a)ma(*ṇe ghuda)[25]m(*e) dharedu ajavaghreṇa yavajivu praṇouviade śaraṇo <*ghade> abhiprasaṇe ◦ i(*dam u) <*bhayavadu> (*atamaṇo) [26] dhoṇe bramaṇe bhayavadeṇa bhaṣido abhiṇadi ○

The Dhoṇa sūtra (Dhoṇa-sutra)

[1] . . . [The Bhagavat], [2] having traveled on the road to *-hoṭo,* stepped off the road. (*Seated near) the root of a tree, [3] he spent the day. And at the same time a brahman named Dhoṇa (*had started out on) that road. [4] The brahman Dhoṇa (*saw) the wheel-marks on the footprints of the Bhagavat, thousand-spoked, (*with rim and nave), [5] with all parts entire, brilliant, resplendent. . . . [following] (*the wheel-marks) on the footprints of the Bhagavat, [he saw the Bhagavat] . . . [6] [who,] having traveled on the road to *-hoṭo* . . . , had stepped off the road [and] (*had sat down) near the root of a tree, [his appearance] (*fair, [7] pleasing), his faculties calm, his mind calm, having attained the highest training and calm . . . , [8] a protector, (*trained), controlled, with faculties restrained, like a clear, translucent, serene pond. . . . (*Having seen him), [9] he approached the Bhagavat. Having approached, he said this to the Bhagavat: "Venerable sir, would you be a (*god)?" "Brahman, (*I) [10] would not be a god." "Venerable sir, would you be a *gandharva?"* "Brahman, I would not be a *gandharva."* "Venerable sir, would you be a *yakṣa?"* "[11] Brahman, (*I) would (*not) be a *yakṣa."* "Venerable sir, would you be a human?" "Brahman, I would not be a human." [12] "Being asked thus, '(*Venerable sir), would you be (*a god)?' you say this, 'Brahman, I would not be a god.' Being asked thus, 'Venerable sir, would you be a *gandharva?'* [13] you say this, 'Brahman, I would not be a *gandharva.'* Being asked thus, '(*Venerable sir), would you be a *yakṣa?'* [14] you say this, 'Brahman, I would not be a *yakṣa.'* Being asked thus, 'Venerable sir, would you be a human?' [15] you say this, 'Brahman, I would not be a human.' Who, then, venerable sir, would you be?" "Brahman, I am the Enlightened One. I am the Enlightened One." . . . [16] The Bhagavat said (*this). Having said this, the Sugata, the Teacher, further said this:

> "(*The *āsavas*) by which there would be rebirth (*as a god) or [by which I would be] (*a *gandharva*) [17] flying in the air [or] by which I would become a *yakṣa* or would become human, (*these) [18] have been destroyed (*by me), eradicated, cut off.
>
> "Just as a flowering lotus is not (*defiled in) water, so [19] I am not defiled in the world. Therefore, Brahman, I am the Enlightened One.
>
> "Having realized what is to be realized, what is to be developed has also been developed. [20] What is to be destroyed has been destroyed by me. All-knowing, all-seeing, therefore, Brahman, I am the Enlightened One."

"(*Wonderful), [21] venerable Gotama! Wonderful! Just as, venerable Gotama, one would set upright what has been overturned or uncover what has been covered [22] or show the path to one who is lost or (*bring) light into the darkness, so that those with eyes might see forms, [23] even so has the monk Gotama declared, revealed, and proclaimed the dharmas, bright and dark. (*I) [24] go to the monk Gotama as a refuge and to the Dharma and to the Saṅgha. May the monk (*Gotama) accept me as a layman, [25] who with faith (*has gone) [to him] as a refuge from today onward, for as long as there is life, until [my] last breath." (*The Bhagavat said this. Pleased), [26] the brahman Dhoṇa rejoiced at what was said by the Bhagavat.

7.2.2. The "Budhabayaṇa-sutra"

[26] eva me rśoda eka (*samaya (◦)) bhayav(*a)[27]du śavastie viharadi jedavaṇo aṇasapiḍiasa aramu ◦ tatra ya bhaya(*va)d(*u) bhi(*khu a)[28]matredi te bhikhu bhayavadu pracarśoṣu ◦ bhayava<*d>u eghad uya ◦ su(*karo bhi)[29]kṣave budhabayaṇo tatu paḍideṇa ṇa baleṇa ◦ sato kamatu ghachateṇa ṇa sukaro ka(*tu ◦) [30] budhabayaṇata bhikṣave ghachateṇa sukaro katu tatu paḍideṇa ṇa baleṇa ◦ sa(*to ka)[31]matu ṭ́hideṇa ṇa sukaro katu ◦ budhabayaṇata bhikṣave ṭ́h(*ide)ṇa suk(*a)ro k(*atu ta)[32]to paḍideṇa ṇa baleṇa ◦ satu kamatu ṇiṣaṇeṇa ṇa sukaro katu ◦ [33] budhabayaṇata bhikṣave ◦ ṇiṣaṇeṇa sukaro katu tatu paḍide(*ṇa ṇa baleṇa ◦) [34] sato kamato śeaṇeṇa jagharadu ṇa sukaro kato ◦ budhabayaṇata (*bhikṣave śe)[35]aṇeṇa jagharadu sukaro kato ◦ tatu paḍideṇa ṇa baleṇa ◦ sukar(*u bhikṣave) [36] budhabayaṇo tatu paḍideṇa ṇa baleṇa ◦ idam u <*bhayavadu> atamaṇa te bhikh(*u bhayavadeṇa bhaṣido) [37] abhiṇadi ○

7.2.3. The "Prasaṇa-sutra"

[37] eva me rśodu eka samaya ◦ bhaya<*va>du śavastie viharadi jedavaṇ(*o aṇasapi)[38]ḍiasa aramu ◦ tatra ya bhayavadu bhikhu amatredi <*te> bhikhu (*bhayavadu pracarśoṣu ◦ bhayavadu) [39] eghad oya ◦ catvarime bhikṣave prasaṇa ◦ satu savijamaṇa loghaśpi ◦ (*kadara/kadama catvari/catvaro ◦) [40] sabaraprasaṇe aṇorakṣaṇaprasaṇe bhavaṇaprasaṇo ◦ prasaṇaprasaṇo ◦

kada(*ra bhikṣave sa)[41]baraprasaṇe ◦ aï bhikṣave bhikhu cakṣuṇa ruvo dhriśpaṇa ◦ ṇa ṇimitighrahe (*bhavadi (◦) ṇa aṇo)[42]vejaṇaghrahi ◦ yavad eva asiaraṇam e(*va (◦)) cakṣidhri asabrodu viharadi ◦ abhija domaṇastu pavea aku(*śala dha)[43]rma ◦ citam arśaveti ◦ tada sabarae pradivajadi rakṣadi cakṣidhri ◦ cakṣidhri saba(*ram a)[44]vajadi ◦ ṣudeṇa chado ṣutvaṇa ṇa ṇimitighrahe bhavadi ◦ ṇa aṇovejaṇaghra(*hi ◦ yavad e)[45]va asiaraṇam eva ◦ sudidhri asabrodu viharadi ◦ abhija domaṇastu pa(*vea akuśala dha)[46]rma ◦ citam arśaveti ◦ tada sabarae pradivajadi rakṣadi sudidhri su(*didhri sabaram avaja)[47]di ◦ ghaṇeṇa ghadhro ghaïta ṇa ṇimitighrahe bhavadi ṇa aṇovejaṇaghra(*hi ◦ yavad eva) [48] asiaraṇam eva ◦ ghaṇidhri asabrodu viharadi ◦ abhija doma(*ṇa)stu p(*a)v(*e)a ak(*uśala) [49] dharma ◦ citam arśaveti ◦ tada sabarae pradivajadi rakṣadi (*ghaṇidhri) ◦ [50] ghaṇidhri sabaram avajadi ◦ jibh(*a) rasu śp(*ay)ita ṇa ṇimitighrahe bhavadi (*(◦) ṇa aṇove)[51]jaṇaghrahi ◦ yavad eva asiaraṇam eva ◦ jibhidhri asabrodo viharadi (*◦ abhija do)[52]maṇastu pavea akuśala dharma ◦ citam arśaveti ◦ tada

The Sūtra on the Buddha's Teaching (Budhabayaṇa-sutra)

[26] Thus I heard at one (*time): The Bhagavat [27] dwelt in Śavasti (Śrāvastī) in the Jedavaṇa (Jetavana), in Aṇasapiḍia's (Anāthapiṇḍada's) park. And there the Bhagavat addressed the monks. [28] Those monks responded to the Bhagavat. The Bhagavat said this: [29] "Monks, the Buddha's teaching is easy [to perform], but only by a wise man, not a fool. Good action[1] is not easy to perform while going. [30] Monks, on account of the Buddha's teaching it is easy to perform while going, but only by a wise man, not a fool. Good action [31] is not easy to perform while standing. Monks, on account of the Buddha's teaching it is easy to perform while standing, [32] but only by a wise man, not a fool. Good action is not easy to perform while sitting. [33] Monks, on account of the Buddha's teaching it is easy to perform while sitting, but only by a wise man, (*not a fool). [34] Good action is not easy to perform while lying down awake. (*Monks), on account of the Buddha's teaching [35] it is easy to perform while lying down awake, but only by a wise man, not a fool. (*Monks), [36] the Buddha's teaching is easy [to perform], but only by a wise man, not a fool." The (*Bhagavat) said this. Pleased, those monks [37] rejoiced (*at what was said by the Bhagavat).

The Sūtra on Effort (Prasaṇa-sutra)

[37] Thus I heard at one time: The Bhagavat dwelt in Śavasti (Śrāvastī) in the Jedavaṇa (Jetavana), in [38] Aṇasapiḍia's (Anāthapiṇḍada's) park. And there the Bhagavat addressed the monks. (*Those) monks (*responded to the Bhagavat. The Bhagavat) [39] said this: "Monks, these four efforts are found existing in the world. (*What four?) [40] The effort of restraint, the effort of protecting, the effort of development, the effort of abandoning.

"What, (*Monks), is the [41] effort of restraint? Here, Monks, a monk, seeing a form with the eye, does not grasp at its general characteristics, does (*not) [42] grasp at its secondary characteristics. Because the evil, unprofitable states of covetousness and grief overpower the mind when one dwells with eye faculty unrestrained, [43] then he takes up restraint, he protects the eye faculty, he exercises restraint in the eye faculty. [44] Hearing a sound with the ear, he does not grasp at its general characteristics, does not grasp at its secondary characteristics. [45] Because the evil, (*unprofitable) states of covetousness and grief overpower the mind when one dwells with ear faculty unrestrained, [46] then he takes up restraint, he protects the ear faculty, he exercises (*restraint) in the ear (*faculty). [47] Smelling a scent with the nose, he does not grasp at its general characteristics, does not grasp at its secondary characteristics. Because [48] the evil, unprofitable states of covetousness and grief overpower the mind when one dwells with nose faculty unrestrained, [49] then he takes up restraint, he protects the (*nose faculty), [50] he exercises restraint in the nose faculty. Tasting a flavor with the tongue, he does not grasp at its general characteristics, does (*not) grasp at its secondary characteristics. [51] Because the evil, unprofitable states of (*covetousness) and grief [52] overpower the mind when one dwells with tongue faculty unrestrained, then (*he takes up) restraint,

[1] An alternative translation for "good action" is "the practice of mindfulness."

sabarae (*pradivajadi) [53] rakṣadi jibhidhri ∘ jibhidhri sabaram avajadi ∘ [54] kayeṇa proṭhabu phuṣita ṇa ṇimitighrahe bhavadi ṇa aṇove(*jaṇaghrahi ∘ yavad e)[55]va asiaraṇam eva kayidhri asabrodo viharadi ∘ abhija domaṇastu pa(*vea akuśa)[56]la dharma ∘ citam arśaveti ∘ tada sabarae pradivajadi rakṣadi kayidh(*ri (∘) kayidhri) [57] savaram avajadi ∘ maṇase dharmu añadu ṇa ṇimitighrahe bhavadi ṇa a(*ṇovejaṇaghrahi ∘) [58] yavad eva asiaraṇam eva maṇidh(*r)i asabrodu viharadi ∘ abhi(*ja domaṇastu pavea aku)[59]śala dharma citam arśaveti ∘ tada sabarae pradivajadi ∘ rakṣadi ma(*ṇidhri (∘) maṇi)[60]dhri sabaram avajadi ∘ aï bucadi sabaraprasaṇo ∘

kadara bhikṣave a(*ṇorakṣaṇaprasa)[61]ṇe ∘ aï bhikṣave bhikhuṇa añadara añadara samasiṇimiti (*sughrahido ???) [62] bhavadi ∘ sayasavi viṇilaü vipuao a ∘ aṭ́hisaña va p(*uḍavayasaña va ???) [63] tae aṇorakṣae sapadedi idi vucadi aṇorakṣaṇaprasaṇo ∘

ka(*dara bhikṣave bha)[64]vaṇaprasaṇe ∘ aï bhikṣave bhikhu śpadisabujaghu bhavedi ∘ vi(*veaṇiṣide vi)[65]raghaṇiṣide ∘ ṇirusaṇiṣide vivasaghapariṇame ∘ dharmaviesa(*bujaghu bha)[66]vedi ∘ viveaṇiṣide viraghaṇiṣide ∘ ṇirusaṇiṣide vivasagha(*pariṇame ∘ vi)[67]riasabujaghu bhavedi viveaṇiṣida ∘ viraghaṇiṣide ṇirusaṇiṣid(*e vivasagha)-[68]pariṇamu ∘ prid(*i)sabujaghu bhavedi viveaṇ(*i)ṣid(*e) viraghaṇiṣide ṇi(*rusaṇiṣi)-[69]de vivasaghaprariṇamu ∘ praṣadhasabujaghu bhavedi ∘ viveaṇiṣide (*viraghaṇi)-[70]ṣide ṇirusaṇiṣide ∘ vivasaghapariṇamu ∘ samasisabujaghu bhav(*edi (∘) vive)[71]aṇiṣide viraghaṇ<*i>ṣide ṇirusaṇiṣide vivasaghaprariṇamu ∘ uekṣa(*sabuja)[72]gh(*u) bhavedi viveaṇiṣide viraghaṇiṣide ṇirusaṇiṣide vivasagha(*pariṇamu (∘)) [73] aï vucadi bhavaṇaprasaṇe ○

[Lost text:] (*kadara bhikṣave prasaṇaprasaṇe ∘ aï bhikṣave bhikhu ??? ??? ∘ aï bucadi prasaṇaprasaṇe ∘ ime catvari/catvaro prasaṇa ∘ idam u bhayavadu ida vadita sughadu hasavaro idam avaï śastu ∘ ??? ??? idam u bhayavadu atamaṇa te bhikhu bhayavadeṇa bhaṣido abhiṇadi ○)

[53] he protects the tongue faculty, he exercises restraint in the tongue faculty. [54] Touching a tangible with the body, he does not grasp at its general characteristics, does not (*grasp at) its secondary characteristics. Because [55] the evil, unprofitable states of covetousness and grief [56] overpower the mind when one dwells with body faculty unrestrained, then he takes up restraint, he protects the body faculty, [57] he exercises restraint (*in the body faculty). Cognizing an idea with the mind, he does not grasp at its general characteristics, does not (*grasp at its secondary characteristics). [58] Because the (*evil), unprofitable states of covetousness (*and grief) overpower the mind when one dwells with mind faculty unrestrained, [59] then he takes up restraint, he protects the mind (*faculty), [60] he exercises restraint in the (*mind) faculty. This is called the effort of restraint.

"What, Monks, is the effort of protecting? [61] Here, Monks, one or other sign of concentration is (*well grasped) . . . by a monk, [62] namely, the [perception of] a blue-black corpse or the [perception of] a corpse full of pus or the perception of a skeleton (*or the perception of a worm-eaten corpse). . . . [63] He causes [it] to succeed through that protection. This is called the effort of protecting.

"What, (*Monks), [64] is the effort of development? Here, Monks, a monk develops the enlightenment factor of mindfulness, which is (*dependent) on seclusion, [65] dependent on dispassion, dependent on cessation, ripening in release. He develops the enlightenment factor of the investigation of dharmas, [66] which is dependent on seclusion, dependent on dispassion, dependent on cessation, (*ripening in) release. [67] He develops the enlightenment factor of energy, which is dependent on seclusion, dependent on dispassion, dependent on cessation, ripening (*in release). [68] He develops the enlightenment factor of joy, which is dependent on seclusion, dependent on dispassion, dependent on cessation, [69] ripening in release. He develops the enlightenment factor of calm, which is dependent on seclusion, dependent (*on dispassion), [70] dependent on cessation, ripening in release. He develops the enlightenment factor of concentration, [71] which is dependent on seclusion, dependent on dispassion, dependent on cessation, ripening in release. He develops the enlightenment factor of equanimity, [72] which is dependent on seclusion, dependent on dispassion, dependent on cessation, (*ripening in) release. [73] This is called the effort of development.

[Lost text:] (*"What, Monks, is the effort of abandoning? Here, Monks, a monk. . . . This is called the effort of abandoning. These are the four efforts." The Bhagavat said this. Having said this, the Sugata, the Teacher, further said this: . . . The Bhagavat said this. Pleased, those monks rejoiced at what was said by the Bhagavat.)

CHAPTER 8

The "Dhoṇa-sutra"

This chapter and chapters 9–10 each present an introductory discussion outlining the contents of the sūtra, extant versions of the sūtra in other languages, other background information, and a detailed commentary on the text. Within the commentary, the text of each sūtra has been divided into distinct events for ease of discussion, for example, "Lines 1–3: The Buddha leaves the road he is traveling on and sits down at the root of a tree" and "Lines 3–5: Dhoṇa sees the wheel-marks on the Buddha's footprints." These divisions usually correspond to distinct formulas. The discussion of each event is headed by a transcription of the text from the manuscript, the reconstruction, and the translation. This is followed by general comments on the wording of the particular event, discussion of the parallels, if any, in Gāndhārī or other languages, and comments on specific words and phrases. The main concern of the commentary is the reading, reconstruction, and interpretation of the text rather than matters of grammar and phonology as such. For these, the reader is referred to § 4.8 (orthography), chapter 5 (phonology), and chapter 6 (morphology), as well as the word index, where a brief description of the form is given.

8.1. Introduction

8.1.1. Summary of Contents

The first of the three sūtras preserved on this Gandhāran scroll records an interaction between a brahman named Dhoṇa and the Buddha. The beginning of the sūtra is fragmentary and the exact sequence of events is not fully clear. Nonetheless, the overall course of events depicted is the following: The Buddha is traveling on a road. He leaves the road and sits under a tree. The brahman Dhoṇa is traveling on the same road. He sees the wheel-marks on the Buddha's footprints. He follows them and sees the Buddha, who is seated under a tree and has a calm appearance. He approaches the Buddha and asks him four questions: is the Buddha a god (*deva*), a *gandharva,* a *yakṣa,* or a human (*manuṣya*) (to use their Skt. forms)? The Buddha answers in the negative. Dhoṇa asks the Buddha what he is if none of these. The Buddha claims that he is the Enlightened One, then utters several verses summarizing why. Dhoṇa expresses his faith in the Buddha. Dhoṇa rejoices in the Buddha's words.

8.1.2. Extant Versions of the Sūtra/Sutta and Their Titles

Five versions of a sūtra depicting this interaction between a brahman and the Buddha are known: our G sūtra, a P version, and three Chinese translations. No Skt. or Tib. version has so far come to light.

As noted earlier (§ 1.2) our manuscript does not preserve titles for the three sūtras.

The P parallel to the G sūtra was first identified by Richard Salomon (1999: 24, 48). It is sutta 36 in the Catukka-nipāta, the Section of Fours, of the AN (II 37.23–39.9). The Manorathapūraṇī (Mp) contains a commentary on this sutta (III 75–9), and there is also a ṭīkā on this commentary (only the Burmese edition has been published to date: Mp-ṭ [B^e] II 291–3).

Of the published editions of the P version of the sutta, the European edition (E^e) records a title for neither the sutta nor the commentary on it. Although the Thai edition (S^e) also does not give a title to the sutta, the commentary on it is entitled Doṇasutta-vaṇṇanā, while the B^e gives the title Doṇasuttaṃ to the sutta and Doṇasutta-vaṇṇanā to the commentary.

The entry for this sutta in the uddāna to this vagga in the E^e of the AN is *loke,* following the Sinh. manuscripts, perhaps taken from the phrase *loke jāto loke saṃvaḍḍho* (AN II 39.1–2). Woodward (1933: 43) uses this entry as the basis for the title he gives his English translation: "As to the world." The entry in the uddāna in the B^e and S^e is *doṇo,* which is given as a v.l. (Burmese mss. B.K.) in the E^e. In other words, as is commonly the case, the title Doṇasuttaṃ in the B^e and S^e has been taken from the uddāna entry (see also §§ 1.2 and 10.1.2).

Another P sutta records a different interaction between a brahman named Doṇa and the Buddha; this sutta occurs in the Pañcaka-nipāta, the Section of Fives, of the AN (III 223–30). As with the first sutta, the E^e and S^e do not give it a title, but in the B^e it is called the Doṇabrāhmaṇasuttaṃ. The B^e and S^e of the commentary are entitled Doṇabrāhmaṇa-suttavaṇṇanā. Just to complicate matters, this second sutta is referred to in the Sn commentary (Pj II 318.20, 325.15) as the Doṇasuttaṃ (*doṇasutte* in all three editions: E^e, B^e, and S^e), which is not surprising considering that the uddāna entry for this second sutta is *doṇo* (all three editions), the same as that for the first sutta in the B^e and S^e. The presence of this title in a commentary indicates that this second sutta, at least, has been so referred to for some time. It is probable that both suttas were referred to as the Doṇasuttaṃ, but that faced with two suttas in the AN collection depicting an encounter between the brahman Doṇa and the Buddha, the B^e and S^e chose to give the title Doṇasuttaṃ to the first and Doṇabrāhmaṇasuttaṃ to the second.

Three Chinese translations of this sūtra have been identified by Tien-Chang Shih. The first occurs in the EĀ, the Zengyi ahan jing (T 2 no. 125 [sūtra 38.3] fasc. 31, pp. 717c18–718a12), translated by Dharmanandin in A.D. 384–5 and revised by Gautama Saṅghadeva in A.D. 397–8 (see Mayeda 1985: 102; Waldschmidt 1980: 137 n. 4, 169 n. 168). The second is found in the SĀ, the Za ahan jing (T 2 no. 99 [sūtra 101] p. 28a20–b18), attributed to Guṇabhadra (fl. A.D. 435–68), and the third occurs in the second translation of the SĀ, the Beiyi za ahan jing (T 2 no. 100 [sūtra 267] p. 467a26–b24). None of these Chinese translations of the sūtra bears a title.

In summary, it is only in the P sources that a title is preserved. Despite the lack of a title in the G text, for the sake of convenience it will be referred to throughout this study as the "Dhoṇa-sutra." The P sutta will be referred to as the Doṇa-sutta.

8.1.3. The Brahman's Name and His Place in Buddhist Literature

In the G sūtra the brahman is referred to as *dhoṇa bramaṇa*. This is the only attestation of this name in a G source to date. In the P parallel, and in the P tradition in general, this brahman is referred to as *doṇa brāhmaṇa* (see DPPN, s.v.). In the Mahāparinibbāna-suttanta of the DN (II 166–7) he resolves the dispute over the remains of the Buddha after his cremation by dividing them among the contending parties, with his own share being the urn that contained the Buddha's ashes. The Doṇa of these two suttas and the Doṇa of the other AN sutta recording an encounter between the brahman of this name and the Buddha (AN III 223–30, mentioned above) are most likely the same person.

In Skt. texts, or at least in the Skt. Mahāparinirvāṇa-sūtra (MPS), the name of this brahman is Dhūmrasagotra (MPS §§ 51.1 ff.), and the village where he builds a stūpa for the urn is, interestingly, Droṇagrāmaka (MPS §§ 51.2, 6, 17). In a further interesting and perhaps merely coincidental parallelism, the Skt. form of the name of the village to which the Buddha is traveling in the P sutta, Ukkaṭṭhā, is *utkaṭaṃ nāma droṇamukhaṃ* (see BHSD, s.v. *Utkaṭa*), that is, Utkaṭa-at-the-Mouth-of-a-Valley. The P tradition does not know a form parallel to Dhūmrasagotra, nor does it record the name of the village where this brahman built his stūpa for the urn.[1] Further, *doṇamukha* is not associated with the name Ukkaṭṭhā.

P *doṇa* is equivalent to Skt. *droṇa,* "a wooden vessel, bucket, trough, . . . a measure of capacity," as well as being the name of various brahmans and mountains (MW, s.v. *droṇa;* cf. PTSD, s.v. *doṇa*). A play upon the "measure" meaning of this word occurs in the concluding statement to the P Mahāparinibbāna-suttanta: *aṭṭhadoṇaṃ cakkhumato sarīraṃ sattadoṇaṃ jambudīpe mahenti. ekañ ca doṇaṃ purisavaruttamassa rāmagāme nāgarājā mahenti;* "The remains of the one who possessed the eye (of understanding) consisted of eight portions. In the Rose-apple continent they honor seven portions. And in Rāmagāma the kings of the nāgas honor one portion of the very best of men" (DN II 167.22–5).[2]

In the Skt. form of the brahman's name, Dhūmrasagotra, the initial element, *dhūmra-,* means "smokey" (adj.) or "incense" (m.), derived from *dhūma,* "smoke" (MW, s.vv. *dhūma, dhūmra*). In his detailed study of the Skt. MPS and discussion of this brahman's name, Waldschmidt (1944–8: 321–4) renders *Dhūmrasagotra* as *"zur Familie 'Rauchig' gehörig,"* an interpretation that is reflected in a number of the Chinese sources investigated by him. A summary of the Chinese material presented by Waldschmidt (1944–8: 321–2) is as follows: (1) Sarvāstivādin Vinaya: 姓烟, *"Sippe Rauch,"* which Waldschmidt considers to be the same as or similar to the name in the Sanskrit; (2) Dīrghāgama: 香姓, *"der Brahmane 'Weihrauch-Sippe,'"* which he renders as *Dhūpa-gotra;* (3) Fo ban nihuan jing of Bo Fazu: *Tunqu:* 屯屈, which he takes to probably represent *Dhūm(a)got(ra);* (4) T 1 no. 6 p. 190b: 毛蹶, *"der brahmane Mao-chüeh,"* whose Skt.

[1] The P material does not know a village equivalent in name to Droṇagrāmaka. The closest is Doṇavatthu(brāhmaṇagāma), a village near Kapilavatthu (DPPN, s.v. *Doṇavatthu*), which is probably not the place where Doṇa built his stūpa.

[2] The commentator (Sv II 615.16–7) considers this conclusion to have been added by the theras of Tambapaṇṇi. (All translations are mine unless otherwise noted.)

equivalent is problematic; and (5) Da banniepan jing of Faxian: *Tuluna:* 徒盧那, which he takes to represent *Droṇa,* the same as P *Doṇa.*

Of the three Chinese translations of the Dhoṇa-sutra, one translates his name as 豆磨, the brahman "Dhomo" (T no. 99); one translates his name as 煙氏, the brahman "Smoke" (T no. 100); and the third (T no. 125) does not give him a name but merely refers to him as "a brahman."

Finally, the form of his name preserved in the Tib. translation of the MPS (Waldschmidt 1950–1: §§ 51.1 ff.), *bram-ze'i rigs bre-bo daṅ mñam-pa,* reflects an original *doṇa/droṇa* rather than *dhūmra-* or the like.

To return now to the G version, G *dhoṇa* is undoubtedly the equivalent of P *doṇa*/Skt. *droṇa* ("wooden trough," "a measure") of the P version, of the Tib. translation, and of Faxian's Chinese translation of the Mahāparinirvāṇa-sūtra rather than of the "smokey," "smoke," "incense" (*dhūmra, dhūma, dhūpa*) words encountered in the Sanskrit and in the majority of the Chinese translations mentioned above. As first noted by Salomon (1999: 127), scribe no. 1, the scribe of this and two other scrolls in the BL collection, frequently wrote *dh-* for *d-* in both initial and medial positions, most commonly in environments with original *r/r̥;* for example, *dhriśpaṇa* = P *disvāna, dhrekṣatu* = Skt. **drakṣyantu* or P *dakkhantu, -idhri* = P/Skt. *indriya* in this manuscript (see § 4.8.1). Although such a development is well attested, the retention of postconsonantal *-r* as seen in *-idhri* for *indriya,* which is the norm in Gāndhārī (see § 5.2.3.4), indicates that the G form would most likely have been **dhroṇa* or **droṇa* had the "trough"/ "measure" word (Skt. *droṇa*) been recognized. In other words, the first G translators evidently retained *doṇa,* the MIA form they received in their archetype text, and the development to *dhoṇa* most likely took place during copying, perhaps even by our scribe. However, it is intriguing that this G spelling *dhoṇa* lends itself to confusion with such words as *dhūmra, dhūma,* and *dhūpa.*

8.1.4. The Setting and Place-Names

In the P version the Buddha and Doṇa are traveling on the road between Setavyā and Ukkaṭṭhā in Kosala. Setavyā (Skt. Śvetikā; see BHSD, s.v.) was the first stop outside Sāvatthi (Skt. Śrāvastī) on the Sāvatthi–Kapilavatthu–Kusīnārā–Vesāli–Rājagaha road.[3] At Jā II 259.26 the Buddha went from Ukkaṭṭhā to Vesāli, but it is unclear whether Ukkaṭṭhā also lay on the road that went to Kapilavatthu and beyond.[4]

---

[3] Setavyā is the setting for the Pāyāsi-suttanta (DN III 316–58), which presents a discussion between Kumāra Kassapa and Pāyāsi rājañña (Skt. Padāśva; cf. MKV 80.4–7: *yathā padāśvasya rājaputrasya yaḥ kumārakāśyapena śvetikāyāṃ vinīto lokāyatikaḥ*; Lévi's n. 3 reads: *"A écrit, évidemment par distraction:* Śvetavipākākābhyām"). King Pasenadi of Kosala had given the town to the brahman Pāyāsi (DN II 316), as he had given Ukkaṭṭhā to the brahman Pokkharasātī (Skt. Puṣkarasārī) (DN I 87; cf. Divy 620–1). Setavyā was also associated with Kassapa Buddha, although the Buddhist Skt. tradition associates him with Vārāṇasī (Divy 54.14–5). There is also some confusion in the P material on this point.

[4] The DPPN (s.v., *Ukkaṭṭhā*) states that a road connected Ukkaṭṭhā with Setavyā and with Vesāli, which is somewhat ambiguous. Ukkaṭṭhā is not mentioned in the list of towns on the Ujjeni–Kosambi–Sāvatthi–Setavyā–Kapilavatthu, etc., route given at Sn 1011–3.

Due to the fragmentary condition of the beginning of the scroll, no place-name is clearly preserved in the G version. The most likely contender is *hoṭo,* which occurs in the phrase *-hoṭo magheṇa ghatva* (ll. 2 and 6), where *hoṭo* represents an incomplete word. The Skt. form of the P *ukkaṭṭhā* is *utkaṭa* (m./n.) or *utkaṭā* (f.) (see BHSD, s.v.),[5] and it is therefore tempting to see *-hoṭo* as the remnant of the G form of this word. (See the text commentary to ll. 1–3 for full discussion.) If so, the phrase *-hoṭo magheṇa ghatva* would then mean "having traveled on the road to *-hoṭo*."

The three Chinese translations of the Dhoṇa-sutra are not in full agreement as to the setting of this interaction between the Buddha and the brahman. Although both SĀ translations have the Buddha traveling in Kośala, in the first (T 2 no. 99 p. 28a21) he is traveling between the villages of You cong jia di 有從迦帝, which corresponds to P *ukkaṭṭhā* according to the Japanese editors of T, and Duo jiu luo 墮鳩羅, which the Japanese editors of T think is a variant of Sui 隨, corresponding to P Setavyā; and in the second (T 2 no. 100 p. 467a27) he is traveling to Sha lin 沙林. In the EĀ translation (T 2 no. 125 p. 717c18) the Buddha is traveling in Magadha along the You jia zhi 憂迦支 River, which the Japanese editors of T think corresponds to P *ukkaṭṭhā.*

If *-hoṭo* of the G text is the equivalent of P *ukkaṭṭhā,* Skt. *utkaṭa/utkaṭā,* then the Gāndhārī would parallel the Pali on this point.

8.1.5. The Frame and Component Elements of This Sūtra in Buddhist Literature

The overall frame of this sūtra, that is, the sequence of events described, is encountered in at least one other place in P literature. The verse Candanamāliyatthera-apadāna (Ap 423–5; quoted at Th-a II 44 for the verses of Valliyatthera) describes the following course of events: The Buddha approaches Candana. Candana asks the Buddha about his "name" (*nāma*) and "clan" (*gotta*) and whether he is a *devatā, gandhabba, Sakka purindada,* or *Mahābrahmā,* remarking that thousand-spoked wheel-marks are seen on the Buddha's feet (*sahassārāni cakkāni, pāde dissanti mārisa;* Ap 424.1). The Buddha replies that he is none of these but is superior to them; Candana is then converted.

Although differing in some details—for example, the list of the four types of beings in the Doṇa-sutta is *deva, gandhabba, yakkha,* and *manussa*—the frame of the Ap version is virtually identical to that of the Doṇa-sutta, and this apadāna could have been modeled on the Doṇa-sutta.

Similarly, the motif of the Buddha traveling along a road at the same time as other individuals, the former then leaving the road and sitting under a tree, and the latter approaching the Buddha in order to question him is encountered a number of times throughout the P canon (AN II 57; DN II 128–30). Again, the scenario of someone asking the Buddha a series of questions (in this case four) and the Buddha answering each in the negative, which is followed by the one asking the questions then repeating each question

---

[5] Mvy 5285 lists *utkaṭo nāma droṇamukhaṃ,* which occurs as such, but in the acc., at Divy 620.12 and as *utkaṭadroṇamukhyaṃ* at Divy 620.28. The word *utkaṭiyaka* is found in a fragment of the Ambāṣṭa-sūtra (= P Ambaṭṭha-suttanta): *(*ava)śiṣṭān utkaṭiyakāṃ brāhmaṇāṃ . . .* (Hartmann 1989: 63 = Frag. DĀ e R3).

and answer before finally asking for clarification, forms the basis for two other suttas within the Catukka-nipāta section of the AN (II 161–3).

Further, a number of the component elements and individual events of this sūtra/sutta are utilized in other Buddhist sūtras/suttas and texts, with the wording of these events and concepts being formulaic, as is typical of this class of literature. For example, several sūtras/suttas begin with the depiction of the Buddha traveling through certain districts, and events such as the Buddha sitting beneath a tree for meditation or a brahman or other individual proclaiming his conversion are all encountered elsewhere in Buddhist literature in identical or similar wording. (See the studies of each section and phrase in the text commentary below.) In other words, although some of the features of the G Dhoṇa-sutra are unique, the majority belong to the vast stock of building blocks utilized by the Buddhists in the creation of their literature.

8.2. Text Commentary

The beginning of the sūtra is missing. Since the second and third sūtras on this scroll have complete opening nidānas, we can safely assume that this sūtra did also. The formula that begins the second and third sūtras is the G equivalent of the very common Śrāvastī-Jetavana nidāna:

eva me rśoda eka samaya (◦) bhayavadu śavastie viharadi jedavaṇo aṇasapiḍiasa aramu ◦ tatra ya bhayavadu bhikhu amatredi te bhikhu bhayavadu pracarśoṣu ◦ bhayavadu eghad uya ◦. (ll. 26–8, 37–9)

Although the Dhoṇa-sutra does not concern the Buddha addressing the monks and therefore would not have opened in this way, we can nonetheless utilize some of the above wording in our reconstruction.

The printed editions of the P sutta open with

ekaṃ samayaṃ bhagavā antarā ca ukkaṭṭhaṃ antarā ca setabbyaṃ addhāna-maggapaṭipanno hoti. doṇo pi sudaṃ brāhmaṇo antarā ca ukkaṭṭhaṃ antarā ca setabbyaṃ addhānamaggapaṭipanno hoti. (AN II 37.23–6)

The omission of the *evaṃ me sutaṃ* opening phrase in the E^e, B^e, and S^e of the Doṇa-sutta merely represents an abbreviation, for it appears in the very first sutta of the Catukka-nipāta in all editions (AN II 1.5). It goes without saying that all suttas begin in this way.

My reading and reconstruction of lines 2 and 3 (see below) is

*(*ho)ṭo magh(*e)ṇa ghatva maghade abhikrami ◦ aña(*daro) rokṣ(*a)mul(*o ṇiṣae ṇiṣaṇo diva)s(*a) vihari ◦ teṇa ceva samaeṇa dhoṇo ṇama bramaṇo to magho (*pradivaṇo bhavadi ◦).*

[The Bhagavat] having traveled on the road to *-hoṭo,* stepped off the road. (*Seated near) the root of a tree, he spent the day. And at the same time a brahman named Dhoṇa (*had started out on) that road.

Based on the opening formulas of the other two sūtras on this scroll and on the P parallel, it is almost certain that the Dhoṇa-sutra opened with *(*eva me rśoda eka samaya (◦) bhayavadu),* with *rśoda* possibly appearing as *rśodu,* as in line 37.[6] The wording following this would have depicted the Buddha traveling on the road from a particular place to another place. It may have included the phrase *(*to magho pradivaṇo bhavadi ◦),* the opening of the sūtra being something like "(*Thus I heard at one time: The Bhagavat had started out on the road from place *x* to place *y*)" (see below).

Lines 1–3: The Buddha leaves the road he is traveling on and sits down at the root of a tree

Edition:

|25h |D6i |25i |25i+25j |25j+ 25h |25j+ 25h+ 25bb |25h+ 25bb |25g

[1] /// ? ? ? ? ? ? ? *ta s.* ? /// [2] ? *ṭo magh.ṇa ghatva ma[ghade] abhi[kra]mi* ◦ *a[ña]* ? +

|25h+ 25g |D6i |25i+25j |25j

[r]okṣ.mul. /// [3] *[s. vi]hari* ◦

Reconstruction:
[1] *(*???) ta s. (*??? [2] ho)ṭo magh(*e)ṇa ghatva maghade abhikrami* ◦ *aña(*daro) rokṣ(*a)mul(*o ṇiṣae ṇiṣaṇo diva)*[3]*s(*a) vihari* ◦

Translation:
[1] [The Bhagavat], [2] having traveled on the road to *-hoṭo,* stepped off the road. (*Seated near) the root of a tree, [3] he spent the day.

Much of the wording of this passage is repeated in line 6: */// hoṭo magheṇa ghatva magha[de abhi]k[r]ami añadaro rokṣamulo ṇiṣa[e] ///.* Based on this latter passage we can reconstruct some of the wording missing from the end of line 2. Although the grammatical subject of the sentence is missing, it must be the Buddha, as the next sentence (l. 3) introduces the brahman Dhoṇa for the first time (see below).

/// ? ? ? ? ? ? ? ta s. ? ///: For the most part only the bottoms of the akṣaras of this line remain. The exact number of akṣaras preserved and their reading are uncertain. The two legible akṣaras, *ta s.,* do not match any of the initial missing wording of the sūtra mentioned above: *(*eva me rśoda eka samaya (◦) bhayavadu).*

? ṭo magh.ṇa ghatva: Due to the peeling of the bark, the area to the right of *ṭo* on line 2 is blank except for a small remnant of an akṣara. Given that the reading of the word preceding *magheṇa* in line 6 is *hoṭo,* we would anticipate that the akṣara preceding *ṭo* in line 2 was likewise *ho,* and that we should therefore reconstruct *(*ho)ṭo magh(*e)ṇa ghatva* for this phrase. Although the remnant of this akṣara does not seem to match any part of *ho,* the lack of match may be due to the peeling. Besides, given that both occurrences of *ṭo* are part of the phrase *magheṇa ghatva*, and that these are the only examples

[6] It is possible that a punctuation mark occurred after *eka samaya,* following the reading on l. 37 (see text commentary to ll. 26–8).

of retroflex *ṭ* in this sūtra (and this manuscript), it is likely that *ṭo* was preceded by the same akṣara in each case.

It is not fully clear what *hoṭo* represents, or whether in fact it is a complete word. Since no obvious equivalent to *hoṭo* is available, it is probably the latter part of a word. The context suggests that the Buddha is "going by the road" either to or from a particular place (or both). As *-ṭo* is unlikely to be an ablative termination, we should therefore take this phrase to mean that the Buddha is traveling on the road to *-hoṭo* rather than from it.

As mentioned in § 8.1.4, in the P version the Buddha is traveling between Setavyā and Ukkaṭṭhā. The word order indicates that he is traveling from Setavyā to Ukkaṭṭhā. The latter place-name is found in Buddhist Skt. texts in the forms *utkaṭa* (m. n.) and *utkaṭā* (f.), which, as noted by the BHSD (s.v.), are "verbally" (i.e., phonetically) close to the P form. The argument for taking G *-hoṭo* as being somehow equivalent to P *ukkaṭṭhā* or Skt. *utkaṭă* is admittedly weak, based as it is solely on the fact that they have in common a retroflex consonant in the final syllable. And even this is complicated by the fact that *-ṭ-* must here represent a geminate *-ṭṭ-*, as single intervocalic *-ṭ-* would be expected to be voiced to *-ḍ-*, parallel to *-t-* > *-d-* elsewhere in this manuscript. Further, *-ho-* and particularly the *o* vowel present major difficulties, indicating that *-hoṭo* is not likely to be related to P *ukkaṭṭhā* and Skt. *utkaṭă*. For the moment, then, all that can be said is that *hoṭo* probably represents the latter part of a place-name in the accusative case. The Chinese translations do not help in the interpretation of *-hoṭo* (see § 8.1.4).

The G phrase *maghena ghatva* differs markedly from the phrase used in the P version to describe the Buddha traveling along a road:

> *ekaṃ samayaṃ bhagavā antarā ca ukkaṭṭhaṃ antarā ca setabbyaṃ* [v.l. *setavyaṃ*] *addhānamaggapaṭipanno hoti.* (AN II 37.23–4)[7]

This formula—[person: nom.] *antarā ca* [place 1: acc.] *antarā ca* [place 2: acc.] *addhānamaggapaṭipanno hoti*—is the standard way of expressing such an event in P suttas. The phrasing of parallel passages in Buddhist Skt. texts is virtually identical, as seen in the following example:

> *tena khalu samayenāyuṣmān mahākāś(*yapaḥ) pañcaśataparivāro 'ntarā ca pāpaṃ antarā ca kuśinagarīm atrāntarādhvapratipan(*no).* (MPS § 48.3)[8]

---

[7] *Addhānamaggapaṭipanno hoti:* literally, "entered on the high road" (see CPD, s.v. *addhāna-magga-paṭipanno*). The commentarial gloss (Mp III 76.21–2) is *addhānasaṅkhātaṃ . . . dīghamaggaṃ*.

[8] Cf. also *atha bhagavān malleṣu janapadeṣu caryāṃ caran ta(*trāntarā ca pāpam) ant(*a)rā ca nadīṃ hi(*raṇyavatīm adhvapratipanno mārgād avakramya)* (MPS § 27.4–5); *tena khalu samayena upaga ājīvikas tasminn eva mārge adhvapratipanno 'bhūt* (listed as such for CPS § 10.1^{G} [cf. § 2.2], by SWTF, s.v. *adhva-pratipanna*); *kāntārādhvānamārgapratipannaḥ* (Mvu I 132.7). The Divy formula is . . . *antarā ca* [place: acc.] *antarā ca* [place: acc.] *atrāntarāt* (see BHSD, s.v. *antarā*, for references). For further occurrences in the Central Asian material, see SWTF, s.v. *antarā*.

However, an alternative form is also encountered. For example, the P parallel to this MPS passage is

tena kho pana samayena āyasmā mahākassapo pāvāya kusināraṃ addhānamagga-paṭipanno hoti. (DN II 162.6–7; cf. Vin II 284.4–5)[9]

The P equivalent of the G phrase *maghen̩a ghatva* is *maggena gantvā.* Although this phrase is not uncommon in Pali, it seems to be restricted to commentarial texts (e.g., Ps I 254.22, II 38–40; Jā II 154.19–20, V 132.10). For example, Ps II 40.25–8 reads *yathā so puriso maggārūḷhaṃ disvā va jānāti 'ayaṃ iminā maggena gantvā . . . rukkhamūle nisīdissati . . . ' ti.* Similarly, the DN ṭīkā (Sv-pṭ II 244) paraphrases the encounter between Doṇa and the Buddha with words that are similar to the G: *bhagavā maggaṃ gacchanto 'pacchato āgacchanto doṇo brāhmaṇo yāva . . . ' ti.*[10] In Buddhist Skt. texts of the sūtra genre the expression *mārgeṇa gatvā* is likewise unusual.[11] It therefore seems that the G text represents an independent tradition in regard to the wording used to express this particular event, which is closer to the forms preserved in the P commentaries.

The example cited above from DN II 162 suggests that, if *-hoṭo* does represent the name of the place to which the Buddha is traveling, it may have been preceded by the name of the town from which he came, in the ablative case.

ma[ghade] abhi[kra]mi ∘ a[ña] ? + [r]okṣ.mul. /// [3]*[s. vi]hari ∘:* As already noted, part of this unit is repeated in line 6: *magha[de abhi]k[r]ami añadaro rokṣamulo ṇiṣa[e] ///.* The corresponding Pali is *atha kho bhagavā maggā ukkamma* [B^{e} and S^{e} *okkamma*] *aññatarasmiṃ rukkhamūle nisīdi* (AN II 38.1–2), which occurs further on in the narrative in the P Doṇa-sutta.

Maghade is the ablative singular formed with the suffix *-de,* which corresponds to the Skt. *-tas* suffix. This is the normal ablative singular form in Gāndhārī, in contrast to P *maggā* and Skt. *mārgāt.*[12] The corresponding *maggato* is found in Pali, but its use is restricted to the commentaries. For example, both of the P commentaries on the phrase

---

[9] Cf. *tena kho pana samayena sambahulā bhikkhū ca bhikkhuniyo ca sāketā sāvatthiṃ addhānamaggaṃ paṭipannā honti* (Vin IV 65.1–3; cf. 120.3–5).

[10] I have encountered only one example so far of such an event being expressed in a P sutta text in approximately similar terms: *tena kho pana samayena khemā bhikkhunī kosalesu cārikaṃ caramānā antarā ca sāvatthiṃ ca antarā ca sāketaṃ ca toraṇavatthusmiṃ vāsām upagatā hoti. atha kho rājā pasenadi kosalo sāketā sāvatthiṃ gacchanto antarā ca sāketaṃ ca antarā ca sāvatthiṃ ca toraṇavatthusmiṃ ekarattivāsam upagacchi* (SN IV 374.5–10).

[11] The SWTF (s.v. *gam*) lists only a few examples of the root *gam* combined with *mārga-.* See also the verses *adhvānamārgaṅ gatvā tu* (Turfan AG-Skt. XX.7) and *[m]ār[g]eṇāgacchaṃ[ti]* (SHT VIII 1858 B2).

[12] The examples of the phrase *mārgād avakramya* in the MPS, which are the only examples in the Central Asian (Turfan) material, were reconstructed by Waldschmidt based on the Pali and Tibetan (see SWTF, s.v. *ava-kram*).

maggā okkamma have paraphrased with this form: *maggā okkammā ti maggato apakkamitvā* (Ud-a 241.4–5) and *maggā okkammā ti maggato okkamma* (Spk II 199.13).[13]

Abhikrami seems to be the third-person singular preterite of *abhi* + √*kram,* contrasting with the nonfinite form in the P and Skt. expressions. This is somewhat problematic in this context because *abhi* + √*kram* does not mean "step down," as does P *okkamma/ukkamma* and Skt. *avakramya,* but rather "advance," "approach." The meaning "he advanced from the road" for *maghade abhikrami* is possible but is unattested in other Buddhist texts to my knowledge. Further, in P texts at least, this verb does not seem to be constructed with the ablative (see CPD, s.v. *abhikkamati*). Thus, because the context so clearly demands a form such as the P *okkamma, apakkamitvā*/Skt. *avakramya,* it seems likely that this is an instance of the confusion of prefixes, encountered elsewhere in Buddhist manuscripts with *abhi/ati, abhi/api,* and *ava/apa.*[14] This is further supported by the punctuation mark after *abhikrami,* which suggests that *maghade abhikrami* is to be taken as one unit parallel to P *maggā okkamma* (although the punctuation mark is missing in the parallel in l. 6). I therefore take *abhikrami* to be semantically equivalent to these P and Skt. forms and translate accordingly.

a[ña] ? + [r]okṣ.mul. ///: Less likely readings for *[ña]* are *[p.]* or *[bh.]*. Fragment 25g, which contains the remnants of *? + [r]o,* has flipped over and covers part of fragment 25h, with the verso appearing on the recto of the frame. Although fragment 25h obscures most of the recto of fragment 25g when viewed from the verso, remnants of some akṣaras are visible on the verso image (see reconstruction), while the *r* of *[r]o* is visible on fragment 25g when a fiber-optic light is shone from behind.

Based on the parallel phrase in line 6, this and the remainder of the line can be reconstructed as *aña(*daro) rokṣ(*a)mul(*o ṇiṣae ṇiṣaṇo).* (See text commentary to ll. 5–6 for further discussion.)

[s. vi]hari ∘: Although there is no *i, e,* or *u* diacritic on the *s* akṣara, an *o* diacritic could have been present. However, the likely reading is *[sa]*. It is possible that the reading is *[ve]* rather than *[vi]*. There is a horizontal ink mark under the *ha* that cannot be a diacritic on an akṣara in the line below. It is probably an accidental mark. A small section of bark containing the top of the *i* diacritic of *ri* has split off from fragment 25i but is not separated from it. The right-hand tip of this chip has the remnant of an ink mark. This could be part of the upper hook of the preceding *h* (although perhaps appearing a little high when realigned). Also, above this mark on fragment 25i there appears a dot of ink that cannot be the remnant of a vowel diacritic on *h*. It is probably merely an accidental mark.

Several P and Skt. parallel phrases indicate that these words are to be taken as part of the sentence under discussion, representing P *divāvihāra-,* "the daytime abiding," or some

---

[13] Cf. *maggato ukkamitvā* (Sv II 405.1); *maggato ukkamāpento* (v.l. *ukkamento*; Sv II 499.5); *maggato apagametvā* (B^e^ *apakkamitvā;* Vv-a 212.19); *maggato okkamitvā* (Nett-a [B^e^] 228); *maggā uyyāhī ti samma sārathi maggato apagaccha* (Jā II 4.23–4).

[14] G *api-* for the Skt. prefix *abhi-* appears in the Senavarma inscription in *apisavudha, apisavujita,* and *apisavuj̄ita* (Salomon 1986: 276–7, notes on 6a and 6c). I am indebted to Richard Salomon for bringing this example to my attention.

closely related form. DN II 130.11–3, for example, reads *bhūtapubbaṃ bhante āḷāro kālāmo addhānamaggapaṭipanno maggā okkamma avidūre aññatarasmiṃ rukkhamūle divāvihāre nisīdi*. In this example *divāvihāre* is the locative singular (the reading of the E^e only), meaning "he sat down in the daytime abiding (place)," as indicated by Pj II 483.26–7 in its gloss of a parallel occurrence in Sn 679: *divāvihāre ti divāvihāraṭṭhāne*.[15] Normally, however, in such a context *divāvihāra-* is in the accusative, which is the reading in the B^e and S^e for this DN II 130 passage. Occurrences of *divāvihāra-* in the dative singular, *divāvihārāya,* are also not uncommon, but only with verbs such as *upa-saṃ* + √*kam,* "approach," never with *rukkhamūla-* and *ni* + √*sad*. For example, both the dative and accusative are used in Vin III 208.1–5, which reads *sāvatthiyaṃ piṇḍāya caritvā . . . yena andhavanaṃ ten' upasaṅkami divāvihārāya. andhavanaṃ ajjhogāhetvā aññatarasmiṃ rukkhamūle divāvihāraṃ nisīdi*.[16] In such passages *divāvihāraṃ* is an adverbial accusative, the passages meaning "he sat down at the root of a tree for the daytime abiding"/"to spend the day." This use of the accusative is not reflected in Buddhist Skt. texts, where the dative *divāvihārāya* is used throughout. Thus, apart from *yena cāpālaṃ cetiyaṃ tenopasaṃkrānto divāvihārāya* (Mvu I 300.2), we find examples such as *vaiśālīṃ piṇḍāya caritvā . . . upasaṃkramyānyatamaṃ vr̥kṣamūlaṃ niśritya niṣaṇṇo divāvihārāya* (Divy 200–1)[17] and *vr̥kṣamūle niṣaṇṇo divāvihārāya* (Avś I 246.6–7).[18]

The reading of the Gāndhārī, however, is *[s. vi]hari*. Although the split in the manuscript completely divides the akṣara that precedes *[vi]*, the top and bottom of this akṣara resemble *s* rather than *v*. This suggests a form such as P *divasa,* "day," perhaps in compound with the following *vihari* or representing the P adverbials *divasā* or *divasaṃ* (*divasassa* seems unlikely). If we are in fact dealing with a *divāvihāra*-type word, a number of interpretations are possible for *vihari*. First, the fact that it ends the sentence suggests that it may be dative, parallel to the Skt. examples quoted above. However, the termination for the dative singular masculine in this text is normally *-ae,* as in *sabarae* = Skt. *saṃvarāya* (see § 6.1.1.2; see also Salomon 2000: § 7.1.1.2). The regular accusative singular masculine terminations are *-u, -a, -o,* or *-am,* plus one example in *-e* (§ 6.1.1.1.3). Final *-i* as an accusative ending may therefore be possible as a weak form of *-e*. Although this is not supported by the manuscripts so far studied in the BL collection (see Salomon 2000: § 7.1.1.1), a few examples are found in the Dhp-G^K (Brough 1962: § 77). It is also possible that it represents a locative singular parallel to the few locative examples quoted above from P sources, the sense being "he sat down in the daytime abiding place, near the root of a tree."

---

[15] Occurrences of the locative are rare. Apart from the above, it occurs at Ap 259.9 (with v.l. *divāvihāraṃ*), and a few times in commentaries.

[16] Cf. MN I 108, 109, 447, 501; SN I 129, 130, etc. The reading at SN I 129.9–10, *rukkhamūle divāvihāratthāya nisīdi* (against *divāvihāraṃ* of the B^e), with *-attha,* "purpose," as final member, may have been taken from or influenced by the commentarial tradition, where this is a common form. Sv II 598 contains an interesting explanation of why *divāvihāraṃ* was not included with the phrase *rukkhamūle nisīdi* at DN II 162.

[17] Cf. Divy 202.2; MSV I 15.5–6.

[18] Further references are given in BHSD, s.v. *divāvihāra*.

More likely is *[vi]hari* as a third-person singular preterite, parallel to *abhikrami* in this very sentence where the P parallel has an absolutive, *ukkamma/okkamma*. Further examples of third-person singular preterites are *abhiṇadi* (l. 26) = P *abhinandi* and *uasakrami* (l. 9) = P *upasaṅkrami*. The preceding word was therefore probably the adverb *(*diva)[s](*a),* the equivalent of either P *divasā* or *divasaṃ;* that is, the most likely reconstruction is *(*diva)s(*a) vihari,* "he dwelt for the day" or "he spent the day."[19] The akṣara count for line 2 in this reconstruction is thirty-one (the average being thirty-two; see p. 45).

In the P parallel the phrase depicting the Buddha sitting down under a tree is followed by a description of his beginning to meditate:

> *atha kho bhagavā maggā ukkamma aññatarasmiṃ rukkhamūle nisīdi pallaṅkaṃ ābhujitvā ujuṃ kāyaṃ paṇidhāya parimukhaṃ satiṃ upaṭṭhapetvā.* (AN II 38.1–3)[20]

No remnant of the latter series of nonfinite clauses is found in the G text, either here or in the repetitive passage in line 6. It seems that the phrase *(*diva)s(*a) vihari* relays much the same information.

Line 3: The brahman Dhoṇa is traveling on the same road

Edition:

| 25j | 25j+25bb

[3] *teṇa ceva samaeṇa dhoṇo ṇama bramaṇo to magho ///*

Reconstruction:

[3] *teṇa ceva samaeṇa dhoṇo ṇama bramaṇo to magho (*pradivaṇo bhavadi ◦)*

Translation:

[3] And at the same time a brahman named Dhoṇa (*had started out on) that road.

The context and wording of this line indicate that the brahman Dhoṇa is being introduced for the first time in the narrative. The corresponding text in the Doṇa-sutta is *doṇo pi sudaṃ brāhmaṇo antarā ca ukkaṭṭhaṃ antarā ca setabbyaṃ addhānamaggapaṭipanno hoti* (AN II 37.25–6). Once again, the G and P texts differ in how they express the same idea, though the component elements of the Gāndhārī are common enough in Pali, particularly in certain types of P texts.

In the P canon, the examples of the *antarā ca . . . antarā ca* passage vary in the wording of the second sentence, which introduces the second individual. In contrast to *doṇo pi sudaṃ brāhmaṇo antarā ca* of the P Doṇa-sutta, we find *suppiyo pi kho paribbājako*

---

[19] It is also possible that *vihari* represents P *vihārī,* the nom. sg. of *vihārin,* constructed with the equivalent of P *divasā* or *divasaṃ,* meaning "dwelling for the day."

[20] Skt. versions of this formula are found at, e.g., Divy 162.11–3, 294.1–4; MPS § 5.3; CPS §§ 6.1–2, 24a.9; Mvu II 131.14–6; Lal 289.16–8.

antarā ca (DN I 1.7–8),[21] *saṃbahulā ca kho gahapatī* (AN II 57.16–7),[22] and, in the passage already quoted in note 10, *atha kho rājā pasenadi kosalo sāketā sāvatthiṃ gacchanto antarā ca* (SN IV 374.8–9). However, there are no examples of the second person being introduced with the phrase *tena samayena* or some variant of it, as seems to be the case in the Gāndhārī.

The G phrase *teṇa ceva samaeṇa dhoṇo ṇama bramaṇo* would correspond to a P **tena ceva samayena* [person's name] *nāma* [person's social status] and a Skt. **tena caiva samayena* [person's name] *nāma* [person's social status]. There are no examples in P canonical texts of *tena ceva samayena* or *tena ca samayena.* Rather, the P expression is *tena kho pana samayena,* with the parallel formula being *tena kho pana samayena* [person's name] *nāma* [person's social status], as in *ekaṃ samayaṃ bhagavā kosalesu cārikaṃ carati mahatā bhikkhusaṅghena saddhiṃ. tena kho pana samayena dhānañjānī nāma brāhmaṇī caṇḍalikappe paṭivasati* (MN II 209.20–3; cf. SN I 177, 179, 182; Sn p. 59).[23] This example provides an instance of such a formula being used immediately after a formula that depicts someone on a journey, though not of the *antarā ca . . . antarā ca* variety. Similarly, in the Buddhist Skt. texts of a similar genre, the regular expression corresponding to P *tena kho pana samayena* is either *tena khalu samayena* or *tena khalu punaḥ samayena,* with an example parallel to the Pali just quoted being *atha bhagavañ chūraseneṣu janapadeṣu cārikāṃ caran . . . viharati . . . tena khalu samayena . . . agnidatto nāma brāhmaṇarājo* (MSV I 25.14–6).[24]

Although the phrase *tena ceva (/caiva) samayena* (or the variant *tena ca samayena*) is not encountered in P canonical texts and those Buddhist Skt. texts of the same genre so far researched, the formula *tena ca samayena* (or *tena samayena*) [person's name] *nāma*

---

[21] *ekaṃ samayaṃ bhagavā antarā ca rājagahaṃ antarā ca nāḷandaṃ addhānamaggapaṭipanno hoti. . . . suppiyo pi kho paribbājako antarā ca rājagahaṃ antarā ca nāḷandaṃ addhānamaggapaṭipanno hoti.*

[22] *ekaṃ samayaṃ bhagavā antarā ca madhuraṃ antarā ca verañjiṃ addhānamaggapaṭipanno hoti. saṃbahulā ca kho gahapatī ca gahapatāniyo ca antarā* [*ca* is missing in E[e]] *verañjiṃ antarā ca madhuraṃ addhānamaggapaṭipannā honti.*

[23] The phrase *tena samayena* is also found in the canon (especially in the Vinaya, e.g., *tena samayena buddho bhagavā uruvelāyaṃ viharati,* Vin I 1) but not in combination with *nāma.* Further examples of the P formula *tena kho pana samayena* [person's name] *nāma* [person's social status] are found at, e.g., DN I 86, 123, II 7, 148; MN I 256, 469, II 91, 97. Many of these follow the formula stating where the Buddha dwelt, e.g., *ekaṃ samayaṃ bhagavā rājagahe viharati. . . . tena kho pana samayena gulissāni nāma bhikkhu . . . hoti* (MN I 469).

[24] Cf. *buddho bhagavān . . . śrāvastyāṃ viharati jetavane 'nāthapiṇḍadasyārāme. tena khalu samayena śrāvastyāṃ pañcamātrāṇi gāndharvikaśatāni goṣṭhikānāṃ prativasanti. tatra ca kāle supriyo nāma gāndharvikarājo 'bhyāgataḥ* (Avś I 93.2–7) and *buddho bhagavān . . . śrāvastyāṃ viharati jetavane 'nāthapiṇḍadasyārāme. tena khalu punaḥ samayena devānāṃ trayastriṃśānām upoṣadho nāma devaputro* (Avś I 336.2–6; cf. I 302.2–6, II 118.2–6). The reading in the Avś fluctuates between *tena khalu samayena* and *tena khalu punaḥ samayena.* In texts such as the MPS, MAV, and MSV, the expression seems to be the former (von Simson 1965: §§ 14.8,14). Further examples of *tena khalu samayena* [person's name] *nāma* are seen at MSV I 8.2–3, 93.15. Some texts omit *nāma* in such passages, e.g., the Avś I 228.3 and MPS § 40.1, which are parallels to DN II 148.28–9. Cf. also *tena khalu samayena* [name: nom.] *rājābhūt* (MAV § 3f.4–6).

[person's social status] is common in P commentarial texts, as is the phrase *tena ca samayena* in other contexts. The commentary on the Uttarāvimāna of the Vv, for example, opens with *uttarāvimānaṃ. tassa kā uppatti. bhagavā rājagahe viharati veḷuvane kalandakanivāpe. tena ca samayena puṇṇo nāma . . . jīvati* (Vv-a 62–3). This formula begins many of the individual commentaries in the Vv-a.[25] In other words, the phrasing of our G sūtra text parallels P commentarial usage rather than that found in P and Skt. sutta/sūtra and canonical texts.

The P and Skt. equivalents of G *to magho* would be *taṃ maggaṃ* and *taṃ mārgaṃ*, respectively; that is, *to magho* is in the accusative singular, meaning "that road." This most likely represents the remnant of a phrase that expresses the same idea as P *addhānamaggapaṭipanno hoti* or, more closely, that found in the Skt. Catuṣpariṣat-sūtra: *tena khalu samayena upaga ājīvikas tasminn eva mārge adhvapratipanno 'bhūt.*[26] In the paraphrase of Doṇa's actions, the P commentary uses the expression *tam eva maggaṃ paṭipajji* (Mp III 77.11–2), and *addhānamaggapaṭipanno hoti* is glossed as *addhānasaṅkhātaṃ maggaṃ paṭipanno hoti* (Mp III 76.21–2). The accusative of G *to magho* thus contrasts with the locative *tasminn eva mārge* in the Skt. CPS passage but parallels the usage of the P commentaries.

Possible reconstructions of the missing portion at the end of line 3 are (1) *(*pradivaṇo bhavadi)* or a preterite phrase following the Skt. example *adhvapratipanno 'bhūt;*[27] (2) *(*adhvaṇapradivaṇo bhavadi);* or (3) *(*pradivaji),* the preterite of a Skt. *prati* + √*pad* (the variant *paḍi-* is possible here and in the previous examples), following the P commentarial example of *tam eva maggaṃ paṭipajji* just quoted. The meaning of these would be much the same.

In the Dhp-G^{K}, G *adhvaṇa* is attested. *Pradivajadi* = P *paṭipajjati* in our manuscript (ll. 46, 49, etc.) suggests that the form of the past participle would have been *(*pradivaṇa)* and the third-person singular preterite would have been *(*pradivaji),* with the variant *paḍi-* being possible in both cases. *Bhavadi* occurs numerous times in this manuscript, whereas the preterite form is not attested in this manuscript, in the Dhp-G^{L}, or in the AG-G fragment written by the same scribe who wrote the text being presented here. Line 3 contains twenty-three akṣaras, including the punctuation mark. The next line (l. 4) is a new sentence, which may have begun either on line 4 or at the end of line 3 (see discussion below). As the number of akṣaras per line ranges from twenty-eight to thirty-eight, with an average of thirty-two, the number of akṣaras missing from line 3 is between five

[25] E.g., Vv-a 108–9, 114, 131, 156, 220, 229, 270. An example from the Dhp-a reads *tadā pana satthā . . . veḷuvane viharati. tena ca samayena . . . mahāli nāma licchavi tāyaṃ parisati nisinno hoti* (III 438.5–9). Cf. Pv-a 4.24, 169.10; Ap-a 569.26; Pj II 327.6, 355.3. Examples of *tena samayena* [person's name] *nāma* are found at Th-a I 79.22, III 91.12; Ap-a 207.26–7; Pv-a 112.10–11. Examples of the phrase *tena ca samayena* used in other contexts are Pv-a 215.13; Th-a II 57.1–2; Ap-a 190.1–2, 567.20–1, 569.31–2. E.g., Ap-a 190.1–2, reads *so ekadivasaṃ uyyānaṃ gacchati. tena ca samayena davaḍāho uṭṭhāsi.*

[26] Listed as such for CPS § 10.1^{G}, by SWTF, s.v. *adhva-pratipanna*; cf. CPS § 2.2.

[27] Examples of past participles of √*pad,* such as *sabarṇo* = Skt. *saṃpannaḥ* (Dhp-G^{K} 6, 7) and *samavarṇo* = Skt. *samāpannaḥ* (Dhp-G^{K} 188), suggest that the spelling *(*pradivarṇo)* is also possible.

and fifteen. This would provide enough room for any of the above suggested reconstructions. I arbitrarily adopt the first.

Lines 3–5: Dhoṇa sees the wheel-marks on the Buddha's footprints

Edition:

| 25j
[4] /// *dhoṇe bramaṇe bhayavadu padeṣu cakra ∘ sahasahara [s.]* /// [5] /// *savarova-*
| 25j+25c
ghada ∘ aceata prabh.[śp.]ra [∘]

Reconstruction:
[3] *(*adhrekṣi)* [4] *dhoṇe bramaṇe bhayavadu padeṣu cakra ∘ sahasahara s(*aṇemia saṇabhia)* [5] *savarovaghada ∘ aceata prabh(*a)śp(*a)ra ∘*

Translation:
[3–4] The brahman Dhoṇa (*saw) the wheel-marks on the footprints of the Bhagavat, thousand-spoked, (*with rim and nave), [5] with all parts entire, brilliant, resplendent.

The P parallel is

> *addasā kho doṇo brāhmaṇo bhagavato padesu cakkāni sahassārāni sanemikāni sanābhikāni sabbākāraparipūrāni disvān' assa etad ahosi.* (AN II 37.26–9)

The initial part of this passage, that preserved on line 4, is virtually identical with the Pali. Due to damage to the manuscript, there is no remnant of the verb expressing the idea of seeing. As in Pali, it is the norm in Buddhist texts of this class for the finite verb to appear at the beginning of the sentence in passages that describe someone seeing another person; the usual structure is *addasā kho . . . disvā (/disvāna)* in P and *adrākṣīt . . . dṛṣṭvā ca punar* in Buddhist Skt. texts.[28] Therefore, a preterite form of the verb √*dṛś* probably also occurred in the G text at the end of line 3 or possibly straddling lines 3–4. The only finite form of √*dṛś* found in this manuscript is *dhrekṣatu* (l. 22), which is either the third-person plural future imperative (= Skt. **drakṣyantu*) or the present imperative (= P *dakkhantu*). The first-person singular preterite of √*dṛś* appears in the AG-G, written by the same scribe, as *adhrikṣe* (l. 35) and *adhrekṣe* (l. 38) (Salomon's [1999: 133] provisional reading of *adhrekṣema* needs amending). It is therefore likely that the third-person singular preterite was **adhrekṣi* in this scribe's orthography, which I adopt in the reconstruction. In view of P *addasā kho,* it is possible that the verb was followed by the G equivalent of P *kho*/Skt. *khalu,* although this indeclinable seems to be generally lacking in these G sūtras (see pp. 35–6, 169–70, and cf. G *teṇa ceva samaeṇa* for P *tena kho pana samayena*). As *dhoṇe* is probably the first word of line 4, I reconstruct *(*adhrekṣi)* as the only word missing from the end of line 3 that belonged to this sentence.

---

[28] See, e.g., von Simson 1965: 156.

/// dhoṇe bramaṇe bhayavadu padeṣu cakra: The bark containing the tops of the two akṣaras of *dhoṇe,* which could be the original first word of the line, needs to be moved to the left (not done in the reconstruction).

Like the following elements that qualify it, *cakra* is in the accusative plural (see § 6.1.1.1.5). The remainder of this passage consists of a string of attributes of the wheel (*cakra*). Descriptions of the wheel-marks on the soles of the Buddha's feet (one of the thirty-two characteristics of a Great Man, P *mahāpurisalakkhaṇa*/Skt. *mahāpuruṣa-lakṣaṇa*) are relatively common in Buddhist literature (Skilling 1992b, 1996). Although most of these descriptions share a basic core of attributes, some important differences are observed. The G form of the formula preserved here is no exception. As found in the P Doṇa-sutta, the standard P form is

> *bhagavato padesu cakkāni sahassārāni sanemikāni sanābhikāni sabbākāra-paripūrāni.* (AN II 37.27–8)[29]

A slight variant is found in

> *mahāpurisassa hetthā pādatalesu cakkāni jātāni honti sahassārāni sanemikāni sanābhikāni sabbākāraparipūrāni suvibhattantarāni.* (DN III 143.9–11)

Examples from Buddhist Skt. literature are[30]

> *adha(*s ta)sya pādayoś cakre jāte sahasrāre san(*ābhike sanemi)ke sar-vānt(*aparipū)rṇ(*e).* (MAV § 6b.3; cf. SHT VI 1453 V3: *[re sanābh]ike [s](*a) + ///*)[31]

> *pādatalayoś cāsya cakrāṇi jātāni sahasrārāṇi sanābhīni sanemikāni sarvākāra-paripūrṇani* [read *-āṇi*] *surucirāṇi darśanīyāni.* (Gv 399.22–4)

> *dīrghāṅgulir adhaḥkramatalayor mahārāja sarvārthasiddhasya kumārasya cakre jāte citre (arciṣmatī prabhāsvare site)*[32] *sahasrāre sanemike sanābhike.* (Lal 106.1–3)

---

[29] Further P examples are DN II 17.13–5, III 148.7–9; MN II 136.9–10. The DN III 149.4–6, verse summary reads *cakkāni pādesu duvesu vindati, samantanemīni sahassārāni ca, vyākaṃsu veyyañjanikā samāgatā*. Cf. the verses at Ap 20.18–9 (= Th-a III 95, abbreviated in E[e]) and Ap 424.1 (quoted at Th-a II 44, abbreviated in E[e], for the verses of Valliya thera). Commentaries on the elements of this phrase in various contexts are found at Sv II 617–20; Ps IV 215–7; Ap-a 225; Bv-a 41.

[30] Discussion of the Buddhist Skt. references to the wheel-marks as one of the *mahāpuruṣa-lakṣaṇa* can be found in BHSD, s.v. *lakṣaṇa,* p. 459. Further examples are *adhastāt pādatalayoś cakre jāte sahasrāre sanābhike sanemike sarvākāraparipūrṇe* (BBh 375.11–3) and the verse *lākṣārasa-prasekavarṇā sahacakrā maharṣiṇāṃ. heṣṭā pādatālā jātā svastikair upaśobhitāḥ* (Mvu II 304.15–6). Cf. Lamotte 1944–80: 272–3.

[31] See SWTF, s.v. *cakra,* for further fragments of this phrase in the Central Asian (Turfan) material.

[32] The parentheses indicate that these epithets are missing in one of the mss. (A) used by Lefmann. Vaidya's edition (1958: 75.3–4) follows Lefmann's edition. Mitra's edition (1877: 121) does not

The wheel-treasure, one of the seven treasures of a cakravartin (P *cakkavatti*), is usually qualified by a similar set of epithets. The P version of the description of the wheel-treasure is

> *dibbaṃ cakkaratanaṃ pāturahosi sahassāraṃ sanemikaṃ sanābhikaṃ sabbākāra-paripūraṃ.* (DN II 172, III 60, 61; MN III 172; Mil 285)

Examples from Buddhist Skt. texts are

> *cakraratnaṃ prādurbhavati sahasrāraṃ sanemikaṃ sanābhikaṃ suvarṇavarṇa-karmālaṃkr̥taṃ.* (Lal 14.10–1; cf. Lal 415.10 ff.)

> *cakraratnaṃ prādurbhavati sahasrāraṃ sanābhikaṃ sanemikaṃ sarvākārapari-pūrṇaṃ śubham akarmārakr̥taṃ divyaṃ [sarva]sauvarṇaṃ.* (MSV I 31.19–32.1)[33]

> *cakravartino 'yasmayaṃ* [*/rājataṃ/(*sanābhi)kaṃ sanemikaṃ divyaṃ (*sar)va-sauvarṇaṃ*] *cakraṃ prādurbhavati samantakrośam* [*dvis◦/tris◦/(*catuḥs)◦*]. (MPS § 31.32)[34]

The sequence *sahassāra sanemika sanābhika* in Pali and *sahasrāra sanābhika sanemika* or *sahasrāra sanemika sanābhika* in Sanskrit is common to all of the above examples, as epithets both of the wheel-marks on the Buddha's feet and of the cakravartin's wheel-treasure. The first epithet, P *sahassāra*/Skt. *sahasrāra,* means "thousand-spoked." The second and third, *sanemika* and *sanābhika* (Pali and Sanskrit), mean, respectively, "with rim" and "with nave."

The wording following *cakra* on line 4 in the Gāndhārī is ◦ *sahasahara [s.] ///.* The punctuation mark between *cakra* and *sahasahara* is of no great significance (see § 4.8.2). There is a horizontal ink mark at the lower left of this punctuation mark which was probably made as the scribe moved on to write the following *sa* (see § 4.6.1).

Sahasahara clearly corresponds to P *sahassāra*/Skt. *sahasrāra.* In the Dhp-G^{K}, Skt. *sahasra* appears as *sahasa,* while *sahasra* is the form found in the Niya documents (Boyer, Rapson, and Senart 1920–9) and the Kharoṣṭhī inscriptions (Konow 1929). The compound should apparently be understood as *sahasa-h-ara,* with *-h-* at the compound boundary representing a sandhi consonant (see § 5.6.5). Although not exactly parallel, *sahasrahani* = Skt. *sahasrāṇi* in the Niya documents (see Burrow 1937: § 28) is nonetheless an interesting coincidence.

All that remains of the following epithet is *[s.],* which is the final surviving akṣara on this line. Given the stability of the three epithets mentioned above, it is highly likely that

---

present them in parentheses. Hokazono's edition (1994: 486.4) prints them in parentheses. According to Hokazono's notes, the Tokyo mss. all insert *arciṣmatī prabhāsvare site,* whereas one of the Nepalese mss. used by him omits it, as does the Tibetan. (I am indebted to Jonathan Silk for checking these Hokazono references for me.)

[33] Virtually identical wording is found in the AKBh(P) 184.15–6; see Pāsādika 1989: no. 251.

[34] The text is presented here following the entry in the SWTF, s.v. *cakra.*

this represents the initial *sa* of either *sanemika* or *sanābhika* (to use their P and Skt. forms). Although the P order is fixed as *sanemika sanābhika,* the order of these two epithets varies in the Skt. material. We therefore cannot be certain in what order they appeared in our G text. The likely G spellings of the missing epithets are **saṇemia* and **saṇabhia,* with *-ṇ-* for both *-n-* and *-ṇ-* in this scribe's orthography and with elision of suffixal *-k-* as seen in such words in our manuscript as *aṇasapiḍiasa* = P *anātha-piṇḍikassa* and *viṇilaü* = P/BHS *vinīlakaṃ-* (see § 5.2.2.1).

One or two akṣaras may be missing from the beginning of line 4, although as the first visible akṣara (*[s.]*) of line 3 appears to be the first akṣara of that line, *dhoṇe* may also have been the first word of line 4. Line 4 contains twenty-one akṣaras, including the punctuation mark. The tentatively reconstructed phrase *(*ṇemia saṇabhia)* represents seven akṣaras. This would make a total of twenty-eight, which is at the lower end of the normal range. It is therefore possible that further epithets appeared on this line, though given that *savarovaghada* begins the next line, this is unlikely.

/// savarovaghada ∘ aceata prabh.[śp.]ra [∘]: Most of line 5 appears to be taken up by further attributes of the wheel-marks, none of which match those found in the corresponding Pali. *Savarovaghada,* which may have been the first word of the line, is probably a compound, representing an alternative to the P *sabbākāraparipūrāni,* the epithet that follows *sanābhikāni* in the P list. Although the akṣaras are reasonably clear, the third akṣara could be read as *ro* or *so.*

If this word is read as *savarovaghada,* it would represent a Skt. *sarva-rūpa-kṛta-*. The sense would be "with all its form made" or "complete," corresponding to *sabbākārapari-pūra-* of the P examples and *sarvākāraparipūrṇa-* and *sarvānt(*aparipū)rṇa-* of the Skt. examples. *Sava* for Skt. *sarva* is a regular G spelling, besides *sarva. Rova* for Skt. *rūpa* would similarly present no problems. However, although examples of the alternation of *u* and *o* are well documented (§ 5.1.8), the spelling *rova* is unattested to date in Gāndhārī, and we might have expected *ruva,* conforming to *[r]u[v]o* = Skt. *rūpam* and *ruaṇa* = Skt. *rūpāṇi* in this manuscript. Although *ghada* could also represent Skt. *gata, gada* for *kṛta* is attested elsewhere (e.g., Dhp-G^{K} 171b), and *sarva-rūpa-gata* would not fit the context as well. Pali does not seem to know an expression such as **sabba-rūpa-kata* (or *-gata*), nor do the P commentaries give any assistance.[35] I have not encountered such a compound in BHS material.[36] This lack of a parallel and the spelling *rova* for Skt. *rūpa* are limitations of this interpretation.

Alternatively, we could read *savasovaghada* and propose that an akṣara has been omitted, that is, that the intended reading was *savasova<*ṇa>ghada*, which would be equivalent to a Skt. *sarva-sauvarṇa-gata-* or, better, *sarva-sauvarṇa-kṛta-* or *sarva-suvarṇa-kṛta-*. This interpretation is supported by the Lal passage quoted above (14.10–1), which describes the wheel-treasure as *suvarṇavarṇakarmālaṃkṛta* rather than as

[35] See, e.g., the commentary on *sabbākāraparipūrāni* at Sv II 445 = Ps III 375.

[36] A less likely interpretation is that an akṣara was omitted, that is, that we should read *sava<*ka>rovaghada.* This word would be equivalent to a Skt. *sarvākāropagata,* which is not attested to my knowledge. This interpretation raises two problems: *upagata* does not have the meaning of P *paripūra,* and the prefix *upa-* appears as *ua-* elsewhere in this text.

sarvākāraparipūrṇa as in the Gv and MSV Skt. passages, and in contrast to *sabbākāraparipūra* of the P passages. Similarly, the MSV and MPS passages quoted above (MSV I 31 and MPS § 31.32) include *sarvasauvarṇa* as an epithet of the wheel-treasure. Although these describe the wheel-treasure of a cakravartin rather than the wheel-marks of the Buddha's feet (or the impressions left by them), the following epithets in the G text, which similarly express radiance (discussed below), are applied to the wheel-treasure in some Skt. texts. This interpretation is further supported by a fragment of the Pretāvadāna found in the Central Asian (Turfan) material where, in a verse description of a preta, *sarvasauvarṇa* is linked with *arciṣmant* (*su*)*prabhāsvara,* the two epithets that seem to follow in our G text: *(*kā)[yo]=sya sarvvasauvarṇṇaṃ hy=arcci[ṣmā](*ṃ) [s]upra-[bh](*āsva)[ra]ḥ* (SHT IV 49 f R4).[37]

As already mentioned, *sava* for *sarva* is regular in Gāndhārī. If an akṣara has been omitted, then *sova<*ṇa>* would represent either *suvarṇa,* "golden" (adj.) or "gold" (n.), or *sauvarṇa,* "golden" (adj.). The compound occurs as *sarvasovarnaṃ* in a recently published G fragment belonging to the Schøyen collection (44a v2; see Allon and Salomon 2000). Given the context, *-ghada* probably represents *-kr̥ta* rather than *-gata* (discussed above).[38] If this word is taken to represent Skt. *sarva-sauvarṇa-kr̥ta,* then the meaning would be "made all golden," that is, of golden appearance. The limitations of this interpretation are that it requires an amendment and that the presence of the punctuation mark separating this word from the following epithets describing the radiance of the wheel-marks suggests that this word is being grouped with the preceding epithets. I therefore tentatively adopt the first interpretation, though I find the latter as convincing.

aceata prabh.[śp.]ra [◦]: G *aceata* = P *accimantāni*/Skt. *arciṣmanti* (for the elision of intervocalic *-m-,* see § 5.2.2.6). *Prabh.[śp.]ra* can be reconstructed as *prabh(*a)śp(*a)ra-* = P *pabhassara-*/BHS *prabhāsvara-* (for *śp* for original *sv,* see p. 96).

The Lal 106 passage quoted above suggests that these words are further epithets of the wheel-marks. Some Lal manuscripts include *arciṣmatī prabhāsvare site,* though when this phrase is included, it appears before the *sahasrāre sanemike sanābhike* sequence rather than after it as in the Gāndhārī. A partially parallel phenomenon is seen in the Gv 399 passage quoted above, where two epithets of related meaning, *surucirāni darśanīyāni,* are included after *sarvākāraparipūrṇāni* in the description of the wheel-treasure.

In Pali the combination *accimanta pabhassara* is used to describe such entities as heavenly mansions, a stake, fire, and so on. MN I 337.25–6 (= Th 1190), for example, reads *vimānā kappaṭhāyino, veḷuriyavaṇṇā rucirā accimanto pabhassarā.*[39] But neither epithet seems to occur in combination with *cakka.*

---

[37] Cf. *kāya* ⏓ ⏓ ⏑ – ⏓ ⏓ *(*a)[rc](*c)[i]ṣ(*m)āṃ [s](*u)[p](*ra)[bh](*āsva)raḥ* in the same verse; and see SHT IV 49 f R6.

[38] *Sabba-sovaṇṇa-kata* does not occur in Pali, though *sabba-sovaṇṇa-maya* and *sabba-suvaṇṇa-maya* are fairly common expressions.

[39] See also *sattiyo teladhotāyo accimantā pabhassarā, vijjotamānā tiṭṭhanti sataraṃsīva tārakā* (Jā VI 448); *evaṃ sabbaṅgasampannaṃ accimantaṃ pabhassaraṃ, odhisuṅkaṃ mahārāja, passa tvaṃ dvipaduttama* (Jā VI 279); *te accimanto va pabhāsayanti* (Th 527).

In summary, the first three words or compounds on line 5 represent further epithets of the wheel-marks. The first may be a synonym of Skt. *sarvākāraparipūrṇa*/P *sabbākāra-paripūra,* found in Skt. and P texts as an epithet of both the wheel-marks and the cakravartin's wheel-treasure, or it may refer to the golden color of the impressions left by the wheel-marks, an epithet found in some Skt. texts and applied only to the wheel-treasure.[40] The appearance of punctuation after this element suggests that it should be grouped with the preceding epithets rather than with those that follow. This tends to support the first interpretation. The second and third epithets, *aceata prabh(*a)śp(*a)ra,* which describe the wheel-marks' bright appearance, have a direct parallel only in the Lal, where they are applied to the wheel-marks on the Buddha's feet, not their impressions left on the road. Such epithets are echoed in the similar *surucira* and *darśanīya,* with which the Gv describes the wheel-marks on the Buddha's feet.

In view of the simplicity of the P examples, it is possible that descriptions of both the wheel-marks on the Buddha's feet and the cakravartin's wheel-treasure initially lacked any reference to color or brightness. It seems likely that the "golden" epithet was later applied to the wheel-treasure as seen in such texts as the Skt. MPS and Lal, and that, by extension, epithets meaning "bright" and "shining" were then applied to the wheel-marks on the Buddha's feet as seen in such texts as the Lal and Gv. It appears that such a developed stock description of the wheel-marks on the soles of the Buddha's feet was then automatically applied to the impressions left by them on the road, as seen in our G sūtra, even though it appears a little odd to describe such impressions in the dust of the road as being "brilliant" and "resplendent," and perhaps also "golden." It is thus noteworthy that the G text parallels a comparatively elaborate text like the Lal in including these epithets meaning "brilliant" and "resplendent."

The Chinese translations lack any description of the wheel-marks that would correspond to "golden," "brilliant," or "resplendent."

Lines 5–6: Dhoṇa follows the Buddha's footprints and sees him seated under a tree

Edition:

|25j+25c |25j |25j+25e |25e |25e+25c |25c

[5] *[bha]yavadu p.[.e] /// [6] /// hoṭo magheṇa ghatva magha[de abhi]k[r]ami añadaro*

|25c+25gg

rokṣamulo ṇiṣa[e] ///

Reconstruction:

[5] *bhayavadu p(*ad)e(*ṣu cakra ???)* [6]*hoṭo magheṇa ghatva maghade abhikrami añadaro rokṣamulo ṇiṣae (*ṇiṣaṇe ◦)*

[40] Cf. the Mahāprajñāpāramitāśāstra (Lamotte 1944–80: 274), where the tops of the Buddha's feet are described as golden and the soles are described as being the color of the red lotus.

Translation:
[5] . . . [following] (*the wheel-marks) on the footprints of the Bhagavat, [he saw the Bhagavat] . . . [6] [who,] having traveled on the road to *-hoṭo* . . . , had stepped off the road [and] (*had sat down) near the root of a tree

In the P Doṇa-sutta, the sequence of events after Doṇa has seen the wheel-marks on the road is (1) he expresses amazement and wonders whether such footprints could belong to a human; (2) the Buddha leaves the road, sits under a tree, and begins to meditate; (3) Doṇa follows the Buddha's footprints and sees him seated calmly under the tree. If my reconstruction and interpretation of lines 1–3 are correct, in the G sūtra the description of the Buddha sitting under a tree in order to meditate is placed before the description of Dhoṇa seeing the Buddha's footprints. All three Chinese translations parallel the Gāndhārī in this ordering. Immediately after the brahman sees the Buddha's footprints, the P sutta and the three Chinese translations include a description of his thoughts. Although the content of the brahman's thoughts differ slightly in each text, they all essentially relay his amazement. In contrast, the G text seems to lack such a passage.[41] Finally, in the three Chinese translations, as in the P text, the brahman follows the Buddha's footprints and sees him seated under the tree in meditation.

In the G text the description of the characteristics of the wheel-marks ends with *prabha(*a)śp(*a)ra* on line 5. This is followed by a punctuation mark, then by *[bha]yavadu* (only faint traces of the punctuation mark and *bha* remain on frag. 25j and on the top of frag. 25c). It thus seems likely that *bhayavadu* begins a new sentence. Line 7 is taken up with a description of the Buddha's calm appearance. Based on the P and Chinese parallels, it is reasonable to assume that the G text from *bhayavadu* at the end of line 5 to the end of line 6 describes Dhoṇa following the Buddha's footprints and seeing him seated under the tree.

Although what remains of the wording is legible, the loss of text at the beginning and end of each line and the resulting lack of certain key words mean that the relationship between the parts that do remain is not absolutely clear. As a result this passage has several possible reconstructions and interpretations.

The first, and most likely, interpretation is that this section of the G text is similar to, but not identical with, the following passage in the P parallel:

> *atha kho doṇo brāhmaṇo bhagavato padāni anugacchanto addasā bhagavantaṃ aññatarasmiṃ rukkhamūle nisinnaṃ.* (AN II 38.3–5)

---

[41] The P passage is *addasā kho doṇo brāhmaṇo . . . disvān' assa etad ahosi: acchariyaṃ vata bho abbhutaṃ vata bho na vat' imāni manussabhūtassa padāni bhavissantī ti* (AN II 37.26–30). The Buddhist Skt. parallel to the P phrase *addasā kho* [person: nom.] [object: acc.] *disvān' assa etad ahosi* is *adrākṣīd* [person: nom.] [object: acc.] *dṛṣṭvā ca punar asyaitad abhavat* (MPS §§ 34.124–5, 34.126; the edition has *dṛṣṭvā punar* in both passages, but the reading of the ms. is *dṛṣṭvā ca punar*). Similar *adrākṣīd . . . dṛṣṭvā ca punar* passages occur at MPS §§ 5.3, 10.7, 20.5 (read *dṛṣtvā ca punar* with the ms.), 48.4, 49.12–3; Divy 197.2–4, 463.14–5). The BHS parallels to the P [person: dat./gen.] *etad ahosi* seem to standardly be [person: gen.] *etad abhavat* (CPS §§ 24a.22, 24k.12; for MPS examples, see MPS index, s.v. *bhav°*).

This passage continues in Pali with a long description of the Buddha's calm appearance, corresponding in part to the G text of lines 7 and 8.

As already noted, *bhayavadu* at the end of line 5 probably begins the G sentence. But it is noteworthy that the G text lacks the initial indeclinables corresponding to the P *atha kho* that are so favored by P prose texts as the indicators of a new moment in the narrative, as well as the subject of the sentence corresponding to *doṇo brāhmaṇo* of the Pali (although this may have appeared later). Although we have only this small and fragmentary narrative portion of this G sūtra upon which to base an opinion, the absence of both of these elements may be characteristic of the G texts of this genre, though this seems "uncanonical" by the standards of P and Buddhist Skt. sutta/sūtra texts (see pp. 35–6).

The last more or less complete akṣara of line 5 is *p.,* which, following the P parallel *bhagavato padāni anugacchanto,* most likely is the initial akṣara of *pada-*. To the left of *p.* is a small diagonal stroke which seems to represent the upper right portion of the *e* diacritic of the akṣara *(*d)e* rather than the remnant of a *da*. P *padāni* is the accusative plural neuter. In this manuscript the accusative plural neuter ending is *-a,* with *-aṇa* = Skt. *-āni* appearing once only (see § 6.1.1.1.5). The Gāndhārī therefore seems to have differed from the Pali, with the likely reconstruction being *bhayavadu p(*ad)[e](*ṣu cakra).*

If the G text did parallel the Pali in general structure at this point, then the words missing from the remainder of line 5 would correspond to P *anugacchanto addasā bhagavantaṃ*. The G equivalent of P *anugacchanto* would be **aṇoghachatu* in this scribe's orthography. In this manuscript the prefix *anu-* always appears as *aṇo-* (see § 5.1.8), and the form of the present participle appears as *ghachata-* in *ghachateṇa* (ll. 29, 30). The choice of *-u* for the nominative singular masculine termination is, of course, arbitrary (see § 6.1.1.1). The G equivalent of P *addasā* would be *adhrekṣi* in this scribe's orthography, as discussed above (see text commentary to ll. 3–5). Finally, the accusative singular masculine *bhayavadu* appears in line 9. The reconstructed text would therefore be *bhayavadu p(*ad)[e](*ṣu cakra aṇoghachatu adhrekṣi bhayavadu),* "(*following the wheel-marks) on the footprints of the Bhagavat, (*he saw the Bhagavat)."

Line 5 contains twenty-two akṣaras, including the punctuation marks and the remnant of *(*d)e,* the final akṣara of the line. The proposed reconstruction has fifteen akṣaras, which would make a total of thirty-seven akṣaras in this line. This is at the upper limit for the number of akṣaras encountered per line in this manuscript. If this reconstruction is correct, then the grammatical subject *dhoṇe bramaṇe* must have been absent in the Gāndhārī.

Again, if this reconstruction is correct, then line 6 must correspond to P *aññatarasmiṃ rukkhamūle nisinnaṃ,* which is the object of the verb *addasā* in the P passage. As already noted, part of line 6 corresponds to line 2, which describes the Buddha traveling on the road, leaving the road, and sitting down under a tree to meditate. The inclusion in line 6, however, of the element *hoṭo magheṇa ghatva maghade abhikrami* finds no parallel in the Pali, although similar passages are found elsewhere in Pali; for example, *addasa kho bhagavā . . . te bhikkhū taṃ bhikkhuṃ pariggahetvā uccāram pi* *passāvam pi nikkhāmente, disvāna* . . . (Vin I 187–8).[42] In other words, it seems that we are to understand this G passage as "[he saw the Bhagavat] . . . [who,] having traveled on the road to *-hoṭo* . . . , had stepped off the road [and] (*had sat down) near the root of a tree."

/// hoṭo magheṇa ghatva magha[de abhi]k[r]ami: The word *hoṭo* could be the original first word of the line. For the discussion of this phrase, see text commentary to lines 1–3.

añadaro rokṣamulo ṇiṣa[e] ///: The bottom of the tail of *lo* appears at the top left of fragment 25d.

Some comments on the first two words have also already been given. Based on the presence of *ṇiṣa[e]* it seems that the G phrase corresponds to the Buddhist Skt. form rather than that found in P texts, which have *aññatarasmiṃ rukkhamūle nisinnaṃ,* "(the brahman Doṇa saw the Bhagavat) seated at the root of a tree." In examples with the finite form of the verb *ni* + √*sad, aññatara- rukkhamūla-* is similarly constructed in the locative. For example, the phrase used in the P Doṇa-sutta to describe the Buddha leaving the road and sitting at the root of a tree is *atha kho bhagavā maggā ukkamma aññatarasmiṃ rukkhamūle nisīdi* (AN II 38.1–2). In other words, in canonical Pali the expression is always *aññatarasmiṃ rukkhamūle ni* + √*sad.*

In contrast, the form of the phrase encountered in Buddhist Skt. texts is *anyataraṃ vr̥kṣamūlaṃ niśritya niṣaṇṇa-,* with minor variations in the readings of some words. SBhV I 149.20–30, for example, reads *atha bhagavān . . . anyatarad vr̥kṣamūlaṃ niśritya niṣaṇṇo divāvihārāya . . . adrākṣuḥ ṣaṣṭir bhadravargīyāḥ pūgā bhagavantam anyatarad vr̥kṣamūlaṃ niśritya <niṣaṇṇaṃ>.*[43] Some texts, such as the Mvu, have *niśrāya* rather than *niśritya* (e.g., III 53.13), while in others the reading is *niśr̥tya* or *niḥśritya* (see BHSD, s.vv. *niśrāya* and *niśritya*). Minor variations are also seen in *'nyatamad vr̥kṣamūlaṃ* (MSV I 139.15; besides *anyatarad vr̥kṣamūlaṃ* in MSV I 15.5), *anyatamaṃ vr̥kṣamūlaṃ* (Divy 201.2), and *anyatama-vr̥kṣamūlaṃ* (Divy 202.1–2). As in the SBhV example just quoted, all the examples of this phrase I have identified in Buddhist Skt. texts are based on the past participle of *ni* + √*sad* rather than on a finite form of the verb.[44]

BHS *niśrāya/niśritya,* along with the corresponding P *nissāya,* is a postposition constructed in both Sanskrit and Pali with the accusative (see BHSD, s.vv. *niśrāya* and *niśritya,* and PTC, s.v. *nissāya*). The G form *ṇiṣa[e]* corresponds to BHS *niśrāya* and P

---

[42] Cf. *so evaṃ pabbajito samāno addhānamaggapaṭipanno addasaṃ bhagavantaṃ antarā ca rājagahaṃ antarā ca nāḷandaṃ bahuputte cetiye nisinnaṃ, disvāna me etad ahosi* (SN II 220) and *addasa kho upako ājīviko bhagavantaṃ antarā ca gayaṃ antarā ca bodhiṃ addhānamagga-paṭipannaṃ, disvāna* (Vin I 8 = MN I 170).

[43] CPS § 22.1–3 was reconstructed by Waldschmidt on the basis of this Gilgit ms. passage. The Gilgit ms. omits *niṣaṇṇaṃ,* which was included by Waldschmidt (and followed by Gnoli in his edition of this SBhV passage) on the basis of parallels and as required by the context.

[44] Examples so far encountered are CPS §§ 6.1, 22.1–3 (reconstructed); MPS § 15.7; NidSa §§ 22.10, 17; MSV I 9.1–2, 15.5–6; Divy 201.2–3, 25–6, 202.1–2, 516.6–7; cf. MSV I 139.15–6; Mvu III 53.13.

nissāya rather than to the more Sanskritized *niśritya* (for the development *śr* > *ṣ,* see § 5.2.3.6; for *ya* > *e,* see § 5.1.1). The ending *-o* in *añadaro rokṣamulo* is ambiguous, as is common in Gāndhārī, but given that in Buddhist Skt. and P texts the postpositions BHS *niśrāya/niśritya* and P *nissāya* take the accusative, it is likely that *añadaro rokṣamulo* in the G text is in the accusative singular also.

In P texts the postposition *nissāya* is quite common, and examples of [object: acc.] *nissāya ni* + √*sad* are encountered, with the object including such things as pillars, walls, and the like (for examples, see PTC, s.v. *nissāya*). An example is found in a passage that is repeated a number of times in the canon: *atha kho bhagavā . . . āvasathāgāraṃ pavisitvā majjhimaṃ thambhaṃ nissāya puratthābhimukho nisīdi. bhikkhusaṅgho pi kho . . . āvasathāgāraṃ pavisitvā pacchimaṃ bhittiṃ nissāya puratthābhimukho nisīdi bhagavantaṃ yeva purakkhatvā* (DN II 85, III 208–9, etc.). However, there are no examples of the phrase *rukkhamūlaṃ nissāya ni* + √*sad* in Pali, although *nissāya* does occur in combination with *rukkhamūlaṃ* once in a verse in the Th: *rukkhamūlaṃ va nissāya muṇḍo saṅghāṭipāruto, paññāya uttamo thero upatisso 'va jhāyati* (998).[45]

Given that G *añadaro rokṣamulo ṇiṣae* corresponds to Buddhist Skt. *anyataraṃ vṛkṣamūlaṃ niśrāya niṣaṇṇaṃ,* the *ṇiṣa[e]* at the end of line 6 must have been followed by the G equivalent of Skt. *niṣaṇṇam*/P *nisinnaṃ*. The G form of the past participle appears in this manuscript as *ṇiṣaṇa-* in *ṇiṣaṇeṇa* (ll. 32, 33). The reconstruction of the G phrase is therefore *añadaro rokṣamulo ṇiṣae (*ṇiṣaṇo)* (the ending *-o* in **ṇiṣaṇo* for the acc. sg. m. is arbitrarily chosen).

As will be discussed in the next section, the end of line 6 must have contained at least one of the terms describing the Buddha's calm appearance. Therefore, from *bhayavadu* on line 5 to *(*ṇiṣaṇo)* at the end of line 6, a likely reconstruction is

> [5] *bhayavadu p(*ad)e(*ṣu cakra aṇoghachatu adhrekṣi bhayavadu ???)* [6]*hoṭo magheṇa ghatva maghade abhikrami añadaro rokṣamulo ṇiṣae (*ṇiṣaṇo).*

> [5] (*Following the wheel-marks) on the footprints of the Bhagavat, (*he saw the Bhagavat), [6] [who,] having traveled on the road to *-hoṭo* . . . , had stepped off the road [and] (*had sat down) near the root of a tree.

The alternative, and less likely, interpretation for this section of the text is to take the brahman Dhoṇa as the grammatical subject of the phrase *-hoṭo magheṇa ghatva maghade abhikrami*. In this interpretation the reconstruction of the text missing at the end of line 5 would be much the same as that proposed above. That is, it would be *bhayavadu p(*ad)[e](*ṣu cakra aṇoghachatu),* though another possibility is *bhayavadu p(*ad)[e](*ṣu cakra dhriśpaṇa ta(/taṇi ?) aṇoghachatu),* "having seen the wheel-marks on the footprints of the Bhagavat, [and] following them," or the like. This latter reconstruction would reflect the tendency in P and Buddhist Skt. texts to begin one sentence with the finite form of the verb and to begin the following clause with the corresponding absolut-

---

[45] In commentaries, *rukkhaṃ nissāya* is enountered a number of times, e.g., *rukkhaṃ nissāya ṭhapethā ti* (Ps III 161.21) and *ekaṃ rukkhaṃ nissāya dārakaṃ nipajjāpetvā* (Mp II 250.6–7).

ive: *addasā kho . . . disvāna* in Pali and *adrākṣīd . . . dr̥ṣṭvā ca punar* in Sanskrit. Then the word or words expressing the idea of the brahman's seeing the Buddha would have occurred at the end of line 6. The reconstruction of this section of the text would thus be

> [5] *bhayavadu p(*ad)e(*ṣu cakra aṇoghachatu ???)* [6]*hoṭo maghena ghatva maghade abhikrami añadaro rokṣamulo ṇiṣae (*ṇiṣaṇo bhayavadu adhrekṣi)* [7] . . .

> [5] [The brahman Dhoṇa], (*following the wheel-marks) on the footprints of the Bhagavat, [6] traveling on the road to *-hoṭo* . . . , stepped off the road [and] (*saw the Bhagavat seated) near the root of a tree.

In this reconstruction, lines 5 and 6 would have had thirty and thirty-five akṣaras, respectively, both of which are around the norm. However, as discussed below, line 6 must have also contained the equivalent of the P *pāsādikaṃ* (probably **prasadiu* or the like), the first word of the stock description of the Buddha's calm appearance. In other words, the text missing from the end of line 6 would have been *(*ṇiṣaṇo bhayavadu adhrekṣi prasadiu)*. The akṣara count for line 6 would then be thirty-nine, which is at the upper extreme of the number of akṣaras per line. I have therefore adopted the first reconstruction for the presentation at the beginning of this section but have excluded the phrase *(*aṇoghachatu adhrekṣi bhayavadu)* on the grounds that it remains quite speculative.

Lines 6–8: The Buddha's calm appearance

Edition:

|25j |25e |25d |25d+ 25f |25d |25d+ 25f |25v |25d+ 25f |25d |25gg
[7] *? + + ṇi śatidhri śatamaṇa[s. ◦ utamada]masaśamasap[r]atu ◦ p. r. [m.]* /// [8] ///
|25e+25f |25f |25z
[gh]u[t]u [vu]didhrio ṇasu rada ṇam=i ◦ [va] achu aṇa[vela v]ip..[s.]ṇ. [◦] ? ? + ? ///

Reconstruction:
[6] *(*prasadiu* [7] *prasada)ṇi śatidhri śatamaṇas(*a) ◦ utamadamasaśamasapratu ◦ p(*a)r(*a)m(*a ???* [8] *datu) ghutu vudidhrio ṇasu rada ṇam iva ◦ achu aṇavela vip(*ra)s(*a)ṇ(*a) ◦ (*???)*

Translation:
[6] [his appearance] (*fair, [7] pleasing), his faculties calm, his mind calm, having attained the highest training and calm . . . , [8] a protector, (*trained), controlled, with faculties restrained, like a clear, translucent, serene pond. . . .

Lines 7 and 8 represent the bulk of the description of the Buddha's calm appearance, which began at the end of line 6 (now lost). This consists of a long string of epithets in the accusative singular in apposition with *(*ṇiṣaṇo)*, "[he saw the Bhagavat] . . . [who] . . . (*had sat down)," which, based on the P and Skt. parallel phrases, must have occurred immediately after *ṇiṣae* at the end of line 6. The formula concludes at the end of line 8 with a simile, comparing the Buddha's appearance to a serene pond.

The P text corresponding to lines 6–9 of the Gāndhārī is

> *addasā bhagavantaṃ aññatarasmiṃ rukkhamūle nisinnaṃ pāsādikaṃ pasādanīyaṃ santindriyaṃ santamānasaṃ uttamadamathasamatham anuppattaṃ dantaṃ guttaṃ santindriyaṃ nāgaṃ disvā yena bhagavā ten' upasaṅkami.* (AN II 38.4–8)[46]

Line 9 of the Gāndhārī begins with */// yavadu teṇa uasakrami,* which corresponds to the latter part of *yena bhagavā ten' upasaṅkami* in the P passage above and describes Dhoṇa's approach to the Buddha. As will be discussed in greater detail below, *dhriśpaṇa yeṇa,* corresponding to *disvā yena* of the Pali, must have occurred at the end of line 8, immediately following the description of the Buddha's appearance.

Buddhist Skt. texts provide a number of examples of such a description of the Buddha in the same or in a parallel setting wherein someone sees the Buddha seated under a tree or in an assembly of monks or walking along a road. A passage in the SBhV of the MSV, for example, reads

> *adrākṣuḥ . . . bhagavantam anyatarad vṛkṣamūlaṃ niśritya <niṣaṇṇaṃ prāsādikaṃ prasādanīyaṃ>*[47] *śāntendriyaṃ śāntamānasaṃ parameṇa cittadamavyupaśamena samanvāgataṃ suvarṇayūpam iva śriyā jvalantaṃ. dṛṣṭvā ca punar yena bhagavāṃs tenopasaṅkrāntāḥ.* (I 149.29–150.2; cf. CPS § 22.3)

The Mvu contains at least two such passages, both much expanded. The one at Mvu III 63.18–64.10 reads (with relevant sections underlined)

> *adrākṣīc chāriputro parivrājako bhagavantaṃ . . . brahmacaryaṃ saṃprakāśayantaṃ dvātriṃśatīhi mahāpuruṣalakṣaṇehi samanvāgataṃ aśītīhi anuvyaṃjanehi upaśobhitaśarīraṃ aṣṭādaśehi āveṇakehi buddhadharmehi samanvāgataṃ daśahi tathāgatabalehi balavāñ caturhi vaiśāradyehi viśārado śāntendriyo śāntamānaso uttamadamathaśamathapāramitāprāpto nāgo yathā kāritakāraṇo antargatehi indriyehi avahirgatena mānasena susthitena dharmatāprāptena ṛjunā yugamātraṃ prekṣamāṇaḥ gupto nāgo jitendriyo hradam iva accho anāvilo viprasanno ratanayūpam iva abhyudgato suvarṇabimbam iva bhāsamānaṃ tejarāśim iva śriyā jvalamānaṃ dvitīyaṃ ādityam iva udayantaṃ asecanakaṃ apratikūlaṃ darśanāye mukto.*

The passage at Mvu I 237.7–14 is slightly shorter and differs in the order of the components as well as in its readings. The relevant section is

---

[46] This formula is also found at Ud 7.24–7, 58.22–5; Vin I 195.26–9.

[47] *Niṣaṇṇaṃ prāsādikaṃ prasādanīyaṃ* (the reading is *prasādanīyaṃ* in Gnoli's edition) is missing in the ms. but was included by Gnoli following Waldschmidt's reconstruction of the CPS parallel (§ 22.3), which in turn was based on the Gilgit ms. Waldschmidt included *niṣaṇṇaṃ prāsādikaṃ prasādanīyaṃ* on the basis of the Tibetan and following his reconstruction of the Sanskrit of MPS § 28.2, the latter being reconstructed on the basis of the Tib. and P parallel.

vaiśāradyehi samanvāgataṃ. nāgo viya kāritakārano antogatehi indriyehi avahirgatamānasena sthito dharmāvasthāprāptaḥ śāntendriyo śāntamānaso uttamadamaśamathapāramiprāpto gupto nāgo jitendriyo hradam iva accho anāvilo viprasanno prāsādiko darśanīyo āsecanako apratikūlo darśanāye yojanagatāye prabhāye obhāsayanto. dr̥ṣtvā ca punar.[48]

/// ? + + ṇi śatidhri śatamaṇa[s. ◦ utamada]masaśamasap[r]atu ◦: Only the very tip of the first akṣara of the line, which is probably the original first akṣara of the line, remains. In the P parallel *santindriyaṃ* is preceded by the two epithets *pāsādikaṃ pasādanīyaṃ* [v.l. *pāsādanīyaṃ*]. Of the Skt. examples, only Avś I 101.1–4 (quoted in n. 48) provides a secure example of the inclusion of *prāsādikaṃ prasādanīyaṃ* in such a formula, since Gnoli includes them in the SBhV passage only on the basis of a reconstruction by Waldschmidt (see n. 47). Nonetheless, because the second visible akṣara of line 7 is *ṇi,* which was probably originally the fourth akṣara of the line, it is likely that the epithet preceding *śatidhri* in the G text corresponded to P *pasādanīyaṃ*/Skt. *prasādanīyaṃ.* The G form of this word would have been **prasadaṇi,* with loss of the final *ya* syllable parallel to *śatidhri* for P *santindriyaṃ* (see § 5.5).[49] This reconstruction is at least partially supported by the fact that the remnant of the initial akṣara is consistent with the top of the *p* of the first syllable of *(*prasada)ṇi.* It is also possible that the remnant is the top of the second akṣara, *sa,* which, due to the alignment of the akṣaras, would mean that the initial *pra* occurred at the end of the preceding line. However, the height of the remnant indicates that it is more likely to be the top of *pra.* Given this interpretation, the first epithet, the G equivalent of P *pāsādikaṃ*/Skt. *prāsādikaṃ,* must have occurred at the end of line 6. The most likely spelling of this word is *(*prasadiu),* with elision of original *-k-* (see § 5.2.2.1). The reconstruction of the text missing from the end of line 6 and the beginning of line 7, containing the beginning of the description of the Buddha's calm appearance, is therefore *(*prasadiu prasada)ṇi,* "(*fair, pleasing)."

The next two epithets, *śatidhri śatamaṇa[s. ◦],* correspond to *santindriyaṃ santamānasaṃ* in Pali and *śāntendriyaṃ śāntamānasaṃ* in Sanskrit. Due to damage to the manuscript (the left-hand edge of frag. 25e is compressed), the final akṣara of *śatamaṇa[s.]* could be *sa, se,* or perhaps *si,* though the first is the most likely. Further, what has been read as a punctuation mark could also be interpreted as the top of the *u* of the following *utama,* the bottom of which appears on fragment 25d.

---

[48] Similar passages are *atha sa rājā . . . dadarśa bhagavantaṃ prabodhanaṃ samyaksaṃbuddhaṃ prāsādikaṃ prasādanīyaṃ śāntamānasaṃ parameṇa cittadamavyupaśamena samanvāgataṃ suvarṇayūpam iva śriyā jvalantaṃ dr̥ṣṭvā ca punaḥ prasādajātaḥ sa rājā* (Avś I 101.1–4); *dadarśa rājā prasenajitkauśalo bhadrikaṃ śāntendriyaṃ śāntamānasaṃ parameṇa ca cittadamavyupaśamanasamanvāgataṃ . . . dr̥ṣṭvā ca punar* (Avś II 114.11–3); *sa nirgato yāvat paśyati bhagavantaṃ dvātriṃśatā mahāpuruṣalakṣaṇaiḥ samalaṃkr̥taṃ aśītyā cānuvyañjanair virājitagātraṃ vyāmaprabhālaṃkr̥taṃ sūryasahasrātirekaprabhaṃ jaṅgamam iva ratnaparvataṃ samantato bhadrakaṃ dr̥ṣṭvā ca punar* (Divy 75.1–5); *adrākṣīd bodhisattvas taṃ bhikṣuṃ śāntaṃ dāntaṃ saṃyataṃ brahmacāriṇaṃ avikṣiptacakṣuṣaṃ yugamātraprekṣiṇaṃ prāsādikenairyāpathena saṃpannaṃ* (Lal 191.14–6).

[49] Cf., e.g., *prasadasa* = Skt. *prasādasya,* "of one who has faith," at Dhp-G^{K} 310c.

[utamada]masaśamasap[r]atu ◦: Only a hairline of the bottom of *ma* in *[utama]* remains on fragment 25d. The placement of fragment 25v in the hole where the *r* in *p[r]atu* once appeared is confirmed by the reading on the verso. The recto contains a large, dark mark, perhaps ink, that does not correspond to the missing part of *pra* of the recto. The recto of this fragment therefore seems to have peeled. The dark mark may be a blemish in the inner bark.

The G expression differs from the P *uttama-damatha-samatham anuppattaṃ* only in that the past participle is *pratu,* the equivalent of P *patta-* (Skt. *prāpta-*) rather than *anupattaṃ,* though interestingly, the P commentary (Mp III 78.13) glosses *anupattaṃ* with *pattaṃ*. The forms in the Mvu, *uttamadamathaśamathapāramitāprāpto* (III 64.6) and *uttamadamaśamathapāramiprāpto* (I 237.11–2), are slightly expanded forms, although they parallel the Gāndhārī in the use of *prāpta* instead of *anupatta* of Pali. In contrast, *paramena cittadamavyupaśamena samanvāgataṃ* (or *~vyupaśamanasamanvāgataṃ*) of SBhV (I 149.30–150.1) and Avś (I 101.2–3, II 114.12), as well as the Tibetan upon which Waldschmidt based his reconstruction of the Sanskrit of CPS § 22.3 and MPS § 28.2, represents a different tradition, though these expressions are virtually synonymous with the G and P forms.

Because the accusative singular masculine can end in *-a* (see § 6.1.1.1.3), it is impossible to tell whether the Gāndhārī represents one compound or whether *utama-damasa-śamasa* is in the accusative, as the object of *pratu*. That is, this could be understood as either *utama-damasa-śamasa-pratu* or *utama-damasa-śamasa pratu*. In the Pali, *anuppattaṃ* is not compounded with *uttamadamathasamatham,* its object, though the E^e of the commentary (Mp III 78) records *uttamadamathasamathānuppattaṃ* as a v.l., whereas in the Mvu examples *-prāpta* is the final member of the compound. In other words, both forms are attested in the wider Buddhist tradition. I make the rather arbitrary choice of treating it as one compound.[50]

◦ *p. r. [m.] ///:* There is a space for two akṣaras between the punctuation mark and *p.* The reading and interpretation of the final three akṣaras of the line are tentative, as only their tops survive. The first is probably *p,* while the second could be *r* or *s*. The third could be *ma*. This suggests a word like *parama*. The remnants of two akṣaras at the top left of fragment 25f may be the bottoms of *p.* and *r.* However, the bark of fragment 25f is distorted at this point and the akṣaras could belong to the end of line 8.

In the P parallel, *uttamadamathasamatham anuppattaṃ* is followed by *dantaṃ guttaṃ santindriyaṃ*. The Gāndhārī corresponding to this latter string is *[gh]u[t]u [vu]didhrio* at the beginning of line 8. Between three and four akṣaras are missing from the beginning of line 8. The akṣara count for line 7 varies according to how it is calculated. If we take *(*pra)* to be the original first akṣara of the line and include the space where the second and third akṣaras occurred and the two punctuation marks (the first of which could also be interpreted as the top of the following *u* of *[utama]*), then the akṣara count is twenty-eight. But this figure could be increased by two if we count the two blank spaces between the second punctuation mark and what I am here reading as *p. r. [m.]*.

[50] Cf. the similarly ambiguous *prata ṇiamo* in the Khvs-G, which could be understood as *prata-ṇiamo* (Salomon 2000: 169).

About eight akṣaras are probably missing from the end of line 6, and at least five are missing from line 8. If this is used as a measure, then, based on the alignment of the final surviving akṣaras of lines 6, 7, and 8, approximately five or six akṣaras are missing from the end of line 7. The akṣara count for line 7 would then be between thirty-three and thirty-four (by the first count).

Based on the P parallel, at least two of the three or four akṣaras missing from the beginning of line 8 may have been taken up with the G equivalent of the P *dantaṃ* (see below). If this is the case, then either the final akṣara or the final two akṣaras of the expression or epithet that began with *parama* at the end of line 7 must have occurred at the beginning of line 8. In other words, the expression beginning with *parama* at the end of line 7 could have contained another six to eight akṣaras. If the equivalent of P *dantaṃ* is not reconstructed at the beginning of line 8, then it could have contained another eight to ten.

The word *parama* suggests *parameṇa cittadamavyupaśamena samanvāgataṃ* in the SBhV and Avś. But as this is the equivalent in these texts for *utama-damasa-śamasa-pratu* of the Gāndhārī, it is unlikely to have occurred in the G text. An alternative is the following. In descriptions of the beauty of various individuals found in P and Skt. texts, the three synonymous terms *abhirūpa, darśanīya,* and *prāsādika,* meaning "beautiful," are followed by *paramaśubhavarṇapuṣkalatayā samanvāgata*, "endowed with the greatest excellence of beautiful color," to use the Skt. form. This stock description is applied on a number of occasions to the Buddha, in P sources at least. For example, *samaṇo khalu bho gotamo abhirūpo dassanīyo pāsādiko paramāya vaṇṇapokkharatāya samannāgato* (DN I 115.21–2, 131.33–5).[51] The G equivalent of P *vaṇṇapokkharatāya* appears in Dhp-G^{K} 186b, *varṇapuṣkalarṇaï va,* where P Dhp 262b has *vaṇṇa-pokkharatāya vā* and Uv XXIX.10b has *varṇapuṣkalayā na ca*. Unfortunately, *puṣkalarṇaï* with its unusual suffix is left unexplained by Brough.[52] The equivalent of Skt. *puṣkariṇī* appears in a new G fragment from the Schøyen collection as *puṣkirini* (44a v2; see Allon and Salomon 2000: 247, 261–2). Based on the Dhp-G^{K} and Schøyen examples, the likely G equivalent in our text for P *paramāya vaṇṇapokkharatāya samannāgata-* would be *parama(*e varṇapuṣkaladae samaṇaghada)*—rendering the instrumental feminine of the abstract suffix *-tayā* with *-dae* rather than with the anomalous *-rṇaï* of the Dhp-G^{K} example. The reconstructed portion of the phrase contains thirteen akṣaras, which is more than the six to ten proposed above. Unfortunately, we have no way of confirming this reconstruction. In the latter part, the Chinese translations differ from the G in the description of the Buddha's appearance, and they appear to have no equivalent of this phrase.

/// [gh]u[t]u [vu]didhrio ṇasu: The sequence *dantaṃ guttaṃ santindriyaṃ nāgaṃ* in the P parallel suggests that *ghutu* (P *gutta-*/Skt. *gupta-*) may have been preceded by the G

---

[51] See PTC, s.v. *parama,* for further P references. Skt. examples are found at RP 37.5–6, Mvy 5216–9, and MSV I 136.2–3.

[52] The character that Brough transcribes as *rṇa* in *puṣkalarṇaï* is unusual, and in the photograph at least, it almost appears as though the reading of the previous akṣara should be *li*. It is possible that the transcription of this word needs to be reconsidered.

equivalent of P *dantaṃ*. If so, the form of the word in this scribe's orthography would have been *(*datu)*, in contrast to *dadu/dada* found in the Dhp-G^{K} (80b, 341d). Of the Skt. passages so far encountered, only the Mvu (quoted above) includes a similar sequence: *gupto nāgo jitendriyo*. As this lacks *dānta-* it is also possible that the G text similarly did not have the equivalent term and that *ghutu* was directly preceded by the expression that began with *parama* at the end of line 7.

The Skt. equivalent of *[vu]didhrio* would be *vr̥tendriyam*, "having controlled faculties." The corresponding Pali has *santindriyaṃ*, "having calm faculties," while the Mvu parallels have *jitendriyo*, "having conquered faculties."[53] There are no occurrences of *vutindriya* in P texts, but *saṃvutindriya* is quite common.[54] Similarly, in the Dhp-G^{K} we find *savudidrio* (53b) and *idrieṣu asavudu* (217b, cf. 218b)—the latter for P *indriyesu asaṃvutaṃ* (Dhp 7b)—as well as *savudu, savrudo,* and *savrudo* in other contexts where Pali has *saṃvuto* or *saṃvutaṃ* (Dhp-G^{K} 23c, 51a–c, 259b, 326a). But there are no examples of *vudidrio* or the like. It is therefore possible that the prefix *sa-* (= Skt. *saṃ-*) was omitted by the scribe.

The variety of forms encountered in the G, P, and Skt. examples is reflected in the diversity of readings for this word in this formula encountered within the P canon itself. Besides *santindriyaṃ*, we find *yatindriyaṃ* and *saṃyatindriyaṃ*, both meaning "having restrained faculties" (the v.l. *satindriyaṃ* in the E^{e} is of a different status), and the European and Oriental editions often preserve different forms in parallel passages found in different canonical texts, or the commentary preserves a different form from the canonical text (for details, see the note to this word in the edition of the P text in appendix 3).

The word following *[vu]didhrio* in the G text is *ṇasu*. Although the P parallel has *nāgaṃ*, "elephant" (acc. sg.), and the Mvu passage has *nāgo* (nom. sg.), *ṇasu* cannot represent this word, which appears in the Dhp-G^{K} (329a) as *nako* (where the Pali has *nāgo*, Dhp 320a) and in the Khvs-G as *ṇago* (32 and udd. 4a). The most likely interpretation is that *ṇasu* represents *nātha-*, "protector," "refuge." This seems awkward in this context. In the P and Skt. parallels the Buddha is likened or referred to as a bull elephant (*nāga*) because of his calm and controlled appearance. However, support for this interpretation comes from a v.l. in Sn 1131, where the E^{e} has *nātho* with v.l. *nāgo*, against B^{e}, S^{e}, and the commentary of Nidd II, which read *nāgo*, which according to Norman (1992a: 386) is the earlier reading. In other words, as the P example attests, *nāga* and *nātha* were liable to alternation in some contexts. I therefore translate this word as "protector."

rada ṇam=i ∘ [va] achu aṇa[vela v]ip..[s.]ṇ. [∘] ? ? + ? ///: The left-hand portion of the manuscript containing lines 8 and 9 is in poor condition, and the overlying fragments (frags. 25z and 25y), containing the remnants of several akṣaras, obscure several akṣaras of these lines. In consequence, the reading of these sections of the manuscript is problematic. In fact, it was the Mvu's description of the Buddha's calm appearance that revealed

---

[53] *Jitindriya* occurs only twice in the P canon (Vv 1035; Th 1096; cf. Sn 250a: *sotesu gutto vijitindriyo care*) but is common in Buddhist Skt. texts.

[54] E.g., *sampajānā samāhitā ekaggacittā saṃvutindriyā* (AN I 70; cf. AN I 266, III 391, 392; It 91). Verse examples are *satimā saṃvutindriyo* (Ap 97.25) and *anuddhato acapalo nipako saṃvutindriyo* (Th 682, etc.).

the correct reading and interpretation of this portion of line 8. For, in contrast to the P parallel where the sequence *dantaṃ guttaṃ santindriyaṃ nāgaṃ* is followed by the description of Doṇa's approach to the Buddha, in Mvu III 63–4, *gupto nāgo jitendriyo* is followed by a series of similes, the first of which is *hradam iva accho anāvilo viprasanno,* "(the Bhagavat) was like a clear, translucent, serene pond."[55] As is typical of Buddhist literature of this class, although this simile is not part of the P version of the stock description of the Buddha's calm appearance, it is found elsewhere in the P canon in illustration of what can be seen when the mind is concentrated and pure. The P form of this simile is *seyyathāpi . . . pabbatasaṅkhepe udakarahado accho vippasanno anāvilo* (e.g., DN I 84.13–4), "like a clear, translucent, serene pond of water in mountain environs,"[56] or simply *seyyathāpi . . . udakarahado accho vippasanno anāvilo* (AN I 9.17–8), the Skt. parallel of which is *tadyathā udakahradaḥ accho viprasannaḥ anāvilaḥ* (EĀ-Skt.$^{Gil.}$ § 11.21). Further, *udakarahada, rahada,* and the alternative P form also corresponding to Skt. *hrada,* namely *daha,* are found in combination with the same or alternative adjectives in other contexts, while the adjectives *accha, vippasanna,* and *anāvila* are also applied to such things as a cakravartin's jewel-treasure, a pot of water, and so on. Examples are *yathāpi rahado gambhīro vippasanno anāvilo* (Dhp 82a–b) and *seyyathāpi . . . udapatto accho vippasanno anāvilo āloke nikkhitto* (SN V 125; AN III 236).[57]

Finally, the G forms of several of these terms are found in two verses in the Dhp-G^{K}. The first is *yatha vi rada gammiro viprasano aṇavilo* (225a–b), corresponding to the Dhp 82a–b verse just quoted, where the Uv has *yathā hradaḥ sugambhīro viprasanno hy anāvilaḥ* (XVII.11a–b). The second is *viprasana aṇavila cadra ba vimali śudhu* (40b–c), where the Pali has *candaṃ va vimalaṃ suddhaṃ vippasannam anāvilaṃ* (Dhp 413a–b) and the Uv has *candro vā vimalaḥ śuddho viprasanno hy anāvilaḥ* (XXXIII.31Aa–c).

The reading of the beginning of the G simile appears to be *rada ṇam=i ◦ [va].* The reading *[va]* is not definite; the akṣara appears as a faint addition below the line to the left of the punctuation mark. Although the text should be understood as *iva ◦*, the scribe probably added *[va]* after the punctuation mark due to the lack of space between *mi* and

---

[55] The simile is also applied to the Buddha at SBhV II 219.10–2. The other four similes in the Mvu passage are *ratanayūpam iva abhyudgato suvarṇabimbam iva bhāsamānaṃ tejarāśim iva śriyā jvalamānaṃ dvitīyaṃ ādityam iva udayantaṃ.* In the SBhV passage quoted above (I 149–50) the Buddha is likened to a golden pillar: *suvarṇayūpam iva śriyā jvalantaṃ.* Similar similes likening the Buddha to something golden occur in the two Chinese SĀ translations of the Dhoṇa-sutra (T nos. 99 and 100).

[56] Further examples are found at DN I 209 (abbreviated in the E^{e}); MN I 279, II 22.

[57] Further examples are *seyyathāpi . . . pabbatasaṅkhepe udakarahado nivāto vigata-ūmiko* (AN III 396); *seyyathāpi . . . maṇi veḷuriyo subho jātimā aṭṭhaṃso suparikammakato accho vippasanno anāvilo sabbākārasampanno* (DN I 76, 208 [abbrev. in E^{e}], II 13, 175; MN II 17); cf. *seyyathāpi . . . udakarahado [gambhīro] ubbhidodako* (DN I 75, 207 [abbrev. in E^{e}]; MN I 276–7, II 15, III 93 [abbrev. in E^{e}], etc.); *seyyathāpi . . . udakarahado uttāno gambhīrobhāso* (AN II 105). For similes based on *rahado,* see Rhys Davids 1906–7: 127–8. Examples from Skt. texts are *rājñaś cakravartino maṇir bhavati aṣṭāṃśo vaiḍūryaḥ śubho jātimān accho viprasannaḥ anāvilaḥ* (MSV I 36.4–6; cf. IV 213.5–6 = SBhV II 245.29–30); *śrāddhaṃ prājñaṃ tu seveta hradaṃ yadvaj jalārthikaḥ, acchodakaṃ viprasannaṃ śītatoyaṃ anāvilam* (Uv X.15).

the punctuation mark. Because the following word is *achu,* which corresponds to *accho* in the P and Skt. forms of the simile, the text up to *achu* must correspond to *hradam iva* of the Sanskrit.

Several interpretations are possible for *rada ṇam iva* ◦. *Rada* is most likely the equivalent of Skt. *hrada-*/P *rahada-* (the spelling is *rada* in the Dhp-G^{K} 225 passage). G *ṇam* could be the emphatic particle found in Pali as *na* and *naṃ,* which can be used in a comparative sense meaning "like," "as" (see PTSD, s.v. *na* 1). This sense is illustrated by the commentary's gloss of *na* in Jā V 341.19, as *nā ti ettha nakāro upamāne,*[58] a meaning also encountered in Vedic (Macdonell 1916: 236) as well as in other MIA and NIA languages.[59] If this interpretation is correct, then the following *iva* would probably be the equivalent of Skt. and P *eva* rather than *iva,* for although two comparative particles cannot be ruled out, it would be unexpected. P seems to know no examples of *nam eva* or *nam iva*. It is possible to take *iva* as the particle of comparison and *ṇam* as an emphatic with no independent meaning. Alternatively, we could assume that the text is faulty at this point, with *ṇa* representing an additional, erroneous akṣara. We would then read *rada-m=iva,* which would correspond to *hradam iva* of the Sanskrit, which likewise should be edited as *hrada-m-iva,* treating *-m-* as a sandhi consonant following the suggestion by Edgerton (BHSD, s.v. *hrada*). Or finally, if *ṇa* is not a scribal error, then it is possible that *radaṇa* is an alternative, perhaps extended, G form of *rada,* though unattested to date. The reading would then be *radaṇa-m=iva*.

Yet another interpretation is that the Buddha's appearance is being likened, not to a pond, but to a jewel, P *ratana*/Skt. *ratna*. This word appears in a G fragment of the Mahāparinirvāṇa-sūtra as *ratana* (44a v2; see Allon and Salomon 2000). In the orthography of our scribe it would appear as *radaṇa*. The string of adjectives that follow (P *accha vippasanna anāvila*) is applied to various jewels in both P and Skt. texts. Examples are *seyyathāpi . . . maṇi veḷuriyo subho jātimā aṭṭhaṃso suparikammakato accho vippasanno anāvilo sabbākārasampanno* (DN I 76, 208 [abbrev. in E^{e}], II 13, 175; MN II 17) and *rājñaś cakravartino maṇir bhavati aṣṭāṃśo vaiḍūryaḥ śubho jātimān accho viprasannaḥ anāvilaḥ* (MSV I 36.4–6; cf. IV 213.5–6 = SBhV II 245.29–30). It is therefore possible that this passage should be edited as *radaṇam=i* ◦ *[va] achu aṇa[vela v]ip..[s.]ṇ.* and reconstructed as *radaṇam iva* ◦ *achu aṇavela vip(*ra)s(*a)ṇ(*a),* "like a clear, translucent, faultless jewel."[60] Although I have not found examples of such a simile applied to the Buddha, the Buddha is likened to a jeweled pillar in the Mvu III 63–4 passage quoted above: *ratanayūpam iva abhyudgato*.

The sequence of three virtually synonymous adjectives that follows, *achu aṇa[vela v]ip..[s.]ṇ.,* which corresponds to P *accha vippasanna anāvila*/Skt. *accha anāvila viprasanna* (or *accha viprasanna anāvila*), presents no real problems, although several of the

---

[58] For discussions of this verse, including the comparative sense of *ṇa,* see CPD, s.v. *kañcanadepiccha,* and Norman 1994: 217–20 (= CP, vol. VI, pp. 53–6).

[59] For a discussion of Apa. *ṇaṃ, ṇâim,* and related forms in other languages meaning "like," see Schwarzschild 1959: 48–9 (= *Collected Articles* 1991: 86–7).

[60] This interpretation was suggested to me by Richard Salomon.

akṣaras are damaged or distorted. The reading seems to be *aṇa[vela]* but could also be *aṇa[vila]*. The manuscript has split, and the upper section has moved to the left. A small, dark chip sitting on top of the *la* looks like a diacritic. The bottoms of the akṣaras *p..[s.]ṇ. [◦]* are covered by fragments 25z and 25y. As original *pr* virtually always remains in this manuscript, and as the form in the Dhp-G^K^ is *viprasana,* it is likely that the reading was *viprasaṇa* in our manuscript also.

[v]ip..[s.]ṇ. is followed by a punctuation mark, which possibly indicates the beginning of a new sentence. Following this on fragment 25f are what appear to be the remnants of two more akṣaras. However, the bark is distorted at this point and it is possible that these are the bottoms of *p.* and *r.* of line 7. The remnant of another akṣara of the line appears on fragment 25z. Line 9 begins */// yavadu teṇa uasakrami,* which describes Dhoṇa approaching the Buddha. In the P the corresponding phrase *yena bhagavā ten' upasaṅkami* follows immediately after the description of the Buddha's appearance. There is room for only one akṣara at the beginning of line 9, which must be the *bha* of *(*bha)yavadu.* The last word on line 8 must therefore have been *yeṇa,* which may have been preceded by *dhriśpaṇa.* That is, the reading of the end of line 8 and beginning of line 9 was probably *(*dhriśpaṇa yeṇa* [9] *bha)yavadu teṇa uasakrami,* corresponding to *disvā yena bhagavā ten' upasaṅkami* of the Pali. Line 8 contains twenty-eight akṣaras (not counting the subscript *[va]*). Two akṣaras are probably missing from the beginning of the line (= thirty akṣaras). This means that up to eight or nine akṣaras are missing from the end of this line. Although badly distorted, the remnants of the two akṣaras that follow the final punctuation mark of line 8 do not seem to match *(*dhriśpaṇa yeṇa),* which indicates that these akṣaras may be the bottoms of the final akṣaras of the previous line or that *dhriśpaṇa* was preceded by other words.

To summarize, the relationship between the G version of the description of the Buddha's calm appearance and the version encountered in P and Skt. texts is complex. The G version is closer to the P in the first half of the description but parallels several of the Skt. examples in its latter half, including at least one simile. This simile, which likens the Buddha's appearance to that of a serene pond, finds a direct parallel in the Mvu version. Although missing in the P version, this simile is nonetheless encountered in P texts in other contexts, which thus provides another illustration of the flexible use of "fixed" units of meaning, or formulas, that is characteristic of Buddhist literature. Further, with its more elaborate description than the P version, the G version is more in keeping with the general character of Buddhist Skt. texts, though it does not approach the elaborateness of the description found in the Mvu.

Lines 8–9: Dhoṇa approaches the Buddha and speaks to him

Edition:

| 25f

[9] */// yavadu teṇa uasakrami uasakramita bhaya[vad]u egha[d=u]* + +

Reconstruction:
[8] *(*dhriśpaṇa yeṇa* [9] *bha)yavadu teṇa uasakrami uasakramita bhayavadu eghad u(*ya ∘)*

Translation:
[8] (*Having seen him), [9] he approached the Bhagavat. Having approached, he said this to the Bhagavat.

What survives of this passage corresponds exactly to the P parallel: *disvā yena bhagavā ten' upasaṅkami upasaṅkamitvā bhagavantaṃ etad avoca* (AN II 38.8–9).

In the discussion of the previous section of the text, it was noted that there is room for one akṣara at the beginning of line 9, the *bha* of *(*bha)yavadu,* and that, based on the context and on the P parallel, the end of line 8 must have contained *(*yeṇa)*, probably preceded by *(*dhriśpaṇa)*. The reading for the first part of the phrase, down to the absolutive that begins the second clause, is thus *(*dhriśpaṇa yeṇa bha)yavadu teṇa uasakrami uasakramita,* "(*having seen him), he approached the Bhagavat. Having approached . . ." Similar approach formulas occur in the Senior manuscripts. Examples are . . . *aña(*aro) bhikhu yeṇa bhayava teṇa uasakami uasakramita* . . . (19 r1); . . . *y[e]ṇa bhayava teṇa uasakrami uasakamita* . . . (19 v2); and . . . *[yeṇa] bhayava teṇa uasakami uasakamita* . . . (19 v8).

bhaya[vad]u egha[d=u] + +: Two other examples of this phrase occur in this manuscript. The first is in line 28, where the reading is *bha[ya]va[ṣu] egha[d=uya ∘],* which is to be amended to *bhayava<*d>u eghad uya ∘*. The second occurs at the beginning of line 39, where only *eghad oya ∘* remains. Both of these examples occur at the beginning of a sūtra and describes the Buddha speaking to the monks, corresponding to P *bhagavā etad avoca*. In contrast, the example under discussion, which corresponds to P *bhagavantaṃ etad avoca,* describes someone speaking to the Buddha. In this text *bhayavadu* can represent both the nominative and the accusative singular, besides the dative/genitive singular (see § 6.1.4.5).

The section of bark following *egha[d=u]* is obscured by an overlying fragment (frag. 25z). Since the readings in the other two examples are *eghad uya ∘* (l. 28) and *eghad oya ∘* (l. 39), the likely reconstruction for this section of the text is *bhayavadu eghad u(*ya ∘)*.

G *eghad uya* and *eghad oya* for P *etad avoca* are unusual, to say the least. The corresponding phrase in Buddhist Skt. texts is *idam avocat* (see von Simson 1965: §§ 12.13 ff.). It is probably best to understand the word division in the G version to come after *-d,* that is, to read *eghad uya* and *eghad oya*, as presented above. In this case *-d-* represents an organic sandhi consonant, as in Pali (see § 5.6.4).

Further G versions of this phrase are found in the Senior manuscripts. The form *eḋaḋ aya* appears in *asa o añaare bhikhu bhayavada eḋaḋ=aya* (5 v8–9); *so bhikhu bhayavada eḋaḋ=aya* (19 r7); *bhayavada eḋaḋ=aya* (19 v3,9); and *so bramaṇo bhayavada eḋaḋ=aya* (20 r2). *Eḋavaya* is found in *asa añaaro bhikhu bhayavada eḋavaya* (20 r15), while *eḋavayi* appears in *sa bhikhu bhayavada eḋavayi* (19 r2).[61]

Eghad uya/eghad oya of our manuscript and *eḋaḋ aya, eḋavaya,* and *eḋavayi* of the Senior manuscripts provide interesting examples of radical contractions of the common fixed locution that appears in Pali as *etad avoca* and in Sanskrit as *idam avocat*. A parallel phenomenon is seen in the G equivalent of the P phrase *idam avoca bhagavā*. In our manuscript this appears as *(*ida)m=u bhayavadu* (ll. 15–6) and *idam=u* <**bhayavadu*> (l. 36), while in the Senior manuscripts studied to date it appears as *iḋam=oyi bhayava* (20 r11), *iḋam=eyi bhayava* (5 r20, v5), *iḋam=aya bhayava* (20 v13), and *iḋa bhayava* (19 v14; this may be a scribal error); see the text commentary to lines 25–6 for further discussion of these forms.

Eḋaḋ in *eḋaḋ aya* of the Senior manuscripts is unproblematic as the G equivalent of P and Skt. *etad,* but *eghad* of our manuscript presents serious problems. As noted previously (§ 4.8.1), the scribe of our manuscript does not distinguish between *g* and *gh,* writing *gh* throughout. G *eghad* for original *etad* seems unlikely, because the development of original *-t-* to *-g-* or *-gh-* is without precedent in Gāndhārī. This word might represent *eka,* "one," corresponding to a previously unattested expression **ekam avoca* (to give it a P form), literally, "he said one (thing)," but meaning in effect "he said."[62] In this case *-d-* would represent an inorganic sandhi consonant as in the P expression *eka-d-atthu* (ind.), "certainly."[63] But this interpretation seems unlikely for several reasons. First, as just stated, such an expression is not attested elsewhere in Buddhist literature, or in Gāndhārī. Second, the word is spelled *eka* elsewhere in this manuscript (ll. 26, 37), and *ega* for *eka* is not very common in Gāndhārī.[64] Finally, *eḋaḋ* and *eḋa* in the Senior manuscript examples of this phrase (*eḋaḋ aya*, *eḋavaya*, *eḋavayi*) clearly represent the demonstrative pronoun.

If we reject *eghad* as equivalent to *eka,* we are left with the unsatisfactory solution of treating *eghad* as a peculiar development of *etad,* perhaps specific to this text or scribe, or at least to this expression. It is probably not a coincidence that such a development has occurred in a fixed locution that was subjected to contraction and other unusual developments in Gāndhārī. This word is one of a small, but significant, number of words in this manuscript that remain to be explained. Others are *dihagama* (l. 17), where the P parallel has *vihaṅgamo,* and *bhiriḍigama* (l. 18), where the P has *vinaḷīkatā*.

With reference to the second element, the forms *uya* and *oya* in our manuscript probably represent the thematic aorist *avaca,* which is found in both P and BHS, with the

---

[61] These provisional readings were provided by Richard Salomon. Further examples may appear in the Senior scrolls not yet studied.

[62] No such expression is found, e.g., among the glosses of this phrase in the P commentaries (Sv I 297, III 820, 833, 943; Ps II 53, 195, III 280, 446).

[63] Cf. *ekodaṭṭho/~aṃ* at Paṭis I 17.16, 18.2, II 120.23, 121.22. The Bᵉ of Paṭis I 18.2 reads *ekadaṭṭha*. See Geiger 1994: § 73 for further examples in Pali.

[64] E.g., in the Niya documents *eǵa* occurs once and *aneǵa* a handful of times. It also appears once in the Khvs-G as *ege* (Salomon 2000: § 6.2.1.1). In the AG-G (l. 26) we find *eghaputrao* = Skt. *ekaputrakaḥ*. See Burrow 1937: §§ 16, 89.

contraction of *ava* to *o,* with a secondary weakening to *u,* and with elision of *-c-* (*-c-* > *-y-*). The latter developent is common in Gāndhārī (see Salomon 2000: § 6.2.1.2), as is the reduction of the prefix *ava-* and of the sequence *-ava-* in internal position to *o* (see § 5.1.10). However, such a contraction of the augment plus root syllable of √*vac* (or √*vad*) is attested in Gāndhārī only in the BL and Senior manuscripts. But again, this may be explained by the fact that this is a fixed locution (as is P *etad avoca*), with *-ava-* of **etad avaca* thus being treated as if in internal position.

Preterites of √*vac* have hitherto been rare in Gāndhārī. The single example of *avaci* in the Niya documents is exceptional for those documents.[65] In line 16 of our text we find *idam a[va]ï,* and a G fragment of the Mahāparinirvāṇa-sūtra (additional fragment r3; see Allon and Salomon 2000) has *idam avaci*. Both of these examples correspond to P *etad avoca* in the stock phrase . . . *athāparaṃ etad avoca satthā* and to *etad uvāca* in some Skt. parallels (see the text commentary to ll. 15–6 below for the full discussion). As mentioned previously, the preterite form of the verb found in the G equivalent of the P phrase *idam avoca bhagavā* appears as *u* in this manuscript (*idam=u bhayavadu*, ll. 16, 36) and as *oyi, eyi,* and *aya* in the Senior manuscripts (*idam=oyi bhayava,* 20 r11; *idam=eyi bhayava,* 5 r20, v5; *idam=aya bhayava,* 20 v13).

The verbal elements in the phrase *edad aya, edavaya,* and *edavayi* in the Senior manuscripts, which correspond to P *etad avoca,* can be interpreted in a number of ways. In the case of *edad aya,* the latter element must represent an alternative contraction of the thematic aorist *avaca*. In this case it appears that the root syllable *va* has been omitted, and *-c-* has been elided. In contrast, it appears that the syllable *da* has been omitted in *edavaya* and *edavayi,* although we could also understand *-v-* to be a sandhi consonant, reading *eda-v-aya* and *eda-v-ayi*. The final *i* vowel in the latter example indicates that the underlying form may be the same as that of G *avaï, avaci, oyi,* and *eyi* listed above, corresponding to BHS *avaci* or *avacī* (see text commentary to ll. 15–6 for full discussion). Since these *i* forms are as common as the *a* forms (*uya, oya, aya*), an *i* form may underlie the latter spellings, but with final vowel not written.

An interesting point with regard to this passage is that, as in the P text of the Doṇa-sutta in the AN, the brahman is not depicted showing respect to the Buddha or adopting a posture. In contrast to, say, the DN, where a visitor is always depicted showing respect to the Buddha, the absence of phrases depicting the showing of respect and the adopting of a posture is not uncharacteristic of the diction of the P AN (see Allon 1997: 163–5). This indicates that such a distinction between the diction of the AN and of the DN collections may be very old.

Further, the G form of this formula, (**yeṇa*) . . . *teṇa uasakrami uasakramita,* which coincides completely with the P form, represents what von Simson (1977: 481) in his detailed discussion of this phrase classes as the *"Mittelindische Fassung,"* the "Middle Indic version," showing no signs of the developments and innovations that occurred with the Sanskritization of Buddhist texts, such as the change of the finite verb to the past

[65] See Boyer, Rapson, and Senart 1920–9, no. 511. The past tense is normally expressed in the Niya documents and in Kharoṣṭhī inscriptions by means of the periphrastic construction (Burrow 1937: §§ 105 ff.).

participle *upasaṃkrānta,* the replacement of the MIA absolutive with *upasaṃkramya,* or the complete replacement of the verb forms with *upajagāma upetya* in certain texts affiliated with the Sarvāstivādins.

Finally, in the Chinese translations of this sūtra there is no mention of the brahman's approach to the Buddha at this point. Rather, the brahman is depicted seeing the Buddha, then speaking to him.

Lines 9–15: Dhoṇa's questions and the Buddha's response

Edition:

| 25f | 25z | 25f
[9] + *[v. bhu bha] ? [śasi ṇa]* + *bra[ma]ṇ. [d.]* /// [10]*ve bhaviśe* ◦ *ghadhrarvo bhu*

| 25f+25a | D6b | 25f
bhaviśa[s]i ṇaho bramaṇa [gha]dharvo bhaviśe ◦ *yakṣu [bh. bh.vi]* /// [11]*maṇa yakṣu*

| 25f+25a | 25a | 25f+25a | 25aa+25a
bhaviśe ◦ *maṇośu bhu bhaviśasi ṇaho bramaṇa maṇośu bhaviśe [◦]* /// [12] /// + *si idi*

| 25a+ | 25cc+ | D6m+
| 25f | 25a | 25cc | D6m | 25ee | 25ee+25dd
proṭhu samaṇa ema vadesi ṇaho bramaṇa dev[e bhaviśe] ◦ *gh.dh.[rv.] bhu bhaviśa[si]* ///

| 25a
[13]*di p[r]oṭhu samaṇa ema vadesi ṇaho bramaṇa ghadharvo bhaviśe* ◦ *ya[kṣ.]* + +

| D6m+
| D6m | 25dd | 25dd | 25a
[vi]śasi idi proṭh[u sama] /// [14] *ema vadesi ṇaho bramaṇa yakṣ[u] bhaviśe [◦] maṇośu*

| 25dd | 25a+24a | 25a
bhu bhaviśasi [id.] proṭhu samaṇa [e] /// [15] /// *s[i] ṇaho bramaṇa maṇośu bhaviśe ku*

re bhu bhaviśasi budho mi b[r]amaṇa budho [mi] ///

Reconstruction:
[Dhoṇa:] [9]*(*de)v(*e) bhu bha(*vi)śasi*
[Buddha:] *ṇa(*ho) bramaṇ(*a) d(*e)*[10]*ve bhaviśe* ◦
[Dhoṇa:] *ghadhrarvo bhu bhaviśasi*
[Buddha:] *ṇaho bramaṇa ghadharvo bhaviśe* ◦
[Dhoṇa:] *yakṣu bh(*u) bh(*a)vi(*śasi)*
[Buddha:] *(*ṇaho bra)*[11]*maṇa yakṣu bhaviśe* ◦
[Dhoṇa:] *maṇośu bhu bhaviśasi*
[Buddha:] *ṇaho bramaṇa maṇośu bhaviśe* ◦
[Dhoṇa:] *(*deve bhu bhavi*[12]*śa)si idi proṭhu samaṇa ema vadesi ṇaho bramaṇa deve bhaviśe* ◦ *gh(*a)dh(*a)rv(*o) bhu bhaviśasi (*i)*[13]*di proṭhu samaṇa ema vadesi ṇaho bramaṇa ghadharvo bhaviśe* ◦ *yakṣ(*u bhu bha)viśasi idi proṭhu sama(*ṇa)* [14] *ema vadesi ṇaho bramaṇa yakṣu bhaviśe* ◦ *maṇośu bhu bhaviśasi id(*i) proṭhu samaṇa e(*ma va*[15]*de)si ṇaho bramaṇa maṇośu bhaviśe ku re bhu bhaviśasi*
[Buddha:] *budho mi bramaṇa budho mi (*???)*

Translation:
[Dhoṇa:] [9] "Venerable sir, would you be a (*god)?"

[Buddha:] "Brahman, (*I) [10] would not be a god."
[Dhoṇa:] "Venerable sir, would you be a *gandharva?"*
[Buddha:] "Brahman, I would not be a *gandharva."*
[Dhoṇa:] "Venerable sir, would you be a *yakṣa?"*
[Buddha:] "[11] Brahman, (*I) would (*not) be a *yakṣa."*
[Dhoṇa:] "Venerable sir, would you be a human?"
[Buddha:] "Brahman, I would not be a human."
[Dhoṇa:] [12] "Being asked thus, '(*Venerable sir), would you be (*a god)?' you say this, 'Brahman, I would not be a god.' Being asked thus, 'Venerable sir, would you be a *gandharva?'* [13] you say this, 'Brahman, I would not be a *gandharva.'* Being asked thus, '(*Venerable sir), would you be a *yakṣa?'* [14] you say this, 'Brahman, I would not be a *yakṣa.'* Being asked thus, 'Venerable sir, would you be a human?' [15] you say this, 'Brahman, I would not be a human.' Who, then, venerable sir, would you be?"
[Buddha:] "Brahman, I am the Enlightened One. I am the Enlightened One."

Line 9: + *[v. bhu bha] ? [śasi]:* The first akṣara of this passage is obscured by fragment 25z, which belongs at the end of this line. The upper left hook of *si* is covered by a small chip where the *s* intersects with the *i* diacritic, making it appear like *li* rather than *si.*

bra[ma]ṇ.: The remnant of ink at the top of fragment D6b could represent the bottom of *bra*. The *ma* akṣara is damaged, appearing as a "laminate."

Line 10: *bramaṇa [gha]dharvo:* The splitting and shifting of the manuscript between *ṇa* and *[gha]* have meant that the right arm of *gha* has been covered, making it appear like a *ga*. However, as this scribe writes only *gha* (= *gha* or *ga*), the reading is certain.

[bh.vi] ///: Fragment D6h contains the akṣara *[si],* which could belong at the end of this line, representing the *si* of *bhaviśasi*. However, there is no way of confirming this placement.

Fig. 4. Reconstruction of line 10 (left side).

Line 12: *proṭhu:* The tops of these akṣaras are obscured by fragment 25r, which remains unplaced.

The bark is split from *vadesi* to the left margin, with the upper portion riding over the lower portion and obscuring the tops of some of the akṣaras of this line. The two portions have been separated in the reconstruction.

dev[e]: The *e* diacritic of *ve* is hidden by the bark from above the split (which also obscures most of *viśe* of the following *[bhaviśe]*). However, the presence of the *e* diacritic is assured by a small mark below the horizontal stroke of the *v* where the diacritic has crossed the horizontal.

Line 13: *p[r]oṭhu:* A small, blank chip of bark sits over the bottom of *pro.*

Line 14: *ema:* A loose, blank chip of bark partially covers these two akṣaras.

[id.]: The section of fragment 25dd containing the *d.* has now broken off. It is clearly visible in the old black-and-white photo.

[e] ///: Only a small remnant of the right-hand horizontal of *e* remains.

Line 15: */// s[i]:* The top of the *i* vowel is obscured by a loose, blank chip of bark.

[mi] ///: Although only the right arm of this akṣara remains, its shape is characteristic of *mi*.

The P parallel (AN II 38.10–24), with abbreviated passage reconstructed and underlined, is

> *devo no bhavaṃ bhavissatī ti. na kho ahaṃ brāhmaṇa devo bhavissāmī ti. gandhabbo no bhavaṃ bhavissatī ti. na kho ahaṃ brāhmaṇa gandhabbo bhavissāmī ti. yakkho no bhavaṃ bhavissatī ti. na kho ahaṃ brāhmaṇa yakkho bhavissāmī ti. manusso no bhavaṃ bhavissatī ti. na kho ahaṃ brāhmaṇa manusso bhavissāmī ti. devo no bhavaṃ bhavissatī ti iti puṭṭho samāno na kho ahaṃ brāhmaṇa devo bhavissāmī ti vadesi. gandhabbo no bhavaṃ bhavissatī ti iti puṭṭho samāno na kho ahaṃ brāhmaṇa gandhabbo bhavissāmī ti vadesi. yakkho no bhavaṃ bhavissatī ti iti puṭṭho samāno na kho ahaṃ brāhmaṇa yakkho bhavissāmī ti vadesi. manusso no bhavaṃ bhavissatī ti iti puṭṭho samāno na kho ahaṃ brāhmaṇa manusso bhavissāmī ti vadesi. atha kho ko carahi bhavaṃ bhavissatī ti*

The conclusion to the Buddha's long prose response to these questions is *buddho ti maṃ brāhmaṇa dhārehī ti* (AN II 39.3).

A tentative reconstruction and translation of this section of the G text was first presented in Salomon 1999: 25–6. The highly repetitive structure of this passage enables virtually all the missing wording and partial akṣaras to be reconstructed with a high degree of certainty. Further, due to the consistency in orthography of words in this section of the text, in only one instance are alternative spellings possible for the reconstructed element. This is *gh.dh.[rv.]* in line 12, where the original could have been either *ghadharvo* or *ghadhrarvo*. Although the former spelling dominates throughout, the latter is found in line 10. I therefore reconstruct this as *gh(*a)dh(*a)rv(*o)*, following the majority.

Having followed the wheel-marks on the Buddha's footprints, and seeing the Buddha seated under a tree, Dhoṇa asks the Buddha whether he would be a *deva,* "god" (P and Skt. *deva*), a *ghadharva* (P *gandhabba*/Skt. *gandharva*), a *yakṣa* (P *yakkha*/Skt. *yakṣa*),[66] or *maṇośa,* "human" (P *manussa*/Skt. *manuṣya*). To each of these questions the Buddha responds in the negative. As is typical of Buddhist sūtra literature, the structure of each question and answer is identical.

The questions asked and the order in which they are asked correspond to the P version. The logic to this order—G and P *deva, ghadharva/gandhabba, yakṣa/yakkha, maṇośa/manussa*—seems to be the following. Given that the Buddha's footprints contain wheel-marks and that his appearance is so amazing, Dhoṇa naturally first asks the Buddha whether he would be a *deva,* "god." When the Buddha answers in the negative, Dhoṇa

[66] For lack of suitable English equivalents, I leave *ghadharva* and *yakṣa* untranslated.

then asks whether he would be a *ghadharva/gandhabba*, which is a more this-worldly being. This is repeated for a *yakṣa/yakkha,* evidently a slightly more worldly being than a *ghadharva/gandhabba*.[67] Finally, Dhoṇa asks the Buddha whether he would be *maṇośa/ manussa,* "human," the state of being he must have thought was least likely given the Buddha's appearance and wheel-marked footprints.

Although basically the same in structure, order of questions, and overall wording, the G and P versions differ slightly in details of wording. To use the last question and answer, which along with the second is complete in the Gāndhārī, as an illustration, Dhoṇa asks the Buddha, *maṇośu bhu bhaviśasi,* to which the Buddha responds, *ṇaho bramaṇa maṇośu bhaviśe*. In the P the corresponding question is *manusso no bhavaṃ bhavissatī ti,* and the Buddha's response is *na kho ahaṃ brāhmaṇa manusso bhavissāmī ti.* First, the indeclinable *no* found in the P version of Doṇa's questions is missing in the Gāndhārī. This particle does not occur in this manuscript or in the P Saṃvara-sutta, which is the parallel to the third sūtra of this G collection, the Prasaṇa-sutra (its presence in the P sutta and absence in the G sūtra would allow a provisional evaluation of its use in Gāndhārī); the sūtras of the Senior manuscripts are yet to be properly studied. We therefore cannot tell whether other prose G sūtras consistently omitted *no* when the P parallel included it. The similar indeclinable *nu* is preserved in Dhp-G^K 143a, corresponding to Dhp 146a, while several Dhp-G^K verses have *nu* where the corresponding P verses do not. But this flexibility is to be expected in verse.

Second, in Dhoṇa's question, the G uses the contracted vocative form *bhu* in combination with the second-person singular of the verb, *bhu bhaviśasi,* "venerable sir, would/will you be?" in contrast to the Pali, which constructs *bhavant* in the nominative singular in combination with the third-person singular of the verb, *bhavaṃ bhavissati,* "would/will the venerable sir be?"

Third, whereas the G version of the Buddha's answers opens with *ṇaho bramaṇa,* the P begins with *na kho ahaṃ brāhmaṇa*. Here it is difficult to tell whether the G lacks the indeclinable or the personal pronoun, for although G *ho* could be the equivalent of P *kho* (Skt. *khalu*), G *ṇaho* could also be a sandhi combination of the negative particle and the first-person pronoun corresponding to a Skt. *nāham*. The G equivalents of P and Skt. *ahaṃ* found in the Dhp-G^K are *ahu, aho,* and *aha,* the last in *dhamaha* (98c), corresponding to P *dhammāhaṃ* (SN I 33), while P *kho*/Skt. *khalu* appears as *hu, ho,* and *gu* in that text. In other words, we could understand the G to be either *ṇaho,* corresponding to Skt. *nāham,* or *ṇa ho,* the equivalent of P *na kho*/Skt. *na khalu*. However, examples such as *karomaho* = Skt. *karomy aham* found in the AG-G (e.g., l. 78), which is written by the same scribe, suggest that *ṇaho* of our text is to be understood as the equivalent of Skt. *nāham*. Further, in three instances where the G corresponding to a P passage containing *kho* is preserved, the G lacks the equivalent of *kho*. They are (1) G *ku re bhu bhaviśasi* (l. 15) against *atha kho ko carahi bhavaṃ bhavissatī ti* (AN II 38.23–4), though E^e

[67] This hierarchy may also be supported by the fact that *ghadharva/gandhabba* has three syllables and precedes *yakṣa/yakkha,* which has two syllables, for normally the ordering of the elements of lists is determined by word length, with the shorter preceding the longer unless this is overridden by conceptual factors (Allon 1997: 191 ff.).

records the v.l. *atha ko* (Burmese mss. B.K.), the reading found in B^e and S^e; (2) G *evam eva* (l. 23) against P *evam eva kho* of the parallel formula found at AN I 56.7, though again B^e and S^e lack *kho;* and (3) G *tatra ya* (ll. 27 and 38) against P *tatra kho* of the parallel formula found at AN II 20.3.[68] This suggests that G sūtras may have tended to omit the equivalent of P *kho* (the indeclinable particle so favored by P texts among several indeclinables used to mark the commencement of a new sentence or clause), although these examples are too few to be conclusive, especially since two of the P examples themselves have variant readings that omit *kho*. If there was a tendency to omit the equivalent of P *kho,* then this omission would be parallel to the lack of the equivalent of P *no* mentioned above and to the absence of the equivalent of P *ti* discussed below (see also pp. 35–6). Influenced by such examples as *karomaho* = Skt. *karomy aham* mentioned above and the possible absence of the equivalent of the P *kho* particle in these G sūtras, I tentatively interpret *ṇaho* of our text as the equivalent of Skt. *nāham* and edit accordingly.

A further difference between the P and G is *bhaviśe* in the Gāndhārī, which appears to be the ātmanepada (Ā.) form of the verb, in contrast to the parasmaipada (P.) form, *bhavissāmi,* of the Pali. In Pali the corresponding Ā. form **bhavisse* is not recorded, nor does it seem to appear in other Prakrits. An alternative interpretation is that this represents the contracted first-person singular parasmaipada future in *-am,* as in P *bhavissaṃ,*[69] with final *-e* for *-aṃ*.

Finally, in both the questions and the answers, the G text lacks *idi* or *di,* corresponding to P *iti* and *ti*. In fact, this absence of the equivalent of *iti* seems to be characteristic for this collection of G sūtras. Whereas in the P versions of these sūtras, and in P canonical texts in general, the end of direct speech or a thought is always marked with *ti,* the corresponding G generally lacks it. Examples from the three G sūtras in this manuscript are *ku re bhu bhaviśasi* (l. 15) against P *atha kho ko carahi bhavaṃ bhavissatī ti* (AN II 38.23–4), and *u(*asaghu) mi ṣ(*a)ma(*ṇe ghuda)m(*e) dharedu . . . śaraṇo <*ghade> abhiprasaṇe* ◦ (ll. 24–5) against P *upāsakaṃ maṃ bhavaṃ gotamo dhāretu . . . saraṇaṃ gatan ti* (AN I 56.9–11). Also, the conclusion to the first two sūtras reads *bhayavadeṇa bhaṣido abhiṇadi* O (ll. 26, 36–7) against the parallel P formula *bhagavato bhāsitaṃ abhinandun ti* (e.g., AN I 276.24).[70] Finally, although *idi* in the next section, where Dhoṇa repeats his question within a statement, could correspond to *ti* of the Pali, which marks the end of the quote, it is more likely to correspond to *iti* of *iti puṭṭho samāno,* meaning "thus," because the following statement, *ṇaho bramaṇa maṇośu bhaviśe,* lacks the quotative particle *idi/di* (e.g., ll. 14–5 read *maṇośu bhu bhaviśasi id(*i) proṭhu*

---

[68] The passages in the P Doṇa-sutta that contain *kho* where the corresponding Gāndhārī is lost are *addasā kho doṇo brāhmaṇo* (AN II 37.26–7); *atha kho bhagavā maggā ukkamma* (AN II 38.1); *atha kho doṇo brāhmaṇo* (AN II 38.3–4).

[69] For discussions of this form in Pali and Prakrit, see Geiger 1994: § 150; Pischel 1965: § 520; von Hinüber 1986: §§ 463 ff.

[70] Cf. also the introductions to the second and third sūtras, where the Gāndhārī has *tatra ya bhayavadu bhikhu amatredi te bhikhu bhayavadu pracarśoṣu* ° (ll. 27–8, 38) against the parallel P formula *tatra kho bhagavā bhikkhū āmantesi bhikkhavo ti bhadante ti te bhikkhū bhagavato paccassosuṃ* (AN II 20.3–4). The Gāndhārī omits the vocative-plus-*ti* units altogether.

*samaṇa e(*ma vade)si ṇaho bramaṇa maṇośu bhaviśe,* where the corresponding P is *manusso no bhavaṃ bhavissatī ti iti puṭṭho samāno na kho ahaṃ brāhmaṇa manusso bhavissāmī ti vadesi,* AN II 38.21–3). Further research is needed to clarify whether this lack of *idi/di* is characteristic of other prose sūtras within the BL collection, or whether it is peculiar to this manuscript, for *di* is found throughout the Dhp-G^{K} (e.g., 1, 6, 7) and in the Dhp-G^{L} (2, 9).

The G and P texts agree in their use of the future tense of the verb √*bhu* throughout this and the following passages. The future in this context can be interpreted in two ways. The first, which is the most obvious, is that Dhoṇa is asking about the future state of the Buddha. In this interpretation Dhoṇa's question *maṇośu bhu bhaviśasi* would be translated as "Venerable sir, will you be (or become in the future) a human?" to which the Buddha answers, *ṇaho bramaṇa maṇośu bhaviśe,* "Brahman, I will not be a human." This is the interpretation adopted by the P commentary on this passage, which states *ayaṃ pana brāhmaṇo anāgate mahesakkho eko devarājā bhavaṃ bhavissatī ti anāgatavasena pucchaṃ karonto*[71] *evam āha* (Mp III 78.21–3), "But this brahman said thus, forming the question in the future (tense): 'Will the venerable sir be a powerful leader of gods in the future?'" Woodward (1933: 44) follows this in his translation of the Pali, translating, for instance, the first question, *devo no bhavaṃ bhavissatī ti,* as "Your worship will become a deva?" arguing for this interpretation on the grounds that the following verses "clearly imply that he [the Buddha] will not again 'become' any one of these creatures" (1933: 44 n.).[72]

In the P version of the sutta, the Buddha's response to the brahman's final question, *atha kho ko carahi bhavaṃ bhavissatī ti,* translated by Woodward as "Who then, pray, will your worship become?" (1933: 44) consists of two parts: a prose passage, which concludes with a simile and a final statement that he is the Buddha, and verses that express the same ideas as the prose passage. In the G version, as in the Chinese translations, only a very brief prose response stating that he is the Buddha and the following verses are given. The main part of the Buddha's prose response in the Pali reads (with abbreviated sections restored and underlined)

> *yesaṃ kho ahaṃ brāhmaṇa āsavānaṃ appahīnattā devo bhaveyyaṃ te me āsavā pahīnā ucchinnamūlā tālāvatthukatā anabhāvakatā āyatiṃ anuppādadhammā. yesaṃ kho ahaṃ brāhmaṇa āsavānaṃ appahīnattā gandhabbo bhaveyyaṃ te me āsavā pahīnā ucchinnamūlā tālāvatthukatā anabhāvakatā āyatiṃ anuppādadhammā. yesaṃ kho ahaṃ brāhmaṇa āsavānaṃ appahīnattā yakkho bhaveyyaṃ te me āsavā pahīnā ucchinnamūlā tālāvatthukatā anabhāvakatā āyatiṃ anuppādadhammā. yesaṃ kho ahaṃ brāhmaṇa āsavānaṃ appahīnattā manusso bhaveyyaṃ te me āsavā pahīnā ucchinnamūlā tālāvatthukatā anabhāvakatā āyatiṃ anuppādadhammā.* (AN II 38.25–30)

[71] The B^{e} reads *pucchāsabhāgeneva kathento.*

[72] In her introductions to Woodward's and Hare's translations of the AN (vols. 2–3), Rhys Davids (1933: vi; 1934: vi–vii, xiv) gives further support to this interpretation.

The simile that follows is *seyyathāpi brāhmaṇa uppalaṃ vā padumaṃ vā puṇḍarīkaṃ vā udake jātaṃ udake saṃvaḍḍhaṃ udakā accuggamma ṭhāti anupalittaṃ udakena evam eva kho brāhmaṇa loke jāto loke saṃvaḍḍho lokaṃ abhibhuyya viharāmi anupalitto lokena* (AN II 38.30–39.3),[73] concluding with *buddho ti maṃ brāhmaṇa dhārehī ti* (AN II 39.3). The first of the concluding verses is *yena devūpapatty assa gandhabbo vā vihaṅgamo, yakkhattaṃ yena gaccheyyaṃ manussattañ ca abbaje* (AN II 39.4–5).

In the prose passage the Buddha seems to be clearly stating that the *āsava*s by which he would be or would become (the optative is used throughout) a god, or the like, have been cut off, while in the first of the concluding verses the idea of not becoming (in the future) one of the four classes of being seems to be even more forcefully stated: *yena devūpapatty assa . . . yakkhattaṃ yena gaccheyyaṃ,* "(the *āsava*s) by which there would be rebirth as a god . . . (or) by which I would become a *yakkha."* The G verse, though fragmentary, parallels the P in wording and in the use of the optative (see below). These P passages therefore seem to support the idea that Doṇa is asking about the Buddha's future state rather than his current status.

Despite this, given the Buddha's appearance and the presence of wheel-marks on his footprints, it does seem more natural for the brahman to be asking about the Buddha's present status. This interpretation is, in fact, the more likely one in light of several parallels in other Buddhist texts and in the Mahābhārata (MBh), and because the future tense can, as noted by Whitney (1889: § 948a), be used "for the expression of a conjecture or presumption."[74] In illustration of this "presumptive" use of the future, Whitney quotes a verse from the Nala story of the MBh: *ko 'yaṃ devo gandharvo vā bhaviṣyati,* which he translates as "who is this? he is doubtless a god, or a Gandharva." The context and full version of this verse are as follows. When Damayantī and her friends first see Nala when he comes to the palace to deliver a message, they are so amazed at his appearance and beauty that they are unable to speak. Instead they think: *aho rūpam aho kāntir aho dhairyaṃ mahātmanaḥ, ko 'yaṃ devo 'tha vā yakṣo gandharvo vā bhaviṣyati* (Bombay ed. 3.55.16; the Critical Edition reads . . . *ko 'yaṃ devo nu yakṣo nu gandharvo nu bhaviṣyati,* 3.52.16), translated by van Buitenen (1975: 326) as "*Aho,* what shape, *aho,* what beauty, *aho,* the poise of the great-spirited man! Would he be a God, or a Yakṣa, or a Gandharva?" This provides an interesting parallel to the brahman Dhoṇa's questions in our Buddhist sūtra, with the difference in the number and order of beings listed no doubt due to metrical factors. Further, Dhoṇa's questions and Damayantī and her friends' thoughts arise from parallel contexts: both are a response to someone's amazing appearance. This motif seems to be relatively common in Indian literature, as indicated by its occurrence in such diverse texts as a Buddhist canonical sūtra and the MBh.

---

[73] This simile also occurs at AN V 152; SN III 140; cf. Mil 375.

[74] In the case of Pali, the PTSD (s.v. *bhavati,* p. 500) list this idiomatic usage of the future *bhavissati* as "is certainly," "must be." See also Warder 1974: 55: "The future also expresses perplexity, surprise, and wonder, for example in: *kiṃ ev' idaṃ bhavissati*, 'what can this be?' 'what is this (stuff)?'"

The MBh itself contains several further examples.[75] At MBh 3.40.30–2 Arjuna, astonished that his arrows are unable to make any impression on the Kirāta, who is in fact Śiva, exclaims:

ko 'yaṃ devo bhavet sākṣād rudro yakṣaḥ sureśvaraḥ
vidyate hi giriśreṣṭhe tridaśānāṃ samāgamaḥ
na hi madbāṇajālānām utsr̥ṣṭānāṃ sahasraśaḥ
śakto 'nyaḥ sahituṃ vegam r̥te devaṃ pinākinam
devo vā yadi vā yakṣo rudrād anyo vyavasthitaḥ
aham enaṃ śarais tīkṣṇair nayāmi yamasādanam.

Similarly, at MBh 3.147.22, Bhima asks Hanuman, whose tail he is unable to lift: *siddho vā yadi vā devo gandharvo vātha guhyakaḥ, pr̥ṣṭaḥ san kāmayā brūhi kas tvaṃ vānararūpadhr̥k* (note that *pr̥ṣṭaḥ san* parallels *proṭhu ṣamaṇa* of the Gāndhārī and *puṭṭho samāno* of the Pali). At 3.177.4, Yudhisthira asks the snake in whose coils Bhima is caught: *devo vā yadi vā daitya urago vā bhavān yadi, satyaṃ sarpa vaco brūhi pr̥cchati tvāṃ yudhiṣṭhiraḥ.* And at 5.119.15c–16, the assembly of kings ask Yayāti, who has suddenly descended from heaven into their midst: *ko bhavān kasya vā bandhur deśasya nagarasya vā, yakṣo vāpy atha vā devo gandharvo rākṣaso 'pi vā, na hi mānuṣarūpo 'si ko vārthaḥ kāṅkṣitas tvayā.*

In the P Mahāparinibbāna-suttanta the Buddha describes how, when he preached to various assemblies, their thoughts were *ko nu kho ayaṃ bhāsati devo vā manusso vā ti.* And when he disappeared, the thought was *ko nu kho ayaṃ antarahito devo vā manusso vā ti* (DN II 109–10; the Skt. parallel reads *antarhi(*tasya) me na jānanti ka eṣa antarhito devo vā manuṣyo vā,* MPS § 23.5). At Jā VI 76 the bodhisatta is seen by a king who thinks: . . . *devo ce ākāse uppatissati. nāgo ce bhūmiyaṃ pavekkhati* (the B^{e} reads *devo ce bhavissati ākāsaṃ uppatissati. nāgo ce bhūmiyaṃ pavissati*). Similarly, the P canon also contains several verse examples. As mentioned in the introduction to the discussion of this sūtra, in the Candanamāliyatthera-apadāna, Candana, after inquiring about the Buddha's name and clan, asks him:[76]

devatā nu 'si gandhabbo uda sakko purindado
ko vā tvaṃ kassa vā putto mahābrahmā idhāgato
vorocesi disā sabbā udayaṃ suriyo yathā

---

[75] I am indebted to John Smith of Cambridge University for the following examples from the MBh.

[76] Further parallel examples are the following. At Jā V 260 (cf. Jā VI 13; Vv 1210) a girl, on seeing Prince Dīghāvu, asks him: *devatā nu 'si gandhabbo ādu sakko purindado, ko vā tvaṃ kassa vā putto kathaṃ jānemu taṃ mayaṃ.* At Jā V 317 King Manoja asks Sonananda, a previous incarnation of the Buddha: *devatā nu 'si gandhabbo adu sakko purindado, manussabhūto iddhimā kathaṃ jānemu taṃ mayan ti.* At Jā VI 98 Salomahaṭṭha asks Sakka: *devatā nu 'si gandhabbo ādu sakko purindado, na ca me tādiso vaṇṇo diṭṭho vā yadivā suto.* At Vv 971 a deva is asked (cf. Pv 673, where a king asks a peta): *devatā nu 'si gandhabbo ādu sakko purindado, ajānantā taṃ pucchāma kathaṃ jānemu taṃ mayan.* Cf. also Pv 266, 268; Cp-a 118.8–9.

sahassarāni cakkāni pāde dissanti mārisa
ko va tvaṃ kassa vā putto kathaṃ jānemu taṃ mayaṃ. (Ap 423–4)

Two verses in the Gilgit version of the AG-Skt. (vv. 173–4; Bechert 1961: 143) provide yet another possible example: *devo manuṣyo ya[kṣo] (*vā), + + tvaṃ brūhi me laghu. tava putro 'ham asmy amba, mānuṣo 'smi na rākṣasaḥ.*[77] In Lal 240.6–7 the people of Rājagṛha, who are amazed on seeing the Buddha, think: *kiṃ svid ayaṃ brahmā bhaviṣyati śakro devānām indro 'ho svid vaiśravaṇo 'ho svit kiṃcid giridaivataṃ.* A passage in the Chinese EĀ translated by Bareau (1999: 43–4) relates that King Śuddhodana, on seeing the monk Udaya flying through the air, utters the words: "Who is this? A man or a non-human [spirit] (*amanuṣya*)? A god or a demon? A Yakṣa or a Rakṣasa? A god or a Nāga? A demon or a spirit?" He then asks Udaya, "Are you a man?" addressing him with the verse "Are you a god? Are you a demon? Or else a Gandharva?" The Chinese Fo ben xing ji jing (T no. 190), translated by Beal (1875) as *The Romantic Legend of Sākya Buddha,* contains a passage in which some sages, while flying through the air, see Prince Siddhartha seated "underneath a tree, sitting with his legs crossed, his whole person so bright with glory that they could with difficulty behold him. Then these Rishis began to consider—'Who can this be?' 'Is it Brahma . . . Krishna Deva . . . Sākra [*sic*] . . . Vaisravana . . . Chandradeva . . . Sūrya Deva—or is it some Chakravartin Rāja?—or is it possibly that this is the person of a Buddha born into the world?'" (Beal 1875: 75).[78] Swearer relates an episode in the Thai *Chronicle of the Haripuñjaya Relic* where some villagers, on seeing the Buddha, were "amazed by his beauty and inquired whether he was a *deva, nāga* king, Indra or Brahma" (1976: 7).[79]

There are undoubtedly many more examples in Indian literature (in the widest sense), and the motif is certainly worthy of further research, but these examples suffice to illustrate the point that such questions are asked by someone, or such thoughts occur to someone, as the result of seeing a person whose appearance is amazing or who is doing something extraordinary, and that the questions are not concerned with the future but rather with the present status of the person. In fact, in all of the examples quoted above, only our Dhoṇa-sutra passage, the B^{e} of the Jā VI 76 passage, the Lal 240 passage, and the MBh 3.52.16 example employ the future tense of the verb √*bhū,* and it is of interest that the MBh 3.40.30–2 example quoted above employs the optative: *ko 'yaṃ devo bhavet,* etc.

Finally, one further piece of internal evidence within the narrative in the P sutta supports this interpretation. That is, when Doṇa sees the Buddha's footprints, he thinks: *acchariyaṃ vata bho abbhutaṃ vata bho na vat' imāni manussabhūtassa padāni bhavissantī ti* (AN II 37.29–30), which is lacking in the G sūtra. Here clearly the future tense cannot refer to a future state but is used to express surprise or wonder.

Turning now to the Chinese translations of the Dhoṇa-sutra and the form of the questions asked by the brahman, in the EĀ translation (T 2 no. 125 p. 717c22–9), the brahman,

---

77 Thanks are due to Richard Salomon for this reference.

78 I am indebted to Timothy Lenz for this reference.

79 This reference was brought to my attention by Richard Salomon.

on seeing the Buddha's footprints, wonders whether they could belong to a (1) *deva* 天, (2) *nāga* 龍, (3) *yakṣa* 鬼神, (4) *gandharva* 乾沓和, (5) *asura* 阿須倫, (6) human 人, (7) nonhuman 非人, or (8) my ancestor Brahmā 先祖梵天. When he sees the Buddha, however, he asks only five of these questions: Is he a (1) *deva,* (2) *gandharva,* (3) *nāga,* (4) *yakṣa,* or (5) Brahmā 祖父? In the first SĀ translation (T 2 no. 99 p. 28a29–b8), the brahman asks the Buddha ten questions: Is the Buddha a (1) *deva* 天, (2) *nāga* 龍, (3) *yakṣa* 夜叉, (4) *gandharva* 乾闥婆, (5) *asura* 阿修羅, (6) *garuḍa* 迦樓羅, (7) *kiṃnara* 緊那羅, (8) *mahoraga* 摩睺羅伽, (9) human 人, or (10) nonhuman 非人? In the Buddha's verse response the list is (1) *deva,* (2) *nāga,* (3) *gandharva,* (4) *kiṃnara,* (5) *yakṣa,* (6) *asura,* (7) *mahoraga,* (8) human, and (9) nonhuman. In the second SĀ translation (T 2 no. 100 p. 467b5–13), the brahman asks eight questions: Is the Buddha a (1) *deva* 天, (2) *asura* 阿修羅, (3) *nāga* 龍, (4) *gandharva* 揵闥婆, (5) *yakṣa* 夜叉, (6) *kiṃnara* 緊那羅, (7) *mahoraga* 摩睺羅伽, or (8) human 人? In the repetition of these questions that follows, the order of *asura* and *nāga* is reversed, while in the Buddha's verse response the order is (1) *deva,* (2) *nāga,* (3) *asura,* (4) *kiṃnara,* (5) *mahoraga,* (6) *gandharva,* (7) *yakṣa,* and (8) human.

Thus none of the Chinese translations corresponds to the G and P texts, which list only four types of beings: *deva, ghadharva/gandhabba, yakṣa/yakkha,* and *maṇośa/manussa*. Rather, all preserve more expanded lists, with five to ten elements. This is of course significant, because it is the four questions that qualify the P Doṇa-sutta, and perhaps also the G Dhoṇa-sutra, for inclusion in a Section of Fours in the AN/EĀs. Further, it is also noteworthy that such expanded lists are generally rare in P sutta texts; one of the examples is *devā manussā asurā nāgā gandhabbā* (DN III 148.19–20), which is presented in verse as *deva-manussāsura-sakka-rakkhasā, gandhabba-nāgā vihagā catuppadā* (DN III 149.16–7).[80] Such lists are more commonly encountered in later canonical texts such as the Ap and Bv and in the commentaries; examples are *devatā nāga-gandhabba-rakkhasā, kumbhaṇḍā dānavā garuḷā* (Ap 19.15–6); *sadeva-gandhabba-manussa-rakkhasā, nāgā supaṇṇā athavāpi kinnarā* (Bv I 20); and *nāgā supaṇṇā gandhabbā asurā yakkhā mahārājāno tāvatiṃsādayo devā mahābrahmā ti* (Ps I 16.6–8; Spk II 4.7–8).[81] Similarly and not surprisingly, such expanded lists are quite common in Buddhist Skt. texts and particularly Mahāyāna texts. For example, the avadānas of the Avś all begin with *buddho bhagavān satkṛto gurukṛto mānitaḥ pūjito . . . devair nāgair yakṣair asurair garuḍaiḥ kinnarair mahoragair* (I 1.5–6, 8.2–3, 13.2–3, etc.), while in the Lal we find such compounds as *nāga-yakṣa-gandharvāsura-garuḍa-kinnara-mahoraga-rākṣasa-preta-bhūta-kumbhāṇḍa-pārṣada-gaṇapati-piśāca* (249.16–7).[82] A G version of

---

[80] Further examples of the list *devā manussā asurā nāgā gandhabbā* are DN II 269, 276, III 153, 169.

[81] Further examples are *devā . . . nāgā . . . garuḷā . . . kumbhaṇḍā . . . yakkhā . . . gandhabbā . . .* (Ap 71–2, quoted at Th-a II 56); *nāgo supaṇṇo devo māro brahmā* (Mp IV 36.8); *nāgā supaṇṇā yakkhā asurā devā brahmāṇo ti* (Sv II 656.20); *manussa-deva-nāga-garuḷa-kumbhaṇḍa-yakkha-gandhabba* (Th-a II 56.18–9).

[82] See also the list at Mvy 3215–25. Cf. */// (*a)[s]ura-garuḍa-kinnara-mahoragā* (MPS, ms. no. 102.5); *nara-devāsura-yakṣa-rākṣasa* (MSV I 12.3). Further references are found in BHSD, s.v. *kumbhāṇḍa*. See also SHT III 842 Bl.10.

such a list is found in the Senavarma inscription (l. 13b; Salomon 1986: 266): *deve va maṇuśe va yakṣe va ṇage va suvaṇi va gadharve va kuvhaḍe va.*

On receiving a negative reply to each of his questions, Dhoṇa then repeats his questions and the Buddha's responses in the form of a statement, the fourth section of which is *maṇośu bhu bhaviśasi id(*i) proṭhu samaṇa e(*ma vade)si ṇaho bramaṇa maṇośu bhaviśe* (ll. 14–5), corresponding to the P *manusso no bhavaṃ bhavissatī ti iti puṭṭho samāno na kho ahaṃ brāhmaṇa manusso bhavissāmī ti vadesi* (AN II 38.21–3). As noted earlier, I take *idi* in the Gāndhārī to correspond to the *iti* of the P phrase *iti puṭṭho samāno,* "being asked thus." Also worthy of note is that in the Pali *vadesi* occurs after the quote, whereas in the G text *ema vadesi,* which corresponds to a P *evaṃ vadesi,* occurs before it. Here *vadesi* of both the Gāndhārī and Pali could be either the second-person singular present or preterite. Thus, a literal translation of the Pali (taking *vadesi* as a present form rather than preterite) would be "being asked thus, 'Would the venerable sir be a human?' you say, 'Brahman, I would not be a human,'" in contrast to the G "being asked thus, 'Venerable sir, would you be a human?' you say this, 'Brahman, I would not be a human.'" This same structure or format is encountered in the P canon a number of times in the AN, MN, and SN, but the reading is the same in all instances: [quote] *ti iti puṭṭho samāno* [quote] *ti vadesi.*[83]

Concluding his statement, Dhoṇa then asks the Buddha *ku re bhu bhaviśasi* (l. 15), "Who, then, venerable sir, would you be?" The corresponding P is *atha kho ko carahi bhavaṃ bhavissatī ti* (AN II 38.23–4), "then who, pray, would the venerable sir be?" Here the G lacks the introductory indeclinables *atha kho* of the Pali (the E^e records the v.l. *atha ko* in the Burmese mss. B.K., which is the reading found in B^e and S^e) and has *re* rather than P *carahi* (the Skt. equivalent of which is *tarhi*). In canonical P the indeclinable *re* and the uncontracted form *are* are fairly common, mostly occurring in exclamations or commands,[84] but in only two instances is this word constructed with the interrogative pronoun: *ko n'eva re m'ayaṃ dāsiputto . . . dhītaraṃ yācati* (DN I 96.8–9) and *ko re tuvaṃ hohisi adakkhiṇeyyo ti* (Jā IV 380.4; quoted at Ps III 79.7, Pj II 189.14, and Cp-a 156.14). In contrast, the expression *atha ko carahi* is far more frequent.[85] Although there are canonical examples, the indeclinables *re* and *are* are far more com-

---

[83] See AN II 161–3, IV 383–6, V 197; MN I 147, 486–7, III 9–11; SN II 20, 22–3, III 239, IV 378, 385, 402. The exception is MN II 212, where the reading in the E^e, B^e, and S^e is [quote] *ti puṭṭho samāno* rather than [quote] *ti iti puṭṭho samāno.*

[84] E.g., *aho vata re amhākaṃ paṇḍitaka, aho vata re amhākaṃ bahussutaka, aho vata re amhākaṃ tevijjaka* (DN I 107.18–20); *no vata re kiñci pāpi dāsi divā uṭṭhāsī ti* (MN I 125.19–20); *aho vatā re aham eva dajjaṃ* (Pv 302a); *gila re gila pāpadhuttaka* (DN II 349.6); *cara pi re mallike vinassā ti* (MN II 108.1–2). *Re* is very common in the Kv in the expressions *tena vata re vattabbe* and *no ca vata re vattabbe* (Kv 1, etc.).

[85] Occurrences are *atha ko carahi devamanussaloke rato mano kassapa brūhi me tan ti* (Vin I 36.24–5); *atha ko carahi uposathaṃ sakkarissati* (Vin I 105.28–9); *atha ko carahi upaṭṭhahissati* (Vin I 302.18–9); *atha ko carahi amhākaṃ dassati* (Vin III 265.12–3; cf. IV 155–6); *atha ko carahi me attā ti* (SN III 133.7, 134.8); *atha ko carahi jānāti* (Sn 990a); *atha ko carahi devamanussaloke, atāri jātiñ ca jarañ ca mārisa* (Sn 1047, 1081).

mon in noncanonical literature (as a search on the P CD-ROMs will reveal; see also CPD, s.v. *are*).

budho mi b[r]amaṇa budho [mi] ///: In the P version the Buddha replies to Doṇa's question by stating that the *āsava*s by which he would be a god, etc., had been cut off. As already noted, the G version lacks a parallel to this long prose passage. The Buddha's prose response in the Pali concludes with the statement *buddho ti maṃ brāhmaṇa dhārehī ti,* "know me, Brahman, as the Enlightened One" (AN II 39.3). In both versions the Buddha then utters some verses, the concluding pāda of which is *taśpi budho mi bramaṇa* (ll. 19 and 20) in the Gāndhārī and *tasmā buddho 'smi brāhmaṇā ti* in the Pali (AN II 39.8–9), a translation of both being "therefore, Brahman, I am the Enlightened One."[86]

The G version of the Buddha's prose response to Dhoṇa's question, *budho mi b[r]amaṇa budho [mi] ///*, which seems to differ from the Pali, may be incomplete. Line 15 currently contains twenty-eight akṣaras. One or two akṣaras (*va* or *vade* of *vadesi*) are missing from the beginning of line 15, which would bring the akṣara count for the line up to twenty-nine or thirty. Given that a line may contain up to thirty-eight or thirty-nine akṣaras, up to ten akṣaras may be missing from the end of line 15, though the number is likely to be less (l. 14 had thirty-four akṣaras; l. 16 had thirty-six) and the alignment of the akṣaras on the reconstructed manuscript suggests about five. If my reconstruction of the phrase that occurs on line 16 is correct (see below), then two akṣaras belonging to that phrase must have occurred at the end of line 15 and may have been preceded by a punctuation mark. It is therefore possible that *budho mi bramaṇa budho mi* of the Gāndhārī may be the Buddha's complete response. The G version of the Buddha's response can be interpreted in two ways. The first is to take *mi* as the first-person singular present of the verb √*as,* equivalent to P *'smi* (Skt. *asmi*), as in the following pāda, *taśpi budho mi bramaṇa,* which is identical to *tasmā buddho 'smi brāhmaṇā ti* of the Pali. If complete, the Buddha's statement *budho mi bramaṇa budho mi* would then mean "Brahman, I am the Enlightened One. I am the Enlightened One." Given that in P canonical sutta texts symmetry is preferred, it is also possible that the complete response was *budho mi bramaṇa budho mi (*bramaṇa)*, "Brahman, I am the Enlightened One. Brahman, I am the Enlightened One." But the example of *bhu ghodama abhikantu* (l. 21), where the P parallel has *abhikkantaṃ bho gotama abhikkantaṃ bho gotama* (see below), suggests that this may not have been a characteristic of these G texts (see pp. 35–6).

A less likely interpretation is to take the G *budho mi bramaṇa budho mi* as parallel to the P *buddho ti maṃ brāhmaṇa dhārehī ti,* but with repetition. In this case the G equivalent of the P *dhārehi* (possibly **dharehi*) would have occurred after the second *mi,* and *mi* would in both cases be the accusative singular of the first-person pronoun, equivalent to P *maṃ* (see §§ 6.2.1 and 5.1.6). The reconstruction would then be *budho mi bramaṇa budho mi (*dharehi),* "(*know) me, Brahman, as the Enlightened One, [know me] as the Enlightened One."

---

[86] Rhys Davids (1933: vi) comments on these verses in her introduction to Woodward's translation of AN II, and in her introduction to Hare's translation of AN III (Rhys Davids 1934: vi–viii) she argues that the orginal reading was *suddha* rather than *buddha* both here and in the following verse, and that the change occurred due to the appearance of *buddha* in the previous sutta.

Lines 15–6: The introduction to the Buddha's verses

Edition:

|24a+25hh |24a |25a |25a+25b |25b+24e+25t |25b+24e

[16]*m=u bhayavadu ida vadita sugha[du] hasavaro idam=a[va]ï ś[astu ◦]*

Reconstruction:

[15]*(*ida)*[16]*m u bhayavadu ida vadita sughadu hasavaro idam avaï śastu ◦*

Translation:

[15–6] The Bhagavat said (*this). Having said this, the Sugata, the Teacher, further said this.

Fragment 25t, which contains only the remnant of a *u* diacritic, overlies the middle of the vertical stroke of *va* in *a[va]ï,* thus confusing the reading. The *u* diacritic of fragment 25t has been tentatively taken to be the bottom of *st* (making the reading *ś[astu]*), in part because of the proximity of fragment 25t to the *st* akṣara in the original frame. It could also belong to *yakṣ(*u)* in line 13. The full length of fragment 25t can be seen on the verso of the frame. If my alignment of the fragments is correct, the first remnant of ink at the top of fragment 24e is the bottom of *st.* The second remnant on fragment 24e is thus taken to be the bottom of the following punctuation mark (see p. 189). Although we would expect the G equivalent of nominative singular P *satthā*/Skt. *śāstā* to be *śasta* rather than *śastu* (just as the nom. sg. f. ending in Gāndhārī is normally *-a;* see § 6.1.2 and Salomon 2000: § 7.1.2), in the AG-G (l. 64) the nominative singular is *śaste* and the accusative singular is *śastu.*

Although not found in the printed editions of the P Doṇa-sutta, this phrase is commonly encountered elsewhere in the P canon, including the first sutta of the Catukkanipāta of the AN (II 1.25–6):[87] *idam avoca bhagavā idaṃ vatvā sugato athāparaṃ etad avoca satthā.* Some occurrences of this phrase in the PTS editions read *vatvāna* instead of *vatvā* or have *vatvāna* as a v.l.[88]

Occurrences in Sanskrit are not particularly frequent. An example from the Dharmaskandha (Dhsk) reads *idam avocad bhagavān idam uktvā sugato hy athāparam etad*

---

[87] This phrase is found in the AN at I 63, II 1, III 34, IV 106, V 173. In addition to these occurrences, the B^e includes the phrase before the verses at AN IV 26 (E^e records this as the reading in its Burmese manuscripts). This formula is also found in the MN, SN, and Sn and once in the Cullavagga of the Vin. All occurrences in the P canon can be found by searching the CD-ROMs for combinations of key words. In the E^e of P texts the reading alternates between *athāparaṃ* and *athāparam.* Some occurrences are abbreviated.

[88] E.g., throughout vol. I of the SN (I 69, 152, 189, 220). Similarly, a CPD listing of this formula (s.v. *aparaṃ*) reads *vatvāna.* The B^e reads *vatvāna* in all occurrences except those corresponding to MN I 227 and SN V 217, where the reading is *vatvā.* SN II 158, III 83, and V 217 read *idaṃ vatvā ca* (as do the vv.ll. to SN II 185, V 6; AN IV 106, V 173; Sn pp. 140, 148). This reading is found once in the B^e (corresponding to SN V 217). SN IV 127 reads *athāparam pi.*

uvāca śāstā (17 v2).[89] The Saddharmapuṇḍarīka-sūtra (SP) occurrences (203.3, 286.11, 357.9) have *vaditvā* instead of *uktvā*. Most Skt. occurrences read *sugato hy athāparam*. The exception is the Central Asian manuscripts of the SP (Toda 1983) where the reading is (with some minor variation) *sugato 'thāparam* (Kashgar ms. 194 a6, 273 a3, 344 a5; Farhād-Bēg ms. 20 b8), a variant reading recorded in the Kern and Nanjio edition for SP 203.3. Finally, the reading in the Central Asian manuscripts of the SP is (with some minor variation) *idam avocac chāstā* (Kashgar ms. 194 a6–7, 273 a3, 344 a5; Farhād-Bēg ms. 20 b8–21 a1) rather than *etad uvāca śāstā*.

A portion of a second G version of this phrase has recently been identified on a Kharoṣṭhī fragment of a G version of the Mahāparinirvāṇa-sūtra (Allon and Salomon 2000). It reads (additional fragment, r3) *idam=avaci bhagava idaṃ vaditva ? ///*. From the two incomplete G versions, we can reconstruct the following complete G forms of the phrase—the first following the orthography of our BL manuscript, the second following the more Sanskritic orthography and morphology of the G Mahāparinirvāṇa-sūtra fragment:

1. *(*ida)m u bhayavadu ida vadita sughadu hasavaro idam avaï śastu* (or *śasta*)
2. *idam avaci bhagava idaṃ vaditva (*sugato athaparaṃ idam avaci śasta)*

m=u bhayavadu: This clearly corresponds to *idam avaci bhagava* of the G Mahāparinirvāṇa-sūtra version and to P *idam avoca bhagavā* and Skt. *idam avocad bhagavān*. On first appearances *u* for G *avaci,* P *avoca,* and Skt. *avocad* seems unlikely. However, the same expression occurs in the formula that concludes the Budhabayaṇa-sutra (ll. 36–7): *idam=u atamaṇa te bhi[kh.] /// /// + + + ? ///* [37] *[a]bhiṇadi,* which corresponds to the P *idam avoca bhagavā. attamanā te bhikkhū bhagavato bhāsitaṃ abhinandun ti* (e.g., AN I 276.23–6). For reasons presented below in my commentary on the phrase in lines 36–7, the initial section of this example should be emended to *idam=u <*bhayavadu>*. Further G versions of this phrase, occurring as part of the formula that concludes sūtras, are found in the Senior manuscripts. These were mentioned previously in the commentary on *eghad uya, eghad oya* (l. 9) = P *etad avoca,* and further details are given in the commentary on lines 25–6 below. The G versions are *id́am=oyi bhayava, id́am=eyi bhayava, id́am=aya bhayava,* and *id́a bhayava* (the last may represent a scribal error). Parallel examples with the contraction of the verbal element in such fixed locutions consisting of a demonstrative pronoun (*etad* or *idam*) followed by a preterite form of the verb √*vac* were mentioned in the commentary on *eghad uya, eghad oya* (l. 9). The forms of the verb recorded to date in Gāndhārī are *avaci, avaï, avaya, avayi,*[90] *oyi, eyi, aya, uya, oya,* and finally *u* of the example under discussion. It thus appears that *u* in

---

[89] Further examples are SP 203.3, 286.11, 357.9 and Avś I 174.1, 194.2. I have been able to find only two other occurrences in the Central Asian (Turfan) material: SHT V 1171 R7–8; cf. VI 1458 R8 n. 9 (a Mahāyāna comm.). The phrase does not seem to occur in the MSV, Divy, Lal, or Mvu, although examples may have escaped me.

[90] The verbal elements in *avaya* and *avayi* could be *aya* and *ayi;* i.e., the reading could be *ed́a-v-aya* and *ed́a-v-ayi* with *-v-* as a sandhi consonant (see p. 165).

idam u is yet a further contraction of the *uya/oya* form, which is derived from the thematic aorist *avaca* (see pp. 164–5), with the dropping of the final syllable (see § 5.5).

vadita: The reading in the G Mahāparinirvāṇa-sūtra version of this formula (quoted above) is *vaditva*. Being an absolutive of √*vad,* the G form thus parallels the SP version, which reads *vaditvā* and contrasts with *vatvā* and *vatvāna* of the P version and *uktvā* of most Skt. versions (see above for references), which are absolutives of √*vac*.

hasavaro: The Pali has *athāparaṃ*. Most Skt. examples have *hy athāparam.* The phonetic changes *-th-* > *-s-*, *-p-* > *-v-*, and *-o* for *-aṃ* are regular in Gāndhārī, but the initial *h-* is of interest, particularly in light of Skt. *hy athāparam.* As in *sugato hy athāparaṃ* of the Skt. version of the phrase under discussion, Buddhist Skt. texts commonly employ *hy* to avoid hiatus or sandhi, where the MIA versions have no problem with the hiatus. In these cases the usual causal or emphatic meanings of the word are absent (see MW, s.v. *hi*). The Uv, for example, contains numerous examples: *ārāt te hy āsravakṣayāt* (Uv IV.19f), where the G has *ara te asavakṣa(*ya)* (Dhp-G^K 339f) and P has *ārā so āsavakkhayā* (Dhp 253d); *praśaṃsanti, hy anuyujya* (Uv XXIX.47a–b), where the G has *praśaj̄adi, aṇuïja* (Dhp-G^K 241a–b) and P has *pasaṃsanti, anuvicca* (Dhp 229a–b); *apāraṃ, hy urago* (Uv XXXII.80c–d, etc.), G *orupara, urako* (Dhp-G^K 82c–d, etc.); compare G *oraparo, uragha* (Dhp-G^L 11c–d, etc.) and P *oraparaṃ, urago* (Sn 1b–c, etc.). A similar phenomenon is seen in *pañca, tv anighaś* (Uv XXXII.76a–b), where the G has *paca, [aṇi] ///* (Dhp-G^L 13a–b), and P has *pañca, anigho* (Sn 17a–b).

The *h-* in *hasavaro* could represent a similar use of *hi* as suggested by the Sanskrit, although we might expect the sandhi form **hisavaro* on the basis of *hisa* (*hi asya*) in Dhp-G^K 233d, 234d; but compare *hi aviaṇada* (Dhp-G^K 256a), where hiatus remains. Alternatively, in view of examples in Pali and Aśokan Prakrit, *h* could be taken as a sandhi consonant or as an "easternism." Geiger (1994: § 73.7) expresses doubt as to whether the *h* in such P forms as *mā-h-evaṃ* and *na-h-eva* should be understood as a sandhi consonant but leaves the question open. Norman (1992b: 85 = CP, vol. V, p. 79; n. 5 to Geiger 1994: § 73.7) entertains the possibility that these and other such examples in Pali represent *hi,* especially when in enclitic position, but prefers to interpret these as eastern forms, citing as evidence Aśokan Pkt. *hida, heḍisa/hedisa, heta, hemeva, hevaṃ,* and *hesā,* which are frequent in eastern versions of the inscriptions. Von Hinüber's statement (1986: § 166) that *h-* in these Aśokan examples as well as in P *hetaṃ, hevaṃ,* and *halaṃ* is *"emphatisches"* (his quotes) needs further clarification.

Several parallel examples are encountered in Gāndhārī. In the Niya documents (Boyer, Rapson, and Senart 1920–9) we find *heḍi,* possibly for *eḍā* "sheep"; *hadehi,* which the editor takes as a scribal error for the more regular *adehi* (Skt. *ataḥ*), "from here";[91] and *huda* for *uta* (ind.). Thomas (Boyer, Rapson, and Senart 1920–9: index, s.v. *harga*) interpreted *harga* to represent *argha,* but this is a less likely case, considering Burrow's (1937: index, s.v. *harga*) provisional Iranian etymology for this word. Among the Kharoṣṭhī inscriptions edited by Konow (1929, see index, s.v.) we find *hida* for *iha,* "here" (cf. P *idha*). Further examples appear in the Senior manuscripts: *himaspi* (5 r16) =

[91] For *hadehi* and *heḍi,* see Burrow 1937: § 28.

P *imasmiṃ; hirdhaa[da](*ṇa)* (5 v11) and *hirdha[a]padaṇa* (5 v15) = P *iddhipādānaṃ; hiṣivadaṇa* (7 r7) = P *isipatane* (see p. 227); and *hidriaṇa* (5 v11) and *idriaṇa* (5 v16) = P *indriyānaṃ*.

Apart from *harga* in the Niya documents, which may not be an example of this phenomenon, and *heḍ́i* = Skt. *eḍā* (?) also in the Niya documents, in all of the G examples listed here prothetic *h* occurs in words with initial short vowel followed by either a dental stop or the labial nasal *m,* though this may only be coincidental. In the case of *hasavaro* of our text, *-s-* is the reflex of an original dental stop (*-th-*), while in *hidriaṇa* = P *indriyānaṃ* in the Senior manuscripts, we may be dealing with a nasal plus dental stop.

Given that such forms are sporadic in Gāndhārī, and examples of the equivalents of such Skt. words as *atha* and *athāparam* with initial *h-* are generally lacking in the G documents studied to date, it is unlikely that *h-* in *hasavaro* represents a sandhi consonant, for we would have expected many more examples of this phenomenon if it were.[92] And although it remains possible that eastern forms were preserved in G Buddhist manuscripts, probably as a secondary borrowing from noneastern exemplars, it is also unlikely that *hasavaro* and the other G examples quoted here are "easternisms," for, apart from the one example of *hida,* the equivalents of such eastern forms as *hedisa, heta, hevaṃ,* and *hesā* of Aśokan Pkt. are absent in Gāndhārī to date. Further, although *hasavaro* could represent Skt. *hy athāparam* (with assimilation of *y* to the preceding consonant; Burrow 1937: § 41), this is unlikely in light of the above G examples. Rather, the *h-* in *hasavaro* most likely is another example of the sporadic, and as yet to be fully understood, appearance of prothetic *h-* in Gāndhārī.

idam=a[va]ï: The same phrase (pronoun plus verb) appears at the beginning of this formula: *(*ida)m u* in our manuscript (showing alternative development of the verb) and *idam avaci* in the G Mahāparinirvāṇa-sūtra version (quoted above). This contrasts with the P version, where the pronouns in the first and second occurrences differ: *idam avoca . . . etad avoca*. In the Skt. version a different pronoun and a different tense of the same verb are used: *idam avocad . . . etad uvāca*. The exceptions are the Central Asian manuscripts of the SP, which, as noted above, read *idam avocad . . . idam avocac chāstā* (Kashgar ms. 273 a2–3, 344 a4–5; Farhād-Bēg ms. 20 b8–21 a1; Kashgar ms. 194 a6 has . . . *tad uvoca(c)*).

G *avaï, avaci,* is the preterite third-person singular of √*vac*. It is also attested once in the Niya documents in the phrase *yo aṭha varna abhani muni sa͚tamasya so sahasrākṣa avaci* (Boyer, Rapson, and Senart 1920–9: no. 511, rev. 3).[93] Although such a form does not appear to be attested in other MIA dialects, both *avaci* and *avacī* are found in BHS (see BHSG, § 32.24). Despite their similarity to the Skt. passive aorist *avāci,* which is acknowledged by Edgerton as a possible source (BHSG, § 32.22), it is preferable to follow Edgerton (BHSG, § 32.24) in seeing BHS *avaci/avacī* and G *avaï/avaci* as adaptations of the thematic aorist *avaca* (common in both BHS and Pali) to the *i/ī* aorists (or, perhaps better, blends of the thematic aorist with the *i/ī* aorists). An alternative but less

---

[92] Examples of *h* used as a sandhi consonant in internal position are found in this manuscript: *sahasa-h-ara* (l. 4) = P *sahassārāni* and *abhiñehi* (l. 19) = Skt. *abhijñeyam*.

[93] Not translated by Burrow (1940) due to the fragmentary state of this side of the document.

convincing explanation, at least for the G form, would be to see the final *-i* as a development of *-a* > *-i/e* in a palatal environment, although this phenomenon does not seem to be attested in such a position with verbs (see § 5.1.1; Brough 1962: § 22a).

As illustrated by the G, P, and Skt. forms of this phrase, variations in the form of the verb (and even the root) for "speak" are quite common in Buddhist texts. Even within the P tradition itself, *avaca* is commonly encountered as an alternative for *avoca* in both canonical and commentarial texts,[94] and at least one P commentarial passage provides an example of its use in a phrase similar to that under discussion: *idaṃ āvuso thero avaca. idañ ca pana vatvā idaṃ suttaṃ āhari* (Sv II 514.31–2). Similar variations are also encountered in the common *ye dhammā* formula, but in this case the contrast is between the form of the verb found in canonical texts and that found in inscriptions (and even colophons). Thus, according to Skilling (1999: 173, 178 ff.), in contrast to *āha* in the texts of the Theravādins, Lokottaravādins, and Central Asian Sarvāstivādins, *avaca* is encountered in a number of "hybrid Pali" inscriptions from South and Southeast Asia, *hy avadat* is found in Indian inscriptions in Sanskrit as well as in the colophons of Indian Pāla period manuscripts and Pāla artifacts from Thailand, and *uvāca* (as well as *avadat*) is encountered in an inscription on a gold plate from Java.

Several authors have noted that this prose stock phrase, or at least the P and Skt. versions of it, seems to have some sort of metrical pattern. The CPD (s.v. *aparaṃ*) notes that the *athāparaṃ etad avoca satthā* portion of this phrase has a ⏑ – ⏑ – – ⏑ ⏑ – ⏑ – – pattern (i.e., it represents a triṣṭubh verse) and that the preceding unit, *idaṃ vatvāna sugato,* represents a śloka pāda (⏑ – – – ⏑ ⏑ ⏑ –). Oldenberg (1917: 51–2) also hinted at the verselike nature of this phrase, and Speyer, referring to the Skt. version of the phrase in his edition of the Avś (I 174, n. 1), suggested that it seems to represent a "mutilated fragment of some triṣṭubh." However, as I have indicated elsewhere (Allon 1997: 248), the meter of the P phrase (*idam avoca bhagavā idaṃ vatvā sugato athāparaṃ etad avoca satthā*) seems rather to be the veḍha, a type of rhythmical prose, or at least a loose variety of it: ⏓ ⏓ | ⏑ – ⏑ | ⏑ ⏑ – | ⏓ – | – – | ⏑ ⏑ – | ⏑ – ⏑ | ⏓ – ⏑ | ⏑ – ⏑ | – – |. In this case the initial short *i* of *idaṃ* is taken as long, illustrating a not uncommon license (see Warder 1967: 81 = § 111). It is interesting to note that here the v.l. *vatvāna* would be problematic in the P version.

Surprisingly for a Skt. translation, the Skt. version, *idam avocad bhagavān idam uktvā sugato hy athāparam etad uvāca śāstā,* would also scan: ⏓ ⏑ ⏑ | – – | ⏑ ⏑ – | ⏓ ⏓ | – – | ⏑ ⏑ – | ⏑ – ⏑ | ⏓ – ⏑ | ⏑ – ⏑ | – – |, with the SP's reading *idaṃ vaditvā* being scanned as ⏓ – ⏑ | – – |.

Reading the metrical pattern of the G version is more problematic due to the absence of vowel length indication and due to our lack of understanding of G metrics. The G Mahāparinirvāṇa-sūtra version, which adopts the reading *bhagava,* probably scans if we follow the model of the P and Skt. versions. The contracted *u* and the extended *bhayavadu* in our manuscript may present problems.

---

[94] Occurrences of *avaca* can be found by searching the P CD-ROMs.

It was noted earlier that this important phrase is absent in the P parallel of the Doṇa-sutta. This would at first seem surprising considering that this metrical prose phrase seems to have had the important function in Buddhist texts of connecting the (nonmetrical) prose speech of the Buddha with the following verses uttered by him, which usually summarize the ideas of the prose passage. However, as already noted, this stock phrase is so used in the first sutta of this Catukka-nipāta collection. It would appear then that the absence of this phrase from subsequent suttas in the Catukka-nipāta that end with verses uttered by the Buddha, including sutta 36, the Doṇa-sutta, is merely due to abbreviation. In other words, this phrase would have been included when these mixed prose-verse suttas of the AN were recited, just as the full nidānas would have been added (see text commentary to ll. 37–9). This is supported by examples of AN suttas that have parallels in other nikāyas. For example, this formula is lacking in the E[e], B[e], and S[e] of AN sutta 4.48 (II 51), but it is included in the E[e] of the parallel at SN II 280.

Lines 16–20: The Buddha's verses

Edition:

| 24e | D6r | 24e+ D6r | D6r | 25hh+ 24a | 24a | 24a+25u+25a | 25k+ 24e | 24e
[16] *? ? [a.a.vati] yeṇa ? ///* [17] *va dihaghama ◦ [ma] yakṣatu yeṇa [ghache maṇ.]śata [ba*
| 24a | 24g | 24g+24b | 24b
abaji] ◦ [a.] /// [18] *kṣiṇa virbhasta bhiriḍighama ◦ pu[ḍar.] + [yasa phulo] + [yo ṇ.] + + +*
| D6p | D6p+ D6v | D6p | 24a | 24b | 24g+24b | 24b
+ + [◦] eva [l.] /// [19]*ghu alitu śpi taśpi budho mi brama[ṇa] + [a]bhiñae abhiñehi*
| D6a | D6v | 24a | 24a+24b
bhavidavu [p.] bh.[vi] /// [20] *prahadavu prahiṇo mi sarvañu sa[rvadaśa]vi taśpi budho [mi*
| 24b
bramaṇa] ///

Reconstruction:
[16] *(*devo u)avati yeṇa (*ghadharvo)* [17] *va dihaghama ◦*
*yakṣatu yeṇa ghache maṇ(*o)śata ba abaji ◦*
*(*ede mi asava)* [18] *kṣiṇa virbhasta bhiriḍighama ◦*

*puḍar(*io) yasa phulo (*to)yo ṇ(*a ualipadi) ◦*
*eva l(*o)*[19]*ghu alitu śpi taśpi budho mi bramaṇa (*◦)*

*abhiñae abhiñehi bhavidavu p(*i) bh(*a)vi(*du ◦)*
[20] *prahadavu prahiṇo mi sarvañu sarvadaśavi taśpi budho mi bramaṇa (*◦)*

Translation:
1. "[16] (*The *āsava*s) by which there would be rebirth (*as a god) or [by which I would be] (*a *gandharva*) [17] flying in the air [or] by which I would become a *yakṣa* or would become human, (*these) [18] have been destroyed (*by me), eradicated, cut off."

2. "Just as a flowering lotus is not (*defiled in) water, so [19] I am not defiled in the world. Therefore, Brahman, I am the Enlightened One."

3. "Having realized what is to be realized, what is to be developed has also been developed. [20] What is to be destroyed has been destroyed by me. All-knowing, all-seeing, therefore, Brahman, I am the Enlightened One."

The first major difference between the G sūtra and the P sutta with reference to the verses uttered by the Buddha is that in the former the verses, which constitute the bulk of the Buddha's response to Dhoṇa's question, clarify or state for the first time the reasons the Buddha is not a god, etc., but rather an Enlightened One. (The critical section of the verse containing the word corresponding to P *āsava,* on account of which he would be a god, etc., has been lost, but based on the P parallel, and as demanded by the meaning of the verse, we can safely assume that the G version contained it.) In contrast, in the P sutta the verses summarize what was already stated in the Buddha's comparatively long prose response, which, as already noted earlier (see pp. 171–2), consists of two sections: (1) a passage stating that the *āsava*s on account of which he would be a god, etc., have been destroyed, cut off at the root; and (2) a simile in which he likens himself to a lotus growing in water (just as a lotus born in the water, growing in the water, and emerging out of the water is undefiled by the water, so also, though born in the world and growing up in the world, he has transcended it and lives undefiled by it). The P sutta is therefore a true *geyya* in that the verses repeat the ideas expressed in the prose (see p. 19, n. 38).

The second major difference is the number of verses spoken by the Buddha. In the G version he utters three śloka verses, perhaps four, the first consisting of three lines, the second two lines, and the third an irregular two and a half lines, while in the P version he utters the first two verses only. It is not surprising, however, that P parallels to the two and a half lines that make up the third G verse are found elsewhere in the P canon.

The P verses in the Doṇa-sutta are

1. *yena devūpapatty assa, gandhabbo vā vihaṅgamo*
   yakkhattaṃ yena gaccheyyaṃ, manussattañ ca abbaje
   te mayhaṃ āsavā khīṇā, viddhastā vinaḷīkatā
2. *puṇḍarīkaṃ yathā vaggu, toye na upalippati*
   na upalippāmi lokena, tasmā buddho 'smi brāhmaṇā ti. (AN II 39.4–9)

The first of these two verses was quite popular in the P tradition at least, as it is quoted in many commentaries and ṭīkās: Ps I 61; Mp II 183; Ud-a 176; It-a I 114; Sv-pṭ I 7; Ps-pṭ (B^{e}) I 6; Spk-pṭ (B^{e}) I 6; Mp-ṭ I 12; Mp-ṭ (B^{e}) II 67, III 330; Sp-ṭ (B^{e}) I 228, II 34; and Vism-mhṭ (B^{e}) I 227. In contrast, although elements of the third line are encountered in Buddhist Skt. texts, as in the verse *prāptaṃ mayārahatvaṃ kṣīṇā me āśravā niraveśeṣāḥ* (Lal 376.11), I have not found examples of the complete verse in such texts.

The second verse, in which the Buddha likens himself to a lotus, seems to occur only once in P texts, that is, in the Doṇa-sutta, but the image of the lotus being untouched or undefiled by water is relatively common. In the Sn, for example, the first pāda of the

Doṇa-sutta verse, *puṇḍarīkaṃ yathā vaggu toye na upalippati*, occurs in a verse of similar import:

puṇḍarīkaṃ yathā vaggu, toye na upalippati
evaṃ puññe ca pāpe ca, ubhaye tvaṃ na lippasi
pāde vīra pasārehi, sabhiyo vandati satthuno. (Sn 547)

Several verses in the Th parallel both verses of the Doṇa-sutta in that they connect the idea of the destruction of the *āsava*s (or *saṃyojana*s) with the imagery of the lotus growing in water:

saṃyojanaṃ aṇuṃ thūlaṃ, sabbaṃ chetvāna bandhanaṃ
yena yen' eva gacchati, anapekkho 'va gacchati
yathāpi udake jātaṃ, puṇḍarīkaṃ pavaḍḍhati
nopalippati toyena, sucigandhaṃ manoramaṃ
tath' eva ca loke jāto, buddho loke viharati
nopalippati lokena, toyena padumaṃ yathā. (Th 699–701 ≈ AN III 347)

namo te purisājañña, namo te purisuttama
yassa te āsavā khīṇā, dakkhiṇeyyo 'si mārisa
pūjito naradevena, uppanno maraṇābhibhū
puṇḍarīkaṃ va toyena, saṅkhāre nopalippati. (Th 1179–80)[95]

A Buddhist Skt. equivalent of the second verse is found in the Mvu as one of several verses spoken by the Buddha to the *ājīvaka* Upaka (III 326–7). It appears as the second of a sequence of three verses (all of which are rather corrupt in the manuscripts), the third of which provides a parallel to the third verse of the G sūtra:

jinā hi mādṛśā bhonti, ye prāptā āśravakṣayaṃ
jitā me pāpakā dharmā, tasmād ahaṃ upaka jino
pauṇḍarīkaṃ yathā varṇaṃ, anope na pralipyate
evaṃ loke na lipyāmi, tasmād ahaṃ upaka jinaḥ
abhijñeyaṃ abhijñātaṃ, sadvaktavyaṃ ca bhāṣyati
prahātavyaṃ prahīnaṃ[96] *me, tasmād ahaṃ upaka jino.* (III 326.19–327.3)

---

[95] Cf. also *udabindu yathā pi pokkhare, padume vāri yathā na lippati, evaṃ muni nopalippati, yad idaṃ diṭṭhasutaṃ mutesu vā* (Sn 812); *padumaṃ va toyena alippamāno* (Sn 71c, 213e). The imagery of some lotuses remaining in the water while others rise above it, untouched by the water, occurs to the Buddha not long after his enlightenment, illustrating that some people will be able to understand his teaching (Vin I 6; DN II 38; MN I 169, II 93 [abbreviated]; SN I 138; cf. Nidd I 359, 453). For Skt. examples, see Mvu III 317–8 and Lal 399–400. Part of this simile occurs at DN I 75, 208 (abbreviated); MN I 277, II 16, III 93–4; AN III 26.

[96] Read *prahīṇaṃ*.

The structure of the third verse in the G sūtra, consisting as it does of two and a half lines, or five pādas, is rather odd. The basic verse of two regular śloka lines, or four pādas, is well known from P, Skt., Tib., and Chinese sources and thus seems to have been quite popular. The P version of this verse, which is found in a variety of contexts in the P canon and is quoted in various commentaries and paracanonical works, is

abhiññeyyaṃ abhiññātaṃ, bhāvetabbañ ca bhāvitaṃ
pahātabbaṃ pahīnam me, tasmā buddho 'smi brāhmaṇa. (E.g., MN II 143.29–31)

This MN example occurs in the Brahmāyu-sutta (MN, sutta 91) as the second of three verses spoken by the Buddha to the brahman Brahmāyu. The verse is also found in Sn 558 in the Sela-sutta (Sn, pp. 102–12) as one of a number of verses spoken by the Buddha to the brahman Sela, and the Sela-sutta also occurs as sutta 92 of the MN, immediately following the Brahmāyu-sutta just mentioned (the E^{e} of the MN does not give the text of this sutta but refers to the Sn occurrence)—in other words, this verse occurs in two sequential MN suttas. Further, the verses of the Sela-sutta occur in Th 818–41; the verse under discussion is Th 828. Apart from the fact that the Buddha is describing himself, the preceding and following verses of the Brahmāyu- and Sela-suttas are not parallel to the first and second verses of the Dhoṇa-sutra.[97] Finally, besides being commented on at Th-a III 49 (cf. Sp-ṭ [B^{e}] I 229–30), this verse is also quoted in several P commentaries and paracanonical works (Sp I 115; Ud-a 84; It-a I 149; Bv-a 25; Nidd-a I 186; Paṭis-a I 215; Vism 201) and is recorded in several Southeast Asian inscriptions (Skilling 1992a: 83–6, 1997a: 96, 1997b: 123–9). Apart from slight differences in orthography (*-vv-* in the gerundives *bhāvetavvaṃ,* etc., in contrast to *-bb-* of standard Pali) the inscriptional examples are identical to the canonical version of the verse (Skilling 1997b: 128–9).

In the course of discussing these inscriptional examples, Skilling (1997b: 126–8) refers to several Skt., Tib., and Chinese parallels to this verse, including the Mvu example quoted above, which are discussed in greater length in Harrison and Skilling (forthcoming). Of particular interest among these examples is the one in the MSV, found in the Bhaiṣajyavastu within a long sequence of verse spoken by the sage Kaineya to the sage Śaila. The parallel verse, along with the preceding verse, is

yac ca kiṃcid abhijñeyaṃ, sarvaṃ tad vetti tatvavit
sarvajñaḥ sarvadarśī ca, tasmād buddho nirucyate
abhijñeyam abhijñātaṃ, bhāvanīyaṃ ca bhāvitam
prahātavyaṃ prahīṇaṃ[98] *ca, tasmād buddho nirucyate.* (MSV I 268.17–20)

According to Harrison and Skilling these two verses also occur in the first sūtra quoted in the Tib. version of Śamathadeva's Upāyikāṭīkā, but in reverse order (1.6 and

---

[97] It is perhaps only coincidental that the first verse of the Brahmāyu-sutta (*ye te dvattiṃsāti sutā mahāpurisalakkhaṇā, sabbe te mama kāyasmiṃ mā te kaṅkhāhu brāhmaṇa*: MN II 143.27–8) and the second verse of the Sela-sutta (Sn 549) refer to the marks of a great man, one of which is the wheel-marks on the soles of the feet, which features so prominently in the Doṇa-sutta.

[98] The reading is *prahīṇaṃ* in the ms., against *prahīnaṃ* in Dutt's edition.

1.7), as part of a set of six verses spoken by the Buddha to an unnamed brahman as an explanation of the epithet "Buddha." Harrison and Skilling also refer to two Chinese translations of this sūtra, one each in the two SĀs (T 2, no. 99, sūtra 100; and T 2, no. 100, sūtra 266).

A further fragmentary Skt. parallel to this verse is found in a bilingual Toch.-Skt. fragment from Central Asia, published in Sieg and Siegling 1921: 202–3.[99] This fragment preserves the remnants of two verses. The second is the *abhijñeyam* verse, and the first is the verse beginning with *dṛṣṭaṃ hy atītaṃ buddhena* that appears two verses before the *abhijñeyam* verse in the MSV example but immediately before it in Śamathadeva's Upāyikāṭīkā. The Skt. portions of the fragment (no. 362.1–4) read

> [1] *tathā dṛṣṭaṃm anāgatam*| . . . /// [2] . . . | *saṃskārā vyayadharmiṇa* | . . . /// [3] *bhijñātaṃ* | . . . | *bhāvanīyaṃ [ca] bhā[v]i[tam]* | . . . /// [4] . . . *smād buddho smi māṇava* | . . . ///.

This fragment thus preserves the second half of pāda a, all of pāda b, and all but the first akṣara of pāda d. The vocative *māṇava* in pāda d indicates that the verses were spoken to a young brahman, a *māṇava,* in contrast to a brahman as in the G, P, and Upāyikāṭīkā versions, where the vocative is G *bramaṇa,* P *brāhmaṇa,* Tib. *bram ze*. (See below for further discussion of the various versions of this pāda.)

The inclusion of this *abhijñeyam* verse (to use the Skt. form) in the G text is no doubt due to the fact that the final pādas of both this verse (pāda e) and the second verse (pāda d) of the Gāndhārī are identical: G *taśpi budho mi bramaṇa*, "therefore, Brahman, I am the Enlightened One." This is clearly also the basis for the grouping together in the MSV and Upāyikāṭīkā of the two verses quoted above whose fourth pādas are *tasmād buddho nirucyate* in the case of the MSV and *des-na bram-ze saṅs-rgyas brjod* and *des-na bram-ze saṅs-rgyas-so* in the case of the Tib. version of the Upāyikāṭīkā (as given by Harrison and Skilling, forthcoming). The same principle is at work in the grouping together of the three Mvu verses quoted above, which all have *tasmād ahaṃ upaka jino* as their pāda d.

In the P canon only two śloka verses share *tasmā buddho 'smi brāhmaṇa,* or the like,[100] as their final pāda: the second (last) verse of the Doṇa-sutta and the *abhiññeyyaṃ* verse discussed above.[101] Despite this, and in contrast to the several non-P examples we have discussed, the P tradition seems to have never combined these two verses (i.e., according to the P texts that have come down to us).

Into this well-known *abhijñeyam* verse, two equally well known epithets of the Buddha have been inserted as pāda d of the G version—G *sarvañu sarvadaśavi,* "all-knowing, all-seeing"—thus displacing the *taśpi budho mi bramaṇa* pāda, which thereby becomes pāda e. This is problematic. First, *taśpi budho mi bramaṇa* is thus left "hanging" in the G version, and to my knowledge śloka verses of an uneven number of pādas are not usual

---

[99] This reference is recorded in the SWTF, s.v. *abhijñāta*. A cross-reference to MSV I 268 appears in the margin of the SWTF's copy of Sieg and Siegling 1921: 202.

[100] Cf. *so 'haṃ brāhmaṇa buddho 'smi* (Th 830c).

[101] Rhys Davids (1934: vi–viii) argues that the original reading was *suddho* rather than *buddho*.

(ignoring the possibility of gayatrī, etc.). And second, although it could be argued that the correct scansion of the G pāda is problematic due to our current knowledge of G metrics, the identical P version, *tasmā buddho 'smi brāhmaṇa,* as well as the similar forms encountered in non-P Buddhist literature, all appear as posterior, not prior, pādas; namely, as pāda d's. (Of course, the scansion of the P version as a posterior śloka pāda depends on a MIA form of the now Sanskritized *brāhmaṇa,* where the initial Skt. conjunct *br-* appeared as *b-,* thereby not making position.) In other words, this is clearly a posterior pāda.

In P texts the equivalent epithets *sabbaññū sabbadassāvī* are found in both verse and prose. Prose examples are relatively common, being applied to Gotama, Nigaṇṭha Nāthaputta, Pūraṇa Kassapa, and others.[102] Prose examples in Buddhist Skt. texts are also common enough: for example, *sarvajño sarvadarśāvī* (e.g., Mvu I 254.3–4, III 51.9–10). In comparison, verse examples in P texts in which both epithets appear together seem to be few. They appear as pāda a of a śloka verse in the Th (*sabbaññū sabbadassāvī, jino ācariyo mama,* 722a–b, attributed to Abhimutto thero) and in the Jā as the latter part of the second line of a gaṇacchandha (āryā) verse (*tvam evāsi* [B^{e} *eva asi*] *sambuddho, sabbaññū sabbadassāvī,* IV 235.15).[103] Although we have only this one (Th 722a) example of *sabbaññū sabbadassāvī* being used in a śloka verse, it nonetheless indicates that in śloka verse this pair only works as a prior pāda. This is also true of the Skt./BHS examples so far encountered, with the pair appearing as a pāda c in *sarvajñaḥ sarvadarśī ca, tasmād buddho nirucyate* (MSV I 268.18, pādas c–d), quoted above, and in *sarvajño sarvadarśāvī, bhaviṣyaṃ puruṣottamaḥ* (Mvu II 22.5, pādas c–d), although they appear at the end of the second line of an āryā verse in *buddho hohiti loke sarvajño sarvadarśāvī* (Mvu II 13.3). The placement of *sarvañu sarvadaśavi* in the position of a posterior śloka pāda in our G text, like the placement of *taśpi budho mi bramaṇa* as a prior śloka pāda, thus indicates that the G text is faulty at this point and is probably due to a scribal error.

There are two possible explanations. The first is that the scribe of this manuscript, or perhaps a previous scribe, accidentally compressed two similar verses. The most obvious candidates for these two verses are those found at MSV I 268.17–20, discussed above, where the first ends in *sarvajñaḥ sarvadarśī ca, tasmād buddho nirucyate,* and the second, the *abhijñeyam* verse, ends in *prahātavyaṃ prahīṇaṃ ca, tasmād buddho nirucyate*. The G version of these would have been *sarvañu sarvadaśavi, taśpi budho mi bramaṇa* and *prahadavu prahiṇo mi, taśpi budho mi bramaṇa*. This would mean that the G version of the Dhoṇa-sutra which this manuscript represents originally had four verses, rather than three, with the third verse parallel to MSV I 268.17–8,

yac ca kiṃcid abhijñeyaṃ, sarvaṃ tad vetti tatvavit,
sarvajñaḥ sarvadarśī ca, tasmād buddho nirucyate,

---

[102] E.g., MN I 92.36, 482.4–5 ff., II 31.16, 126.33, 218.1; AN I 220.29, IV 428.20, 429.1–2. *Sabbaññū* alone is also found in a variety of contexts: e.g., *bhagavā sabbaññū* (Sv II 606.28–9, 609.5); *sabbaññubuddho hoti* (Mp I 150.15–6).

[103] Cf. also the prior pāda of the verse *sabbaññū sabbavidū ca* (Jā IV 235.21), which has the same meter. (I am grateful to Prof. K. R. Norman for assistance with the meter of these Jā verses.) Cf. the posterior śloka pādas *sabbaññū lokanāyako* (Ap 96.27, etc.); *sabbaññū samaṇuttaro* (Ap 318.3).

or, at least, sharing the second line in common.

Another possibility is that the scribe's exemplar (or an earlier exemplar) contained only three verses, but that the scribe of this manuscript (or even a previous scribe) knew this verse, or at least a verse that ended in *sarvañu sarvadaśavi, taśpi budho mi bramaṇa,* and was thus prompted to write *sarvañu sarvadaśavi, taśpi budho mi bramaṇa* instead of *taśpi budho mi bramaṇa*. It is likely that we will never know which of these two alternatives actually occurred because even if another G manuscript containing a second example of a Dhoṇa-sutra were to come to light, the number of verses that version contained would not necessarily solve the problem, for it may very well have been the case that G versions of this sūtra fluctuated in the number of *taśpi budho mi bramaṇa* verses that were included. That such additions and omissions occurred is immediately evident when the various examples of the *abhijñeyam* verse and its associated verses found in Buddhist literature are compared.

? ? [a.a.vati] yeṇa (v. 1, pāda a): P *yena devūpapatty assa* (v. 1, pāda a), v.l. *devūpapaty* (see appendix 1), avoids the unacceptable three-consonant conjunct. Parallels in Buddhist Skt. and elsewhere have not so far been found.

The alignment of fragment 24e is rather tentative, as is the reading of the remnants of the four akṣaras that appear on its upper edge belonging to line 16 and this pāda. The first remnant of ink on fragment 24e belonging to this line is taken to represent the bottom of the *st.* of *śast.* of the preceding sentence, but it could also be the bottom of the punctuation mark that follows. The next akṣara is very faint. It is probably the bottom of the punctuation mark but could also be the bottom of the first akṣara of the next pāda (possibly *de*). The third remnant could be the bottom of a *d., v., s.,* or *u,* among others. Then there is a space, followed by a small remnant of ink. Fragment D6r contains the tops of further akṣaras belonging to this pāda. The reading of this fragment is */// ? [a.a.vati] yeṇa ? ///*. The first akṣara could be the remnant of the left arm of *v*. The second and third akṣaras are probably the tops of *ua,* while the final akṣara on this fragment could be the upper right arm of the *gha* of *ghadharvo* of the next pāda. Thus, the probable reading of fragment D6r is *[v. uavati] yeṇa [gh.]*. The appearance of *yeṇa* after *uavati* = P *-upapatti* indicates that the word order of this pāda differs from the P *yena devūpapatty assa,* a G version of which would probably be **yeṇa devuavati asa*. Since the reading of the initial remnants of this line is uncertain, there are a number of possibilities for the reconstruction of this pāda. The most likely is *(*devo) uavati yeṇa,* "by which there would be rebirth (*as a god)." This takes the first remnant of ink on fragment 24e as the bottom of *st.* of the previous sentence; the second remnant as the bottom of the punctuation mark; the third, the bottom of a *de,* the first akṣara of the verse; and the fourth (occurring after a space), the bottom of the *u*. The remnant of the top of *v.* of what was probably *vo* occurs at the beginning of fragment D6r. Although there are eight syllables, the metrical pattern is not ideal. A reconstruction that would be metrically more acceptable (with resolution of the first short syllable) is *uavati yeṇa (*deveṣu),* "by which there would be rebirth (*among the gods)," for which compare the ṭīkā's gloss *devūpapattī ti devesu uppatti nibbatti* (Mp-ṭ II [B^{e}] 293). However, although the remnant of the third akṣara on fragment 24e could be read as the bottom of a *u* vowel, it does not seem to match the top of the initial *u* of *uavati* found on fragment D6r, while the remnant of an akṣara at the beginning of fragment D6r does not match a punctuation mark.

In the above reconstruction, the verb equivalent to P *assa* (opt.), which would be **asa* in Gāndhārī, partially attested in the Khvs-G (40a) as *(*a)sa* (Salomon 2000: notes on v. 40, pp. 187–8), has to be understood from the context.

? /// [17] *va dihaghama ◦* (v. 1, pāda b): Based on the meter, this can be understood as *? + + va dihaghama ◦*, with two akṣaras missing from the end of line 16. The P version is *gandhabbo vā vihaṅgamo* (v. 1, pāda b). Again, given that this pāda refers to the second of the four types of being, and in view of the close correspondence with the P verse throughout, the first word of this pāda was undoubtedly the G equivalent of P *gandhabbo*. In this text, this appears twice as *ghadharvo* (ll. 10 and 13) and once as *ghadhrarvo* (l. 10), with the spelling at line 12 unclear. I reconstruct *ghadharvo*. The remnant of the final akṣara on fragment D6r is consistent with the upper right arm of *gh*.

Va is the equivalent of P/Skt. *vā*, "or."

In the P verse *vihaṅgamo* is an adjective meaning "going in the sky," "flying," though the word can also be used as a masculine noun meaning "bird" (PTSD, s.v. *vihaṅgama*). This word is not attested elsewhere in Gāndhārī. In all but the initial *d-* the correspondence between *dihaghama* and P *vihaṅgamo* is straightforward, but *d-* for an original initial *v-* presents serious problems. Throughout this manuscript, as in Gāndhārī generally, initial *v-* remains. The exception is *v-* alternating with *b-* in such words as *bucadi* and *vucadi* = P *vuccati* and *bayaṇa* = P *vacana*, which is not uncommon in Gāndhārī (see § 5.2.1). But this is hardly a precedent for *v- > d-*, which is not attested elsewhere in Gāndhārī or in other Prakrits. (The example of *saṅghādisesa* in P texts versus *saṅghāvaśeṣa* of Buddhist Skt. texts discussed in Norman 1989a: 375 represents a different phenomenon.) It is possible that we are looking at nothing more than a scribal error or even at another example of the type of problem we face later in this verse (and elsewhere in Gāndhārī generally) in explaining *virbhasta* and *bhiriḍighama* in pāda f where the P has *viddhastā* and *vinaḷīkatā;* it is significant that in *bhiriḍighama* for P *vinaḷīkatā,* we have the similar problem of initial *vi-* appearing as *bhi-*. As will be discussed in greater detail below, these latter words appear to be examples of a small group of words that were garbled or confused in transmission (which in effect is another way of saying that they defy satisfactory explanation). Nonetheless, at least two alternative interpretations of *dihaghama* are worth mentioning.

The first is that the initial component of the G compound is based on the root √*ḍī,* which alternates with √*dī,* "to soar," "to fly" (see von Hinüber 1986: § 196 for discussion of this root). This occurs in Pali as *ḍeti* (also with dental in *dayati*), which is defined by the Dhātupāṭha as *ākāsa-gamana* (see PTSD, s.v. *ḍeti*), which in turn is parallel to the commentary's gloss on *vihaṅgamo* of the P Doṇa-sutta with *ākāsacāro* (Mp III 79.10). Although derivatives of this root do not seem to be found in connection with *gandhabba*s in Pali it is applied to birds in the common simile *seyyathā pi . . . pakkhī sakuṇo yena yen' eva ḍeti sapattabhāro va ḍeti* (see PTSD, s.v. *ḍeti,* for references); compare also the verse at Jā II 443.10, *ucce sakuṇa omāna pattayāna vihaṅgama,* where the Burmese vv.ll. for *omāna* are *ḍehanā* and *ḍemānā* (the B[e] has *ḍemāna*). An unattested P form such as

**ḍeha(na)gama,* or **deha(na)gama* with initial dental, would then mean "going by flying." This could appear in Gāndhārī as *dihaghama* in this scribe's orthography.

The second possibility is that *dihaghama* is parallel to Skt. *dīrgha-gāmin,* "going or flying far" (MW, s.v.); *dīha* for *dīrgha* is found in several Prakrits (see Pischel 1965: § 87), though it is not attested in Gāndhārī to date (in the Dhp-G^{K} the form is *drigha*).

Neither of these latter two explanations seems satisfactory.[104] Glosses on *gandhabba* and *vihaṅgama* in the P commentaries give no support nor do they suggest alternatives. Thus, given that the correspondence with P *vihaṅgamo* is so tempting, *dihaghama* as a scribal error for *vihaghama* may have to stand, and for want of a better explanation, my translation of this passage reflects this conclusion.

[ma] yakṣatu yeṇa [ghache] (v. 1, pāda c): The P parallel is *yakkhattaṃ yena gaccheyyaṃ* (v. 1, pāda c). Between the punctuation mark indicating the end of the preceding pāda and *ya,* the initial akṣara of this pāda, a faint akṣara appears that resembles *ma*. This is probably a scribal error that has been erased. The scribe may have begun to write *maṇośata,* the first word of pāda d, but then realized his mistake. The very tips of *ṇa* and *ghache* are at the bottom of fragment 25a. The remainder of the tops of these akṣaras are on fragment 25u. *Che* is badly distorted. The reading is tentative, influenced in part by the P parallel, *gaccheyyaṃ*.

The only word of note is the optative *[ghache],* where the P has *gaccheyyaṃ*. Although this is a regular G parasmaipada optative form (cf. *ukuje* = P *ukkujjeyya,* l. 21), it leaves the pāda one syllable short. Optatives in *-ea* (e.g., *carea* in Khvs-G 25d, where the P has *careyya*) are as common, if not more so, in Gāndhārī (see § 6.3.2), and such a form could have been used in this instance. It is perhaps only coincidental that the reading *gacche* is also found in one Sinh. manuscript used for the E^{e} of the Dīghanikāya-aṭṭhakathāṭīkā's quote of this verse (Sv-pṭ I 7). Similar optative forms are found in the AG-G; for example, *araghae aha b.dho pravaja ya aha labhe* (l. 20), where the P has *ārādhayeyyaṃ sambuddhaṃ pabbajjañ ca labheyy' ahaṃ* (Ap 298.6). Note that the meter is not disturbed in this AG-G example.

[maṇ.]śata [ba abaji] ◦ (v. 1, pāda d): The P parallel is *manussattañ ca abbaje* (v. 1, pāda d). The placement of fragment 25k, which contains a portion of *ma,* is verified by the reading of the verso; that is, the writing on the verso of this fragment forms parts of the akṣaras in the corresponding position. The small mark of ink at the very right of the fragment may be part of the preceding *che.* In its damaged state, the *ṇ.* akṣara looks like a *ṇi,* which is unlikely in this context. The reading of this akṣara is problematic. I therefore reconstruct this word as *maṇ(*o)śata,* corresponding to P *manussattañ*/Skt. *manuṣyatvam,* in view of the spelling *maṇośu* = Skt. *manuṣyaḥ* elsewhere in this text (ll. 11, 14, 15).

Ba for Skt. *vā,* "or," is well attested in the Dhp-G^{K} (see § 5.2.2.7; Brough 1962: § 68). The G text thus differs from the Pali, which has *ca,* "and."

The reading of the final akṣara of pāda d is problematic. Only the upper half of the akṣara survives and the quality of the bark has deteriorated. Further, the upper hook or

[104] Still less likely is confusion with a word that appears in Pali as *dūraṅgama,* "going far," as in Pv 266c–d, where a *yakkha* is so described; or confusion with P *dija/dvija,* Skt. *dvija,* "bird."

horizontal stroke of the letter is rather shallow for a *j-*. Besides *ji,* the reading could therefore be either *ti* or *vi*.

The Pali has *abbaje,* which is the first-person singular optative parasmaipada of *abbajati* (Skt. *ā* + √*vraj*), "to go to," "to come to" (see CPD, s.v. *abbajati, āvajati*; Turner 1966: § 1451; PTSD, s.v. *abbaje*). However, the number of variant readings that are recorded indicates that this word was not always clearly understood. The E^{e} records the v.l. *aṇḍaje* (in Sinh. S.Tr.), which is the reading at Ud-a 176. S^{e} reads *abbhaje;* the S^{e} for Mp II 183 reads *ambuje*. Abandoning his adoption of the reading *aṇḍaje* of his edition of the Ud-a and rejecting the reading *abbaje,* Woodward (1933: 45 n. 2), in his translation of the Doṇa-sutta occurrence, proposes *abbude,* "in the womb," and translates accordingly: "Or go to birth in human womb." No P commentary seems to have concerned itself with this word.

The preferable reading for the Pali is clearly *abbaje*. There are no instances in our manuscript of words containing reflexes of original *-j-*. In the Dhp-G^{K} and in the Khvs-G, intervocalic *-j-* invariably goes to *-y-* (see Salomon 2000: § 6.2.1.2). In the Dhp-G^{K}, for example, are found *vayadi, [pravaya]di,* and *-pravaï* (this last example showing elision of *-j-*), which are all based on the same root, √*vraj*. We would therefore anticipate that the G equivalent of P *abbaje* would be **abaye* or **abayi,* with weakening of the final vowel. However, even though the reading of the final akṣara of this word in the Gāndhārī is problematic, it does not appear to be a *ye* or *yi*. Similarly, the alternative readings *ti* and *vi* are not expected. I therefore tentatively read *[abaji]*.

[a.] /// [18] *kṣiṇa* (v. 1, pāda e): Based on the meter, this can be understood as *[a.]* + + + + + *kṣiṇa*. The P parallel is *te mayhaṃ āsavā khīṇā* (v. 1, pāda e). Although I have not been able to locate an exact parallel to this pāda in Buddhist Skt. texts, verses containing the core components are encountered. For example, the expression "those *āśrava*s have been destroyed by me" or "my *āśrava*s have been destroyed" (depending on the understanding of *mayhaṃ* and *me*) appears in the āryā verse *prāptaṃ mayārahatvaṃ kṣīṇā me āśravā niraveśeṣāḥ* (Lal 376.11), while the compound *kṣīṇāsrava-* appears in the prior pāda of śloka verse in *kṣīṇāsravo visaṃyukta, upaśāntaḥ sunirvr̥taḥ* (MSV I 272.3) and *kṣīṇāsravo vāntadoṣaḥ* (MSV I 174.14, 182.15; Uv XXXIII.23c, cf. XXXI.39e).

The first akṣara of this pāda, which follows the punctuation mark that ends the previous pāda, is the last akṣara preserved on line 17. The final word of the pāda, *kṣiṇa,* appears at the beginning of line 18. Thus five akṣaras are missing at the end of line 17. The first akṣara of this pāda appears to be a vowel, which is not expected if we take the P parallel as guide. Given that the final word of this pāda in both the G and P is the past participle G *kṣiṇa*/P *khīṇā,* and given that the majority of the G verses closely parallel the Pali, we would have expected this verse to have read something like *(*te mi asava) kṣiṇa*. In this case the enclitic form of the first-person pronoun, *me* (instr. or gen.) or, better, *mi* as in line 20, would have appeared where the P has *mayhaṃ* (1st-pers. pron. gen. sg.), despite this leaving the verse one syllable short. (Although P *mayhaṃ āsavā* can mean "my *āsava*s," the context demands that this is the agentive genitive: *yena . . . te mayhaṃ āsavā khīṇā;* cf. the prose passage in the Pali, *yesaṃ . . . āsavānaṃ . . . te me āsavā* *pahīnā . . .*; e.g., AN II 38.25–6.) Further, although the G equivalent of P *āsavā,* Buddhist Skt. *āsravāḥ/āśravāḥ,* may have appeared as *asava* in this scribe's orthography, as in the Dhp-G^K (e.g., 339e; cf. *kṣiṇasavu* 26c), the phrase *citam arśaveti* in this manuscript (ll. 43, 46, etc.), where the verb is cognate with P *āsava,* BHS *āsrava/āśrava,* suggests that the form **arśava* is also possible. I adopt the attested spelling (*asava*).

A possible solution is to assume that the word order differed slightly in the Gāndhārī, with *asava* beginning the sentence. In this reconstruction, the verse would have read *(*asava te mi) kṣiṇa.* Apart from the problem of being one syllable short, this would be metrically less desirable because of the heavy fifth syllable, unless *mi/me* was taken as light, *metri causa.*

An alternative solution is to propose that the first word of the pāda was *(*ede),* the equivalent of P *ete,* "these." In this reconstruction the reading would be *(*ede mi asava) kṣiṇa,* which would avoid the two problems faced by the preceding reconstruction. Neither solution is completely compelling. I have tentatively adopted the second in the reconstruction and translation.[105]

virbhasta bhiriḍighama ◦ (v. 1, pāda f): The P parallel is *viddhastā vinaḷīkatā* (v. 1, pāda f). The correspondence between the G and P forms of these two adjectives presents major problems. The P *viddhastā* and *vinaḷīkatā,* virtually synonymous and meaning "destroyed," occur in a variety of contexts in verse. In a Sn verse they are applied to *upāyāsā,* "troubles": *upāyāsā ca te sabbe, viddhastā vinaḷīkatā* (542a–b). In a verse in the MN they are applied to *pāpimato sotaṃ,* "the Evil One's stream": *chinnaṃ pāpimato sotaṃ, viddhastaṃ vinaḷīkataṃ* (I 227.12, pādas a–b). In the Jā they describe a mango: *phalaṃ ambaṃ hataṃ disvā, viddhastaṃ vinaḷīkataṃ* (VI 60.28, pādas a–b; cf. also Th 216b, *saṃsārā vinaḷīkatā*). It is noteworthy that in all these examples they constitute posterior śloka pādas (pāda b), as in the verse under review (pāda f).

I have not encountered examples of these words being used together in Buddhist Skt. texts, though *parapravādā vihatā, vidhvastā virūḍhīkr̥tāḥ,* in the MSV (I 276.14, pādas c–d) provides an intriguing parallel.[106]

P *viddhasta-* is the past participle of *vi* + √*dhaṃs*/Skt. *vi* + √*dhvaṃs* (pp. *vidhvasta*), meaning "scattered." The P commentaries gloss *viddhastā* with *vidhamitā* (the pp. of *vi* + √*dham/dhmā,* "destroy"; Mp III 79.11) or *vinaṭṭhā* (Vv-a 265.7–8) and *viddhastaṃ* with *vināsitaṃ* (Ps-pṭ [B^e] I 93). Although the first and last syllables correspond, G *virbhasta* cannot represent P *viddhasta-*/Skt. *vidhvasta-*. Rather, it seems to represent Skt.

---

[105] Two Dharmapada verses are tantalizing but of no assistance. The first is *ara te asavakṣa(*ya)* (Dhp-G^K 339f) = *ārāt te hy āsravakṣayāt* (Uv IV.19f), where *ārāt* takes the ablative: "they are indeed far from the destruction of the *āsravas*"; cf. P *ārā so āsavakkhayā* (Dhp 253d). The second is *aprati asavakṣayi* (Dhp-G^K 134b; cf. 66d) = P *appatto āsavakkhayaṃ* (Dhp 272d).

[106] Cf. *sa hata-vihata-vidhvastaḥ pratyāgataḥ* (MSV I 138.9 [cf. 10] = Divy 445.24–5 [cf. 26]). This is the reading of the ms. The reading in Dutt's first edition of the MSV (1947) is *-vidhvastaḥ,* which was changed to *-viddhastaḥ* in the second edition (1984). I am indebted to Klaus Wille for bringing the correct reading to my attention. In the Mahāsāṅghika-Lokottaravādin Bhikṣuṇī-vinaya a corpse, *śava,* is described as *vidhavastañ* [read *vidhvastañ*] *ca vinīlakaṃ* (BhīVin(Mā-L) 119.2–4 [= § 147, v. 5, pāda d]).

vibhraṣṭa-, the past participle of *vi* + √*bhraṅś,* "fallen," "destroyed," etc. The corresponding form does not occur in Pali, but derivatives of this root are recorded: *bhassati, pabhassati,* and the past participle *bhaṭṭha,* "fallen." This word appears in Buddhist Skt. texts in, for example, *prahāṇa-vibhraṣṭaḥ* (Lal 407.19), which the BHSD (s.v. *prahāṇa*) takes as "fallen away from religious exertions." In the same entry Edgerton refers to the same passage at Mvu III 329.4, where the edition reads *prahāṇa-vikrānto* following the manuscripts, but he notes that *-vibhrānto* for *-vibhraṣṭaḥ* was probably intended. As further noted by Edgerton, this appears in Pali as *padhāna-vibbhanto* (Vin I 9.1). It thus seems that in Buddhist texts *vidhvasta, vibhraṣṭa,* and *vibhrānta* (to use the Skt. forms), all of similar meaning, were interchangeable and sometimes confused. Of some significance in this regard is the presence in the Dhp-G^K of the words *bhatsadi* and *batsadi* where the corresponding P has *dhaṃsati* and *dhaṃsate,* respectively: *sagaṭhaṇa i bhatsadi* (Dhp-G^K 268d), where the corresponding Jā verse has *saggaṭṭhānā ca dhaṃsati,* "he is deprived of that heavenly place" (III 457.6, pāda d); and *athadu batsadi balu,* probably "the fool is deprived of the benefit (*arthataḥ*)" (Dhp-G^K 336c), corresponding to the Th verse *sukhā so dhaṃsate ṭhānā,* "he is deprived of the happy state" (225c). In his discussion of this word, Brough (1962: § 63) proposes two possibilities. The first is that the existence of examples which show the development of *dv* and *tv* to the labial stops *b* and *p* "allows the possibility that *bhatsadi, batsadi* is the directly inherited verb representing (*dhvaṃsate*)." The second is that the word could "equally well have been taken over at an earlier period from a Middle Indian *bhaṃsati* < (*bhraṃśate*); and it is not impossible that the Dharmapada form is a compromise between the two verbs of almost identical meaning." In the light of *virbhasta* of our text, it seems that the latter is now more likely.

If G *virbhasta* is the equivalent of Skt. *vibhraṣṭa-* as I propose, then *-rbh-* for original *-bhr-* may be merely graphic or may be an example of metathesis (see § 5.3, and the discussion of *rś* written for *śr,* § 5.2.3.6).

The main problem with taking G *virbhasta* as the equivalent of Skt. *vibhraṣṭa-* is the appearance of the dental cluster *-st-* where we would expect *-ṭh-* or *-ṣṭ-*. In this manuscript original *-ṣṭ-* appears as *-ṭh-* in *proṭhabbu* = BHS *spraṣṭavyam*/P *phoṭṭhabbaṃ,* and in *proṭhu* = Skt. *pr̥ṣṭaḥ*/P *puṭṭho,* while original *-st-* is retained in *śavastie* = Skt. *śrāvastyām*/P *sāvatthiyaṃ,* and in *ś[astu]* = Skt. *śāstā* (see pp. 94–5). As no examples of *st* appear for original *ṣṭ* in Gāndhārī (see, e.g., Brough's discussion of the problem of the development of original sibilant plus dental or retroflex stop and the correct transcription of the characters used to represent them; Brough 1962: § 18–18b), it seems likely that the dental cluster in *virbhasta* of our text has been influenced by the fact that the semantically similar word P *viddhasta*/Skt. *vidhvasta,* with which it alternated in some contexts, contains this conjunct; in Brough's words, this represents "a compromise between the two verbs of almost identical meaning" (1962: § 63).

The Pali corresponding to the problematic *bhiriḍighama* is *vinaḷīkatā,* which is derived from *vi* + *naḷa* + *kata,* meaning, literally, "having the reed or stem removed," hence "destroyed" (PTSD s.v.). The P commentaries gloss *vinaḷīkatā* with *vigatanaḷā vigatabandhanā katā* (Mp III 79.12), *vigatanaḷā katā ucchinnā* (Pj II 435.24), and *vigatāvasesaṃ katan* (Ps-pṭ [B^e] I 93), and they gloss *vinaḷīkataṃ* with *nipattanaḷaṃ* *kataṃ* (Jā VI 61.12), none of which help us with G *bhiriḍighama*. The Skt. equivalent, which would be *vinalīkr̥ta* or **vinālīkr̥ta,* is not recorded in any of the standard Skt. dictionaries, including the BHSD, although *vināla,* with the same meaning, is recorded in MW and PW (s.v. *vināla*) for the MBh.

Of some interest for our discussion is the pairing of *vidhvasta* with *virūḍhīkr̥ta,* "overcome," "expelled," in the MSV's description of the disputes of others (*parapravādā vihatā, vidhvastā virūḍhīkr̥tāḥ,* quoted above), and with *vinīlaka,* "blue," in the Bhikṣuṇī-vinaya's description of a corpse as being *vidhvastañ ca vinīlakaṃ* (see n. 106). Although these examples do not explain *bhiriḍighama* of our text, they indicate that similarly sounding words, **vinā̆līkr̥ta, virūḍhīkr̥ta,* and *vinīlaka* (to use the Skt. forms), were all paired with *vidhvasta,* which might lead to confusion under certain circumstances.

The least problematic element in *bhiriḍighama* for P *vinaḷīkatā* is the second member of the compound, *-ghama*. This must be the equivalent of *-gama,* "going to," as in P *vihaṅgama,* "going in the sky," which appears in pāda b of verse 1 as *dihaghama*. It is in fact possible that the occurrence of *dihaghama* at the end of the first line of verse has influenced the development of an original *-ghada,* the G equivalent of P *-kata*/Skt. *-kr̥ta,* to *-ghama* in *bhiriḍighama* at the end of the third line of verse. This also suggests that the problems seen in the initial members of the compounds *diha-ghama* and *bhiriḍi-ghama* are somehow linked, although exactly how is unclear.

The third syllable, *-ḍi-,* presents no problems (see § 5.2.2.3).

Of a different category, however, is initial *bhi-* where the P has *vi-*. As noted in the discussion of *dihaghama* above, initial *v-* (including the prefix *vi-*) remains throughout this manuscript, as in Gāndhārī generally, except for initial *v-* > *b-* in some cases. Further, intervocalic *-v-* remains in this manuscript, as it does in other G texts, except for *-v-* > *-m-* in *ema* = *evaṃ,* as elsewhere in Gāndhārī and in the common *b/v* alternation (see § 5.2.1). In intervocalic position and not uncommonly in the prefix *abhi-, -bh-* can appear as *-v-, -vh-,* and *-h-* in Gāndhārī (Brough 1962: §§ 12, 44; von Hinüber 1986: § 191). Examples of such alternations in initial position are discussed by Norman (1989a: 374); for example, *bhajati* (Dhp 303c) and *bhajate* (Patna Dhp 332c) in the P and Patna Dharmapadas compared to *vrajate* (Uv X.8c) and *vayadi* (Dhp-G^K 323c) in the Uv and Dhp-G^K and *vajati* in a similar verse in the Sn (1143c). However, these examples differ from *bhiriḍighama* in that the alternation of *bh* and *v* has given rise to the employment of two different words that make sense in the same context.

Although encountered elsewhere in Gāndhārī, examples of *-bh-* appearing as *-v-, -vh-,* or *-h-* do not occur in this manuscript or in other texts written by the same scribe to my knowledge, apart from the possible instance of the word under review. Again, the reverse development of *-bh-* for original *-v-* is unattested in Gāndhārī, although, of course, the opposite of any development is always technically possible. A graphic *bhi* for *vhi*/*vi* is not impossible, although it would be unexpected, given that *-vh-* for original *-v-* appears in such words as *makavha* = P/Skt. *maghavā* in the Dhp-G^K and *(*bha)gavha* = *bhagavā* (?) in the Peshawar Museum inscription listed in Brough 1962: § 12 (cf. Burrow 1937: § 20), where *vh* in turn can appear as a reflex of original *bh* as noted above. The development *vhi/vi* > *bhi* could have occurred if *vi* was treated in this context (P *viddhastā vinaḷīkatā*) as if it were intervocalic. A further influence, which could be an explanation in itself, may have been the presence of the voiced labial aspirate in the previous word, *virbhasta,* with the fact that these two words commonly occur as a fixed pair having some influence.

Alternatively, as noted, there are a number of examples of *b-* for original initial *v-* in this manuscript. A further development of the aspiration of *b-* to *bh-* could then have taken place (Brough 1962: § 49), perhaps influenced by *virbhasta,* the previous word. (For the alternation and confusion of aspirates and nonaspirates, see Boucher 1998: 477–81.)

Finally, the problematic second akṣara is not clearly written, and a blob of ink obscures the juncture of the horizontal and vertical strokes at the upper right. It is difficult to tell whether the scribe intended to write *ri, li,* or even *ṇi.* Although the shape of the upper horizontal stroke finds a parallel in *le* in line 29, the lack of a tail turning up to the left is uncharacteristic of this scribe's *l* (cf. *li* in l. 19). As the horizontal and tail of the vertical are consistent with an *r,* this is the most likely reading. It is also possible that an akṣara of uncertain reading has been corrected to *ṇi,* the scribe perhaps having accidentally written the horizontal of an *r* or *l* and then continued by writing *ṇi* over it. However, the vertical stroke is rather long and the tail too sharp for an *ṇ.* If this word does correspond to P *vinaḷīkata,* then the nasal *ṇ* rather than *r* or *l* would be expected in this position. Yet, examples of *r* for *n* are found in Pali (Geiger 1994: § 43), and *n* and *ṇ* occasionally appear as *l,* and *ṇ* appears as *ḷ,* in Pali and Prakrit (Geiger 1994: §§ 43, 45; Pischel 1965: §§ 243, 247, 260). The *r/l* alternation is also well attested in both Pali and Prakrit (Geiger 1994: §§ 44–5; Pischel 1965: §§ 256–9). An example in Gāndhārī is *saleloa* = P *saroruhaṃ,* "lotus" (Dhp-G[L] 8b). (For *r* for *d* in Gāndhārī, see Brough 1962: § 64; for *l* for *d,* see Burrow 1937: § 50.) Further, such phonemes are liable to transposition, for example, Pkt. *āṇāla* = Skt. *ālāna* (Pischel 1965: § 354). At least two similar examples are found in the Senior manuscripts: G *bilaḍa-* (20 r6), "cat," = Skt. *biḍāla,* P *biḷāra, biḷāla,* Pkt. *biḍāla, bilāḍa,* etc., and G *oraḍi* (20 r6), where the P parallel (AN V 195.6) has *oḷārikā* = Skt. *audārika-,* "large." Given the above, it is therefore possible that *n, ṇ, l,* or *r* could appear for original *n.* Further, it is possible that such phonetic changes lie behind the confusion we see in this word, with the scribe's writing of this akṣara in an unclear manner being somehow connected. It is thus significant that we find *virūḍhīkr̥tāḥ* paired with *vidhvastā* (*vidhvastā virūḍhīkr̥tāḥ*) in the MSV example quoted above.

The above argument is somewhat thwarted by the fact that this consonant, whatever the reading may be, is combined with an *i* vowel. *Bhiriḍighama* as representing P *vinalīkata-* thus appears even less likely, unless one proposes that the scribe accidentally wrote an *i* vowel on the second akṣara in anticipation of *i* in the next syllable, *ḍi.*

In summary, it is obvious that a number of the above explanations for *bhiriḍighama* (and to a lesser extent for *virbhasta*) are desperate ones. As with *dihaghama* in line 17, corresponding to P *vihaṅgamo* (or even *eghad oya/eghad uya* encountered elsewhere in this text and corresponding to P *etad avoca*), *virbhasta* and *bhiriḍighama* seem to be examples of a small, but significant, number of words that have undergone changes in the course of transmission that are yet to be satisfactorily explained. Further, since the final element of *bhiriḍi-ghama* seems to have been influenced by *diha-ghama,* which is also the final word of a pāda, it is possible that the problems presented by the initial members of these compounds are connected in a way that is yet to be fully understood.

pu[ḍar.] + [yasa phulo] (v. 2, pāda a): The P parallel is *puṇḍarīkaṃ yathā vaggu* (v. 2, pāda a). Only the upper right shoulder of *r.* remains. As intervocalic *-k-* is elided in most instances in this manuscript (see § 5.2.2.1), the G equivalent of the stem form of P *puṇḍarīka-* would probably be *puḍar(*ia)* in this scribe's orthography. The nominative singular could be *puḍar(*io), puḍar(*iu),* or even *puḍar(*ia)* (§ 6.1.1.1.2). I reconstruct *puḍar(*io).*

The surface of fragment 24g, on which *[yasa phulo]* appears, is rather worn. There seems to be a faint *o* diacritic on the *s*. A small chip covers the area where the upper portion of an *o* diacritic would have touched the *s* akṣara. The same word appears once more in this manuscript in the compound and sandhi combination *sayasavi* = P *seyyathāpi*. In the Khvs-G the spelling is *yaṣa* and, once, *yasa* (e.g., 4a, 5a), while in the Dhp-G^K it is *yadha, yatha,* and *yada*. In the Niya documents (Boyer, Rapson, and Senart 1920–9) the spelling is *yatha* and *yathā*. Although a final *o* vowel is thus unexpected in this word, there are examples in Gāndhārī of final *-o* appearing as *-ā,* for example, *sado* = P/Skt. *sadā* in the Dhp-G^K (see Brough 1962: § 22; Salomon 2000: § 6.1.3). I take the mark as an illusion and edit it as *[yasa]*.

For *[phulo]* the corresponding P has *vaggu* (= Skt. *valgu*), "beautiful," though the S^e has *uggaṃ,* "strong." The P commentaries gloss *vaggu* with *sundaraṃ* (Mp III 79.13) and *abhirūpaṃ* (Pj II 436.7). The G word, however, clearly corresponds to P and Skt. *phulla-,* an adjective meaning "blossoming," "flowering," which is commonly applied to lotuses, though apparently not to *puṇḍarīka*. Examples are *ath' ettha padumā phullā* (Jā VI 534.31, pāda a of śloka verse) and *padumaṃ yathā kokanadaṃ sugandhaṃ, pāto siyā phullam avītagandhaṃ* (SN I 81.13–4; AN III 239.23–4, pāda b of triṣṭubh verse).[107] The word is also applied to other plants and trees, for example, *sālaṃ va na ciraṃ phullaṃ* (DN II 267.12, pāda a of śloka verse), *navapattavanaṃ phullaṃ* (Jā V 158.17, pāda c of śloka verse), and *dumāni phullāni manoramāni* (Th 528, pāda a of triṣṭubh verse). In the majority of examples where it appears in śloka verse, it is the final word of a prior pāda, as in this G verse.

Also of interest is the parallel to this verse in Mvu III 326.21–327.1, where Senart's reading for pādas a and b, which are corrupt in the manuscripts, is *pauṇḍarīkaṃ yathā varṇaṃ, anope na pralipyate*. This provides a further illustration of the tendency for the final word of this pāda to be substituted, which in the case of this Mvu verse has completely changed the meaning.

+ [yo ṇ.] + + + + + [◦] (v. 2, pāda b): The P parallel is *toye na upalippati* (v. 2, pāda b). There is some variation in the reading of this and similar pādas in P texts. Apart from *upalimpati* (the active form) as a common v.l. of *upalippati,* the locative singular *toye,* as here, alternates with the instrumental singular *toyena*. The B^e and S^e of this AN passage read *toyena nupalippati*. The E^e of Sn 547b reads *toye na upalippati* but records the v.l. *toyena na* in two Burmese manuscripts. The B^e here has *toye na*. The CPD (s.v. *upalip-*

[107] This verse is quoted in many P commentaries. A parallel is found in the MPS § 11.17, where only *(*phu)llam upetagandham* is preserved.

pati) suggests reading *toyena nopalippati* in both locations. The CPD takes the instrumental constructions to mean "to be stained, defiled by," and the locative constructions to mean "to stick to."

In his discussion of the Sn verse, arguing against von Hinüber's attempt to take *toye* as an instrumental plural, Norman (1992a: 253) notes that the parallel words in the next line of verse, *evaṃ puññe ca pāpe ca, ubhaye tvaṃ na lippasi* (Sn 547c–d), are all in the locative singular, and he suggests that *toye* should likewise be taken as a locative singular. In contrast, in most of the other pādas of similar meaning quoted at the beginning of my discussion of these verses above, we find instrumental singular forms, for example, *nopalippati toyena, . . . nopalippati lokena, toyena padumaṃ yathā* (Th 700c, 701c–d ≈ AN III 347; see above for further references). Similarly, while pāda b of the AN verse under discussion reads *toye na upalippati* in the E[e], pāda c is *na upalippāmi lokena,* which suggests that the instrumental singular reading is the preferable one for pāda b also. Finally, in Mvu III 327.1, parallel to pāda c, we have the locative singular with no possibility of emending to the instrumental: *evaṃ loke na lipyāmi* (unless we were to propose *naivaṃ lokena lipyāmi*). In other words, it appears that in Buddhist texts the passive verb (P *upalippati, lippati*) was constructed with either the locative or the instrumental singular when connecting lotuses and water, on the one hand, and the Buddha and the world, on the other, without differentiation in meaning. A suitable translation for both contexts would be "defiled by" in the case of the instrumental and "defiled in" for the locative.

All that remains of this pāda in the Gāndhārī are the bottoms of the second and third akṣaras, which appear at the top of fragment 24b, and the punctuation mark at the beginning of fragment D6p. The first remaining akṣara appears to be the lower left arm of *yo,* and the second is consistent with *ṇ*. I therefore take the first three akṣaras to be *(*to)[yo ṇ](*a)* and, based on the P parallel, reconstruct the complete pāda as *(*to)yo ṇ(*a ualipadi)* ◦. In this case *(*to)yo* represents the locative singular as seen in the locative singular neuter *jedavaṇo* elsewhere in this manuscript (see § 6.1.1.2).

eva [l.]ghu alitu śpi (v. 2, pāda c): The parallels are P *na upalippāmi lokena* (v. 2, pāda c) and Skt. *evaṃ loke na lipyāmi* (Mvu III 327.1, pāda c). The P pāda is hypermetric, requiring resolution of the first syllable. The B[e] reads *nupalippāmi.*

Although the meaning is the same, the wording of the Gāndhārī differs from the Pali, being closer to the Mvu version, though not identical with it. The Gāndhārī, which can be reconstructed as *eva l(*o)ghu alitu śpi,* "so I am not defiled in the world," shares with the Mvu version *eva/evaṃ* and the locative singular *loghu/loke* as the first and second words but differs from it in using the negated past participle *alitu* = Skt. *aliptaḥ* in combination with the copula *śpi* = P/Skt. *'smi/asmi* in contrast to *na lipyāmi*. The Skt. equivalent of this verse would thus be **evaṃ loke 'lipto 'smi,* which would leave the pāda one syllable short and render the verse liable to misinterpretation (although the context would rule against this, it could nonetheless be misunderstood as "so I am defiled in the world"). It is possible that the Skt. version of the Mvu represents a secondary modification that occurred as a result of the Sanskritization of the text, designed to avoid these two problems, though, of course, it is equally possible that the MIA version or versions upon which the current BHS Mvu is based also had the negative particle plus finite verb. Such an example is found in Sn 547, which has pādas a and b in common with the AN verse, but whose pādas c and d are constructed similarly to the Mvu's pāda c: *puṇḍarīkaṃ yathā vaggu, toye na upalippati, evaṃ puññe ca pāpe ca, ubhaye tvaṃ na lippasi.*

A P equivalent of the G verse would read **evaṃ loke alitto 'smi,* which would make a perfectly good śloka pāda c. Apart from its verse occurrence in *alittam upalimpati* (It 68.6; Jā IV 435.26, VI 236.2), P *alitta-,* the equivalent of G *alita-,* does not occur in canonical texts but is not uncommon in P commentarial literature, especially as a gloss on *anŭpalitta-* (e.g., *anūpalitto ti . . . alitto:* Sp V 964.12–3; Pj II 409.9–10; Jā IV 332.11–2) in a long list of synonyms commonly found in the Niddesa's gloss on this and similar phrases: *na limpati na saṃlimpati* [v.l. *palimpati*] *na upalimpati alitto asaṃlitto* [v.l. *apalitto*] *anŭpalitto* (e.g., Nidd I 55, 90, 135, 203, 332). In contrast, besides its occurrence in the prose response of the Buddha found only in the P Doṇa-sutta (*viharāmi anupalitto lokena,* AN II 39.2–3), *anŭpalitta-* is the form normally found in canonical verse (e.g., *kāme ca loke ca anūpalitto,* Sn 845f). As in Sn 845f, it frequently occurs as the last word of a triṣṭubh pāda (e.g., Sn 392c, 790c; Dhp 353b).

taśpi budho mi brama[ṇa] + (v. 2, pāda d): The P parallel is *tasmā buddho 'smi brāhmaṇā ti* (v. 2, pāda d); compare Skt. . . . *smād buddho smi māṇava* (Toch.-Skt. bilingual fragment [Sieg and Siegling 1921], no. 362.4), *tasmād buddho nirucyate* (MSV I 268.17–20, pāda d), and *tasmād ahaṃ upaka jino* (Mvu III 326.19–327.3, pāda d).

The small remnant of ink at the far right of fragment 24b probably is the bottom of *ṇa* of *brama[ṇa].* If so, there is a space between *brama[ṇa]* and *[a]bhiñae,* perhaps where the anticipated punctuation mark once occurred. I therefore reconstruct *taśpi budho mi bramaṇa (*○).*

This pāda is identical with the final pāda of the next verse: *taśpi budho [mi bramaṇa].* Although only the Pali provides a parallel to the full verse, Skt. versions of this pāda appear as pāda d in the Skt. parallels to the following *abhijñeyaṃ* verse. Among the verses listed above, the one in the Toch.-Skt. bilingual fragment is the closest to the Gāndhārī and Pali, being parallel in all but the vocative.

As required by the meaning of the verse, the demonstrative pronoun is in the ablative singular in the P and Skt. parallels: P *tasmā*/Skt. *tasmād.* Although G *taśpi* is phonetically the equivalent of Skt. locative singular *tasmin,* its function here is ablative. Such a use of the locative ending for the ablative was previously unattested in Gāndhārī, but several further examples in the BL and Senior manuscripts prove that this did occur. In the Senior manuscripts we find *taspi* (with *sp* as a graphic variant of *śp*) so used: *asti bhade taspi paraḍa[e] a[ña] paraḍae aṣi mahadaro* (20 r16; cf. v1,2), where the P parallel (SN V 451.9–10) has *atthi nu kho bhante etamhā pariḷāhā añño pariḷāho mahantataro,* "Is there, Lord, another hell greater than this hell?" In the AG-G, written by the scribe who wrote the text presented here, we find *samasiśpi me cavae* (l. 38), which can be compared with P *samādhimhā cāvetukāmo* (e.g., SN I 129.12–3).[108] It seems that the pronominal declen-

---

[108] The example from the AG-G was provided by Richard Salomon. *Me* is the acc. sg. of the 1st-pers. pron., and *cavae* is a preterite of the causative of the verb √*cyu.* In *taśpi citu prasadesa* (AG-G, l. 85), *taśpi* represents the loc.; cf. *tasmiṃś cittaṃ prasādyāhaṃ* (MSV I 175.3). Abl. forms appear in the AG-G as *taśpa* (ll. 94, 96, 120).

sion has collapsed to the point where the locative and ablative singular have become interchangeable. In the Dhp-G^K the ablative, genitive, and locative singulars of the demonstrative pronoun (Skt. *tasmāt, tasya,* and *tasmin*) appear as *tasa,* with assimilation of *-sm-* and *-sy-* (Brough 1962: § 53) and apparently with weakening of the final vowel in the case of the locative (Fussman 1989: 456, 458, 471–2 [= §§ 18.1, 18.4, 31.1–3]; Salomon 1999: 132).[109] However, in light of the examples of the locative *taśpi/taspi* being used for the ablative in our manuscript and in the Senior manuscripts, phonetic "decay" is not the only explanation for such ambiguity in case inflection. A shift in case function is probably also a factor, though it is impossible to separate the two. It appears that the ablative, genitive, and locative singulars have collapsed so that any historical form could be used for any of these three oblique cases, representing a further stage of development of a phenomenon that is already evident in Pali and other Prakrits, while phonetic decay has resulted in ambiguity of case ending.

[a]bhiñae abhiñehi (v. 3, pāda a): The P parallel is *abhiññeyyaṃ abhiññātaṃ* (e.g., Sn 558a); Skt. parallels are *abhijñeyaṃ abhijñātaṃ* (Mvu III 327.2, pāda a; MSV I 268.19, pāda a) and the incomplete *bhijñātaṃ* (Toch.-Skt. bilingual fragment [Sieg and Siegling 1921], no. 362.3).

As discussed at some length above, the P Doṇa-sutta lacks this third verse, though the equivalent verse is found elsewhere in the canon. Both P and Skt. versions consist of a gerundive, *abhiññeyyaṃ/abhijñeyaṃ,* and a past participle, *abhiññātaṃ/abhijñātaṃ,* "what is to be realized has been realized," which is also the structure of pādas b and c of this verse (e.g., P *bhāvetabbañ ca bhāvitaṃ, pahātabbaṃ pahīnam me*). Although pāda c, and probably also pāda b, of the Gāndhārī are the same as the corresponding P and Skt. pādas (with the exception of the Mvu's pāda b), the syntax of pāda a of the Gāndhārī seems to differ from the corresponding Pali and Sanskrit, though the words are etymologically connected.

The form G *abhiñae,* which is unlikely to be a gerundive, seems to be the absolutive corresponding to P *abhiññāya*/Skt. *abhijñāya,* "having realized," though it could also be the feminine noun G *abhiña*/P *abhiññā,* declined in the instrumental singular or other oblique case (= P *abhiññāya*), "by means of knowledge." Similarly, G *abhiñehi* cannot be a past participle but must represent the gerundive corresponding to P *abhiññeyyaṃ*/Skt. *abhijñeyaṃ,* "what is to be realized," with *-i* for *-yaṃ* resulting from the palatalization of the vowel (see § 5.1.1) and with sandhi consonant *-h-* "written in place of alif or *-y-* as a syllable-divider" (Brough 1962: § 39). This finds a direct parallel in *ramahi* and *deśehi* in the Dhp-G^K, which Brough (1962: § 39) takes to be the present participle (the P version has *damayam*) and the optative (*deśayet;* the P version has *bhāsaye*), respectively.

In view of the above interpretation, a translation of the G *abhiñae abhiñehi* would be "having realized what is to be realized," which contrasts with the P and Skt. versions, "what is to be realized has been realized." The P and Skt. equivalents of the G pāda would be *abhiññāya abhiññeyyaṃ* and *abhijñāyābhijñeyaṃ.* Only the P version would work as a prior pāda of śloka verse. The pāda would also scan if the word order in the P

[109] Similar examples are seen in *cakṣusa* and *maṇosa* in the Senior mss. (20 r8), where the P parallel (SN IV 85.23–4) has the loc., *cakkhusmiṃ* and *manasmiṃ*.

and Skt. is reversed—P *abhiññātam abhiññeyyaṃ*/Skt. *abhijñātam abhijñeyaṃ*—though this seems a little awkward and changes the emphasis. It is no doubt this flexibility of word order that gave rise to the reading in the G verse. Further, given that the reading of this pāda is the same in both the P and the Skt. traditions, it is possible that *abhiñae* of our text arose when a form such as **abhiñaya(ṃ)* or **abhiñaï/*abhiñae* (with elision of *-t-* and possibly also with palatalization of the vowel) was not recognized as a past participle, which could have occurred in the course of oral or written transmission. And it is probably the case that *abhiñae* would not have been recognized by the scribe of our manuscript as a past participle, for there are no examples of elision of *-t-* or *-d-* in this manuscript, although there are examples in the other two manuscripts written by him (see § 5.2.2.4). This indicates that this verse at least, and perhaps this text also, passed through a dialect or scribal hand in which intervocalic *-t-* was occasionally elided, and where *-ya(ṃ)* most likely underwent further development to *-i/-e*. This could be seen as problematic because the elision of original intervocalic *t* or *d* is generally taken to be a characteristic of a later stage in the G language (see Salomon 1999: 126, 152; 2000: § 6.2.1.4; Brough 1962: § 33). However, examples of the elision of *-t-* or *-d-* are found in early documents. Salomon (1999: 126) lists several examples in the BL collection, including two from the AG-G, which is written by the same scribe as our text (*piu* = Skt. *pitur* and *ṇaï[ti]ru* = Skt. *nadītiram*), while examples such as *añaaro* = P *aññataro* appear in the Senior manuscripts (20 r1,15). In other words, the elision of original dental stops (*t* and *d*) may be more widespread in early G documents than previously thought.

bhavidavu [p.] bh.[vi] /// (v. 3, pāda b): The P parallel is *bhāvetabbañ ca bhāvitaṃ* (e.g., Sn 558b); the Skt. parallels are *bhāvanīyaṃ ca bhāvitam* (MSV I 268.19, pāda b), *bhāvanīyaṃ [ca] bhā[v]i[tam]* (Toch.-Skt. bilingual fragment [Sieg and Siegling 1921], no. 362.3), and *sadvaktavyaṃ ca bhāṣyati* (Mvu III 327.2, pāda b).[110] The main difference between the G version and the P and Skt. versions (excluding the Mvu passage) is the use of the conjunctive particle *p(*i)* = P *pi/api* (if my reconstruction is correct) rather than *ca,* which is of no great significance.

The akṣaras *bh.[vi] ///* must represent the past participle. The word can be restored with some degree of certainty to *bh(*a)vi(*du)* or *bh(*a)vi(*do)*. Adopting the former, the reconstruction of this pāda is therefore *bhavidavu p(*i) bh(*a)vi(*du ◦),* "what is to be developed has also been developed."

prahadavu prahiṇo mi (v. 3, pāda c): The upper part of *pra* in *prahadavu* is covered by a blank chip of bark. The parallels are P *pahātabbaṃ pahīnam me* (e.g., Sn 558c); Skt. *prahātavyaṃ prahīnaṃ* [read *prahīṇaṃ*] *me* (Mvu III 327.3, pāda c) and *prahātavyaṃ prahīṇaṃ ca* (MSV I 268.20, pāda c). The G and P versions and the Skt. version of the

---

[110] Compared to the G, P, and the other Skt. versions, which all more or less agree, the reading of the Mvu (*sadvaktavyaṃ ca bhāṣyati*; v.l. *sarvetavyañ ca bhāṣati* in two mss.) is exceptional. This reading and its variant are clearly closely connected with an MIA form such as the Pali. An MIA form such as the P *bhāvetabbañ ca bhāvitaṃ* and an MIA equivalent of Skt. *sadvaktavyaṃ ca bhāṣyati* or, even better, of *sarvetavyañ ca bhāṣati* would be virtually identical except for the initial *sa-* of the first word and the final *-ṣati* of the last. However, the process by which these initial and final elements changed is not at all clear.

Mvu are identical. The MSV version differs only in having *ca* in place of P/Skt. *me,* G *mi,* the enclitic first-person pronoun.[111]

sarvañu sa[rvadaśa]vi (v. 3, presented as pāda d): The akṣara *[rva]* is distorted by the splitting and expansion of the manuscript edge. Although the *śa* akṣara in the seventh syllable is badly distorted, there seems to be no remnant of a subscript *r*. The reading thus seems to be *daśavi* rather than *darśavi*. Both spellings are found in the Dhp-G^{K} (31c, 273c), while *sarvadarśiṇa* = Skt. *sarvadarśinā* appears in the AG-G (ll. 95–6). (See also Salomon 2000: § 6.2.2.3.) The parallels are P *sabbaññū sabbadassāvī* (e.g., Th 722a) and Skt. *sarvajñaḥ sarvadarśī ca* (MSV I 268.18, pāda c). This pāda and the reasons for its intrusion into the third verse of the Gāndhārī were discussed at length above. In form the G version is closer to the P version than to the MSV version. The reading of the MSV version may have arisen in the process of Sanskritization, where *sarvadarśī* was felt to be preferable to the BHS *sarvadarśāvī* (corresponding to P *sabbadassāvī*), which is found, for example, in the Mvu (I 254.3–4, II 13.3, 22.5, III 51.9–10). Although *sabbadassin* is found in the P canon, it is rare, occurring in such texts as the Ap (six times: e.g., II 406.4, 560.5), once in the Jā (III 349.4), and once as a proper name in the Bv (XIV.20). For the most part it is restricted to the commentarial literature, as are most examples of compounds with *-dassin* as final member. Because the Skt. form *sarvadarśī* left the pāda one syllable short, *ca* was inserted to make it scan.

A similar development may be seen in Uv XVI.4c, where the older manuscripts have *bhayadarśāvī,* while the younger ones have *bhayadarśino* (BHSD, s.v. *darśāvin*). However, the P Dhp (317a and b) has *bhayadassino* and *cābhayadassino* where the Dhp-G^{K} (273c and d) has *bhayadarśavi* and *abhayadarśaṇo*, indicating that the situation may be more complex.

taśpi budho [mi bramaṇa] (v. 3, presented as pāda e): The top of the *i* diacritic of *mi* only barely crosses the *m* stroke, making it appear like *kṣa* or *kṣu,* which would, however, be inappropriate in this context. The top of *bra* is distorted. The P parallel is *tasmā buddho 'smi brāhmaṇa* (e.g., Sn 558d); Skt. parallels are . . . *smād buddho smi māṇava* (Toch.-Skt. bilingual fragment [Sieg and Siegling 1921], no. 362.4) and *tasmād buddho nirucyate* (MSV I 268.17–20, pāda d); cf. *tasmād ahaṃ upaka jino* (Mvu III 326.19–327.3, pāda d).

For the discussion of the misplacement of this pāda due to the insertion of the preceding *sarvañu sa[rvadaśa]vi* pāda, see pp. 187–9. See also the above discussion of the identical pāda in verse 2.

[111] Although unlikely given the P and Skt. parallels, and given that the construction of pādas a and b in Pali and Sanskrit indicates otherwise, G *prahadavu prahiṇo mi* could theoretically be a periphrastic perfect construction (where *mi* represents P and Skt. *'smi/asmi*), with active meaning for the transitive verb: "I have destroyed what is to be destroyed" (cf. Geiger 1994: § 173; Burrow 1937: §§ 105 ff.).

Lines 20–5: Dhoṇa expresses his conversion to lay status

Edition:

[21] [|24a] *bhu ghodama abhikatu* ∘ *suyasavi [bhu] ghudama ṇiujidu ukuje* ∘ *paḍ[i]*[|D6u+ D6x] *c*[|D6x]*haṇo a viv.* ///
[22] [|24a] *muḍhasa va maghu praghaśe ?* ∘ *[adhagha]ro [a]l[oka va]* ∘ *ya[va]d=eva cakṣu[a]tu ruaṇa dhrekṣatu* ∘ [23] *[eva]m=eva ṣamaṇeṇa gho[da]meṇa krirṇo śukro dharmu akhade vivaḍe [s.]*[|24a+ D6dd |24a]*praghaśi[d]e* /// [24] *ṣamaṇo ghudamu śaraṇo ghachami dhama ca bhikhusagha ca* ∘ *u ? ? ?* [|D6dd] *[mi ṣ.]ma* /// [|24a] [25]*[m.] dharedu ajavaghreṇa yavajivu praṇouviade śaraṇo abhiprasaṇe* ∘

Reconstruction:
[20] *(*abhikatu)* [21] *bhu ghodama abhikatu* ∘ *suyasavi bhu ghudama ṇiujidu ukuje* ∘ *paḍichaṇo a viv(*are* ∘*)* [22] *muḍhasa va maghu praghaśe* ∘ *adhagharo aloka va* *<*dharae>* ∘ *yavad eva cakṣuatu ruaṇa dhrekṣatu* ∘ [23] *evam eva ṣamaṇeṇa ghodameṇa krirṇo śukro dharmu akhade vivaḍe s(*a)praghaśide (*∘ eṣaho)* [24] *ṣamaṇo ghudamu śaraṇo ghachami dhama ca bhikhusagha ca* ∘ *u(*asaghu) mi ṣ(*a)ma(*ṇe ghuda)-* [25]*m(*e) dharedu ajavaghreṇa yavajivu praṇouviade śaraṇo <*ghade> abhiprasaṇe* ∘

Translation:
[20] "(*Wonderful), [21] venerable Gotama! Wonderful! Just as, venerable Gotama, one would set upright what has been overturned or uncover what has been covered [22] or show the path to one who is lost or (*bring) light into the darkness, so that those with eyes might see forms, [23] even so has the monk Gotama declared, revealed, and proclaimed the dharmas, bright and dark. (*I) [24] go to the monk Gotama as a refuge and to the Dharma and to the Saṅgha. May the monk (*Gotama) accept me as a layman, [25] who with faith (*has gone) [to him] as a refuge from today onward, for as long as there is life, until [my] last breath."

The P version of the sutta ends with the two verses uttered by the Buddha, with no mention of Doṇa's conversion. The commentary (Mp III 76–7) states that the Buddha had taken this road because he foresaw that the following course of events would happen (main verbs in the future tense): Doṇa will be traveling on that road; Doṇa will follow his footprints and ask him questions; he will teach Doṇa the four truths (*catusaccadhammaṃ*) (this is not explicitly related in the sutta; the vv.ll. are *ekaṃ saccadhammaṃ* and *evaṃ saccadhammaṃ*); realizing the three fruits of an ascetic (*tīṇi sāmaññaphalāni paṭivijjhitvā*), Doṇa will "roar the praise called the Doṇa-roar consisting of 12,000 words" and resolve the dispute over the Buddha's remains after his *parinibbāna*; then Doṇa will divide his remains.[112] The commentary on this sutta ends (Mp III 79) by stating that, at the end of the discourse, which concluded with the words *tasmā buddho 'smi brāhmaṇa,* the last pāda of the second verse, Doṇa attained the "fruits of the path" (*tīṇi maggaphalāni*), uttered the Doṇa-roar, then resolved the dispute and distributed the Buddha's remains (all in the past tense) after the Buddha attained the *parinibbāna.*[113]

Doṇa's "roar" and his resolution of the dispute over the Buddha's remains are recorded in the Mahāparinibbāna-suttanta (DN II 166–7), but there is no canonical record of Doṇa's spiritual attainment. The commentarial statement *desanāpariyosāne tīṇi maggaphalāni pāpuṇitvā* implies that he attained the "three fruits of the path" at the end of his interaction with the Buddha, though the wording of the commentary makes the temporal relationship between his attainment and his uttering of the Doṇa-roar a little ambiguous. We would have expected that, if his attainment had resulted from this conversation, then his declaration of conversion would have immediately followed.

The Doṇabrāhmaṇa-sutta[114] (AN III 223–30), which records a fairly long discussion between the Buddha and "Doṇa brāhmaṇa" (who is generally assumed to be the same Doṇa), ends with Doṇa being converted to lay status (AN III 230; the formula is abbreviated in the E^e and B^e), parallel to the conversion recorded at the end of the G Dhoṇa-sutra. His conversion on this occasion is confirmed by the fact that the respect he shows the Buddha when he first approaches him (*saddhiṃ sammodi*) is typical of those who do not have faith, for if he had already been a convert, he would have shown the *abhivādetvā* form of respect and addressed him as *bhante*. Thus, if this Doṇabrāhmaṇa-sutta does concern the same brahman who features in the Doṇa-sutta, then the P tradition is implying that the events described in the Doṇabrāhmaṇa-sutta occurred after those depicted in the Doṇa-sutta, and that Doṇa's attainment (and obviously his conversion) occurred after his second recorded interaction with the Buddha. Unfortunately, the commentary on this latter sutta (Mp III 307–10) provides no relevant information.

The absence at the end of the P Doṇa-sutta of a record of Doṇa's conversion is a little odd, for this event forms a standard conclusion to suttas that record the Buddha debating or in discussion with someone who is not already a convert, as in the Doṇabrāhmaṇa-sutta. In fact, the lack of any conclusion to the P sutta renders it incomplete, though this is typical of many suttas in the editions and in most manuscripts of the AN. The absence of a statement at the end of the P Doṇa-sutta regarding Doṇa's conversion may have resulted from the fact that the AN collection contained two separate suttas recording an interaction

---

[112] *kasmā paṭipanno ti. taṃ divasaṃ kira bhagavā idaṃ addasa mayi taṃ maggaṃ paṭipanne doṇo brāhmaṇo mama padacetiyāni passitvā padānupadiko hutvā mama nisinnaṭṭhānaṃ āgantvā pañhaṃ pucchissati ath' assāhaṃ catusaccadhammaṃ desissāmi brāhmaṇo tīṇi sāmaññaphalāni paṭivijjhitvā dvādasapadasahassaparimāṇaṃ doṇagajjitaṃ nāma vaṇṇaṃ gajjitvā mayi parinibbute sakala-jambudvīpe uppannaṃ mahākalahaṃ vūpasametvā dhātuyo bhājessatī ti iminā kāraṇena paṭipanno* (Mp III 76–7).

[113] *tasmā buddho 'smi brāhmaṇā ti desanāpariyosāne tīṇi maggaphalāni* [S^e v.l. *phalāni*] *pāpuṇitvā dvādasahi padasahassehi doṇagajjitaṃ nāma vaṇṇaṃ kathesi, tathāgate ca parinibbute jambudīpatale uppannaṃ mahākalahaṃ vūpasametvā dhātuyo bhājesī ti* (Mp III 79).

[114] Pj II 318.20 and 325.15 refer to this sutta as the Doṇasuttaṃ (see § 8.1.2 for the discussion of the sutta titles).

between the Buddha and a brahman called Doṇa, both of which could not conclude in the same way if the brahman in both was the same individual. Why the compilers of the P material chose to associate his conversion with the interaction depicted in the second sutta is not clear (unless we regard these records as historically accurate). His conversion could have been attached to the Doṇa-sutta, and the introduction to the Doṇabrāhmaṇa-sutta could have depicted him exhibiting the gestures of a convert. It is therefore possible that the two brahmans were not the same individual, and that the conversion formula was omitted from the Doṇa-sutta under the assumption that they were.

In contrast to the P tradition, the G tradition as represented by our manuscript records Dhoṇa's conversion as having occurred after the events depicted therein. Along with the concluding formula (see below), the G version thus presents a more complete sūtra. No G parallel to the P Doṇabrāhmaṇa-sutta currently exists, but were it to turn up, its conclusion would be of interest.

The three Chinese translations of this sūtra parallel the P in making no mention of the brahman's conversion. In the version found in the EĀ (T no. 125), the sūtra ends with the brahman's gaining insight and expressing his delight at the Buddha's words, while both SĀ translations (T nos. 99, 100) end with the brahman's delighting in the Buddha's words and departing.

A second G version of the conversion formula appears in the Senior manuscripts. A provisional reading by Richard Salomon is

> [9] *i�́[i] vute s̱o bramaṇo bhayava[ta] e[d́a] ? [ya]* [10] *eṣao bha g[a]d́a[m. śara]ṇo gachami dhrarma ja bhikhusa[ga] ja uasao me bh[i] god́am[o] dharei ajavag[r]eṇa yavajiv. p.ṇued́.* [11] *śaraṇa gada.* (20 r9–11)

Although the conversion formula does not occur in the P Doṇa-sutta, conversion formulas, whether depicting conversion to lay status or to the state of becoming a monk, do occur innumerable times in P texts. The P formula depicting conversion to lay status is

> *abhikkantaṃ bho gotama abhikkantaṃ bho gotama. seyyathāpi bho gotama nikkujjitaṃ vā ukkujjeyya paṭicchannaṃ vā vivareyya mūḷhassa vā maggaṃ ācikkheyya andhakāre vā telapajjotaṃ dhāreyya cakkhumanto rūpāni dakkhintī ti evam eva kho bhotā gotamena anekapariyāyena dhammo pakāsito. esāhaṃ bhagavantaṃ gotamaṃ saraṇaṃ gacchāmi dhammañ ca bhikkhusaṅghañ ca. upāsakaṃ maṃ bhavaṃ gotamo dhāretu ajjatagge pāṇupetaṃ saraṇaṃ gatan ti.* (E.g., AN I 56.3–11)[115]

The corresponding formula in Buddhist Skt. texts is also quite common. Although there are variations in the reading, even within the same text, the basic structure and wording of the examples encountered in various Buddhist Skt. texts are essentially the same. Catuṣpariṣat-sūtra § 16.16, for example, reads

---

[115] For occurrences of this common conversion formula in Pali, see PTC, s.v. *abhikkamati*.

abhikrānto 'haṃ bhadantābhikrāntaḥ. eṣo 'haṃ bhagavantaṃ śaraṇaṃ gacchāmi dharmañ ca bhikṣusaṃghaṃ ca. upāsakaṃ ca māṃ dhārayādyāgreṇa yāvajjīvaṃ prāṇopetaṃ śaraṇaṃ gatam abhiprasannam.[116]

In the Divy examples (e.g., 53.6–9, 71.27–72.3, 311.5–8, 462.13–6) the reading alternates between *atikrānto* and *abhikrānto*[117] (the alternation between the *abhi-* and *ati-* prefixes is common in Buddhist texts; see Divy 707, n. to p. 311; BHSD, s.vv. *atikrānta, abhikrānta;* CPD, s.v. *abhi-*).[118] Numerous examples are also found in the MSV (e.g., I 54.5–7, 58.16–8, 70.3–5, 231.1–4, II 46.21–47.1, III 143.4–6).[119] The reading throughout the MSV is *śaraṇagatam* instead of *śaraṇaṃ gatam.*[120]

The relationship between the G, P, and Skt. versions of the conversion formula will be discussed in the course of the analysis of each phrase below and summarized in the conclusion to this section. But it is worthy of note here that one of the most striking differences between the G, P, and Skt. versions is the complete absence in the Skt. version, and in Buddhist Skt. texts in general it seems, of the similes likening the Buddha's words to the uncovering of what was covered, to showing the path to one who is lost, and to the bringing of light into darkness. The complex relationship among the various versions of this formula is further complicated by the absence of these similes and of the initial exclamation of amazement in the G version of the formula in the Senior manuscripts.

The first word or words of the conversion formula are missing in our manuscript. They must have occurred at the end of line 20. Based on a comparison with the second G

---

[116] Further examples are CPS §§ 17.13, 18.9, 22.15, 23.12, 27f.22. Cf. also KaVā §§ 4.5,7,9, 6.3. (For further references, see SWTF, s.v. *abhikrānta.*) Of the vv.ll. worthy of mention in the CPS, the manuscript of § 16.16 reads *bhadantaḥ abhikrāntaḥ . . . apiprasannam,* while the reading at § 27f.22 is *e(*ṣo) 'haṃ bhadanta bhagavantaṃ śaraṇaṃ.* The Skt. BimbSū (Waldschmidt 1932: 143) has *e(*ṣo) 'haṃ bhadanta bhagavantaṃ.* Parallels to the §§ 22.15, 23.12, and 27f.22 CPS occurrences are found in the Gilgit ms. of the Saṅghabhedavastu. The vv.ll. of interest in the Gilgit ms. noted by Waldschmidt in his footnotes to these sections of the CPS are *atikrānto* for *abhikrānto; copāsakaṃ* for *ca upāsakaṃ* throughout; *śaraṇagatam atiprasannam* to § 27f.22.

[117] Edgerton (BHSD, s.v. *atikrānta*) notes that *atikrānta* is an erroneous reading for *abhikrānta* at Divy 462.13 at least. Other vv.ll. in the Divy are *eṣo 'haṃ buddhaṃ bhagavantaṃ śaraṇaṃ* (311.6); *eṣo 'haṃ bhagavantaṃ buddhaṃ śaraṇaṃ* (462.13–4). The 311.5–8 occurrence omits *śaraṇaṃ gatam* (i.e., the reading is *prāṇopetam abhiprasannam*), while the 53.6–9 occurrence has *ca upāsakāṃ* (with appropriate f. gender), compared with *copāsakaṃ* elsewhere.

[118] Cf. the P commentarial gloss on *abhikkantaṃ* from another context: *atha vā abhikkantan ti atikkantaṃ ati-iṭṭhitaṃ atimanāpaṃ atisundaran ti* (e.g., Sp I 170.27–8; Ud-a 286.10–1; Pj II 155.14–6; Sv I 228.14–5; see CPD, s.v. *abhikkanta,* for references), with some occurrences reading *atikantaṃ* or *abhikantaṃ* for *atikkantaṃ.*

[119] See also Mvu III 268.8 ff.; BhīVin(Mā-L), §§ 10, 11, 153; Avś I 82.5.

[120] The vv.ll. are *buddhaṃ śaraṇaṃ* (I 58.16–7); *dhāraya adyāgreṇa* (I 58.17–8, 70.4–5); the second *abhikrāntā* is omitted at I 231.2. Gnoli's (1978) reading at Śayanāsanavastu 17.26–9, which parallels MSV III 143.4–6 of the Dutt edition, has *ca upāsakam māṃ ca dhāraya adyāgreṇa* rather than *ca upāsakaṃ māṃ dhārayādyāgreṇa* and *śaraṇāgatam* for *śaraṇagatam,* but Wille (1990: 117) reads *copāsakaṃ ca mān dhārayādyāgreṇa . . . śaraṇagatam.*

version and with the parallel P and Skt. versions (see below for discussion), the missing portion probably comprised four or five akṣaras. Preceding this formula and providing a connection between the verses spoken by the Buddha and this declaration of conversion spoken by the brahman Dhoṇa, we would have expected wording parallel to P *evaṃ vutte* [name] *brāhmaṇo bhagavantam etad avoca,* as found, for example, throughout the Brāhmaṇa-saṃyuttaṃ within the Sagātha-vagga of the SN (I 160–84; e.g., I 161.8–9, 163.1–2, 164.1–2) functioning in the same way. Such a formula precedes the second G version of the conversion formula quoted above: *iḋ[i] vute ṣo bramaṇo bhayava[ta] e[ḋa] ? [ya]*. Since the equivalent of P *ti*/Skt. *iti*, in its function as quotative particle, does not seem to be common in G texts (see pp. 170–1), it is most likely that the initial *iḋi* of this formula is functioning in the sense of *evaṃ*, "thus"; that is, G *iḋ[i] vute* is the equivalent of P *evaṃ vutte* rather than *ti* (*evaṃ*) *vutte*. The final *e[ḋa] ? [ya]* of the Senior manuscript version would appear in our manuscript as *eghad oya* or *eghad uya,* which corresponds to P *etad avoca* (see pp. 163–5). A possible reading of the formula were it to occur in our text would then be *(*idi vute dhoṇe bramaṇe bhayavadu eghad oya ◦)*, which is eighteen akṣaras long.

Line 20 currently has twenty-four akṣaras, but a punctuation mark would have marked the end of the verses, making twenty-five. As mentioned above, the words missing from the beginning of the conversion formula at the end of line 20 consisted of four or five akṣaras (see below for details), taking the count up to twenty-nine or thirty. As a line may contain up to thirty-eight or -nine akṣaras, and given that lines 18 and 19, consisting of verse, both had thirty-one akṣaras, it seems that the **idi vute dhoṇe bramaṇe bhayavadu eghad oya* phrase of seventeen akṣaras (or eighteen with final punctuation) was not included in our manuscript, since its inclusion would make the line too long. This is somewhat unexpected given that the G version of this sūtra (and of the following two sūtras) is more complete than the P version preserved in manuscripts and presented in published editions. For example, our G text includes the phrase that connects the Buddha's prose speech with his verses (*(*ida)m u bhayavadu ida vadita sughadu hasavaro idam avaï śastu*, ll. 15–6), whereas the P text omits it (though it was probably included when chanted). The G text includes a standard sūtra conclusion (see below), which the P editions omit, and the second and third sūtras of this manuscript include complete versions of the standard sūtra opening, which is missing in the P parallel to the third.

The inclusion of some phrase such as *bhagavantam idam avocat* introducing the speech of the one who is professing his or her conversion is common to Buddhist Skt. texts also (e.g., CPS §§ 16.15, 17.12, 18.8, 22.14, 23.11, 27f.21). However, as in these CPS examples, it seems to be the norm that, after the Buddha's discourse and before the individual's declaration of conversion, the individual is depicted as attaining a certain spiritual insight. In some cases the individual's declaration of conversion immediately follows the statement about his or her spiritual attainment without a *bhagavantam idam avocat* phrase (e.g., Divy 71, 462; MSV I 53–4, 69–70). But examples of the conversion formula occurring immediately after the Buddha's speech with no phrase indicating change of speaker are not encountered, in either Sanskrit or Pali. It is therefore possible that a phrase indicating a change of speaker was accidentally omitted in our manuscript.

bhu ghodama abhikatu ◦*:* The corresponding P is *abhikkantaṃ bho gotama abhikkantaṃ bho gotama,* and the Buddhist Skt. version is *abhikrānto 'haṃ bhadantābhikrāntaḥ,* with v.l. *atikrānto . . . atikrāntaḥ*. These introductory words of exclamation are missing in the second G version in Senior manuscript no. 20.

Although similar in overall wording (i.e., leaving aside the different vocatives, *bho gotama* in the Pali and *bhadanta* in the Sanskrit), the P and Skt. versions differ in an interesting way. P *abhikkantaṃ* is nominative singular neuter, meaning "it is wonderful," "it is excellent," and is used as an exclamation, "wonderful!" "excellent!" a use that is articulated in the P commentaries as *abbhanumodana* (see CPD, s.v. *abhikkanta* 4; PTSD, s.v. *abhikkanta* 3). The Pali can be translated "Wonderful, venerable Gotama! Wonderful, venerable Gotama!" In the Sanskrit, however, *abhikrāntaḥ* is predicated to *(a)haṃ,* and the meaning seems rather to be "I am advanced," "I am successful" (see BHSD, s.v. *abhikrānta* 1). This, in fact, suits the context of the examples of this formula so far encountered in Buddhist Skt. texts in that these normally follow a statement about the individual's attainment of a particular spiritual insight as a result of hearing the Buddha's words. A possible translation of the Sanskrit is "I am successful, Lord. (I am) successful." The v.l. *atikrāntaḥ* would be even more forceful in this context, as illustrated in a recent translation of the Divy 53.6 occurrence, which reads *atikrāntāhaṃ bhadantātikrāntā,* as "I have gone beyond [the cycle of birth-and-death], Venerable, I have gone beyond!" (Tatelman 2000: 79).

As vocatives do not normally occur at the beginning of a sentence in sūtra/sutta texts, it is highly likely that *bhu ghodama abhikatu* ◦ does not represent the full phrase. If the Gāndhārī paralleled the Pali, then it is likely that *abhikatu* = P *abhikkantaṃ* is all that is missing. The reconstruction would then be *(*abhikatu) bhu ghodama abhikatu* ◦. In this case the Gāndhārī lacked the second vocative. But if the Gāndhārī paralleled the Sanskrit, then the missing phrase would be *(*abhikatu ho)* = Skt. *abhikrānto 'haṃ,* and the reconstruction would be *(*abhikatu ho) bhu ghodama abhikatu* ◦. It is also possible, but less likely, that the reading was *(*aha) bhu ghodama abhikatu* ◦, equal to a Skt. *ahaṃ . . . abhikrāntaḥ*.

G *abhikatu* is ambiguous. It could represent the nominative singular masculine or neuter. Although, perhaps, ultimately not significant, the lack of the second vocative ending in the G phrase could be taken as an indication that the Gāndhārī was parallel to the Sanskrit. However, as no statement concerning Dhoṇa's spiritual attainment precedes Dhoṇa's declaration of conversion, I am inclined to think that the Gāndhārī was closer to the Pali. Further, although the Gāndhārī parallels the Sanskrit on other points, the inclusion in the Gāndhārī of the simile parallel to the Pali suggests that the first half of the G formula was closer to the Pali. I therefore rather tentatively reconstruct *(*abhikatu) bhu ghodama abhikatu* ◦, taking *abhikatu* as the nominative singular neuter = P *abhikkantaṃ*. The translation is "(*Wonderful), venerable Gotama! Wonderful!"

It is worthy of note that the G form is *abhikatu,* reflecting P *abhikkantaṃ,* rather than the expected G **abhikratu* with the cluster *-kr-* retained from OIA. Apart from one example in the Niya documents (Burrow 1937: § 37b) and the examples of *kudhu, kodha, kothu* = Skt. *krodha* and *kodhaṇa* = Skt. *krodhana* in the Dhp-G^K, original *kr* virtually always appears as *kr* in Gāndhārī (see Burrow 1937: §§ 36b, 37b; Brough 1962: § 51; Salomon 2000: § 6.2.2.2). This is also the case in this manuscript (see § 5.2.3.4). In fact, if *abhikatu* is the equivalent of Skt. *abhikrānta-,* then it would be the only example of *-k(k)-* for *-kr-* in this manuscript and apparently also in the other BL manuscripts written by this scribe, although the spelling *uasakamita* = BHS *upasaṃkramitvā* is found in the Senior manuscripts in the passage quoted above (see commentary on ll. 8–9). According to the CPD (s.v. *abhikkanta*), in at least two of its meanings P *abhikkanta* also allows a derivation from *abhi* + √*kam* (CPD, s.v. *abhikkanta* 2, "excellent," and 3, "beautiful, splendid"), a derivation that Geiger (1994: § 33.1) favored for P *abhikkantaṃ* in the phrase under review. It is therefore possible that the word was so understood by the G translators, although it cannot be ruled out that the spelling was taken over from the source dialect (see § 2.6).

suyasavi [bhu] ghudama ṇiujidu ukuje ◦: The P parallel is *seyyathāpi bho gotama nikkujjitaṃ vā ukkujjeyya*. The structure of the simile in the Gāndhārī, that is, *suyasavi* [vocative] . . . *evam eva* [vocative], parallels the P *seyyathāpi* [vocative] . . . *evam eva* [vocative], "just as . . . even so."

The reading of the first akṣara in *suyasavi* is clearly *su-,* which is unexpected. The word appears again on line 62 as *sayasavi*. The initial *se-* element of the corresponding P *seyyathāpi* is an eastern feature, representing the nominative singular neuter *tad* (Lüders 1954: § 2; Norman 1976: 22 [= CP, vol. II, p. 97], cf. 1989a: 370 [= CP, vol. IV, p. 47]; von Hinüber 1986: § 375), found in the corresponding Skt. expression *tadyathā* encountered in Buddhist texts whose language is less hybrid.[121] *Sayathāpi* is recorded once in the P canon (Th 412), as the reading in the E^e only, but because this reading was adoped by the editor from the commentary, against *seyyathāpi* of the manuscripts (also the reading of the B^e and S^e of text and commentary), Lüders (1954: § 2) expressed some uncertainty as to its status.[122] The G form *sayasavi* (l. 62) does not exhibit the full eastern *se-* (Amg. *se,* Mg. *śe*) but rather parallels the modified BHS form *sayyathāpi*. If *suyasavi* is a valid G spelling (rather than a scribal whim), then it is possible that it originated by replacing the *se-* of a received MIA form such as P *seyyathāpi* with *so-/su-* based on an erroneous assumption that *se-* represented the nominative singular masculine, G and P *so,* Skt. *saḥ*. Of course, it is also possible that *suyasavi* arose as a secondary development from a G *sayasavi* for the same reasons. Alternatively, *suyasavi* may be nothing more than a scribal error for *sayasavi,* where the scribe mistook a more curved tail on the *sa-* of his exemplar as a *u* diacritic. Further examples are needed to adequately evaluate this spelling. (See also § 5.1.4.)

In view of the P and BHS forms, it is likely that *-y-* represents a geminate (*yy*).

---

[121] The western (and Sanskritic) form *taṃyathā* (in the sense of "as") is found once in Pali in the Mil (1.11), which, as Norman (1976: 22 = CP, vol. II, p. 97) notes, is of interest considering the supposed origins of this text.

[122] Norman (1969a: 191, n. to v. 412) notes that the meter is better with *sayathāpi*.

The first image depicted in the simile is that of setting upright what has been overturned. Although the simile itself does not seem to occur in Buddhist Skt. texts, a similar image utilizing similar words is encountered in the MSV: *sa bhikṣūṇāṃ dūtam anupreṣayati. āgacchantv āryāḥ pātraṃ nikubjam utkubjāpayiṣyatha* (IV 140.14–5).

The G past participle *ṇiujidu,* with elision of single intervocalic *-k-,* reflects the P spelling *nikujjitaṃ,* also *nikujjati,* etc., rather than *nikkujjitaṃ, nikkujjati,* etc., of which they are a common v.l. The latter spellings are based on analogy with *ukkujja, ukkujjati,* and derivatives (see PTSD, s.vv. *nikujjati, nikkujjati,* etc.).

G *ukuje* represents a regular parasmaipada optative equivalent of P *ukkujjeyya* (see § 6.3.2). The akṣara *je* could possibly be read as *mi,* but the reading *ukumi* is unlikely in this context.

The Gāndhārī differs from the Pali only in lacking the disjunctive *vā,* "or." The disjunctive appears in each of the four images in the first half of the P simile: *nikkujjitaṃ vā ukkujjeyya, paṭicchannaṃ vā vivareyya, mūḷhassa vā maggaṃ ācikkheyya, andhakāre vā telapajjotaṃ dhāreyya.* The G phrases corresponding to the second, third, and fourth images contain *a/va,* but further examples are needed to determine whether the lack of the disjunctive in the first clause is a scribal omission or reflects a stylistic feature of G texts of this class.

paḍ[i]chaṇo a viv.: The P parallel is *paṭicchannaṃ vā vivareyya.* The vowel diacritic on the second akṣara (*ḍ[i]*) appears to be *o,* as no remnant of ink appears above the horizontal. However, as the bark is badly worn at this point, and because *ḍo* would be unexpected in view of the P parallel, I adopt the above reading.

The likely reconstruction of the verb is *viv(*are).* Examples of forms of *vi* + √*vṛ,* "uncover," from the present system are so far lacking in Gāndhārī.

muḍhasa va maghu praghaśe ? ∘: The P parallel is *mūḷhassa vā maggaṃ ācikkheyya.* An akṣara of uncertain reading (possibly a vowel) appears below the line before the final punctuation mark. This is normally the position for the addition of corrections, although none seems warranted here. If it does represent an intentional correction, it is possible that the scribe has "corrected" *praghaśe* to *praghaśea,* although this is not the regular optative form in this manuscript. I therefore ignore this mark.

The Gāndhārī differs from the Pali only in the verb used. Both are third-person singular parasmaipada optatives. G *praghaśe* is from *pra* + √*kāś.* The etymology of P *ācikkhati* is complex, but the word is generally considered to be connected with both *ā* + √*khyā* and *ā* + √*cakṣ* (see CPD, s.v., for references to the various discussions). The BHS form corresponding to P *ācikkhati* is *ācikṣati,* which according to the BHSD (s.v.) occurs only in the Mvu (but it also appears in the BhīVin(Mā-L), see index, s.v. *ācakṣ,* for references). The Skt. form is *ācakṣati* (e.g., *ācakṣva,* MSV I 268.8,12; cf. SWTF, s.v *ācakṣati*).

The P form corresponding to G *praghaśe* is *pakāseyya,* which is found in a list of synonyms given in the old commentarial section of the Vinaya as a gloss on *āvikareyya: so deseyya so vivareyya so uttānikareyya so pakāseyya* (Vin I 103.25–6). The same commentarial section contains an even longer list of synonyms that appears as a gloss on (*pātimokkhaṃ*) *uddisissāmi,* in which the future forms of *ācikkhati* and *pakāseti* are the first and last members, respectively: *ācikkhissāmi desessāmi paññāpessāmi paṭṭhapessāmi vivarissāmi vibhajissāmi uttānikarissāmi pakāsessāmi* (Vin I 103.15–7). This list also occurs in the Vibh (259; cf. Ud-a 308.26–7), with each member commented on in Vibh-a 371, and in the Niddesa as a gloss on *pabrūmi* and *brūmi* (e.g., Nidd I 274.21–3, 290.3–5), where the reading is more commonly *uttānīk~*. A shorter list of synonyms consisting of past participles occurs in the SN (IV 166–7): *akkhāto vivaṭo pakāsito,* with the G version of this list (*akhade vivaḍe s(*a)praghaśide*) appearing in the latter part of the conversion formula where the corresponding P has *pakāsito* only (see below). The G text thus uses a similar verb (*maghu praghaśe . . . dharmu s(*a)praghaśide*) in both places within the conversion formula where the P uses different, though synonymous, ones (*maggaṃ ācikkheyya . . . dhammo pakāsito*).

It is of some interest that all the longer lists of synonyms found in canonical sutta texts lack the final *pakāseti: ācikkhati deseti paññāpeti paṭṭhapeti vivarati vibhajati uttānīkaroti* (e.g., SN II 26.1–2).[123] The reading at AN II 160.24–5, *ācikkhāmi desemi* <u>*pakāsemi*</u> *paññāpemi paṭṭhapemi vivarāmi vibhajāmi uttānīkaromi,* where both the B^e^ and the commentary (Mp III 149) omit *pakāsemi,* indicates that *pakāsemi* is an insertion based on familiarity with lists containing this word. *Pakāseti,* and related forms, are included only in the longer lists of synonyms in the commentarial and Abhidhamma sections of the P canon, and here as the final member of the list, thus indicating that it probably represents a later addition. The Skt. equivalent of these lists within sūtra texts (NidSa § 14.3; MPS § 9.18; cf. SWTF, s.v. *ākhyā-*) is *ākhyāti prajñāpayati prasthāpayati vibhajati vivaraty uttānīkaroti deśayati saṃprakāśayati*. If we ignore the slight change in word order (*deśayati* as the penultimate member), it is worthy of note that *ākhyāti* appears as the equivalent of P *ācikkhati* (to which P *ācikkhati* is in part related), while *saṃprakāśayati* appears as the final member, parallel to *pakāseti* in the same position in the commentarial/Abhidhamma versions of the P list.

Apart from the past participial form just referred to, finite forms of P *pakāseti* are quite common in canonical sutta texts. In verse, for example, we find *te imaṃ dhammaṃ pakāsenti* (AN II 52.26), and in prose, *tassa bhikkhū dhammaṃ desenti . . . brahmacariyaṃ pakāsenti* (AN I 130.11–4). However, there are no examples of this verb being connected with *maggaṃ* as in the G phrase.[124] In this regard a verse in the MSV, which echoes the simile under discussion, provides an interesting parallel to the G usage: *satvānām andhabhūtānāṃ, mūḍhānām utpathacāriṇām, ṛjumārgaṃ prakāśayati, kṣemaṃ nirvāṇagāminam* (I 271.5–6).[125]

Of course, as a comparison of parallel versions of particular Buddhist texts quickly reveals, the substitution of synonyms is common. With reference to verbs meaning "teach," "show," etc., for example, the P Dhp has *atthaṃ dhammañ ca dīpeti* (363c) where the Dhp-G^K^ has *deśedi* (24c, 54c), the Patna Dhp has *deśeti* (54c, ed. Roth 1980),

---

123 Each synonym is explained at Spk II 40.

124 The closest examples are *paṭipadā samaṇena pakāsitā* (Sn 714) and *atha yā buddhānaṃ sāmukkaṃsikā dhammadesanā taṃ pakāsesi dukkhaṃ samudayaṃ nirodhaṃ maggaṃ* (MN I 380.2–3).

125 Cf. *āryaṃ dharmaṃ prakāseyaṃ* (Mvu I 42.7, 53.4) and *evaṃ ca mahyaṃ asyā prakāśanā deśanā ca dharmasya* (Mvu I 42.10, 53.5).

and the Uv has *deśayati* (VIII.10c). The Dhp-G^{K} has *deśehi jodaï dhamu* (236a) where the P has *bhāsaye jotaye dhammaṃ* (AN II 51.31, pāda a), and the Uv has *bhāṣayed dyotayed dharmam* (XXIX.44a). Similarly, the expression *sāvakānaṃ dhammaṃ deseti* found in the P Lohicca-suttanta (DN I 230.11) appears as *samānaśrāvakānāṃ dharmam ākhyāsi* in the Skt. parallel (SHT IV 495 c V1). The example under review of a G text reading *maghu praghaśe* where the P has *maggaṃ ācikkheyya* thus provides yet another instance of this phenomenon, while the P list of synonyms *akkhāto vivaṭo pakāsito* is a reflection of the potential for *pakāsita*/*pakāseti* to be used instead of *akkhāta*/*ācikkhati*.

[adhagha]ro [a]l[oka va] ◦ ya[va]d=eva cakṣu[a]tu ruaṇa dhrekṣatu ◦: The P parallel is *andhakāre vā telapajjotaṃ dhāreyya cakkhumanto rūpāni dakkhintī ti*. The first two akṣaras of *[adhagha]ro* are very faint, but the reading appears to be *[adha]*, as expected given that the third and fourth akṣaras are *[gha]ro* and the P parallel is *andhakāre*. The initial vowel of *[a]l[oka]* could be read as a *u*, though this would be unexpected. The top of *[ka]* is missing; the reading could be *[bha]*, but this is also unlikely. The akṣara after *[a]l[oka]* appears to be a *[va]* but could also be a vowel.

Horner's literal translation of the Pali captures the P idiom: "or might bring an oil lamp into the darkness, thinking, 'Those with eyes may see shapes' " (1951: 24). A less literal translation is provided by Norman (1992a: 10): "or bring an oil-lamp into the darkness, so that those with eyes might see shapes."

The G phrase *[adhagha]ro [a]l[oka va]* ◦ can be interpreted in several ways. The first is to understand this as equivalent to an unattested P *andhakāre ālokaṃ vā* (*dhāreyya*), "or (bring) light into the darkness," with the verb either accidentally omitted by the scribe or to be understood. The G equivalent of P *dhāreyya*/Skt. *dhārayet* appears as *dharaï* in the Dhp-G^{K} (275) and as *dharei* in a Senior manuscript (where the corresponding P and Skt. have *dhāretu* and *dhāraya*, respectively; see below). In our manuscript it would probably appear as **dharae* (see § 6.3.2; Salomon 2000: § 7.3.2). In this interpretation *adhagharo* is locative singular. Although the P parallel has *telapajjotaṃ*, *āloka-* is found in similar phrases in Pali as the opposite of *andhakāra-* (e.g., *andhakāraṃ vā ālokaṃ karoti . . . idaṃ andhakāraṭṭhānaṃ ālokajātaṃ hotū ti*, Vism 390.15–9).[126] Besides the lack of a verb, the placement of the disjunctive *va* = P/Skt. *vā* is somewhat peculiar. We would have expected *adhagharo va aloka <*dharae>*.

Alternatively, the G could be equivalent to a P *andhakāre āloko va*, with *va* representing Skt. *iva*, which would better suit its placement after *aloka*. The meaning would be "like a light in darkness." Although this makes sense in itself, it seems a little awkward in this context, and given that the previous three clauses contained third-person singular optative verbs, we would expect one here also. We should therefore assume that the verb **dharae* was omitted. The meaning would then be "[or] as if one were to bring light into darkness."

Finally, given that the verb *ālokati* appears in BHS in the sense of "furnishes light," "provide illumination" (BHSD, s.v.), for which compare also *ālokaya-*, *"Licht versorgen;*

---

[126] Cf. *andhakāro āloko kato* (Mil 130.19, 154.16, 160.19–20, 170.11); *andhakāraguhāyaṃ āloko udapādi* (DN II 269.29); *seyyathāpi vā pan' . . . jāneyyāsi tvaṃ ānanda 'āloko antarahito andhakāro pātubhūto' ti . . . evam eva . . .* (AN III 407 ff.).

erleuchten," in the SWTF (s.v.), it is possible that my reading of the final akṣara is wrong and that the reading is *alokae,* representing the third-person singular optative of the denominative verb. In this case *adhagharo* would be accusative rather than locative, and the translation would be "would illuminate the darkness." Although technically possible, the fact that this use of the verb is quite rare tends to count against this interpretation. I therefore tentatively adopt the first interpretation, which is reflected in the above reconstruction and translation.

At first appearance, the retention of *-k-* in *[a]l[oka],* if my reading of this akṣara is correct, could seem unusual since *-k-* normally appears as *-gh-* or *ø* in this manuscript and in the others written by the same scribe and the word appears as *logha-* in lines 18–9, 39. In this manuscript original *-k-* appears as *-k-* in only three other words: *akuśala, eka,* and *sukaro* (see § 5.2.2.1), that is, at a morpheme boundary or in the word *eka,* which reflects the regular pattern in Gāndhārī generally (see Salomon 2000: § 6.2.1.1; Brough 1962: § 38). However, throughout the Dhp-G^{K}, for example, the only spelling of this word encountered is *loka-,* suggesting that this word may behave differently.

The Gāndhārī further differs from the P in including *yavad eva* = P and BHS *yāvad-eva,* for which the BHSD (s.v. *yāvad-eva*) gives "merely, just simply," and the PTSD (s.v. *yāva*), "up to . . . as far as, in short," etc. In this context we would anticipate a sense of "so that," "in order that." Compare, for example, *yāvad eva dvayatānaṃ dhammānaṃ yathābhūtaṃ ñāṇāyā ti* (Sn p. 140) translated by Norman (1992a: 82) as "So as to know properly the pairs of doctrines."

For *cakṣu[a]tu,* see § 5.2.2.6.

Dhrekṣatu appears to be the third-person plural of the future imperative of √*dṛś,* equivalent to a Skt. **drakṣyantu*. The future imperative is rare in Sanskrit, but a few examples are recorded in Buddhist Sanskrit (BHSG, § 31.37) and in the epics (Whitney 1889: § 938). The Pali has the future form *dakkhinti* (Geiger 1994: § 152; Norman 1992a: 142, 338; the PTSD, s.v. *dassati,* wrongly takes this as a present). An alternative explanation (suggested to me by Professor K. R. Norman) is that G *dhrekṣatu* is a present imperative based on a form such as P *dakkhantu*. In Pali, *dakkh-* was extracted as a stem and formed the basis for an imperative (e.g., *dakkha, dakkhantu*), besides a future (*dakkhiss-*), infinitive (*dakkhituṃ*), and gerundive (*dakkhitabba*). The imperative forms appear to be restricted to commentarial and other paracanonical literature, particularly grammatical literature (e.g., *passa abhipassa dakkha olokaya,* Nidd II [B^{e}] 105, on *abhipassa* at Sn 1070d). An imperative, future, or future imperative would work in the context of the simile under review.

[eva]m=eva ṣamaṇeṇa gho[da]meṇa krirṇo śukro dharmu akhaḍe vivaḍe [s.]praghaśi[d]e: The first three akṣaras are distorted by a fold. The P parallel is *evam eva kho bhotā gotamena anekapariyāyena dhammo pakāsito*. There is some variation within P texts in the reading of the initial part of this clause. While the E^{e} reading of this formula at AN I 56 is *evam eva kho bhotā gotamena,* the B^{e} and S^{e} read *evam evaṃ bhotā gotamena*. The E^{e} of most other occurrences similarly omit *kho,* with the exception of MN I 205. Within the E^{e} the reading also alternates between *evam eva, evam evam,* and *evam*

evaṃ, as it does in all similes. The Vin III 6 reading of *evam eva bho gotama bhotā gotamena,* with the inclusion of the vocative, is exceptional.

The basic structure of the G and P sentences is the same, but their wording is quite different. A literal translation of the Pali is "even so the Dhamma has been proclaimed by the venerable Gotama in various ways," and for the Gāndhārī, "even so dharmas, bright and dark, have been declared, revealed, and proclaimed by the monk Gotama" (ignoring the singular number of *dharmu* for the sake of the translation). Where the P has *bhotā gotamena,* the G has *ṣamaṇeṇa ghodameṇa.* Where the P has the adverbial phrase *aneka-pariyāyena,* "in various ways," preceding *dhammaṃ,* the G has two adjectives, *kriṛṇo śukro,* qualifying the noun. And where the P has one past participle, *pakāsito,* the G has three, *akhade vivaḍe s(*a)praghaśide,* all synonyms.

Although an exact P parallel to the G phrase *kriṛṇo śukro dharmu akhade vivaḍe s(*a)praghaśide* does not occur, the component elements are encountered in canonical P texts. G *kriṛṇo* and *śukro* represent Skt. *kr̥ṣṇaḥ* and *śuklaḥ/śukraḥ.* In P we find such phrases as *kaṇha-sukka-sappatibhāgā dhammā* (SN V 66.5, 104.9), *kaṇhaṃ dhammaṃ vippahāya, sukkaṃ bhāvetha paṇḍito* (Dhp 87a–b); *atthi bhikkhave kammaṃ kaṇhaṃ kaṇhavipākaṃ . . . kammaṃ sukkaṃ sukkavipākaṃ* (AN II 230.21 ff.); and the like.[127] Similar passages are found in Buddhist Skt. texts: *ekāntakr̥ṣṇānāṃ karmaṇām ekāntakr̥ṣṇo vipāka ekāntaśuklānām ekāntaśuklo* (Avś I 226.2–3, 245.8–9, etc.; MSV I 109.6–8, 255.6–7); *kr̥ṣṇaśuklāni karmāṇy* (MSV I 207.2; Dutt's edition reads *kr̥ṣṇāśuklāni* but see Wille 1990: 105); and *śuklā hy ete dharmāḥ* (MPS § 30.20; cf. Saṅg-Skt. § VI.24a). Despite this, examples linking *kaṇha/kr̥ṣṇa, sukka/śukla,* and *dhamma/ dharma* with verbs expressing the idea of teaching seem to be lacking in the P and Skt. sources so far researched. It seems, then, that G *kriṛṇo śukro* expresses the same idea of thoroughness as *anekapariyāyena* of the Pali, though no P commentary seems to preserve a gloss that incorporates such words (see, e.g., Pj II 156).

The bottom of the initial *s.* of *[s.]praghaśi[d]e* is missing. The reading could have been *sa* or *su.* This word could therefore be the equivalent of Skt. *saṃprakāśitaḥ* or *suprakāśitaḥ.*

The G string of three synonymous past participles *akhade vivaḍe s.praghaśide* finds a parallel in the P SN (IV 166–7), for example, *ayaṃ kāyo bhagavatā anekapariyāyena akkhāto vivaṭo pakāsito,* which interestingly enough is followed by *ācikkhituṃ desetuṃ paññāpetuṃ paṭṭhapetuṃ vivarituṃ vibhajituṃ uttānīkātuṃ* (SN IV 166.22–5, 27–31), the extended string of synonyms discussed above. It is also worthy of note that in this example these three past participles occur in conjunction with *anekapariyāyena,* parallel to *anekapariyāyena dhammo pakāsito,* the P parallel of the G passage under review. This SN passage is thus essentially the same as the G Dhoṇa-sutra passage but with *kriṛṇo śukro* in the Gāndhārī for *anekapariyāyena* of the Pali.

The P sequence of three past participles differs from the G list only in reading *pakāsito* against *s(*a)praghaśide* or *s(*u)praghaśide* of the Gāndhārī. Whichever reading is adopted, the G differs from P usage for, although *pakāsita-* and the finite verb forms

[127] Cf. *dve 'me bhikkhave sukkā dhammā lokaṃ pālenti* (It 36.5–6); *devadattassa sukko dhammo samucchedam agamā* (SN II 240.28–9).

are common enough in Pali, *sam-pa* + √*kās* occurs only twice in the canon, both times in the Ap: *saccāni sampakāseti* (460.4) and *so me dhammam adesesi, sabbattha-sampakāsayaṃ* (507.21; cf. Bv-a 299.14). Similarly, *supakāsita-* occurs only once, as a gloss in the Culla-niddesa: *sukittitaṃ su-ācikkhitaṃ sudesitaṃ . . . su-uttānīkataṃ supakāsitaṃ* (Nidd II [B^{e}] 81–2). The example from the Buddhist Skt. Nidāna-saṃyukta and MPS (NidSa § 14.3; MPS § 9.18) of *ākhyāti prajñāpayati prasthāpayati vibhajati vivaraty uttānīkaroti deśayati saṃprakāśayati* suggests that the reading of the Gāndhārī may have been *sapraghaśide* = Skt. *saṃprakāśitaḥ*. If so, then because the final synonym of the corresponding P list is *pakāsati* (when it is included; see above discussion), the Gāndhārī would attest a usage closer to the Sanskrit than to the Pali.

ṣamaṇo ghudamu śaraṇo ghachami dhama ca bhikhusagha ca ◦: The parallels are

G (Senior ms.) *eṣao bha g[a]ḋa[m. śara]ṇo gachami dhrarma ja bhikhusa[ga] ja*
P *esāhaṃ bhagavantaṃ gotamaṃ saraṇaṃ gacchāmi dhammañ ca bhikkhusaṅghañ ca*
Skt. *eṣo 'haṃ bhagavantaṃ śaraṇaṃ gacchāmi dharmañ ca bhikṣusaṃghaṃ ca*

There is again some variation among P texts in the reading of this passage. Whereas most occurrences read *esāhaṃ,* the E^{e} of DN I 110 has *esāhaṃ kho*. More important, in the E^{e} the reading alternates between *bhagavantaṃ gotamaṃ,* as in this AN I 56 example (SN I 171 omits *gotamaṃ*), and *bhavantaṃ gotamaṃ* (e.g., MN I 24, 39, 184; AN I 173), despite the following sentence having *bhavaṃ gotamo dhāretu* in all occurrences (in both the E^{e} and B^{e}). B^{e} has *bhavantaṃ gotamaṃ* in all cases. The exception is the B^{e} corresponding to E^{e} SN I 161, which has *esāhaṃ bhante bhagavantaṃ gotamaṃ* despite *bho gotama* occurring as the form of address throughout the full passage.

The beginning of the G version, which would have occurred at the end of line 23, is missing. In view of the reading *eṣao* in the G version in the Senior manuscripts, *esāhaṃ* of the Pali, and *eṣo 'haṃ* of the Skt. parallels, the missing word must have been *(*eṣaho),* for which compare *ṇaho* (ll. 10–5). This reconstruction is based on the assumption that *eṣao* of the Senior manuscript version is the equivalent of P *esāhaṃ* rather than of *eso kho,* which is also possible. Although the P parallel to *ṇaho* (ll. 10–5) has *na kho ahaṃ,* in my commentary on this phrase (see p. 169) I argued that *ṇaho* was more likely to represent P *nāhaṃ* than *na kho* because the equivalent of P *kho* seems to be absent in the BL texts.

The *bh* akṣara of *bha g[a]ḋa[m.]* in the Senior version appears to have no vowel diacritic. Despite resembling vocatives, *bha gaḋam.* must be accusative singular masculines as demanded by the context and as found elsewhere in the Senior manuscript version and the P and Skt. parallels. The nominative singular appears as *bh[i] goḋam[o]* in the Senior manuscript in the next sentence (see below). *Bha* = P *bhavantaṃ* and *bhi* = P *bhavaṃ* in the Senior manuscript thus represent highly contracted forms of the word.

The only difference between the G, P, and Skt. versions is the term used to refer to the Buddha: G (BL manuscript) *ṣamaṇo ghudamu;* G (Senior ms.) *bha gaḋam.;* P *bhagavantaṃ gotamaṃ* or *bhavantaṃ gotamaṃ;* and Skt. *bhagavantaṃ.*

u ? ? ? [mi ṣ.]ma /// [25][*m.*] *dharedu ajavaghreṇa yavajivu praṇouviade śaraṇo abhiprasaṇe* ◦: The parallels are G (Senior manuscript) *uasao me bh[i] goḋam[o] dharei ajavag[r]eṇa yavajiv. p.ṇue�. śaraṇa gada;* P *upāsakaṃ maṃ bhavaṃ gotamo dhāretu ajjatagge pāṇupetaṃ saraṇaṃ gatan ti;* and Skt. *upāsakaṃ ca māṃ dhārayādyāgreṇa yāvajjīvaṃ prāṇopetaṃ śaraṇaṃ gatam abhiprasannam.*

Only the bottoms of the three akṣaras following the initial *u* remain, with the third appearing on the lower side of the split in the manuscript (above l. 25). The bottoms of these akṣaras are consistent with the reading *u(*asaghu)* or *u(*vasaghu),* the word expected based on the Senior G version and on the P and Skt. parallels. I adopt the first in my reconstruction since intervocalic *-p-* is commonly elided, as in *uasao* in the Senior version (see § 5.2.2.5).

The placement of fragment D6dd, which contains *[mi ṣ.]ma,* is confirmed by the alignment of the text on the verso. The first akṣara on line 25 (*[m.]*), which is the third akṣara of the word *(*ghuda)m.,* could possibly be read as *[ma]* or *[me].* I reconstruct the nominative singular as *(*ghuda)m(*e).*

In view of *uasao me bh[i] goḍam[o] dharei* of the Senior manuscripts and *upāsakaṃ maṃ bhavaṃ gotamo dhāretu* of the P version, the first part of this formula can be reconstructed as *u(*asaghu) mi ṣ(*a)ma(*ṇe ghuda)*[25]*m(*e) dharedu,* with *ṣ(*a)ma(*ṇe)* rather than the G equivalent of P *bhavaṃ,* in accordance with the reading *ṣamaṇeṇa ghodameṇa* (instr. sg.) and *ṣamaṇo ghudamu* (acc. sg.) earlier in this formula.

The reading in the Senior manuscript version of this formula is *me.* The P and Skt. versions have the accusative singular of the first-person pronoun: P *maṃ*/Skt. *māṃ.* G *mi,* or *me,* in this context probably represents the use of the enclitic form of the pronoun (Skt. *me*) for the accusative rather than the accusative singular (Skt. *māṃ*). A further example of such a usage is *samasiśpi me cavae* in the AG-G (l. 38), which can be compared with P *samādhimhā cāvetukāmo* (e.g., SN I 129.12–3).[128] See also § 6.2.1.

Dharedu is the direct equivalent of P *dhāretu,* the third-person singular imperative of the causative verb, "may the monk Gotama accept me." This contrasts with the Skt. version, which has the second-person singular *dhāraya,* "may you accept me." The form *dharei* in the Senior manuscript seems to differ from both. It appears to represent Skt. *dhārayet,* the third-person singular optative, with *ay* > *e* and with weakening of final vowel, as regularly in Gāndhārī. The same word appears in Dhp-G^{K} 275b as *dharaï* where the P parallel has *dhāraye* (Dhp 222b) and the Sanskrit has *dhārayet* (Uv XX.22b). It could possibly represent Skt. *dhāraya,* the second-person singular, but *goḍam[o]* appears to be a nominative singular.

In both *ajavaghreṇa* here and in *ajavag[r]eṇa* of the Senior version, *-v-* is a sandhi consonant (see § 5.6.5). In P *ajjatagge* and its variant *ajjadagge* we find *-t-* and *-d-* functioning in the same way (see Geiger 1994: § 73.5; BHSD, s.v. *adyāgre*), as explained by the P commentaries in the case of *-d-: tattha da-kāro pada-sandhikaro* (e.g., Ud-a 288.14–5). However, the CPD (s.v. *ajjatagge*) proposes **ajjato agge;* compare also the commentaries, for example, Sp I 173.5 ff. and Ud-a 288.14.

The G form *ajavaghreṇa/ajavagreṇa* parallels the Skt. *adyāgreṇa* with its instrumental termination, in contrast to the seeming locative of the P *ajjatagge.* Although *adyāgre*

[128] This example was provided by Richard Salomon. *Cavae* is a preterite of the causative of the verb √*cyu.*

is found in Buddhist Skt. texts, it is comparatively rare (see BHSD, s.v. *adyāgre*, cf. *agre* and *-agreṇa*).

The G parallels the Skt. version in the inclusion of *yavajivu* (Skt. *yāvajjīvaṃ*). The word is absent in the P version but is common in other contexts in P literature, particularly in the context of living the *brahmacariya* life, or the virtuous life: for example, *dukkaraṃ kho soṇa yāvajīvaṃ . . . brahmacariyaṃ* (Ud 57.20–1).[129] It occurs in a context similar to the conversion formula in a number of Ap verses: for example, *sutvā sumadhuraṃ dhammaṃ, pasanno jinasāsane, sugataṃ saraṇaṃ gantvā, yāvajīvaṃ namass' ahaṃ* (509.11–2); and *tadā 'haṃ muditā hutvā, yāvajīvaṃ tadā jinaṃ, mettacittā paricariṃ, sasaṅghaṃ lokanāyakaṃ* (558.7–8). More interesting is the appearance of a similar phrase in the P commentarial gloss on *pāṇopetaṃ,* the next word in the formula, namely, *pāṇupetan ti pāṇehi upetaṃ yāva me jīvitaṃ pavattati tāva upetaṃ . . .* (e.g., Ud-a 288.16–7),[130] which occurs in Sinh. sannayas (P-Sinh. bilingual versions of P texts) as *pānupetaṃ jīvatāntaya dakvā* (Somadasa 1987: 71 [Or.6600(2)], 74 [Or.6600(8)], etc.). No doubt *yāvajjīvaṃ,* which is a synonym of *prāṇopetaṃ* and which appears as a gloss on *pāṇopetaṃ* in P commentarial literature, was included in the G and Skt. versions of the conversion formulas in accordance with the common tendency of Buddhist sūtra texts to proliferate similar word elements.

The second akṣara of *uviade* could be read as *ve* or even *ti*. The reading in the Senior manuscript example is *p.ṇueḋ.,* which can be reconstructed as *p(*ra)ṇueḋ(*a)* or *p(*ra)ṇueḋ(*u)*. G *p(*ra)ṇueḋ(*a)* (to use the first as example), P *pāṇupetaṃ,* and Skt. *prāṇopetaṃ* represent the same word, namely, a compound of *prāṇa-* and *-upeta* used adverbially (to use the Skt. forms). Given that the G version in the Senior manuscripts and the P and Skt. are all in agreement, *uviade* could be a misspelling for *uvide* (or *uvede*) = Skt. *upetam,* with the *a* in *uviade* representing a mistaken, extra syllable. This word appears in the Dhp-G^{K} as *uveda* and *uvidu.*

The presence of the *o* vowel in *praṇo* is also problematic. In contrast to G *p(*ra)ṇueḋ(*a),* P *pāṇupetaṃ,* and Skt. *prāṇopetaṃ,* it appears that *praṇouviade* of our manuscript may not be a compound (*praṇo uviade*), with *praṇo* being the accusative singular, the object of the past participle *uviade*. However, this interpretation does not suit the usual understanding of *-upeta* in the context of *pāṇupetaṃ/prāṇopetaṃ,* where it means "furnished with" (CPD, s.v. *upeta*) and is constructed with the instrumental, as seen in P commentarial glosses; for example, *pāṇupetan ti pāṇehi upetaṃ* (e.g., Ud-a 288.16; for the seeming example of *upeta* plus acc. in the Dhp, see Brough 1962: 80). It therefore seems that it is a pseudocompound (*praṇo-uviade* or, in my preferred reading, *praṇo-uvide*). A similar example is seen in *ṇidhaṃto-kaṣaya-mrakṣo* (Khvs-G 33b), where the P parallel has *niddhanta-kasāva-moho* (Sn 56b). As noted by Salomon (2000: 173–4), it is unclear whether the apparent nominative ending in *ṇidhaṃto* is the mark of a type of pseudocompound found in BHS or is a scribal error.

Finally, it is also possible that *uviade* is not an error but represents P *upayāta-,* "reached," "arrived at" (see CPD, s.v. *upayāta*), which coincides with *upeta* in at least

[129] For further examples, see DN III 9; MN II 5; SN I 228–30; AN I 211–2.

[130] *Yāvajīvaṃ,* in turn, is glossed as *yāva jīvitaṃ pavattati* (e.g., Ps II 72.22).

some of its meanings, and takes *praṇo* (accusative singular) as object. But given that the G version in the Senior manuscript and the P and Skt. versions are all in agreement, I tentatively take *uviade* as a scribal error for *uvide* and interpret *praṇouvide* as a pseudo-compound (*praṇo-uvide*).

The reading of the G Senior version is *śaraṇa gada,* and the Sanskrit is *śaraṇaṃ gatam abhiprasannam,* with *śaraṇagatam* as v.l. The Pali has *saraṇaṃ gatan,* with the v.l. *saraṇagatan* in some occurrences (e.g., MN I 24, 184; II 213). The past participle *gata-* in the P and Skt. versions and the equivalent *gada* in the G Senior version, as well as the context, suggest that the equivalent *ghade* (or *ghadu, ghado*) has been accidentally omitted in our manuscript. I therefore emend the text to *śaraṇo* <**ghade*> *abhiprasaṇe* ◦, adopting the ending *-e* in **ghade* to match the following past participle, *abhiprasaṇe*.

It is noteworthy that the G version of our manuscript again parallels the Skt. version and contrasts with the P in including *abhiprasaṇe* = Skt. *abhiprasannam* in the formula. Yet just to complicate matters, the G Senior version omits this word (although this could be a scribal omission parallel to the omission of *ghade* in the BL manuscript). Of course, although the P version omits the equivalent *abhippasannaṃ,* which is common enough in canonical texts (see PTC, s.v. *abhippasīdati*; CPD, s.v. *abhippasanna*), the idea expressed by this term, that is, "out of faith," is inherent in the act of going for refuge to the Buddha. The G and Skt. texts have merely articulated this explicitly. It is thus not surprising that we find such an articulation in texts such as the P Ap: *sutvā sumadhuraṃ dhammaṃ, pasanno jinasāsane, sugataṃ saraṇaṃ gantvā, yāvajīvaṃ namass' ahaṃ* (509.11–2); *saddhā mātāpitā mayhaṃ, buddhassa saraṇaṃ gatā* (439.5); *saraṇaṅgatā ca te buddhaṃ, saddahanti tathāgataṃ* (56.3); and the like. Similarly, the beginning of the P commentary on the declaration of conversion reads *evaṃ desanaṃ thometvā tāya desanāya ratanattaye pasannacitto pasannākāraṃ karonto esāhan ti ādim āha* (e.g., Ud-a 287.13–4).

In summary, the G version of this conversion formula preserved in this manuscript is not identical with either the P or the Skt. parallels or even, more surprisingly, with the G version in the Senior manuscripts (although this may be due for the most part to scribal omission). In including the long simile, the Gāndhārī of our manuscript parallels the Pali rather than the Sanskrit, which omits it, although there are some important differences in wording. But in the wording of the final request by the brahman for the Buddha to accept him as an upāsaka, the Gāndhārī parallels the Sanskrit rather than the Pali.

Lines 25–6: Dhoṇa shows his appreciation. The sūtra ends.

Edition:

[25] *[i] /// ///* |D6j *? ///* [26] |24a *dhoṇe bramaṇe bhayavade[bha]ṇa bhaṣido abhiṇadi* ○

Reconstruction:

[25] *i(*dam u)* <**bhayavadu*> *(*atamaṇo)* [26] *dhoṇe bramaṇe bhayavadeṇa bhaṣido abhiṇadi* ○

Translation:
[25] (*The Bhagavat said this. Pleased), [26] the brahman Dhoṇa rejoiced at what was said by the Bhagavat.

The penultimate akṣara in *bhayavade[bha]ṇa* has been erased, and I read *bhayavadeṇa*. The scribe probably began to write the next word, *bhaṣido,* but then realized his mistake, which may suggest that he was familiar with a form such as *bhayavada* as found in the Senior manuscript example.

The reading of the Senior manuscript example, which occurs as the conclusion to a sūtra that similarly depicts a brahman questioning the Buddha and then being converted, is

id́am=oyi bhayava atamaṇo s[o] bhamaṇa bhayavada bhaṣid́a aviṇadi ◦. (20 r11)

The same formula, but depicting the monks rejoicing in the Buddha's speech, occurs at the end of the second sūtra in our manuscript, the Budhabayaṇa-sutra:

idam=u atamaṇa te bhi[kh.] /// /// + + + ? /// [37] [a]bhiṇadi ○. (Ll. 36–7)

This formula has been reconstructed as

*idam u <*bhayavadu> atamaṇa te bhikh(*u bhayavadeṇa bhaṣido) abhiṇadi* ○.

This form of the formula commonly occurs at the end of suttas/sūtras depicting the Buddha giving a discourse to the monks. Further G examples of this version of the formula, most of which are abbreviated, are found in the Senior manuscripts. Provisional readings made by Richard Salomon are the following:[131]

1. *id́am=eyi bhayava* (5 r20): the formula is incomplete
2. *[i]d́am=e[yi] bhayava* (5 v5 and margin; *bhayava* is written vertically in the right margin between ll. 4 and 5): the formula is incomplete
3. *[id́a] bhayava atamaṇa ṣi bhikhu aiśpaya [ṇa]da bhayava ? + ? aviṇadi* (19 v14; the *i* of *aiśpaya* has been added above the line)
4. *id́am=aya bhayava atamaṇa te bhikhu* (20 v13): the formula is incomplete

The P Doṇa-sutta lacks the concluding formula as found in the G Dhoṇa-sutra, though similar formulas are encountered in other contexts in P texts. Interestingly, although many P suttas end with a brahman, ascetic, householder, or the like being converted, no examples then add a concluding "pleased at the words of the Buddha" formula (the

---

[131] Comparable abbreviations of the formula are common in P manuscripts and editions. E.g., the formula is abbreviated in the E[e] of SN V 400.19, 401.15, and 402.7, with *idam avoca bhagavā,* where the Sinh. manuscripts used by the E[e] (S[1–3]) read *idam avoca bhagavā . . . pe . . . etad avoca satthā.* Waldschmidt (1957: 375 n. 2) draws attention to the omission of both the introductory and the concluding formulas in some of the manuscripts of the NidSa. For the comparable abbreviation of the introductory formula, see my discussion of the opening nidāna of the Budhabayaṇa-sutra.

attamana formula). Such suttas in Pali end with the last words of the conversion formula (*saraṇaṃ gatan ti*), as seen, for example, in the Subha- (DN I 210), Lohicca- (DN I 234), Tevijja- (DN I 252), and Siṅgālovāda- (DN III 193) suttantas of the DN (cf. also the Ambaṭṭha-suttanta: DN I 110). However, at least two examples of P suttas depict an individual proclaiming his conversion, expressing his delight at the Buddha's words, and departing, with the sutta then continuing with the depiction of other events. In the Subha-sutta of the MN (sutta 99), for example, Subha declares his conversion, then states that he is busy and must go. This is followed by *atha kho subho māṇavo todeyyaputto bhagavato bhāsitaṃ abhinanditvā anumoditvā uṭṭhāy' āsanā bhagavantaṃ abhivādetvā padakkhiṇaṃ katvā pakkāmi,* after which the sutta continues (II 208; cf. Ud 49).

A formula comparable to that found in the G Dhoṇa-sutra is encountered as a conclusion to at least one P sutta, the Kevaddha-suttanta of the DN (no. 11), which depicts a conversation between the Buddha and the householder Kevaddha. After the Buddha's long discourse, the sutta concludes with

> *idam avoca bhagavā. attamano kevaddho gahapatiputto bhāsitaṃ abhinandī ti* [read *gahapatiputto bhagavato bhāsitaṃ* following the vv.ll. and the B^{e}]. (DN I 223)

The P version of the more common version of the formula, which occurs as the standard conclusion to suttas that depict the Buddha preaching to monks or nuns, is

> *idam avoca bhagavā. attamanā te bhikkhū bhagavato bhāsitaṃ abhinandun ti.* (E.g., AN I 276.23–6; see PTC, s.v. *attamana,* for further references)

Although the majority of suttas that depict the Buddha addressing the monks in, say, the first volume of the E^{e} of the AN lack this formula, it is found as the conclusion to the last sutta of that volume, which is the last sutta of the Tika-nipāta (AN I 299). Further, although not appearing in the last suttas of the Eka-nipāta and Duka-nipāta in the E^{e}, the one Burmese manuscript used for the E^{e} and the B^{e} both include it. This indicates that the formula was probably included when such suttas were chanted. Similarly, the three Chinese translations of the Doṇa-sutta (T nos. 99, 100, and 125) all end with the brahman delighting in the words of the Buddha (although there is no mention of his conversion), with the two SĀ translations (T nos. 99 and 100) then depicting his departure. It is therefore possible that the *attamana* formula was included when the P Doṇa-sutta was chanted.

The Skt. version of the formula that depicts the monks delighting in the Buddha's words is

> *idam avocad bhagavān. āttamanasas te bhikṣavo bhagavato bhāṣitam abhyanandan.* (E.g., Divy 24.6–7, 55.13–5; Avś I 7.12, 12.20)

An example of the singular form is *idam avocad bhagavān. āttamano āyuṣmān mahāmaudgalyāyano bhagavato bhāṣitam abhyanandat* (Mvu I 61.8–9). The formula found in Central Asian sūtra texts differs only in reading *āptamanasas* against *āttamanasas* (see SWTF, s.v. *āptamanas,* vol. 1, pp. 265, 591, for references; cf. BHSD, s.v. *āttamanas*).[132]

The inclusion of the unit *idam oyi bhayava* in the formula concluding a sūtra in a Senior manuscript (20 r11) that, like our G Dhoṇa-sutra, also depicts a brahman questioning the Buddha seems to be a scribal error, for the last one to speak in that sūtra is the brahman, not the Buddha. The phrase "the Buddha said this" therefore seems out of place. It appears that the scribe unthinkingly included this unit on the basis of its usual occurrence in the concluding formula employed when the Buddha is the last to speak. The fact that all other sūtras in the Senior manuscripts so far read are addressed to monks may have played a part. The alternative interpretation is that the full formula may have in fact formed the standard conclusion to G sūtras which contained the Buddha's words, whether the Buddha was the last to speak or not, even though such a usage is not encountered in Pali and probably also not in Sanskrit.

Since the overall wording of the G, P, and Skt. versions of this formula agree, the only word missing from the beginning of this formula in the version of our manuscript may have been the equivalent of P *attamano*/Skt. *āttamanas, āptamanas*. The plural form *atamaṇa* occurs on line 36. The singular would appear as *atamaṇo* (with variable final vowel), the spelling also encountered in Senior 20 r11. The first akṣara of this concluding formula occurs after the punctuation mark at the end of line 25. It appears to be the top of an independent vowel and could very well be the initial *a* of the missing *atamaṇo*. There are twenty-eight akṣaras on line 25 up to and including the punctuation mark. If *atamaṇo* is all that is missing, then the akṣara count for this line would be a perfectly acceptable thirty-two. The reconstruction of the conclusion to the sūtra would thus be *a(*tamaṇo) dhoṇe bramaṇe bhayavadeṇa bhaṣido abhiṇadi* O, "Pleased, the brahman Dhoṇa rejoiced at what was said by the Bhagavat." However, there appears to be a small remnant of ink (representing the right tip of the horizontal stroke of an *i* vowel) between this akṣara and the preceding punctuation mark, which indicates that the reading of the independent vowel was probably *[i]*. This suggests that the formula may have begun with something like the *iḋam=oyi bhayava* of the Senior 20 r11 example, which I have argued may have been included in that example by mistake. As mentioned, the reading of the beginning of the formula that concludes the next sūtra in our manuscript, the Budhabayaṇa-sutra, which depicts the Buddha giving a discourse to the monks, begins with *idam=u atamaṇa te bhi[kh.]* (ll. 36–7). Based on the various parallels it is likely that *bhayavadu,* the G equivalent of Skt. *bhagavān,* was accidentally omitted in this location, and that the text should be emended to *idam u* <**bhayavadu*> *atamaṇa.* As already discussed in my commentary on *eghad uya* (l. 8) and *idam u* (ll. 14–5), it appears that G *idam u* of our

[132] In some Mahāyāna texts the concluding formula is much extended. The Vajracchedikā-prajñāpāramitā-sūtra, for example, concludes with *idam avocad bhagavān āttamanāḥ sthavira-subhūtis te ca bhikṣubhikṣuṇyupāsakopāsikās te ca bodhisattvāḥ sadevamānuṣāsuragandharvaś ca loko bhagavato bhāṣitam abhyanandann iti* (Conze 1974: 62; cf. Schopen 1989: 107). As discussed by Kajiyama (1977: 94–9), traditional commentaries on this phrase reflect uncertainty as to whether the term *āttamanāḥ* qualifies *bhagavān* or *sthavirasubhūtis* (or the like). Such an ambiguity does not arise in the G, P, and Skt. examples discussed here.

manuscript and *ídam oyi, ídam eyi,* and *ídam.ya* (possibly to be read as *ídam=(*a)ya*) of the Senior manuscripts represent a highly contracted form of P *idam avoca*/Skt. *idam avocad.* If the reading of the akṣara that follows the punctuation mark at the end of line 25 is *i* rather than *a,* then the reading of the first part of the formula may have been either *[i](*dam u atamaṇo) dhoṇe bramaṇe* or *[i](*dam u bhayavadu atamaṇo) dhoṇe bramaṇe,* with both representing examples of the mistaken inclusion of the *idam u (bhayavadu)* phrase (though *bhayavadu* was actually omitted in the first). The remnant of at least one of the akṣaras of the wording missing from the end of line 25 is found at the top of fragment D6j. It could be the bottom of either *a* or *ṇa* of the missing *atamaṇo.* The small, dark mark at the upper left of fragment D6j could be the remnant of the bottom of another akṣara. The akṣara count for line 25 with these two reconstructions would be thirty-five and thirty-nine, respectively. As the latter is a little too high (the following two lines have an akṣara count of thirty-two and thirty-four, respectively), the reading of the manuscript was most likely *i(*dam u atamaṇo) dhoṇe bramaṇe,* with *bhayavadu* omitted by the scribe as in the line 36 example. The reconstruction for the first half of the formula is therefore *i(*dam u) <*bhayavadu> (*atamaṇo) dhoṇe bramaṇe.*

In all versions of the formula the final finite verb is a preterite of *abhi* + √*nand:* G *abhiṇadi* of our manuscript and *aviṇadi* of the Senior manuscripts for both the third-person singular and plural; P *abhinandi* (sg.), *abhinanduṃ* (pl.); and Skt. *abhyanandat* (sg.), *abhyanandan* (pl.).[133] Based on the third-person plural preterite *pracarśoṣu* (= P *paccassosuṃ*/Skt. *pratyaśrauṣuḥ*) elsewhere in this text (l. 28), we would have expected **abhiṇadu* as the third-person plural preterite of *abhi* + √*nand* in lines 36–7, where the actual reading is *abhiṇadi.* However, the appearance of *aviṇadi* in the Senior manuscripts in both the singular and plural forms of the formula confirms that *abhiṇadi* in line 37 is not a scribal error. Rather, based on the G examples gathered so far, it appears that the singular form of the formula, in which the final verb is *abhiṇadi/aviṇadi,* became the fixed form used in Gāndhārī for both the singular and the plural.

The syntax of the G version (of our manuscript at least) differs from the P and Skt. Although the past participle *bhāsitaṃ/bhāṣitam* could in the P and Skt. versions of this expression (P *bhagavato bhāsitaṃ*/Skt. *bhagavato bhāṣitam*) be taken as a verbal adjective qualifying an unstated pronoun and constructed with the agentive genitive, "he/they rejoiced at what was spoken by the Bhagavat," it is normally understood to be a substantive (see, e.g., PTSD, s.v. *bhāsita*) constructed with the possessive genitive, "he/they rejoiced at the speech of the Bhagavat," as seen in the glosses of the P commentaries: *bhagavato bhāsitaṃ abhinandun ti . . . brahmassarena bhāsato bhagavato vacanaṃ abhinandiṃsu* (Spk II 10.28–31); and *bhagavato bhāsitaṃ abhinandun ti idaṃ dukkhassa antakiriyapariyosānaṃ bhagavato bhāsitaṃ sukathitaṃ sulapitaṃ . . . abbhanumodiṃsu* (Ps I 87.20–4).[134] In contrast, in the G version (or at least in the version of our manuscript)

---

[133] The spelling is usually *abhyanandam* for the 3rd pl. impf. in the Central Asian Skt. mss. (see SWTF, s.v. *abhi-nand*, vol. 1, pp. 118–9, 532–3).

[134] Examples of *bhāsita* functioning as a verbal adj. constructed with the instr. in Pali are many: *saḷāyatananirodhaṃ kho āvuso bhagavatā sandhāya bhāsitaṃ* (SN IV 100.11–2); *idaṃ kho taṃ mahārāja tena bhagavatā . . . bhāsitaṃ . . . subhāsitaṃ c' idaṃ tena bhagavatā* (MN II 69); *sace taṃ*

the past participle *bhaṣido* is constructed with the agentive instrumental *bhayavadeṇa,* thus making it a verbal adjective qualifying an unstated pronoun.[135] Unfortunately, *bhayavada* of the Senior manuscript is ambiguous, representing either a genitive singular (= Skt. *bhagavataḥ*) or the instrumental singular (= Skt. *bhagavatā*). Interestingly, the Tibetan also uses the instrumental as seen, for example, throughout the Tib. parallel to this and similar phrases in the MPS and CPS: *bcom-ldan-'das-kyis gsuṅs-pa-la/bśad-pa-la/bka' stsal-pa-la* (MPS §§ 1.43, 11.27, 26.7, 28.49; CPS §§ 3.14, 22.16).[136]

---

mahārāja bhagavatā bhāsitaṃ (MN II 107–8); *bhāsitā nu kho bhante bhagavatā esā vācā* (MN II 108.9–10); *yaṃ bhagavatā bhāsitaṃ suttaṃ geyyaṃ . . . taṃ sabbaṃ* (e.g., Sv I 66.19–20); *yaṃ buddhena bhagavatā bhāsitaṃ navaṅgaṃ satthusāsanaṃ taṃ* (Mil 372.7–8). Cf. also similar constructions with other verbs for speaking, preaching, and so on: *brāhmaṇagahapatikā bhagavatā dhammiyā kathāya sandassitā . . .* (e.g., MN II 55.32–3); *yathā yathā khvāhaṃ bhagavatā dhammaṃ desitaṃ ājānāmi* (e.g., MN II 55.27–8); *imā tisso vedanā vuttā bhagavatā* (SN IV 216.16). For the agentive instr. and gen. in Pali, see von Hinüber 1968: §§ 113, 234–7.

[135] The word is missing in the l. 36 example due to damage to the ms. At the very top of frag. 24i there is a remnant of an akṣara that could be the bottom of *de* of the missing *bhayavadeṇa;* the reading *du* is also possible. If the latter, then the reading would have been *bhayavadu,* the gen. sg. parallel to the P and Skt. examples.

[136] I am indebted to Gregory Schopen for bringing this Tib. usage to my attention.

CHAPTER 9

The "Budhabayaṇa-sutra"

9.1. Introduction

9.1.1. Summary of Contents

In depicting a dialogue between the Buddha and a brahman, the first sūtra of this collection, the Dhoṇa-sutra, is an example of a popular sūtra type: those in which the Buddha debates with a brahman or ascetic or is questioned by such an individual. The second and third sūtras on this scroll belong to the most common type of sūtra, particularly in the AN/EĀs and SN/SĀ: sūtras that depict the Buddha giving a discourse to monks. The main topic of the Buddha's discourse in this second sūtra is *budhabayaṇa* (P/Skt. *buddhavacana*), "the word, instruction, or teaching of the Buddha," which the Buddha considers easy to perform under certain conditions, but only by a wise man, not by a fool. Like the third sūtra, and like the vast majority of sūtras of this class, in which the place where the discourse was given is of secondary importance, the setting of this sūtra is the Jetavana in Śrāvastī (*śavastie viharadi jedavaṇo aṇasapiḍiasa aramu*).

9.1.2. Extant Versions of the Sūtra/Sutta and Their Titles

Although much of the wording of this sūtra is common enough, no parallel to it has yet been identified in P or Skt. sources or in Tib. or Chinese translations.[1] This state of affairs is particularly unfortunate when dealing with G fragments because, unlike Skt. fragments, where the language and meaning are usually clear enough, the peculiarities of the language, script, and orthography of G texts mean that a G text is often completely comprehensible only with the help of an Indic parallel. In the case of the present sūtra, the lack of a parallel means that the interpretation of a number of key terms and their syntactic status remain provisional.

The structure of this G sūtra is provided by the four postures: good action or the practice of mindfulness (depending on how we interpret *sato kamatu*) is easy or difficult to do by one going (*ghachateṇa*), standing (*ṭ́hideṇa*), sitting (*ṇiṣaṇeṇa*), or lying down awake (*śeaṇeṇa jagharadu*). The four postures feature in a number of contexts in Buddhist literature (see below), but particularly worthy of mention here are suttas 11 and 12 of the Catukka-nipāta of the AN (II 13–5 = It 115–21), whose basic structure is provided by the four postures (*carato . . . ṭhitassa . . . nisinnassa . . . sayānassa jāgarassa*), which thereby qualifies these suttas for inclusion in the Section of Fours, the Catukka-nipāta. Although neither of these P suttas provides a parallel to the G sūtra, the third sūtra in this G collec-

---

[1] I am indebted to Paul Harrison and Tien-chang Shih for their attempts to find a Chinese parallel.

tion, the Prasaṇa-sutra, whose topic is the four efforts (G *catvara prasaṇa*/P *cattāri padhānāni*), corresponds to sutta 14 of the Catukka-nipāta; sutta 13 deals with the same topic but in different wording. It is interesting that suttas 11 and 12 of the Catukka-nipāta and the second G sūtra on this scroll have as their foundation the four postures, though they deal with different topics, while suttas 13 and 14 of the Catukka-nipāta and the third G sūtra of this collection deal with the same topic, namely, the four efforts, and sutta 14 of the Catukka-nipāta is a direct parallel to the third G sūtra.

The topic of suttas 11 and 12 of the Catukka-nipāta is *viriya,* “energy,” which is synonymous with *padhāna,* “effort,” the topic of suttas 13 and 14; much of the wording of suttas 11 and 12 corresponds to that found in suttas 13 and 14. This was undoubtedly the reason these two pairs of suttas were grouped together in the Catukka-nipāta collection. Such an overt thematic relationship between the second and third sūtras of the G collection seems to be lacking, although there may be a more subtle underlying connection (see § 1.3).

Since the main topic and one of the key words of the second G sūtra is *budhabayaṇa,* this sūtra will be referred to as the “Budhabayaṇa-sutra.”

9.2. Text Commentary

Lines 26–8: The introductory nidāna

Edition:

[26] |24a *eva me [rśoda eka] /// ///* |D6j+D6e *bhaya[v.] ///* |24a [27]*du śavastie viharadi jedavaṇo aṇasapiḍiasa aramu ◦ ta[tra] ya bha[ya] +* |D6e *[d.] bhi ///* |24a [28]*matredi te bhikhu bhayavadu pracarśoṣu ◦ bha[ya]va[ṣu] egha[d=uya ◦]*

Reconstruction:

[26] *eva me rśoda eka (*samaya (◦)) bhayav(*a)*[27]*du śavastie viharadi jedavaṇo aṇasapiḍiasa aramu ◦ tatra ya bhaya(*va)d(*u) bhi(*khu a)*[28]*matredi te bhikhu bhayavadu pracarśoṣu ◦ bhayava<*d>u eghad uya ◦*

Translation:

[26] Thus I heard at one (*time): The Bhagavat [27] dwelt in Śavasti (Śrāvastī) in the Jedavaṇa (Jetavana), in Aṇasapiḍia’s (Anāthapiṇḍada’s) park. And there the Bhagavat addressed the monks. [28] Those monks responded to the Bhagavat. The Bhagavat said this.

The same introductory nidāna occurs at the beginning of the third sūtra of this collection (ll. 37–9):

> [37] *eva me rśodu eka sama[ya ◦] bhayadu śavastie viharadi [jedavaṇ.] ///* [38]*ḍiasa aramu ◦ tatra ya bhayavadu bhikhu amat[r]edi bhikhu ? ? ? ? ? ///* [39] *eghad=oya ◦*

The lacunae in lines 26–8 can be restored with the help of this second occurrence. The only element whose reconstruction is uncertain is the punctuation mark in the reconstructed *(*samaya (◦))* on line 26, for although the reading seems to be *sama[ya ◦]* on line 37, this scribe is not consistent in his employment of punctuation marks (see § 4.8.2). Further, a split in the manuscript renders the reading of the text on line 37 imperfect. Based on the text of lines 26–8, the lacunae in lines 37–9 can be reconstructed:

> *eva me rśodu eka samaya ◦ bhaya<*va>du śavastie viharadi jedavaṇ(*o aṇasapi)ḍiasa aramu ◦ tatra ya bhayavadu bhikhu amatredi <*te> bhikhu (*bhayavadu pracarśoṣu ◦ bhayavadu) eghad oya ◦*

Apart from the obvious scribal errors in *bhayavaṣu* (l. 28) and *bhayadu* (l. 37) for *bhayavadu* and the omission of *te* between *amatredi* and *bhikhu* on line 38, the only difference between the two passages is orthographic: (1) *rśoda* in line 26 and *rśodu* in line 37; and (2) *eghad uya* in line 28 and *eghad oya* in line 39.

No further examples of the introductory nidāna to sūtras has so far come to light among the BL Kharoṣṭhī manuscripts. However, most of the stories in the avadāna-type texts within the collection begin with the phrase *evo śuyadi (/śruyadi/ṣuyadi)*. For example, line 2 of the avadāna text that appears at the bottom of the recto side of this scroll (= l. 74 according to the line numbering of the scroll) reads *evo śuyadi ◦ anaṣapiḍigasa grahavadisa puni[g.] ///*. A likely translation is "Thus it is heard. Puniga was the . . . of the householder Anaṣapiḍiga" (for further discussion, see appendix 2).

Fortunately, several examples of the Śavasti (= Skt. *śrāvastī*) and other nidānas, mostly in abbreviated form, are found in the Senior manuscripts. The following is a provisional reading made by Richard Salomon of the examples encountered in the manuscripts that have been read to date.

Examples of the Śavasti nidāna are

1. *eva [me śuḋa eka] ṣamae śavasti ṇidaṇa* (20 r11)
2. *śava[sti] ṇ[i]daṇa* (5 r15a; added above the line)
3. *śava[sti] ṇi* (5 v0; written in the blank space above l. 1; note that the word *ṇidaṇa* has not been completed)
4. *bhayava śavasti v.hara* (5 v5a; added above the line; note that the word *viharadi* has not been completed)
5. *śavasti ṇiḋaṇe* (17 r5)
6. *bhayava śavast[i] viharadi teṇa ho va ṇidaṇa samaha aṇaṣapi[ḍi] ///* (7 r18; this may not be the same nidāna as that in the Budhabayaṇa-sutra)

Examples of other nidānas containing relevant wording are

7. *[eva me] ṣuda eka [sama] ? ///* (13 r1)

8. *bhayava baraṇasia viharadi hiṣivadaṇa [rmi]adava tatra da ///* (7 r7; the P equivalent is . . . *bhagavā bārāṇasiyaṃ viharati isipatane migadāye. tatra kho bhagavā,* etc., e.g., SN I 105.2–6, cf. III 172 ff.)
9. *eva me śuda eka ṣamae bhayava ayajae* (or read *avojae*) *viharadi gagae ṇadia tira* (19 r1; this is followed by *aña + + bhikhu* with *te[ṇa] ho [va] + [s.m.]eṇa* added above the line; cf. P *ekaṃ samayaṃ bhagavā ayojjhāyaṃ* [v.l. *ayujjhāyaṃ*] *viharati gaṅgāya nadiyā tīre,* e.g., SN III 140.22–3)

Of these examples only no. 9 appears to be a complete nidāna, though even here the scribe has added the *teṇa ho [va](*ṇa) s(*a)m(*a)eṇa* phrase (= P *tena kho pana samayena*) above the line, probably as a later correction. In all other cases the scribe has abbreviated the nidāna, even leaving words incomplete on occasion: *ṇi* for *ṇidaṇa; v(*i)hara* for *viharadi*. The tendency of the scribes of P and Skt. manuscripts to give only a partial entry for the nidāna is well known. In the case of P manuscripts, abbreviations of this Sāvatthi-Jetavana nidāna include *sāvatthinidānaṃ* (e.g., AN II 54.19), *sāvatthiyaṃ* (e.g., SN I 2.2), *sāvatthi* (e.g., SN II 2.12, in the Sinh. mss.), *sāvatthiyaṃ viharati* (*la*) (e.g., SN II 2.12), and the full phrase minus the initial *evaṃ me sutaṃ* (e.g., AN II 20.2–5), to cite but a few examples. And here it must be noted that *sāvatthinidānaṃ, sāvatthiyaṃ,* and the like are not used as abbreviations for the alternative Sāvatthi nidāna, the Sāvatthi-Pubbārāma nidāna, which is *evam me sutaṃ. ekaṃ samayaṃ bhagavā sāvatthiyaṃ viharati pubbārāme migāramātupāsāde,* etc. (e.g., SN V 222.5–7).[2]

In Skt. manuscripts, examples of such abbreviations are *śrāvastyāṃ nidānaṃ,* as found in the EĀ fragments edited by Tripāṭhī (EĀ-Skt.[Gil.] § 14.01) and in the SĀ fragments edited by de La Vallée Poussin (SĀ(LVP)), and *śrāvastyāṃ nidānaṃ tatra bhagavān bhikṣūn āmaṃtrayati sma,* encountered occasionally in the same SĀ fragments (SĀ(LVP), pp. 575 ff.: 10 r3,7–8, 10 v1,5,8–9).[3] As in P manuscripts, full and abbreviated forms may appear together; for example, in the NidSa the abbreviated form appears at § 1.1 (cf. § 2.1) and the full form at § 5.1, although one of the manuscripts (76.1) used for § 5.1 has the abbreviated form *((*śrāva)styā(*ṃ) nidānaṃ)*.

The full P version of the Sāvatthi-Jetavana nidāna is

evaṃ me sutaṃ. ekaṃ samayaṃ bhagavā sāvatthiyaṃ viharati jetavane anāthapiṇḍikassa ārāme. tatra kho bhagavā bhikkhū āmantesi bhikkhavo ti. bha-

---

[2] This nidāna is relatively common in the canon, but it occurs in combination with wording parallel to the Śrāvastī-Jetavana nidāna (*tatra kho bhagavā bhikkhū āmantesi bhikkhavo ti. bhadante ti te bhikkhū bhagavato paccassosuṃ. bhagavā etad avoca*) only four times (SN V 222–3; cf. AN I 63.15–21). In these four suttas, only the first gives the nidāna in full. The other three suttas abbreviate the formula with *taṃ yeva nidānaṃ*.

[3] Examples in the Central Asian (Turfan) mss. can be found by using the indexes to the SHT, s.vv. *Śrāvastī* and *nidāna*. For discussions of the use and abbreviation of this and other nidānas in Skt. mss., see Tripāṭhī 1962: 11. Cf. Waldschmidt 1957: 375 n. 2, who refers to the habit of the Chinese SĀ of generally giving the nidāna in full.

dante ti te bhikkhū bhagavato paccassosuṃ. bhagavā etad avoca. (E.g., AN II 102.2–5)[4]

The full Skt. version of the same nidāna is

evaṃ mayā śrutam. ekasmin samaye bhagavān śrāvastyāṃ viharati sma jetavane 'nāthapiṇḍadasyārāme. tatra bhagavān bhikṣūn āmantrayati sma. (E.g., DbSū(1) = BBS 209; Dhsk 17 r3; NidSa § 5.1)

A number of variant readings are encountered in the Skt. version. The following list also includes variant readings encountered in the same units in other nidānas: *ekasmiṃ* for *ekasmin* (common in Central Asian manuscripts given in the SHT); *ekasamayaṃ* for *ekasmin samaye* (see SWTF, s.v. *eka-samayam*);[5] *bhagavān śrāvastyāṃ* (e.g., Lal 1.4) is commonly written as *bhagavāṃ śrāvastyāṃ* (e.g., in Central Asian manuscripts given in the SHT), although the readings *bhagavāṃś chrāvastyāṃ* (e.g., Dhsk 17 r3) and *bhagavāṃ cchrāvastyāṃ* (EĀ-Skt.Gil. § 28.01) are also found; *viharati sma* (e.g., NidSa § 5.1; SHT I 620 R1, III 816 V1, 881 V1, V 1332+1476 a V4, VI 1256 a V1, 1493 V4; DbSū(1) = BBS 209; Lal 1.4; RP 1.6; SP 1.5; ŚSPP(G) 2.8–9; DBhS 1.9) alternating with *viharati* (e.g., MPS §§ 1.2, 4.2; see e.g., indexes to SHT, s.v. *viharati*); *anātha-piṇḍadārāme* for *(a)nāthapiṇḍadasyārāme* (see SWTF, s.v. *Anāthapiṇḍada* and *Anātha-piṇḍadārama*, vol. 1, pp. 51, 494); *tatra khalu* for *tatra* (e.g., SHT VI 1256 a V1); and variation among *āmantrayati, āmantrayati sma, āmantrayate,* and *āmantrayate sma* (see SWTF, s.v. *āmantraya,* for references).

eva me [rśoda] (l. 26); *eva me rśodu* (l. 37): The Senior manuscripts have *eva me śuḋa* (19 r1, 20 r11) and *eva me ṣuda* (13 r1). The P is *evaṃ me sutaṃ;* the Skt., *evaṃ mayā śrutam.*

In the line 26 occurrence, only a small remnant of the *o* diacritic of the *rśo* akṣara in *[rśoda]* remains.

G *rśoda* and *rśodu* in this manuscript and *śuḋa* and *ṣuda* in the Senior manuscripts are G reflexes of OIA *śrutam* (see § 5.2.3.6). Further examples of this word in Gāndhārī are *-rśodu* in *baho-rśodu* (= Skt. *bahu-śrutaḥ*) in the AG-G (l. 96), written by the same scribe as our text; *śruta, śruda* (Niya documents; see Boyer, Rapson, and Senart 1920–9: index, s.vv.); and *ṣuda* (Dhp-GK 254, 255), also *ṣuda* in *baho-ṣuda, bahu-ṣuda* (= Skt. *bahu-śruta;* Khvs-G 24b; Dhp-GK 244, 245, etc.); cf. *śrudi* = Skt. *śruti* (Dhp-GK 249). (For the discussion of *rś* written for original *śr,* see § 5.2.3.6; for the writing of *o* for original *u,* see § 5.1.8.)

[eka] /// (l. 26); *eka sama[ya ◦]* (l. 37): The reading based on these two examples is *eka samaya ◦*. For the reasons given above, the example on line 26 may or may not have included the punctuation mark. The examples in the Senior manuscripts are *[eka] ṣamae*

[4] For two Indian epigraphical versions of the formula in "Pali," see von Hinüber 1985: 188, 193. They differ from the standard P version only on points of orthography.

[5] SWTF, s.v. *eka*, vol. 1, p. 431, suggests that the reading of *eka[ṃ] samayaṃ* at MPS § 1.2, may be *ekasamayaṃ*.

(20 r11), *eka ṣamae* (19 r1), and *eka [sama] ? ///* (13 r1; which can be reconstructed as *eka sama(*e)*). The Pali is *ekaṃ samayaṃ*. The most common Skt. form is *ekasmin samaye,* frequently written *ekasmiṃ samaye,* but *ekasamayaṃ* and possibly *eka[ṃ] samayaṃ* are also recorded (see above for references). The form *eka sama[ya]* of our manuscript undoubtedly represents the accusative singular rather than the locative singular. Although *eka ṣamae* and *eka sama(*e)* of the Senior manuscripts could be locative singular, they probably also represent an accusative singular with final *-e* for *-yaṃ* or *-ya* (see § 5.1.1; cf. *samudae* = P *samudayo,* Senior 5 v7,8, as a nom. sg. m.).[6]

In light of the Skt. example of *ekasamayaṃ,* it is possible that G *eka sama[ya], eka ṣamae*, and *eka sama(*e)* represent a compound and therefore should be edited as *ekasamaya, ekaṣamae,* and *ekasama(*e)*, respectively. However, given that the P form is not in compound and that the compound form is rare, the noncompound form seems more likely.

The reading *eva me rśodu eka sama[ya ◦]* in line 37, with the punctuation mark after *eka samaya* rather than after *eva me rśodu,* is of some interest because the punctuation of this formula has been discussed by several scholars (Brough 1950; Samtani 1964–5; Kajiyama 1977; Silk 1989; Galloway 1991; Tola and Dragonetti 1999).[7] The debate has centered on the problem of whether the phrase *ekaṃ samayaṃ/ekasmin samaye* (to use the P and Skt. forms) is to be taken with the preceding *evaṃ me sutaṃ/evaṃ mayā śrutam* or with the following phrase describing where the Buddha dwelt (*bhagavā/bhagavān . . . viharati,* etc.). That is, is the opening of Buddhist suttas/sūtras to be understood as "Thus have I heard: At one time the Bhagavat dwelt in such and such a place" or as "Thus at one time I heard: The Bhagavat dwelt in such and such a place"?

The presence of the punctuation mark after *eka samaya* in line 37 indicates that the scribe of this manuscript probably understood the phrase to mean "Thus at one time I heard: The Bhagavat dwelt. . . ."[8] But caution needs to be exercised here, first because the manuscript is split at this point, which throws some doubt on the reading, and second because this scribe is not always consistent in his use of punctuation marks (see § 4.8.2). Further, we have only this one example, so that we cannot be certain this scribe would have included the punctuation mark in the same location in other sūtras that he copied. Nor can we conclude on the basis of one example that this was the common understanding of the phrase in this scribe's monastery or in the Gandhāran region as a whole. It is unfortunate that further examples of the opening sūtra nidāna have not so far been encountered in the BL manuscripts. It is also unfortunate that the scribe of the Senior manuscripts studied to date rarely used punctuation marks. Finally, the appearance of a punctuation mark after many examples of the phrase that begins the stories in the avadāna

---

[6] The use of the acc. in P *ekaṃ samayaṃ* and loc. in Skt. *ekasmin samaye* is discussed by Brough (1950: 421–3) and Galloway (1991: 96 ff.).

[7] The most comprehensive bibliography is given by Daniel Boucher in Bongard-Levin et al. 1996: 90 n. 1, to which can be added an unpublished paper by Konrad Klaus read at the XXVI Deutscher Orientalistentag, Leipzig, 1995; and Tola and Dragonetti 1999.

[8] However, Galloway (1991: 90 ff.) suggests that the daṇḍa after *dus gcig na* (Skt. *samaye*) in Tib. mss. may be no more than a comma.

texts in the BL collection, *evo śuyadi/śruyadi/ṣuyadi* (see appendix 2), does not necessarily imply that the scribe of these texts would have punctuated the *eva me rśoda eka samaya bhayavadu* phrase after *eva me rśoda* were he writing a sūtra text, for *evo śuyadi/śruyadi/ṣuyadi* is the set phrase used in the avadāna genre (though it may have originated from a formula that included an *eka samaya*-type unit).[9]

/// bhaya[v.] /// [27]*du śavastie viharadi jedavaṇo aṇasapiḍiasa aramu* ∘ (ll. 26–7); *bhayadu śavastie viharadi [jedavaṇ.] ///* [38]*ḍiasa aramu* ∘ (ll. 37–8): The combined reading is *bhayavadu śavastie viharadi jedavaṇo aṇasapiḍiasa aramu* ∘. Although less likely, the reading could be *jedaaṇo* in line 27. Examples of the same nidāna from the Senior manuscripts are *bhayava śavasti v.hara,* which has been left incomplete (5 v5a), and possibly *bhayava śavast[i] viharadi* (7 r18). The P version is *bhagavā sāvatthiyaṃ viharati jetavane anāthapiṇḍikassa ārāme*. The Sanskrit is *bhagavān śrāvastyāṃ viharati sma jetavane 'nāthapiṇḍadasyārāme* with the vv.ll. *viharati* for *viharati sma* and *anāthapiṇḍadārāme* for *anāthapiṇḍadasyārāme* (see above for references).

The G spelling *aṇasapiḍia* for the name of this well-known householder who gave the Jetavana to the Buddhist community is equivalent to P *anāthapiṇḍika,* with elision of intervocalic *-k-,* rather than to *anāthapiṇḍada* of the Skt., a form that seems to be universal in Skt. texts (see BHSD and SWTF, s.v.; the spelling *anāthapiṇḍika* is recorded once: see BHSD, s.v.) and is reflected in the standard Tib. translation, *mgon-med-zas-sbyin* (Mvy 4111). This proper name also appears in Gāndhārī as *anaṣapiḍiga* in the first avadāna story at the bottom of our scroll (see appendix 2), while *aṇaṣapi[ḍi] ///* (7 r18) and *aṇasapiḍi g.ahava[d]i* (7 r4) are encountered in the Senior manuscripts. The spelling *anaṣapiḍiga* reflects the P form of the word, whereas *aṇasapiḍi* of the second Senior example may be a scribal error or possibly an example of the loss of the final syllable (see § 5.5).

As expected, the G version of the phrase lacks the *sma* encountered in some Skt. versions, and the reading *aṇasapiḍiasa aramu* reflects the noncompounded form rather than the compounded form of some Skt. examples (*anāthapiṇḍadārame*).

ta[tra] ya bha[ya] + [d.] bhi /// [28]*matredi* (ll. 27–8); *tatra ya bhayavadu bhikhu amat[r]edi* (l. 38): The lower part of *tra* (l. 27) appears as a diagonal line on a splinter just to the left of the akṣara, thereby distorting its appearance. Based on these two examples the combined reading for this phrase is *tatra ya bhayavadu bhikhu amatredi*. There are no certain examples of this phrase in the Senior manuscripts studied to date.[10] The P version is *tatra kho bhagavā bhikkhū āmantesi bhikkhavo ti*. The Sanskrit is *tatra bhagavān bhikṣūn āmantrayati sma,* with variation between *tatra* (rarely, it seems) and *tatra khalu* and among *āmantrayati, āmantrayati sma, āmantrayate,* and *āmantrayate sma* (see above for references).[11]

---

[9] However, punctuation is implied after *anuśrūyate* in the comparable phrase *evam anuśrūyate yadā bhagavān* found in the Divy (e.g., 348.20–1; the Cowell and Neil edition has a daṇḍa).

[10] It is unclear whether the fragmentary *tatra da ///* (Senior 7 r7) represents the beginning of this phrase. If so, then *da,* where the reading is *ya* in our ms., is problematic, for *ya* = Skt./P *ca*.

[11] See von Simson 1965: §§ 12.2 ff., 14.1 ff., 14.11–2, 17.2–3, for a discussion of the Central Asian Skt. examples of *tatra . . . āmantrayate*.

The reading *tatra ya* (= Skt./P *tatra ca*) in Gāndhārī, where the Pali has *tatra kho* and the Skt. *tatra* or rarely *tatra khalu,* finds no parallel elsewhere in such a context, although the combination is common enough in other contexts in Buddhist literature.[12]

The Gāndhārī parallels the Sanskrit in lacking an equivalent of *bhikkhavo ti* of the Pali, the Buddha's vocative of address to the monks. The Gāndhārī similarly lacks the equivalent of the monks' response *bhadante ti* of the Pali in the following phrase. However, it is possible that further G examples may turn up that contain the vocatives in both places, indicating that the omission is a scribal error or abbreviation.

The Gāndhārī also parallels the Sanskrit in using the present indicative form of the verb (G *amatredi*/Skt. *āmantrayati sma,* etc.) where the P has the preterite *āmantesi.*[13]

te bhikhu bhayavadu pracarśoṣu ◦ (l. 28); *bhikhu ? ? ? ? ? ///* (l. 38): The line 28 example provides the complete text. The scribe seems to have accidentally omitted *te* in line 38. There are no examples of this phrase in the Senior manuscripts studied to date. The P is *bhadante ti te bhikkhū bhagavato paccassosuṃ,* including a vocative phrase. All Skt. versions of "the Buddha addresses the monks" formula at the beginning of sūtras lack the equivalent of both this and the following phrase (G *bhayavadu eghad uya;* P *bhagavā etad avoca*). In other words, the Skt. version ends with *tatra bhagavān bhikṣūn āmantrayati sma.* However, the Skt. equivalents of both of these phrases are common in other contexts. An example of the first phrase is *tatra bhagavān āyuṣmantam ānandam āmantrayate. āgamayānanda yena mathurā iti. evaṃ bhadanta ity āyuṣmān ānando bhagavataḥ pratyaśrauṣīt* (MSV I 3.12–3; cf. I 24.8–9, 48.5–6, etc.; MPS §§ 3.1–2, 4.1–2, 8.1–3, etc.). The reading is *bhadantety* in a number of examples in the MSV and throughout the MPS and elsewhere. Note that the initial vocative is included in the Skt. version of this phrase, indicating that the omission of the vocatives in the G text may be a deliberate act of abbreviation. For examples of Skt. equivalents of the second phrase, see below.

The omission in Skt. texts of these two units (G *te bhikhu bhayavadu pracarśoṣu* ◦ *bhayavadu eghad uya* ◦; P *bhadante ti te bhikkhū bhagavato paccassosuṃ. bhagavā etad avoca*) in the opening nidāna of sūtras and the simplification of this formula may have resulted from the fact that the simpler form, Skt. *tatra bhagavān bhikṣūn āmantrayati sma*/P *tatra kho bhagavā bhikkhū āmantesi,* is the one commonly encountered within other sections of sūtras, both in Skt. and in P texts (e.g., DN II 94.28, the parallel to MPS § 10.7; cf., e.g., MPS § 8.5). Further, it may have been felt that these units added no new information. Nonetheless, the omission is a little surprising considering that the phrases

---

[12] Examples are *atha kho ahaṃ . . . yena so bhavaṃ gotamo ten' upasaṅkamiṃ. tatra ca so bhavaṃ gotamo anekapariyāyena jhānakathaṃ kathesi* (MN III 13.28–30); *buddho bhagavān . . . śrāvastyāṃ viharati jetavane 'nāthapiṇḍadasyārāme. tena khalu samayena śrāvastyāṃ pañcamātrāṇi gāndharvikaśatāni goṣṭhikānāṃ prativasanti. tatra ca kāle supriyo nāma gāndharvikarājo 'bhyāgataḥ* (Avś I 93.4–7); cf. MSV I 47.10.

[13] In Buddhist Skt. texts the historical present seems to dominate (see, e.g., SWTF, s.v. *āmantraya*). The only example of a preterite form in the Central Asian (Turfan) mss. is one periphrastic perfect, *āmantrayāmāsa,* in a fragment of the Mahāparinirvāṇa-sūtra attributed to the Dharmaguptakas (see Waldschmidt 1968: 10; cf. 1980: 167–8).

express the formal and ceremonial character of the interchange that opens the sūtra. In this connection it is interesting that in editions and manuscripts of P texts a common abbreviation of the full opening passage (*tatra kho bhagavā bhikkhū āmantesi bhikkhavo ti. bhadante ti te bhikkhū bhagavato paccassosuṃ. bhagavā etad avoca*) is *tatra kho bhagavā bhikkhū āmantesi*. In some instances the abbreviation is indicated with *pe, la,* or the like (e.g., the E^e and B^e of SN IV 143.33–4, 144.20, etc.), but in many cases the indicator of abbreviation is lacking. Examples are SN V 222.7, where only the Sinh. manuscripts used for the E^e indicate that abbreviation has occurred (the E^e, the one Burmese ms. used there, and the B^e lack the indication), and SN III 140.24, where the Sinh. manuscripts give the complete wording, while the E^e, the one Burmese manuscript used there, and the B^e lack the abbreviation indicator.[14] It is thus possible that the tendency to abbreviate this phrase in manuscripts led to the eventual standardization of the simpler formula in the Skt. textual traditions.

bha[ya]va[ṣu] egha[d=uya ◦] (l. 28); *eghad=oya* ◦ (l. 39): As noted above, *bha[ya]va[ṣu]* is a scribal error for *bhayavadu*. The complete phrase is *bhayavadu eghad uya* (or *eghad oya*) ◦. A similar phrase occurs on line 9, *bhaya[vad]u egha[d=u] + +,* which I reconstruct as *bhayavadu eghad u(*ya ◦),* though in this case *bhayavadu* represents the accusative rather than the nominative (= P *bhagavantaṃ etad avoca*). None of the nidānas in the Senior manuscripts contain this phrase, but equivalents of the line 9 phrase, which describes someone speaking to the Buddha, are encountered. The P is *bhagavā etad avoca*. The Sanskrit lacks this unit in this context, but equivalents are found in other contexts, where the standard form is *bhagavān idam avocat* (e.g., MSV II 74.5–6).

The *bhayavadu eghad uya* phrase, along with the examples from the Senior manuscripts and Skt. equivalents, is discussed in my analysis of the line 9 example.

In summary, in overall wording the G version of the opening nidāna is closer to the P than to the Skt., though it is not identical with it. It differs from the P in omitting the vocatives of address (though I have argued that this may be a scribal abbreviation), in reading *tatra ya* (= *tatra ca*) against *tatra kho,* and in having the present indicative *amatredi,* parallel to *āmantrayati* of the Skt., where the P has the preterite *āmantesi*.

Lines 28–36: The Buddha's discourse

Edition:

| 24a
[28] *[su] ///* [29]*kṣave budhabayaṇo tatu paḍideṇa [ṇa] baleṇa ◦ sato kamatu*

[ghacha]teṇa ṇa sukaro ka /// [30] *budhabayaṇata bhikṣave ghachateṇa s[u]karo katu*

tatu paḍideṇa ṇa bal[eṇa] ◦ [sa] /// [31]*matu ṭ́hideṇa ṇa sukaro katu ◦ budhabayaṇata*

| 25o | 25o+ D6bb | D6bb | 24a
bhikṣave [ṭ́h.] + ṇa s[u]k.ro k. /// [32]*to [pa]ḍideṇa ṇa baleṇa ◦ satu kama[t]u ṇiṣaṇeṇa*

ṇa sukaro kat[u] ◦ [33] *budhabayaṇata bhikṣave ◦ ṇiṣaṇeṇa sukaro katu tatu paḍide ///*

[14] Other instances where this or similar phrases are found at the beginning of suttas in the E^e and B^e without an indication of abbreviation are SN II 241.4–5, IV 19.25, 20.32, 124.26.

[34] *sato kamato śeaṇeṇa jaghara[du] ṇa sukaro kato ◦ budhabayaṇa[ta] ///* [35]*aṇeṇa jagharadu sukaro kato ◦ ta[tu] paḍideṇa ṇa [ba]l[e]ṇa ◦ sukar. ///* [36] *budhabayaṇo tatu paḍideṇa ṇa ba[le]ṇa ◦*

Reconstruction:
[28] *su(*karo bhi)*[29]*kṣave budhabayaṇo tatu paḍideṇa ṇa baleṇa ◦ sato kamatu ghachateṇa ṇa sukaro ka(*tu ◦)* [30] *budhabayaṇata bhikṣave ghachateṇa sukaro katu tatu paḍideṇa ṇa baleṇa ◦ sa(*to ka)*[31]*matu ṭhideṇa ṇa sukaro katu ◦ budhabayaṇata bhikṣave ṭh(*ide)ṇa suk(*a)ro k(*atu ta)*[32]*to paḍideṇa ṇa baleṇa ◦ satu kamatu ṇiṣaṇeṇa ṇa sukaro katu ◦* [33] *budhabayaṇata bhikṣave ◦ ṇiṣaṇeṇa sukaro katu tatu paḍide(*ṇa ṇa baleṇa ◦)* [34] *sato kamato śeaṇeṇa jagharadu ṇa sukaro kato ◦ budhabayaṇata (*bhikṣave śe)*[35]*aṇeṇa jagharadu sukaro kato ◦ tatu paḍideṇa ṇa baleṇa ◦ sukar(*u bhikṣave)* [36] *budhabayaṇo tatu paḍideṇa ṇa baleṇa ◦*

Translation:
[28–9] "Monks, the Buddha's teaching is easy [to perform], but only by a wise man, not a fool. Good action[15] is not easy to perform while going. [30] Monks, on account of the Buddha's teaching it is easy to perform while going, but only by a wise man, not a fool. Good action [31] is not easy to perform while standing. Monks, on account of the Buddha's teaching it is easy to perform while standing, [32] but only by a wise man, not a fool. Good action is not easy to perform while sitting. [33] Monks, on account of the Buddha's teaching it is easy to perform while sitting, but only by a wise man, (*not a fool). [34] Good action is not easy to perform while lying down awake. (*Monks), on account of the Buddha's teaching [35] it is easy to perform while lying down awake, but only by a wise man, not a fool. (*Monks), [36] the Buddha's teaching is easy [to perform], but only by a wise man, not a fool."

Line 30: *s[u]karo:* The bottom of *s[u],* which is partially covered by a loose chip, is distorted, making the akṣara appear like a *rsa*.

paḍideṇa: A thin, transparent section of bark sits over the bottom of *ḍide*. The remnants of two akṣaras (*da ?*) from the verso are visible through the transparent bark, upside down and in mirror image.

Line 32: *ṇiṣaṇeṇa:* Two small chips, containing small remnants of ink, sit above *ṣa*. These chips have been left unnumbered.

The final punctuation mark on the line must be the end of the line, as there are no words missing between this and *budhabayaṇata,* which begins the next line.

As the manuscript is preserved, there is a large empty space between lines 32 and 33, representing the overlay area where two sections of bark were originally glued together.

Line 33: A large ink mark in the right margin appears to be merely a smudge.

A space the width of an akṣara has been left blank between *katu* and *tatu.* A similar space has been left blank directly below in the next line (l. 34) after *kato* ◦.

---

[15] An alternative translation for "good action" is "the practice of mindfulness."

paḍide ///: The bark containing *de* has begun to break up. The akṣara is clearly visible in the old black-and-white photo.

Line 35: *sukar. ///:* The bottom of *r.* is partially missing. The vowel could not have been *o,* so the reading probably is *ru.*

The reconstruction of the lacunae in this section of the text is straightforward due to the repetitiveness of the text. The only uncertainty lies in the reconstruction of final vowels of some words. As the final vowel alternates between *-u* and *-o* in *sukaro/sukaru, kato/katu,* and *sato/satu*, the choice of one or the other in the reconstruction of these words is based on the majority.

Although I have not found a parallel to this discourse elsewhere in Buddhist literature, a number of passages, chiefly from the P canon, provide guidance in understanding the G text. Apart from suttas 11 and 12 of the Catukka-nipāta of the AN (II 13–5 = It 115–21), whose structure, as mentioned in § 9.1.2, is also based on the four postures, a number of passages within suttas/sūtras provide parallels to some of the key phrases of the G sūtra and possibly to the general sentiment of the text.

The first example is in the description of four of the eight "grounds for slackness" (P *kusītavatthu*/Skt. *kausīdyavastu*) and "grounds for undertaking effort" (P *āraddhavatthu*/ Skt. *vīryārambhavastu*), which appears in Pali in the AN (IV 332–5) and Saṅgīti-suttanta (DN III 255–8), and in Sanskrit in the Daśottara-sūtra (§§ VIII.5–6; the Skt. text of the Saṅgīti-sūtra parallel has not survived; see Saṅg-Skt. §§ VIII.4–5).

The first *āraddhavatthu* in P is

> *idha bhikkhave bhikkhunā kammaṃ kattabbaṃ hoti. tassa evaṃ hoti kammaṃ kho me kattabbaṃ bhavissati, kammaṃ kho pana me karontena na sukaraṃ buddhānaṃ sāsanaṃ manasikātuṃ, handāhaṃ paṭigacc' eva viriyaṃ ārabhāmi appattassa pattiyā . . . ti. so viriyaṃ ārabhati appattassa pattiyā . . .. idaṃ bhikkhave paṭhamaṃ ārabbhavatthuṃ.* (AN IV 334.3–11; DN III 256.24–32)

> Here, Monks, there is work that is to be done by a monk. It occurs to him: "I am to do work, but in doing that work it will not be easy for me to attend to the instruction of the Buddhas. Well then, in preparing for that I'll exert myself for the attainment of the unattained. . . ." He exerts himself for the attainment of the unattained. . . . This, Monks, is the first ground for undertaking effort.

The second *āraddhavatthu* differs from the first only in that the first half (up to *manasikātuṃ*) is in the past tense. The tenses of the third and fourth *āraddhavatthu*s parallel the first and second, respectively, but the wording of the first half of the third is

> *puna ca paraṃ bhikkhave bhikkhunā maggo gantabbo hoti. tassa evaṃ hoti maggo kho me gantabbo bhavissati, maggaṃ kho pana me gacchantena na sukaraṃ buddhānaṃ sāsanaṃ manasikātuṃ.* (AN IV 334.20–5; DN III 257.5–11)

Again, Monks, there is a journey that is to be undertaken by a monk. It occurs to him: "I am to go on a journey, but in going on a journey it will not be easy for me to attend to the instruction of the Buddhas."

The Skt. Daśo (§ VIII.6.[3]) parallel to the first P passage, which appears as the third *vīryārambhavastu*, is the following (edited here on the basis of the repetitive wording preserved in VIII.6.(3) and (4), as well as the other *vīryārambhavastus*):

punar aparaṃ bhikṣuṇā śvaḥ karma kartavyaṃ bhavati. tasyaivaṃ bhavati. mayā khalu śvaḥ karma kartavyam. na śakyaṃ mayā karma ca kartuṃ śāstuś ca śāsane yogam āpattum. yannv ahaṃ pratiyaty'eva vyāyateyam. sa pratiyaty'eva vyāyatate . . . idaṃ tṛtīyaṃ vīryārambhavastu.

The Skt. parallel to the second P passage quoted above (i.e., the third *āraddhavatthu* of the Pali) is quite fragmentary (Daśo § VIII.6.[5]). The opening is *punar aparaṃ bhikṣuṇā śvo mārgo gantavyo bhavati.*

Passages similar to these are found in an AN sutta that describes the five "fears concerning the future" (*anāgatabhaya*), perceiving which a monk makes effort (III 103–5). In the first he perceives that he is now young but will one day be old, when it will be difficult for him to attend to the instruction of the Buddhas (*na sukaraṃ buddhānaṃ sāsanaṃ manasikātuṃ*) and it will not be possible for him to live in secluded places (*na sukarāni araññavanapatthāni pantāni senāsanāni paṭisevituṃ*). He therefore exerts himself in the present. Similar wording is used for the fear concerning future sickness, famine, war, and schism in the Buddhist community, when it will also be difficult to attend to the instruction of the Buddhas.

In another AN sutta (V 332–4), which repeats much of the wording of the sutta that precedes it (AN V 328–32), the Buddha instructs the Sakka Mahānāma in how he should live. He states that the successful one (*ārādhaka*) has faith (*saddha*) and is energetic (*āraddhaviriya*), mindful (*upaṭṭhitasati*), concentrated (*samāhita*), and wise (*paññavā*), but that as support for these he should bring to mind the Buddha, Dhamma, Saṅgha, virtue, abandoning, and the gods, developing this practice when going, standing, sitting, lying down, doing work, and spending time with family. The passage most relevant for our purposes is

imaṃ kho tvaṃ mahānāma buddhānussatiṃ gacchanto pi bhāveyyāsi, ṭhito pi bhāveyyāsi, nisinno pi bhāveyyāsi, sayāno pi bhāveyyāsi, kammantaṃ adhiṭṭhahanto pi bhāveyyāsi, puttasambādhasayanaṃ ajjhāvasanto pi bhāveyyāsi. (AN V 333.29–33)

Energy—exerting oneself and applying oneself to the Buddha's/Buddhas' teaching—is the theme common to all these passages, including suttas 11 and 12 of the Catukka-nipāta of the AN, with their foundation of the four postures, and suttas 13 and 14 of the Catukka-nipāta, which define *padhāna,* "effort," the topic of the G Prasaṇa-sutra. It is therefore possible that this is the underlying sentiment of the G Budhabayaṇa-sutra also.

In the G sūtra the Buddha's discourse opens and closes with an identical statement. For the purpose of the following study, these will be labeled A and B. Between the opening and closing statement are four parallel statements that differ only in that a different posture is referred to. These will be numbered I–IV. Each of these four statements is further divisible into two parts: Ia, Ib, IIa, IIb, etc. The four "a" units (Ia, IIa, etc.) are parallel in overall wording, as are the four "b" units (Ib, IIb, etc.). The reconstructed discourse can thus be presented as follows:

A. *su(*karo bhi)kṣave budhabayaṇo tatu paḍideṇa ṇa baleṇa* ◦
Ia. *sato kamatu ghachateṇa ṇa sukaro ka(*tu* ◦*)*
Ib. *budhabayaṇata bhikṣave ghachateṇa sukaro katu tatu paḍideṇa ṇa baleṇa* ◦
IIa. *sa(*to ka)matu ṭ́hideṇa ṇa sukaro katu* ◦
IIb. *budhabayaṇata bhikṣave ṭ́h(*ide)ṇa suk(*a)ro k(*atu ta)to paḍideṇa ṇa baleṇa* ◦
IIIa. *satu kamatu ṇiṣaṇeṇa ṇa sukaro katu* ◦
IIIb. *budhabayaṇata bhikṣave* ◦ *ṇiṣaṇeṇa sukaro katu tatu paḍide(*ṇa ṇa baleṇa* ◦*)*
IVa. *sato kamato śeaṇeṇa jagharadu ṇa sukaro kato* ◦
IVb. *budhabayaṇata (*bhikṣave śe)aṇeṇa jagharadu sukaro kato* ◦ *tatu paḍideṇa ṇa baleṇa* ◦
B. *sukar(*u bhikṣave) budhabayaṇo tatu paḍideṇa ṇa baleṇa* ◦

The meaning of the opening and closing statement (A and B) is fairly straightforward: "Monks, the Buddha's teaching is easy [to perform], but only by a wise man, not a fool."

[su] /// (l. 28); *sukar. ///* (l. 35): Although the reading is *sukaro* wherever the word is complete, there is no *o* diacritic on the final *r.* in *sukar.* at the end of line 35. The reading therefore must have been *sukar(*u).*

This word is the equivalent of P/Skt. *sukaraṃ,* used as a predicative adjective to *budhabayaṇo* = P/Skt. *buddhavacanaṃ.* In statements I–IV it is constructed with the infinitive *katu/kato* (= P *kātuṃ*/Skt. *kartum*) in *ṇa sukaro katu* and *sukaro katu.* In P, *sukara* is usually constructed with the infinitive, in both canonical and paracanonical texts, as in *na sukaraṃ buddhānaṃ sāsanaṃ manasikātuṃ* and *na sukarāni araññavana-patthāni pantāni senāsanāni paṭisevituṃ* quoted above.[16] Although instances are found in the P canon where *sukara* occurs without an infinitive, these are relatively rare, mostly occurring in verse. Most examples of *sukara* without infinitive are in paracanonical texts. A canonical verse example is *sukaraṃ sādhunā sādhu, sādhu pāpena dukkaraṃ, pāpaṃ pāpena sukaraṃ, pāpam ariyebhi dukkaran ti* (Ud 61 = Vin II 198), but even here the infinitive *kātuṃ* is understood, as seen in the commentarial gloss: <u>*sukaraṃ sādhunā*</u>

[16] Further canonical examples are *(ariyasāvakassa) na sukaraṃ puññassa pamāṇaṃ gahetuṃ* [v.l. *gaṇetuṃ*] (AN II 55, III 52, 337; SN V 400 ff. [some are abbreviated in E^e]); *(ākāse) tattha na sukaraṃ rūpaṃ likhituṃ rūpapātubhāvaṃ kātuṃ* (MN I 127); *na kho taṃ sukaraṃ sukhaṃ adhigantuṃ* (e.g., MN I 247); *na kho bhikkhu sukaro so bhagavā amhehi upasaṅkamituṃ* (SN I 11); *so (kappo) na sukaro saṅkhātuṃ* (SN II 181–2; cf. II 183–4); *ayaṃ hi bhante mahāpaṭhavī gambhīrā appameyyā. sā na sukarā apaṭhavī kātuṃ* (MN I 127); *vālikā sā na sukarā saṅkhātuṃ* (SN II 184).

sādhū ti . . . sukaraṃ sukhena kātuṃ sakkā . . . pāpaṃ pāpena sukaran ti . . . sukaraṃ sukhena kātuṃ sakkuṇeyya (Ud-a 317–8).[17]

Although *tatu/tato* resembles an infinitive, it more likely represents Skt. *tat-tu,* as shown by a passage in a Central Asian Skt. fragment of a sūtra collection:

> + + *saṃskārā [ni]rudhyante ākh(*y)ātāhaṃ bhikṣoḥ tat tu tvayā na sukaram ājñātum labhyaṃ bha* (SHT II 504 V5)

The editor of this fragment reconstructs *(*āyuḥ)saṃskārā* based on the P parallel *tato sīghataraṃ āyusaṅkhārā khīyanti* (SN II 266.19–20). The translation is therefore likely to be "I declare that the constituents (*of life) cease. But that, Monk, is not easy for you to understand."[18] That *tatu/tato* is not an infinitive is also supported by its appearance after the infinitive *katu/kato* in the "b" passages, where two infinitives would be awkward. Also note that a punctuation mark appears between the two words in the IVb example. I therefore take *tatu/tato* to be the equivalent of Skt. *tat-tu,* presenting it as *tatu/tato* rather than *ta tu/ta to.*

Based on the above, it is therefore likely that the infinitive *katu/kato* is to be understood in the opening and closing statements.

budhabayaṇo (ll. 29 and 36): This is the equivalent of P and Skt. *buddhavacanaṃ.* Despite its apparent familiarity, the expression *buddhavacana* is actually quite rare in P canonical texts and in comparable Skt. literature, though it is commonly encountered in P commentaries and other paracanonical works. When it does appear in the P canon, it is often in the later layers (e.g., in the Bv and Ap); Skt. examples are rarely from sūtras. Its seeming familiarity comes from the fact that it appears in the much-discussed passage of the Culla-vagga of the Vin that depicts two monks, who were brahmans, asking the Buddha for his consent to allow them to change the *buddhavacana* into *chandaso* because it is being defiled by monks who recite it in their own dialects: *etarahi bhante bhikkhū nānānāmā nānāgottā nānājaccā nānākulā pabbajitā, te sakāya niruttiyā buddhavacanaṃ dūsenti. handa mayaṃ bhante buddhavacanaṃ chandaso āropemā ti . . .* (Vin II 139).[19]

---

[17] Cf. *sukarāni asādhūni, attano ahitāni ca, yaṃ ve hitañ ca sādhuñ ca, taṃ ve paramadukkaraṃ* (Dhp 163). A prose canonical example is *'. . . yāvañ cidaṃ bhikkhave upamā pi na sukarā yāva dukkhā nirayā' ti* (MN III 165). Paracanonical examples are *paribhogo pi tena saddhiṃ sukaro hoti* (Sv III 928); *so 'dukkaraṃ khuradhārūpamaṃ sāsane paṭipattipūraṇaṃ* [Bᵉ adds *dukkhaṃ*], *tāpasapabbajjā pana sukarā c' eva bahujanasammatā cā' ti vibbhamitvā* (Sv I 269).

[18] See the editor's note (SHT II p. 31). Other occurrences of *tat tu* are *yady api cānyair āryasubhūtiprabhṛtibhir api kiṃcid uktaṃ tat tu bhagavadādhipatyād evety adoṣaḥ* (Abhisamayālaṃkārālokā, Vaidya ed., pp. 556–7), quoted in Kajiyama 1977: 98. According to Klaus Wille (personal communication) Dutt's reading *kadācit syāt tat tu tu laghunipāti* at MSV II 56.9–10 should be emended to *syāt taṃttra laghu nipāti.*

[19] Other canonical occurrences in P are *sutvāna buddhavacanaṃ* (Sn 202a); *karotha buddhavacanaṃ* (Th 403a); *navaṅgabuddhavacanaṃ* (Ap 44.12, pāda c); *sussāma buddhavacanaṃ* (Ap 143.24, pāda c); *nipuṇe buddhavacane* (Ap 503.4, pāda c); *idh' ekaccassa buddhavacanaṃ pariyāputaṃ hoti suttaṃ geyyaṃ,* etc. (Nidd II [Bᵉ] 224, 278); *lābhā te gahapati . . . yassa te gambhīre buddhavacane paññācakkhu kamatī ti* (SN IV 283.18–9, 292.31–2; the Bᵉ also includes it at

Examples from Buddhist Skt. literature are *tena buddhavacanaṃ lekhayitavyam . . . buddhavacanapustakā . . . prakṣeptavyāḥ* (MSV II 143.3–6; cf. ll. 13–4) and *atha sa brāhmaṇadārako 'nāthapiṇḍadasaṃsargāj jetavanaṃ gatvā buddhavacanaṃ śṛṇoti* (Avś I 296.3; cf. I 217.2).[20]

Although the term *buddhavacana* is rare in canonical P and in comparable Skt. texts, alternative expressions for the same idea are, not surprisingly, relatively common. Examples are the following:

1. P *bhagavato vacana-* is encountered in the well-known Mahāpadesa-sutta, in which the Buddha sets out the method for determining the authenticity of claims about what is "the word of the Buddha" (DN II 123 ff.; AN II 167 ff.). The Skt. parallel has *(na) bhagavatā bhāṣitāḥ* (MPS §§ 24.7 ff.).[21]
2. P *buddhānaṃ sāsana-* and Skt. *buddhānāṃ śāsana-* are found in the passages quoted above that parallel the G text on a number of points (AN IV 332–5; DN III 255–8). The Skt. Daśo parallel (§ VIII.6.[3–6]) has *śāstuś ca śāsane*. The expression *buddhānāṃ śāsana-* also occurs at MSV II 75–6 in a similar context. The singular *buddhassa sāsana-* also occurs in Pali.
3. For P *bhagavato sāsana-* and Skt. *bhagavataḥ śāsana-*, see, for example, *idam pi bhagavato sāsanaṃ niccakappaṃ manasikātabbaṃ* (MN III 266); *bhagavataś ca śāsane pravajya* (MSV I 55.3, 72.8); and *tena bhagavacchāsane prasādaḥ pratilabdhaḥ* (Avś I 296.3–4).
4. P *satthu sāsana-* and Skt. *śāstuḥ śāsana-/śāt̥rśāsana-* are encountered in *ayaṃ dhammo ayaṃ vinayo idaṃ satthu sāsanaṃ* (in the Mahāpadesa-sutta: DN II 123 ff.; AN II 167 ff.; cf. Vin II 73–4, 203); *ayaṃ dharmo 'yaṃ vinaya idaṃ śāstuḥ śāsanam* (MPS §§ 24.5, 11, etc.); *saddhassa . . . sāvakassa satthu sāsane pariyogāya vattato rumhaniyaṃ satthu sāsanaṃ hoti ojavantaṃ* (MN I 480 [cf. 481]; cf. MN I 150.12,31); *tato 'haṃ pravrajitveha vyaharaṃ* [Wille (1990: 100) reads *vyāhāraṃ*] *śāt̥rśāsane* (MSV I 202.7); *śāstuḥ śāsane* (MSV II 46.18–9). For *śāstuḥ śāsana-* see also SHT II 51 a Bl.(1)41 V1,3; III 994 a R2.
5. Other examples are *pravrajyā ca mayā labdhā śākyasiṃhasya śāsane* (MSV I 177.3, 184.13, 188.3), the G version of which is *paba[ja] ya mae ladha śakasihasa śaśaṇe* (AG-G l. 81; also on ll. 109–10), and *śraddhayā pravrajitvā ca yukto 'haṃ jinaśāsane* (MSV I 208.16). Expressions such as *jinavacana, tathāgatavacana,* and so on are also relatively common in P commentarial and other paracanonical works.

The passages *kammaṃ kho pana me karontena na sukaraṃ buddhānaṃ sāsanaṃ manasikātuṃ* and *maggaṃ kho pana me gacchantena na sukaraṃ buddhānaṃ sāsanaṃ*

---

the end of the sutta that ends on p. 297). Cf. also *buddhassa vacanaṃ sutvā* (Ap 318.4, pāda c, 553.25, pāda a).

[20] The example *(*nirāmiṣ)eṣu (*buddhavacaneṣu)* at MPS § 30.26, was reconstructed by the editor on the basis of the Tibetan.

[21] Other examples of *bhagavato vacanaṃ* are SN III 121–2, IV 62; AN IV 163–4.

manasikātuṃ in Pali and *na śakyaṃ mayā karma ca kartuṃ śāstuś ca śāsane yogaṃ āpattuṃ* in Sanskrit, which seem to express an idea similar to *sukaro bhikṣave budhabayaṇo* and *budhabayaṇata bhikṣave ghachateṇa sukaro katu* of the G text, indicate that in this context *budhabayaṇo* of the G text is to be understood as synonymous with *buddhānaṃ sāsana-* of the Pali (or, better, the singular *buddhassa sāsana-*, as *buddhavacana* is generally so understood) and *śāstuḥ śāsana-* of the Sanskrit, all meaning the word, instruction, or training of the Buddha, Buddhas, or teacher. This is all very much in keeping with the alternation of synonyms and parallel expressions that is common in Buddhist literature. Nonetheless, the use of the term *budhabayaṇa* in the G sūtra is interesting because in Pali, at least, the equivalent, *buddhavacana,* is more characteristic of paracanonical texts.

paḍideṇa ṇa baleṇa: The P and Skt. equivalent would be *paṇḍitena na bālena*. Both *paṇida-* (besides *paṇada*) = Skt. *paṇḍita-* and *bala-* = Skt. *bāla-* are encountered a number of times in the Dhp-G^K, and *paḍida-* occurs in the AG-G (l. 96) and in the Senior manuscripts (7 r14). Both terms are common enough in Buddhist literature, frequently in verses or prose passages where the two are contrasted, as in the Dhp-G^K (230cd) verse *paṇidaṇa prio bhodi balaṇa bhodi aprio,* "He is dear to the wise, he is not dear to fools," and the P Jā (VI 225.30–1) verse *bālehi dānaṃ paññattaṃ, paṇḍitehi paṭicchitaṃ, avasā denti dhīrānaṃ, bālā paṇḍitamānino,* and in such prose passages as *tīhi bhikkhave dhammehi samannāgato bālo veditabbo . . . tīhi bhikkhave dhammehi samannāgato paṇḍito veditabbo* (AN I 102–4) and *tīṇ' imāni bhikkhave bālassa bālalakkhaṇāni . . . tīṇ' imāni bhikkhave paṇḍitassa paṇḍitalakkhaṇāni* (AN I 102). However, I have not so far encountered the expression *paṇḍitena na bālena* (or P *paṇḍitehi na bālehi*/Skt. *paṇḍitair na bālaiḥ*) in P or Skt. texts.[22]

sato kamatu/satu kamatu/sato kamato: This expression begins each of the four "a" units. The interpretation of this unit is problematic. First, it is unclear whether these two words are in compound or not. The presence of the final vowel in *sato/satu* and its variation suggests that the phrase is not a compound (though this is not conclusive); the presence of *k* is no help, for although original intervocalic *-k-* is normally voiced or elided in this text, it generally remains unchanged at compound juncture (see § 5.2.2.1).

The examples quoted at the beginning of this section suggest that *kamatu/kamato* probably represents P *kammanta-*/Skt. *karmānta-,* "acting," "work," "occupation," "deed," "action" (= *kamma/karma*). The word was previously unattested in Gāndhārī, though P *kamma-*/Skt. *karma-* appears as *karma/karmu* throughout the AG-G (e.g., ll. 75, 84, 87), written by the same scribe as our text, and as *karma/kama* in the Dhp-G^K. The less likely alternative is that it is connected with P and Skt. *kāma,* "desire," which appears as *kama-* in the Dhp-G^K and Khvs-G (17a, 18b).

There are a number of possible interpretations for *sato/satu*. The presence of *-t-* rather than *-d-* indicates that we are dealing with a geminate or nasal plus stop, as must also be the case in *kamatu/kamato* = Skt. *karmānta-*. For this reason it is less likely that *sato/satu* represents P *sāta*/Skt. *śāta-, sāta-,* "pleasant," which appears in the Dhp-G^K (186c) as

---

[22] Cf. *paccattaṃ veditabbā viññūhī ti paṇḍitehi attano attano santāne yeva jānitabbā, bālehi pana dujjānā* (Mp II 333.18–9).

sada- (see Brough 1962: 240). The most likely possibility is that it corresponds to P *santa-*/Skt. *sant,* "good." The word appears several times in the Dhp-G^K as *sada,* as in *sada du dharma na jara (*u)vedi, sado hi ṣa sabhi praverayadi* (160cd), where the P has *satañ ca dhammo na jaraṃ upeti, santo have sabbhi pavedayanti* (Dhp 151cd). (Although *sada* [= P *sataṃ*] in the Dhp-G^K verse for the gen. pl. m. is expected, *sado* [= P *santo*] for the nom. sg. m. with the development of *-nt-* > *-d-* is also a characteristic of the Dhp-G^K; see Brough 1962: §§ 46–8.) The meaning of *sato kamatu ghachateṇa ṇa sukaro ka(*tu ∘)* would then be "Good action is not easy to perform while going."

Another possibility, which is somewhat more problematic, is that *sato/satu* represents P *sata-*/Skt. *smr̥ta-,* "mindful." The word does not appear elsewhere in this scroll or in other texts written by this scribe, but the spelling *śpadi* (= P *sati*/Skt. *smr̥ti*) in this text (l. 64) and *[śpa]rami* (= Skt. *smarāmi*) in the AG-G fragment (l. 124) written by our scribe (cf. *svadi* in Dhp-G^K 98, 100–3, 340, and *spaḋi-* in Senior 8 r6 for Skt. *smr̥ti;* and *[s]v(*a)[d](*ima)* in Khvs-G 25d for P *satīmā*) suggests that the word should appear as **śpada* in our text. However, the appearance of the spelling *sada-* for original *smr̥ta-* in the Dhp-G^K (340e) in *sadaṇa sabrayaṇaṇa,* which corresponds to P *satānaṃ sampajānānaṃ* (Dhp 293e), raises the possibility that *sato/satu* is an example of a borrowed dialect form,[23] though the spelling *sato/satu* rather than *sado/sadu* remains problematic. If this correspondence is correct, then the meaning of *sato kamatu ghachateṇa ṇa sukaro ka(*tu ∘)* would be "Action is not easy to perform mindfully when going" (giving *sato* a quasi-adverbial status), which seems in keeping with a number of the P passages quoted at the beginning of this section. Further, in view of such expressions as *satokārin,* "the cultivator of mindfulness," and *satokārita,* "with mindfulness performed," found in P paracanonical words (e.g., Paṭis I 162)—the sutta version being *sampajānakārin* in such common phrases as *gate ṭhite nisinne sutte jāgarite bhāsite tuṇhībhāve sampajānakārī hoti* (DN I 70, II 95, 292; MN I 57, etc.)—it is even possible that *satokamatu/satukamatu/satokamato* is a compound: "the action of mindfulness" or, perhaps, "the practice of mindfulness." The meaning of *satokamatu ghachateṇa ṇa sukaro ka(*tu ∘)* would then be "The practice of mindfulness is not easy to perform while going."

Other, less likely possibilities are P *satta*/Skt. *sapta,* "seven," which appears in the Dhp-G^K (196a) as *sata,* and P *satta*/Skt. *sakta,* "clung to." The compound *sattakamma* appears in Pali as the title of several suttas that deal with a particular set of seven actions constituting basic morality.[24] However, it is unlikely that this is the topic of our G sūtra.

budhabayaṇata: This term begins each of the four "b" units. Once again, several interpretations are possible. It is unclear whether this represents one or two words; that is, are we to understand *budhabayaṇata* or *budhabayaṇa ta?* If the former, then the word

[23] See § 2.6; Brough 1962: 48–9, cf. 102 (= § 52).

[24] The B^e gives the title Sattakamma-suttaṃ to sutta 203 of the Catukka-nipāta (AN II 218–9), for which the E^e does not have a title. The uddāna entry in the B^e for this sutta is *sattakammaṃ,* where the E^e has *sattanāso* (AN II 225.22). The E^e gives the title Sattakammapathā to the fourth sutta of the Kammapatha-vagga of the Dhātu-saṃyutta (SN II 167) following the uddāna entry, while the B^e calls it the Sattakammapatha-suttaṃ. The expressions *sattakammapathacetanā* and *sattakammapathavasena* are also found in a number of P commentaries.

could represent either Skt. *buddhavacanatvam* or *buddhavacanatvāt* (or possibly *buddhavacanānta-; buddhavacanatā* would appear as **budhabayaṇada*), expressions that are unattested to my knowledge. If it is the equivalent of Skt. *buddhavacanatvam,* then *budhabayaṇata bhikṣave ghachateṇa sukaro katu tatu paḍideṇa ṇa baleṇa* (Ib) would mean "Monks, it is easy to perform the state of the Buddha's teaching while going." If it is the equivalent of Skt. *buddhavacanatvāt*, the meaning would be "Monks, on account of the state of the Buddha's word/instruction [good action] is easy to perform while going" (the grammatical subject would be *sato kamatu* of the previous phrase). Both interpretations are awkward.

If we are to read *budhabayaṇa ta* as two words, *budhabayaṇa* could be singular neuter nominative, accusative, or ablative (Skt. *buddhavacanam/buddhavacanāt*), though we would expect *budhabayaṇo* for the nominative/accusative, as elsewhere in the text, and *budhabayaṇade* with the suffix *-de* for the ablative. *Ta* would then represent the pronoun *tad,* declined in either the nominative singular neuter to qualify *budhabayaṇa* or the accusative singular masculine referring back to *sato kamatu* in the previous phrase (or perhaps acc. n., depending on the gender of *kamatu*). In the Dhp-G^{K} *ta* represents Skt. *tam* and *tat* (cf. *to* in Khvs-G 14a, 15a, 29a; see also Burrow 1937: § 80). The alternative is that it represents Skt. *tu,* "but," despite the lack of *u* vowel (if my interpretation is correct, the word appears as *tu* in *tatu/tato* = Skt. *tat tu* in this passage). The enclitic position of *ta* supports this interpretation.

The possibilities for interpreting *budhabayaṇata* are therefore (using the Skt. forms): (1) *buddhavacanaṃ tat;* (2) *buddhavacanāt tat,* with *tat* referring back to *sato kamatu;* (3) *buddhavacanaṃ tu;* and (4) *buddhavacanāt tu*. The meaning of *sato kamatu ghachateṇa ṇa sukaro ka(*tu ◦) budhabayaṇa ta bhikṣave ghachateṇa sukaro katu tatu paḍideṇa ṇa baleṇa* (Ia–b) in each of these interpretations would be the following (taking *sato kamatu* to mean "good action"): I(1) "Good action is not easy to perform while going. Monks, that teaching/instruction of the Buddha is easy to perform while going, but only by a wise man, not a fool." (2) "Good action is not easy to perform while going. Monks, on account of the Buddha's teaching/instruction, that [good action] is easy to perform while going, but only by a wise man, not a fool." (3) "Good action is not easy to perform while going. But, Monks, the Buddha's teaching/instruction is easy to perform while going, but only by a wise man, not a fool." (4) "Good action is not easy to perform while going. But, Monks, on account of the Buddha's teaching/instruction, [good action] is easy to perform while going, but only by a wise man, not a fool." None of these interpretations is fully convincing, since one is left wondering what the point of the sūtra is.

For each of these four interpretations, "good action" can be replaced by "the practice of mindfulness" or "(to perform) action mindfully," as outlined above. To take no. 2, for example, the translation would then be "The practice of mindfulness is not easy to perform while going. Monks, on account of the Buddha's teaching/instruction, that [practice of mindfulness] is easy to perform while going, but only by a wise man, not a fool." Although, as already noted, this interpretation too has its problems, it seems to be the most credible, especially as the practice of mindfulness is so commonly associated with the four postures. However, I adopt the second (no. 2) translation as the main translation of this passage because it involves the least number of problems and present this latter translation as the most likely alternative at the beginning of this section.

ghachateṇa . . . ṭ́hideṇa . . . ṇiṣaṇeṇa . . . śeaṇeṇa jagharadu: These four postures have a direct parallel in suttas 11 and 12 of the Catukka-nipāta of the AN (II 13–5): *carato/caraṃ . . . ṭhitassa/ṭhito . . . nisinnassa/nisinno . . . sayānassa jāgarassa/sayāno jāgaro.* The only problematic element in the G is *jagharadu.* We would have expected **jaghareṇa* for the instrumental singular, based on the P genitive singular *jāgarassa.* Although *jagharadu* appears to represent P *jāgarato,* the genitive singular of the present participle of P *jāgarati* (cf. *puññapāpapahīnassa n' atthi jāgarato bhayaṃ,* Dhp 39cd; *dīghā jāgarato rattī,* Dhp 60a), the context demands the instrumental singular. It therefore appears that *jagharadu* corresponds to an unattested P instrumental singular **jāgaratā,* with final *-u* for *-ā* as occasionally encountered in Gāndhārī (see § 5.1.4–5; Salomon 2000: § 6.1.3). The alternative is that it represents a genitive used for the instrumental.[25]

In canonical P texts the four postures are usually associated with meditative practice, as in the oft repeated passage describing the development of mindfulness (DN II 292 = MN I 56–7 = MN III 89 = Nidd I 491).[26] But here, as elsewhere, the combination is *gacchanto + ṭhito + nisinno + sayāno,* with *jāgaro* lacking. It is therefore of some significance that suttas 11 and 12 of the Catukka-nipāta of the AN provide the only instance in canonical P where, parallel to the G *śeaṇeṇa jagharadu,* the term *sayāna,* "lying down," is qualified by *jāgara,* "awake," in the context of the four postures.[27] In other words, although the sūtra that precedes the G Prasaṇa-sutra in our collection and the sutta that precedes the parallel Saṃvara-sutta (AN, no. 4.14) in the P AN are not parallel, they nonetheless share identical structures.

Lines 36–7: The conclusion to the sūtra

Edition:

[36] [|24a] *idam=u* [|24a+ 24v] *atamaṇa* [|24a] *te bhi[kh.] /// ///* + + + [|24i] *? ///* [37] [|24a] *[a]bhiṇadi* ○

[25] It could possibly represent an adverb in *-tas.*

[26] DN I 90 (*gacchantena . . . ṭhitena . . . nisinnena . . . sayānena*) provides the only instance of the instr. construction in Pali. Other examples of these four postures in Pali are *imaṃ kho tvaṃ mahānāma buddhānussatiṃ gacchanto pi bhāveyyāsi . . . ṭhito pi . . . nisinno pi . . . sayāno pi . . . kammantaṃ adhiṭṭhahanto pi . . .* (AN V 333); *gaccheyya . . . tiṭṭheyya . . . nisīdeyya . . . seyyaṃ kappeyya* (Nidd I 157); *gaccheyya . . . tiṭṭheyya . . . nisīdeyya . . . nipajjeyya* (e.g., MN I 120). In the context of meditative practice and often following the above passages, we find the combination *gate ṭhite nisinne sutte jāgarite bhāsite tuṇhībhāve sampajānakārī hoti* (DN I 70, II 95, 292; MN I 57, etc.). Skt. examples of this formula are found at MPS § 10.12; ŚBh(T) 20.7–8, 182, 186.8–9; SBhV II 241.4–6.

[27] Cf. the following phrase, where three of the four are given: *carato ca me tiṭṭhato ca suttassa ca jāgarassa ca satataṃ samitaṃ ñāṇadassanaṃ paccupaṭṭhitaṃ* (MN I 92–3, 482, 519, 523, II 31, 218; AN I 220, IV 428–9).

Reconstruction:
[36] *idam u <*bhayavadu> atamaṇa te bhikh(*u bhayavadeṇa bhaṣido)* [37] *abhiṇadi* ○

Translation:
[36] The (*Bhagavat) said this. Pleased, those monks [37] rejoiced (*at what was said by the Bhagavat).

The remnant of the final akṣara of line 36 (*? ///*), which appears at the top left of fragment 24i, is consistent with the bottom of *de* or *du.*

The reconstruction is based on the occurrence of the same formula at the end of the Dhoṇa-sutra (ll. 25–6). For the discussion of this formula, see the commentary on lines 25–6.

CHAPTER 10

The "Prasaṇa-sutra"

10.1. Introduction

10.1.1. Summary of Contents

Like the second sūtra in this collection, the third sūtra depicts the Buddha giving a discourse to the monks. The topic on this occasion is, to use the G spelling, the four *prasaṇa*s. The G text is incomplete, ending with the third *prasaṇa*. The fourth *prasaṇa,* along with the conclusion to the sūtra, would have appeared on the next scroll of the text, which unfortunately has not survived.

The P term corresponding to G *prasaṇa* is *padhāna,* "endeavor," "exertion," "effort." In Buddhist Skt. texts this word appears as either *pradhāna/prahāṇa,* with the same meaning, or *prahāṇa,* "abandoning." The latter meaning is reflected in the usual Tib. translation of the term, *spoṅ-ba,* and in some Chinese translations. The correct interpretation of G *prasaṇa,* which could represent both *pradhāna* and *prahāṇa,* or just *prahāṇa,* will be discussed below.

The four *prasaṇa*s as presented in this G text are (1) *sabara,* "restraint" (P/Skt. *saṃvara*); (2) *aṇorakṣaṇa,* "protecting" (P *anurakkhaṇā, anurakkhanā*/Skt. *anurakṣaṇā*); (3) *bhavaṇa,* "development" (P/Skt. *bhāvanā*); and (4) *prasaṇa,* "abandoning" (P *pahāna*/Skt. *prahāṇa*). Following the more general definition found elsewhere in Buddhist texts (see below), these can be summarized as (1) endeavoring to prevent unprofitable states of mind from arising; (2) endeavoring to maintain profitable states of mind that have arisen; (3) causing profitable states of mind that have not arisen to arise; and (4) endeavoring to abandon unprofitable states of mind that have arisen.

The setting of this sūtra is *Śavasti,* corresponding to P *Sāvatthi*/Skt. *Śrāvastī,* which is the most common location for discourses given by the Buddha to the monks (see below).

10.1.2. Extant Versions of the Sūtra/Sutta and Their Titles

The formulaic presentation of the four *padhāna*s or *pradhāna/prahāṇa*s, "efforts" (or "abandonings"), is relatively common in Buddhist literature, since the concept of "effort," which is synonymous with "energy" (P *viriya*/Skt. *vīrya*), forms a fundamental component of the Buddhist path, appearing in a variety of contexts and in a number of lists. It appears, for example, as P *samma-ppadhāna*/Skt. *samyak-pradhāna, ~prahāna,* "right effort," or simply as *padhāna/pradhāna/prahāṇa,* "effort" (as in this G sūtra), as a topic of discussion in its own right or as one of the seven sets that make up the "limbs of enlightenment," P *bodhipakkhiya-dhamma*/Skt. *bodhipākṣika-dharma. Samma-ppadhāna/ samyak-pradhāna* in turn is synonymous with P *samma-vāyāma*/Skt. *samyag-vyāyāma,* the sixth limb, or factor, of the Noble Eightfold Path, while the four *padhāna*s or *pradhāna/prahāṇa*s appear in the definition of "the faculty of energy," P *viriyindriya*/Skt. *vīryendriya,* on occasion.[1]

At least four suttas in the P canon are devoted exclusively to the elaboration of the four efforts (*padhānāni*) or the four right efforts (*sammappadhānā(ni)*). Three appear in the Catukka-nipāta, the Section of Fours, of the AN as sutta numbers 13, 14, and 69 (AN II 15, 16–7, 74); the fourth appears in the SN as the first sutta of the Sammappadhāna-saṃyutta (SN V 244–5). A comparison of these four suttas provides an excellent illustration of the way in which the same topic could be elaborated in different ways and presented within different frames.

Essentially, the four *padhāna*s could be elaborated in two ways, representing a general definition and a specific one (see Gethin 1992: 74). I will refer to these as series A and B, respectively. There are no examples in Pali (or in Buddhist Skt. literature) of the mixing of these two series. In other words, in any one sutta, or wherever this concept is presented within a larger sutta or text, the four *padhāna*s are defined in terms of series A1–4 or B1–4, never A1 plus B2, and so on. Each series of four is presented below in the order in which it is found in P texts, that is, (1) *saṃvara,* "restraint"; (2) *pahāna,* "abandoning"; (3) *bhāvanā,* "development"; and (4) *anurakkhaṇā,* "protecting."

Series A (e.g., DN III 221; MN II 11; AN II 15, 74, IV 462–3; Vibh 208):
idha bhikkhave [or other vocative] *bhikkhu*

1. *anuppannānaṃ pāpakānaṃ akusalānaṃ dhammānaṃ anuppādāya chandaṃ janeti vāyamati viriyaṃ ārabhati cittaṃ paggaṇhāti padahati.*
2. *uppannānaṃ pāpakānaṃ akusalānaṃ dhammānaṃ pahānāya chandaṃ janeti vāyamati viriyaṃ ārabhati cittaṃ paggaṇhāti padahati.*
3. *anuppannānaṃ kusalānaṃ dhammānaṃ uppādāya chandaṃ janeti vāyamati viriyaṃ ārabhati cittaṃ paggaṇhāti padahati.*
4. *uppannānaṃ kusalānaṃ dhammānaṃ ṭhitiyā asammosāya bhiyyobhāvāya vepullāya bhāvanāya pāripūriyā chandaṃ janeti vāyamati viriyaṃ ārabhati cittaṃ paggaṇhāti padahati.*

Series B (DN III 225–6; AN II 16–7):

1. *idha bhikkhave bhikkhu cakkhunā rūpaṃ disvā na nimittaggāhī hoti nānuvyañjanaggāhī yatvādhikaraṇaṃ enaṃ cakkhundriyaṃ asaṃvutaṃ viharantaṃ abhijjhādomanassā pāpakā akusalā dhammā anvāssaveyyuṃ tassa saṃvarāya paṭipajjati rakkhati cakkhundriyaṃ cakkhundriye saṃvaraṃ āpajjati. sotena saddaṃ sutvā . . . ghānena gandhaṃ ghāyitvā . . . jivhāya rasaṃ sāyitvā . . . kāyena phoṭṭhabbaṃ phusitvā . . . manasā dhammaṃ viññāya . . .*
2. *idha bhikkhave bhikkhu uppannaṃ kāmavitakkaṃ nādhivāseti pajahati vinodeti vyantikaroti anabhāvaṃ gameti. uppannaṃ vyāpādavitakkaṃ . . . uppannaṃ vihiṃsāvitakkaṃ . . . uppannuppanne pāpake akusale dhamme . . .*

[1] A detailed discussion with references can be found in Gethin 1992: 72 ff.

3. *idha bhikkhave bhikkhu satisambojjhaṅgaṃ bhāveti vivekanissitaṃ virāganissitaṃ nirodhanissitaṃ vossaggapariṇāmiṃ. dhammavicayasaṃbojjhaṅgaṃ bhāveti . . . viriyasambojjhaṅgaṃ bhāveti . . . pītisambojjhaṅgaṃ bhāveti . . . passaddhisambojjhaṅgaṃ bhāveti . . . samādhisambojjhaṅgaṃ bhāveti . . . upekhāsambojjhaṅgaṃ bhāveti . . .*
4. *idha bhikkhave bhikkhu uppannaṃ bhaddakaṃ samādhinimittaṃ anurakkhati aṭṭhikasaññaṃ puḷavakasaññaṃ vinīlakasaññaṃ vipubbakasaññaṃ vicchiddakasaññaṃ uddhumātakasaññaṃ.*

The four P suttas mentioned above that deal exclusively with the *padhāna*s each present one or other of these definitions within a different frame. Only the SN V 244–5 sutta includes an introductory nidāna, consisting merely of the word *Sāvatthi* (E^{e}, B^{e}, and S^{e}), but a nidāna, most likely the Sāvatthi-Jetavana nidāna, was probably prefixed to the three AN suttas when a nidāna was necessary. SN V 244–5 presents series A within the opening and closing frame of *cattāro 'me bhikkhave sammappadhānā. katame cattāro . . . ime kho bhikkhave cattāro sammappadhānā*. This is followed by a simile likening the four right efforts to the river Ganges, then a repetition of series A without the opening and closing frame. The sutta concludes by stating that, when developed, the four efforts lead to nibbāna.

Sutta 13 of the Catukka-nipāta (AN II 15) presents series A within the opening and closing frame of *cattār' imāni bhikkhave sammappadhānāni. katamāni cattāri . . . imāni kho bhikkhave cattāri sammappadhānāni* and concludes with four lines of verse of uncertain meter (or, perhaps, prose).

Sutta 14 of the Catukka-nipāta (AN II 16–7) opens with

cattār' imāni bhikkhave padhānāni. katamāni cattāri. saṃvarappadhānaṃ pahānappadhānaṃ bhāvanappadhānaṃ anurakkhanappadhānaṃ;

that is, each *padhāna* is named. Series B is then presented with each *padhāna* framed by *katamañ ca bhikkhave saṃvarappadhānaṃ. . . . idaṃ vuccati bhikkhave saṃvarappadhānaṃ* (with replacement of key terms for each *padhāna*). The sutta concludes with *imāni kho bhikkhave cattāri padhānāni,* followed by three lines of śloka verse (different from those in sutta 13).

Finally, sutta 69 of the Catukka-nipāta (AN II 74) differs from sutta 14 only in presenting series A rather than B, with virtually the same frames (the *idaṃ vuccati* phrase is omitted throughout) and the same verse.

Of these four P suttas, sutta 14 of the Catukka-nipāta (AN II 16–7) provides the closest parallel to the G sūtra, although, as the latter part of the G sūtra is missing, it is uncertain whether the G version paralleled the P in having a concluding verse or verses and, if so, what the form of that verse or verses was. The G Dhoṇa-sutra has three (possibly four) verses where the P Doṇa-sutta has only two. Since sutta 4.14 of the AN and two Chinese parallels (see below) end with what is essentially the same verse, and since both sutta 4.14 of the AN and the P Doṇa-sutta occur in the initial section of the Catukka-nipāta where all the suttas are *sagāthā,* "with verses," it is highly likely that the G

Prasaṇa-sutra included at least one verse, which probably was similar to that found in the P and Chinese parallel sūtras.

None of the four P suttas discussed here bears a title in the E^e of either the text or the commentaries, but titles for each are found in the B^e and S^e (the C^e was not available to me). The B^e, for example, gives the title Padhānasuttaṃ to both suttas 13 (AN II 15) and 69 (AN II 74) of the Catukka-nipāta, following the uddāna entries of *padhānāni* (B^e and S^e; E^e reads *padhānaṃ*) and *padhānaṃ* (all three editions), respectively, and the B^e gives the title Padhānasuttavaṇṇanā to the commentaries on them (as does the S^e). Sutta 14 of the Catukka-nipāta (AN II 16–7) bears the title Saṃvarasuttaṃ in the B^e, following the uddāna entry of *saṃvaraṃ* (as such in the E^e, B^e, and S^e), while the commentary is called the Saṃvarasuttavaṇṇanā (so also the S^e). Besides these, three other suttas (two in the AN, one in the Sn) are entitled Padhānasuttaṃ in the B^e, following their uddāna entries, while one further sutta in the SN is called Saṃvarasuttaṃ.[2] Thus several suttas that deal with the topic of the *padhāna*s either exclusively or in part bear the title Padhānasuttaṃ (or Saṃvarasuttaṃ) in the Burmese and Thai traditions at least, though as usual it is difficult to know how old this tradition is, especially because only the Padhāna-sutta of the Sn is referred to by name in a commentary.[3] Sutta 14 of the Catukka-nipāta was not given the title Padhānasuttaṃ, because the composer of the P uddāna chose to give suttas 13 and 14 of the Catukka-nipāta the distinct entries *padhānaṃ* and *saṃvaraṃ* rather than a paired entry such as *dve padhānāni* or the like as is commonly done in uddānas for two or more suttas that deal with the same topic.

Given that the G version of this sūtra is not preceded by a sūtra dealing explicitly with the topic of *prasaṇa* (as is the case with suttas 13 and 14 of the Catukka-nipāta), it is highly likely that, if this collection of G sūtras contained uddānas, which it probably did, the uddāna entry for this sūtra would have been *prasaṇa,* and that therefore this sūtra would have been referred to as the **Prasaṇa-sutra*, which is the title I give it. Throughout this study the P parallel, sutta 4.14 of the AN (II 16–7), will be referred to as the Saṃvara-sutta following the tradition of the P Oriental editions (B^e and S^e, at least) of the P canon.

A likely Skt. parallel to sutta 4.14 and therefore to our G sūtra is given by Harrison (1997: 272) in his study of An Shigao's EĀ translations, which contain a sūtra dealing with this topic (see below). This Skt. example appears on two Central Asian (Turfan) fragments, parts of a single leaf, published in 1985 by Sander and Waldschmidt (SHT V

---

[2] The B^e gives the title Padhānasuttaṃ (not in S^e) to the following: (1) AN, no. 2.2 (= II.I.2 in E^e; AN I 49), following the uddāna entry (*padhānā* in B^e, *(vajja)ppadhānā* in E^e); (2) AN, no. 4.71 (AN II 76), where the uddāna entry is *padhāna-,* though the word does not actually occur in the sutta (only *āraddhaviriyo*); and (3) Sn 425–49 (pp. 74–8)—also given this title in the E^e and S^e and referred to as such in the comm. (Pj II 386.8: in E^e, B^e, and S^e)—following the uddāna entry *padhānañ ca* (E^e, B^e, and S^e). The B^e gives the title Saṃvarasuttaṃ to a sutta in the SN corresponding to SN IV 79–80 following the uddāna entry of *saṃvaro* (in E^e, B^e, and S^e). The E^e merely reproduces the uddāna entry as the title.

[3] Pj II 386.8; Ap-a 115.13. The reading in the B^e and S^e of the latter is *padhānasutte,* which both editions consider to be a reference to Padhāna-sutta of the Sn, but the E^e reads *mahāpadhānasutte,* which the editor (wrongly) takes to refer to the Mahāpadāna-suttanta of the DN.

1445+1447). Unfortunately, little more than the bare listing of the four *prahāṇa*s remains of the text. Waldschmidt considered the text to represent one sūtra and identified it as a *"Fragment aus dem Prahāṇasūtra (II) des Saṃyuktāgama"* on the basis of the Chinese parallels, noting at the same time a possible parallel in either AN II 16–7 or 74. In fact, this leaf contains the remnants of two sūtras, one on the recto and one on the verso. Based on what little remains of the elaboration of each of the four *prahāṇa*s, it is also likely that the text on what the editor presented as the recto is parallel to sutta 4.14 of the AN (II 16–7), while that presented as the verso is parallel to either sutta 13 or sutta 69 of the Catukka-nipāta (AN II 15, 74). Based on the Chinese parallels in the SĀ (T 2 no. 99 [sūtras 875–9] p. 221a–c), Klaus Wille (SHT VIII, p. 205) suggests that what was formerly identified as the recto is likely to be the verso. No titles to these Skt. sūtras are preserved. The order of the four *prahāṇa*s is (1) *prahāṇa-prahāṇa,* (2) *saṃvara-prahāṇa,* (3) *anurakṣaṇā-prahāṇa,* and (4) *bhāvanā-prahāṇa*.[4]

Apart from this Central Asian (Turfan) fragment there seem to be no other examples of "canonical" Skt. sūtras that deal exclusively with the four *prahāṇa*s and present them in the manner in which they are found in our G sūtra. Further, although presentations of the four (*samyak*)-*prahāṇa*s are found in Buddhist Skt. texts as part of larger sūtras or texts, they seem never to be defined in terms of the series B of the G sūtra and its P parallel. (Particular *prahāṇa*s are, however, presented separately according to series B; these examples will be discussed in the following commentary.) In other words, it appears that there is no complete Skt. parallel to our G sūtra.

A number of sūtras in Chinese translation deal with this topic:[5]

1. T 2 no. 150a p. 877b27–c15. This is sūtra 26 (according to the numbering in Harrison 1997: 272; sūtra 11 according to the T edition) of the Za jing sishisi bian, An Shigao's translation of an EĀ (or an anthology of EĀ sūtras). It bears no title. The topic is the four "abandonings" (*she* 舍 = Skt. *prahāṇa*). The order of the four, to use their Skt. equivalents, is (1) *prahāṇa-prahāṇa* (*she-she* 舍舍); (2) *saṃvara-prahāṇa* (*shou-she* 守舍); (3) *anurakṣaṇā-prahāṇa* (*hu-she* 護舍); (4) *bhāvanā-prahāṇa* (*xing-she* 行舍). The elaborations of the four *prahāṇa*s are those of series B, parallel to the G and to AN sutta 4.14 (II 16–7) and DN III 225–6. The sūtra ends with a verse closely parallel to that in the P text.

2. T 2 no. 99 p. 221a–c, sūtras 875–9. Guṇabhadra's translation of the SĀ, the Za ahan jing, contains a series of five sūtras dealing with the topic of the four "right abandonings," *samyak-prahāṇa*s (正斷), none of which bears a title. The amount of information given in each varies, and some contain verses. The order of the four *samyak-prahāṇa*s is the same as in T no. 150a. The first sūtra, sūtra 875, merely lists the four *samyak-prahāṇa*s. The second, sūtra 876, is identical but adds a verse that is parallel to

---

[4] Harrison (1997: 272) suggests that the ascription of these sūtras to the SĀ may need rethinking.

[5] The following references along with a summary of the order in which the *pradhāna/prahāṇa*s are presented in each were kindly provided to the EBMP team by Jan Nattier. Tien-chang Shih gave further information on the content of each, and Paul Harrison provided a translation of T 2 no. 150a p. 877b27–c15. Further references were provided by Collett Cox.

the first two lines of the three-line verse in AN sutta 4.14. In the third and fourth sūtras, 877 and 878, the four *samyak-prahāṇa*s are elaborated in terms of series A, with sūtra 878 differing from sūtra 877 only in adding the same two lines of verse found in sūtra 876. Finally, in sūtra 879 the four *samyak-prahāṇa*s are first listed, then defined for the most part in terms of series B. The exception seems to be the elaboration of the first *prahāṇa* (*prahāṇa-prahāṇa*), which is a repetition of the general definitions of all four *prahāṇa*s, that is, series A1–4. This is rather odd and may result from a confusion. The sūtra then ends with three lines of verse that parallel the full three lines of the P version (AN sutta 4.14). This last sūtra (T 2 no. 99 p. 221b16–c5) thus is parallel to the G text, to AN sutta 4.14 (II 16–7), and to T 2 no. 150a p. 877b27–c15 (see Harrison 1997: 272).

3. T 2 no. 125 pp. 635b–636a. Dharmanandin's translation of the EĀ, the Zengyi ahan jing, contains four sūtras on the topic of the four *prahāṇa*s, "mind-abandonings" (四意斷), none of which has a title. The order of the four *prahāṇa*s, which are not individually named, is (1) *saṃvara;* (2) *prahāṇa;* (3) *bhāvanā;* (4) *anurakṣaṇā*. The four *prahāṇa*s are elaborated in terms of the definitions of series A and therefore are parallel to AN sutta 4.13 rather than 4.14. None contains a verse.

No doubt many further discussions of the four *prahāṇa*s occur in Chinese sources—for example, in the Saṅgīti-sūtra of the DĀ the four are defined in general terms (series A) in the sequence *saṃvara, prahāṇa, bhāvanā, anurakṣaṇā* (T 1 no. 1 p. 50c13–6), as also at T 15 no. 603 pp. 173c25, 174a10–8—but they are found within the context of larger sūtras or texts, not as separate sūtras with a concluding verse. Of the examples mentioned above, nos. 150a and 99 provide the closest parallels to the G text. Although a detailed comparison of these Chinese translations, both with each other and with the G and P texts, is desirable, it is a separate project that is beyond the skills of the present writer. The translations will nonetheless be referred to in the course of the following study where appropriate.

10.1.3. The Order of the Four "Efforts" or "Abandonings" in Buddhist Texts

As apparent from the above examples, the order in which the four "efforts" or "abandonings" (G *prasaṇa*/P *padhāna*/Skt. *pradhāna, prahāṇa*) are listed in Buddhist texts varies greatly. A complete study of all occurrences of this concept in Buddhist literature is a desideratum but beyond the scope of the present study. I present here examples from a very limited selection of Buddhist texts in a variety of languages to make a provisional evaluation of the G order.

As there are four items in this list, there are twenty-four possible combinations. Despite this potential, the examples so far encountered in Buddhist literature attest only five combinations. They are (to use their Skt. forms for convenience):

I. (1) *saṃvara* (2) *anurakṣaṇā* (3) *bhāvanā* (4) *prahāṇa*

This is the sequence in the G sūtra. No other examples of this combination have been found.

II. (1) *saṃvara* (2) *prahāṇa* (3) *bhāvanā* (4) *anurakṣaṇā*

This combination is found in the following texts: P sources (references above); Mahāvyutpatti (§§ 957–65);[6] Daśabhūmika-sūtra (38.26–32);[7] Pañcaviṃśatisāhasrikā Prajñāpāramitā (PSPP(D)) (207.15–21)[8] and Śatasāhasrikā Prajñāpāramitā (ŚSPP(G)) (1435–6);[9] a v.l. in the Dharmasaṅgraha (Dhsgr) (§ 45, frag. F);[10] SHT VII 1763 c V3–R2 (text unidentified); the Chinese Ekottarikāgama, the Zengyi ahan jing (T 2 no. 125 pp. 635b–636a); the Chinese Dīrghāgama, the Chang ahan jing (T 1 no. 1 p. 50c13–6); and T 15 no. 603 p. 174a10–8.[11]

III. (1) *prahāṇa* (2) *saṃvara* (3) *bhāvanā* (4) *anurakṣaṇā*

This sequence is found in the following texts: Abhidharmakośavyākhyā (AKV) (599.22–8);[12] Mahāparinirvāṇa-sūtra (§ 10.10), which Waldschmidt reconstructed largely on the basis of the Mvy, but with a change in order; Saṅgīti-sūtra (§ IV.2) and Saṅgītipariyāya, both largely reconstructed on the basis of the Chinese translation (T 26 no. 1536 p. 391c6–25) and the AKV; sūtra 26 (according to Harrison's numbering) of An Shigao's

---

[6] *catvāri prahāṇāni.* (1) *anutpannānāṃ pāpakānām akuśalānāṃ dharmāṇām anutpādāya cchandaṃ janayati.* (2) *utpannānāṃ pāpakānām akuśalānāṃ dharmāṇām prahāṇāya cchandaṃ janayati.* (3) *anutpannānāṃ kuśalānāṃ dharmāṇām utpādāya cchandaṃ janayati.* (4) *utpannānāṃ kuśalānāṃ dharmāṇām sthitaye bhūyobhāvatāyai asaṃpramoṣāya paripūraṇāya cchandaṃ janayati. . . . vyāyacchate vīryam ārabhate cittaṃ pragṛhṇāti samyak pradadhāti.*

[7] (Rahder ed.) (1) *so 'nutpannānāṃ pāpakānām akuśalānāṃ dharmāṇām anutpādāya cchandaṃ janayati vyāyacchate vīryam ārabhate cittaṃ pragṛhṇāti samyak praṇidadhāti.* (2) *utpannānāṃ pāpakānām akuśalānāṃ dharmāṇāṃ prahāṇāya* (etc. in full). (3) *anutpannānāṃ kuśalānāṃ dharmāṇām utpādāya* (etc. in full). (4) *utpannānāṃ kuśalānāṃ dharmāṇāṃ sthitaye 'saṃpramoṣāya vaipulyāya bhūyobhāvāya bhāvanāya paripūraye* (etc. in full).

[8] *catvāri samyakprahāṇāni. katamāni catvāri. iha . . . mahāsattvo* (1) *'nutpannānāṃ pāpakānām akuśalānāṃ dharmāṇām anutpādāya chandaṃ janayati vyāyacchate vīryam ārabhate cittaṃ pratigṛhṇāti samyak praṇidadhāti.* (2) *utpannānāṃ pāpakānām akuśalānāṃ dharmāṇāṃ prahāṇāya chandaṃ janayati* (etc. in full). (3) *anutpannānāṃ kuśalānāṃ dharmāṇām utpādāya chandaṃ janayati* (etc. in full). (4) *utpannānāṃ kuśalānāṃ dharmāṇāṃ sthitaye bhūyobhavāya* (read *~bhāvāya*) *asaṃpramoṣāya aparihāṇāya chandaṃ janayati* (etc. in full).

[9] *catvāri samyakprahāṇāni. katamāni. idaṃ . . .* (1) as PSPP(D) but *cittaṃ pragṛhṇāti samyak pradadhāti.* (2) As PSPP(D). (3) As PSPP(D). (4) *utpannānāṃ kuśalānāṃ dharmāṇāṃ sthitaye bhūyotāvanatāyai asaṃmoṣāya paripūraye chandaṃ janayati* (etc. in full).

[10] *catuḥsamyakprahāṇāni. tadyathā.* (1) *anutpannānāṃ pāpakānāṃ viramaṇāya.* (2) *utpannānāṃ pariharaṇāya.* (3) *anutpannānāṃ kuśa[la]mūlānam* (read *~ām*) *utpādanāya.* (4) *utpannānāṃ kuśalamūlānāṃ buddhatvaṃ pariṇāmanāya bhavati.*

[11] According to Collett Cox this order is also found in a sūtra quotation in the Śāriputrābhidharma-śāstra (T 28 no. 1548 p. 633b20–5).

[12] *catvāri samyakprahāṇāni.* (1) *utpannānāṃ pāpakānām akuśalānāṃ dharmāṇāṃ prahāṇāya chandaṃ janayati vyāyacchate vīryam ārabhate cittaṃ pragṛhṇāti pradadhāti.* (2) *anutpannānāṃ pāpakānām akuśalānāṃ dharmāṇām anutpādāya chandaṃ janayatīti pūrvavat.* (3) *anutpannānāṃ kuśalānāṃ dharmāṇām utpādāya chandaṃ janayatīti pūrvavat.* (4) *utpannānāṃ kuśalānāṃ dharmāṇāṃ sthitaye asaṃmoṣāya bhāvanāparipūraye bhūyobhāvāya vṛddhivipulatājñānasākṣātkriyāyai chandaṃ janayatīti pūrvavat.*

Za jing sishisi bian (T 2 no. 150a p. 877b27–c15); and the Chinese SĀ, the Za ahan jing (T 2 no. 99 [sūtras 875–9] p. 221a–c).[13]

IV. (1) *prahāṇa* (2) *saṃvara* (3) *anurakṣaṇā* (4) *bhāvanā*

This order appears in the two sūtras of the Central Asian fragment SHT V 1445+1447.[14]

V. (1) *anurakṣaṇā* (2) *bhāvanā* (3) *prahāṇa* (4) *saṃvara*

This order is found only in the Dharmasaṅgraha (§ 45; see sequence II above for a v.l.).[15]

Each of the four *pradhāna/prahāṇa*s is directed toward what is either *akuśala,* "unprofitable," or *kuśala,* "profitable"; *saṃvara* and *prahāṇa* are directed toward the *akuśala,* and *bhāvanā* and *anurakṣaṇā* are directed toward the *kuśala*. The basic principle of arrangement in sequences II, III, and IV is to place the pair associated with *akuśala* first, either in the order *saṃvara, prahāṇa* or *prahāṇa, saṃvara,* followed by the pair associated with *kuśala: bhāvanā, anurakṣaṇā* or *anurakṣaṇā, bhāvanā*. This conforms to the general tendency in Buddhist texts to place the morally negative (particularly *akuśala*) before the positive (see Allon 1997: 241–2; Tripāṭhī 1995: 25, 231–4). In this respect, sequence V, the order found in the Dhsgr, is at variance with all other examples so far encountered, with the exception of the Gāndhārī.

In sequences II and III, which represent the schemas found in the majority of examples, the order of the second pair is *bhāvanā, anurakṣaṇā*. The logic in this ordering seems to be that one first develops the *kuśala* and then protects it. However, the difference between sequences II and III in the first pair speaks against a temporal principle underlying the sequence: one does not necessarily first stop (*saṃvara*) unarisen *akuśala* from arising and then destroy (*prahāṇa*) arisen *akuśala,* or vice versa. In this regard the Abhidharmakośa's comment (328.2–5) quoted by Gethin (1992: 69 n) is telling:

> *keṣāṃcid utpattyanukūlā deśanā yathā smr̥tyupasthānadhyānādīnām. keṣāṃcit prarūpaṇānukūlā deśanā yathā samyakprahāṇānāṃ. na hy eṣa niyamo yat pūrvam utpannānāṃ prahāṇāya cchandaṃ janayati paścād anutpannānām anutpādāyeti.*

Gethin translates:

> For certain things, like the *smr̥ty-upasthānas,* the *dhyānas,* etc., the [order of] teaching conforms with arising; for certain things, like the *samyak-prahāṇas,* it

---

[13] This order is also found in the Prakaraṇapāda (T 26 no. 1542 p. 712a24–8, and T 26 no. 1541 p. 645a19–22) and Dharmaskandha (T 26 no. 1537 pp. 467c25–468a3) (information supplied by Collett Cox).

[14] According to Collett Cox, this order is found at T 1 no. 18 p. 256b6–8.

[15] *katamāni catvāri samyakprahāṇāni. tadyathā.* (1) *utpannānāṃ kuśalamūlānāṃ saṃrakṣaṇaṃ.* (2) *anutpannānāṃ samutpādaḥ.* (3) *utpannānām akuśalānāṃ dharmāṇāṃ prahāṇaṃ.* (4) *anutpannānāṃ punar anutpādaś ceti.*

conforms with explanation, for it is not a fixed rule that one first generates desire for the abandoning of arisen things and afterwards for the non-arising of unarisen things.

From the above it can be seen that, with the exception of the G version, all examples of passages dealing with the four *padhāna/prahāṇa*s so far encountered in Buddhist literature group the four into two pairs, one directed at the *akuśala* and the other at the *kuśala,* with all but the Dharmasaṅgraha example adopting the *akuśala, kuśala* ordering of the pairs. It is not clear what conclusions can be drawn from the uniqueness of the G version, especially as this is the only example of the four *prasaṇa*s found in a G text and our present understanding of G literature is still in its infancy. We currently do not know, for example, whether this represents "the" G sequence of the four *prasaṇa*s or a peculiarity of this manuscript. Hopefully our understanding of the general principles of the ordering of topics in G texts will improve with the study and publication of further documents in the recently discovered collections of G manuscripts.

The order in which particular concepts appear in Buddhist texts has sometimes been used as a basis for drawing conclusions about the school affiliation of those texts. The whole question of the school affiliation of texts, particularly the Chinese translations, is, of course, as Harrison puts it "a Buddhological minefield" (1997: 279). With reference to the ordering of the four *pradhāna/prahāṇa*s, three observations are worthy of note. The first is that most texts in which sequence III appears—the AKV, the MPS, the Saṅg-Skt., and the Saṅgītipariyāya—are generally considered to be Sarvāstivādin works[16] (with An Shigao's Za jing sishisi bian—T no. 150a—possibly also being of this affiliation; Harrison 1997: 280–1), whereas the Chinese SĀ (T no. 99) is generally considered to belong to the Mūlasarvāstivādins (Harrison 1997: 280).[17] However, it is interesting that the sequence (IV) in Central Asian fragment SHT V 1445+1447, whose affiliation must surely also be Sarvāstivādin or Mūlasarvāstivādin, is different. Second, the sequence in Müller and Wenzel's edition of the Skt. Dharmasaṅgraha (§ 45) is V, and that of Cambridge fragment F used by them for their edition is II. In other words, although the majority of manuscripts of texts belonging to a particular school may generally attest a certain sequence, variant orderings are occasionally found within a school's literature. Finally, since the sequence of concepts in the G fragment of the Saṅgīti-sūtra and its commentary within the BL collection closely matches that in the Chinese translation of the Saṅgīti-sūtra in the DĀ, which is often considered to be a Dharmaguptaka work, Salomon (1999: 171–5) used this match as one of a number of indications of the Dharmaguptaka affiliation of the BL manuscripts. However, the sequence of the four *prasaṇa*s of the G Prasaṇa-sutra under review (sequence I) does not match that found in the Chinese Saṅgīti-

[16] The same order is found in the Prakaraṇapāda (T 26 no. 1542 p. 712a24–8 and T 26 no. 1541 p. 645a19–22) and Dharmaskandha (T 26 no. 1537 pp. 467c25–468a3).

[17] Waldschmidt (1980: 136) attributes the Chinese SĀs (T nos. 99 and 100) to the Sarvāstivādins.

sūtra of the DĀ (T 1 no. 1 p. 50c13–6) (sequence II). Unfortunately, the four *prasaṇa*s are not preserved in the Saṅg-G fragment in the BL collection. In conclusion, all that can be said for now is that the sequence of the four *prasaṇa*s found in the G Prasaṇa-sutra is unique, and further research is required to fully evaluate this.

10.2. Text Commentary

Lines 37–9: The introductory nidāna

Edition:

|24a |24w |24a+ 24v |24v |24v+ 24u |24u |24u+ 24i |24i |24a

[37] *eva me rśodu eka sama[ya ◦] bhayadu śavastie viharadi [jedavaṇ.] ///* [38]*ḍiasa*

|24u |24a

aramu ◦ tatra ya bhayavadu bhikhu amat[r]edi bhikhu ? ? ? ? ? /// [39] *eghad=oya ◦*

Reconstruction:
[37] *eva me rśodu eka samaya ◦ bhaya<*va>du śavastie viharadi jedavaṇ(*o aṇasa-pi)*[38]*ḍiasa aramu ◦ tatra ya bhayavadu bhikhu amatredi <*te> bhikhu (*bhayavadu pracarśoṣu ◦ bhayavadu)* [39] *eghad oya ◦*

Translation:
[37] Thus I heard at one time: The Bhagavat dwelt in Śavasti (Śrāvastī) in the Jedavaṇa (Jetavana), in [38] Aṇasapiḍia's (Anāthapiṇḍada's) park. And there the Bhagavat addressed the monks. (*Those) monks (*responded to the Bhagavat. The Bhagavat) [39] said this.

A detailed discussion of the opening formula is given in the commentary on the second sūtra of this collection (ll. 26–8).

Line 37: The tops of *me rśodu eka* are obscured by an overlying splinter of bark.

sama[ya]: Fragment 24w, containing the bottom left arm of *ya,* has broken off and obscures part of the same *ya* akṣara. The bark containing the remainder of the line has shifted to the left.

bhayadu: Read *bhaya<*va>du.*

Line 38: Only a faint trace of the subscript *r* of *tra* in *mat[r]edi* remains. It appears on the section of bark below the split, which has shifted slightly to the right.

? ? ? ? ? ///: The remnants of four akṣaras following *bhikhu* at the end of line 38 are probably the bottoms of the expected *bhayavadu.* The remnant of an akṣara at the bottom of fragment 24u may be the top of the *pra* of the following missing *pracarśoṣu.*

The corresponding P Saṃvara-sutta lacks the introductory nidāna in the E^{e}, B^{e}, and S^{e} and in the manuscripts utilized by them. Of the suttas preceding the Saṃvara-sutta in the Catukka-nipāta, only the first (AN II 1) has a nidāna. In this case the location for the discourse given by the Buddha to the monks is the village of Bhaṇḍagāma in the Vajjī districts (*ekaṃ samayaṃ bhagavā vajjīsu viharati bhaṇḍagāme*). The first sutta to include a nidāna after the Saṃvara-sutta is sutta 21 (AN II 20), where the nidāna is the Sāvatthi-Jetavana nidāna parallel to that which heads the G Prasaṇa-sutra. But this does not imply that suttas 2–20, which do not include nidānas, were also understood to have occurred in Bhaṇḍagāma like the first sutta. Within the P AN (according to the reading of the E^e and B^e), and based on an analysis of the Catukka-nipāta in particular, the criteria for the inclusion of a nidāna in a sutta seem to be the following. A full nidāna is given to the first sutta of each nipāta (AN I 1, 47, 101, II 1, III 1, 279, IV 1, 150, 351, V 1). Although the initial unit *evaṃ me sutaṃ. ekaṃ samayaṃ bhagavā sāvatthiyaṃ viharati jetavane anāthapiṇḍikassa ārāme* is omitted in the E^e of the Ekādasaka-nipāta (AN V 311), it is included in B^e and S^e. All of these nidānas are of the Sāvatthi-Jetavana type except for the first sutta of the Cattukka-nipāta (AN II 1), which, as mentioned, sets the scene in Bhaṇḍagāma.

Within the Catukka-nipāta at least, and probably also within the other nipātas, another general principle seems to be that a nidāna is given when the setting of the sutta is other than Sāvatthi-Jetavana. Of the 271 suttas of the Catukka-nipāta (according to the E^e numbering) only 31 have nidānas.[18] Of these, only seven are of the Sāvatthi-Jetavana type (suttas 21, 45, 48, 51, 67, 101, 197), of which three begin vaggas (21, 51, 101). Those suttas that lack a nidāna in the editions and manuscripts (which are generally in agreement) would have the Sāvatthi-Jetavana nidāna restored when the sutta was recited or when it was placed in a special collection, the full Sāvatthi-Jetavana nidāna being:

> *evaṃ me sutaṃ. ekaṃ samayaṃ bhagavā sāvatthiyaṃ viharati jetavane anāthapiṇḍikassa ārāme. tatra kho bhagavā bhikkhū āmantesi bhikkhavo ti. bhadante ti te bhikkhū bhagavato paccassosuṃ. bhagavā etad avoca.* (E.g., AN II 102.2–5)

The restoration of nidānas is demonstrated by an examination of P manuscripts of anthologies of favored suttas that include suttas from the AN. For example, the Dasadhamma-sutta lacks a nidāna (as well as a conclusion) in its setting in the AN (V 87–8), but whenever this popular sutta occurs in manuscripts as part of an anthology, it is given the Sāvatthi-Jetavana nidāna (and the *idam avoca bhagavā. attamanā te bhikkhū bhagavato bhāsitaṃ abhinandun ti* conclusion). Examples of this are seen in the two Sinh. manuscripts Or.6599(10) and Or.6601(22) in the BL listed in Somadasa's catalog (Somadasa 1987: 22, 277). This is also the case in its setting in the novice's training manual, the Catubhāṇavāra (Pategama-Walpita 1956: 5–7).[19]

Although further detailed research is needed to verify the above findings and to fully understand the principles for nidāna composition that are operational in the P canon,[20]

---

[18] Sutta nos. 1, 21, 24, 30, 35, 36, 45, 48, 51, 53, 55, 57, 67, 68, 76, 80, 101, 159, 170, 180, 183, 185, 187, 188, 190, 193, 194, 195, 196, 197, 241.

[19] For a discussion of the Dasadhamma-sutta and the reasons for its popularity, see Blackburn 1999.

[20] See also Schopen's discussion of the principles for nidāna composition set out in the MSV (Schopen 1997).

from this cursory study of the AN it is highly likely that the nidāna that would normally be attached to the P Saṃvara-sutta would be the Sāvatthi-Jetavana nidāna, as would be the case for most suttas of this class that present the Buddha giving a discourse to the monks where place is irrelevant.

Like the G Prasaṇa-sutra, and probably also the P Saṃvara-sutta, the two Chinese translations (T 2 no. 150a p. 877b27–8 and 99 p. 221b16–7) both set this sūtra in Śrāvasti-Jetavana.[21]

Lines 39–40: The Buddha lists the four *prasaṇa*s

Edition:

[39] *catvarime bhikṣave pra[sa]ṇa ∘ sat[u] savijamaṇa [lo]gha[śpi ∘] ///* |24a [40]

sabaraprasaṇe aṇorakṣaṇaprasa[ṇe] bhavaṇaprasaṇ[o ∘ pra]saṇaprasa[ṇo] ∘

Reconstruction:
[39] *catvarime bhikṣave prasaṇa ∘ satu savijamaṇa loghaśpi ∘ (*kadara/kadama catvari/ catvaro ∘)* [40] *sabaraprasaṇe aṇorakṣaṇaprasaṇe bhavaṇaprasaṇo ∘ prasaṇaprasaṇo ∘*

Translation:
[39] "Monks, these four efforts are found existing in the world. (*What four?) [40] The effort of restraint, the effort of protecting, the effort of development, the effort of abandoning."

The P parallel is

cattār' imāni bhikkhave padhānāni. katamāni cattāri. saṃvarappadhānaṃ pahānappadhānaṃ bhāvanappadhānaṃ anurakkhanappadhānaṃ. (AN II 16.2–4)

Only the latter part of this unit is preserved on the Central Asian (Turfan) Skt. fragment. It reads:

*/// (*pra)[h](*ā)ṇaṃ a(*nurakṣa)ṇāpra[h]ā + + + + (*pra)[hā]ṇam.* (SHT V 1445+1447 V1)

Based on the repetition of the wording on this fragment, the list can be reconstructed:[22]

prahāṇaprahāṇaṃ saṃvaraprahāṇam anurakṣaṇāprahāṇaṃ bhāvanāprahāṇam.

---

[21] Waldschmidt (1980: 171) gives a number of examples of P AN suttas that lack nidānas whose Chinese parallels include nidānas. Tripāṭhī (1962: 11) also comments on the tendency in Skt. mss.

[22] The spelling *sanvara-* of the ms. has been emended to *saṃvara-* here and wherever this passage is quoted.

catvarime bhikṣave pra[sa]ṇa: A loose splinter of bark obscures the bottoms of the three akṣaras of *pra[sa]ṇa.*

In the many passages dealing with the four *padhāna*s or *sammappadhāna*s in Pali, the terminations of these words and their associated numeral and pronoun alternate between the nominative plural neuter and masculine. For example, all elements are declined in the nominative plural neuter in the opening prose section of the P Saṃvara-sutta: *cattār' imāni bhikkhave padhānāni. katamāni cattāri* (AN II 16). But in the concluding verse we find nominative plural masculines: *ete padhānā cattāro* (AN II 17.9, pāda c). Again, while neuter terminations are found at AN II 15 (*cattār' imāni bhikkhave sammappadhānāni. katamāni cattāri;* cf. *sammappadhānā* in the verses AN II 15.27), AN II 74, and DN III 225, masculine terminations are found at SN V 244–5 (*cattāro 'me bhikkhave sammappadhānā. katame cattāro*), DN III 221, and AN IV 463; and so on. Such examples can be described as instances of either the shifting of gender or the flexible use of terminations belonging to different genders and are not uncommon in Pali (see Geiger 1994: § 76; Norman 1992a: 149, 153), BHS (BHSG, § 6), Gāndhārī (see Salomon 2000: §§ 7.1.1, 7.1.1.1.7), and MIA in general. The neuter plural ending *-aṇi* is found in the related *-prah(*a)ṇaṇi* in the Dhp-G^{K} (135c). The Buddhist Skt. examples of these passages so far encountered all have the neuter termination (Mvy 957; Dhsgr § 45; AKV 599.22; PSPP(D) 207.15; ŚSPP(G) 1435.22; DBhS 38.24). Since both masculine and neuter nominative and accusative terminations are virtually always *-a* in this text (§ 6.1.1.1.5), *pra[sa]ṇa* in this G passage could represent either the masculine or neuter plural. The pronoun *ime* suggests that the terminations in the G phrase *catvarime bhikṣave pra[sa]ṇa* are masculine, though inscriptional evidence indicates that *ime* may also be a neuter plural (see § 6.2.2.2). Further evidence that *prasaṇa* is masculine in this text is also supported by the expression *aï bucadi sabaraprasaṇo* (l. 60), where *aï* = Skt. *ayam.*

sat[u] savijamaṇa [lo]gha[śpi ◦]: A loose splinter of bark obscures parts of the first six akṣaras.

This corresponds to P *santo saṃvijjamānā lokasmiṃ,* which is lacking in the P parallel but common elsewhere. In P texts this phrase is most commonly encountered in the following opening and concluding statements (with differences in the numeral and vocative according to context):

> *cattāro 'me bhikkhave puggalā santo saṃvijjamānā lokasmiṃ. katame cattāro.*
> *. . . ime kho bhikkhave cattāro puggalā santo saṃvijjamānā lokasmiṃ.* (E.g., AN II 5–6)

Although occasionally found in other nikāyas, this phrase seems to be most characteristic of the AN.[23] As in the example cited above where it is applied to the four individuals

[23] In the Catukka-nipāta it is found in the following suttas (with change of vocative according to who is addressed): suttas 5 (II 5), 6 (II 6), 43 (II 46), 65 (II 71), 66 (II 71), 85–100 (II 85–101), 123–6 (II 126–30), 131–8 (II 133–8), 169 (II 155–6), 178 (II 165–7), 198 (II 205–11); cf. suttas 101–10 (II 102–11). See Rhys Davids 1933: xi. Examples found in other nikāyas sometimes have parallels in the AN: MN I 24–5 (no AN parallels), 341 (cf. MN I 411; DN III 234; AN II 205; Pp 55), 411 (cf. AN II

(*puggalā*), the phrase *santo saṃvijjamānā lokasmiṃ* only occurs in P texts in association with animate things, for example, the three *kāmabhogino* (SN IV 331), *tapassino lūkhajīvino* (SN IV 337), and *puttā* (It 62–4); the four *bhaddā assājāniyā* and *bhaddā purisājāniyā* (AN II 114–6); the five *satthāro* (Vin II 186–7, 194) and *mahācorā* (Vin III 89–90). Thus, in applying the expression *satu savijamaṇa loghaśpi* to the abstract concepts of the four "efforts" (*prasaṇa*), the G text attests a usage that is alien to the P tradition.

I have not found the corresponding phrase in the Buddhist Skt. texts so far investigated. Among the Central Asian sūtra fragments that have parallels to P suttas containing this phrase, that is, among those sūtras that discuss types of "individuals" (*pudgala*), the sections of the text where the phrase would normally occur are missing (e.g., SHT V 1142; VII 1736). The closest example is SHT VII 1701, which parallels AN IV 11–3.[24] Although the beginning and end of the sūtra are missing, in the description of each individual we find *audakopamaḥ pudgalaḥ san saṃvidyamāna ārye dharmavinaye* (SHT VII 1701 V1,4, R4); in the P parallel *udakūpamā puggalā santo saṃvijjamānā lokasmiṃ* is found at the beginning and end of the sutta. This suggests that the corresponding Skt. phrase *pudgalaḥ san saṃvidyamāno loke,* or the like, may have been employed in Skt. versions of such sūtras.[25]

The Gāndhārī probably included the equivalent of P *katamāni cattāri* (followed by a punctuation mark) at the end of line 39. As will be seen in the discussion below, it is difficult to know whether the interrogative pronoun was *kadara* (= Skt./P *katara*) or *kadama* (= Skt./P *katama*). In the rhetorical question that begins each of the three *prasaṇa*s constructed in the singular, *kadara* is encountered (l. 60; ll. 40 and 63 are damaged) where the Pali has *katamaṃ* (nom. sg. n.). In view of Buddhist Skt. and P usage (see below) we would expect *kadama* where the plural is used and *kadara* for the singular. However, in the Senior manuscripts *kadara* is also used in plural contexts (see below). I therefore offer both in the reconstruction *(*kadara/kadama).* Based on *catvarime* at the beginning of the unit, the stem of the numeral corresponding to P *cattāri* would have been *catvara-*. But it is unclear whether *catvarime* represents the sandhi combination of *catvaro/carvaru + ime* or *catvari + ime* (see § 5.6.2). We would expect *catvaro* or *catvaru* for the masculine and *catvari* for the neuter (cf. *catvari* in Dhp-G^K 172c, 270a). However, *catvari* for the masculine and neuter in the Saṅg-G (Salomon 1999: 172) suggests that *catvari* may have been so used here also. I present both in the reconstruction: *(*catvari/catvaro).* Line 39 has twenty-seven akṣaras. The addition of *(*kadara/kadama catvari/catvaro ◦)* would bring the count to thirty-four.

205–6; Pp 56–61), 453–4 (no AN parallels), 477 ff. (no AN parallels), II 159 (AN II 205; Pp 55), III 209 (no AN parallel); SN I 93–6 (cf. AN II 85–6; Pp IV 19), IV 331 (no AN parallel), 337 (no AN parallel); It 62–5 (no AN parallels); Vin II 186–7, 194 (no AN parallel), III 89–90 (cf. AN I 153, III 128).

[24] This fragment was brought to my attention by Siglinde Dietz. I am also indebted to her for verifying my suspicion that the phrase is generally absent in the Central Asian (Turfan) material.

[25] Cf. RP 18.17, where the phrase is absent: *catvāra ime rāṣṭrapāla pudgalā bodhisatvena na sevitavyāḥ. katame catvāraḥ.*

sabaraprasaṇe aṇorakṣaṇaprasa[ṇe] bhavaṇaprasaṇ[o ◦ pra]saṇaprasa[ṇo] ◦: The final akṣara *[ne]* in *aṇorakṣaṇaprasa[ṇe]* (l. 40), of which only the upper part remains, appears as a poorly written addition below the line. The inclusion of the punctuation mark between the third and fourth elements is unexpected. But as discussed elsewhere (§ 4.8.2), this scribe is not consistent in his use of punctuation marks in such lists.

The P word corresponding to G *prasaṇa* is *padhāna,* "effort," as in the "four efforts" (*cattāri padhānāni*) or the "four right efforts" (*cattāri sammappadhānāni*). Although the corresponding form *pradhāna* is encountered in Skt. texts (see BHSD, s.v.; Gethin 1992: 70–2), the more usual form is *prahāṇa,* similarly understood as "effort" in most sources (BHSD, s.v.) but taken to mean "abandoning" in others (Ruegg 1998: 125; Gethin 1992: 70–2).[26] This dual interpretation is reflected in Tib. and Chinese translations. In Tib. sources, although (*yaṅ-dag-par*) *rab-tu 'jog-pa,* reflecting Skt. *pra* + √*dhā,* is occasionally found, the standard translation is (*yaṅ-dag-par*) *spoṅ-ba,* "right abandoning," reflecting Skt. *pra* + √*hā* (Ruegg 1998: 125).[27] Similarly, the Chinese renderings found in the translations listed above (pp. 248–9) are *si yi duan* (四意斷), the "four mind-abandonings" (T 1 no. 1 p. 50c13; T 2 no. 125 pp. 635b9 ff.; T 15 no. 602 p. 164b18; T 15 no. 603 p. 173c25); *si zheng duan* (四正斷), the "four right abandonings" (T 2 no. 99 p. 221a10); and *si she* (四舍), the "four abandonings" (T 2 no. 150a p. 877b28); all reflecting Skt. *pra* + √*hā*. But there are examples where, within the same text, the translation reflects *pradhāna* in one location and *prahāṇa* in another. For example, whereas the SĀ example just referred to (T 2 no. 99 p. 221a10) reflects *prahāṇa,* the translation reflects *pradhāna* at p. 14a7 and p. 19c5. Again, in the Madhyamāgama (T no. 26) *pradhāna* is reflected at p. 476c21, but *prahāṇa* at p. 519c13.[28] Further, Collett Cox has brought to my attention a passage in the Mahāvibhāṣā that shows an awareness of the two meanings of *prahāṇa* (T 27 no. 1545 p. 724b25–c2). She translates:

> (Question) For what reason are these four said to be *samyakprahāṇa*? (Answer) Due to the fact that these four kinds are capable of correct abandonment. (Question) This can be said of the first two, but how is this said of the last two? (Answer) There is no error due to the fact that the name is [correctly] applied to the first two. Or else, these four all have the meaning of abandonment: that is to say, the first two abandon the obstruction of defilement; the last two abandon the obstruction of knowledge. There are other places which state that these are referred to as *samyakpradhāna*. . . .

---

[26] Examples of *pradhāna* and *prahāṇa* in the Central Asian (Turfan) mss. can be found by seaching the indexes of the SHT (in vols. IV, V, VII, and VIII) and the indexes to such texts as the MPS and Daśo.

[27] I am indebted to Ulrich Pagel for bringing this reference to my attention.

[28] These latter examples were supplied by Collett Cox. Further examples supplied by her are, in the Saṅgītiparyāya (T 26 no. 1536), *pradhāna* at p. 436b24, but *prahāṇa* at p. 425c19–20. An example of two different translations of the same text reflecting different forms is seen in the two translations of the Prasaraṇapāda: *prahāṇa* at T 26 no. 1542 p. 712a23 ff.; *pradhāna* at T 26 no. 1541 p. 645a19.

In his entry for *pradhāna* in the BHSD, Edgerton notes that the older Chinese translations render "effort," while the later ones have "abandonment," as if translating Skt. *prahāṇa* (cf. Lamotte 1944–80: 1123). However, according to Jan Nattier (personal communication) the picture is more complex:

> All of the as-yet documented pre-Kumārajīva translators beginning with An Shigao use some form of "abandon/cut-off"; around Kumārajīva's time, the translation "exertion" comes into fashion; and with Xuanzang, the tide turns back toward understanding the term as "cutting off." There are, of course, interesting blips here and there, but it seems fair to say that there are three major phases, not two, and that what Edgerton described as "early" and "late" are really the "middle" and "late" phases of this sequence.

The P corresponding to G *prasaṇa-prasaṇo,* the fourth *prasaṇa* in the G list, is *pahāna-padhāna,* the "effort of abandoning." Of the Skt. occurrences so far encountered, only the Central Asian (Turfan) fragment (SHT V 1445+1447) names each of the four *prahāṇa*s. Each is referred to as a *-prahāṇaṃ;* the one corresponding to G *prasaṇa-prasaṇo* is *prahāṇa-prahāṇaṃ* (V1; the manuscript reads *-prahaṇaṃ*). Of the Tib. references so far encountered, none name the four. Of the Chinese sources mentioned above only two give names. In both texts each is referred to as an "abandoning" (斷 or 舍); the one corresponding to the G *prasaṇa-prasaṇo* is *duan duan* (斷斷) in T 2 no. 99 pp. 221a11 ff., and *she-she* (舍舍) in T 2 no. 150a p. 877b29, both meaning the "abandoning of abandoning."

Given that the spelling is the same throughout the Gāndhārī, that is, *prasaṇa* for the overall concept and *prasaṇa-prasaṇo* for one of the four *prasaṇa*s, it is tempting to see the Gāndhārī as parallel to the Skt. texts that have *prahāṇa/prahāṇa-prahāṇaṃ,* which, as suggested by the standard Tib. translation and many Chinese renderings, may have been understood as "abandoning" and the "abandoning of abandoning." However, this interpretation is problematic, for throughout this manuscript and in the two other manuscripts written by the same scribe in the BL collection, *-s-* is the standard reflex of original intervocalic *-th-* and *-dh-* (see § 5.2.2.4), never *-h-*. The one glaring exception is the initial *prasaṇa-* in *prasaṇa-prasaṇo,* which must be the equivalent of P *pahāna-*/Skt. *prahāṇa-*. The general pattern in Gāndhārī is that *-th-* and *-dh-* appear as *s,* also written *s̱* (Salomon 2000: § 6.2.1.4; Brough 1962: § 43), or as *-dh-* (Brough 1962: § 42), whereas *-h-* remains (Salomon 2000: § 6.2.1.7) or is occasionally elided (Brough 1962: § 39). There thus seem to be no examples of original *-h-* appearing as *-s-* or *-s̱-* elsewhere in Gāndhārī. It is therefore more likely that G *prasaṇa* as the main topic and *-prasaṇa* as the second member of each compound representing the names of the four reflect the P and Skt. spellings *padhāna* and *pradhāna,* "effort," while the spelling *prasaṇa-* for P *pahāna-*/Skt. *prahāṇa-* in the compound *prasaṇa-prasaṇo* has developed by association and "contamination." This is further supported by the spelling *-prah(*a)ṇaṇi* for original *-prahāṇāni* in the Dhp-G[K] (135c); and by the spelling of the G equivalent of P *sammappadhānānaṃ* as *samepas̱aṇaṇa* in the Senior manuscripts (5 v11,15). Nonetheless, the leveling of the spelling of these two words (*pradhāna* and *prahāṇa* to *prasaṇa*) in this G manuscript is a further illustration of the fact that the word *pradhāna* in Buddhist literature generally behaves irregularly.

The order of the four "efforts" or "abandonings" in the Gāndhārī in relationship to the order found in other Buddhist texts was discussed above.

Lines 40–60: The effort of restraint (*sabaraprasaṇa*)

Edition:

[40] [|24a]*ka[da]* /// [41]*baraprasaṇe ∘ aï bhikṣave bhikhu cakṣ[u]ṇa [r]u[v]o [dh]r[iśpa]ṇa ∘ ṇa ṇ[i]miti*[|24a+24x]*ghra[he]* /// [42][|24a]*vejaṇaghrahi ∘ yavad=eva [asi]araṇa[m=e] + cakṣi[dhri asabro]du viharad[i] ∘ a*[|24a+24q]*bhija domaṇa*[|24q+24j+24o]*stu* [|24j]*pavea aku* /// [43][|24a]*rma ∘ citam=arśaveti ∘ ta[da saba]ra[e pra]divajad[i] rakṣadi ca*[|24a+24q]*kṣi*[|24q]*dhri ∘* [|24q+24o]*ca*[|24o]*kṣi*[|24o+24j]*dhri* [|24j]*sa[ba]* /// [44][|24a]*[va]jadi ∘ ṣudeṇa chado ṣutvaṇa ṇa ṇimitighrahe bhavadi ∘ ṇa* [|24a+24r]*aṇo*[|24a+24s]*[ve]*[|24s+D6c+24h]*jaṇa*[|D6c+24h]*ghra* /// [45][|24a]*va asiaraṇam=eva ∘ sudidhri asabrodu viharadi ∘ [a]bhi[ja do]maṇa*[|24a+24y]*stu* [|24a+24aa]*[pa]* /// [46][|24a]*rma ∘ citam=arśaveti ∘ tada sabarae pradivajadi rakṣadi sudidhri s[u]* /// [47]*di ∘ ghaṇeṇa ghadhro gha[ï]ta ṇa ṇimitighrahe bhavadi ṇa aṇovejaṇa[ghra]* /// [48] *asiaraṇam=eva ∘ ghaṇidhri asabro[d]u viharadi ∘ abhija doma ?* [|24p]*stu* [|24n]*[p.v.a a*[|24m]*k.]* /// [49] [|24a]*dharma ∘ citam=arśaveti ∘ tada sabarae pradivajadi rakṣadi* [|24n]*? ? + [∘]* /// [50] [|24a]*ghaṇidhri sabaram=avajadi ∘ ji[bh.] rasu [śp.].i[ta ṇa ṇimiti]ghrahe bhavadi* /// [51]*jaṇaghrahi ∘ yavad=eva asiaraṇam=eva ∘ jibhidhri asabrodo viharadi ?* /// [52]*maṇastu pavea akuśala dharma ∘ citam=arśaveti ∘ tada saba*[|24a+24cc]*[ra]*[|24cc]*e* /// [53] [|24a]*rakṣadi ji[bhi]dhri ∘ ji[bhi]dhri sabaram= avajadi ∘* [54] [|28a]*kayeṇa proṭhabu phuṣita ṇa ṇimitighrahe bhavadi ṇa a*[|28a+28c]*ṇo*[|28a+28b]*[ve]* /// [55][|28a]*va asiaraṇam=eva kayidhri asabrodo viharadi ∘ abhija domaṇastu [pa]* /// [56]*la dharma ∘ citam=arśaveti ∘ tada sabarae pradivajadi rakṣadi kayi[dh..]* /// [57] *savaram=avajadi ∘ maṇase dharmu añadu ṇa ṇimitighrahe bhavadi ṇa [a]* /// [58] *yavad=eva asiaraṇam=eva maṇidh.i asabrodu viharadi ∘ abh[i]* /// [59]*śala dharma citam=arśa[veti ∘] tada sabarae pradivajadi ∘ rakṣadi ma ?* /// [60]*dhri sabaram=avajadi ∘ aï bucadi sabaraprasaṇo ∘*

Reconstruction:
[40] *kada(*ra bhikṣave sa)*[41]*baraprasaṇe ◦ aï bhikṣave bhikhu cakṣuṇa ruvo dhriśpaṇa ◦ ṇa ṇimitighrahe (*bhavadi (◦) ṇa aṇo)*[42]*vejaṇaghrahi ◦ yavad eva asiaraṇam e(*va (◦)) cakṣidhri asabrodu viharadi ◦ abhija domaṇastu pavea aku(*śala dha)*[43]*rma ◦ citam arśaveti ◦ tada sabarae pradivajadi rakṣadi cakṣidhri ◦ cakṣidhri saba(*ram a)*[44]*vajadi ◦ ṣudeṇa chado ṣutvaṇa ṇa ṇimitighrahe bhavadi ◦ ṇa aṇovejaṇaghra(*hi ◦ yavad e)*[45]*va asiaraṇam eva ◦ sudidhri asabrodu viharadi ◦ abhija domaṇastu pa(*vea akuśala dha)*[46]*rma ◦ citam arśaveti ◦ tada sabarae pradivajadi rakṣadi sudidhri su(*didhri sabaram avaja)*[47]*di ◦ ghaṇeṇa ghadhro ghaïta ṇa ṇimitighrahe bhavadi ṇa aṇovejaṇaghra(*hi ◦ yavad eva)* [48] *asiaraṇam eva ◦ ghaṇidhri asabrodu viharadi ◦ abhija doma(*ṇa)stu p(*a)v(*e)a ak(*uśala)* [49] *dharma ◦ citam arśaveti ◦ tada sabarae pradivajadi rakṣadi (*ghaṇidhri) ◦* [50] *ghaṇidhri sabaram avajadi ◦ jibh(*a) rasu śp(*ay)ita ṇa ṇimitighrahe bhavadi (*(◦) ṇa aṇove)*[51]*jaṇaghrahi ◦ yavad eva asiaraṇam eva ◦ jibhidhri asabrodo viharadi (*◦ abhija do)*[52]*maṇastu pavea akuśala dharma ◦ citam arśaveti ◦ tada sabarae (*pradivajadi)* [53] *rakṣadi jibhidhri ◦ jibhidhri sabaram avajadi ◦* [54] *kayeṇa proṭhabu phuṣita ṇa ṇimitighrahe bhavadi ṇa aṇove(*jaṇaghrahi ◦ yavad e)*[55]*va asiaraṇam eva kayidhri asabrodo viharadi ◦ abhija domaṇastu pa(*vea akuśa)*[56]*la dharma ◦ citam arśaveti ◦ tada sabarae pradivajadi rakṣadi kayidh(*ri (◦) kayidhri)* [57] *savaram avajadi ◦ maṇase dharmu añadu ṇa ṇimitighrahe bhavadi ṇa a(*ṇovejaṇaghrahi ◦)* [58] *yavad eva asiaraṇam eva maṇidh(*r)i asabrodu viharadi ◦ abhi(*ja domaṇastu pavea aku)*[59]*śala dharma citam arśaveti ◦ tada sabarae pradivajadi ◦ rakṣadi ma(*ṇidhri (◦) maṇi)*[60]*dhri sabaram avajadi ◦ aï bucadi sabaraprasaṇo ◦*

Translation:
"[40] What, (*Monks), is the [41] effort of restraint? Here, Monks, a monk, seeing a form with the eye, does not grasp at its general characteristics, does (*not) [42] grasp at its secondary characteristics. Because the evil, unprofitable states of covetousness and grief overpower the mind when one dwells with eye faculty unrestrained, [43] then he takes up restraint, he protects the eye faculty, he exercises restraint in the eye faculty. [44] Hearing a sound with the ear, he does not grasp at its general characteristics, does not grasp at its secondary characteristics. [45] Because the evil, (*unprofitable) states of covetousness and grief overpower the mind when one dwells with ear faculty unrestrained, [46] then he takes up restraint, he protects the ear faculty, he exercises (*restraint) in the ear (*faculty.) [47] Smelling a scent with the nose, he does not grasp at its general characteristics, does not grasp at its secondary characteristics. Because [48] the evil, unprofitable states of covetousness and grief overpower the mind when one dwells with nose faculty unrestrained, [49] then he takes up restraint, he protects the (*nose faculty), [50] he exercises restraint in the nose faculty. Tasting a flavor with the tongue, he does not grasp at its general characteristics, does (*not) grasp at its secondary characteristics. [51] Because the evil, unprofitable states of (*covetousness) and grief [52] overpower the mind when one dwells with tongue faculty unrestrained, then (*he takes up) restraint, [53] he protects the tongue faculty, he exercises restraint in the tongue faculty. [54] Touching a tangible with the body, he does not grasp at its general characteristics, does

not (*grasp at) its secondary characteristics. Because [55] the evil, unprofitable states of covetousness and grief [56] overpower the mind when one dwells with body faculty unrestrained, then he takes up restraint, he protects the body faculty, [57] he exercises restraint (*in the body faculty). Cognizing an idea with the mind, he does not grasp at its general characteristics, does not (*grasp at its secondary characteristics). [58] Because the (*evil), unprofitable states of covetousness (*and grief) overpower the mind when one dwells with mind faculty unrestrained, [59] then he takes up restraint, he protects the mind (*faculty), [60] he exercises restraint in the (*mind) faculty. This is called the effort of restraint."

Line 41: *[dh]r[iśpa]ṇa:* The reading of the akṣara *[dh]r[i]* is difficult because the split in the manuscript divides its upper section. There seems to be the remnant of an *i* diacritic, but *dhra* is a possible reading.

ṇ[i]mitighra[he]: Fragment 24x contains the bottom left of the *i* diacritic of *ti,* the middle section of *ghra,* and the right arm of the *e* diacritic of *he.* The lower part of fragment 24x is obscured by fragment 24a. The left side of *he* is missing. The reading *hi* is also possible but less likely considering that the reading is *-ghrahe* before *bhavadi* in the other parallel phrases (see ll. 44, 47, 50, 54, 57).

Fig. 5. Reconstruction of line 41 (left side).

Line 42: *Asiaraṇam=e(*va),* which the scribe initially omitted by homoeoteleuton because of the *eva* ending of *yavad eva,* has been added below the line. The final akṣara (*va* of *eva*) and a possible punctuation mark have been lost due to the split in the manuscript.

Line 43: A loose splinter of bark obscures the tops of *ta[da saba].* Also, the scribal correction of the addition of *asiaraṇam=e(*va)* to the previous line appears above these akṣaras, further complicating the reading.

[pra]divajad[i]: The bark containing the bottoms of *vajadi* has peeled off and shifted to the left.

Line 44: *[va]jadi:* A fold obscures the tops of *va* and *ja.*

Line 45: Fragment 24aa, which contains part of the final akṣara of the line, *[pa],* is attached to fragment 24a in the old black-and-white photo.

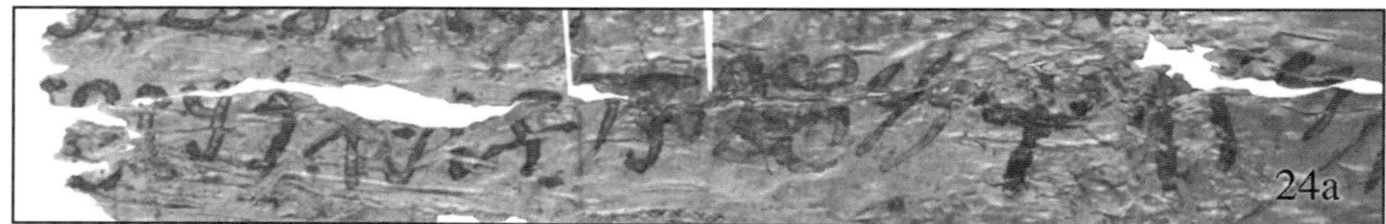

Fig. 6. Reconstruction of line 47 (left side).

Line 48: *[p.v.a ak.]:* The tops of *[p.v.a a]* on fragment 24n are more complete in the old black-and-white photo. Fragment 24m, which contains the bottom of *k.,* sits off fragment 24n in the old black-and-white photo. The fragment has since moved and can no longer be located.

Line 49: *? ? +:* Although these two akṣaras are very faint, they are consistent with *ghaṇa* of the expected *ghaṇidhri*.

Line 50: *ji[bh.]:* There is no *o* or *u* diacritic on *[bh.]*. Besides *jibha,* the reading could therefore be *jibhe*.

[śp.].i[ta]: The reading of these three akṣaras is influenced by the expected wording (P *sāyitvā,* BHS *svādayitvā*). The first akṣara is consistent with *śpa*. The *i* diacritic of the next akṣara is clearly visible on the section of bark above the crack. The remnant of the third akṣara is consistent with the reading *ta.*

Line 51: *jibhidhri:* The akṣara *ji* is not clearly written. It almost appears as though the scribe wrote *ci* but then corrected it.

? ///: The final akṣara, of uncertain reading, is probably the expected punctuation mark. Fragment D6k, with the reading */// ◦ abhi ///,* could belong at the end of this line, but the verso gives no confirmation of this.

Line 52: *tada saba[ra]e:* The bottoms of *da* and *sa* are found on the bark below the split.

Line 53: It seems that the line ends with *avajadi ◦,* as there is no trace of any akṣara on the remaining bark. There is space on this line for about eleven further akṣaras. The decision to end the line at this point may have been influenced by the fact that two sections of bark were joined below this line. The scribe avoided the raised line created by the overlapping bark. The two sections have now separated, leaving a large blank area of bark. Fragment 24t, which is blank, belongs to this section of the manuscript.

Line 54: *aṇo[ve] ///:* Fragment 28b, which contains the left portion of *ve,* is attached to fragment 28a in the old black-and-white photo.

Line 55: A small ink mark to the upper right of the initial *va* does not belong to the akṣaras above. It probably represents an accidental stroke of the pen.

[pa]: Only the right shoulder of *pa* remains.

Line 56: *kayi[dh..]:* Only the tip of the upper right arm of the *dh.* remains.

Line 58: *maṇidh.i:* A section of bark containing the bottoms of *ṇidhri* has peeled off and flipped over, obscuring some of the akṣaras in the line below. A remnant of ink on the recto side of the peel is visible on the verso image (appearing between the crack in the two sections of bark).

Line 59: *arśa[veti ◦]:* A section of bark from the line above has peeled off and flipped over, obscuring most of *rśave,* all but part of the *i* of *ti,* and all of the following punctuation mark. However, the akṣaras *veti ◦* are visible when a fiber-optic light is directed at the back of the manuscript.

The P parallel is

katamañ ca bhikkhave saṃvarappadhānaṃ. idha bhikkhave bhikkhu cakkhunā rūpaṃ disvā na nimittaggāhī hoti nānuvyañjanaggāhī yatvādhikaraṇaṃ enaṃ cakkhundriyaṃ asaṃvutaṃ viharantaṃ abhijjhādomanassā pāpakā akusalā dhammā anvāssaveyyuṃ tassa saṃvarāya paṭipajjati rakkhati cakkhundriyaṃ cakkhundriye saṃvaraṃ āpajjati. sotena saddaṃ sutvā . . . pe . . . ghānena gandhaṃ ghāyitvā . . . pe . . . jivhāya rasaṃ sāyitvā . . . pe . . . kāyena phoṭṭhabbaṃ phusitvā . . . pe . . . manasā dhammaṃ viññāya na nimittaggāhī hoti nānuvyañjanaggāhī yatvādhikaraṇaṃ enaṃ cakkhundriyaṃ asaṃvutaṃ viharantaṃ abhijjhādomanassā pāpakā akusalā dhammā anvāssaveyyuṃ tassa saṃvarāya paṭipajjati rakkhati manindriyaṃ manindriye saṃvaraṃ āpajjati. idaṃ vuccati bhikkhave saṃvarappadhānaṃ. (AN II 16.5–19)

The core of this description of the restraint of the faculties is quite common in the P canon, occurring in a variety of contexts and under a number of headings, thus indicating the importance of this practice. Apart from its occurrence in the Saṅgīti-suttanta (DN III 225–6) in the parallel description of the four efforts, it is the standard description of how a monk guards his sense faculties (*indriyesu guttadvāro*), which is often referred to in such passages as the "noble restraint of the sense faculties" (*ariya indriyasaṃvara*).[29] Many of these occurrences appear in a standard description of the path to nibbāna, which finds a parallel in numerous Skt. sources, some of which are listed below. AN II 39, for example, reads *catuhi bhikkhave dhammehi samannāgato bhikkhu abhabbo parihānāya nibbānass' eva santike. katamehi catuhi. idha bhikkhave bhikkhu sīlasampanno hoti indriyesu guttadvāro hoti bhojane mattaññū hoti jāgariyaṃ anuyutto hoti,* with the elaboration of *indriyesu guttadvāro* being the same as in the AN II 16 passage above. The formula also occurs as the definition of the "taming path" (*damā paṭipadā,* which is one of four paths; AN II 152–3 [abbreviated]) in the description of how a monk dresses or covers a wound (*vaṇaṃ paṭicchādetā:* MN I 223, cf. 221; AN V 351–2, cf. 348–9), in the description of how a monk is a protector (*rakkhitā hoti:* AN III 163), and in the description of how a monk should enter a village or town on his alms rounds, that is, with restrained faculties (*saṃvutehi indriyehi:* AN III 99–100). In the Sabbāsava-sutta (MN I 9) the practice is said to bring about the destruction of the *āsava*s. Finally, in the Vism (15–6) the practice is referred to as *indriyasaṃvarasīlaṃ* and is commented on at length at Vism 20–2.[30]

Parallel examples in Buddhist Skt. literature are relatively common also, most often given as the definition of *indriyasaṃvara* or *indriyeṣu guptadvāra*. Although the basic wording and overall structure of these examples are essentially the same, each text seems to preserve interesting variations in reading. I present below a selection of texts with variations worthy of note:

tasmād iha te kāśyapa evaṃ śikṣitavyaṃ. kiṃ tv ahaṃ ṣaṭsu indriyeṣu guptadvāro vihariṣyāmīti ārakṣāsmṛti nidhyāpanasmṛtiḥ samavasthāvihārī ādīnavadarśāvī niḥśaraṇaḥ prājño araktena cetasā samanvāgataḥ. so cakṣuṣā rūpaṃ dṛṣṭvā na

[29] DN I 70, 207 (abbreviated); MN I 180–1, 269, 273, 346, 355, II 162 (abbreviated), 226 (abbreviated), III 2, 34–5; SN IV 104, 112, 176, 178; AN I 113, II 39–40, 210, V 206. Cf. Dhs 230–1; Vibh 248–9, 360, 372; Pp 20–1, 24–5, 58–9.

[30] A variant of this standard formula is found at MN III 225–6; cf. AN IV 166–7. Cf. also the different definition of *saṃvara* at SN IV 189–90.

*ca nimittagrāhī bhaviṣyan na cānuvyaṃjanagrāhī. yato adhikaraṇaṃ ca me cakṣvindriyeṇa asaṃvr̥tasya viharantasya abhidhyā daurmanasyam aneke pāpakāḥ akuśalā dharmāḥ cittaṃ anuprāvensuḥ teṣāṃ saṃvarāya pratipadiṣyāmi rakṣiṣyāmi (*cakṣvindriyaṃ)*[31] *cakṣvindriyeṇa saṃvaram āpadiṣyāmi iti. evan te kāśyapa śikṣitavyaṃ. śrotreṇa śabdāṃ śrutvā ghrāṇena gandhāṃ ghrāyitvā jihvayā rasāṃ svādayitvā kāyena praṣṭavyāṃ spr̥śitvā manasā dharmāṃ vijñāya na ca nimittagrāhī vihariṣyāmi na cānuvyaṃjanagrāhī vihariṣyāmi. yato adhikaraṇaṃ ca me bhavendriyeṇa asaṃvr̥tasya viharato abhidhyā daurmanasyaṃ aneke pāpakāḥ akuśalā dharmā cittam anuprāvensuḥ teṣāṃ saṃvarāya pratipadiṣyāmīti rakṣiṣyāmi manindriyaṃ manindriyeṇa saṃvaram āpadyiṣyāmīti. evan te kāśyapa śikṣitavyaṃ.* (Mvu III 52.3–15)

*so 'nena āryeṇa śīlaskandhena samanvāgataḥ adhyātmam anavadyasukhaṃ prativedayate. sa indriyair guptadvāro bhava(*ti nipakasmr̥tir guptasmr̥ti) mānasaḥ sahāvasthāvacārakaḥ. sa cakṣuṣo* [read *cakṣusā?*] *rūpāṇi dr̥ṣṭvā na nimittagrāhī bhavati nānuvyañjanagrāhī. yato 'dhikaraṇam eva cakṣurindriyeṇa asaṃvarasaṃvr̥tasya viharataḥ abhidhyādaurmanasye loke pāpakā akuśalā dharmāś (*cittam anusravanti teṣām saṃvarāya prati)padyate rakṣati cakṣurindriyam cakṣurindriyena* [read *~eṇa*] *saṃvaram āpadyate. śrotrendriyeṇa śabdān ghrāṇendriyeṇa gandhān jihvayā rasān kāyena spraṣṭavyāni manasā dharmān vijñāya na nimittagrāhī bhavati nānuvyañjanagrāhī. yato 'dhikaraṇam eva mana(*indriyāsaṃvarasaṃvr̥ta)sya viharataḥ abhidhyādaurmanasye loke pāpakā akuśalā dharmāś cittam anusravanti teṣām saṃvarāya pratipadyate rakṣati (*mana-indriyam) mana-indriyena* [read *~eṇa*] *saṃvaram pratipadyate.* (SBhV II 240.18–31)

sa cakṣuṣā rūpāṇi dr̥ṣṭvā na nimittagrāhī bhavati nānuvyañjanagrāhī. yato 'dhikaraṇam asya cakṣurindriyeṇāsaṃvarasaṃvr̥tasya viharato 'bhidhyādaurmanasye anye vā pāpakā akuśalā dharmāś cittam anuprāpnuyuḥ teṣāṃ saṃvarāya pratipadyate rakṣati cakṣurindriyam. evaṃ śrotreṇa śabdān śrutvā ghrāṇena gandhān ghrātvā jihvayā rasān āsvādya kāyena spraṣṭavyāni spr̥ṣṭvā manasā dharmān vijñāya na nimittagrāhī bhavati nānuvyañjanagrāhī. yato 'dhikaraṇam asya mana-indriyeṇāsaṃvarasaṃvr̥tasya pāpakāś cittam anuprāpnuyuḥ teṣāṃ saṃvarāya pratipadyate rakṣati mana-indriyaṃ. (Śikṣ 202.9–15; cf. 357.1–3)

indriyasaṃvaraḥ katamaḥ. sa tam eva śīlasaṃvaraṃ niśrityārakṣitasmr̥tir bhavati nipakasmr̥tiḥ smr̥tyārakṣitamānasaḥ samāvasthāvacārakaḥ. sa cakṣuṣā rūpāṇi dr̥ṣṭvā na nimittagrāhī bhavati nānuvyaṃjanagrāhī yato 'dhikaraṇam asya pāpakā akuśalā dharmāś cittam anusraveyuḥ teṣāṃ saṃvarāya pratipadyate

[31] *Cakṣvindriyaṃ* should be restored on the basis of *manindriyaṃ manindriyeṇa* below.

rakṣati [32]*(*cakṣurindriyaṃ cakṣurindriyeṇa saṃvaram āpadyate). sa śrotreṇa śabdān ghrāṇena gandhān jihvayā rasān kāyena spraṣṭavyāni manasā dharmān vijñāya na nimittagrāhī bhavati nānuvyaṃjanagrāhī yato 'dhikaraṇam asya pāpakā akuśalā dharmāś cittam anusraveyuḥ teṣāṃ saṃvarā(*ya pratipadyate)*[33] *rakṣati mana-indriyaṃ mana-indriyeṇa saṃvaram āpadyate. ayaṃ ucyate indriyasaṃvaraḥ.* (ŚBh(T), pp. 16–8; cf. pp. 104 ff.; cf. ŚBh(S) 9.13–10.3 and Wayman 1961: 61)

In contrast to the G, P, and Skt. versions just given, the description of *saṃvaraprahāṇa* preserved on the Central Asian Skt. fragment SHT V 1445+1447 V2–3, the only Skt. parallel to the G Prasaṇa-sutra, presents a more succinct articulation of the same idea:

*sanvaraprahāṇaṃ kata[r](*at) [i]ha bhikṣuś=cakṣurindriyasya* [3] */// + sya ārakṣāya guptaye damathā[ya] pratipanno bhavati idam=u[cya]*

A remnant of the standard series B definition is found in SHT VI 1226 fragment 3 Rw–y:

*ta[t](*r)=e(*da)ṃ + /// + + + + + ... nuvya + /// /// .=[c](*i)ttam=anusravanti [tataḥ] /// /// + [tta]grāhī bhavati n=ānu[vy]. ///*

The structure of the G passage, like that of the P parallel and the version in the ŚBh, consists of an opening rhetorical question, the answer to that question, which constitutes a definition, and a concluding statement confirming that the answer is the definition. This structure, which is also utilized in the elaboration of the second and third *prasaṇa*s (and undoubtedly also in the fourth, which is now missing) of the G sūtra, is one commonly encountered in Buddhist literature.

The opening rhetorical questions and concluding statements of the three *prasaṇa*s that are preserved in the G text are best discussed together. Below, the questions are presented in the left column, and the concluding statements are on the right:

[40] *ka[da] ///* [41]*baraprasaṇe* ◦	[60] *aï bucadi sabaraprasaṇo* ◦
[60] *kadara bhikṣave [a] ///* [61]*ṇe* ◦	[63] *idi vucadi aṇorakṣaṇaprasaṇo* ◦
[63] *[ka] ///* [64]*vaṇaprasaṇe* ◦	[73] *aï vuca[di] bhava[ṇapra]saṇe* ○

On the basis of the repetitions, the lacunae can be restored as follows:

*kada(*ra bhikṣave sa)baraprasaṇe* ◦	*aï bucadi sabaraprasaṇo* ◦
*kadara bhikṣave a(*ṇorakṣaṇaprasa)ṇe* ◦	*idi vucadi aṇorakṣaṇaprasaṇo* ◦
*ka(*dara bhikṣave bha)vaṇaprasaṇe* ◦	*aï vucadi bhavaṇaprasaṇe* ○

---

[32] The ms. reads *rakṣati mana-indriyaṃ*. The editors of the Taishō University edition (ŚBh(T)) reconstruct the following based on the same phrase further on.

[33] Reconstructed on the basis of the parallel phrase.

The questions and concluding statements in the P parallel differ from each other only in the *padhāna* listed. The opening question and concluding statement for *saṃvara-ppadhāna* will therefore suffice as illustration:

katamañ ca bhikkhave saṃvarappadhānaṃ	*idaṃ vuccati bhikkhave saṃvara-ppadhānaṃ*

The corresponding phrases in the Central Asian Skt. fragment SHT V 1445+1447 (V2–3, R2–3, plus parallel repetitions) are[34]

saṃvaraprahāṇaṃ katarat	*idam ucyate saṃvaraprahāṇaṃ*

The only significant difference between the three opening questions and concluding statements in the G is *idi vucadi* in the concluding statement of the second *prasaṇa* against *aï bucadi/vucadi* of the first and third. As discussed above (see text commentary to ll. 39–40), the terminations in the opening statement in this sūtra, *catvarime bhikṣave pra[sa]ṇa,* seem to be masculine rather than neuter. The form *aï,* which is nominative singular masculine (= P/Skt. *ayaṃ*), where the P and Skt. parallels have the nominative singular neuter *idaṃ/idam,* indicates that the use of the masculine termination is continued in the concluding statement of the second and third *prasaṇa*s at least, and perhaps elsewhere also. The divergent *idi* in the concluding statement of the second *prasaṇa* can be interpreted in several ways. The first is to take it as a scribal error: the scribe accidentally wrote *idi,* representing P/Skt. *iti,* "thus," rather than *aï.* Alternatively, it is not an error but an example of free variation or inconsistency in phrasing: *idi* = Skt. *iti* thus being a valid reading. Finally, it could represent P/Skt. *idaṃ.* Although *idi* for original *idam* has not been attested in Gāndhārī before now (it appears as *ida* throughout the Dhp-G^{K}), two examples of *id́i* in the new Senior manuscripts where the corresponding P has *idaṃ* may support this correspondence. They are *id́i dukha arias̱aṇja da yas̱abhuda ṇaprayaṇadi* (20 v3), corresponding to P *idaṃ dukkhan ti yathābhūtaṃ nappajānanti* (SN V 451.15–6), and *id́i dukha arias̱aca di yoge karaṇi[o]* (20 v11), corresponding to P *idaṃ dukkhan ti yogo karaṇīyo* (SN V 452.3–4). However, the correspondence of *idi/id́i* for *idaṃ* is weakened by the fact that *id́i* could in these two latter passages also represent original *iti.* If *idi* of our G text does represent P/Skt. *idaṃ,* as I am inclined to believe, then it would attest an inconsistency in the employment of genders in parallel passages.

The G version of the opening questions and concluding statements differs from the P and Skt. parallels on a number of points. In the questions the G employs the interrogative pronoun *kadara,* parallel to *katarat* of the Skt., in contrast to *katamaṃ* of the P, which is the regular form encountered in P canonical texts. *Katara* is found in Pali, but as noted by the CPD (s.v.) it is predominantly postcanonical and is only used in the singular. The CPD further notes that "in some cases *katara* and *katama* are used interchangeably." In Buddhist Skt. texts both *katara* and *katama* are encountered, although *katara* only seems

---

[34] The reading in the ms. is *sanvara-.* I have emended this to *saṃvara-.*

to occur in the singular, as in Pali (SWTF, s.v. *katama* and *katara*; BHSD, s.v. *katara*). Further, some texts favor one or the other form, while others employ them interchangeably. In the CPS (§ 14.1–11), for example, we find the following passage:

> *catvārīmān(*i) bh(*i)kṣava āryasatyāni. katamāni catvāri . . . (*d)uḥkham āryasatyaṃ kata(*rat) . . . du(*ḥhasa)muda(*ya ā)ryasatyaṃ katarat . . . duḥkhanirodha āryasatyaṃ katarat . . . (*duḥkha)nirodhagāminī prati(*pad āryasatyaṃ kata)rat.*

In contrast to this use of *katama* in the initial plural question but *katara* for the following singulars, *katama* is employed in both contexts in the parallel passages found in the Mvu (III 331.17–332.12) and Lal (417.2–15).[35] The Dhsk provides an example of a text that employs both forms interchangeably (SWTF, s.v. *katama*, vol. 2, p. 10), as the following passage illustrates:

> *yāvajjīvaṃ prāṇātipātād viratir upāsakasya śikṣāpadam iti. tattra kataraḥ prāṇātipātaḥ. kataraḥ prāṇī. katamā prāṇātipātād vairamaṇiḥ(!).* (Dhsk 19 v8–9, p. 80)

The G equivalents of *katara* and *katama* (i.e., *kadara* and *kadama*) were not attested in G sources before the appearance of the BL Kharoṣṭhī scrolls. Apart from the present manuscript, in the BL scrolls so far studied, *katama* has been recorded a number of times in a sūtra dealing with meditation, *dhyāna* (BL Frag. 29 [frame 54], provisional line numbers r16, v14), and in an Abhidharma text currently being edited by Collett Cox (BL Frag. 28, ll. 21, 22, 39, 51, 118, 131). Among the Senior manuscripts read to date, *kadara* rather than *kadama* seems to dominate: *kadaro* (20 v1) where the P parallel has *katamo* (SN V 451.12), and *kadareṣa* in *kadareṣa caḋoṇa* (20 v10) where the parallel P phrase (not found in the corresponding P sutta) is *katamesaṃ catunnaṃ* (e.g., SN V 439.28). Other examples are *kadara* (Senior 5 r1,7; 8 r4 [three times]; 20 r3, which lack P parallels, at least to the individual phrases) and *kadareṣa* in *kadareṣa kuśalaṇa dharma[ṇa] abhavida[tva]* (5 v15), which is lacking in the P parallel (SN III 179) but which would be **kadamesaṃ kusalānaṃ dhammānaṃ abhāvitattā*.

These examples suggest that the usage of *kadara* and *kadama* in G texts in the BL and Senior texts so far studied in part parallels that encountered in Buddhist Skt. texts. Both forms are encountered in "canonical" texts, with one or other form tending to dominate in a particular text. But there is insufficient evidence to determine whether both forms were used interchangeably within a given text or by a particular scribe. In the Senior manuscripts so far studied, *kadara* seems to have been used throughout, even in the plural forms, which is contrary to the usage found in P (postcanonical) and Buddhist Skt. texts. In this regard, it is unfortunate that the section of bark that contained the rhetorical question that began our G sūtra (end of l. 39), where the P parallel has *katamāni cattāri,* is missing. We therefore cannot determine whether the form used for the plural in our G Prasaṇa-sutra would have been *kadama* or *kadara*.

---

[35] Cf. MSV II 109 ff., where *katama* is used throughout in a passage parallel in structure to these passages and to the G text under discussion.

Further differences between the G, P, and Skt. (SHT V 1445+1447) versions are the following: (1) in the questions the Gāndhārī generally parallels the Pali in word order, in contrast to the Sanskrit, which places the interrogative pronoun last (*saṃvaraprahāṇaṃ katarat*), although the G and P word order is found in other Skt. texts; (2) in the questions the Gāndhārī lacks *ca* of the Pali (*katamañ ca*), as does the Sanskrit; and (3) the Gāndhārī parallels the Pali in including the vocative *bhikṣave* (P *bhikkhave*) in the opening questions but differs from it in omitting the vocative in the concluding statements, whereas the Sanskrit omits it in both the question and the answer.

The definition of *sabaraprasaṇa* (P *saṃvarappadhāna*/Skt. *saṃvarapradhāna, saṃvaraprahāṇa*) consists of six parallel structures differing only in that certain key words and phrases are changed in each repetition according to which of the six senses is being referred to. Each of these six parallel structures in turn consists of distinct units. For the purpose of this study I will group these into four main subunits. Of all the examples so far collected of this formula, only in our G manuscript is each repetitive structure written out in full. The Skt. and P examples give the first and last (concerned with the visual and mental) in full and abbreviate the second to fifth by merely giving the opening phrase of each (*śrotreṇa śabdān śrutvā,* etc.), although in contrast to the Skt. examples, the P editions and manuscripts used for the editions explicitly indicate that the abbreviations are to be filled out with *pe* (= *peyyāla*) and the like.

As the structures are virtually identical, we can discuss the whole by analyzing the first structure of the G, P, and Skt. versions, which is concerned with the visual. In the following discussion the six parallel structures are numbered 1–6 and the four subunits of each are labeled a–d, as in the following presentation of lines 41–4 of the Gāndhārī:

1a. *aï bhikṣave bhikhu cakṣuṇa ruvo dhriśpaṇa ◦ ṇa ṇimitighrahe (*bhavadi (◦) ṇa aṇo)vejaṇaghrahi ◦*
1b. *yavad eva asiaraṇam e(*va (◦)) cakṣidhri asabrodu viharadi ◦*
1c. *abhija domaṇastu pavea aku(*śala dha)rma ◦ citam arśaveti ◦*
1d. *tada sabarae pradivajadi rakṣadi cakṣidhri ◦ cakṣidhri saba(*ram a)vajadi ◦*

The reconstruction of the lacunae in the G version can be considered as certain in view of the repetitiveness of the formula and the consistency in orthography throughout. The same is true of the reconstructions in the SBhV and ŚBh(T) examples given by the editors of those texts. In the following lists, specific textual references will not be given, as these are listed above.

Section 1a:
G: *aï bhikṣave bhikhu cakṣuṇa ruvo dhriśpaṇa ◦ ṇa ṇimitighrahe (*bhavadi (◦) ṇa aṇo)vejaṇaghrahi ◦*
P: *idha bhikkhave bhikkhu cakkhunā rūpaṃ disvā na nimittaggāhī hoti nānuvyañjanaggāhī*
Mvu: *so cakṣuṣā rūpaṃ dr̥ṣṭvā na ca nimittagrāhī bhaviṣyan na cānuvyaṃjanagrāhī*

SBhV: *sa cakṣuṣo* [read *cakṣusā*?] *rūpāṇi dṛṣṭvā na nimittagrāhī bhavati nānuvyañjanagrāhī*
Śikṣ: *sa cakṣuṣā rūpāṇi dṛṣṭvā na nimittagrāhī bhavati nānuvyañjanagrāhī*
ŚBh: *sa cakṣuṣā rūpāṇi dṛṣṭvā na nimittagrāhī bhavati nānuvyaṃjanagrāhī*

The absence of *iha bhikṣavo bhikṣuś* at the beginning of the Skt. examples is due merely to the different contexts in which these passages occur. Each of the definitions of the three surviving *prasaṇa*s in the G text begins with *aï bhikṣave bhikhu* (ll. 41, 64) or *aï bhikṣave bhikhuṇa* (l. 61), where the Pali has *idha bhikkhave bhikkhu*. It is unlikely that G *aï* represents original *idha* or *iha*. In the Dhp-G^{K}, for example, this word appears as *idha* (e.g., 205, 206, 333) where the corresponding Pali also has *idha*. Rather, *aï* may be the demonstrative pronoun corresponding to P/Skt. *ayaṃ*. If so, then it would qualify *bhikhu*, the translation being "O Monks, this monk, having seen a form with the eye," etc. However, this is rather strained and is contrary to the typical phrasing of such passages in P and Skt. Buddhist texts, where *idha* and *iha* are the norm, meaning "here," "in this case" (CPD, s.v. *idha* 3; SWTF, s.v. *iha* 1c). Further examples may indicate that, although formerly representing the demonstrative pronoun, G *aï* is semantically equivalent to P *idha*/Skt. *iha* in such contexts in certain texts. I adopt this interpretation in my translation.

cakṣ[u]ṇa [r]u[v]o [dh]r[iśpa]ṇa ◦: Because this is a nonrepetitive phrase, it is presented here as per the edition. The only uncertain akṣara is *dhri*, in which only a very small remnant of an *i* diacritic is visible. However, the reading *dhriśpaṇa* rather than *dhraśpaṇa* is confirmed by the forms *dhriśpa* and *dhriśpaṇa* in the AG-G, which was written by the same scribe as our manuscript.[36] For discussion of the phonetic features of *dhriśpaṇa*, see §§ 4.8.1, 5.1.9, 5.2.3.6.

Worthy of note is the use of the extended form *dhriśpaṇa*, corresponding to P *disvāna*, rather than *dhriśpa* = P *disvā*. This is parallel to *ṣutvaṇa* in line 44 where the P parallel has *sutvā*, although these are the only examples of extended absolutives in our text. (For a discussion of these extended forms, see Geiger 1994: §§ 208–9; von Hinüber 1986: § 498.)

Also worthy of note is the fact that the G version of this phrase, *cakṣuṇa ruvo dhriśpaṇa*, parallels *cakkhunā rūpaṃ disvā* of the P and *cakṣuṣā rūpaṃ dṛṣṭvā* of the BHS Mvu in constructing the grammatical object (*ruvo, rūpaṃ*) in the singular rather than the plural; the plural is used in *cakṣuṣā rūpāṇi dṛṣṭvā* of the Skt. versions of the SBhV, Śikṣ, and ŚBh. In the parallel phrases dealing with the other five senses, the Gāndhārī and Pali both have singular forms (G *chado, ghadhro, rasu, proṭhabu, dharmu;* P *saddaṃ, gandhaṃ, rasaṃ, phoṭṭhabbaṃ, dhammaṃ*), but the Skt./BHS versions, including the Mvu, have plural forms (*śabdān, gandhān, rasān, spraṣṭavyāni/praṣṭavyāṃ, dharmān*).[37]

---

[36] See Salomon 1999: 133, where these words were initially transcribed as *dhrispa* and *dhrispaṇa*. We now read these as *dhriśpa* and *dhriśpaṇa;* see § 5.2.3.6 for the discussion of this character. The line numbers given by Salomon for the occurrence of these examples still remain provisional.

[37] See also Daśo § VI.2, where the plural forms are found (the fifth sense object is *spraṣṭavyān*).

*ṇa ṇimitighrahe (*bhavadi (◦) ṇa aṇo)vejaṇaghrahi ◦:* For the discussion of the spelling *ṇimiti-* = P/Skt. *nimitta-,* see § 5.1.2; for the phonetic features of *aṇovejaṇa,* see §§ 5.1.1, 5.1.8, 5.2.3.4. Except for the punctuation mark, the reconstruction is secure, since the spelling is uniform throughout the remaining repetitions; see, for example, the almost complete phrase in the second parallel phrase (l. 44), *ṇa ṇimitighrahe bhavadi ◦ ṇa aṇovejaṇaghra(*hi ◦).* Although the punctuation mark after *bhavadi* is present in line 44, it is absent in the other parallel phrases. Its reconstruction is therefore optional in the first structure (1a) and also in the fourth (4a), on line 50. As the reconstruction of these repetitive sections is secure, the reconstructed reading is presented as the pattern for discussion here and in the following passages.

The G version of this phrase is identical with the P, SBhV, Śikṣ, and ŚBh versions and differs from the Mvu version only in that the Mvu includes *ca: na ca nimittagrāhī bhaviṣyan na cānuvyaṃjanagrāhī.*[38]

Sections b and c are best discussed together:

Section 1b:

G:	*yavad eva asiaraṇam e(*va (◦)) cakṣidhri asabrodu viharadi ◦*
P:	*yatvādhikaraṇaṃ enaṃ cakkhundriyaṃ asaṃvutaṃ viharantaṃ*
Mvu:	*yato adhikaraṇaṃ ca me cakṣvindriyeṇa asaṃvr̥tasya viharantasya*
SBhV:	*yato 'dhikaraṇam eva cakṣurindriyeṇa asaṃvarasaṃvr̥tasya viharataḥ*
Śikṣ:	*yato 'dhikaraṇam asya cakṣurindriyeṇāsaṃvarasaṃvr̥tasya viharato*
ŚBh:	*yato 'dhikaraṇam asya*

Section 1c:

G:	*abhija domaṇastu pavea aku(*śala dha)rma ◦ citam arśaveti ◦*
P:	*abhijjhādomanassā pāpakā akusalā dhammā anvāssaveyyuṃ*
Mvu:	*abhidhyā daurmanasyam aneke pāpakāḥ akuśalā dharmāḥ cittaṃ anuprāvensuḥ*
SBhV:	*abhidhyādaurmanasye loke pāpakā akuśalā dharmāś (*cittam anusravanti)*
Śikṣ:	*'bhidhyādaurmanasye anye vā pāpakā akuśalā dharmāś cittam anuprāpnuyuḥ*
ŚBh:	*pāpakā akuśalā dharmāś cittam anusraveyuḥ*

All six versions listed here begin with an adverbial expression in section 1b, but whereas this is similar in the P and Skt. versions (for P *yatvādhikaraṇaṃ,* cf. MN III 2.15, 2.22, 34.32, 35.5–6, where the reading is *yato 'dhikaraṇam*),[39] the Gāndhārī has *yavad eva asiaraṇam,* which is equivalent to a Skt. **yāvad eva adhikaraṇam* (ignoring sandhi). The P and Skt. expressions mean "because," "by reason of which" (BHSD, s.v. *adhikaraṇa* 2; CPD, s.v. *adhikaraṇa*). The Vism (21.11–2) gloss is *yaṃ kāraṇā yassa cakkhundriyasaṃvarassa hetu. Yāvad eva* generally means "merely," "just simply"

---

[38] Cf. SHT VI 1226, frag. 3, Ry *(/// + [tta]grāhī bhavati n=ānu[vy]. ///),* which lacks the conjunctive particle.

[39] At MN I 9 the pattern is *yaṃ hi 'ssa . . . viharato.*

(BHSD, s.v. *yāvad-eva*), or "up to," "as far as," "in short" (PTSD, s.v. *yāva*),[40] which seems somewhat out of place in this context, but its employment here in place of *yato-* probably changes the meaning little. The same word appears in the conversion formula that ends the Dhoṇa-sutra in a context that demands the meaning "so that," "in order that" (see p. 213). It is therefore possible that the use of this word in Gāndhārī may differ from its use in P and Buddhist Skt. texts. Further, the G expression appears to be constructed with *tada* (= P/Skt. *tadā*) at the beginning of section d, which seems to have the meaning "therefore."

In the Pali, the remainder of section b consists of a noun phrase, *enaṃ cakkhundriyaṃ asaṃvutaṃ viharantaṃ,* which is the direct object of the optative verb *anvāssaveyyuṃ* that appears at the end of section c. The translation of sections b and c of the Pali is "because the evil, unprofitable states of covetousness and grief would overpower one who dwells with his eye faculty unrestrained." The Skt. versions similarly have the finite verb at the end of section c, but here the latter part of section b consists of a genitive phrase governed by the direct object (*cittam*) of the verb. Thus, the translation of the SBhV passage is "because the evil, unprofitable states of covetousness and grief concerning the world would overpower the mind of one who dwells unrestrained in the restraint of the eye faculty."[41]

The syntax of the Gāndhārī is a little ambiguous due to the uncertain status of *viharadi* at the end of section b. The words *citam arśaveti* at the end of section c in the Gāndhārī suggest that the overall syntax is parallel to the Sanskrit rather than the Pali, but *viharadi* is not likely to represent the genitive singular of the present participle (Skt. *viharataḥ*), or the accusative singular for that matter (P *viharantaṃ*). Two interpretations seem possible. It could be the locative singular of the present participle (= Skt. *viharati*/P *viharati, viharantasmiṃ,* etc.), representing a locative absolute construction. The meaning of *yavad eva asiaraṇam e(*va (◦)) cakṣidhri asabrodu viharadi ◦ abhija domaṇastu pavea aku(*śala dha)rma ◦ citam arśaveti ◦* would then be "because the evil, unprofitable states of covetousness and grief overpower [one's] mind when one dwells with eye faculty unrestrained." The alternative is to take *viharadi* as a third-person singular present indicative. The meaning would be "because [or perhaps "as long as"] one dwells with eye faculty unrestrained, the evil, unprofitable states of covetousness and grief overpower [one's] mind." Since the P and Skt. parallels tend to support taking *viharadi* as a present participle, I tentatively adopt the first alternative and translate accordingly. (The punctuation mark after *viharadi* cannot be used as support for either interpretation.)

Before leaving section b, it is worth noting that considerable variation is seen in the element or elements that follow *asiaraṇam* in the Gāndhārī and *adhikaraṇaṃ* in the Pali

---

[40] In P, *yāvad eva* is often constructed with the dat./gen., e.g., Vin IV 143.18 (comm. at Sp IV 876); DN II 292.5–10 (comm. at Sv III 766); AN I 145.8 (comm. at Mp II 237); Dhp 72 (comm. at Dhp-a II 73); Sn p. 140.7–8 (comm. at Pj II 503); cf. the comm. at Vism 30–1.

[41] Cf. MN I 9.26–7: *yaṃ hi 'ssa bhikkhave cakkhundriyasaṃvaraṃ asaṃvutassa viharato uppajjeyyuṃ āsavā.*

and Sanskrit: the G and SBhV versions have *eva;* the Mvu, *ca me;* the P, *enaṃ;*[42] and the Śikṣ and ŚBh, *asya.*

abhija domaṇastu: In Pali, *abhijjhādomanassā* is a dvandva compound declined in the nominative plural neuter (see CPD, s.v.), while *abhidhyādaurmanasye* of the Skt. SBhV and Śikṣ is a dvandva in the dual neuter.[43] Since the termination *-u* is unlikely to be a G plural, *abhija domaṇastu* of the Gāndhārī cannot represent a dvandva but must parallel the Mvu version, which has the noncompounded form *abhidhyā daurmanasyam.*[44]

Besides the current example of *domaṇastu,* the spelling *dormanasta* is found in the Kurram casket inscription, and *domaṇasta* appears in the Senior manuscripts (20 v6,8). With reference to the Kurram casket example, Konow (1929: 153–4) was unable to explain the "apparent substitution of *st* for *sy,*" stating that "it seems as if we have before us a barbaric *daurmanastā.*" But now it is more likely that G *dormanasta-/domaṇasta-* represents an unattested Skt. **daurmanastva-,* with the abstract suffix *-tva. Daurmanasyatā* in *vivekaṃ śrutvā buddhasya na teṣāṃ daurmanasyatā* (Mvu II 355.17) is worthy of note here (cf. BHSD, s.v. *daurmanasyita*) since it represents a somewhat similar formation.

citam arśaveti ◦*:* There is considerable variation in the verb employed in each version to express the idea of the unprofitable states of mind overpowering the unrestrained person. The Pali has *anvāssaveyyuṃ,* which is the third-person plural optative of *anu-ā* + √*sru* (see CPD, s.v. *anvāssavati*), a verb that does not seem to occur in such contexts in Buddhist Skt. texts. The P is the only version not to construct the verb with *cittam* as its direct object.[45] The SBhV and ŚBh examples employ the synonymous *anu-* + √*sru,* with *cittam* as direct object: *cittam anusravanti* (SBhV II 240.23–4,29) and *cittam anusraveyuḥ* (ŚBh(T) 16.24, 18.4). The same expression appears in two Central Asian fragments: *cittaṃ nānusravaṃti* (SHT V 1099 R2) and *[c](*i)ttam anusravanti* (SHT VI 1226 frag. 3 Rx). This verb is, in fact, found in two similar phrases in Pali. The first is *yathā carantaṃ viharantaṃ*[46] *abhijjhādomanassā pāpakā akusalā dhammā nānusavanti* (SN IV 188.9–11, 189.8–9, 190.23–4), where the B^e reads *nānusenti* in the first occurrence (a Burmese v.l. recorded in the E^e) but *nānussavanti* in the second and third. The second phrase is *yathāsataṃ viharantaṃ āsavā nānusavanti* (SN II 54.2–3; the B^e reads *nānussavanti*). Finally, the Mvu and Śikṣ examples employ the verb *anu-pra* + √*āp,* "reach," "attain" (MW, s.v.), "obtain" (BHSD, s.v. *anuprāpunati*), but in this context it must mean "overpower," "take hold of": *cittam anuprāpnuyuḥ* (Śikṣ 202.11,15) and *cittaṃ anuprāvensuḥ* (Mvu III 52.8,13). The Mvu example shows the Pkt. *v* for *p* (see

---

[42] The reading *etaṃ* in the E^e of DN III 225–6 may be a misreading based on the *n/t* confusion in Sinh. script.

[43] For a discussion of the term, see Gethin 1992: 48 ff.

[44] See also *vinīyābhidhyā loke daurmanasyam* at MPS § 14.25, and cf. § 10.14 (reconstructed). See also SWTF, s.v. *abhidhyā.*

[45] No P commentaries seem to include *cittaṃ* in their glosses on this passage (e.g., Vism 21).

[46] *Viharantaṃ* is missing in the SN IV 188 example.

BHSD, s.v. *anuprāpunati*). This verb is not recorded in Pali in such a usage, or in the SWTF (s.v.).

The G expression *citam arśaveti* finds no parallel elsewhere. G *arśaveti* is to be derived from *ā* + √*sru,* with the G spelling exhibiting the confusion between the roots √*sru* and √*śru* and their derivatives that is commonly encountered in Buddhist Skt. (e.g., in the spellings *āsrava* and *āśrava;* see BHSD, s.v. *āsrava;* BHSG, § 2.58). (For the conjunct *rś* for *śr* in this and related words, see § 5.2.3.6.) In Pali this verb is found in the commentary on the SN II 54 passage (*viharantaṃ āsavā nānusavanti*) quoted above (*āsavā nānussavantī ti cakkhuto rūpe savanti āsavanti sandanti pavattantī ti,* Spk II 64.25–6)[47] and in a gloss on the word *āsava* (*āsavantī ti āsavā,* Ud-a 176.2 = As 48).[48] Although *anu-ā* + √*sru* of the Pali, *anu* + √*sru* of some Skt. versions, and *ā* + √*sru* of the Gāndhārī are synonymous, the G *arśaveti* expresses a direct connection with *āsava/āśrava; pavea akuśala dharma* (= Skt. *pāpakā akuśalā dharmāś*) of this passage may be synonymous.

In the P and Skt. versions, with the exception of the SBhV, the finite verb is in the optative. But *arśaveti* of the G is unlikely to be an optative, having only superficial resemblance to optatives of the *-eyati* and *-eati* type (see Burrow 1937: §§ 97, 100; Salomon 1986: 277). It is also unlikely that we are to understand this to consist of two words (*arśave ti*) with *ti* representing the quotative particle *iti,* for *arśave* could not represent a plural form as required here. Rather, *arśaveti* appears to be the third-person plural present causative form of the verb, but without a specifically causative sense, as this would not suit the context. The employment of the verb in the present indicative rather than the optative finds a parallel in the SBhV version: *cittam anusravanti.*

Section 1d:

G:	*tada sabarae pradivajadi rakṣadi cakṣidhri ∘ cakṣidhri saba(*ram a)vajadi ∘*
P:	*tassa saṃvarāya paṭipajjati rakkhati cakkhundriyaṃ cakkhundriye saṃvaraṃ āpajjati*
Mvu:	*teṣāṃ saṃvarāya pratipadiṣyāmi rakṣiṣyāmi (*cakṣvindriyaṃ) cakṣvindriyeṇa saṃvaram āpadiṣyāmi iti*
SBhV:	*(*teṣām saṃvarāya prati)padyate rakṣati cakṣurindriyam cakṣurindriyena* [read ~*eṇa*] *saṃvaram āpadyate*
Śikṣ:	*teṣāṃ saṃvarāya pratipadyate rakṣati cakṣurindriyam*
ŚBh:	*teṣāṃ saṃvarāya pratipadyate rakṣati (*cakṣurindriyaṃ cakṣurindriyeṇa saṃvaram āpadyate)*

The six versions listed here exhibit only minor variations in section d. G *tada* represents P/Skt. *tadā.* The Pali has *tassa,* which Buddhaghosa (Vism 21.15–6) takes to refer to the eye faculty (*tassa cakkhundriyassa*). The Skt. versions have *teṣāṃ,* which, being plural, must refer to all six faculties, since it cannot refer to the *pāpakā akuśalā dharmāś.* In a Central Asian (Turfan) fragment of this formula (SHT VI 1226 frag. 3 Rx) we also

[47] For the expression *cakkhuto rūpe savanti āsavanti sandanti pavattanti,* cf. Sv III 989.4–7; Nidd II (B^{e}) 29 ff. Cf. also *cakkhuto rūpataṇhā savati* [B^{e} *āsavati*] *pasavati sandati pavattati* (Nidd I 233–4).

[48] Cf. *śuṣkā āśravā na puna śravanti* (Lal 351.1).

find *[c](*i)ttam anusravanti [tataḥ] ///,* where Skt. *tataḥ* provides a parallel to the use of *tada* in the Gāndhārī.

Whereas the Pali has *cakkhundriye saṃvaraṃ āpajjati,* with *cakkhundriye* representing a locative singular (cf. Vism 21–2), the Skt. versions have *cakṣurindriyeṇa saṃvaram āpadyate* (with minor variations), with the instrumental.[49] In G *cakṣidhri saba(*ram a)vajadi* the case of *cakṣidhri* is ambiguous, as it is elsewhere, since the loss of the final syllable makes it unclear whether *idhri* (= Skt. *indriya-*) is treated as an *a*-stem or an *i*-stem noun. In the preceding phrase, *rakṣadi cakṣidhri,* the form is the accusative singular, as it is in *śatidhri* (l. 7), corresponding to P *santindriyaṃ*. In the section b phrase *cakṣidhri asabrodu viharadi,* where the Pali has *cakkhundriyaṃ asaṃvutaṃ viharantaṃ* and Sanskrit has *cakṣvindriyeṇa asaṃvr̥tasya viharantasya* (Mvu) or *cakṣurindriyeṇa asaṃvarasaṃvr̥tasya viharataḥ* (SBhV), its status is also ambiguous, representing the nominative or locative singular. As *cakṣidhri* is unlikely to represent an instrumental, I am inclined to take it as locative singular in the phrase *cakṣidhri saba(*ram a)vajadi.* However, it is also possible that *cakṣidhrisabaram* is a compound. But since the other versions do not have the compounded form, I tentatively take it as the locative singular parallel to the Pali.

Sections 2–6:

The wording of the remaining five repetitive sections of the G formula dealing with the other five senses differs from section 1 only in that the initial nonfinite clause of section 1a (*cakṣuṇa ruvo dhriśpaṇa*) is replaced by the corresponding phrase relevant to each of the other five senses, while *cakṣidhri* of sections 1b and 1d is replaced by *sudidhri, ghaṇidhri, jibhidhri, kayidhri,* and *maṇidhri,* respectively.

The initial nonfinite clauses of section a dealing with each sense (with the first included for comparison) are

1. *cakṣ[u]ṇa [r]u[v]o [dh]r[iśpa]ṇa*
2. *ṣudeṇa chado ṣutvaṇa*
3. *ghaṇeṇa ghadhro gha[ï]ta*
4. *ji[bh.] rasu [śp.].i[ta]*
5. *kayeṇa proṭhabu phuṣita*
6. *maṇase dharmu añadu*

The corresponding nonfinite clauses in the G, P, and Skt. are

Section 2:	G	*ṣudeṇa chado ṣutvaṇa*
	P	*sotena saddaṃ sutvā*
	Skt.	*śrotreṇa śabdān śrutvā* (Mvu, Sikṣ)
		śrotreṇa śabdān (ŚBh)
		śrotrendriyeṇa śabdān (SBhV)

[49] For a discussion of the use of the instr. and loc. with *(a)saṃvuta* in Pali and with *(a)saṃvr̥ta* in Buddhist Skt. texts, see Lüders 1954: § 224; see also Norman 1997: 117 (notes on Dhp 225).

The only difference worthy of note is that the Gāndhārī and Pali agree in constructing the sense object (and grammatical object) in this and in the following parallel phrases in the singular rather than the plural as in the Skt. examples. The absolutive is omitted in the SBhV and ŚBh versions in this and the following four sections (cf. Daśo § VI.2: *iha bhikṣuś cakṣuṣā rūpāṇi dr̥ṣṭvā . . . śrotreṇa śabdān ghrāṇena gandhāñ jihvayā rasān kāyena spraṣṭavyān manasā dharmān vijñāya . . .*). For a discussion of the phonetic features of *chado,* see § 5.2.1; for *ṣudeṇa,* and *ṣutvaṇa,* see § 5.2.3.6.

Section 3: G *ghaṇeṇa ghadhro gha[ï]ta*
P *ghānena gandhaṃ ghāyitvā*
Skt. *ghrāṇena gandhāṃ ghrāyitvā* (Mvu)
ghrāṇena gandhān ghrātvā (Śikṣ)
ghrāṇena gandhān (ŚBh)
ghrāṇendriyeṇa gandhān (SBhV)

For the phonetic features of *ghaṇeṇa, ghadhro,* and *gha[ï]ta,* see §§ 5.2.3.4 and 5.3.

Section 4: G *ji[bh.] rasu [śp.].i[ta]*
P *jivhāya rasaṃ sāyitvā*
Skt. *jihvayā rasāṃ svādayitvā* (Mvu)
jihvayā rasān āsvādya (Śikṣ)
jihvayā rasān (SBhV, ŚBh)

The top of the *bh* of *ji[bh.]* is missing. As there is no *o* or *u* diacritic, the reading could be *jibha* or *jibhe,* though the former is more likely (and is adopted in the reconstruction). We would have expected **jibhae* or **jibhaï,* corresponding to P *jivhāya,* for the instrumental singular feminine of an *ā* stem, for which compare *vayaï* = P *vācāya* (Dhp-G^{K} 23, 51, 52, 232). However, the same word appears as *[jibha]* and *cibha* in the Senior manuscripts in what appears to be a locative absolute construction: *cakṣusa . . . [sa]d́a . . . [s.]d. gaṇo [jibha kaya maṇasa . . . sad́.]* (20 r3–4) and *cakṣusa . . . [sad́i] . . . sodo gaṇo cibha kaya manasa . . . sad́a* (20 r8), which parallels the P phrase *cakkhusmiṃ sati . . . sotasmiṃ . . . ghānasmiṃ . . . jivhāya . . . kāyasmiṃ . . . manasmiṃ sati* (SN IV 171, abbreviated). If these Senior manuscript examples of *[jibha]* and *cibha* do represent locative singulars, then it would seem that the reading of our example is in fact *jibh(*a)* and that this represents another example of the dropping of final *-ya* (see § 5.5).

The portion of the manuscript containing the absolutive is badly damaged. The reading of the remnants of the akṣaras of this word as *[śp.].i[ta]* is influenced by the expected wording: P *sāyitvā* (AN II 16.12) and BHS *svādayitvā* (Mvu III 52.10).[50] The first akṣara is consistent with *śp.*; the *i* diacritic on the next akṣara is clearly visible on the section of bark above the horizontal split in the manuscript, indicating that the reading was most

[50] For discussion of this and related words, see BHSD, s.v. *sātīyati, svādīyati,* cf. *āsvādanīya;* Geiger 1994: §§ 36, 176; Lüders 1954: § 111.

likely *yi* (𐨩𐨁) rather than *di* (𐨡𐨁); the remnant of the third akṣara is consistent with the reading *ta*. I therefore tentatively reconstruct this word as *śp(*ay)ita*.

Section 5: G *kayeṇa proṭhabu phuṣita*
P *kāyena phoṭṭhabbaṃ phusitvā*
Skt. *kāyena praṣṭavyāṃ spr̥śitvā* (Mvu)
kāyena spraṣṭavyāni spr̥ṣṭvā (Śikṣ)
kāyena spraṣṭavyāni (SBhV, ŚBh)

Cf. Daśo § VI.2, for the form *kāyena spraṣṭavyān*.

Section 6: G *maṇase dharmu añadu*
P *manasā dhammaṃ viññāya*
Skt. *manasā dharmān vijñāya* (Mvu, SBhV, Śikṣ, ŚBh)

The form *maṇase* as instrumental singular is problematic. We would have expected **maṇaseṇa* (only *maṇeṇa* appears in the Dhp-G^{K}: 51, 52, 232) or *maṇasa* (Dhp-G^{K} 23, 201, 202).[51] Although *maṇase* could be a locative singular, this is unlikely in this context unless this is an example of the locative termination used for the instrumental. It is possible that the syllable *ṇa* was accidentally omitted from the end of the word and that we should emend to *maṇase*<**ṇa*>.

G *añadu* where the Pali has *viññāya* and the Skt. versions have *vijñāya* is also unusual. Although this seems at first glance to be a past participle, Skt. *ājñāta-*, the fact that the other parallel phrases have absolutives suggests that it is also an absolutive. It must therefore be an absolutive in *-tu* of *ā* + √*jñā;* the Dhp-G^{K} has *añaï* (250c) where the corresponding P parallel has *aññāya*. The regular absolutive endings in our text are *-ita, -tva,* or *-tvaṇa* as in *ṣutvaṇa, gha[ï]ta,* and *phuṣita* in the parallel sections (see also § 6.3.7). Von Hinüber (1986: § 498; see also Geiger 1994: § 210B) lists as examples of absolutives in *-tu* Aśokan *sutu/śrutu* (= Skt. *śrutvā*) and P *daṭṭhu* (= Skt. *dr̥ṣṭvā*), the former given as an example of samprasāraṇa by Norman (1958: 46 = CP, vol. I, p. 3). However, others suggest that it may be preferable to see P *daṭṭhu,* which normally has the v.l. *daṭṭhuṃ* (Sn 424, 681, 1098), as an infinitive used as an absolutive (Geiger 1994: § 210B; Norman 1992a: 226 [notes to Sn 424], 277 [notes to Sn 681], 380 [notes to Sn 1098]).[52] The employment of this uncommon absolutive in *-tu* in our G text is parallel to the use of the uncommon absolutive in *-ti* in the Dhp-G^{K}, the latter based on the Vedic *-tvī* absolutive (see von Hinüber 1986: § 498).

Finally, although the use of the verb *ā* + √*jñā* in this context, where *vi* + √*jñā* seems to be the form found throughout Buddhist literature, is indeed exceptional, the basis for this substitution of synonyms is seen in such canonical expressions as *atha kho brahmā sahampati bhagavato cetasā cetoparivitakkam aññāya* (e.g., MN II 458.12–3) and in

[51] In the Senior mss. (20 r8) *manasa* is a loc. sg.

[52] The comms. to Sn 424 (Pj II 385.20), 681 (Pj II 485.23–4), and 1098 (Pj II 598.15–7) gloss *daṭṭhu(ṃ)* as *disvā*.

commentarial lists of synonyms, for example, *jānāmi ājānāmi vijānāmi paṭijānāmi paṭivijjhāmi* (Nidd II 223.4; cf. Nidd I 41.16–7; Nidd II 92.28, 189.24, etc.).[53]

Lines 60–3: The effort of protecting (*aṇorakṣaṇaprasaṇa*)

Edition:

| 28a
[60] *kadara bhikṣave [a] ///* [61]*ṇe ◦ [a] aï bhikṣave bhikhuṇa añadara añadara samas[i]ṇimi[ti] ///* [62] *bhavadi ◦ sayasavi viṇilaü v[i]puao a ◦ aṭhisaña [va] p. ? ///* [63] *tae aṇorakṣa[e] sapadedi idi vucadi aṇorakṣaṇaprasaṇo ◦*

Reconstruction:
[60] *kadara bhikṣave a(*ṇorakṣaṇaprasa)*[61]*ṇe ◦ aï bhikṣave bhikhuṇa añadara añadara samasiṇimiti (*sughrahido ???)* [62] *bhavadi ◦ sayasavi viṇilaü vipuao a ◦ aṭhisaña va p(*uḍavayasaña va ???)* [63] *tae aṇorakṣae sapadedi idi vucadi aṇorakṣaṇaprasaṇo ◦*

Translation:
[60] "What, Monks, is the effort of protecting? [61] Here, Monks, one or other sign of concentration is (*well grasped) . . . by a monk, [62] namely, the [perception of] a blue-black corpse or the [perception of] a corpse full of pus or the perception of a skeleton (*or the perception of a worm-eaten corpse). . . . [63] He causes [it] to succeed through that protection. This is called the effort of protecting."

In this *prasaṇa* one strives to protect arisen profitable states of mind. As in other sections of the G text, the phrasing of the G version of this *prasaṇa* is not identical with any one known Indic version, though most of the component elements are encountered elsewhere in Buddhist literature in similar contexts.

kadara bhikṣave [a] /// [61]*ṇe ◦* and *idi vucadi aṇorakṣaṇaprasaṇo ◦:* The structure and most of the wording of the opening question and concluding statement of this *prasaṇa* are the same as in the previous *prasaṇa*. Based on the concluding statement (and *aṇorakṣaṇaprasa[ṇe]* in l. 40), the opening question can be reconstructed as *kadara bhikṣave a(*ṇorakṣaṇaprasa)ṇe ◦*. The corresponding Pali has *katamañ ca bhikkhave anurakkhanappadhānaṃ* (AN II 17.1) and *idaṃ vuccati bhikkhave anurakkhana-ppadhānaṃ* (AN II 17.5–6), with the B^{e} reading *anurakkhaṇāppadhānaṃ*. (I adopt the reading *anurakkhaṇā* throughout this study for the noncompounded word.)

[a] aï bhikṣave bhikhuṇa añadara añadara samas[i]ṇimi[ti] /// [62] *bhavadi ◦:* The word *aï* is preceded by a faint, smudged vowel sign, perhaps an *a, o,* or *i,* caused by the ink's having run due to a defect (perhaps a knot) in the bark. It appears that the scribe

[53] Cf. also Mvu I 172.14, where the Buddha's voice (*vācā*) is described as *ājñeyā vijñeyā. Viññāya* is glossed as *jānitvā* at Sv III 949.30; Dhp-a III 240.21–2; Jā II 314.5.

rubbed out the first attempt at writing the *a* of *aï* when the ink ran, then started again. The alternative explanation is that he wrote the wrong vowel, rubbed it out, and started again.

The P version, though containing a similar list of perceptions of the body in various states of decomposition, is fundamentally different from the G version in its the overall structure:

idha bhikkhave bhikkhu uppannaṃ bhaddakaṃ samādhinimittaṃ anurakkhati aṭṭhikasaññaṃ puḷavakasaññaṃ vinīlakasaññaṃ vipubbakasaññaṃ vicchiddaka-saññaṃ uddhumātakasaññaṃ. (AN II 17.2–5 = DN III 226.28–31)

Here, Monks, a monk guards an arisen favorable sign of concentration . . .

The P parallel to the structure of the G version is found in the description of the fifth of the five *vimuttāyatanas* (Skt. *vimuktyāyatana*), "occasions of being released," which appear in the Saṅgīti- and Dasuttara-suttantas and elsewhere:

api ca kho assa aññataraṃ samādhinimittaṃ suggahītaṃ hoti sumanasikataṃ supadhāritaṃ suppaṭividdhaṃ paññāya. yathā yathā āvuso bhikkhuno aññataraṃ samādhinimittaṃ . . . (DN III 242, 279; AN III 23)

Further, of this one a certain sign of concentration is well grasped, well attended to . . .

The Skt. parallel in the Daśottara-sūtra is quite fragmentary but seems to differ only slightly:

*'(*p)i ca khal(*v asya bhikṣor anyataraṃ sam)ādhinimi(*ttaṃ bhavati sugṛ)hītaṃ sumanasik(*ṛtaṃ supradhāritaṃ) s(*u)pratividdhaṃ yathā yath(*ā) khal(*v asya bhikṣor* . . . (Daśo § V.9 [5a–b])[54]

In the P and the reconstructed Skt. we have the agentive genitive (P *assa . . . bhikkhuno*/Skt. *asya bhikṣor*) while in the G text *bhikhuṇa* is most likely instrumental, equivalent to a P *bhikkhunā*. This finds a parallel in an expanded version of this *vimuktyāyatana* found in the AKV (see de Jong 1966: 19) where the agentive instrumental is used:

api tv anenānyatamaṃ bhadrakaṃ samādhinimittaṃ sādhu ca suṣṭhu ca sūdgṛhītaṃ bhavati sumanasikṛtaṃ subhāvitaṃ sujuṣṭaṃ supratividdhaṃ. tadyathā vinīlakaṃ vā vipūyakaṃ vā vyādhmātakaṃ vā vipaṭumakaṃ vā vilohitakaṃ vā vikhāditakaṃ vā vikṣiptakaṃ vā asthi vā asthisaṃkalikā vā. yathā yathā . . . (AKV 54.31–55.2)

---

[54] The text was reconstructed by Mittal following the Pali. I have edited it here using 5a and b. Based on a number of similar phrases in the mss., Mittal (1957: 73 n. 7) notes that *sujuṣṭaḥ* may be preferable to *supradhāritaṃ*.

Unfortunately, the Skt. fragment SHT V 1445+1447 preserves only remnants of the description of *anurakṣaṇāprahāṇa:*

> *///* + + .. + *.ā* .. .. *.[i]r* .. *.ā .i* .. + *ṣ[ṭha] ca anurakṣi[ta]vyaṃ manyate* + + (V4, possibly continued on V5)

In this case, what remains of the wording seems to differ from all other versions.

Based on these parallels, and given that *bhavadi* (= Skt. *bhavati*) begins line 62, the text missing at the end of line 61 of the G must have contained one or more past participles. The line currently contains twenty-five akṣaras (including the punctuation mark). Line 60 contains twenty-eight akṣaras and is missing six, making a total of thirty-four akṣaras. As lines 63 to 72 had between thirty and thirty-two akṣaras per line, line 61 may be missing between five and nine akṣaras, though I am inclined to think that the former is more likely. Although we cannot say what the missing wording was, the P and Skt. parallels suggest that it probably included the G equivalent of the past participle P *suggahītaṃ*/Skt. *sugr̥hītaṃ, sūdgr̥hītaṃ* (even though in the Daśo version this seems to have followed *bhavati*). This word is found in the Dhp-G^{K} (216a) as *sugahido* and would have been written **sughahido* or more likely **sughrahido* in our manuscript (cf. *kirṇo* = Skt. *kr̥ṣṇaḥ, proṭhu* = Skt. *pr̥ṣṭaḥ,* and *-ghrahi/-ghrahe* = Skt. *-grāhī* elsewhere in this manuscript). But because this represents only four akṣaras, it is therefore likely that either another past participle was present or that an adverb, such as *sādhu* or *suṣṭhu* as found in the AKV parallel, preceded *(*sughrahido).* If two past participles were present, then the G equivalent of P *sumanasikataṃ, supadhāritaṃ,* or *suppaṭividdhaṃ,* or of Skt. *sujuṣṭaṃ,* are possible contenders.[55] I tentatively include *(*sughrahido)* in my reconstruction.

aï: See discussion on page 270.

añadara añadara samas[i]ṇimi[ti] ///: The parallels are P *aññataraṃ samādhinimittaṃ* (e.g., DN III 242.23–4); Skt. *anyatamaṃ bhadrakaṃ samādhinimittaṃ* (AKV 54.32); *(*anyataraṃ sam)ādhinimi(*ttaṃ)* (Daśo § V.9 [5a–b]); and *anyatamānyatamaṃ bhadrakaṃ samādhinimittaṃ* (ŚBh(T) 154.22). The P parallel and the Skt. AKV parallel differ from the Gāndhārī in not repeating *aññataraṃ/anyataraṃ* (the Daśo occurrence is reconstructed). The Pali, for example, means "a certain sign of concentration," whereas the meaning of the Gāndhārī is "one or other sign of concentration."[56] But a parallel to the repeated pronominal adjective in the Gāndhārī is seen in *anyatamānyatamaṃ* of the ŚBh(T) example. The inclusion of the adjective *bhadrakaṃ,* "favorable," in the AKV and ŚBh versions is parallel to the inclusion of this word in the definition of *anurakkhaṇappadhāna* in the P Saṃvara-sutta (AN II 17.2–3).

G *añadara añadara* probably represents two separate words, the equivalent of a P *aññataraṃ aññataraṃ* (which does not seem to occur), both declined in the nominative singular neuter in agreement with *samasiṇimiti*. However, as the compound form *aññata-*

---

[55] In Pali, *suggahī̆ta* occurs in another, slightly different, common list: *sussutaṃ suggahī̆taṃ sumanasikataṃ sūpadhāritaṃ* (MN I 252–3, III 104; AN IV 370, etc.).

[56] See CPD, s.v. *aññatarāññatara.*

raññatara is the regular form in P canonical texts,[57] and as the ŚBh example similarly knows the compound form (*anyatamānyatamaṃ*), this may be an example of a compound with vowel hiatus tolerated at the compound juncture. Although similar vowels at compound juncture are normally contracted in the Prakrits, as in P *aññataraññatara,* examples are found, particularly in Ardhamāgadhī, where hiatus is permitted (see Pischel 1965: § 156).[58] Further examples in Gāndhārī are needed to clarify this issue. It is also possible to treat this as one long compound: *añadara-añadara-samasiṇimiti.* Similar phrases are encountered in Pali in both the compound and noncompound forms, with one sometimes the variant reading of the other. For example, the E[e] of AN IV 56.5–6, reads *aññataraññataraṃ methunasaṃyogaṃ,* while the B[e] reads *aññataraññataramethunasaṃyogaṃ.*

As previously discussed (see § 5.1.2), the G text reads *ṇimiti* throughout this sūtra in all instances where P and Skt. parallels have *nimitta,* with change of *-a* to *-i* in the *i* environment of *samasi-* in this instance and of *-grahe* (= Skt. *-grāhī*) in previous occurrences. *Samasiṇimiti* is therefore taken to be the G equivalent of P/Skt. *samādhinimittaṃ,* declined in the nominative singular neuter.

sayasavi viṇilaü v[i]puao a ◦ aṭ́hisaña [va] p. ? ///: The list of *samādhinimitta*s that are to be attended to is introduced by *sayasavi* (P *seyyathāpi*/BHS *sayyathāpi*). The absence of this element in the P parallel may be due to the difference in structure. The AKV parallel, which is closer to the Gāndhārī in its overall structure, has *tadyathā,* the regular Skt. form.

In canonical Pali, lists are normally introduced by *seyyathĭ̄daṃ* rather than *seyyathāpi,* for example, *te evarūpaṃ visūkadassanaṃ anuyuttā viharanti seyyathīdaṃ naccaṃ gītaṃ vāditaṃ pekkhaṃ akkhānaṃ . . .* (DN I 6.10–8), whereas in Buddhist Skt. texts they are introduced by *sayyathīdaṃ* or *tadyathā.* P *seyyathāpi*/BHS *sayyathāpi* usually means “as,” “just as,” and is commonly employed in similes, forming a part of the structure P *seyyathāpi . . . evaṃ eva,* “just as . . . even so.” Such a usage occurs in this G manuscript also: *suyasavi . . . evam eva* (ll. 21–3). However, the BHSD (s.v. *yathāpi* 3, p. 443) notes that on rare occasions *sayyathāpi* is used in Buddhist Skt. texts like *sayyathīdaṃ,* “namely,” just as occasionally *seyyathāpi* is so used in Pali (e.g., DN III 218–9). The G text thus attests this less common usage. See p. 209 for further discussion of *sayasavi/ suyasavi.*

The list of *samādhinimitta*s (G *samasiṇimiti*), “signs of concentration,” is a list of perceptions (G *saña*/P *saññā*/Skt. *saṃjñā*) of the body in various states of decay. As in the Skt. parallel in the AKV and in the corresponding passage in the P Saṃvara-sutta, these perceptions are often referred to as “favorable” or “good” (P *bhaddaka*/Skt. *bhadraka*)—a designation missing in the Gāndhārī—because their presence brings about the destruction of *rāga,* “lust,” or *kāmacchanda,* “sensual desire,” and ensures their absence.[59] These *samādhinimitta*s are therefore an important subject of meditation.

---

[57] See PTC and CPD, s.v. *aññataraññatara.*

[58] Cf. P *akkhara-akkharāya,* representing *akkharā-akkharā,* “every syllable” (Vin IV 15.12, 22.28, 200.16, etc.).

[59] See CPD and PTC, s.v. *asubha,* for further references.

Such lists of terms describing the body in decay are encountered in a variety of contexts in Buddhist literature, with the number of component elements included ranging from two to ten. Some of the component elements, particularly *vinīlaka,* are of course also found individually in other contexts.

The simplest list in the P material is probably that found in Sn 200, containing two elements: *yadā ca so mato seti uddhumāto vinīlako, apaviddho susānasmiṃ anapekhā honti ñātayo.* A more common list contains three terms: *passeyya sarīraṃ . . . uddhumātakaṃ vinīlakaṃ vipubbakajātaṃ.*[60] A list of five forms the second half of a list of ten subjects of meditation: *dasa yimā bhikkhave saññā bhāvitā . . . anicca-saññā anatta~ maraṇa~ āhāre paṭikkula~ sabbaloke anabhirata~ aṭṭhika~ puḷavaka~* [v.l. *puḷuvaka*] *vinīlaka~ vicchiddaka~ uddhumātaka~* (AN V 106).[61]

A similar list of ten dhammas given at AN V 310 inserts *vipubbaka-saññā* before *vicchiddaka-saññā,* thus making six in total referring to a corpse, with *maraṇa-saññā* omitted from the first half of the list to maintain a total of ten (three Sinh. manuscripts read *vicchiddaka~ vipubbaka~*). This is the same list as that in the P Saṃvara-sutta: *aṭṭhikasaññaṃ puḷavakasaññaṃ*[62] *vinīlakasaññaṃ vipubbakasaññaṃ vicchiddakasaññaṃ uddhumātakasaññaṃ* (AN II 17.3–5). However, the E^e, B^e, and S^e of the parallel passage found at DN III 226.30–1, omit *vipubbakasaññaṃ,* as does the B^e of this AN II 17 passage. Given that the commentary to the AN II 17 passage specifically refers to five perceptions,[63] it seems that *vipubbakasaññaṃ* has been included in some manuscripts and editions due to its inclusion in longer lists, for instance, the Vism list below.

Finally, a list with ten elements found in later P texts (the Dhs, Paṭis, Vism, and Mil) is the most extensive one. These are called the ten impure (things to be contemplated), the *dasa asubhā,* which are the same as the *asubhabhāvanā:*

> *uddhumātakaṃ vinīlakaṃ vipubbakaṃ vicchiddakaṃ vikkhāyitakaṃ vikkhittakaṃ hatavikkhittakaṃ lohitakaṃ puḷuvakaṃ*[64] *aṭṭhikan ti ime dasa asubhā.* (Vism 110.29–31)[65]

The P tradition thus preserves lists with two, three, five, six, and ten elements, with the manuscripts and editions of some occurrences showing additions or omissions, and at least one example where several manuscripts reverse the order of two elements.[66]

---

[60] DN II 295; MN I 58, 88, III 91, 182; AN I 140, III 324.

[61] Cf. AN I 41–2; SN V 131. As elsewhere, these references have the v.l. *puḷuvaka-* for *puḷavaka-*.

[62] The E^e records the v.l. *paḷuvaka.* B^e and S^e read as E^e (*puḷavaka*), though the B^e to DN III 226 reads *puḷuvaka~*.

[63] The comm. (Mp III 20.6–8) states that although five are listed here, the ten given in the Vism should be understood: *ettha ca aṭṭhiksaññādikā pañc' eva saññā vuttā. imasmiṃ pana ṭhāne dasa pi asubhāni vitthāretvā kathetabbāni; tesaṃ vitthāro visuddhimagge vutto yeva.*

[64] V.l. *puḷavakaṃ* in the Vism (Warren 1950: 145).

[65] Cf. Paṭis I 49, 95; Dhs 55; Mil 332.19–22. The full description of each element is found at Vism 178–9.

[66] Three of the Sinh. mss. used for AN V 310 read *vicchiddaka~ vipubbaka~* rather than the reverse.

Parallel lists with a similar range in the number of elements are encountered in Buddhist Skt. texts, with greater divergence in ordering due to their disparate origins. In the Śikṣ, for example, a list is found that merely adds one item to the list of three found in the P (DN II 295, etc.):

> *paśyati nānārūpāṇi mṛtaśarīrāṇi . . . vyādhmātakāni vinīlakāni vipūyakāni vipaṭmakāni*. (Śikṣ 210.15–211.1)

A parallel passage found in the ŚSPP(G) adds three new terms to the initial three:

> *paśyati . . . vyādhmātakāni vā vinīlakāni vā vipūtikāni vā vikhāditakāni vā vilohitakāni vā vikṣiptakāni vā.* (1431.17–21)

Under the heading *aśubhabhāvanāḥ,* the Mvy (1155–64) lists nine elements, a list which closely parallels the Vism's *dasa asubhā* list:

> *aśubhabhāvanāḥ* (1) *vinīlaka-saṃjñā* (2) *vidhūtika-(vipūyaka)~*[67] (3) *vipaḍumaka~* (4) *vyādhmātaka~* (5) *vilohitaka~* (6) *vikhāditaka~* (7) *vikṣiptaka~* (8) *vidagdhaka~* (9) *asthi~*.

Similar lists of nine are also found, though with divergences in ordering and reading as well as in the actual terms included:[68]

> *navasaṃjñā bhāvayitavyā dhyātaka-saṃjñā bhāvayitavyā . . . vipadāka~ . . . vipūtika~ . . . vilohita~ . . . vinīlaka~ . . . vikhāditaka~ . . . vikṣiptaka~ . . . asthi~ . . . vidagdhaka~*. (ŚSPP(G) 59.1 ff.)[69]

> *tadyathā vinīlakaṃ vā vipūyakaṃ vā vyādhmātakaṃ vā vipaṭumakaṃ vā vilohitakaṃ vā vikhāditakaṃ vā vikṣiptakaṃ vā asthi vā asthisaṃkalikā vā.* (AKV 54.33–55.2)

The BhīKaVā(R/LVP) preserves a list containing eight members, in which the ninth, *vidagdhaka-,* has been accidentally omitted according to Edgerton (BHSD, s.v. *aśubhabhāvanā*):[70]

> *lābhy aham asmy anityasaṃjñāyā . . . aśubhasaṃjñāyā vinīlaka-saṃjñāyā vipūyaka~ vipaṭumaka~ vyādhmātaka~ vikhyāditaka~ vilohitaka~ vikṣiptaka~ asthi~*. (27 a2, quoted in SWTF, s.v. *aśubha-saṃjñā,* vol. 1, p. 565)

---

[67] BHSD (s.v. *aśubhabhāvanā*) reads *vipūyaka~.*

[68] Cf. ŚBh(T) 154.20–2. Further Skt. references are given in Lamotte 1944–80: 34 n. 2.

[69] Cf. *laukikā navasaṃjñāḥ yaduta vyādhatika-saṃjñā niruttamaka~ vipūtika~ vilohitaka~ vilīnaka~ vivādika~ vikṣiptaka~ asmi~ vidagnaka~* (ŚSPP(G) 1258.5–8).

[70] Given that the number of elements included in these lists varies greatly (unless a specific number has been specified), it is possible that *vidagdhaka-* was not omitted but that the reading is valid.

Finally, several fragments from Central Asia have been published that contain such lists; most important is a fragment of the Daśabala-sūtra (DbSū(2) Y 906^{9} 5–7 and 906^{11} V1–2) edited by Waldschmidt (1958: 383–4):[71]

> *(*vidagdhakasaṃ)jñā* | *vinīlakasaṃjñā* | *vipūyakasa(*ṃ)jñā* | *[vi](*pa)ṭmakasaṃjñā* | *vyādhmātakasaṃjñā* | *vikhāditakasaṃjñā* | *vil[oh](*i)takasa[ṃ]jñā vikṣiptakasa(*ṃ)jñā* | *asthisaṃjñā* | *śunyatāpratyavekṣaṇasaṃ-*.[72]

The two Chinese translations of this sūtra (T nos. 99 and 150a) differ from each other in the number of elements listed in this passage. No. 150a (p. 877c8–9) lists six: oozing red and bloated (紅汁膖脹), half-eaten by foxes and dogs (狐犬半食), running red with blood (若血流赤), putrid greenish black (若青黑腐), white bones (若骨白), and a skull (若髑髏). No. 99 (p. 221b27–8) lists five: blue (青瘀), swollen (脹), pussy (膿), rotten (壞食), impure (不盡, v.l. 淨).[73]

The diversity encountered in these lists in terms of both the number of elements included and their ordering is quite typical of certain classes of lists commonly found in Buddhist literature. In contrast to lists such as the four truths or the Noble Eightfold Path that are fixed by their very nature, the description of a decomposing corpse allows for much flexibility. There is a natural tendency for such flexible lists to expand with time. In the P material the list containing ten elements is found only in the later strata of the canon or in paracanonical material, that is, in the canonical Paṭis and Dhs and in the paracanonical Vism and Mil, as well as in commentarial texts. We can see this process at work in the addition of a sixth element in some manuscripts and editions of the P parallel (AN II 17) to our G text, perhaps on the basis of its inclusion in the Vism list, even though the commentary (Mp III 20.6) states that there are only five. And as already mentioned above (see n. 63), this commentary considers the list of five to be an abbreviation of the ten given in the Vism, or at least implies that the list should be so expanded (Mp III 20.7–8). Shorter lists, however, may not always be earlier. For example, the function of a passage may not require the expanded list. This is clearly the case with the Sn verse that lists only two elements and the common P canonical passage with three elements (both quoted above). Neither of these passages has as its purpose the full description of possible subjects of meditation. Besides, even the most expansive list is not exhaustive in its description. It is therefore not surprising that some Skt. lists include *vidagdhaka,* "a corpse that is burnt," instead of *hatavikkhittaka,* "a corpse that is broken up and scattered," of the P list; the latter designation is merely an expansion of the previous term *vikkhittaka*.

---

[71] Cf. the fragmentary SHT VI 1420 A1–2 and VII 1689 f V1 and see Schlingloff 1964: 59–62.

[72] Considering that the SHT VI 1420 A1–2 fragment containing this list begins with *vinīlaka* and that *vidagdhakasaṃjñā* normally ends the list when it does occur in Sanskrit, Waldschmidt's reconstruction of *(*vidagdhakasaṃ)jñā* at the beginning of this list (no doubt in order to make nine elements) may not be correct.

[73] See Lamotte 1944–80: 1311–3 for further Chinese examples. The Mahāprajñāpāramitāśāstra discusses each of these terms (Lamotte 1944–80: 1314 ff.).

As for the ordering of the terms, the variability seems to be in part the result of the nature of the list. Given that the list in the Vism begins with *uddhumātaka,* "a bloated corpse," and ends with *aṭṭhika,* "a skeleton" (an order that is reversed in a number of the other P lists), and the Mvy list begins with *vinīlaka-saṃjñā,* "perception of a blue-black corpse," and ends with *asthi-saṃjñā,* "perception of a skeleton," it is tempting to see these lists as a description of a corpse in decay, presented in either progressive or reverse order. However, a closer examination of these lists reveals that this is not the case. For example, in the Vism list (which begins with *uddhumātaka,* "a bloated corpse"), *vikkhittaka,* "a corpse scattered or dispersed," precedes *lohitaka,* "a bloody corpse," and *puḷavaka,* "a worm-eaten corpse." Further, the order of certain terms seems to remain stable regardless of whether *aṭṭhika* begins or ends the list. In the P material, for example, *vinīlaka,* "a blue-black corpse," always precedes *vicchiddaka,* "a corpse with cuts or fissures" (sometimes with *vipubbaka,* "a corpse full of pus," interposed between the two). Similarly, in the Skt. material the grouping *vinīlaka vipūyaka* (where *vipūyaka* = P *vipubbaka*) seems to remain stable, with *vyādhmātaka* (= P *uddhumātaka*) preceding this pair in some lists and following in others.

Turning to the G list, the first three terms are clear. *Viṇilaü* represents P/Skt. *vinīlaka,* "a blue-black corpse." The word is also found in the AG-G as *viṇi[la.o]* (l. 35). *Vipuao,* not attested elsewhere in Gāndhārī, represents BHS *vipūyaka,*[74] with elision of intervocalic *-y-* and *-k-,* rather than *vipubbaka* of the Pali, "a corpse full of pus."[75] These two terms are then followed by an *a,* which must be a separate word (of which more below) since it is followed by a punctuation mark. The third term is *aṭ́hisaña,* which represents P *aṭṭhika-saññā*/Skt. *asthi-saṃjñā,* "the perception of a skeleton." *Aṭhi* or *aṭ́hi* for Skt. *asthi,* "bone," appears elsewhere in Gāndhārī.[76]

As noted above, *a,* which must be a separate word, occurs between the second and third elements of the list. It could represent either the conjunctive Skt. *ca,* "and," or the disjunctive *vā,* "or." Original *ca* appearing as *a* is attested in other G documents.[77] Although *a* for original *vā* has not so far been recorded in Gāndhārī, the appearance of what is probably *[va]* rather than *[a]* (the reading in this portion of the text is not fully clear) after *aṭ́hisaña,* the third member of the list, suggests that the word represents original *vā.* This is supported by the fact that in the AKV and ŚSPP(G) occurrences of such lists (quoted above), which are the only ones among the Skt. and P parallels to

[74] BHS also knows *vipūtika* (see BHSD, s.v.).

[75] Geiger (1994: § 46.1) lists P *pubba,* "pus," as an example of P *v* for Skt. *y,* with short V + CC/long V + C alternation: Vedic *pūya* > **pūva* > **puvva* > *pubba.* See also Norman 1979a: 43 (= CP, vol. II, p. 120).

[76] See Burrow 1937: § 49; Dhp-G^{K} 155, 284. The problem of the correct transcription and understanding of the G group *ṭh/ṭ́h* has been discussed in detail by Brough (1962: §§ 18, 18a, 18b); see also pp. 94–5.

[77] It has been recorded once in the BL scrolls so far studied (Khvs-G 6b). According to Boyer, Rapson, and Senart (1920–9: index, s.v., *ko a*), *a* for *ca* occurs twice in the Niya documents in the expression *ko a* (besides *ko ca*), though Burrow (1937: § 92) preferred to interpret this *a* as the preposition *ā* because "*c* is never otherwise omitted." It is also found in the Indravarman (Avaca) casket inscription (see Salomon and Schopen 1984: 108).

include such particles, the particle is *vā*. Besides, in the G text "one or other sign of concentration" (*añadara añadara samasiṇimiti*) is protected, and in the AKV a "certain favorable sign of concentration" (*anyatamaṃ bhadrakaṃ samādhinimittaṃ*) is protected, rather than each and every sign of concentration.

The remnants of two more akṣaras appear at the end of this line (l. 62). The first is the top of a *p.*, which could represent *p(*a)*, *p(*u)*, or *p(*o)*. This is followed by the remnant of an illegible akṣara. Given that *tae aṇorakṣa[e] sapadedi* begins the next line (l. 63), these two akṣaras may be the remnant of the first of one or more further perceptions (*-saña*) that occupied the remainder of this line. If so, the initial *p.* suggests *puḷavaka-(saññaṃ)* of the Pali (with v.l. *puḷuvaka~*), "the perception of a worm-eaten corpse." This appears in the Skt. examples as *vipaṭumaka, vipaḍumaka,* and *vipaṭmaka*. The BHS forms suggest that the akṣara preceding *p.*, which I have read as *[va]*, could be part of this word. However, there seems to be no *i* diacritic present. Although the scribal omission of vowels does occur in this manuscript (*-ṇaṣide* and perhaps also *-ṇiṣida* for *-ṇiside* and *praṣadha-* for BHS *praśrabdhi-*), it would be unusual in the prefix *vi-*. I therefore take *[va]* to represent Skt. *vā*.

The G equivalent of P *puḷavaka/puḷuvaka* and BHS *vipaṭumaka/vipaḍumaka/ vipaṭmaka* is not recorded. It would probably be **puḍavaya* or **puḍuvaya* based on the Pali (or possibly **vipaḍumaya* based on the BHS). This may have been combined with *-saña* (= Skt. *-saṃjñāṃ*) as in *aṭhisaña* or have simply occurred alone as in the first two elements in the list, *viṇilaü v[i]puao*. It is also possible that the particle *a* or *va* (= Skt. *vā*) occurred again after this word, given the pattern of the previous wording. Line 62 has twenty-five akṣaras, including the punctuation marks. The repetitions in the following text enable us to calculate that lines 63–72 had thirty to thirty-two akṣaras each. Line 62 is therefore probably missing five to seven (perhaps more) akṣaras. Reconstructing *p(*uḍavaya)* or *p(*uḍuvaya)* would only bring the akṣara count up to twenty-seven (or twenty-eight if followed by a disjunctive particle), while *p(*uḍavayasaña)* or *p(*uḍuvayasaña)* would make twenty-nine (or thirty with the particle). The reconstruction *p(*uḍavayasaña va ◦)* would produce a count of thirty-one akṣaras for the line, completing the expected number of missing akṣaras. Alternatively, a reconstruction of a noncompounded *p(*uḍavaya)* would leave room for at least one further member of the list, perhaps the equivalent of P *uddhumātaka* or *uddhumātaka-saññaṃ,* "the (perception of) a bloated corpse" (cf. *udh[u]maü* in the AG-G, l. 35), or *vicchiddaka* or *vicchiddaka-saññaṃ,* "the (perception of) a corpse with cuts or fissures." Particles and punctuation marks may or may not have been present.

Thus, as it stands, the G list has only three certain members: *viṇilaü,* "the [perception of] a blue-black corpse"; *vipuao,* "the [perception of] a corpse full of pus"; and *aṭhisaña,* "the perception of a skeleton." The presence of further members remains uncertain. If the reconstruction above is correct, then the list contained at least four members, possibly five.

The order of the first two members of the G list, *viṇilaü vipuao,* is encountered in the majority of the P and Skt. examples given above. However, in the P examples *aṭṭhika-saññā* appears as either the first or final member of the list, while in the Skt. examples *asthi-(saṃjñāṃ)* is the final or penultimate member. Of the two Chinese translations of this sūtra, only T no. 150a includes this word. In this case it appears as the penultimate member of the list, while the last is the perception of a skull (p. 877c9). If *p(*uḍavaya)* did come after *aṭhisaña,* then the G order *aṭhisaña va p(*uḍavayasaña)* would reflect the pairing seen in the P *aṭṭhikasaññaṃ puḷavakasaññaṃ* (AN II 17.3, V 106.6–7).

The fact that *aṭṭhikasaññā/asthisaṃjñā* occurs at either the beginning or the end of all lists so far encountered suggests an alternative interpretation for this G passage: this passage may be abbreviated, with only the first, second, and last members given out of a longer list of an uncertain number. In this case the *a* that follows the second member (*v[i]puao a* ◦) may be the preposition *ā,* "as far as," used to indicate that abbreviation has taken place. This is not the usual term employed to indicate abbreviation in Buddhist texts,[78] but according to Norman (1969b: 227–31 = CP, vol. I, pp. 87–90), in the Aśokan inscriptions *a* and *ā* can represent a dialect variant of *(y)āva* (Skt. *yāvat*), with both *a/ā* and *āva* used to indicate an abbreviation. In this context the words that precede and follow it are in the same case. He suggests, for example, that the phrase *coḍa-paṃḍiyā āva taṃbapaṃniyā* at Rock Edict XIII(Q), where Mānsehrā has *a* for *āva,* Shāhbāzgaṛhī has *ava,* Kālsī has *avaṃ,* and Ye[ṛṛ]aguḍi has *ā,* should be translated as "the *Coḍas,* the *Pāṇḍyas* (and so on, down to) the inhabitants of *Taṃbapaṃnī."* The theory that the G text is abbreviated may be supported by the fact that neither of the first two elements in the list are in compound with *-saña* (= Skt. *saṃjñā*), unlike all other parallel lists. According to this interpretation the translation would be "namely, [the perception of] a blue-black corpse, [the perception of] a corpse full of pus, and so on, down to the perception of a skeleton."

There are two major problems with this interpretation, however. The first is that this would be the only instance of abbreviation of this kind in this manuscript. Throughout this manuscript repetitive passages are always given in full. Second, if we are to take *aṭhisaña* as the end of the list, then the following wording would represent a new syntactic unit. The inclusion of such a unit would find no equivalent in the parallel P, Skt., or Chinese passages. I therefore adopt the reconstruction *p(*uḍavayasaña va)* as the equivalent of a P *puḷavakasaññaṃ vā,* leaving open the possibility that there was one further member of the list.

tae aṇorakṣa[e] sapadedi: The final *[e]* in *aṇorakṣa[e]* appears as a faint addition below the line and thus is a correction. This phrase affords several possible interpretations. Although *sapadedi* = P *sampādeti* has no parallel in the P or Skt. versions of either the description of *anurakkhaṇā/anurakṣaṇā* or the fifth *vimuttāyatana/ vimuktāyatana* as presented above, in the P canon we do find *sampādeti* used in similar contexts. For example:

> *chahi bhikkhave dhammehi samannāgato bhikkhu bhabbo anadhigataṃ vā kusalaṃ dhammaṃ adhigantuṃ adhigataṃ vā kusalaṃ dhammaṃ phātikātuṃ. katamehi chahi. idha bhikkhave bhikkhu āyakusalo ca hoti apāyakusalo ca hoti upāyakusalo ca hoti anadhigatānaṃ kusalānaṃ dhammānaṃ adhigamāya*

[78] Such a usage is not recorded in CPD (s.v. *ā*).

chandaṃ janeti adhigate kusale dhamme sārakkhati[79] sātaccakiriyāya sampādeti. (AN III 431–2)

Although *sātaccakiriyāya* in this passage could be in the dative singular feminine, in P *sampādeti* most often takes the instrumental, for example, *idha . . . kulaputtassa bhogā honti uṭṭhānaviriyādhigatā . . . te ārakkhena guttiyā sampādeti 'kinti me ime bhoge neva rājāno hareyyuṃ . . .'* (AN IV 281–2, 286, 323),[80] ". . . he causes them to succeed through protection and guarding. . . ."[81] We would thus translate *sātaccakiriyāya sampādeti* as "he causes (them) to succeed through perseverance" or simply "he perseveres." This suggests that *aṇorakṣae* of the Gāndhārī should also be taken as an instrumental singular feminine.

In canonical Pali *anurakkhā* (f.) is quite rare. Examples are *anurakkhaṃ vaṇṇeti* (SN IV 323.22, ff.) and *attānurakkhāya bhavanti h' ete* (Jā V 486.18).[82] Further, in contrast to the more common and synonymous *ārakkhā̆* (m. or f.), it is not recorded in conjunction with *sampādeti.*[83] A few examples of *anurakṣā* are also encountered in Buddhist Skt. texts (see BHSD, s.v.),[84] but again, none of the occurrences so far researched are constructed with *saṃpādayati*. The Central Asian fragment of the Prahāṇa-sūtra, SHT V 1445+1447, contains the similar phrase */// + sya ārakṣāya guptaye damathā[ya] pratipanno bhavati* (V3). It therefore seems that in this G text we have a substitution of synonyms in this phrase: *aṇorakṣae sapadedi* of the Gāndhārī for *ārakkhena sampādeti* of the Pali.

Although *tae,* which begins the line, could be the end of a word which started on the previous line (a dat. sg. m., n., or oblique f.), it is more likely to be the instrumental singular feminine of the demonstrative pronoun (= P *tāya*) qualifying *aṇorakṣae:* "he causes [it] to succeed through that protection."[85]

The alternative interpretation is to read this as *ta e,* representing *taṃ ca*. In the Khvs-G, *e* for original *ca* occurs once in *asevamaṇa mutita e kalo* (36b), where the Pali has *āsevamāno muditañ ca kāle* (Sn 73b), and there are numerous examples of *i* for *ca* in the

---

[79] V.l. *ārakkhati* (also the reading of B^e). The comm. (Mp III 412.26) glosses *rakkhati.*

[80] Cf. *yaṃ bhattā āharati dhanaṃ vā dhaññaṃ vā rajataṃ vā jātarūpaṃ vā taṃ ārakkhena guttiyā sampādeti* (AN IV 266, 268, 270), which Hare (1935: 179) translates as "she keeps it secure by watch and ward"; *taṃ kho pana dhammaṃ sutvā dvayena vūpakāsena sampādeti* (DN III 285 = AN IV 152, 154), which Rhys Davids and Rhys Davids (1921: 260) translate as "succeeds in obtaining. . . ." For the inf. with instr. constructions, see, e.g., SN II 29.17–8 = AN IV 134.30–1. The abs. only occurs in the Vin and Jā, where it is constructed with the acc., e.g., *imaṃ maṃsaṃ sampādetvā* (Vin I 217.15).

[81] Hare (1935: 188) translates this as ". . . such he husbands by watch and ward. . . ."

[82] A few examples are found in later layers of the canon, e.g., *kulānurakkhāya* (Nidd I 496.7) and *tassānurakkhāya* (Vin V 167.37), or in commentarial or other paracanonical texts.

[83] Examples of *ārakkha* + *sampādeti* have already been given. An example of *ārakkha* in a similar phrase, but without *sampādeti,* is *evam eva kho bhikkhave bhikkhu imesaṃ channaṃ indriyānaṃ ārakkhāya sikkhati* (SN IV 176.21–2).

[84] The SWTF has no entry, but a few examples are listed in the index to SHT VII.

[85] In the Niya documents, *tae* occurs as the gen. sg. f., along with *taya, tayā* (Burrow 1937: § 80), *tāya,* and *taṣa* (= Skt. *tasyāḥ*/P *tassā*) (Boyer, Rapson, and Senart 1920–9: index, s.vv.).

Dhp-G[K], for example, *dhira hi prańa i* (177a), where the Pali has *dhīrañ ca paññañ ca* (Dhp 208a). This would parallel the P examples *te ārakkhena guttiyā sampādeti* (AN IV 281–2) and *taṃ ārakkhena guttiyā sampādeti* (AN IV 266, etc.) already mentioned. The translation of *ta e aṇorakṣae sapadedi* would then be "and he causes that to succeed through protection."

Lines 63–73: The effort of development (*bhavaṇaprasaṇa*)

Edition:

|28a

[63] *[ka] ///* [64]*vaṇaprasaṇe ◦ aï bhikṣave bhikhu śpadisabujaghu bhavedi ◦ [vi] ? ///*

[65]*raghaṇiṣide ◦ ṇirusaṇiṣide vivasaghapariṇame ◦ dharmavie[sa] ///* [66]*vedi ◦ viveaṇiṣide*

viraghaṇiṣide ◦ ṇirusaṇiṣide vivasagha /// [67]*riasabujaghu bhavedi viveaṇiṣida ◦*

viraghaṇiṣide ṇirusaṇi[ṣid.] /// [68]*pariṇamu ◦ [prid.sabujaghu bhave]di [viveaṇ.ṣid.*

vira]ghaṇiṣide [ṇi] /// [69]*de vivasaghaprariṇamu ◦ praṣadhasabujaghu bhavedi ◦ viveaṇiṣide*

/// [70]*ṣide ṇirusaṇiṣide ◦ vivasaghapariṇamu ◦ samasisabujagh[u] bhav. ///* [71]*aṇiṣi[de]*

viraghaṇaṣide ṇirusaṇiṣide vivasaghap[r]ariṇamu ◦ uekṣa /// [72]*gh. [bhave]di viveaṇiṣide*

viraghaṇiṣide ṇirusaṇiṣide vivasa[gha] /// [73] *aï vuca[di] bhava[ṇapra]saṇe* ○

Reconstruction:

[63] *ka(*dara bhikṣave bha)*[64]*vaṇaprasaṇe ◦ aï bhikṣave bhikhu śpadisabujaghu bhavedi ◦ vi(*veaṇiṣide vi)*[65]*raghaṇiṣide ◦ ṇirusaṇiṣide vivasaghapariṇame ◦ dharmaviesa(*bujaghu bha)*[66]*vedi ◦ viveaṇiṣide viraghaṇiṣide ◦ ṇirusaṇiṣide vivasagha(*pariṇame ◦ vi)*[67]*riasabujaghu bhavedi viveaṇiṣid<*a> ◦ viraghaṇiṣide ṇirusaṇiṣid(*e vivasagha)*[68]*pariṇamu ◦ prid(*i)sabujaghu bhavedi viveaṇ(*i)ṣid(*e) viraghaṇiṣide ṇi(*rusaṇiṣi)*[69]*de vivasaghaprariṇamu ◦ praṣadhasabujaghu bhavedi ◦ viveaṇiṣide (*viraghaṇi)*[70]*ṣide ṇirusaṇiṣide ◦ vivasaghapariṇamu ◦ samasisabujaghu bhav(*edi (◦) vive)*[71]*aṇiṣide viraghaṇ<*i>ṣide ṇirusaṇiṣide vivasaghaprariṇamu ◦ uekṣa(*sabuja)*[72]*gh(*u) bhavedi viveaṇiṣide viraghaṇiṣide ṇirusaṇiṣide vivasagha(*pariṇamu (◦))* [73] *aï vucadi bhavaṇaprasaṇe* ○

Translation:

[63] "What, (*Monks), [64] is the effort of development? Here, Monks, a monk develops the enlightenment factor of mindfulness, which is (*dependent) on seclusion, [65] dependent on dispassion, dependent on cessation, ripening in release. He develops the enlightenment factor of the investigation of dharmas, [66] which is dependent on seclusion, dependent on dispassion, dependent on cessation, (*ripening in) release. [67] He develops the enlightenment factor of energy, which is dependent on seclusion, dependent on dispassion, dependent on cessation, ripening (*in release). [68] He develops the enlightenment factor of joy, which is dependent on seclusion, dependent on dispassion,

dependent on cessation, [69] ripening in release. He develops the enlightenment factor of calm, which is dependent on seclusion, dependent (*on dispassion), [70] dependent on cessation, ripening in release. He develops the enlightenment factor of concentration, [71] which is dependent on seclusion, dependent on dispassion, dependent on cessation, ripening in release. He develops the enlightenment factor of equanimity, [72] which is dependent on seclusion, dependent on dispassion, dependent on cessation, (*ripening in) release. [73] This is called the effort of development."

Line 64: *vaṇaprasaṇe:* The akṣaras *ṇapra* are partly obscured by an overlying splinter of bark.

An ink smudge, which probably represents the erasure of a wrong akṣara, appears after *bhikhu.*

Line 65: *dharmavie[sa] ///:* The akṣara *e* looks like *he* due to an overlying loose splinter. Slightly more of final *[sa]* is visible in the old black-and-white photo.

Line 66: *ṇirusaṇiṣide:* The akṣara *de* has been added below the line (see l. 71).

Line 67: The left edge of the manuscript containing the final *ṇiṣid(*e)* has broken up into a number of microfragments. The old black-and-white photo shows this section of the manuscript in a better state of preservation.

Line 68: *[prid.sabujaghu bhave]di:* A section of bark containing much of *pri* and all of *di* and the tops of many of the following akṣaras has peeled away and folded over. The bottom of *pri* and part of *bu* are seen on the verso image. The remnant of the *d.* akṣara is visible when fiber-optic light is shone through from the verso.

[viveaṇ.ṣid. vira]: The tops of these akṣaras are obscured by a fold of bark.

Line 69: *vivasagha: Vasa* is written over a smudge. This probably represents a correction, although it is unclear what the scribe initially wrote.

Line 71: *aṇiṣi[de]:* The akṣara *de* appears as a faint addition below the line (see l. 66).

ṇaṣide: Read *ṇ<*i>ṣide.*

p[r]ariṇamu: Although the bottom of *pra* is missing, the angle of the lower part of the vertical indicates that the subscript *r* was present.

Line 72: *[bhave]di:* The akṣaras *bha* and *ve* are badly smudged.

ṇirusaṇiṣide: The initial *ṇi* and the final *de* are smudged.

Line 73: *aï:* The akṣara *a,* which lines up correctly as the beginning of the line, is smudged. A small ink mark appears to its right in the margin, representing an accidental stroke of the pen.

vuca[di]: The akṣara *[di]* is badly smudged.

bhava[ṇapra]saṇe: The akṣaras *[ṇapra]* are badly smudged.

○: This punctuation mark indicates the end of this text on the scroll. It is the largest punctuation mark on the recto side of this manuscript, consisting of three circles, one inside the other (see § 4.5). The two outer circles seem to have been made by the scribe of the following avadāna text, which occupies four more lines of the manuscript, then continues on the verso.

The P parallel is

> *katamañ ca bhikkhave bhāvanappadhānaṃ. idha bhikkhave bhikkhu satisambojjhaṅgaṃ bhāveti vivekanissitaṃ virāganissitaṃ nirodhanissitaṃ vossaggapariṇāmiṃ. dhammavicayasambojjhaṅgaṃ bhāveti . . . pe . . . viriyasambojjhaṅgaṃ bhāveti . . . pe . . . pītisambojjhaṅgaṃ bhāveti . . . pe . . . passaddhisambojjhaṅgaṃ bhāveti . . . pe . . . samādhisambojjhaṅgaṃ bhāveti . . . pe . . . upekhāsambojjhaṅgaṃ bhāveti vivekanissitaṃ virāganissitaṃ nirodhanissitaṃ vossaggapariṇāmiṃ. idaṃ vuccati bhikkhave bhāvanappadhānaṃ.* (AN II 16.28–37)[86]

As was the case with the practice of the restraint of the faculties (*sabara/saṃvara*), the listing and description of the seven *bojjhaṅga*s, or "factors of awakening or enlightenment," are quite common in P canonical texts, occurring in a variety of contexts, sometimes in wording that differs from the above. Apart from its occurrence in the parallel passage in the Saṅgīti-suttanta (DN III 226), the formula occurs, for example, in the Sabbāsava-sutta (MN I 11) as a definition of the (mental) development that brings about the destruction of the *āsava*s. At MN III 88 the practice is said to lead to the fulfillment of knowledge and liberation (*vijjāvimuttiṃ paripūrenti*), while in the Mahāparinibbāna-suttanta (DN II 79) the Buddha lists this practice as one of the "conditions of welfare" (*aparihāniyā dhammā*) that, if developed, will ensure the growth and welfare of the monks.[87] A detailed study of the seven *bojjhaṅga*s in P sources (including some reference to Skt. occurrences) appears in Gethin 1992: 146–89.

Lamotte (1944–80: 1128) gives the Skt. version of the formula as

> *sa smṛtysaṃbodhyaṅgaṃ* [read *smṛti~*] *bhāvayati vivekaniśritaṃ virāganiśritaṃ nirodhaniśritaṃ vyavasargapariṇatam. dharmapravicayasaṃbodhyaṅgaṃ bhāvayati . . . vīryasaṃbodhyaṅgaṃ bhāvayati . . . prītisaṃbodhyaṅgaṃ bhāvayati . . . praśrabdhisaṃbodhyaṅgaṃ bhāvayati . . . samādhisaṃbodhyaṅgaṃ bhāvayati . . . upekṣāsaṃbodhyaṅgaṃ bhāvayati . . .*

The references given by Lamotte for this formula are PSPP(D) 208 [208.8–12], ŚSPP(G) 1438 [1437.9–1438.12], DBhS 39 [39.6–8], and Mvy 989–95. Due to the manner in which the text is abbreviated in each of these references, none match Lamotte's wording exactly. The reading of the PSPP(D), for example, is

> *. . . yaduta saptabodhyaṅgāni. katamāni sapta. smṛtisaṃbodhyaṅgaṃ dharmapravicayasaṃbodhyaṅgaṃ vīryasaṃbodhyaṅgaṃ prītisaṃbodhyaṅgaṃ prasrabdhisaṃbodhyaṅgaṃ samādhisaṃbodhyaṅgaṃ upekṣāsaṃbodhyaṅgaṃ. tatra katamat smṛtisaṃbodhyaṅgaṃ yāvad upekṣāsaṃbodhyaṅgaṃ. iha . . .*

---

[86] Only minor variations in the reading of this formula are encountered: (1) for *bhāvanappadhānaṃ*, B[e] and S[e] read *bhāvanāpp~;* (2) for *viriyasambojjhaṅgaṃ*, B[e] reads *vīriya~;* and (3) for *upekhāsambojjhaṅgaṃ*, B[e] and S[e] read *upekkhā~*.

[87] The E[e] lacks the phrase *vivekanissitaṃ virāganissitaṃ nirodhanissitaṃ vossaggapariṇāmiṃ*, but B[e] and S[e] indicate that abbreviation has occurred and that this phrase should be read throughout.

smṛtisaṃbodhyaṅgaṃ yāvad upekṣāsaṃbodhyaṅgaṃ bhāvayati vivekaniśritaṃ virāganiśritaṃ nirodhaniśritaṃ vyavasargaparigatam.

Further, in the Mvy and DBhS the phrase *vivekaniśritaṃ virāganiśritaṃ nirodhaniśritaṃ vyavasargapariṇataṃ* is given only with the previous description of the *ṛddhipāda*s (Mvy 972–5; DBhS 39.1–2). Despite this, the version given by Lamotte is probably correct, at least as an "ideal" version.

Apart from the above, several fragments of this formula or components of it used in other contexts survive among the Central Asian (Turfan) manuscripts. The formula occurs twice in the MPS (§§ 2.27, 30.11–2), though the original Skt. survives for only a portion of § 30.11–2. The full text of § 2.27 and most of § 30.11–2 were reconstructed by Waldschmidt on the basis of the Tib., P, and Mvy parallels. Similarly, only a fraction of the original of the Skt. Saṅgīti-sūtra survives (§ VII.1). Other Central Asian (Turfan) fragments dealing with the *bodhyaṅga*s, some of which are given in the SWTF (s.v. *upekṣā-sambodhyaṅga*), are SHT IV 162 c 4–5,9; V 1427;[88] VI 533 (p. 215) Bl.106; 533 (p. 216) Bl.(10)8; 1226, frag. 21; VII 1763 b R4–5. Fragments of the *viveka-niśrita* formula employed in other contexts are found at SHT V 1119 a V5, R1, and VI 533 (p. 216) Bl.114 R3. Finally, a more or less complete list occurs in the EĀ-Skt.[Gil.] fragment (§ 25.6). Significant variant readings encountered in these and the other passages mentioned so far will be discussed in the course of the following analysis of the G text. The Central Asian (Turfan) fragment SHT 1445+1447 of two "Prahāṇa-sūtras," one of which is probably parallel to our G Prasaṇa-sutra, has no remnant of the specific definition of *bhāvanāprahāṇa* parallel to the G and P texts; only the initial wording of the general definition survives (R4).

Apart from minor differences in the opening and concluding statements, the P and G versions are essentially identical. Again, although the manner in which the seven *bodhyaṅga*s are presented in Skt. texts varies, and although there are minor differences between the Skt. and G versions in the form of certain words, the Skt. version (particularly Lamotte's "ideal" version) and the G version are virtually identical. As seen in the comparison of the G, P, and Skt. versions of the *sabaraprasaṇa/saṃvaraprahāṇa,* this stability in the wording is typical of passages that depict key Buddhist concepts, standing in sharp contrast to narrative passages, which often exhibit greater variation. But in contrast to the *sabaraprasaṇa/saṃvaraprahāṇa* passage, the *bhavaṇaprasaṇa/bhāvanāprahāṇa* passage exhibits no differences in syntax.

The opening rhetorical question, *[ka] ///* [63]*vaṇaprasaṇe,* which can be reconstructed as *ka(*dara bhikṣave bha)vaṇaprasaṇe,* the concluding statement, *aï vuca[di] bhava[ṇapra]saṇe,* and the opening wording of the definition, *aï bhikṣave bhikhu,* were discussed above in the study of the first *prasaṇa* (*sabaraprasaṇa*) (see pp. 266–70) and will not be dealt with again here.

The definition of *bhavaṇaprasaṇa* consists of eight parallel structures, differing only in that the first word of each, that is, the initial member of the compound *-sabujaghu* (= P

---

[88] SHT V 1427 is a fragment of Dhsgr that merely lists the seven *bodhyaṅga*s and excludes the *viveka-niśrita* formula (cf. Dhsgr § 49).

-sambojjhaṅgaṃ/Skt. *-saṃbodhyaṅgam*), is changed to match the factor of enlightenment. These eight structures are numbered 1–8 in the present study. The first of the eight in the G, P, and Skt. deals with the enlightenment factor of mindfulness:

G: *śpadisabujaghu bhavedi ◦ vi(*veaṇiṣide vi)raghaṇiṣide ◦ ṇirusaṇiṣide vivasaghapariṇame ◦*

P: *satisambojjhaṅgaṃ bhāveti vivekanissitaṃ virāganissitaṃ nirodhanissitaṃ vossaggapariṇāmiṃ.*

Skt.: *smr̥tisaṃbodhyaṅgaṃ bhāvayati vivekaniśritaṃ virāganiśritaṃ nirodhaniśritaṃ vyavasargapariṇataṃ.*

As in the *sabaraprasaṇa* passage, there is only minor variation in orthography among the repetitive elements in the Gāndhārī. Apart from the insignificant nonwriting of the final vowel in *viveaṇiṣida* in line 67 where all other occurrences have *viveaṇiṣide* and the omission of the vowel in *viraghaṇaṣide* for *viraghaṇiṣide* in line 71, the only difference (apart from the placement of the punctuation marks) is in the last word of each structure: *-pariṇame* (l. 65), *-pariṇamu* (ll. 68, 70), and *-prariṇamu* (ll. 69, 71). The reconstructions *(*pariṇame)* in line 66 and *(*pariṇamu)* in line 72 are therefore tentative.

śpadisabujaghu: The P equivalent is *satisambojjhaṅgaṃ*. The Sanskrit is *smr̥tisaṃbodhyaṅgaṃ*. Although not previously attested in Gāndhārī, the spelling *śpadi* for Skt. *smr̥ti*/P *sati* is one of several possible G spellings for this word. In this manuscript *śp* regularly occurs as a reflex of an original *sm* (see p. 95). In the Dhp-G[K], Skt. *smr̥ti* (P *sati*) appears as *svadi* (98, 100–3, 340), while *smr̥tānām* (P *satānaṃ*) appears as *sadaṇa* (340e), the latter reflecting the received dialect form rather than the true G spelling. In the Senior manuscripts original *smr̥ti* appears as *spadi* (8 r6), while in the Khvs-G (25d) we find *[s]v.[d.]* + for P *satīmā*.

In the Senior manuscripts the equivalent of P *bojjhaṅgānaṃ*/Skt. *bodhyaṅgānām* appears as *(*bojhaga)ṇa* and *bo[jha]gaṇa* (5 v11,16).

The string of four compounds that follow *bhavedi* in each of the eight parallel sentences and their P and Skt. parallels are

G: *viveaṇiṣide viraghaṇiṣide ṇirusaṇiṣide vivasaghapariṇame*

P: *vivekanissitaṃ virāganissitaṃ nirodhanissitaṃ vossaggapariṇāmiṃ.*

Skt.: *vivekaniśritaṃ virāganiśritaṃ nirodhaniśritaṃ vyavasargapariṇatam.*

This *viveka-nissita/niśrita* formula consisting of a set of four compounds is encountered in P and Buddhist Skt. texts in contexts other than the *bojjhaṅga/bodhyaṅga*s. In Buddhist Skt. sources the formula is also applied to the *r̥ddhipāda*s, *indriya*s, *bala*s, and *mārgāṅga*s (Lamotte 1944–80: 1124–30; see, e.g., DBhS 38–9). This formula is also occasionally applied in the P nikāyas to some of these concepts, but that is more characteristic of later P texts. Based on his study of this formula Gethin concluded that "in the Nikāyas the formula is in the first place to be associated with the *bojjhaṅgas* alone; it should be seen as being applied to other sets of items by a process of attraction, that is to say, by virtue of their association or affinity with the seven *bojjhaṅgas*" (1992: 165). For an analysis of this formula and for a discussion of the meaning of the key terms, see Gethin 1992: 162–8.

G *ṇiṣide* corresponds to P *nissitaṃ*/Skt. *niśritam,* "depending on," the past participle of *ni* + √*śri*. The G spelling finds a parallel in the related *niṣaï* (= P *nissāya*) in the Dhp-G^K (258d), with *ṣ* one of the possible reflexes of original *śr* (see § 5.2.3.6).

vivasagha-: The P equivalent is *vossagga* (also *vavassagga;* see PTSD, s.vv.). The Sanskrit is *vyavasarga* (see BHSD, s.v.), "release," "abandonment." In contrast to the P form *vossagga,* which shows the assimilation of the initial *vy-* and contraction of *ava* to *o* (*vyava-* > **vvo-* > *vo-*), the G form shows initial palatalization of the vowel before assimilation: *vyava-* > **vyeva-* > **vveva-* > *viva-*/**veva-,* for which see also *aṇovejaṇa* (= P/Skt. *anuvyañjana*) in this manuscript (see p. 271).[89] A parallel development is seen in *-viṃjaṇaṇi* (= P *-vyañjanāni*) in the Khvs-G (19a) and perhaps also in *vivedi* (Dhp-G^K 226a; cf. *vajanti* in Dhp 83a and *bhavanti* in Uv XXX.52a and Patna Dhp 80a), which Brough (1962: 245) took as possibly equivalent to Skt. *vyapenti*. However, the same development is not seen in G *vosido* (= Skt. *vyavasita*) in the Dhp-G^K (5d), where the Dhp has *vosito* (423d).

-pariṇame, pariṇamu, prariṇamu: The P parallel has *-pariṇāmiṃ.* With the exception of *vyavasarga-parigatam* (PSPP(D) 208.12) and *vyavasarge parigatam* (PSPP(D) 207.24–5), the reading is *vyavasarga-pariṇataṃ* in all Skt. examples so far collected (see also SHT V 1119 a V5, R1; VI 533 [p. 216] Bl.[10]8 R4, Bl.114 R3). In contrast to P *pariṇāmiṃ,* which is an *in*-stem adjective, and Skt. *pariṇataṃ*, a past participle, G *pariṇame/pariṇamu/prariṇamu* is an *a*-stem noun equivalent to P/Skt. *pariṇāma-* (see PTSD, s.v. *pariṇāma* 3).

For the spelling *prariṇamu*, see § 5.3.

dharmavie-: The P parallel has *dhammavicaya-,* "the investigation or discrimination of dhammas." The most common Skt. form is *dharmapravicaya-* (see BHSD, s.v. *pravicaya*): Mvy 990; Lal 34.4; DBhS 39.7; Dhsgr § 49; PSPP(D) 208.9; ŚSPP(G) 1437.10; and AKV 599.33. In contrast, the form seems to be *dharmavicaya-* in the Central Asian (Turfan) manuscripts: SHT VI 533 (p. 215) Bl.10 6 V2; 533 (p. 216) Bl.(10)8 R4; VII 1763 b R4. The editors reconstruct *(*dharmavica)yo* at MPS § 30.12; and *(*dharmavi)cayo* at SHT VI 533 (p. 216) Bl.(10)8 R2. In light of this, the editors' reconstruction of *(*dharmapravicayo)* at Saṅg-Skt. § VII.1; *dha(*rmapravicaya)* at SHT IV 162 c 9 Ab; *(*dharmapra)[v]icayo* at SHT V 1427 R3–4 (a fragment of the Dhsgr); and *(*dharmapravicayaṃ)* at SHT 1874 V5 (listed in SWTF, s.v. *upekṣā,* vol. 1, p. 615); and the editor's reconstruction and emendment *dharmapravicayasaṃbodhyaṅgaṃ* where the manuscript has *dharmavicaya ///* at SHT VII 1763 b R4 may not be justified. Tripāṭhī's reconstruction of *(*dharma-pravicaya)* in the EĀ-Skt.^Gil. (§ 25.6) seems to be based on the Saṅg-Skt. passage, itself a reconstruction. The Central Asian (Turfan) manuscripts thus seem to parallel the G and P texts in reading *dharmavicaya* in this context rather than *dharmapravicaya* as encountered in the Skt. texts listed above. Although beyond the scope of the present study, this distinction is worthy of further investigation.

---

[89] Cf. *vy-* appearing as *vi-* in *viaṣi* (= Skt./P *vyādhi*) in the Senior mss. (20 v6,8,9).

The basis for the employment of *pravicaya* rather than *vicaya* in this context is seen in P canonical, commentarial, and Abhidhamma glosses. For example, SN V 111.1–6, reads *yad api bhikkhave ajjhattaṃ/bahiddhā dhammesu paññāya pavicinati pavicarati parivīmaṃsam āpajjati tad api dhammavicayasambojjhaṅgo*. Again, in the elaboration of the seven *bojjhaṅga*s found in the Paṭis we find *dhammavicayasambojjhaṅgassa pavicayaṭṭho abhiññeyyo* (I 16.24), *pavicayaṭṭhena dhammavicayasambojjhaṅgo abhiññeyyo* (I 21.13), etc., while in the Mahāniddesa (Nidd I 44.24–45.1, 77.22–3, etc.) we find the following list of synonyms: *paññā pajānanā vicayo pavicayo dhammavicayo,* etc. (see PTC, s.v. *pavicaya,* for further references). The Peṭ has the gloss *dhammānaṃ pavicayena dhammavicayasambojjhaṅgo* (103.3–4).

For the phonetic features of *vie,* see § 5.1.1.

ria- (l. 67): The P equivalent is *viriya-*. The Sanskrit is *vīrya-,* "energy," "strength." The word is incomplete; its first syllable was written on the previous line. From the P and Skt., the G can be safely reconstructed as *(*vi)ria*. This is the common MIA form with resolution of a conjunct by means of epenthesis, as in P *viriya*. The word appears in the verse uddāna to the Khvs-G (udd. 2a) as *virya* in the triṣṭubh pāda *aradhavirya* ◦ *raṣe agridhaṃ* ◦. The actual verse, verse 11, is lost, but the first pāda was probably parallel to P *āraddhaviriyo paramatthapattiyā* (Sn 68a). In this P Jagatī pāda *-viriyo* is to be read as *-vīryo, metri causa,* whereas in the G uddāna (and perhaps also in the verse) *-virya* is conversely to be read as *-viriya* (Salomon 2000: 130, 192). In the Dhp-G^{K} the word appears as *viya* (260b), *virya* (316d), and the equivalent of Skt. *vīryavant* appears as *viyava* (316b) and *viryava* (217d, 218d). In Dhp-G^{K} 316b *viyava* must be read as equivalent to *vīryavā* for the purpose of the meter (the scansion of *viya* in 260b is uncertain due to its position). Examples of *viriya* written as *vīriya* and of *viriya* read as *vīriya* or *vīrya* are not uncommon in P verse. Examples of the former are *kusītaṃ hīnavīriyaṃ* (Dhp 7d) and *saddhaṃ āraddhavīriyaṃ* (Dhp 8d), where the G parallels are *kusidu hiṇaviryava* (Dhp-G^{K} 217d) and *ṣadhu aradhaviryava* (Dhp-G^{K} 218d); note that in these G examples the nonepenthetic form has been maintained, making the sixth syllable heavy, while the eighth syllable is created through the addition of the *-vant* suffix (cf. the spelling of the same pāda at Dhp-G^{K} 316b, *kusidhu hiṇaviyava,* parallel to Dhp 112b). Besides the above example of *āraddhaviriyo paramatthapattiyā* (Sn 68a), examples where *viriya* is to be read as *vīrya* in Pali are *atthi saddhā tato viriyaṃ* (Sn 432a) and *viriyam ārabhato daḷhaṃ* (Dhp 112d); the G parallel to the latter is *virya arahado driḍha* (Dhp-G^{K} 316d).[90]

Among prose examples so far recorded in Gāndhārī the spelling is similarly *virya-,* appearing in the word *viryavaṃta/viryavaṃda* in the Niya documents (see Boyer, Rapson, and Senart 1920–9: index, s.vv.). The form *(*vi)ria* in our prose text thus seems to be the first example of this epenthetic form in Gāndhārī to date. The appearance of both epenthetic and nonepenthetic forms in Gāndhārī (*virya, viya, (*vi)ria*) is what we

---

[90] An example where *viriya* is to be read as *vīriya* is *saddhāya sīlena ca viriyena ca* (Dhp 144a). Cf. the reading *āriyaṃ* for *ariyaṃ* in Dhp 208b and the need to read *āriya-* in Dhp 236d *metri causa.* See Norman 1997: xxxix–xl for examples in the Dhp where epenthetic forms have to be disregarded for the purpose of the meter.

would expect and finds a parallel in the variation in spellings encountered in Gāndhārī for Skt. *ārya,* namely, *arya, ari, aria,* and *ariya.*[91]

praṣadha- (l. 69): The P equivalent is *passaddhi-,* "calm," "tranquility," "serenity." The spelling in Buddhist Skt. texts fluctuates between *prasrabdhi-* and *praśrabdhi-* (see BHSD, s.v. *praśrabdhi*).[92]

The lack of a final *i* vowel in *praṣadha-* at the compound juncture (*praṣadha-sabujaghu*) is another example of the scribal omission of a vowel (see § 5.1.2). The presence of the retroflex sibilant in *praṣadha-* reflects original *śr* rather than *sr* and indicates a derivation from BHS *praśrabdhi-* rather than *prasrabdhi-*. This is of some interest because a similar phenomenon is seen in the Khvs-G (25c, 37c) in *pariṣeaṇi,* which is to be derived from BHS *pariśraya* rather than *parisrava* (see p. 274).

10.3. The Missing Sections of the Sūtra

As noted in § 10.1.1, only the first three of the four *prasaṇa*s are preserved. The remainder of the sūtra, which was written on a separate scroll, now lost, would probably have included the following: (1) the description of the fourth *prasaṇa,* the effort of abandoning (*prasaṇaprasaṇa*); (2) the concluding statement confirming that the previous description constituted the definition of the four efforts; (3) the formula introducing the verse or verses uttered by the Buddha; (4) the Buddha's verse or verses; and (5) the concluding formula describing the monks' delight at the Buddha's words.

The P version as presented in the editions contains units 1 (in this case the description of *anurakkhanappadhāna*), 2, and 4, though units 3 and 5 are to be supplied, as I have argued in connnection with the P Doṇa-sutta (see pp. 178, 183, 219–20). The two Chinese translations, T 2 no. 150a p. 877b27–c15 and T 2 no. 99 (sūtra 879) p. 221b16–c5, both (approximately) contain units 1, 3, 4, and 5. The P versions of these five units constitute 23% of the P sutta when all abbreviations are restored. Although the figure will be

---

[91] Throughout the verses of the Dhp-G^{K} the form is *aria* (116, 177, etc.), while throughout the prose of the Senior mss. so far studied the spelling is *ariya* or *aria* (5 v12,16; 20 v3[twice], 10,11[twice],12). In the Niya documents the word appears as *arya* and *ari* (Boyer, Rapson, and Senart 1920–9: index, s.vv.; see also Burrow 1937: 76; for the preservation of the conjunct *ry* in the Niya documents see Burrow 1937: § 42). *Arya* appears in the Senavarma inscription (Salomon 1986: text 1a, 8c; cf. *ayaseṇa,* 9d).

[92] Among the references listed in BHSD, s.v. *praśrabdhi,* and encountered in the current context the spelling is *praśrabdhi* at Dhsgr § 49; Lal 34.7; and, as a v.l., Mvy 993. In the EĀ-Skt.$^{Gil.}$ (§ 25.6) the spelling is also *praśrabdhi.* In the Central Asian (Turfan) material the only instance of *praśrabdhi* seems to be SHT VII 1763 b R4. Of the references listed in BHSD, s.v. *praśrabdhi,* the spelling *prasrabdhi* is found at Mvy 993 (v.l. *praśrabdhi*) and DBhS 39.8 (so also DBhS(V) 24.28). This spelling is also found at PSPP(D) 208.9 and ŚSPP(G) 1438.2,4 (the reading of *ṛddhi-* at 1437.11 is a misprint) and is the spelling that dominates in the Central Asian mss.: SHT I 624 Z 15; VI 1226, frag. 21, Vb, Ra; 1360 A5; 533 (p. 216) Bl.(10)8 V2,6, R2; MPS § 30.27; Bil b 9a. The editor reconstructs *pra(*srabdhiḥ)* at SHT IV 162 c 4 B8 and *(*pras)[ra]bdhiḥ* at c 5 A2, while the editor of SHT V 1358+1385 reads *praśrabdhī* for *(*pra)srabdhī* of the ms. (R1). The editor reconstructs *(*pra-śra)bdhaśayyo* at SHT V 1279 V1. But these reconstructions of *praśabdhi* rather than *prasrabdhi* may be unjustified.

different for the G Prasaṇa-sutra, it is clear that a substantial portion of the G sutra is missing.

At a minimum, the G sūtra would have included units 1, 2, and 5: 1 and 2 of necessity, and 5, the conclusion to the sūtra, on the grounds that the first two sūtras in this collection include suitable conclusions. But in view of the fact that the P version and the two Chinese translations include verse, it is highly likely that the G version did also, though the number of verses is unknown. It is therefore probably safe to say that the G sūtra included all five units listed here.

The G and other Indic parallels to each of these missing five units will be presented and briefly discussed.

10.3.1. The Effort of Abandoning (*prasaṇaprasaṇa*) (Unit 1)

The P version is

> *katamañ ca bhikkhave pahānappadhānaṃ. idha bhikkhave bhikkhu uppannaṃ kāmavitakkaṃ nādhivāseti pajahati vinodeti vyantikaroti anabhāvaṃ gameti. uppannaṃ vyāpādavitakkaṃ . . . pe . . . uppannaṃ vihiṃsāvitakkaṃ . . . pe . . . uppannuppanne pāpake akusale dhamme nādhivāseti pajahati vinodeti vyantikaroti anabhāvaṃ gameti. idaṃ vuccati bhikkhave pahānappadhānaṃ.* (AN II 16.20–7)[93]

> And what, Monks, is the effort of abandoning? Here, Monks, a monk does not tolerate an arisen thought of sensual pleasure; he abandons, rejects, destroys, eliminates it. (He does not tolerate) an arisen thought of hatred; (he abandons, rejects, destroys, eliminates it. He does not tolerate) an arisen thought of cruelty; (he abandons, rejects, destroys, eliminates it.) He does not tolerate any arisen evil, unprofitable states of mind; he abandons, rejects, destroys, eliminates them. This, Monks, is called the effort of abandoning.

In this passage three specific things are to be abandoned: *kāma-vitakka,* "thoughts of sensual pleasure"; *vyāpāda-vitakka,* "thoughts of hatred"; and *vihiṃsā-vitakka,* "thoughts of cruelty." This is followed by a more general injunction stating that whatever evil, unprofitable states of mind should arise (*uppannuppanne pāpake akusale dhamme*) are to be abandoned.

The same passage is found elsewhere in the P canon. Apart from the parallel passage in the Saṅgīti-suttanta (DN III 226), it is also found in the Sabbāsava-sutta of the MN (I 11 = AN III 390) as the definition of the *āsava*s that are to be abandoned through elimination (*vinodanā*), and elsewhere as the perception of abandoning (*pahānasaññā;* AN V 110) and as the way in which a monk resembles one who removes the egg of an insect (*āsāṭikaṃ sāṭetā hoti;* the B^e reads *hāretā;* AN V 351 = MN I 223; cf. Paṭis II 201). The opposites of these four types of thought are found at AN II 76, III 446–7.

---

[93] The B^e and S^e read *byantīkaroti* for *vyantikaroti* and *byāpādavitakkaṃ* for *vyāpādavitakkaṃ* throughout.

All that remains of the passage dealing with *prahāṇaprahāṇa* in the Skt. fragment SHT V 1445+1447 (V1–2) is part of the opening and concluding statement: *prahāṇa-prahaṇaṃ k[a]* [2] /// *pprahāṇāṃ*. Based on the repetitions within this fragment, this was reconstructed (with corrections) by the editor as *prahāṇaprahāṇaṃ ka(*tarat) . . . (*idam ucyate prahāṇa)prahāṇaṃ*.

I have not been able to find an exact parallel to the P version in other Buddhist Skt. texts, though the component elements are encountered. Examples are *kāmavitarka-prahāṇāya saṃvartate . . . vyāpādavitarkaprahāṇāya saṃvartate* (Lal 32.21–2); *na kāmavitarkam utpādayāmāsa na vyāpādavitarkaṃ na vihiṃsāvitarkam utpādayāmāsa* (Śikṣ 39.14–5); and *(*trayaḥ akuśalavitarkāḥ. kāmavita)rko vyāpā(*davitarko vihiṃsā-vi)tarkaḥ* (Saṅg-Skt. § III.5).[94]

The description of the effort of abandoning in the two Chinese translations, T 2 no. 150a p. 877c1–2 and T 2 no. 99 (sūtra 879) p. 221b19–23, differs from the P only in that the final general injunction is omitted and the definition in T no. 99 is different, as previously noted. Although the P version and one of the two Chinese translations are closely parallel, we cannot thereby conclude that the G version was similar, although this is fairly likely. The only parts of the Gāndhārī that can safely be reconstructed are the opening and concluding statements and probably also the beginning of the definition on the basis of the corresponding units found in the first three efforts (see pp. 266–70):

> *(*kadara bhikṣave prasaṇaprasaṇe ◦ aï bhikṣave bhikhu ??? ??? ◦ aï bucadi prasaṇaprasaṇe ◦)*[95]
>
> What, Monks, is the effort of abandoning? Here, Monks, a monk. . . . This is called the effort of abandoning.

G equivalents of some of the words found in the P version are recorded in this and other G texts.[96]

---

[94] Cf. also *nādhivāsayati* (Mvy 7041) and *na vyantīkaroti* (Mvy 7044).

[95] Besides *prasaṇaprasaṇe,* the reading could also have been *prasaṇaprasaṇo*. In view of the reading in the parallel phrase in the description of the effort of protecting (*aṇorakṣaṇaprasaṇa*), the reading in the concluding statement may have been *idi* rather than *aï,* and *vucadi* rather than *bucadi* (see p. 267).

[96] In the following list of such words, preference is given to examples from this ms. or from the other mss. written by this scribe. Where such examples are found, further examples from other sources are not given. Entries are listed in the order in which they appear in the P:

P *uppanna* (Skt. *utpanna*): G *upaṃna* in the Niya documents (Boyer, Rapson, and Senart 1920–9: index, s.v.); cf. *upada/upaya* (= Skt. *utpāda*) in Dhp-G^{K} 181b, 263d.

P *kāma* (ts.): G *kama* in Khvs-G 17a, 18b; Dhp-G^{K} 9b, 10b, etc.

P *pajahati* (Skt. *prajahāti*): G *jahadi* in Dhp-G^{L} 7d, 8d, etc.; cf. *prahadi* (= P *pahāya* or *pajahati*) in Dhp-G^{L} 13a; cf. *viprayahea* (= P *vippajaheyya*) in Dhp-G^{K} 274a.

P *vinodeti* (Skt. *vinodayati*): G *vavaṇuja* (= Skt. *vyavanudya*) in Khvs-G 37b.

P *pāpaka akusala dhamma* (Skt. *pāpaka akuśala dharma*): G *pavea akuśala dharma* in ll. 42–3, 45–6, 48–9, 52, 55–6, 58–9.

G equivalents to the following P words have not so far been recorded: *adhivāseti, vitakka, vyanti-karoti, anabhāvaṃ, gameti, vyāpāda, vihiṃsā.*

10.3.2. The Concluding Statement (Unit 2)

The introductory statement to the four *prasaṇa*s in the G is *catvarime bhikṣave pra[sa]ṇa* ◦ (l. 39), where the P parallel has *cattār' imāni bhikkhave padhānāni* (AN II 16.2). The masculine gender is found in *cattāro 'me bhikkhave sammappadhānā* (SN V 244.6).

The concluding statements to the three *prasaṇa*s in the G are *aï bucadi sabaraprasaṇo* ◦*, idi vucadi aṇorakṣaṇaprasaṇo* ◦, and *aï vuca[di] bhava[ṇapra]saṇe* O, where the P parallel of the first, for example, is *idaṃ vuccati bhikkhave saṃvarappadhānaṃ* (AN II 16.19) and the parallel phrase in the Skt. fragment SHT 1445+1447 is *(*i)dam ucyate sanvarapprahāṇaṃ* (R3).

The P version of the concluding statement to the description of the four is *imāni kho bhikkhave cattāri padhānānī ti* (AN II 17.6–7). The parallel phrase is missing in the Skt. fragment SHT 1445+1447.[97]

Since the Gāndhārī omits the vocative (*bhikṣave*) in the concluding statement to each of the descriptions of the *prasaṇa*s, it is likely that it was also omitted from the final concluding statement. As the numeral, pronoun, and noun in the opening statement are given the masculine gender (as elsewhere), it is likely that this was also the case in the concluding statement. Finally, as we have seen throughout this study, the equivalent of the P particle *kho* is absent throughout this text. The likely reconstruction is therefore *(*ime catvari/catvaro prasaṇa* ◦*)*, "These are the four efforts."

10.3.3. The Formula Introducing the Buddha's Verse(s) (Unit 3)

The formula introducing the concluding verse or verses spoken by the Buddha occurs in this manuscript in the first sūtra of the collection, the Dhoṇa-sutra (l. 16). The reading of the missing formula in the Prasaṇa-sutra was presumably similar or identical: *(*idam u bhayavadu ida vadita sughadu hasavaro idam avaï śastu* ◦*)*, "The Bhagavat said this. Having said this, the Sugata, the Teacher, further said this."

10.3.4. The Verse(s) (Unit 4)

The P sutta has one concluding verse:

saṃvaro ca pahānañ ca bhāvanā anurakkhanā
ete padhānā cattāro desitādiccabandhuno
yehi bhikkhu idh' ātāpī khayaṃ dukkhassa pāpuṇe ti. (AN II 17.8–10)[98]

Restraint, abandoning, development, and protecting; these are the four efforts which are taught by the kinsman of the sun. Diligent with these, a monk would attain the destruction of suffering.

---

[97] The concluding statement is often missing in Buddhist Skt. texts; e.g., MPS §§ 17.3–22, where the Pali has *ime kho ānanda aṭṭha hetū aṭṭha paccayā mahato bhūmicālassa pātubhāvāyā ti* (DN II 109.4–5), versus MSV II 109.7–13.10 (*aṣṭāv ime bhikṣavo lābhāḥ*). In other cases the numeral is omitted, e.g., *catvāra āhārāḥ . . . ima āhārāḥ* (NidSa § 23.9b).

[98] In pāda b, the B^{e} reads *anurakkhaṇā*. In pāda d, the B^{e} and S^{e} read *~bandhunā*.

As stated earlier, the two Chinese translations both conclude with a single verse, the original Indic version of which was probably basically the same as this P verse (T 2 no. 150a p. 877c13–4; T 2 no. 99 [sūtra 879] p. 221c2–4). A Skt. parallel to this verse has not been found.

Although it is highly likely that the G sūtra contained a verse similar to this, it may have contained more than the one verse, since there are three, possibly four, verses in the G Dhoṇa-sūtra, and the P Doṇa-sutta has two.

A G version of pāda f of the P verse (*khayaṃ dukkhassa pāpuṇe*), which also occurs in two verses in the It as pāda d (30.16, 87.6), appears in the Dhp-G^K (130d) as *kṣaya dukhasa pramuṇi,* where *pramuṇi* = P *pāpuṇe* with *m/v* alternation (see Brough 1962: § 36). Despite the exact correspondence in this pāda, the G version of this verse may very well have differed from the P in other details. For example, the same idea that is expressed in pāda d in the P (*desitādiccabandhuno*) is presented in different wording in the Uv: *yathā buddhena deśitā* (XV.1d).[99] Pāda f of SN III 142.30, reads *desitādiccabandhunā* in the B^e, but the reading in the E^e is *dīpitādiccabandhunā*.[100]

The G equivalents of the majority of the words of the P verse are found in this manuscript (*sabara, prasaṇa, bhavaṇa, aṇorakṣaṇa, catvari, bhikhu*), and the G equivalents of most of those that do not appear in this manuscript are found in other G texts.[101]

10.3.5. The Conclusion to the Sūtra (Unit 5)

Since the first and second sūtras of this collection include formal conclusions (ll. 25–6 and 36–7), it is highly likely that the Prasaṇa-sutra did also. This presumably would have been the same as that found at the end of the Budhabayaṇa-sutra (ll. 36–7). The probable reconstruction is therefore *(*idam u bhayavadu atamaṇa te bhikhu bhayavadeṇa bhaṣido abhiṇadi ○)*, "The Bhagavat said this. Pleased, those monks rejoiced at what was said by the Bhagavat."

The P version of the sutta, the Saṃvara-sutta, presented in printed editions ends with the Buddha's verse. But as we have seen elsewhere, the phrase *attamanā te bhikkhū bhagavato bhāsitaṃ abhinandun ti* (e.g., AN I 276.24) is to be supplied. Both Chinese translations include similar, though not identical, phrases.

---

[99] Cf. *daśa vaśitā ākhyātā buddhenādityabandhunā* (Mvu I 282.15, pādas a–b); *ete upakkilesā vuttā buddhenādiccabandhunā* (Vin II 296.17 = AN II 54.8, pādas c–d); *sudesitā cakkhumatā buddhenādiccabandhunā* (Th 1258a–b, cf. 417a–b); *bud(*dh)enādityabandhunā* (MAV § 1c.3, pāda b). For further P references, see CPD, s.v. *ādicca-bandhu*.

[100] Cf. *ye saṃvarā cakkhumatā desitādiccabandhunā* (AN IV 228.11, pādas c–d).

[101] P *desita* (Skt. *deśita*): G *deśida* in Dhp-G^K 3b, 299d.

P *ādiccabandhu* (Skt. *ādityabandhu*): *[a] + [c.]ba[ṃ]dh[uṣ.]* in Khvs-G 15c, corresponding to P *ādiccabandhussa* in Sn 54c; cf. G *adicu/adico* in Dhp-G^K 50a, 279d.

P *khaya* (Skt. *kṣaya*): G *kṣaya* in Dhp-G^K 5c, 10c, etc.

P *dukkha* (Skt. *duḥkha*): G *dukha/duha/dokhu* in Dhp-G^K (see index, s.vv.); *dukha* in Khvs-G 2b.

P *pāpuṇe*: G *pramuṇi* in Dhp-G^K 130d; cf. *pranodi/panodi* (= Skt. *prāpnoti*) in Dhp-G^K 134d, 255d.

A G equivalent of P *ātāpī* has not been recorded.

APPENDIX 1

Readings of Unlocated Fragments

Unlocated fragments containing only illegible akṣaras are

> Frame 25: 25l, 25m, 25n, 25q, 25r, 25s, 25y, 25ii, 25jj, 25kk
> Frame 24: 24c, 24d, 24f, 24k, 24l, 24z, 24bb
> Frame 28: 28f
> Debris box: D6g, D6l, D6n, D6q, D6w, D6y, D6cc

The following list includes all unlocated fragments that contain remnants of one or more legible akṣaras:

25p: Two small fragments, the larger of which is reproduced from the old black-and-white photo (pl. 8). The small splinter contains part of one illegible akṣara. The large fragment contains the remnant of three akṣaras. The reading appears to be */// ? [v. ṇ.] ? ///*.

25x+25w: These two small fragments have flipped over, with the original recto visible on the verso of the frame. They contain the remnants of two lines. The reading is

1. */// [va a] ? ///*
2. */// ? [j.] ? ? ? ///*

The second akṣara of line 2 appears to be the top of a *j*. The third could be a vowel, while the fourth could be *[ma]*.

25ff: The more complete fragment visible in the old black-and-white photo is reproduced in plate 8. It contains the remnants of the akṣaras belonging to two lines. The reading is

1. */// ? ? ///*
2. */// pra ? ///*

The vowel on the second akṣara on line 2 is either *i* or *e*. The remnant of the consonant matches the right shoulder of an *r* or *v,* although it could also be the top of a *k* or *bh*. The small chip at the bottom left corner of the fragment may not be in its original position; it may originally have occupied the space immediately above its current location. If so, the reading of the second akṣara on line 2 may have been *[te]*.

24dd: Contains parts of two akṣaras. The first is illegible, and the second appears to be the top of an *ṣ*. It is not certain whether these belong to the recto or verso.

28d: Although there appears to be two lines of writing, the akṣaras are jumbled and distorted, with what seems to be a *ja* appearing between the two lines on the right. If *ja* belongs to line 2, the reading of the second line could be *jad.[maṇa],* matching *jadomaṇa,* which is missing from the end of line 58. However, the remnants of the akṣaras of the first line of the fragment do not match *ṇovejaṇa,* which is missing from the end of line 57. The alternative, but more problematic, location for this fragment is at the end of lines 62 and 63. The reading of the latter part of the second line could be *[dara bh.]* rather than *d.[maṇa]* as proposed above, which would match the wording missing at the end of line 63 (*[ka]dara bhikṣave bha*). However, there seems to be too much bark remaining between *[da]* of fragment 28d and the preceding *[ka],* which is the last akṣara on fragment 28a belonging to this line. Further, this would mean that the akṣara *ja,* which seems to be floating between the lines, is on a separate chip, which appears not to be the case. The wording missing from the end of line 62 is a matter of speculation, but possible reconstructions include *[p](*uḍavaya)* and *[p](*uḍavayasaña)* (see text commentary). Due to their jumbled condition it is unclear whether the remnants of akṣaras on the first line of fragment 28d match either of these reconstructions. Fragment 28d thus remains unplaced.

28e: Contains parts of two akṣaras. The reading of the first is uncertain, but it resembles the top of a *ya*. The second could be part of a *bh* or possibly *gh*.

D6d: It is unclear which side is the recto and which the verso. Side A contains parts of two akṣaras. The first appears to be the bottom of an *e*. Side B contains parts of two, possibly three, akṣaras, which may be the tops or bottoms of these akṣaras. If the former, the reading may have been */// ṇ. d. ? ///*.

D6f: The reading is */// p. ///*.

D6h: The reading is */// [si] ? ///*.

D6k: The reading is */// [°] abh[i] ///*. This fragment may belong at the end of line 51.

D6o: The reading probably is */// [di ghr.] ///*.

D6s: Part of one or two akṣaras. If two akṣaras, the reading of the first may be *.i*. The fragment may belong with D6t.

D6t: The reading probably is */// [gh.] ? ///*. The fragment may belong with D6s.

D6z: The reading probably is */// ? .u ///*.

D6aa: The reading probably is */// [a ro] ///*.

D6ee: Probably contains the remnants of two akṣaras belonging to different lines. The one belonging to the first line is illegible. The reading of the second is */// [de] ///*.

APPENDIX 2

The Gāndhārī Avadāna of Puniga

As noted in § 1.1, BL Fragments 12 and 14 contain two distinct texts written by different scribes: a collection of three EĀ-type sūtras and a separate collection of stories, each labeled as an avadāna. The following is a provisional reading and translation of the first of these avadānas, presented by way of giving a sample of the second text on the scroll, which will be published in full at a later date.[1] The avadānas in the BL collection were first discussed by Salomon (1999: 35–9). As illustrated by the story published here, these avadānas are extremely brief, representing the skeletal outlines of stories that are to be filled in by the individual reader or reciter. In contrast to avadānas in other languages, these stories generally concern only the present life of the individual. It was initially thought that these G avadānas lacked parallels in other languages (Salomon 1999: 36–7), but subsequent research, including that presented here, shows that this is not the case for all of them, as some parallels to them have been subsequently discovered in Pali, Sanskrit, and Chinese.

The first avadāna on this scroll occupies the last five lines of the recto (ll. 73–7), illustrated in plate 4. A photo of this section of the manuscript was first published in Salomon 1999: pl. 10. The second avadāna in the collection begins at the top of the verso (not illustrated in this volume). After the first avadāna (recto, l. 77) is written *likhidago sa[rvo],* "all is written," while between lines 75 and 76 (= ll. 3 and 4 of the first avadāna) appears the single word *likhidago.* Both of these notations seem to be in a different hand from that of either the sūtras or the avadāna text. Similar notations appear on several other scrolls in the BL collection. According to Salomon (1999: 71–6), these are probably notations by subsequent copyists to indicate that the text on the scroll had been copied onto a new scroll.

The avadāna presented here is labeled *puniga avadana.* The Puniga of this avadāna most likely is Puṇṇikā or Puṇṇā of the P tradition, known in Sanskrit as Pūrṇikā. She was the daughter of one of Anāthapiṇḍika's domestic slaves, and therefore a slave herself, who became a nun (DPPN, s.v. 3. Puṇṇā Therī; see Salomon 1999: 36–7). The P commentarial tradition (Mp IV 34–5) preserves a story that is probably parallel to this avadāna. In it the Buddha decides to leave Sāvatthi after having spent the rainy season there. Anāthapiṇḍika, King Pasenadi, and other prominent lay followers from Sāvatthi

[1] I am indebted to Timothy Lenz, Richard Salomon, and Andrew Glass for their valuable comments on the reading and interpretation of this avadāna.

unsuccessfully try to convince the Buddha to stay longer, but Puṇṇā manages to convince him to stay by promising that she would take the three refuges and observe the five precepts.

The same story appears in the collection of avadānas referred to as the Sūtrālaṃkāra or Kalpanāmaṇḍitikā, which survives in a complete Chinese translation and in Skt. fragments from Central Asia. The Skt. fragments were edited by Lüders (1926). The Chinese was translated into French by Huber (1908), and a study of the collection was undertaken by Lévi (1908). Fragments of the Skt. version of the Pūrṇikā avadāna are presented in Lüders 1926: 178, frag. 196 R2–5 (quoted below). For the French translation and study of the Chinese version, see Huber 1908: 313–21 and Lévi 1908: 144–5.

In the G version presented here, *anaṣapiḍiga* is the equivalent of P *anāthapiṇḍika*/ Skt. *anāthapiṇḍada,* and *praṣeniga* corresponds to P *pasenadi*/Skt. *prasenajit.* The paleography of this scribe (BL scribe no. 2; see Salomon 1999: 54) has not so far been studied in detail and the proper transcription of some akṣaras is yet to be established. For example, in the material presented here, the consonant *g* has at least four forms, with different types of foot marks: type 1, with no foot mark on the vertical; type 2, with a slight curve off to the left; type 3, with a slight curve to the right; and type 4, with a horizontal foot mark, the bulk of which is to the right of the vertical. As the use of these four types seems to be randomly distributed, I provisionally transcribe all of them as *g,* but further research may show that a distinction needs to be made. As with most of the avadānas in the BL collection, the correct interpretation of this story is not without difficulties, due to the brevity of the text and the fragmentary state of the manuscript.

> [73] *puniga avadano vistara ka ? ? ? ///* [74] *evo śuyadi · anaṣapiḍigasa grahavadisa puni[g.] ///* [75] *da bhagava rayeno p[r]aṣen[i]g[e]no matriadi budho [na uv.ch.] ///* [76] *ya sarv[e]ṣo grahavadino na uv[e]chadi puniga ? ? ///* [77] *vistare avadano* ◦ 1

> The Puniga avadāna. (*This to be done) in full [i.e., filled in]. Thus it is heard. Puniga was the . . . of the householder Anaṣapiḍiga. The Bhagavat was addressed by King Praṣeniga. The Buddha did not agree [to his request] . . . and he did not agree to [the request] of all the householders. Puniga . . . The avadāna [is to be done] in full. 1.

> The relevant sections of the Skt. version are

> [3] *bhagavāñ=śrāvastyāṃ yathābhipretam=uṣitvā prakkramitukāmo=[n]ātha-p[i]ṇḍadena vij(*ñ)āpi(*t)[o]* . . . . . . [4] *bhagavān=vasat[v]=i(*t)i* . . . . *i* . . . . *vatsyām=īty=atha mr̥gāramātr̥pramukhābhir=anyābhiś=c=opāsikābhir= r̥sidattapu(*raskr̥taiś=c= ā)[m]ātyaiḥ kā[l]e* . . . . [5] . . . . *v(*i)[j]ñ[ā]pito bhagavan(*n)=i(*h)=ai(*va)* . . . . *m=iti — na ca (*prat)i-(*j)ā(*nā)ti sma vatsyā(*m)=ī(*t)i (*—).* (Frag. 196 R3–5, Lüders 1926: 178)

Fig. 7. Reconstruction of lines 73–4 (left side).

The parallel section of the P version is

satthā kira vutthavasso pavāretvā dve aggasāvake ohāya dakkhiṇāgiriṃ cārikaṃ gamissāmī ti nikkhami. rājā pasenadikosalo anāthapiṇḍiko gahapati visākhā mahā-upāsikā aññe ca bahujanā dasabalaṃ nivattetuṃ nāsakkhiṃsu. (Mp IV 34.9–13)

Notes on the Text

puniga avadano: This is the title of the avadāna (see § 1.2).

vistara ka ? ? ? ///: The section of bark containing the remnants of part of the second illegible akṣara and all of the third illegible akṣara has deteriorated since the old black-and-white photo was taken. On the model of *karyam ida ti* (BL Frag. 1, part 3 v2) and *karyam ido* (BL Frags. 16+25, r59) in other avadānas in the BL collection, this can be reconstructed as either *ka(*ryam ida ti)* or *ka(*ryam ido),* the equivalent of Skt. *kāryam idam iti* and *kāryam idam,* respectively (see Salomon 1999: 36). Given the space available, the latter is the more likely. The phrase *vistara kāryam idam,* literally, "this is to be done in full," means that the story is to be filled in, given in full.

evo śuyadi ·: There is some variation in the reading of this common phrase throughout the avadāna texts. For example, the reading in the second avadāna in this collection, which is the first on the verso, is *evo ṣuyadi* (v1), while in the third avadāna it is *evo śruyadi* (v9). A similar expression is *evam anuśrūyate* in the Divyāvadāna (e.g., 348.20–1), while Brough (1950: 426) draws attention to the phrase *tadyathānuśrūyate* found in the Jātakamālā and Kalpanāmaṇḍitikā and *taṃ yathānusūyate* in the Milindapañha.

anaṣapiḍigasa grahavadisa puni[g.] /// [75] da: Once again, more of the final akṣara *ga* of line 74 is visible in the old black-and-white photo. Given that *bhagava* probably begins the next sentence, *da* at the beginning of line 75 should be the final syllable of this sentence. In view of the P version, in which Puṇṇā is referred to as *puṇṇā nāma dāsī* (Mp IV 34.14–5), a word meaning "slave" or "servant" is probably missing from the end of line 74. Several avadānas in the BL collection begin with a formula such as *evo ṣuyadi* [name] *nama* [social designation] *hovadi.* For example, the third avadāna in this collection begins with *evo śruyadi kar[n]amagasa rayasa ka ///* [10]*go namo pido hovadi* (v9–10), "Thus it is heard. The father of King Karnamaga was called . . . ," and the fourth begins with *evo ṣuyadi nagare palaḍipu[tre] ? ///* [13] *nama ganiga hova[di]* (v12–3),

"Thus it is heard. In the city of Palaḍiputra [= Pāṭaliputra] there was a courtesan named . . ." We can therefore anticipate that the original reading was *anaṣapiḍigasa grahavadisa punig(*a nama dasi hova)*[75]*d<*i>,* taking *da* at the beginning of line 75 to be the final letter of the verb *hovadi,* with the vowel left unwritten. However, there is space for only two or three akṣaras at most at the end of line 74, whereas *(*nama dasi hova)* contains six. Even if *(*nama)* were omitted, *(*dasi hova)* would be four akṣaras. The correct reconstruction is therefore uncertain.

bhagava rayeno p[r]aṣen[i]g[e]no matriadi: Matriadi is the present passive form corresponding to the more common active form *matredi* = Skt. *mantrayate* (see Salomon 1999: 133–4). The construction is parallel to *bhagavāñ . . . '[n]āthap[i]ṇḍadena vij(*ñ)āpi(*t)[o]* in the Skt. version. King Praṣeniga's words are not quoted in the Gāndhārī, but the P, Skt., and Chinese parallels indicate that the king, like the other lay followers of Śrāvastī, asked the Buddha to remain longer in their town: *bhagavān vasat[v] i(*t)i,* in the words of Anāthapiṇḍada in the Skt. version.

budho [na uv.ch.] /// [76] ya sarv[e]ṣo grahavadino na uv[e]chadi: The final two akṣaras of line 75 are faint but are consistent with the reading *[v.ch.],* as suggested by the apparently parallel phrase *na uv[e]chadi* in line 76. The interpretation of *uv[e]chadi* is problematic. The context suggests that the Buddha is not agreeing to the request of the king and the householders, and that *na uv[e]chadi* is equivalent in meaning to *na ca (*prat)i(*j)ā(*nā)ti sma* of the Sanskrit. Although unattested in Pali or Sanskrit, Turner (1966: § 2320) lists **upecchati* from *upa* + √*iṣ,* "desires," as a form proposed by Morgenstierne (1954: 309) to explain several words in Northwestern languages in this semantic range, such as Waigalī (Nuristani) *weč-,* "wish," and Khowār (Dardic) *wečhik,* "to want." In P canonical prose texts the verb used when someone accepts or agrees to something is *adhivāseti* (*adhivāsesi, adhivāsetvā,* etc.) when it is the Buddha accepting or *paṭissuṇāti* (*paccassosi, paṭissuṇitvā,* etc.) when it is someone else. However, in P commentarial and paracanonical texts the usual verb is *sampaṭicchati* and its derivatives (*sampaṭicchi, sampaṭicchitvā,* etc.), which, like the term under discussion here, is based on the root √*iṣ;* for example, *rājā . . . amaccānaṃ vacanaṃ sutvā evaṃ hotu tātā ti sampaṭicchitvā tathā akāsi* (Sv II 606.4–5) and *te sādhū ti tassa vacanaṃ sampaṭicchitvā* (Jā I 377.20). Further, the most common commentarial gloss of both *adhivāseti* and *paṭissuṇāti* and their derivatives is *sampaṭicchati* (e.g., Sv I 277.6,9–12). I therefore take *na uvechadi* to mean "he did not wish [to stay]," "he did not agree [to the request]." If this interpretation is correct, *uvechadi* would be another example of Northwestern regional vocabulary that is not attested in MIA but encountered in NIA languages of the Northwest and occasionally found in G texts (see Salomon 1999: 133–5).

puniga ? ? ///: Given that there is only space for one, or possibly two, akṣaras after the final two illegible akṣaras of the line, it is uncertain what word or words are missing. The parallel stories suggest that the meaning was something like "Puniga was able to do so" or "Puniga was successful."

vistare avadano ◦ 1: As discussed by Salomon (1999: 36), there is some variation in the wording of the conclusion to these avadānas. The numeral 1 after the circular punctuation sign marks this as the first story in this collection.

APPENDIX 3

The Pali Parallels to the First and Third Gāndhārī Sūtras

The following edition of the P parallels to the first and third G sūtras, the Dhoṇa-sutra and Prasaṇa-sutra, is based on the European PTS edition (E^{e}),[1] which is also found in the Dhammakaya CD-ROM (= Dhk-CD). The readings found in the CD-ROM versions of the Burmese Chaṭṭhasaṅgāyana edition (B^{e}) (= VRI-CD) and Thai King of Siam edition (S^{e}) (= Mah-CD), as well as in the commentary (Mp), have been included. Passages abbreviated in the PTS edition have been restored in italics.

The Pali Doṇa-sutta (AN II 37.23–39.9)

evaṃ me sutaṃ (e.g., AN II 1.5).[2] ekaṃ samayaṃ bhagavā antarā ca ukkaṭṭhaṃ antarā ca setabbyaṃ[3] addhānamaggapaṭipanno[4] hoti. doṇo pi sudaṃ[5] brāhmaṇo antarā ca ukkaṭṭhaṃ antarā ca setabbyaṃ addhānamaggapaṭipanno hoti. addasā kho doṇo brāhmaṇo bhagavato padesu[6] cakkāni sahassārāni sanemikāni sanābhikāni sabbākāraparipūrāni. disvān' assa etad ahosi acchariyaṃ vata bho abbhutaṃ vata bho na vat' imāni manussabhūtassa padāni[7] bhavissantī ti. atha kho bhagavā maggā ukkamma[8] aññatarasmiṃ rukkhamūle nisīdi pallaṅkaṃ ābhujitvā ujuṃ kāyaṃ paṇidhāya parimukhaṃ satiṃ upaṭṭhapetvā. atha kho doṇo brāhmaṇo bhagavato padāni[9] anugacchanto addasā[10] bhagavantaṃ aññatarasmiṃ rukkhamūle nisinnaṃ pāsādikaṃ pasādanīyaṃ[11] santindriyaṃ santamānasaṃ uttamadamathasamatham[12] anuppattaṃ[13]

---

[1] The 1955 reprint of the E^{e} includes corrections, whereas the 1976 reprint is a reprint of the 1888 original edition, without corrections.

[2] This opening phrase is also omitted in B^{e} and S^{e}.

[3] E^{e} records the v.l. *setavyaṃ* (in some Burmese and Sinh. mss.) in this and the next occurrence. B^{e} and S^{e} have *setabyaṃ*. The reading in the E^{e} of the comm. (Mp III 75) is *setavya-*.

[4] B^{e} reads *~ppaṭipanno* here and in the next occurrence.

[5] *Sudaṃ* is missing in S^{e}.

[6] The 1888 original and 1976 reprint of the E^{e} read *pādesu,* which was changed to *padesu* in the 1955 reprint, the reading also found in the Dhk-CD. The reading in the E^{e} of the comm. (Mp III 77) is *padesu*. B^{e} and S^{e} both have *pādesu,* though the former has *padāni* in the following two occurrences.

[7] S^{e} reads *pādāni.*

[8] B^{e} and S^{e} read *okkamma,* as does the E^{e} of the parallel phrase in DN II 128.

[9] S^{e} reads *pādāni.*

[10] B^{e} and S^{e} read *addasa* here but *addasā* in the previous occurrence.

[11] The 1888 original and 1976 reprint of the E^{e} read *pāsādanīyaṃ,* which was changed to *pasādanīyaṃ* in the 1955 reprint, which is also the reading of the Dhk-CD. B^{e} and S^{e} read *pasādanīyaṃ*. However, S^{e} reads *pāsādanīyaṃ* in, e.g., the Udāna occurrences corresponding to Ud 7 and 58.

dantaṃ guttaṃ santindriyaṃ[14] nāgaṃ disvā[15] yena bhagavā ten' upasaṅkami upasaṅkamitvā bhagavantaṃ etad avoca devo no bhavaṃ bhavissatī ti. na kho ahaṃ brāhmaṇa devo bhavissāmī ti. gandhabbo no bhavaṃ bhavissatī ti. na kho ahaṃ brāhmaṇa gandhabbo bhavissāmī ti. yakkho no bhavaṃ bhavissatī ti. na kho ahaṃ brāhmaṇa yakkho bhavissāmī ti. manusso no bhavaṃ bhavissatī ti. na kho ahaṃ brāhmaṇa manusso bhavissāmī ti. devo no bhavaṃ bhavissatī ti iti puṭṭho samāno na kho ahaṃ brāhmaṇa devo bhavissāmī ti vadesi. gandhabbo no bhavaṃ bhavissatī ti iti puṭṭho samāno na kho ahaṃ brāhmaṇa[16] gandhabbo bhavissāmī ti vadesi. yakkho [17]*no bhavaṃ bhavissatī ti iti puṭṭho samāno na kho ahaṃ brāhmaṇa yakkho bhavissāmī ti* vadesi. manusso no bhavaṃ bhavissatī ti iti puṭṭho samāno na kho ahaṃ brāhmaṇa manusso bhavissāmī ti vadesi. atha kho ko[18] carahi bhavaṃ bhavissatī ti. yesaṃ kho ahaṃ brāhmaṇa āsavānaṃ appahīnattā devo bhaveyyaṃ te me āsavā pahīnā ucchinnamūlā tālāvatthukatā anabhāvakatā[19] āyatiṃ anuppādadhammā. yesaṃ kho ahaṃ brāhmaṇa āsavānaṃ appahīnattā gandhabbo bhaveyyaṃ [20]*te me āsavā pahīnā ucchinnamūlā tālāvatthukatā anabhāvakatā āyatiṃ anuppādadhammā. yesaṃ kho ahaṃ brāhmaṇa āsavānaṃ appahīnattā* yakkho bhaveyyaṃ *te me āsavā pahīnā ucchinnamūlā tālāvatthukatā anabhāvakatā āyatiṃ anuppādadhammā. yesaṃ kho ahaṃ brāhmaṇa āsavānaṃ appahīnattā* manusso bhaveyyaṃ te me āsavā pahīnā *ucchinnamūlā tālāvatthukatā anabhāvakatā āyatiṃ* anuppādadhammā. [21]seyyathāpi brāhmaṇa[22] uppalaṃ vā padumaṃ vā puṇḍarīkaṃ vā udake jātaṃ udake saṃvaḍḍhaṃ udakā[23]

---

[12] E^e has the w.r. *~dammatha~* (both reprints). The reading in the E^e of the comm. (Mp III 78) is *~damatha~*. The E^e of Ud 58 reads *uttamaṃ samathadamathaṃ.*

[13] E^e records the v.l. *anuppattaṃ taṃ* (in one Sinh. ms.).

[14] E^e records the v.l. *satindriyaṃ* (in one Sinh. ms.). The E^e of Ud 58 and Vin I 195 read *yat-indriyaṃ* (see editor's notes to Vin I 195, § V.13.5, on I 380). B^e reads *saṃyatindriyaṃ* here but *yatindriyaṃ* in, e.g., the Udāna occurrences corresponding to Ud 7 and 58. S^e reads *santindriyaṃ* here but *yatindriyaṃ* (as in B^e) in the Udāna occurrences corresponding to Ud 7 and 58. The reading in the E^e of the comm. (Mp III 78) is *saṃyatindriyaṃ.*

[15] B^e reads *disvāna.*

[16] E^e omits *brāhmaṇa.*

[17] B^e and S^e do not abbreviate the following repetition.

[18] E^e records the v.l. *atha ko* (in some Burmese mss.), the reading found in B^e and S^e.

[19] B^e reads *anabhāvaṃkatā* throughout. S^e has *anabhāvaṃ gatā.*

[20] E^e abbreviates this and the following parallel units without indicating that abbreviation has occurred. B^e and S^e also abbreviate the next three parallel passages but give the second part of the fourth in full.

[21] The following simile also occurs at AN V 152; SN III 140; cf. Mil 375.

[22] The 1888 original and 1976 reprint of the E^e have the w.r. *bhikkhave,* which was changed to *brāhmaṇa* in the 1955 reprint.

[23] E^e reads *udakāṃ* (in both reprints), which is changed to *udakaṃ* by the Dhk-CD, probably in accordance with the Thai edition. As *accuggamma* takes the acc. or abl., the reading of the E^e should have been *udakā-m-accuggamma* (cf. CPD, s.v. *accuggamma*), though the editor may have intended the acc. E^e records the vv.ll. *udake* and *udakā* (in two Sinh. mss.), as well as *udakā paccuggamma tiṭṭhati* (in some Burmese mss.). B^e reads *udakā accuggamma tiṭṭhati.* S^e reads *udakam accuggamma tiṭṭhati.*

accuggamma ṭhāti[24] anupalittaṃ udakena evam eva kho[25] brāhmaṇa loke jāto loke saṃvaḍḍho lokaṃ abhibhuyya viharāmi anupalitto lokena. buddho ti maṃ brāhmaṇa dhārehī ti. *idam avoca bhagavā idaṃ vatvā*[26] *sugato athāparaṃ etad avoca satthā* (e.g., AN II 1.25–6)[27]

yena devūpapatty[28] assa, gandhabbo vā vihaṅgamo
yakkhattaṃ yena gaccheyyaṃ, manussattañ ca abbaje[29]
te mayhaṃ āsavā khīṇā, viddhastā vinaḷīkatā
puṇḍarīkaṃ yathā vaggu,[30] toye na upalippati[31]
na upalippāmi[32] lokena, tasmā buddho 'smi brāhmaṇā ti.[33]

The following are the P parallels to the extra verses, the conversion formula, and the concluding formula found in the G version:

abhiññeyyaṃ abhiññātaṃ, bhāvetabbañ ca bhāvitaṃ
pahātabbaṃ pahīnam me, tasmā buddho 'smi brāhmaṇa. (e.g., MN II 143.29–31)

sabbaññū sabbadassāvī. (e.g., Th 722a)

abhikkantaṃ bho gotama abhikkantaṃ bho gotama. seyyathāpi bho gotama nikkujjitaṃ vā ukkujjeyya paṭicchannaṃ vā vivareyya mūḷhassa vā maggaṃ ācikkheyya andhakāre vā telapajjotaṃ[34] dhāreyya cakkhumanto rūpāni dakkhintī[35] ti evam eva kho[36] bhotā gotamena anekapariyāyena dhammo pakāsito. esāhaṃ bhagavantaṃ[37] gotamaṃ saraṇaṃ gacchāmi dhammañ ca bhikkhusaṅghañ ca. upāsakaṃ maṃ bhavaṃ gotamo dhāretu ajjatagge pāṇupetaṃ saraṇaṃ gatan ti. (e.g., AN I 56.3–11)

---

[24] See the previous footnote.

[25] B^{e} reads *evamevaṃ kho ahaṃ*. S^{e} has *evameva kho ahaṃ*.

[26] B^{e} and S^{e} of this AN II 1 occurrence of this formula read *vatvāna*.

[27] This formula is missing in all three editions (E^{e}, B^{e}, and S^{e}) but is presumably to be restored (see text commentary to ll. 15–6).

[28] The 1888 original and 1976 reprint of the E^{e} read *devūpapaty,* which was changed to *devūpapatty* in the 1955 reprint, the reading found in the Dhk-CD. B^{e} reads *devūpapaty;* S^{e} reads *devupapaty*. The reading in the E^{e} of the comm. (Mp III 79.9), like that in the B^{e} of the comm., is *devūpapatyassā ti devūpapatti assa*.

[29] E^{e} records the v.l. *aṇḍaje* (in one Sinh. ms.). S^{e} reads *abbhaje*.

[30] S^{e} reads *uggaṃ*.

[31] B^{e} and S^{e} read *toyena nupalippati* (with the former recording the v.l. *upalimpati*).

[32] B^{e} and S^{e} read *nupalippāmi* (with the former recording the v.l. *nupalimpāmi*).

[33] B^{e} adds *chaṭṭhaṃ*.

[34] S^{e} reads *telappajjotaṃ*.

[35] E^{e} records the v.l. *dakkhantī* (in a Burmese ms.), the reading in B^{e} and S^{e}.

[36] B^{e} and S^{e} read *evamevaṃ bhotā*.

[37] B^{e} and S^{e} read *bhavantaṃ*.

idam avoca bhagavā. attamanā te bhikkhū bhagavato bhāsitaṃ abhinandun ti. (e.g., AN I 276.23–6)

The Pali Saṃvara-sutta (AN II 16.2–17.10)

evaṃ me sutaṃ ekaṃ samayaṃ bhagavā sāvatthiyaṃ viharati jetavane anāthapiṇḍikassa ārāme. tatra kho bhagavā bhikkhū āmantesi bhikkhavo ti bhadante ti te bhikkhū bhagavato paccassosuṃ. bhagavā etad avoca (e.g., AN II 20.2–5)[38] cattār' imāni bhikkhave padhānāni. katamāni cattāri. saṃvarappadhānaṃ pahānappadhānaṃ bhāvanappadhānaṃ[39] anurakkhanappadhānaṃ.[40] katamañ ca bhikkhave saṃvarappadhānaṃ. idha bhikkhave bhikkhu[41] cakkhunā rūpaṃ[42] disvā na nimittaggāhī hoti nānuvyañjanaggāhī[43] [hoti][44] yatvādhikaraṇaṃ[45] enaṃ[46] cakkhundriyaṃ[47] asaṃvutaṃ viharantaṃ abhijjhādomanassā pāpakā akusalā dhammā anvāssaveyyuṃ[48] tassa saṃvarāya paṭipajjati rakkhati cakkhundriyaṃ cakkhundriye saṃvaraṃ āpajjati. sotena saddaṃ sutvā [49]*na nimittaggāhī hoti nānuvyañjanaggāhī yatvādhikaraṇaṃ enaṃ sotindriyaṃ asaṃvutaṃ viharantaṃ abhijjhādomanassā pāpakā akusalā dhammā anvāssaveyyuṃ tassa saṃvarāya paṭipajjati rakkhati sotindriyaṃ sotindriye saṃvaraṃ āpajjati.* ghānena gandhaṃ ghāyitvā *na nimittaggāhī hoti nānuvyañjanaggāhī yatvādhikaraṇaṃ enaṃ ghānindriyaṃ asaṃvutaṃ viharantaṃ abhijjhādomanassā pāpakā akusalā dhammā anvāssaveyyuṃ tassa saṃvarāya paṭipajjati rakkhati ghānindriyaṃ ghānidriye saṃvaraṃ āpajjati.* jivhāya rasaṃ sāyitvā *na nimittaggāhī hoti nānuvyañjanaggāhī yatvādhikaraṇaṃ enaṃ jivhindriyaṃ asaṃvutaṃ viharantaṃ abhijjhādomanassā pāpakā akusalā dhammā anvāssaveyyuṃ tassa saṃvarāya paṭipajjati rakkhati jivhindriyaṃ jivhindriye saṃvaraṃ āpajjati.* kāyena phoṭṭhabbaṃ phusitvā *na nimittaggāhī hoti nānuvyañjanaggāhī yatvādhikaraṇaṃ enaṃ kāyindriyaṃ asaṃvutaṃ viharantaṃ abhijjhādomanassā pāpakā akusalā dhammā anvāssaveyyuṃ tassa saṃvarāya paṭipajjati rakkhati kāyidriyaṃ kāyidriye saṃvaraṃ āpajjati.* manasā dhammaṃ viññāya na nimittaggāhī hoti nānuvyañjanaggāhī yatvādhikaraṇaṃ enaṃ manindriyaṃ asaṃvutaṃ viharantaṃ

---

38 The nidāna is lacking in all three editions (E[e], B[e], and S[e]).

39 B[e] and S[e] read *bhāvanāpp~* throughout.

40 B[e] has *anurakkhaṇāpp~* throughout; S[e] has *anurakkhanāpp~*. The E[e] prints a question mark here.

41 E[e] has *bhikkhuno,* but the E[e] of all occurrences of this passage read *bhikkhu,* as do the B[e] and S[e] here and elsewhere.

42 *Rūpaṃ* is lacking in the 1888 ed. and 1976 reprint but restored in the 1955 reprint. B[e] and S[e] read *bhikkhu cakkhunā rūpaṃ disvā,* the reading in the E[e] of all other occurrences of this passage.

43 B[e] and S[e] read *nānabyañjana~* throughout.

44 The E[e] includes *hoti* here but not in the following repetitions. B[e] and S[e] lack this second *hoti* throughout. It is similarly missing in the E[e] of all other occurrences of this passage.

45 B[e] and S[e] read *~am.*

46 The E[e] of DN III 225–6 reads *etaṃ.* The B[e] has *enaṃ* in all such passages.

47 The E[e] of DN III 225–6 has *cakkhindriya-* throughout this passage. The B[e] has *cakkhundriya-* in all such passages.

48 The B[e] of the AN II 152 parallel reads *anvāsaveyyuṃ.* The E[e] of DN III 225–6 reads *anvāyassaveyyuṃ.*

49 B[e] and S[e] agree fully with the E[e] in the abbreviation of repetitive passages throughout this sutta.

abhijjhādomanassā pāpakā akusalā dhammā anvāssaveyyuṃ tassa saṃvarāya paṭipajjati rakkhati manidriyaṃ manindriye saṃvaraṃ āpajjati. idaṃ vuccati bhikkhave saṃvarappadhānaṃ. katamañ ca bhikkhave pahānappadhānaṃ. idha bhikkhave bhikkhu uppannaṃ kāmavitakkaṃ nādhivāseti pajahati vinodeti vyantikaroti[50] anabhāvaṃ gameti uppannaṃ vyāpādavitakkaṃ[51] *nādhivāseti pajahati vinodeti vyantikaroti anabhāvaṃ gameti.* uppannaṃ vihiṃsāvitakkaṃ *nādhivāseti pajahati vinodeti vyantikaroti anabhāvaṃ gameti.* uppannuppanne pāpake akusale dhamme nādhivāseti pajahati vinodeti vyantikaroti anabhāvaṃ gameti. idaṃ vuccati bhikkhave pahānappadhānaṃ. katamañ ca bhikkhave bhāvanappadhānaṃ.[52] idha bhikkhave bhikkhu satisambojjhaṅgaṃ bhāveti vivekanissitaṃ virāganissitaṃ nirodhanissitaṃ vossaggapariṇāmiṃ. dhammavicayasambojjhaṅgaṃ bhāveti *vivekanissitaṃ virāganissitaṃ nirodhanissitaṃ vossaggapariṇāmiṃ.* viriyasambojjhaṅgaṃ[53] bhāveti *vivekanissitaṃ virāganissitaṃ nirodhanissitaṃ vossagga pariṇāmiṃ.* pītisambojjhaṅgaṃ bhāveti *vivekanissitaṃ virāganissitaṃ nirodhanissitaṃ vosaggapariṇāmiṃ.* passaddhisambojjhaṅgaṃ bhāveti *vivekanissitaṃ virāganissitaṃ nirodhanissitaṃ vossaggapariṇāmiṃ.* samādhisambojjhaṅgaṃ bhāveti *vivekanissitaṃ virāganissitaṃ nirodhanissitaṃ vossaggapariṇāmiṃ.* upekhāsambojjhaṅgaṃ[54] bhāveti vivekanissitaṃ virāganissitaṃ nirodhanissitaṃ vossaggapariṇāmiṃ. idaṃ vuccati bhikkhave bhāvanappadhānaṃ. katamañ ca bhikkhave anurakkhanappadhānaṃ.[55] idha bhikkhave bhikkhu uppannaṃ bhaddakaṃ samādhinimittaṃ anurakkhati aṭṭhikasaññaṃ puḷavakasaññaṃ[56] vinīlakasaññaṃ vipubbakasaññaṃ[57] vicchiddakasaññaṃ uddhumātakasaññaṃ. idaṃ vuccati bhikkhave anurakkhanappadhānaṃ. imāni kho bhikkhave cattāri padhānānī ti. *idam avoca bhagavā idaṃ vatvā sugato athāparaṃ etad avoca satthā* (e.g., AN II 1.25–6)

saṃvaro ca pahānañ ca, bhāvanā anurakkhanā[58]
ete padhānā cattāro, desitādiccabandhuno[59]
yehi bhikkhu idh' ātāpī, khayaṃ dukkhassa pāpuṇe ti.[60]

idam avoca bhagavā. attamanā te bhikkhū bhagavato bhāsitaṃ abhinandun ti. (e.g., AN I 276.23–6)

---

[50] B^e and S^e read *byantī~* throughout.

[51] B^e and S^e read *byāpāda~*.

[52] B^e and S^e read *bhāvanāpp~* throughout.

[53] B^e reads *vīriya~*.

[54] B^e and S^e read *upekkhā~*.

[55] B^e reads *anurakkhaṇāpp~* throughout.

[56] *Puḷavaka-:* so E^e, B^e, and S^e. E^e records the v.l. *paḷuvaka* in two Burmese mss.

[57] B^e lacks *vipubbakasaññaṃ,* as does the E^e of the DN III 226 parallel. Though present here in the S^e, it is missing in the parallel list at AN I 42 in all three editions.

[58] B^e reads *~ṇā.*

[59] B^e and S^e read *~unā.*

[60] The 1888 ed. (and 1976 reprint) of E^e reads *pāpuṇoti,* which was corrected to *pāpuṇeti* in the 1955 reprint. S^e reads *pāpuṇeti.* B^e has *". . . pāpuṇe" ti catutthaṃ.*

References

Akanuma, Chizen. 1958. The Comparative Catalogue of Chinese Āgamas and Pāli Nikāyas. Tokyo: Hajinkaku-Shobō.

Allon, Mark. 1997. *Style and Function: A Study of the Dominant Stylistic Features of the Prose Portions of Pāli Canonical Sutta Texts and Their Mnemonic Function.* Studia Philologica Buddhica Monograph Series 12. Tokyo: International Institute for Buddhist Studies.

Allon, Mark, and Richard Salomon. 2000. "Kharoṣṭhī Fragments of a Gāndhārī Version of the Mahāparinirvāṇa-sūtra." In Jens Braarvig, ed., *Manuscripts in the Schøyen Collection I, Buddhist Manuscripts,* vol. 1. Oslo: Hermes Publishing.

Bailey, H. W. 1946. "Gāndhārī." Bulletin of the School of Oriental and African Studies 11: 764–97.

———. 1982. "Two Kharoṣṭhī Inscriptions." *Journal of the Royal Asiatic Society,* pp. 142–55.

Bareau, André. 1999. "The Beginnings of the Buddha's Teaching according to the Ekottarāgama." *Buddhist Studies Review* 16.1: 7–49.

Beal, Samuel, tr. 1875. *The Romantic Legend of Sākya Buddha: From the Chinese-Sanscrit.* London: Trübner and Co.

Bechert, Heinz. 1955–7. "Zur Geschichte der buddhistischen Sekten in Indien und Ceylon." *La Nouvelle Clio* 7–9: 311–60.

———. 1961. *Bruchstücke buddhistischer Verssammlungen aus zentralasiatischen Sanskrithandschriften.* Vol. 1, *Die Anavataptagāthā und die Sthaviragāthā.* Sanskrittexte aus den Turfanfunden 6. Berlin: Akademie-Verlag.

———, ed. 1990. *Abkürzungsverzeichnis zur buddhistischen Literatur in Indien und Südostasien.* Sanskrit-Wörterbuch der buddhistischen Texte aus den Turfan-Funden, Beiheft 3. Göttingen: Vandenhoeck and Ruprecht.

———, ed. 1994. *Sanskrit-Wörterbuch der buddhistischen Texte aus den Turfan-Funden und der kanonischen Literatur der Sarvāstivāda-Schule.* 1 vol. to date. Göttingen: Vandenhoeck and Ruprecht.

Bechert, Heinz, Daw Khin Khin Su, and Daw Tin Tin Myint. 1979. *Burmese Manuscripts.* Pt. 1. Verzeichnis der orientalischen Handschriften in Deutschland 23.1. Wiesbaden: Franz Steiner Verlag.

Bechert, Heinz, and Petra Kieffer-Pülz, eds. 1989. *Ernst Waldschmidt: Ausgewählte kleine Schriften.* Glasenapp-Stiftung 29. Stuttgart: Franz Steiner Verlag.

Bendall, Cecil, ed. 1897–1902. *Çikshāsamuccaya: A Compendium of Buddhistic Teaching Compiled by Çāntideva Chiefly from Earlier Mahāyāna-sūtras.* 4 vols. Bibliotheca Buddhica 1. St. Petersburg: Académie impériale des sciences.

Bernhard, Franz, ed. 1965–8. *Udānavarga.* 2 vols. Abhandlungen der Akademie der Wissenschaften in Göttingen, Philologisch-historische Klasse, ser. 3, no. 54. Sanskrittexte aus den Turfanfunden 10. Göttingen: Vandenhoeck and Ruprecht.

Blackburn, Anne M. 1999. "Looking for the *Vinaya:* Monastic Discipline in the Practical Canons of the Theravāda." *Journal of the International Association of Buddhist Studies* 22.2: 281–309.

Bollée, Willem B. 1998. *Bhadrabāhu Bṛhat-kalpa-niryukti and Sanghadāsa Bṛhat-kalpa-bhāṣya.* 3 vols. Beiträge zur Südasienforschung, Südasien-Institut, Universität Heidelberg, 181. Stuttgart: Franz Steiner Verlag.

Bongard-Levin, Gregory, et al. 1996. "The Nagaropamasūtra: An Apotropaic Text from the Saṃyuktāgama: A Transliteration, Reconstruction, and Translation of the Central Asian Sanskrit Manuscripts." In Gregory Bongard-Levin et al., *Sanskrit-Texte aus dem buddhistischen Kanon: Neuentdeckungen und Neueditionen,* vol. 3, pp. 7–131. Sanskrit-Wörterbuch der buddhistischen Texte aus den Turfan-Funden, Beiheft 6. Göttingen: Vandenhoeck and Ruprecht.

Boucher, Daniel. 1998. "Gāndhārī and the Early Chinese Buddhist Translations Reconsidered: The Case of the *Saddharmapuṇḍarīkasūtra.*" *Journal of the American Oriental Society* 118.4: 471–506.

Boyer, A. M., E. J. Rapson, and E. Senart. 1920–9. *Kharoṣṭhī Inscriptions Discovered by Sir Aurel Stein in Chinese Turkestan.* 3 pts. (pt. 3 by Rapson and P. S. Noble). Oxford: Clarendon Press.

Braun, Heinz, and Daw Tin Tin Myint. 1985. *Burmese Manuscripts.* Pt. 2. Verzeichnis der orientalischen Handschriften in Deutschland 23.2. Wiesbaden: Franz Steiner Verlag.

Braun, Heinz, assisted by Anne Peters. 1996. *Burmese Manuscripts.* Pt. 3. Verzeichnis der orientalischen Handschriften in Deutschland 23.3. Wiesbaden: Franz Steiner Verlag.

Brough, John. 1950. "'Thus Have I Heard. . . .'" *Bulletin of the School of Oriental and African Studies* 13: 416–26.

———, ed. 1962. *The Gāndhārī Dharmapada.* London Oriental Series 7. London: Oxford University Press.

Buddruss, Georg. 1975. "Gāndhārī-Prakrit *chada* 'Ton.'" *Studien zur Indologie und Iranistik* 1: 37–48.

van Buitenen, J. A. B., tr. 1975. *The Mahābhārata.* Vol. 2. Chicago: University of Chicago Press.

Burrow, T. 1937. *The Language of the Kharoṣṭhi Documents from Chinese Turkestan.* Cambridge: Cambridge University Press.

———, tr. 1940. *A Translation of the Kharoṣṭhi Documents from Chinese Turkestan.* James G. Forlong Fund 20. London: Royal Asiatic Society.

Caillat, Colette. 1977–8. "Forms of the Future in the Gāndhārī Dharmapada." *Annals of the Bhandarkar Oriental Research Institute* 58–9: 101–6.

Chêng, Lü. 1963. "Āgama (1)." In G. P. Malalasekera, ed., *Encyclopaedia of Buddhism,* vol. 1, fasc. 2, pp. 241–4. Colombo: Government of Ceylon.

Conze, Edward, ed. and tr. 1974. *Vajracchedikā Prajñāpāramitā.* 2nd ed. Serie orientale Roma 13. Rome: Istituto italiano per il Medio ed Estremo Oriente.

Cousins, Lance. 1998. Review of von Hinüber 1996. *Bulletin of the School of Oriental and African Studies* 61: 155–6.

Cowell, Edward B., and Robert A. Neil, eds. 1886. *The Divyâvadâna: A Collection of Early Buddhist Legends.* Cambridge: n.p.

Dani, Ahmad Hasan. 1963. *Indian Palaeography.* Oxford: Clarendon Press.

Dietz, Siglinde, ed. 1984. *Fragmente des Dharmaskandha: Ein Abhidharma-Text in Sanskrit aus Gilgit.* Abhandlungen der Akademie der Wissenschaften in Göttingen, Philologisch-historische Klasse, ser. 3, no. 142. Göttingen: Vandenhoeck and Ruprecht.

Dutt, Nalinaksha, ed. 1934. *The Pañcaviṃśatisāhasrikā Prajñāpāramitā.* London: Luzac and Co.

———, ed. 1984. *Gilgit Manuscripts.* Vol. 3, pts. 1–4, *Mūlasarvāstivādavinayavastu.* 2nd ed. Bibliotheca Indo-Buddhica 16–9. Delhi: Sri Satguru Publications.

Edgerton, Franklin. 1953. *Buddhist Hybrid Sanskrit Grammar and Dictionary*. 2 vols. William Dwight Whitney Linguistic Series. New Haven: Yale University Press.

Feer, M. Léon, ed. 1884. *The Saṃyutta-nikāya of the Sutta-piṭaka. Pt. 1, Sagātha-vagga*. London: Pali Text Society.

Finot, L., ed. 1901. *Rāṣṭrapālaparipṛcchā: Sūtra du Mahāyāna*. Bibliotheca Buddhica 2. St. Petersburg: Académie impériale des sciences.

Fussman, Gérard. 1989. "Gāndhārī écrite, Gāndhārī parlée." In Colette Caillat, ed., *Dialectes dans les littératures indo-aryennes,* pp. 433–501. Publications de l'Institut de civilisation indienne, ser. in-8°, fasc. 55. Paris: Collège de France.

Galloway, Brian. 1991. "'Thus Have I Heard: At One Time. . . .'" *Indo-Iranian Journal* 34: 87–104.

Geiger, Wilhelm. 1994. *A Pāli Grammar*. Tr. Batakrishna Ghosh, rev. and ed. K. R. Norman. Oxford: Pali Text Society.

Gethin, R. M. L. 1992. *The Buddhist Path to Awakening: A Study of the Bodhi-Pakkhiyā Dhammā*. Brill's Indological Library 7. Leiden: E. J. Brill.

Ghoṣa, Pratāpacandra, ed. 1902–14. *Çatasāhasrikā Prajñāpāramitā*. Calcutta: Asiatic Society of Bengal.

Glass, Andrew. 2000. "A Preliminary Study of Kharoṣṭhī Manuscript Paleography." Master's thesis, Department of Asian Languages and Literature, University of Washington.

Gnoli, Raniero (with T. Venkatacharya), ed. 1977–8. *The Gilgit Manuscript of the Saṅghabhedavastu: Being the 17th and Last Section of the Vinaya of the Mūlasarvāstivādin.* 2 vols. Serie orientale Roma 49.1–2. Rome: Istituto italiano per il Medio ed Estremo Oriente.

Gnoli, Raniero, ed. 1978. *The Gilgit Manuscript of the Śayanāsanavastu and the Adhikaraṇavastu: Being the 15th and 16th Sections of the Vinaya of the Mūlasarvāstivādin*. Serie orientale Roma 50. Rome: Istituto italiano per il Medio ed Estemo Oriente.

Gombrich, Richard F. 1990. "How the Mahāyāna Began." In Tadeusz Skorupski, ed., *The Buddhist Forum,* vol. 1, *Seminar Papers, 1987–1988,* pp. 21–30. London: School of Oriental and African Studies.

Gooneratne, E. R. J., tr. 1913. *The Aṅguttara Nikaya: Of the Sutta piṭaka, eka, duka and tika nipata*. Galle: Lankaloka Press.

Hahn, Michael. 1977. "Das Saptamaithunasaṃyuktasūtra, ein Sūtra des Ekottarikāgama." In *Beiträge zur Indienforschung: Ernst Waldschmidt zum 80. Geburtstag gewidmet,* pp. 205–24. Veröffentlichungen des Museums für indische Kunst Berlin 4. Berlin: Museum für indische Kunst.

Hardy, E., ed. 1900. *The Anguttara-nikāya*. Pt. 5, *Dasaka-nipāta, and Ekādasaka-nipāta*. London: Pali Text Society.

Hare, E. M., tr. 1935. *The Book of the Gradual Sayings (Anguttara-nikāya) or More-Numbered Suttas*. Vol. 4, *The Books of the Sevens, Eights and Nines*. PTS Translation Series 26. London: Pali Text Society.

Harrison, Paul. 1997. "The *Ekottarikāgama* Translations of An Shigao." In Petra Kieffer-Pülz and Jens-Uwe Hartmann, eds., *Bauddhavidyāsudhākaraḥ: Studies in Honour of Heinz Bechert on the Occasion of His 65th Birthday,* pp. 261–84. Indica et Tibetica 30. Swisttal-Odendorf: Indica et Tibetica Verlag.

Harrison, Paul, and Peter Skilling. Forthcoming. "Śamathadeva and the *Saṃyuktāgama* on the Epithet 'Buddha.'"

Härtel, Herbert. 1956. *Karmavācanā, Formulare für den Gebrauch im buddhistischen Gemeindeleben aus ostturkistanischen Sanskrit-Handschriften*. Sanskrittexte aus den Turfanfunden 3. Berlin: Akademie-Verlag.

Hartmann, Jens-Uwe. 1989. "Fragmente aus dem Dīrghāgama der Sarvāstivādins." In Fumio Enomoto et al., *Sanskrit-Texte aus dem buddhistischen Kanon: Neuentdeckungen und Neueditionen,* vol. 1, pp. 37–67. Sanskrit-Wörterbuch der buddhistischen Texte aus den Turfan-Funden, Beiheft 2. Göttingen: Vandenhoeck and Ruprecht.

———. 1994. "Der Ṣaṭsūtraka-Abschnitt des in Ostturkistan überlieferten Dīrghāgama." In Cornelia Wunsch, ed., *XXV. Deutscher Orientalistentag vom 8. bis 13.4.1991 in München, Vorträge,* pp. 324–34. Zeitschrift der Deutschen Morgenländischen Gesellschaft, Supplement 10. Stuttgart: Franz Steiner Verlag.

———. 1999. "Buddhist Sanskrit Texts from Northern Turkestan and Their Relation to the Chinese Tripiṭaka." In Erik Zürcher et al., *Collection of Essays 1993. Buddhism across Boundaries: Chinese Buddhism and the Western Regions*, pp. 107–36. Sanchung: Foguang Cultural Enterprise Co.

———. 2000. "Zu einer neuen Handschrift des Dīrghāgama." In Christine Chojnacki, Jens-Uwe Hartmann, and Volker M. Tschannerl, eds., *Vividharatnakaraṇḍaka: Festgabe für Adelheid Mette*, pp. 359–67. Indica et Tibetica 37. Swisttal-Odendorf: Indica et Tibetica Verlag.

Hazra, Kanai Lal. 1994. *Pāli Language and Literature: A Systematic Survey and Historical Study*. 2 vols. Emerging Perceptions in Buddhist Studies 4–5. New Delhi: D. K. Printworld.

von Hinüber, Oskar. 1968. *Studien zur Kasussyntax des Pāli, besonders des Vinaya-Piṭaka*. Munich: J. Kitzinger.

———. 1982. "Pāli as an Artificial Language." *Indologica Taurinensia* 10: 133–40.

———. 1983. "Sanskrit und Gāndhārī in Zentralasien." In Klaus Röhrborn and Wolfgang Veenker, eds., *Sprachen des Buddhismus in Zentralasien,* pp. 27–34. Veröffentlichungen der Societas Uralo-Altaica 16. Wiesbaden: Otto Harrassowitz.

———. 1985. "Epigraphical Varieties of Continental Pāli from Devnimori and Ratnagiri." In *Bukkyō to ishūkyō: Kumoi Shōzen hakushi koki kinen/Buddhism and Its Relation to Other Religions: Essays in Honour of Dr. Shozen Kumoi on His Seventieth Birthday*, pp. 185–200. Kyoto: Heirakuji Shoten.

———. 1986. *Das ältere Mittelindisch im Überblick*. Österreichische Akademie der Wissenschaften, Philosophisch-historische Klasse, Sitzungsberichte 467. Vienna: Verlag der Österreichischen Akademie der Wissenschaften.

———. 1988. *Die Sprachgeschichte des Pāli im Spiegel der südostasiatischen Handschriftenüberlieferung*. Akademie der Wissenschaften und der Literatur, Mainz, Abhandlungen der geistes- und sozialwissenschaftlichen Klasse 1988, 8. Stuttgart: Franz Steiner Verlag.

———. 1996. *A Handbook of Pāli Literature*. Indian Philology and South Asian Studies 2. Berlin: Walter de Gruyter.

von Hinüber, Oskar, and K. R. Norman, eds. 1994. *Dhammapada* (with a complete word index compiled by Shoko Tabata and Tetsuya Tabata). Oxford: Pali Text Society.

Hitch, D. 1984. "Kharoṣṭhī Influences on the Saka Brāhmī Scripts." In W. Skalmowski and A. van Tongerloo, eds., *Middle Iranian Studies,* pp. 187–202. Orientalia Lovaniensia Analecta 16. Leuven: Uitgeverij Peeters.

Hokazono, Koichi, ed. 1994. *Raritavisutara no Kenkū* [*Lalitavistara*]. Vol. 1. Tokyo: Daitō Shuppansha.

Horner, I. B., tr. 1951. *The Book of the Discipline (Vinaya-piṭaka)*. Vol. 4, *Mahāvagga*. Sacred Books of the Buddhists 14. London: Pali Text Society.

Huber, Édouard, tr. 1908. *Sûtrâlaṃkâra*. Paris: Ernest Leroux.

Huyên-Vi, Thích, tr. 1984–; and Bhikkhu Pāsādika, in collaboration with Sara Boin-Webb, 1993–. "Ekottarāgama." *Buddhist Studies Review* 1.2–.

Jayasundere, A. D. 1925. *The Book of the Numerical Sayings*. Adyar: n.p.

de Jong, J. W. 1966. "The Daśottarasūtra." In *Kanakura Hakushi Koki Kinen: Indogaku Bukkyōgaku Ronshū (Indian and Buddhist Studies in Honour of Professor Kanakura)*, pp. 3–25. Kyoto: n.p. Reprinted in Gregory Schopen, ed., *Buddhist Studies by J. W. de Jong* (Berkeley: Asian Humanities Press, 1979), pp. 251–73.

Kajiyama, Yuichi. 1977. "'Thus Spoke the Blessed One. . . .'" In Lewis Lancaster, ed., *Prajñāpāramitā and Related Systems: Studies in Honor of Edward Conze*, pp. 93–9. Berkeley Buddhist Studies Series 1. Berkeley and Los Angeles: University of California Press.

Kalupahana, David J. 1965. "Aṅga (2)." In G. P. Malalasekera, ed., *Encyclopaedia of Buddhism*, vol. 1, fasc. 4, pp. 616–9. Colombo: Government of Ceylon.

Kern, H., and Bunyiu Nanjio, eds. 1908–12. *Saddharmapuṇḍarīka*. Bibliotheca Buddhica 10. St. Petersburg: Académie impériale des sciences.

Klaus, Konrad. 1998. "*Evaṃ me sutaṃ:* Zur Interpretation des Einleitungssatzes der Suttas des Theravāda-Kanons." In H. Preissler and H. Stein, eds., *XXVI. Deutscher Orientalistentag vom 25. bis 29.9.1995 in Leipzig, Annäherung an das Fremde,* p. 482. Zeitschrift der Deutschen Morgenländischen Gesellschaft, Supplement 11. Stuttgart: Franz Steiner Verlag.

Konow, Sten, ed. 1929. *Kharoshṭhī Inscriptions with the Exception of Those of Aśoka*. Corpus Inscriptionum Indicarum 2.1. Calcutta: Government of India.

Kumoi, Shōzen. 1963. "Āgama (2)." In G. P. Malalasekera, ed., *Encyclopaedia of Buddhism*, vol. 1, fasc. 2, pp. 244–8. Colombo: Government of Ceylon.

Lalou, Marcelle. 1953. "Contribution à la bibliographie du Kanjur et du Tanjur: Les textes bouddhiques au temps du roi khri-sroṅ-lde-bcan." *Journal Asiatique* 241: 313–53.

Lamotte, Étienne, tr. 1944–80. *Le traité de la grande vertu de sagesse de Nāgārjuna (Mahāprajñāpāramitāśāstra)*. 5 vols. Bibliothèque du Muséon 18. Louvain: Institut orientaliste (vols. 1–2). Publications de l'Institut orientaliste de Louvain 2, 12, 24. Louvain: Institut orientaliste de Louvain (vols. 3–5).

———. 1967. "Un sūtra composite de l'*Ekottarāgama*." *Bulletin of the School of Oriental and African Studies* 30: 105–16.

———. 1988. *History of Indian Buddhism: From the Origins to the Śaka Era*. Tr. Sara Webb-Boin. Publications de l'Institut orientaliste de Louvain 36. Louvain and Paris: Peeters Press.

La Vallée Poussin, Louis de, ed. 1913a. "Documents sanscrits de la seconde collection M. A. Stein: Fragments du Samyuktakagama." *Journal of the Royal Asiatic Society,* pp. 569–80.

———, ed. 1913b. "Nouveaux fragments de la collection Stein." *Journal of the Royal Asiatic Society,* pp. 843–55.

Law, Bimala Churn. 1933. *A History of Pāli Literature*. 2 vols. London: Kegan Paul, Trench, Trubner and Co.

Lefmann, S., ed. 1902–8. *Lalita Vistara: Leben und Lehre des Çâkya-buddha*. 2 vols. Halle: Verlag der Buchhandlung des Waisenhauses.

Lenz, Timothy J. 1999. "A New Version of the Gāndhārī Dharmapada: British Library Kharoṣṭhī Fragments 16+25." Ph.D. diss., University of Washington.

Lévi, Sylvain, ed. 1908. "Açvaghoṣa, le Sûtrâlaṃkâra et ses sources." *Journal Asiatique*, ser. 10, vol. 12: 57–184.

———, ed. 1932. *Mahākarmavibhaṅga (la grande classification des actes) et Karmavibhaṅgopadeśa (discussion sur le Mahā Karmavibhaṅga)*. Paris: Librairie Ernest Leroux.

Lüders, Heinrich, ed. 1926. *Bruchstüche der Kalpanāmaṇḍitikā des Kumāralāta*. Kleinere Sanskrittexte 2. Leipzig: Deutsche Morgenländische Gesellschaft.

———. 1954. *Beobachtungen über die Sprache des buddhistischen Urkanons*. Ed. Ernst Waldschmidt. Abhandlungen der Deutschen Akademie der Wissenschaften zu Berlin, Klasse für Sprachen, Literatur und Kunst, 1952, no. 10. Berlin: Akademie-Verlag.

Macdonell, Arthur Anthony. 1916. *A Vedic Grammar for Students*. Oxford: Clarendon Press.

Malalasekera, G. P. 1937–8. *Dictionary of Pāli Proper Names*. 2 vols. London: J. Murray.

Mayeda, Egaku. 1964. *Genshibukkyō seiten no seiritsushi kenkyū* (*A History of the Formation of Original Buddhist Texts*). Tokyo: Sankibo-Busshorin Publishing Co.

———. 1985. "Japanese Studies on the Schools of the Chinese Āgamas." In Heinz Bechert, ed., *Zur Schulzugehörigkeit von Werken der Hīnayāna-Literatur*, vol. 1, pp. 94–103. Symposien zur Buddhismusforschung 3.1. Abhandlungen der Akademie der Wissenschaften in Göttingen, Philologisch-historische Klasse, ser. 3, no. 149. Göttingen: Vandenhoeck and Ruprecht.

Mitra, Rajendra Lal, ed. 1877. *Lalitavistara*. Bibliotheca Indica. Calcutta: Asiatic Society of Bengal.

Mittal, Kusum. 1957. *Dogmatische Begriffsreihen im älteren Buddhismus*. Vol. 1, *Fragmente des Daśottarasūtra aus zentralasiatischen Sanskrit-Handschriften*. Sanskrittexte aus den Turfanfunden 4. Berlin: Akademie-Verlag.

Monier-Williams, Monier. 1899. *A Sanskrit-English Dictionary*. Oxford: Clarendon Press.

Morgenstierne, Georg. 1947. "Metathesis of Liquids in Dardic." *Det Norske videnskapsakademi i Oslo, Skrifter, II, Hist.-filos. klasse* (Festskr. for O. Broch), pp. 145–54. Reprinted in Georg Morgenstierne, *Indo-Dardica* (Wiesbaden: Dr. Ludwig Reichelt Verlag, 1973), pp. 231–40.

———. 1954. "The Waigali Language." *Norsk Tidsskrift for Sprogvidenskap* 17: 146–324.

Morris, Richard, ed. 1888. *The Aṅguttara-nikāya*. Pt. 2, *Catukkanipāta*. London: Pali Text Society.

———, ed. 1961. *The Aṅguttara-nikāya*. Vol 1, *Ekanipāta, Dukanipāta, and Tikanipāta*. 2nd ed. Rev. A. K. Warder. London: Pali Text Society.

Müller, F. Max, and H. Wenzel, eds. 1885. *Buddhist Technical Terms: An Ancient Buddhist Text Ascribed to Nāgārjuna* [*Dharmasaṃgraha*]. Anecdota Oxoniensia, Aryan Series 1.5. Oxford: Clarendon Press.

Nakamura, Hajime. 1980. *Indian Buddhism: A Survey with Bibliographical Notes*. Intercultural Research Institute Monograph Series 9. Hirakata: KUFS Publications.

Norman, K. R. 1958. "Samprasāraṇa in Middle Indo-Aryan." *Journal of the Royal Asiatic Society,* pp. 44–50.

———, tr. 1969a. *The Elders' Verses*. Vol. 1, *Theragāthā*. PTS Translation Series 38. London: Pali Text Society.

———. 1969b. "Middle Indo-Aryan Studies VII." *Journal of the Oriental Institute* (Baroda) 18: 225–31.

———, tr. 1971. *The Elders' Verses*. Vol. 2, *Therīgāthā*. PTS Translation Series 40. London: Pali Text Society.

———. 1976. "The Language in Which the Buddha Taught." In Harish Chandra Das et al., eds., *Buddhism and Jainism*, pt. 1, pp. 15–23. Cuttack: Institute of Oriental and Orissan Studies.

———. 1979a. "Middle Indo-Aryan Studies XV." *Journal of the Oriental Institute* (Baroda) 29: 42–9.

———. 1979b. "Two Pāli Etymologies." *Bulletin of the School of Oriental and African Studies* 42: 321–8.

———. 1983. *Pāli Literature, Including the Canonical Literature in Prakrit and Sanskrit of All the Hīnayāna Schools of Buddhism*. A History of Indian Literature, vol. 7, fasc. 2. Wiesbaden: Otto Harrassowitz.

———. 1984. "The Value of the Pāli Tradition." *Jagajjyoti,* pp. 1–9.

———. 1989a. "Dialect Forms in Pāli." In Colette Caillat, ed., *Dialectes dans les littératures indo-aryennes,* pp. 369–92. Publications de l'Institut de civilisation indienne, ser. in-8°, fasc. 55. Paris: Collège de France.

———. 1989b. "The Pāli Language and Scriptures." In Tadeusz Skorupski, ed., *The Buddhist Heritage,* pp. 29–53. Buddhica Britannica, Series Continua 1. Tring: Institute of Buddhist Studies.

———. 1990–6. *Collected Papers.* 6 vols. Oxford: Pali Text Society.

———. 1991. "Gāndhārī." In Li Zheng et al., eds., *Papers in Honour of Professor Dr. Ji Xianlin on the Occasion of His 80th Birthday,* pp. 1.133–43. Peking.

———, tr. 1992a. *The Group of Discourses (Sutta-Nipāta).* Vol. 2, *Revised Translation with Introduction and Notes.* PTS Translation Series 45. Oxford: Pali Text Society.

———. 1992b. "Pāli Lexicographical Studies IX." *Journal of the Pali Text Society* 16: 77–85.

———. 1993a. "External Sandhi in Pāli (with Special Reference to the *Suttanipāta*)." *Journal of the Pali Text Society* 19: 203–13.

———. 1993b. "The Languages of Early Buddhism." In *Premier colloque Étienne Lamotte (Bruxelles et Liège 24–27 septembre 1989),* pp. 83–99. Publications de l'Institut Orientaliste de Louvain 42. Louvain-la-Neuve: Institut Orientaliste.

———. 1994. "Pāli Lexicographical Studies XII." *Journal of the Pali Text Society* 20: 211–30.

———, tr. 1997. *The Word of the Doctrine (Dhammapada).* PTS Translation Series 46. Oxford: Pali Text Society.

Nyanatiloka, tr. 1969. *Die Lehrreden des Buddha aus der angereihten Sammlung Anguttara-nikāya.* 5 vols. 3rd ed. Cologne: Dumont Schauberg.

Okubo, Yusen, ed. 1982. "The Ekottara-āgama Fragments of the Gilgit Manuscript." *Bukkyō gaku (Buddhist Seminar)* 35: 1–30 (91–120).

Oldenberg, H. 1917. *Zur Geschichte der altindischen Prosa: Mit besonderer Berücksichtigung der prosaisch-poetischen Erzählung.* Abhandlungen der Königlichen Gesellschaft der Wissenschaften zu Göttingen, Philologisch-historische Klasse, new ser. 16, no. 6. Berlin: Weidmannsche Buchhandlung.

Pande, Govind Chandra. 1974. *Studies in the Origins of Buddhism.* 2nd ed. Delhi: Motilal Banarsidass.

Pāsādika, Bhikkhu. 1989. *Kanonische Zitate im Abhidharmakośabhāṣya des Vasubandhu.* Sanskrit-Wörterbuch der buddhistischen Texte aus den Turfan-Funden, Beiheft 1. Göttingen: Vandenhoeck and Ruprecht.

Pategama-Walpita Siri Sumanatissa Nayaka Thero, ed. 1956. *Catubhāṇavārapāḷi.* Simon Hewavitarne Bequest Pāli Text Series 7. Colombo: Tripiṭaka Publication Press.

Pecenko, Primoz, ed. 1996–9. *Aṅguttaranikāyaṭīkā: Catutthā Sāratthamañjūsā.* 3 vols. Oxford: Pali Text Society

Pischel, R. 1965. *Comparative Grammar of the Prākṛit Languages.* 2nd ed. Tr. Subhadra Jhā. Delhi: Motilal Banarsidass.

Pradhan, P., ed. 1975. *Abhidharmakośabhāṣyam of Vasubandhu.* 2nd ed. Rev. Aruna Haldar. Tibetan Sanskrit Works Series 8. Patna: K. P. Jayaswal Research Institute.

Pruitt, William, and Roger Bischoff. 1998. *Catalogue of the Burmese-Pāli and Burmese Manuscripts in the Library of the Wellcome Institute for the History of Medicine.* London: Wellcome Trust.

Rahder, Johannes, ed. 1926. *Daśabhūmikasūtra.* Louvain: J.-B. Istas.

Rhys Davids, C. A. F. 1906–7. "Similes in the Nikāyas." *Journal of the Pali Text Society,* pp. 52–151.

———. 1910. Prefatory Note to Mabel Hunt, *Anguttara-Nikāya,* vol. 6, *Indexes,* pp. v–ix. Rev. and ed. C. A. F. Rhys Davids. London: Pali Text Society.

———. ed. 1920–1. *The Visuddhi-magga of Buddhaghosa.* London: Pali Text Society.

———. 1932. Introduction to F. L. Woodward, tr., *The Book of the Gradual Sayings (Anguttara-nikāya) or More-Numbered Suttas,* vol. 1, *Ones, Twos, Threes,* pp. v–xviii. PTS Translation Series 22. London: Pali Text Society.

———. 1933. Introduction to F. L. Woodward, tr., *The Book of the Gradual Sayings (Anguttara-nikāya) or More-Numbered Suttas*, vol. 2, *The Book of the Fours,* pp. v–xv. PTS Translation Series 24. London: Pali Text Society.

———. 1934. Introduction to E. M. Hare, tr., *The Book of the Gradual Sayings (Anguttara-nikāya) or More-Numbered Suttas*, vol. 3, *The Books of the Fives and Sixes,* pp. v–xiv. PTS Translation Series 25. London: Pali Text Society.

Rhys Davids, T. W., and C. A. F. Rhys Davids, trs. 1921. *Dialogues of the Buddha.* Vol. 3. Sacred Books of the Buddhists 4. London: Pali Text Society.

———, trs. 1959. *Dialogues of the Buddha.* Vol. 2. 4th ed. Sacred Books of the Buddhists 3. London: Pali Text Society.

Rhys Davids, T. W., and William Stede, eds. 1921–5. *The Pali Text Society's Pali-English Dictionary.* London: Pali Text Society.

Ridding, C. M., and Louis de La Vallée Poussin. 1920. "A Fragment of the Sanskrit Vinaya, Bhikṣuṇīkarmavācanā." *Bulletin of the School of Oriental Studies* 1: 123–43.

Roth, Gustav, ed. 1970. *Bhikṣuṇī-Vinaya, Including Bhikṣuṇī-Prakīrṇaka and a Summary of the Bhikṣu-Prakīrṇaka of the Ārya-Mahāsāṃghika-Lokottaravādin.* Tibetan Sanskrit Works Series 12. Patna: K. P. Jayaswal Research Institute.

———. 1980. "Particular Features of the Language of the Ārya-Mahāsāṃghika-Lokottaravādins and Their Importance for Early Buddhist Tradition." In Heinz Bechert, ed., *Die Sprache der ältesten buddhistischen Überlieferung/The Language of the Earliest Buddhist Tradition,* pp. 78–135. Symposien zur Buddhismusforschung 2. Abhandlungen der Akademie der Wissenschaften in Göttingen, Philologisch-historische Klasse, ser. 3, no. 117. Göttingen: Vandenhoeck and Ruprecht.

Ruegg, David Seyfort. 1998. "Sanskrit-Tibetan and Tibetan-Sanskrit Dictionaries and Some Problems in Indo-Tibetan Philosophical Lexicography." In Boris Oguibénine, ed., *Lexicography in the Indian and Buddhist Cultural Field: Proceedings of the Conference at the University of Strasbourg, 25 to 27 April 1996*, pp. 115–42. Munich: Bayerische Akademie der Wissenschaften.

Sakaki, R., ed. 1926. *Mahāvyutpatti.* 2 vols. Kyoto: Shingonshū Kyōto Daigaku.

Salomon, Richard. 1986. "The Inscription of Senavarma, King of Oḍi." *Indo-Iranian Journal* 29: 261–93.

———. 1995. "Three Dated Kharoṣṭhī Inscriptions." *Bulletin of the Asia Institute,* n.s., 9: 127–41.

———. 1998. *Indian Epigraphy: A Guide to the Study of Inscriptions in Sanskrit, Prakrit, and the Other Indo-Aryan Languages.* New York: Oxford University Press.

Salomon, Richard (with contributions by Raymond Allchin and Mark Barnard). 1999. *Ancient Buddhist Scrolls from Gandhāra: The British Library Kharoṣṭhī Fragments.* London: British Library; Seattle: University of Washington Press.

Salomon, Richard (with contribution by Andrew Glass). 2000. *A Gāndhārī Version of the Rhinoceros Sūtra: British Library Kharoṣṭhī Fragment 5B.* Gandhāran Buddhist Texts 1. Seattle: University of Washington Press.

Salomon, Richard, and Gregory Schopen. 1984. "The Indravarman (Avaca) Casket Inscription Reconsidered: Further Evidence for Canonical Passages in Buddhist Inscriptions." *Journal of the International Association of Buddhist Studies* 7: 107–23.

Samtani, N. H. 1964–5. "The Opening of the Buddhist Sūtras." *Bhāratī: Bulletin of the College of Indology (Benares Hindu University)* 8.2: 47–63.

Sander, Lore. 1979. "Buddhist Literature in Central Asia." In Jotiya Dhirasekera, ed., *Encyclopaedia of Buddhism*, vol. 4, fasc. 1, pp. 52–75. Colombo: Government of Sri Lanka.

———. 1980. "Fixed Sequences of Texts in Some Sūtra Collections." In Lore Sander and Ernst Waldschmidt, eds., *Sanskrit-Handschriften aus den Turfan-Funden,* vol. 4, pp. 6–14. Verzeichnis der orientalischen Handschriften in Deutschland 10, no. 4. Wiesbaden: Franz Steiner Verlag.

———. 1987. *Nachträge zu "Kleinere Sanskrit-Texte, Hefte III–IV."* Monographien zur Indischen Archäologie, Kunst und Philologie 3, pp. 123–212. Stuttgart: Franz Steiner Verlag.

Schlingloff, Dieter. 1961. "Zum Mahāgovindasūtra." *Mitteilungen des Instituts für Orientforschung* 8: 32–50.

———. 1962. *Dogmatische Begriffsreihen im älteren Buddhismus.* Vol. 1a, *Daśottarasūtra IX–X.* Sanskrittexte aus den Turfanfunden 4a. Berlin: Akademie-Verlag.

———. 1964. *Ein buddhistisches Yogalehrbuch.* Sanskrittexte aus den Turdanfunden 7. Berlin: Akademie-Verlag.

Schopen, Gregory, ed. and tr. 1989. "The Manuscript of the Vajracchedikā Found at Gilgit." In Luis O. Gómez and Jonathan A. Silk, eds., *Studies in the Literature of the Great Vehicle: Three Mahāyāna Buddhist Texts,* pp. 89–139. Michigan Studies in Buddhist Literature 1. Ann Arbor: University of Michigan.

———. 1997. "If You Can't Remember, How to Make It Up: Some Monastic Rules for Redacting Canonical Texts." In Petra Kieffer-Pülz and Jens-Uwe Hartmann, eds., *Bauddhavidyāsudhākaraḥ: Studies in Honour of Heinz Bechert on the Occasion of His 65th Birthday,* pp. 571–82. Indica et Tibetica 30. Swisttal-Odendorf: Indica et Tibetica Verlag.

Schwarzschild, L. A. 1959. "Some Aspects of the History of Modern Hindi *nahîn* 'no,' 'not.'" *Journal of the Royal Asiatic Society,* pp. 44–50. Reprinted in *Collected Articles of L. A. Schwarzschild on Indo-Aryan, 1953–1979,* comp. Royce Wiles, Faculty of Asian Studies Monographs, n.s., 17 (Canberra: Faculty of Asian Studies, Australian National University, 1991), pp. 82–8.

Senart, Émile, ed. 1882–97. *Mahāvastu avadānaṃ: Le Mahāvastu.* 3 vols. Paris: Société asiatique.

Sengupta, Sudha, ed. 1975. "Fragments from Buddhist Texts." In Ramchandra Pandeya, ed., *Buddhist Studies in India,* pp. 137–208. Delhi: Motilal Banarsidass.

Shukla, Karunesha, ed. 1973. *Śrāvakabhūmi of Ācārya Asaṅga.* Tibetan Sanskrit Works Series 14. Patna: K. P. Jayaswal Research Institute.

Sieg, E., and W. Siegling, eds. 1921. *Tocharische Sprachreste.* Vol. 1, *Die Texte.* Berlin and Leipzig: Walter de Gruyter and Co.

Silk, Jonathan A. 1989. "A Note on the Opening Formula of Buddhist *Sūtras.*" *Journal of the International Association of Buddhist Studies* 12: 158–63.

von Simson, Georg. 1965. *Zur Diktion einiger Lehrtexte des buddhistischen Sanskritkanons.* Munich: J. Kitzinger.

———. 1977. "Zur Phrase *yena . . . tenopajagāma / upetya* und ihren Varianten im buddhistischen Sanskrit." In *Beiträge zur Indienforschung: Ernst Waldschmidt zum 80. Geburtstag gewidmet,* pp. 479–88. Veröffentlichungen des Museums für indische Kunst Berlin 4. Berlin: Museum für indische Kunst.

Sircar, D. C. 1965. *Indian Epigraphy.* Delhi: Motilal Banarsidass.

Skilling, Peter. 1992a. "Preliminary Report on a Recently Discovered Pāli Inscription." *Journal of the Office of the Supreme Patriarch's Secretary* 1.1: 83–6.

———. 1992b. "Symbols on the Body, Feet, and Hands of a Buddha. Part I, Lists." *Journal of the Siam Society* 80.2: 67–79.

———. 1993. "Theravādin Literature in Tibetan Translation." *Journal of the Pali Text Society* 19: 69–201.

———. 1996. "Symbols on the Body, Feet, and Hands of a Buddha. Part II, Short Lists." *Journal of the Siam Society* 84.1: 5–28.

———. 1997a. "The Advent of Theravāda Buddhism to Mainland South-east Asia." *Journal of the International Association of Buddhist Studies* 20: 93–107.

———. 1997b. "New Pāli Inscriptions from South-east Asia." *Journal of the Pali Text Society* 23: 123–57.

———. 1999. "A Buddhist Inscription from Go Xoai, Southern Vietnam, and Notes Towards a Classification of *ye dharmā* Inscriptions." In *80 Years: Prof. Dr. Prasert Na Nagara*, pp. 171–87. Bangkok.

Somadasa, K. D. 1987. *Catalogue of the Hugh Nevill Collection of Sinhalese Manuscripts in the British Library*. Vol. 1. London and Henley-on-Thames: British Library and Pali Text Society.

———. 1996. *Catalogue of the Sinhalese Manuscripts in the Library of the Wellcome Institute for the History of Medicine*. London: Wellcome Institute for the History of Medicine.

Speyer, J. S., ed. 1906–9. *Avadānaçataka: A Century of Edifying Tales Belonging to the Hīnayāna*. 2 vols. Bibliotheca Buddhica 3. St. Petersburg: Académie impériale des sciences.

Śrāvakabhūmi Study Group, ed. 1998. *Śrāvakabhūmi: Revised Sanskrit Text and Japanese Translation*. Vol. 1. Taishō University Sōgō Bukkyō Kenkyūjo Series 4. Tokyo: Sankibo Press.

Stache-Rosen, Valentina ("nach Vorarbeiten von Kusum Mittal bearbeitet"). 1968. *Dogmatische Begriffsreihen im älteren Buddhismus*. Vol. 2, *Das Saṅgītisūtra und sein Kommentar Saṅgītiparyāya*. 2 pts. Sanskrittexte aus den Turfanfunden 9. Berlin: Akademie-Verlag.

Suzuki, D. T., and H. Idzumi, eds. 1934–6. *Gaṇḍavyūha*. Kyoto: Society for the Publication of Sacred Texts.

Swearer, Donald. 1976. *Wat Haripuñjaya: A Study of the Royal Temple of the Buddha's Relic, Lamphun, Thailand*. American Academy of Religion Studies in Religion 10. Missoula, Mont.: Scholars Press.

Tatelman, Joel. 2000. *The Glorious Deeds of Pūrṇa: A Translation and Study of the Pūrṇāvadāna*. Richmond, Surrey, U.K.: Curzon.

Thomas, F. W. 1933. "Some Notes on the Kharoṣṭhī Documents from Chinese Turkestan." *Acta Orientalia* 12: 37–70.

Toda, Hirofumi, ed. 1983. *Saddharmapuṇḍarīkasūtra: Central Asian Manuscripts. Romanized Text*. 2nd ed. Tokushima: Kyoiku Shuppan Center.

Tola, Fernando, and Carmen Dragonetti. 1999. "Ekaṃ Samayam." *Indo-Iranian Journal* 42: 53–5.

Tripāṭhī, Chandrabhāl, ed. 1962. *Fünfundzwanzig Sūtras des Nidānasaṃyukta*. Sanskrittexte aus den Turfanfunden 8. Berlin: Akademie-Verlag.

———, ed. 1995. *Ekottarāgama-Fragmente der Gilgit-Handschrift*. Studien zur Indologie und Iranistik Monographie 2. Reinbek: Verlag für orientalische Fachpublikationen.

Tsukamoto, Keisho. 1996–8. *A Comprehensive Study of the Indian Buddhist Inscriptions*. 2 vols. Kyoto: Heirakuji-Shoten.

Turner, R. L. 1966. *A Comparative Dictionary of the Indo-Aryan Languages*. London: Oxford University Press.

Vaidya P. L., ed. 1958. *Lalitavistara*. Buddhist Sanskrit Texts 1. Darbhanga: Mithila Institute.

———, ed. 1967. *Daśabhūmikasūtra*. Buddhist Sanskrit Texts 7. Darbhanga: Mithila Institute.

Waldschmidt, Ernst, ed. 1932. *Bruchstücke buddhistischer Sūtras aus dem zentralasiatischen Sanskritkanon*. Kleinere Sanskrit-Texte 4. Leipzig: Deutsche Morgenländische Gesellschaft.

———. 1944–8. *Die Überlieferung vom Lebensende des Buddha: Eine vergleichende Analyse des Mahāparinirvāṇasūtra und seiner Textentsprechungen*. Abhandlungen der Akademie der

Wissenschaften in Göttingen, Philologisch-historische Klasse, ser. 3, nos. 29–30. Göttingen: Vandenhoeck and Ruprecht.

———, ed. 1950–1. *Das Mahāparinirvāṇasūtra*. 3 vols. Abhandlungen der Deutschen Akademie der Wissenschaften zu Berlin, Klasse für Sprachen, Literatur und Kunst, 1949, no. 1, 1950, nos. 2–3. Berlin: Akademie-Verlag.

———, ed. 1952–62. *Das Catuṣpariṣatsūtra: Eine kanonische Lehrschrift über die Begründung der buddhistischen Gemeinde*. 3 vols. Abhandlungen der Deutschen Akademie der Wissenschaften zu Berlin, Klasse für Sprachen, Literatur und Kunst, 1952, no. 2, 1956, no. 1, 1960, no. 1. Berlin: Akademie-Verlag.

———, ed. 1953–6. *Das Mahāvadānasūtra: Ein kanonischer Text über die sieben letzten Buddhas*. 2 vols. Abhandlungen der Deutschen Akademie der Wissenschaften zu Berlin, Klasse für Sprachen, Literatur und Kunst, 1952, no. 8, 1954, no. 3. Berlin: Akademie-Verlag.

———. 1955. "Zu einigen Bilinguen aus den Turfan-Funden." *Nachrichten der Akademie der Wissenschaften in Göttingen, Philologisch-historische Klasse*, 1: 1–20

———. 1956. "A Fragment from the Saṃyuktāgama found in Chinese-Turkestan ('Turfan')." *Adyar Library Bulletin* 20: 213–28.

———. 1957. "Identifizierung einer Handschrift des Nidānasaṃyukta aus den Turfanfunden." *Zeitschrift der Deutschen Morgenländischen Gesellschaft* 107: 372–401.

———. 1958. "Ein zweites Daśabalasūtra." *Mitteilungen des Instituts für Orientforschung* 6: 382–405.

———. 1968. "Drei Fragmente buddhistischer Sūtras aus den Turfanhandschriften." *Nachrichten der Akademie der Wissenschaften in Göttingen, Philologisch-historische Klasse*, 1: 1–26.

———. 1980. "Central Asian Sūtra Fragments and Their Relation to the Chinese Āgamas." In Heinz Bechert, ed., *Die Sprache der ältesten buddhistischen Überlieferung/The Language of the Earliest Buddhist Tradition*, pp. 136–74. Symposien zur Buddhismusforschung 2. Abhandlungen der Akademie der Wissenschaften in Göttingen, Philologisch-historische Klasse, ser. 3, no. 117. Göttingen: Vandenhoeck and Ruprecht.

Warder, A. K. 1961. "Preface to the Second Edition." In Morris 1961: xi–xiii.

———. 1967. *Pali Metre: A Contribution to the History of Indian Literature*. London: Pali Text Society.

———. 1974. *Introduction to Pali*. 2nd ed. London: Pali Text Society.

Warren, Henry Clarke, ed. 1950. *Visuddhimagga of Buddhaghosâcariya*. Rev. Dharmananda Kosambi. Harvard Oriental Series 41. Cambridge: Harvard University Press.

Wayman, Alex. 1961. *Analysis of the Śrāvakabhūmi Manuscript*. University of California Publications in Classical Philology 17. Berkeley and Los Angeles: University of California Press.

Webb, Russell, ed. 1991. *An Analysis of the Pali Canon*. 2nd ed. The Wheel, Publication 217–20. Kandy: Buddhist Publication Society.

Whitney, William Dwight. 1889. *Sanskrit Grammar: Including Both the Classical Language, and the Older Dialects, of Veda and Brahmana*. 2nd ed. Cambridge: Harvard University Press.

Wille, Klaus. 1990. *Die handschriftliche Überlieferung des Vinayavastu der Mūlasarvāstivādin*. Verzeichnis der orientalischen Handschriften in Deutschland, Supplementband 30. Stuttgart: Franz Steiner Verlag.

Winternitz, Moriz. 1983. *A History of Indian Literature*. Vol. 2, *Buddhist Literature and Jaina Literature*. Tr. V. Srinivasa Sarma. Rev. ed. Delhi: Motilal Banarsidass.

Wogihara, Unrai, ed. 1930–6. *Bodhisattvabhūmi*. Tokyo: Seigo Kenkyukai.

———, ed. 1932–6. *Sphuṭârthā Abhidharmakośavyākhyā by Yaśomitra*. 2 vols. Tokyo.

Woodward, F. L., tr. 1933. *The Book of the Gradual Sayings (Anguttara-nikāya) or More-Numbered Suttas*. Vol. 2, *The Book of the Fours*. PTS Translation Series 24. London: Pali Text Society.

Woodward, F. L., et al. 1952–84. *Pāli Tripiṭakaṃ Concordance*. 3 vols. Ed. E. M. Hare et al. London: Pali Text Society.

Wright, J. C. 1995. Review of Norman 1992a. *Bulletin of the School of Oriental and African Studies* 58: 221.

van Zeyst, H. G. A. 1965. "Aṅguttara Nikāya." In G. P. Malalasekera, ed., *Encyclopaedia of Buddhism*, vol. 1, fasc. 4, pp. 629–55. Colombo: Government of Ceylon.

Word Index

Each entry consists of the following:

1. The head word according to its form in the reconstructed text. Where there is only one occurrence, akṣaras whose reading is uncertain are bracketed as in the transcribed text.
2. The Pali and Sanskrit equivalents, respectively, as represented in the parallel texts, if any, cited in the text commentary. Where the Pali or Sanskrit equivalent is not found in the parallel Pali or Sanskrit text but occurs in a similar formula or phrase in another Pali or Sanskrit text, the entry is presented in angle brackets < >. Where no such equivalent is found in either the parallel text or in a similar formula or phrase, a presumptive equivalent is given in parentheses ( ). The abbreviation BHS indicates Buddhist Hybrid Sanskrit usage (i.e., the word appears in the BHSD).
3. The English translation.
4. The grammatical status of the Gāndhārī word.
5. Occurrences according to the line number in the reconstructed text.
6. Cross-references, if any.

For convenience, roots cited as head words and in etymologies are given in their Sanskrit forms.

a: *<vā>*; *<vā>*; "or," ind. 21, 62. See also ***[ba]***, ***va***.

aï: (*ayaṃ*) for *idaṃ* (n.); (*ayam*) for *idaṃ* (n.); "this," dem. pron., nom. sg. m. 60, 73.

aï: (*ayaṃ*) for *idha;* (*ayam*) for *iha;* "here," dem. pron. used for ind. (?). 41, 61, 64. See text commentary.

akuśala: *akusalā;* *<akuśalā(ḥ)>*; "unprofitable," adj., nom. pl. m. 42 *aku(*śala),* 48 *[ak](*uśala),* 52, 55–6 *(*akuśa)la,* 58–9 *(*aku)śala.*

akhade: *<akkhāta->*; (*ākhyātaḥ*); "declared," pp., *ā* + √*khyā,* nom. sg. m. 23.

aceata: (*accimantāni*); (*arciṣmanti*); "brilliant," adj., acc. pl. n. 5.

achu: *<accha->*; *<accha->*; "clear," adj., acc. sg. m. 8.

ajavaghreṇa: *<ajjatagge* (adv., loc.)>; *<adyāgreṇa* (adv., instr.)>; "from today onward," adv., instr. 25.

añadara-: "a, one," pron. adj.

añadara: (*aññataraṃ*); (*anyataram*) for *<anyatamaṃ*, etc.>; in ***añadara añadara*** or ***añadara-añadara*** (?); "one or other," nom. sg. n. 61, 61. See text commentary.

añadaro: (*aññataraṃ*) for *aññatarasmiṃ* (loc. sg. n.); *<anyataraṃ* (acc. sg. n.)>; "a," acc. sg. n. 2 *a[ña](*daro),* 6.

añadu: (**aññātu*) for *viññāya;* *<vijñāya>*; "having cognized, cognizing," abs. in *-tu, ā* + √*jñā.* 57.

aṭhi-saña: *aṭṭhika-saññaṃ* (bv., acc. sg. n.); *<asthi* and *asthi-saṃjñā->*; "the perception of a skeleton," bv., nom. sg. n. 62.

aṇa[vela]: *<anāvila->*; *<anāvila->*; "translucent," adj., acc. sg. m. 8.

aṇasapiḍiasa: *<anāthapiṇḍikassa>*; *<anāthapiṇḍadasya>*; "of Aṇasapiḍia," P.N., gen. sg. m. 27, 37–8 *(*aṇasapi)ḍiasa.*

aṇorakṣa[e]: (*anurakkhāya*); (*anurakṣayā*); "through protection," instr. sg. f. 63.

aṇorakṣaṇa-prasaṇa-: "the effort of protecting," m. for n.

~prasaṇe: *anurakkhană-ppadhānaṃ* (nom. sg. n.); *anurakṣaṇā-prahāṇaṃ* (nom. sg. n.); nom. sg. 40 *~prasa[ṇe]*, 60–1 *[a](*ṇorakṣaṇaprasa)ṇe.*

~prasaṇo: (as previous); nom. sg. 63.

aṇovejaṇa-ghrahi: *anuvyañjana-ggāhī;* <*anuvyañjana-grāhī*>; "grasping the secondary characteristics," adj., nom. sg. m. 41–2 *(*aṇo)vejaṇa-ghrahi,* 44 *aṇo[ve]jaṇa-ghra(*hi),* 47 *aṇovejaṇa-[ghra](*hi),* 50–1 *(*aṇove)jaṇa-ghrahi,* 54 *aṇo[ve](*jaṇa-ghrahi),* 57 *[a](*ṇovejaṇa-ghrahi).*

atamaṇa: <*attamanā*>; <BHS *āttamanasas, āptamanasas*>; "pleased," adj., nom. pl. m. 36.

[adhagha]ro: <*andhakāre*>; (*andhakāre*); "in the darkness," loc. sg. m. 22.

[abaji]: see s.v. ***ā* + √*vraj*.**

abhikatu: see s.v. ***abhi* + √*kram*.**

abhi* + √*kram: "step off."

abhikrami: *(abhikkami)* for *ukkamma, okkamma* (abs.); <*avakramya* (abs.)>; 3rd sg. pret. 2 *abhi[kra]mi,* 6 *[abhi]k[r]ami.*

abhikatu: <*abhikkantaṃ*>; <*abhikrāntaḥ* (m.)>; "wonderful!" pp., nom. sg. n. 21.

abhija: *abhijjhā-* in *~domanassā* (nom. pl. n.); <*abhidhyā*>; "covetousness," nom. sg. f. 42, 45 *[a]bhi[ja],* 48, 55, 58 *abh[i](*ja).*

[a]bhiñae: (*abhiññāya*) for <*abhiññātaṃ* (pp., nom. sg. n.)>; (*abhijñāya*) for <*abhijñātaṃ* (pp., nom. sg. n.)>; "having realized," abs. (or pp.?), *abhi* + √*jñā.* 19. See text commentary.

abhiñehi: <*abhiññeyyaṃ* (nom. sg. n.)>; <*abhijñeyaṃ* (nom. sg. n.)>; "what is to be realized," gdv., *abhi* + √*jñā,* acc. sg. n. 19.

abhi* + √*nand: "rejoice."

abhiṇadi: <*abhinandi*>; <*abhyanandat* (3rd sg. impf.)>; "he rejoiced," 3rd sg. pret. 26.

[a]bhiṇadi: <*abhinandun*>; <*abhyanandan* (3rd pl. impf.)>; "they rejoiced," 3rd pl. pret. 37.

abhiprasaṇe: (*abhippasannaṃ*); <*abhiprasannam*>; "with faith," pp., *abhi-pra* + √*sad,* acc. sg. m. 25.

amatredi: see s.v. ***ā* + *mantraya-*.**

-ara: in ***sahasa-h-ara***.

aramu: <*ārāme*>; <*ārāme*>; "in the park," loc. sg. m. 27, 38.

arśaveti: see s.v. ***ā* + √*sru*.**

alitu: (*alitto*) for *upalippāmi* (1st sg. pres.); (*aliptaḥ*); "not defiled," pp., neg., √*lip,* nom. sg. m. 19.

[a]l[oka]: (*āloka-*) for <*telapajjotaṃ* (acc. sg. m.)>; (*āloka-*); "light," acc. or nom. sg. m. (?). 22. See text commentary.

a[va]ï: see s.v. **√*vac*.**

avajadi: see s.v. ***ā* + √*pad*.**

-avaro: in ***hasavaro***.

-avi: <*-api* in *seyyathāpi*>; <*-api* in BHS *sayyathāpi*>; ind.; in ***sayasavi, suyasavi***. See also ***[p](*i)***.

√*as*: "be."

mi: *'smi* and <*'smi*>; (*asmi*); "I am," 1st sg. pres. 15, 15 *[mi],* 19, 20 *[mi].*

śpi: (*asmi*); (*asmi*); "I am," 1st sg. pres. 19.

sat[u]: <*santo*>; (*santaḥ*); "existing," pres. part., nom. pl. m. 39.

samaṇa: *samāno;* (—); "being," pres. part., nom. sg. m. 12, 13, 13 *[sama] ///,* 14.

asabroda-: "unrestrained," pp., neg., *sam* + √*vṛ.*

asabrodu: *asaṃvutaṃ* (acc. sg. m.); <*asaṃvṛtasya*, etc. (gen. sg. m.)>; nom. or loc. sg. m. (?). 42 *[asabro]du,* 45, 48 *asabro[d]u,* 58. See text commentary.

asabrodo: (as previous); nom. or loc. sg. m. (?). 51, 55. See text commentary.

asiaraṇam: *-adhikaraṇaṃ* in *yatvādhikaraṇaṃ;* <*adhikaraṇaṃ* in *yato (a)dhikaraṇaṃ*>; "because," adv., acc. (in ***yavad eva asiaraṇam eva***) 42 *[asi]araṇa[m],* 45, 48, 51, 55, 58.

aho: *ahaṃ* in *na kho ahaṃ;* (*ahaṃ* in *nāhaṃ*); "I," 1st pers. pron., nom. sg. (or ***ho*** = P *kho,* Skt. *khalu* ?). (in ***ṇaho*** or ***ṇa ho***) 9 *[ṇa](*ho),* 10, 11, 12, 13, 14, 15. See text commentary.

ā* + √*pad: "exercises."

avajadi: *āpajjati;* <*āpadyate*>; "he exercises," 3rd sg. pres. 43–4 *(*a)[va]jadi,* 46–7 *(*avaja)di,* 50, 53, 57, 60.

ā + mantraya-: "address" (denom.).
amatredi: <*āmantesi* (3rd sg. aor.)>; <*āmantrayate, ~ti*>; "he addressed," 3rd sg. pres. 27–8 *(*a)matredi,* 38 *amat[r]edi.*
ā + √vraj: "go to, become."
[abaji]: *abbaje* (1st sg. opt. P.); (*āvrajeyam*); "I would become, go to," 1st sg. opt. P. (?). 17. Reading uncertain; see text commentary.
ā + √sru: "overpower."
arśaveti: (**āsaventi/assaventi*) for *anvāssaveyyuṃ* (3rd pl. opt.); (BHS *āśrāvayanti* or *āsrāvayanti*) for <*anusravanti,* etc.>; "they overpower," 3rd pl. pres. caus. 43, 46, 49, 52, 56, 59 *arśa[veti].*

idam: "this," dem. pron.
idi: *idaṃ* or (*iti*); *idam* or (*iti*); "this" or "thus," nom. sg. n. for m. or ind. (?; elsewhere *aï*). 63. See text commentary.
ida: <*idaṃ*>; <*idam*>; acc. sg. n. 16.
idam: (*idaṃ*) for <*etad*>; (*idam*) for <*etad*>; acc. sg. n. (+ ***a[va]ï***). 16.
idam: <*idam*>; <*idam*>; acc. sg. n. (+ ***u***). 15–6 *(*ida)m,* 36.
ime: *imāni* in *cattār' imāni* (n.); <*imāni* (n.)>; dem. pron., nom. pl. m. for n. (in ***catvarime***). 39.
idi: *iti;* (*iti*); "thus," ind. 12, 12–3 *(*i)di,* 13, 14 *[id](*i).*
idi: (*iti*) or *idaṃ;* (*iti*) or *idam.* 63. See ***idam***.
-idhri: in ***kayidhri, ghaṇidhri, cakṣidhri, jibhidhri, maṇidh(*r)i, śatidhri, sudidhri.***
-idhrio: in ***[vu]didhrio.***
i[va]: (*iva* or *eva*); (*iva* or *eva*); "like" or "even," ind. 8. Interpretation uncertain; see text commentary.

u: see s.v. ***√vac***.
(*u)[avati]: *upapatti* in *devūpapatty;* (*upapatti*); "rebirth," nom. sg. f. 16. Reconstruction uncertain; see text commentary.
uasakramita: see s.v. ***upa-sam + √kram***.
u(*asaghu): <*upāsakaṃ*>; <*upāsakaṃ*>; "layman," acc. sg. m. 24. Reconstruction uncertain; see text commentary.
uekṣa-(*sabuja)gh(*u): *upekhā-sambojjhaṅgaṃ;* <BHS *upekṣā-saṃbodhyaṅgaṃ*>; "the enlightenment factor of equanimity," acc. sg. n. 71–2.
ukuje: <*ukkujjeyya*>; (**utkubjaya-*); "would set upright," 3rd sg. opt. P. denom. 21.
[utama-da]masa-śamasa-p[r]atu (or ***[utama-da]masa-śamasa p[r]atu***): *uttama-damatha-samathaṃ;* <*uttama-dama(tha)-śamatha-*>; "having attained the highest training and calm," acc. sg. m. 7. See text commentary.
upa-sam + √kram: "approach."
uasakrami: *upasaṅkami;* <*upasamakramat* and BHS *upasaṃkrāmat,* etc. (3rd sg. impf.)>; 3rd sg. pret. 9.
uasakramita: *upasaṅkamitvā;* (BHS *upasaṃkramitvā*) for <*upasaṃkramya*>; "having approached," abs. 9.
[uya]: see s.v. ***√vac***.
-uviade: in ***praṇo-uviade:*** <*pāṇupetaṃ*>; <*prāṇopetaṃ*>; *-upayātaṃ* or w.r. for *uvide* = *-upetaṃ.* Interpretation uncertain; see text commentary.

eka: <*ekaṃ*>; <*ekasmiṃ* (loc. sg.)>; "one," card., acc. sg. m. 26 *[eka],* 37.
eghad: *etad;* (*etad*) for <*idam*>; "this," dem. pron., acc. sg. n. (+ ***[uya]***, ***oya***). 9 *egha[d],* 28 *egha[d],* 39.
ema: (*evaṃ*) for *iti;* (*evam*); "thus," ind. 12, 13, 14, 14 *[e](*ma).* See also ***eva, [eva]m***.
eva: "so, thus," ind.
eva: (*evaṃ*); (*evam*); 18.
eva: <*evaṃ*>; <*evaṃ*>; 26, 37.
See also ***ema***, ***[eva]m***.
eva: "indeed, even," ind.
In ***asiaraṇam eva:*** (*eva*) for *enaṃ* (dem. pron., acc. sg. m.); (*eva*); 42 *[e](*va),* 45, 48, 51, 55, 58.
In ***[eva]m eva:*** *eva* in *evam eva;* (*eva*); 23.
In ***ceva:*** (*ceva*); (*caiva*); 3.
In ***yavad eva:*** (*eva*); (*eva*); 22.
In ***yavad eva:*** (*yāvad eva*) for *yato;* (*yāvad eva*); 42, 44–5 *(*yavad e)va,* 51, 54–5 *(*yavad e)va.* 58.

[eva]m**: eva* in *evam eva; (eva)*; "so," ind. (in ***[eva]m eva). 23. See also ***ema, eva***.

oya**:* see s.v. **√*vac.

***katu, kato**: (kātuṃ); (kartum)*; "to perform," inf., √*kṛ*. 29 *ka ///*, 30 *katu*, 31 *katu*, 31 *k. ///*, 32 *kat[u]*, 33 *katu*, 34 *kato*, 35 *kato*.

***kadara**: (katara-)* for *katamaṃ* (n.); *katarat* and *<katama->* (n.); "which? what?" interr. pron., nom. sg. m. for n. (?). 40 *ka[da] ///*, 60, 63 *[ka] ///*. See text commentary.

***kamatu, kamato**: (kammanta- ?); (karmānta- ?)*; "action" or "practice" (?). 29 *kamatu*, 30–1 *(*ka)matu*, 32 *kama[t]u*, 34 *kamato*. Interpretation uncertain; see text commentary.

***kayidhri-**:* "body faculty," n.

***kayidhri**: kāyindriyaṃ; <kāyendriyeṇa>;* adv., acc. (?). 55.

***kayi[dh](*ri)**: kāyindriyaṃ; <kāyendriyaṃ>;* acc. sg. n. 56.

***kayeṇa**: kāyena; <kāyena>*; "with the body," instr. sg. m. 54.

***ku**: ko; (kaḥ)*; "who?" interr. pron., nom. sg. m. 15.

-kuśala**:* see s.v. ***akuśala.

***krirṇo**: (kaṇho); (kṛṣṇaḥ)*; "dark," adj., nom. sg. m. 23.

***kṣiṇa**: khīṇā; (kṣīṇāḥ)*; "destroyed," pp., √*kṣĭ̄*, nom. pl. m. 18.

√*gam*: "go."

***ghachami**: <gacchāmi>; <gacchāmi>*; "I go," 1st sg. pres. 24.

***[ghache]**: gaccheyyaṃ; (gaccheyam)*; "I would go," 1st sg. opt. P. 17.

***ghatva**: (gatvā); (gatvā)*; "having gone, traveled," abs. 2, 6.

***ghachateṇa**: (gacchantena); (gacchatā)*; "by one going," pres. part., instr. sg. m. 29 *[ghacha]teṇa*, 30.

***gha[ĭ]ta**: ghāyitvā;* <BHS *ghrāyitvā*, Skt. *ghrātvā*>; "having smelled, smelling," abs., √*ghrā*, 47.

ghachateṇa**:* see s.v. **√*gam.

ghachami**:* see s.v. **√*gam.

[ghache]**:* see s.v. **√*gam.

***ghaṇidhri-**:* "nose faculty," n.

***ghaṇidhri**: ghānindriyaṃ; <ghrāṇendriyeṇa>*; adv., acc. (?). 48. See text commentary.

ghaṇidhri**: ghānindriye* (loc. sg. n.); *<ghrāṇendriyeṇa* (instr. sg. n.)>; loc. sg. n. or in ***ghaṇidhri-sabaram, acc. sg. m. (?). 50. See text commentary.

***ghaṇeṇa**; ghānena; <ghrāṇeṇa>*; "with the nose," instr. sg. n. 47.

ghatva**:* see s.v. **√*gam.

-ghada**:* in ***sava-rova-ghada or ***sava-sova<*ṇa>-ghada*** (?).

***ghadharvo**: gandhabbo; (gandharvaḥ)*; "a *gandharva*," nom. sg. m. 10 *[gha]dharvo*, 12 *gh(*a)dh(*a)[rv](*o)*, 13.

***ghadhrarvo**: gandhabbo; (gandharvaḥ)*; "a *gandharva*," nom. sg. m. 10.

***ghadhro**: gandhaṃ; <gandhān* (acc. pl. m.)>; "scent," acc. sg. m. 47.

-ghama**:* in ***bhiriḍi-ghama.

***[gh]u[t]u**: guttaṃ; <guptaṃ>*; "controlled," pp., √*gup*, acc. sg. m. 8.

***ghudama-**:* "Ghudama/Gotama/Gautama," P.N. m.

***(*ghuda)[m](*e)**: <gotamo>; (gautamaḥ)*; nom. sg. 24–5. Reconstruction uncertain.

***ghudamu**: gotamaṃ; (gautamam)* for *bhagavantaṃ* (acc. sg. m.); acc. sg. 24.

***ghudama**: <gotama>; (gautama)*; voc. sg. 21.

***ghodama-**:* "Ghodama/Gotama/Gautama," P.N. m.

***gho[da]meṇa**: <gotamena>; (gautamena)*; instr. sg. 23.

***ghodama**: <gotama>; (gautama)* for *<bhadanta>*; voc. sg. 21.

-ghrahi**:* in ***aṇovejaṇa-ghrahi.

-ghrahe**:* in ***ṇimiti-ghrahe.

***ca**: <ca>; <ca>*; "and," ind. 24, 24.
In ***ceva**: (ceva); (caiva)*. 3.
See also ***ya***.

***cakra**: cakkāni; <cakrāṇi>*; "wheel-marks," acc. pl. n. 4.

***cakṣidhri-**:* "eye faculty," n.

***cakṣi[dhri]**: cakkhundriyaṃ; <cakṣurindriyeṇa>*; adv., acc. (?). 42. See text commentary.

cakṣidhri: *cakkhundriyaṃ*; <*cakṣurindriyaṃ*>; acc. sg. n. 43.
cakṣidhri: *cakkhundriye* (loc. sg. n.); <*cakṣurindriyeṇa* (instr. sg. n.)>; loc. sg. n. or in ***cakṣidhri-sa[ba](*ram)***, acc. sg. m. (?). 43. See text commentary.

cakṣu[a]tu: <*cakkhumanto* (adj., nom. pl. m.)>; (*cakṣuṣmantaḥ*); "having eyes," adj., nom. pl. m. 22.

cakṣ[u]ṇa: *cakkhunā*; <*cakṣuṣā*>; "with the eye," instr. sg. n. 41.

catvarime (= ***catvaro ime*** ?): *cattār' imāni* = *cattāri imāni* (n.); <*catvāri* (n.)>; card., nom. pl. m. for n. 39. See text commentary.

citam: (*cittaṃ*); (*cittam*); "mind," acc. sg. n. (+ ***arśaveti***). 43, 46, 49, 52, 56, 59.

ceva: see s.v. ***ca***.

chado: *saddaṃ*; <*śabdān* (acc. pl. m.)>; "sound," acc. sg. m. 44.

jagharadu: (**jāgaratā* ?); (—); "by one awake," pres. part., √*jāgṛ*, instr. or gen. sg. m. (?). 34 *jaghara[du]*, 35. See text commentary.

ji[bh](*a): *jivhāya*; <*jihvayā*>; "with the tongue," instr. sg. f. 50.

jibhidhri-: "tongue faculty," n.
jibhidhri: *jivhindriyaṃ*; <*jihvendriyeṇa*>; adv., acc. (?). 51. See text commentary.
ji[bhi]dhri: *jivhindriyaṃ*; <*jihvendriyaṃ*>; acc. sg. n. 53.
ji[bhi]dhri: *jivhindriye* (loc. sg. n.); <*jihvendriyeṇa* (instr. sg. n.)>; loc. sg. n. or in ***ji[bhi]dhri-sabaram***, acc. sg. m. (?). 53. See text commentary.

-jivu: in ***yavajivu***.

jedavaṇo: <*jetavane*>; <*jetavane*>; "in the Jedavaṇa," P.N., loc. sg. n. 27, 37 *[jedavaṇ.] ///*.

-ñu: in ***sarvañu***.

ṭhideṇa: (*ṭhitena*); (*sthitena*); "by one standing," pp., √*sthā*, instr. sg. m. 31, 31 *[ṭh](*ide)ṇa*.

ṇa: *na*; (*na*); "not," ind. 18, 29, 29, 30, 31, 32, 32, 34, 35, 36, 41, 44, 44, 47, 47, 50, 54, 54, 57, 57.
In ***ṇaho***: (*nāhaṃ* or *na khɔ*) for *na kho ahaṃ*; (*nāham* or *na khalu*). 9 *[ṇa](*ho)*, 10, 11, 12, 13, 14, 15.

ṇam: (*naṃ*, *na*); (*nam*); "like" (?), ind. (in ***ṇam iva***). 8. Interpretation uncertain; see text commentary.

ṇama: *nāma*; <*nāma*>; "named," adv., acc. 3.

-ṇaṣide: read ***-ṇ<*i>ṣide***, in ***viragha-ṇ<*i>ṣide***.

ṇasu: (*nāthaṃ*) for *nāgaṃ*; (*nātham*) for <*nāgaṃ*>; "protector," acc. sg. m. 8.

ṇiujidu: (*nikujjitaṃ*) for <*nikkujjitaṃ*>; (**nikubjitam*); pp., denom. **nikubjaya-*, acc. sg. n. 21.

ṇimiti-ghrahe: *nimitta-ggāhī*; <*nimitta-grāhī*>; "grasping its general characteristics," adj., nom. sg. m. 41 *ṇ[i]mitighra[he]*, 44, 47, 50 *[ṇimiti]ghrahe*, 54, 57.

-ṇimi[ti] ///: in ***samas[i]-ṇimi[ti] ///***.

ṇirusa-ṇiṣide: *nirodha-nissitaṃ*; <BHS *nirodha-niśritaṃ*>; "dependent on cessation," adj., acc. sg. n. 65, 66, 67 *~ṇi[ṣid](*e)*, 68–9 *[ṇi](*rusaṇiṣi)de*, 70, 71, 72.

ṇiṣa[e]: (*nissāya*); <BHS *niśrāya*, *niśritya*, *niśṛtya*, etc.>; "near," abs./postposition. 6.

ṇiṣaṇeṇa: (*nisinnena*); (*niṣaṇṇena*); "while sitting," pp., *ni* + √*sad*, instr. sg. m. 32, 33.

-ṇiṣida: in ***vivea-ṇiṣida***.

-ṇiṣide: in ***ṇirusa-ṇiṣide***, ***viragha-ṇiṣide***, ***vivea-ṇiṣide***.

ta-: "he, she, it, this, that," dem. pron.
tat: (*tat*); (*tat*); "that," (in ***tatu/tato*** = *tat tu*). 29, 30, 31–2 *(*ta)to*, 33, 35, 36.
to: <*taṃ*>; (*tam*) for <*tasmin*>; "that," acc. sg. m. 3.
teṇa: (*tena*) for *pi sudaṃ* and <*tena*>; <*tena*>; "at that," instr. sg. m. 3.
teṇa: *tena*; <*tena*>; "to where," instr. sg. n. 9.
taśpi: (*tasmiṃ*) for *tasmā*; (*tasmin*) for <*tasmād*>; "therefore," loc. for abl. sg. 19, 20.
te: <*te*>; <*te*>; "those," nom. pl. m. 28, 36.

/// tae*:* (*tāya* ?); (*tayā* ?); "by that," dem. pron., instr. sg. f. (?). 63. Interpretation uncertain; see text commentary.

tatra*:* <*tatra*>; <*tatra*>; "there," ind. 27 *ta[tra],* 38.

tada*:* (*tadā*) for *tassa* (dem. pron., dat./gen. sg. n.); (*tadā*) for <*teṣāṃ* (dem. pron., gen. pl. n.)>; "then," ind. 43 *ta[da],* 46, 49, 52, 56, 59.

taśpi*:* see s.v. ***ta-***.

tu, ***to****:* (*tu*); (*tu*); "but," ind. (in ***tatu/tato*** = *tat tu*). 29 *tatu,* 30 *tatu,* 31–2 *(*ta)to,* 33 *tatu,* 35 *ta[tu],* 36 *tatu.*

te*:* see s.v. ***ta-***.

teṇa*:* see s.v. ***ta-***.

to*:* see s.v. ***ta-***.

to*:* see s.v. ***tu***.

(*to)[yo]*:* *toye;* (*toye*); "in water," loc. sg. n. 18. Reading and reconstruction uncertain; see text commentary.

-[da]masa-*:* "training"; in ***[utama-da]masa-śamasa-p[r]atu*** (or ***[utama-da]masa-śamasa p[r]atu***).

-[daśa]vi*:* in ***sa[rva-daśa]vi***.

dihaghama*:* *vihaṅgamo;* (*vihaṃgamaḥ*); "flying in the air," nom. sg. m. 17.

√dr̥ś*:* "see."

  dhrekṣatu*:* (Skt. **drakṣyantu* [fut. impv.] or P *dakkhantu* [pres. impv.]); the P parallel has <*dakkhinti* (3rd pl. fut.)>; "they might see" (or "let them see"), 3rd pl. fut. impv. or pres. impv. 22.

  [dh]r[iśpa]ṇa*:* *disvā;* <*dr̥ṣṭvā*>; "having seen, seeing," abs. 41.

deve*:* *devo;* (*devaḥ*); "a god," nom. sg. m. 9 *(*de)[v](*e),* 9–10 *[d](*e)ve,* 12 *dev[e].*

domaṇastu*:* *-domanassā* in *abhijjhā~* (nom. pl. n.); (**daurmanastvam*) for <*daurmanasyaṃ* (nom. sg. n.)>; "grief," nom. sg. n. 42, 45 *[do]maṇastu,* 48 *doma(*ṇa)stu,* 51–2 *(*do)maṇastu,* 55.

dhama*:* <*dhammaṃ*>; <*dharmaṃ*>; "the Dharma," acc. sg. m. 24. See also ***dharma-***.

dharedu*:* see s.v. ***√dhr̥***.

dharma-*:* "state, idea, dharma," m.

  dharmu*:* <*dhammo*>; (*dharmaḥ*); "dharma(s)," nom. sg. 23.

  dharmu*:* *dhammaṃ;* <*dharmān* (acc. pl.)>; "idea," acc. sg. 57.

  dharma*:* *dhammā;* <*dharmāḥ*>; "states," nom. pl. 42–3 *(*dha)rma,* 45–6 *(*dha)rma,* 49, 52, 56, 59.

  See also ***dhama***.

dharma-vie-[sa](*bujaghu)*:* *dhamma-vicaya-sambojjhaṅgaṃ;* <BHS *dharma-(pra)vicaya-saṃbodhyaṅgaṃ*>; "the enlightenment factor of the investigation of dharmas," acc. sg. n. 65.

√dhr̥*:* "hold."

  dharedu*:* <*dhāretu*>; (*dhārayatu*) for <*dhāraya* (impv. 2nd sg. caus.)>; "accept," 3rd sg. impv. caus. 25.

dhoṇa-*:* "Dhoṇa," P.N. m.

  dhoṇe*:* *doṇo;* <*droṇa-, dhūmrasagotra-*>*;* nom. sg. 4, 26.

  dhoṇo*:* (as previous); nom. sg. 3.

[dh]r[iśpa]ṇa*:* see s.v. ***√dr̥ś***.

dhrekṣatu*:* see s.v. ***√dr̥ś***.

paḍ[i]chaṇo*:* <*paṭicchannaṃ*>; (*praticchannam*); "covered," pp., *prati* + *√chad,* acc. sg. n. 21.

paḍideṇa*:* (*paṇḍitena*); (*paṇḍitena*); "by the wise," instr. sg. m. 29, 30, 32 *[pa]ḍideṇa,* 33 *paḍide(*ṇa),* 35, 36.

padeṣu*:* *pădesu;* (*pādeṣu*), "on the footprints," loc. pl. m. 4, 5 *p(*ad)e(*ṣu).*

-pariṇamu, ***-pariṇame****:* in ***vivasagha-pariṇamu***, ***~pariṇame***.

pavea*:* *pāpakā;* <*pāpakā(ḥ)*>; "evil," adj., nom. pl. m. 42, 45 *[pa](*vea),* 48 *[p](*a)[v](*e)[a],* 52, 55 *[pa](*vea).*

[p](*i)*:* (*pi*, *api*) for <*ca*>; (*api*) for <*ca*>; "also," ind. 19. See also ***avi***.

pu[ḍar](*io)*:* *puṇḍarīkaṃ;* (*puṇḍarīkam*); "lotus," nom. sg. n. 18.

pra + √kāś*:* "show."

  praghaśe*:* (*pakāse/pakāseyya*) for <*ācikkheyya*>; (*prakāśet*); "would show," 3rd sg. opt. P. 22.

praghaśe: see s.v. ***pra + √kāś.***

pracarśoṣu: see s.v. ***prati + √śru.***

praṇo-uviade: <*pāṇupetaṃ*>; <*prāṇopetaṃ*>; "until [my] last breath," adv., acc. 25. Interpretation uncertain; see text commentary.

prati + √pad: "take up."

pradivajadi: *paṭipajjati;* <*pratipadyate*>; "he takes up," 3rd sg. pres. 43 *[pra]divajad[i]*, 46, 49, 56, 59.

prati + √śru: "respond."

pracarśoṣu: <*paccassosuṃ*>; <*pratyaśrauṣuḥ*>; "they responded," 3rd pl. pret. 28.

p[r]atu (or in ***[utama-da]masa-śamasa-p[r]atu***): (*pattaṃ*) for *anupattaṃ* (pp., acc. sg. m.); (*prāptam*); "attained," pp., *pra* + *√āp,* acc. sg. m. 7. See text commentary.

pradivajadi: see s.v. ***prati + √pad.***

prabh(*a)[śp](*a)ra: (*pabhassarāni*); (BHS *prabhāsvarāṇi*); "resplendent," adj., acc. pl. n. 5.

-prariṇamu: in ***vivasagha-prariṇamu.***

praṣadha-sabujaghu: *passaddhi-sambojjhaṅgaṃ;* <BHS *praśrabdhi-saṃbodhyaṅgaṃ, prasrabdhi~*>; "the enlightenment factor of calm," acc. sg. n. 69.

pra[sa]ṇa: *padhānāni* (n.); (BHS *pradhānāni* and *prahāṇāṇi* [n.]); "efforts," nom. pl. m. for n. 39.

[pra]saṇa-prasa[ṇo]: *pahāna-ppadhānaṃ* (n.); *prahāṇa-prahāṇaṃ* (n.); "effort of abandoning," nom. sg. m. for n. 40.

-prasaṇe, -prasaṇo: in ***aṇorakṣaṇa~, [pra]saṇa~, bhavaṇa~, sabara~.***

(*prasada)ṇi: *pasādanīyaṃ;* <*prasādanīyaṃ*>; "pleasing," adj., acc. sg. m. 7. Reconstruction uncertain; see text commentary.

prahadavu: <*pahātabbaṃ*>; <*prahātavyaṃ*>; "to be destroyed," gdv., *pra* + *√hā,* nom. sg. n. 20.

prahiṇo: <*pahīnaṃ*>; <*prahīṇaṃ*>; "has been destroyed," pp., *pra* + *√hā,* nom. sg. n. 20.

[prid](*i)-[sabujaghu]: *pīti-sambojjhaṅgaṃ;* <BHS *prīti-saṃbodhyaṅgaṃ*>; "the enlightenment factor of joy," acc. sg. n. 68.

proṭhabu: *phoṭṭhabbaṃ;* <BHS *spraṣṭavyāni, praṣṭavyān* (acc. pl. n./m.)>; "a tangible," gdv., *√spṛś,* acc. sg. n. 54.

proṭhu: *puṭṭho;* (*pṛṣṭaḥ*); "asked," pp., *√prach,* nom. sg. m. 12, 13 *p[r]oṭhu,* 13 *proṭh[u],* 14.

[phulo]: (*phullo*) for *vaggu;* (*phullaḥ*); "flowering," adj., nom. sg. n. 18.

phuṣita: *phusitvā;* <BHS *spṛśitvā,* Skt. *spṛṣṭvā*>; "having touched, touching," abs., *√spṛś.* 54.

[ba]: (*vā*) for *ca;* (*vā*); "or," ind. 17. See also ***a, va.***

-bayaṇata: in ***budha-bayaṇata.***

-bayaṇo: in ***budha-bayaṇo.***

baleṇa: (*bālena*); (*bālena*); "by a fool," instr. sg. m. 29, 30 *bal[eṇa],* 32, 35 *[ba]l[e]ṇa,* 36 *ba[le]ṇa.*

bucadi: see s.v. ***√vac.***

budha-bayaṇata: (*buddha-vacanatā-/~tva-* ?); (*buddha-vacanatā-/~tva-* ?); "on account of the Buddha's teaching" (?), 30, 31, 33, 34 *budhabayaṇa[ta].* Interpretation uncertain; see text commentary.

budha-bayaṇo: (*buddha-vacanaṃ*); (*buddha-vacanaṃ*); "the Buddha's teaching," nom. sg. n. 29, 36.

budho: *buddho;* (*buddhaḥ*); "the Enlightened One," pp., *√budh,* nom. sg. m. 15, 15, 19, 20.

bramaṇa-: "a brahman," m.

bramaṇe: *brāhmaṇo;* (*brāhmaṇaḥ*); nom. sg. 4, 26.

bramaṇo: *brāhmaṇo;* (*brāhmaṇaḥ*); nom. sg. 3.

bramaṇa: *brāhmaṇa;* (*brāhmaṇa*); voc. sg. 9 *bra[ma]ṇ(*a),* 10, 10–1 *(*bra)maṇa,* 11, 12, 13, 14, 15, 15 *b[r]amaṇa,* 19 *brama[ṇa],* 20 *[bramaṇa].*

bhayavada-: "the Bhagavat," m.

bhayavadu: *bhagavā* and <*bhagavā*>; <*bhagavān*>; nom. sg. 9 *///* *yavadu,* 16, 26–7 *bhaya[v](*a)du,* 27 *bha[ya](*va)[d](*u),* 28 w.r. *bha[ya]va[ṣu],* 37 w.r. *bhayadu,* 38.

***bhaya[va]du**: bhagavantaṃ;* <*bhagavantaṃ*>; acc. sg. 9.

***bhayavadeṇa**:* (*bhagavatā/bhagavantena*) for <*bhagavato* (dat./gen. sg.)>; (*bhagavatā*) for <*bhagavato*>; instr. sg. 26.

***bhayavadu**: bhagavato* and <*bhagavato*>; <*bhagavataḥ*>; dat./gen. sg. 4, 5 *[bha]yavadu,* 28.

***bhavaṇa-prasaṇa-**:* "the effort of development," m. for n.

***~prasaṇe**: bhāvanā̆-ppadhānaṃ* (n.); *bhāvanā-prahāṇaṃ* (n.); nom. sg. 63–4 *(*bha)vaṇa~,* 73 *bhava[ṇapra]saṇe.*

***~prasaṇo**:* (as previous); nom. sg. 40 *~prasaṇ[o].*

***bhavadi**:* see s.v. **√*bhū*.**

***bhavidavu**:* see s.v. **√*bhū*.**

***bh(*a)[vi](*du)**:* see s.v. **√*bhū*.**

***bhaviśasi**:* see s.v. **√*bhū*.**

***bhaviśe**:* see s.v. **√*bhū*.**

***bhavedi**:* see s.v. **√*bhū*.**

***bhaṣido**:* <*bhāsitaṃ*>; <*bhāṣitaṃ*>; "said," pp., √*bhāṣ,* acc. sg. n. 26.

***bhikṣave**:* (*bhikkhave*) and *bhikkhave;* <*bhikṣavaḥ*>; voc. pl. m. 28–9 *(*bhi)kṣave,* 30, 31, 33, 39, 41, 60, 61, 64. See also ***bhikhu-**.*

***bhikhu-**:* "monk," m.

***bhikhu**: bhikkhu; bhikṣuḥ*; nom. sg. 41, 64.

***bhikhuṇa**:* (*bhikkhunā*) for *bhikkhu* (nom. sg.); (*bhikṣuṇā*) for <*bhikṣor* (gen. sg.)>; instr. sg. 61.

***bhikhu**:* <*bhikkhū*>; <*bhikṣavaḥ*>; nom. pl. 28, 36 *bhi[kh.] ///,* 38.

***bhikhu**:* <*bhikkhū*>; <*bhikṣūn*>; acc. pl. 27 *bhi ///,* 38.

See also ***bhikṣave**.*

***bhikhu-sagha**:* <*bhikkhu-saṅghaṃ*>; <*bhikṣu-saṃghaṃ*>; "Saṅgha, community of monks," acc. sg. m. 24.

***bhiriḍi-ghama**: vinaḷīkatā* (nom. pl. m.); (**vinālīkr̥ta-/*vinālīgama-*); "cut off," adj., nom. pl. m. 18. Reading and interpretation uncertain; see text commentary.

***bhu**: bho;* (*bhoḥ*); "venerable sir," voc. sg. m. 9 *[bhu],* 10, 10 *[bh](*u),* 11, 12, 14, 15, 21, 21 *[bhu].*

√*bhū*: "be."

***bhavadi**: hoti;* <*bhavati*>; "is," 3rd sg. pres. 44, 47, 50, 54, 57.

***bhavadi**:* (*hoti/bhavati*); <*bhavati*>; "is," 3rd sg. pres. 62.

***bhaviśe**: bhavissāmi* (1st sg. fut. P.); (*bhaviṣye*); "I would be," 1st sg. fut. Ā. 10, 10, 11, 11, 12 *[bhaviśe],* 13, 14, 15.

***bhaviśasi**:* (*bhavissasi*) for *bhavissati* (3rd sg. fut.); (*bhaviṣyasi*); "would you be?" 2nd sg. fut. 9 *[bha](*vi)[śasi],* 10 *bhaviśa[s]i,* 10 *[bh](*a)[vi] ///,* 11, 11–2 *(*bhaviśa)si,* 12 *bhaviśa[si],* 13 *(*bha)[vi]śasi,* 14, 15.

***bhavedi**: bhāveti;* <*bhāvayati*>; "develops," 3rd sg. pres. caus. 64, 65–6 *(*bha)vedi,* 67, 68 *[bhave]di,* 69, 70 *bhav. ///,* 72 *[bhave]di.*

***bh(*a)[vi](*du)**:* <*bhāvitaṃ*>; <*bhāvitam*>; "developed," pp., nom. sg. n. 19.

***bhavidavu**:* <*bhāvetabbaṃ*>; <*bhāvanīyaṃ*>; "to be developed," gdv., nom. sg. n. 19.

***magha-**:* "road, path," m.

***maghu**:* <*maggaṃ*>; (*mārgam*); acc. sg. 22.

***magho**:* <*maggaṃ*>; (*mārgam*); acc. sg. 3.

***magheṇa**:* (*maggena*); (*mārgeṇa*); instr. sg. 2 *magh(*e)ṇa,* 6.

***maghade**: maggā;* <*mārgāt*>; abl. sg. 2 *ma[ghade],* 6 *magha[de].*

***-maṇa[s.]**:* in ***śata-maṇa[s.]**.*

maṇase or read ***maṇase<*ṇa>**: manasā* (instr. sg. n.) (or *mānasaṃ/mānase,* acc. or loc. sg. n.); <*manasā* (instr. sg. n.)>; "with the mind," instr. sg. n. (?). 57. Interpretation uncertain; see text commentary.

***maṇidhri-**:* "mind faculty," n.

***maṇidh(*r)i**: manindriyaṃ;* <BHS *manindriyeṇa, mana-indriyeṇa*>; adv., acc. (?). 58. See text commentary.

***ma(*ṇidhri)**: manidriyaṃ;* <BHS *manindriyaṃ, mana-indriyaṃ*>; acc. sg. n. 59.

***(*maṇi)dhri**: manindriye* (loc. sg. n.); <BHS *manindriyeṇa, mana-indriyeṇa* (instr. sg. n.)>; loc. sg. n. or in

(*maṇi)dhri-sabaram, acc. sg. m. (?). 60. See text commentary.

[maṇ](*o)śata: *manussattaṃ;* (*manuṣyatvam*); "state of being human," acc. sg. n. 17.

maṇośu: *manusso;* (*manuṣyaḥ*); "a human," nom. sg. m. 11, 11, 14, 15.

mi: see s.v. ***√as***.

mi: <*me*>; <*me*>; 1st pers. pron., instr. or gen. sg. enclitic. 20. See also ***me***.

[mi]: (*me*) for <*maṃ*>; (*me*) for <*māṃ*>; 1st pers. pron., acc. sg. enclitic. 24. See also ***me***.

muḍhasa: <*mūḷhassa*>; (*mūḍhasya*); "lost," pp., √*muh*, dat./gen. sg. m. 22.

-mulo: in ***rokṣa-mulo***.

me: <*me*>; (*me*) for <*mayā*>; "by me," 1st pers. pron., instr. sg. enclitic. 26, 37. See also ***mi***.

ya: (*ca*) for <*kho*>; (*ca*); "and," ind. 27, 38. See also ***ca***.

yakṣatu: *yakkhattaṃ;* (*yakṣatvam*); "the state of being a *yakṣa/yakkha,*" acc. sg. n. 17.

yakṣu: *yakkho;* (*yakṣaḥ*); "a *yakṣa*," nom. sg. m. 10, 11, 13 *ya[kṣ](*u),* 14 *yakṣ[u]*.

yavajivu: (*yāvajīvaṃ*); <*yāvajjīvaṃ*>; "for as long as there is life," adv., acc. 25.

ya[va]d: adv.

In ***ya[va]d eva***: (*yāvad eva*); (*yāvad eva*); "so that." 22.

In ***yavad eva***: (*yāvad eva*) for *yato;* (*yāvad eva*); 42, 44–5 *(*yavad e)va,* 51, 54–5 *(*yavad e)va,* 58.

-yasa-: in ***sayasavi***, ***suyasavi***.

[yasa] or ***[yaso]***: *yathā;* (*yathā*); "as," ind. 18. Reading uncertain.

yeṇa: *yena;* (*yena*); "by which," rel. pron., instr. sg. n. 16, 17.

√rakṣ: "protect."

rakṣadi: *rakkhati;* <*rakṣati*>; "he protects," 3rd sg. pres. 43, 46, 49, 53, 56, 59.

rada: <*rahada-*>; <*hrada-*>; "pond," acc. sg. m. 8. See text commentary.

rasu: *rasaṃ;* <*rasān* (acc. pl. m.)>; "flavor," acc. sg. m. 50.

ruaṇa: <*rūpāni*>; (*rūpāṇi*); "forms," acc. pl. n. 22.

[r]u[v]o: *rūpaṃ;* <*rūpaṃ, rūpāṇi*>; "form," acc. sg. n. 41. See also ***-rova-***.

re: (*re, are*); (*are*); ind. 15.

rokṣa-mulo: *rukkha-mūle* (loc. sg.); <*vr̥kṣa-mūlaṃ*>; "at the root of a tree," acc. sg. n. 2 *[r]okṣ(*a)mul. ///,* 6.

-rova- or ***-sova<*ṇa>-***: in ***sava-rova-ghada*** or ***sava-sova<*ṇa>-ghada*** (?).

rśoda-: "heard," pp., √*śru*.

[rśoda]: <*sutaṃ*>; <*śrutaṃ*>; nom. sg. n. 26.

rśodu: <*sutaṃ*>; <*śrutaṃ*>; nom. sg. n. 37.

logha-: "world," m.

[l](*o)ghu: (*loke*) for *lokena* (instr. sg.); <*loke*>; loc. sg. 18–9.

[lo]gha[śpi]: <*lokasmiṃ*>; (*loke*); loc. sg. 39.

va: *vā;* (*vā*); "or," ind. 17, 22, 22 *[va],* 62 *[va]*. See also ***a***, ***[ba]***.

√vac: "speak"

a[va]ï: (*avaca, *avaci*) for <*avoca*>; (BHS *avacĭ*) for <*uvāca, avocat*>; "he said," 3rd sg. pret. (in ***idam a[v]aï***). 16.

u: (*avaca*) for <*avoca*>; (BHS *avaca*) for <*avocat*>; 3rd sg. pret. (in ***idam u***). 16, 36.

[uya]: (*avaca*) for <*avoca*>; (BHS *avaca*) for <*avocat*>; 3rd sg. pret. (in ***eghad uya***). 9 *[u](*ya),* 28 *[uya]*.

oya: (*avaca*) for <*avoca*>; (BHS *avaca*) for <*avocat*>; 3rd sg. pret. (in ***eghad oya***). 39.

bucadi: *vuccati; ucyate;* "is called," 3rd sg. pass. 60.

vucadi: *vuccati; ucyate;* "is called," 3rd sg. pass. 63, 73 *vuca[di]*.

-vaṇo: in ***jeda-vaṇo***.

√vad: "speak."

vadesi: *vadesi* (2nd sg. pres. or pret.); (—); "you say," or "you said," 2nd sg. pres. or pret. 12, 13, 14, 14–5 *(*vade)s[i]*.

vadita: (**vaditvā*) for <*vatvā*>; <BHS *vaditvā* and *uktvā*>; "having said," abs. 16.

vadita: see s.v. ***√vad***.

-vie-: in ***dharma-vie-[sa](*bujaghu)***.

[śp](*ay)i[ta]: *sāyitvā;* <BHS *svādayitvā, āsvādya*>; "having tasted, tasting," abs., √*svad.* 50. Reading and reconstruction uncertain; see text commentary.

-[śp](*a)ra: in ***prabh(*a)[śp](*a)ra.***

śpi: see s.v. **√*as.***

ṣamaṇa-: "monk," m.

[ṣ](*a)ma(*ṇo): <*samaṇo*>; (*śramaṇaḥ*); nom. sg. 24.

ṣamaṇo: <*samaṇaṃ*>; (*śramaṇaṃ*) for *bhagavantaṃ* (acc. sg. m.); acc. sg. 24.

ṣamaṇeṇa: <*samaṇena*>; (*śramaṇena*); instr. sg. 23.

ṣutvaṇa: *sutvā;* <*śrutvā*>; "having heard, hearing," abs., √*śru.* 44.

ṣudeṇa: *sotena;* (BHS *śrotena*) for <*śrotreṇa*>; "with the ear," instr. sg. n. 44.

-sagha: in ***bhikhu-sagha.***

-saña: in ***aṭhi-saña.***

sat[u]: see s.v. **√*as.***

satu, sato: (*santa-* or *sata-* ?); (*sant-* or *smr̥ta-* ?); "good," "mindful," or "mindfully" (?). 29 *sato,* 30 *[sa] ///,* 32 *satu,* 34 *sato.* Interpretation uncertain; see text commentary.

sapadedi: see s.v. ***sam* + √*pad.***

[s](*a)praghaśi[d]e: (*sampakāsito*); (*saṃprakāśitaḥ*); "proclaimed," pp., *sam-pra* + √*kāś,* nom. sg. m. 23.

sabara-: "restraint," m.

sabaram: *saṃvaraṃ;* <*saṃvaram*>; acc. sg. (+ ***avajadi***). 43 *sa[ba] ///,* 50, 53, 60.

sabarae: *saṃvarāya;* <*saṃvarāya*>; dat. sg. 43 *[saba]ra[e],* 46, 49, 52 *saba[ra]e,* 56, 59.

See also ***savaram.***

sabara-prasaṇa-: "effort of restraint," nom. sg. m. for n.

~prasaṇe: *saṃvara-ppadhānaṃ; saṃvara-prahāṇaṃ;* 40, 40–1 *(*sa)bara~.*

~prasaṇo: (as previous). 60.

-sabujaghu: in ***uekṣa~, dharma-vie~, praṣadha~, [prid](*i)~, (*vi)ria~, śpadi~, samasi~.***

-sabrodu, -sabrodo: see s.v. ***asabroda-.***

samaeṇa: <*samayena*>; <*samayena*>; "at [that] time," instr. sg. m. 3.

samaṇa: see s.v. **√*as.***

sama[ya]: <*samayaṃ*>; <*samaye* (loc. sg. m.)>; "at [one] time," acc. sg. m. 37.

samas[i]-ṇimi[ti] ///: *samādhi-nimittaṃ* (acc. sg. n.); <*samādhi-nimittaṃ* (acc. sg. n.)>; "sign of concentration," nom. sg. n. (?). 61. Interpretation uncertain; see text commentary.

samasi-sabujagh[u]: *samādhi-sambojjhaṅgaṃ;* <BHS *samādhi-saṃbodhyaṅgaṃ*>; "the enlightenment factor of concentration," acc. sg. n. 70.

sam* + √*pad: "succeed."

sapadedi: <*sampādeti*>; (*saṃpādayati*); "he causes [it] to succeed," 3rd sg. pres. caus. 63.

sayasavi: (*seyyathāpi*); (BHS *sayyathāpi*) for <*tadyathā*>; "namely," ind. 62. See also ***suyasavi.***

sarvañu: <*sabbaññū*>; <*sarvajñaḥ*>; "all-knowing," adj., nom. sg. m. 20.

sa[rva-daśa]vi: <*sabba-dassāvī*>; <*sarva-darśī/~darśāvī*>; "all-seeing," adj., nom. sg. m. 20.

savaram: *saṃvaraṃ;* <*saṃvaram*>; "restraint," acc. sg. m. (+ ***avajadi***). 57. See also ***sabara-.***

sava-rova-ghada or ***sava-sova<*ṇa>-ghada:*** (*sabba-rūpa-katāni* or *sabba-sovaṇṇa-katāni* ?) for *sabbākāraparipūrāni;* (*sarva-rūpa-kr̥tāni* or *sarva-sauvarṇa-kr̥tāni* ?) for <*sarvākāraparipūrṇāni* or *sarvasauvarṇa-*>; "with all parts entire" or "all golden" (?), acc. pl. n. 5. Reading and interpretation uncertain; see text commentary.

savijamaṇa: <*saṃvijjamāna-*>; <*saṃvidyamāna-*>; "found," pres. part., pass., *sam* + √*vid,* nom. pl. m. 39.

sahasa-h-ara: *sahassārāni;* <*sahasrārāṇi*>; "thousand-spoked," bv., acc. pl. n. 4.

sukaro: (*sukaraṃ*); (*sukaram*); "easy," adj., nom. sg. n. 28 *[su] ///,* 29, 30 *s[u]karo,* 31, 31 *s[u]k(*a)ro,* 32, 33, 34, 35, 35 *sukar. ///.*

sugha[du]: <*sugato*>; <*sugataḥ*>; "the Sughada/Sugata," nom. sg. m. 16.

sudidhri-: "ear faculty," n.
  sudidhri: *sotindriyaṃ*; <*śrotrendriyeṇa*>; adv., acc. (?). 45. See text commentary.
  sudidhri: *sotindriyaṃ*; <*śrotrendriyaṃ*>; acc. sg. n. 46.
  s[u](*didhri): *sotindriye* (loc. sg. n.); <*śrotrendriyeṇa* (instr. sg. n.)>; loc. sg. n. or in ***s[u](*didhri-sabaram)***. 46. See text commentary.
suyasavi: <*seyyathāpi*>; (BHS *sayyathāpi*); "just as," ind. 21. See also ***sayasavi***.
-sova<*ṇa>- or ***-rova-***: in ***sava-rova-ghada*** or ***sava-sova<*ṇa>-ghada*** (?).

hasavaro: <*athāparaṃ*>; <*athāparam*>; "further," adv. 16.

hoṭo: 2 *(*ho)ṭo*, 6. Interpretation uncertain, probably incomplete P.N.; see text commentary.

∘ (punctuation type 1; see § 4.5): 2, 3, 4, 5, 5 *[∘]*, 7 *[∘]*, 7, 8, 8 *[∘]*, 10, 10, 11, 11 *[∘]*, 12, 13, 14 *[∘]*, 16 *[∘]*, 17, 17, 18, 18 *[∘]*, 21, 21, 22, 22, 22, 24, 25, 27, 28, 28 *[∘]*, 29, 30, 31, 32, 32, 33, 34, 35, 35, 36, 37 *[∘]*, 38, 39, 39, 39 *[∘]*, 40 *[∘]*, 40, 41, 41, 42, 42, 43, 43, 43, 44, 44, 45, 45, 46, 46, 47, 48, 48, 49, 49, 49 *[∘]*, 50, 51, 51, 52, 52, 53, 53, 55, 56, 56, 57, 58, 59 *[∘]*, 59, 60, 60, 61, 62, 62, 63, 64, 64, 65, 65, 66, 66, 67, 68, 69, 69, 70, 70, 71.
O (punctuation types 2 and 3; see § 4.5): 26 (type 2), 37 (type 2), 73 (type 3).